DEBIT AND CREDIT RULES

Assets	=	Liabilities	+	Owner's Equity

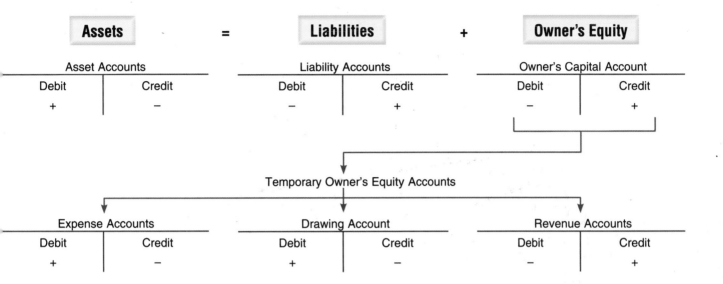

Asset Accounts		Liability Accounts		Owner's Capital Account	
Debit	Credit	Debit	Credit	Debit	Credit
+	−	−	+	−	+

Temporary Owner's Equity Accounts

Expense Accounts		Drawing Account		Revenue Accounts	
Debit	Credit	Debit	Credit	Debit	Credit
+	−	+	−	−	+

Debits		Credits
+	Assets	−
+	Drawing	−
+	Expenses	−
−	Liabilities	+
−	Owner's Capital	+
−	Revenue	+

Account	Increase Side	Decrease Side	Normal Balance
Asset	**Debit**	Credit	**Debit**
Liability	**Credit**	Debit	**Credit**
Owner's Capital	**Credit**	Debit	**Credit**
Revenue	**Credit**	Debit	**Credit**
Drawing	**Debit**	Credit	**Debit**
Expense	**Debit**	Credit	**Debit**

If an account is increased with a debit, it will be decreased with a credit.

If an account is increased with a credit, it will be decreased with a debit.

Since there are usually more increases than decreases in an account, the normal balance is the same as the increase side.

JOURNALIZING AND POSTING

Analyzing a Transaction

Step **1** Identify the accounts involved.
Step **2** Identify the classifications of the accounts involved.
Step **3** Determine if the accounts were increased or decreased.
Step **4** Determine how (debit or credit) the accounts were increased or decreased.

Posting the Debit Part of an Entry

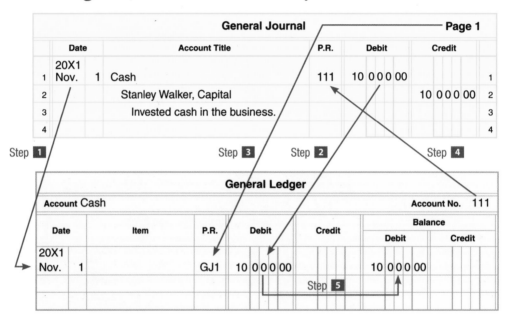

Step **1** Enter the date of the transaction in the ledger account.
Step **2** Enter the amount of the transaction in the ledger account.
Step **3** Enter the page number of the journal in the P.R. column of the account.
Step **4** Enter the number of the account in the P.R. column of the journal.
Step **5** Determine the balance of the account.

THE WORK SHEET

Account Classification	Trial Balance		Adjustments		Adjusted Trial Balance		Income Statement		Balance Sheet	
	Debit	Credit	Debit	Credit	Debit	Credit	Debit	Credit	Debit	Credit
Assets	X				→ X				→ X	
Liabilities		X				→ X				→ X
Capital		X				→ X				→ X
Drawing	X				→ X				→ X	
Revenue		X				→ X		→ X		
Expenses	X				→ X		→ X			

Introductory Accounting

Robert L. Dansby, PhD
Columbus Technical College, Emeritus, and University of Phoenix
Columbus, Georgia

Burton S. Kaliski, EdD
Southern New Hampshire University, Retired
Manchester, New Hampshire

Michael D. Lawrence, MBA, CPA, CMA, CFM
Portland Community College
Portland, Oregon

EMC
Publishing

St. Paul • Los Angeles • Indianapolis

Senior Developmental Editor: Christine Hurney
Copy Editor: Susan Free
Proofreader: Nancy Ahr
Production Editor: Amy McGuire
Indexer: Edwin Durbin

Cover & Text Designer: Leslie Anderson
Photo Researcher: Terri Miller
Production Specialists: Jaana Bykonich, Matthias Frasch, Ryan Hamner, John Valo
Cover Image: © Robert Marien/Corbis

Photo Credits:

AP Images/Cook, Dennis: 32, 191
Corbis: Abrams, Henny Ray/Reuters, 153; *East, Chip/Reuters:* 71; *Ken Seet Photography:* 216; *Pixland:* 504; *PNC/Brand X:* 504
iStockphoto.com: 1, 2, 14, 26, 56, 68, 90, 105, 109, 134, 135, 178, 190, 234, 282, 288, 307, 336, 355, 410, 416, 424, 451, 456, 510, 526, 558

Jupiterimages: BananaStock: 221; *Comstock Images:* 474, 521; *Hola Images/Workbook Stock:* 220; *Image100:* 359; *Image Source Black:* 546; *Polka Dot Images:* 354, 561; *Skelley, Ariel/Blend Images:* 15; *Tetra Images:* 242; *Thinkstock Images:* 91
Newscom: Boyle, Tim/Getty Images: 11; *Sullivan, Justin/Getty Images: 217; Wong, Alex: 505*

We have made every effort to trace the ownership of all copyrighted material and to secure permission from copyright holders. In the event of any question arising as to the use of any material, we will be pleased to make the necessary corrections in future printings. Thanks are due to the aforementioned authors, publishers, and agents for permission to use the materials indicated.

ISBN 978-0-82195-202-3

© 2010 by EMC Publishing, LLC
875 Montreal Way
St. Paul, MN 55102
E-mail: educate@emcp.com
Web site: www.emcp.com

Printed in the United States of America

17 16 15 14 13 12 11 10 09 08 1 2 3 4 5 6 7 8 9 10

BRIEF CONTENTS

Contents

To the Student

Introductory Accounting teaches the key concepts and skills of accounting to prepare you for direct job entry or for further study of accounting and business. Using practical and up-to-date examples, the text's approach blends the *why* with the *how* of accounting. This approach allows you to master accounting procedures (the how) because you understand the underlying theory (the why). Because ethics are so important in business, and especially in accounting practice, ethics are introduced in Chapter 1 and are reinforced and applied throughout the text.

Textbook Features

Use the features found within this text to help you succeed in your accounting course.

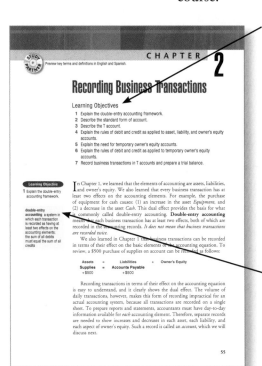

- **Learning Objectives** at the beginning of each chapter list the important concepts or procedures to be mastered in the chapter. They are correlated to the text material, the chapter summary, and all of the end-of-chapter exercises and problems.

> **Study Tip** Use the objectives as a "big picture" preview of the chapter. When you have finished studying the chapter, review the summary, which is organized by objective. If you are confused about a particular objective, find its reference in the text and re-read that section. Prepare for exams by reviewing the chapter objectives.

- **Key terms** are formally defined in the page margins, next to the place where each term is introduced and explained. Experience demonstrates that students who learn these terms score higher on quizzes and exams. The Key Terms element at the end of the chapter lists the terms and the page where each term is defined. A complete glossary appears at the back of the book. Another tool for learning the language of accounting is the Study Partner CD, which provides audio of all of the chapter terms and definitions plus Spanish translations and flash cards.

> **Study Tip** The key terms are the building blocks of accounting. Use the Study Partner CD flash cards to test your memory of the terms and definitions for each chapter.

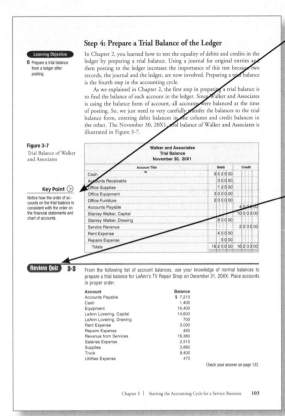

- **Key Point** margin boxes provide further reinforcement of important, testable facts.

  Study Tip Information included in Key Point boxes will probably appear in your chapter quizzes and exams. Make sure you study these points carefully.

- Major topics are reinforced with **Review Quiz** boxes that appear after the topic information. Answer these questions to check your comprehension as you work through the chapter. Quiz answers are found at the end of the chapter.

  Study Tip Use the Review Quiz questions to make sure you understand what you have just read. Or use them as a quick review of the chapter content as you are preparing for quizzes or exams.

- **Remember** notes appear in the margin, next to the corresponding text discussion, to remind you of important concepts learned in previous chapters.

  Study Tip If you do not remember the information discussed in a Remember box, look back to the chapter referenced and review the information. Concepts and skills will build throughout your study of the text. Don't allow gaps to form in your understanding by skipping over these reminders.

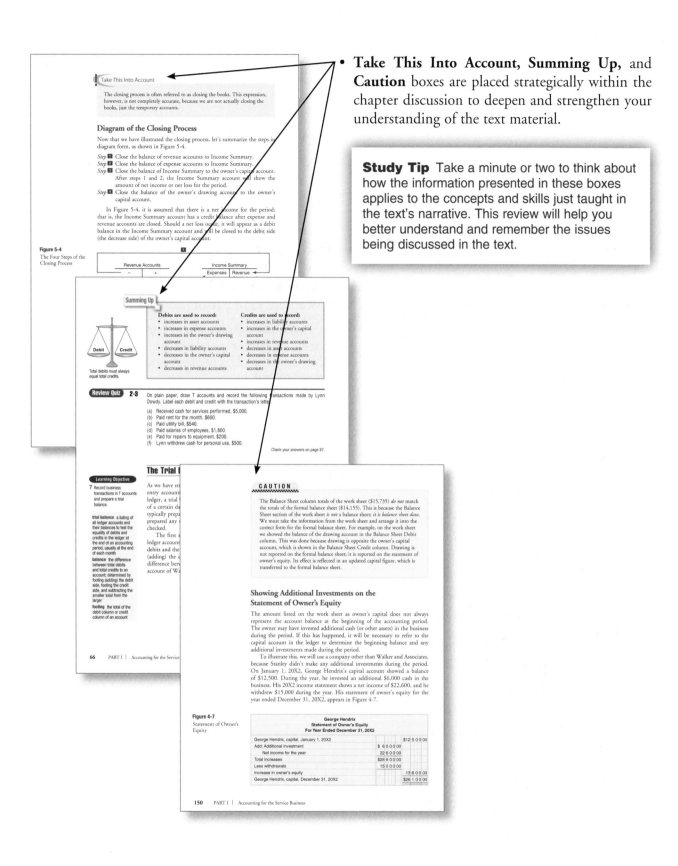

Take This Into Account, Summing Up, and **Caution** boxes are placed strategically within the chapter discussion to deepen and strengthen your understanding of the text material.

Study Tip Take a minute or two to think about how the information presented in these boxes applies to the concepts and skills just taught in the text's narrative. This review will help you better understand and remember the issues being discussed in the text.

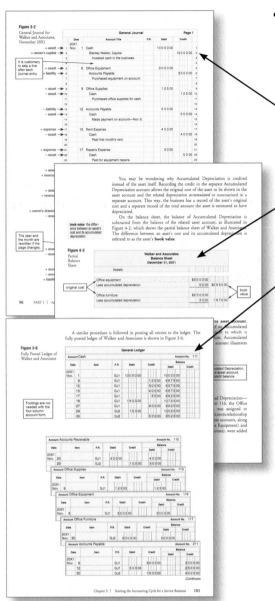

- **Color** is used to help you quickly identify the major accounting documents. In addition, significant entries are identified with labels defining how each entry affects the corresponding account.

Study Tip Yellow is used for all journals, including the general journal, combined journal, sales journal, cash receipts journal, purchases journal, and cash payments journal.

Blue is used for all statements, including the income statement, balance sheet, statement of owner's equity, retained earnings statement, and statement of cash flows.

Green is used for ledgers and other rulings, including the general ledger, trial balance, work sheet, accounts receivable ledger, accounts payable ledger, payroll register, and petty cash payments record.

- **Focus on Ethics** boxes precede the end-of-chapter material. The ramifications of not acting ethically are illustrated in these interesting accounts of crime and corruption.

Study Tip Use these examples to help you better understand how the accounting rules are applied in the business world.

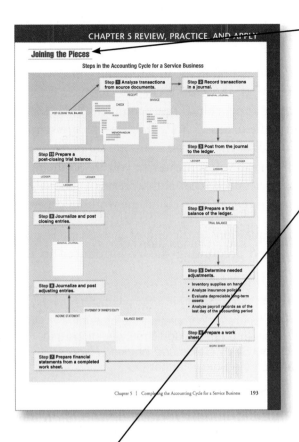

- **Joining the Pieces** presents an at-a-glance summary of the major concepts, entries, or terms contained in the chapter.

Study Tip Review this visual summary to see what you know and what you need to study further in the chapter.

- You may be accustomed to **chapter summaries**, but note that the summaries in this text offer extra value. Each summary restates the chapter's learning objectives and explains the objectives using detailed examples. The end-of-chapter work is also coded with learning objective references.

Study Tip Use the summary to review the chapter's key concepts and complete the corresponding exercises or problems to confirm that you have met the Learning Objectives stated at the beginning of the chapter.

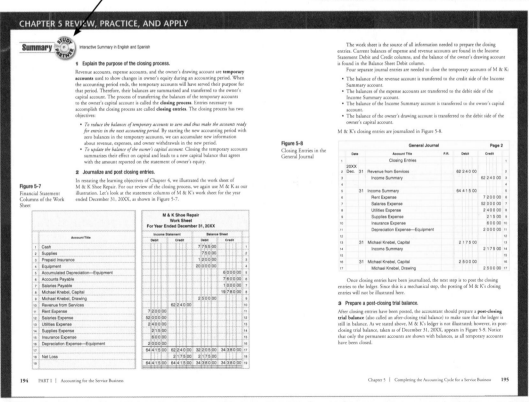

Concept Building Activities, Exercises, and Problems

To learn accounting best practices, it is important to apply the concepts and procedures by completing as many of the end-of-chapter activities in the Review, Practice, and Apply section as possible. Try to complete the work in the order it is presented, because the exercises and problems progress from beginning to mastery level. Almost all of the exercise items are supported with "Check Figures"—partial answers to help you confirm that you are on the right track to achieving the complete answer. All exercises and problems can be solved using either printed working papers or Excel 2007 electronic working papers.

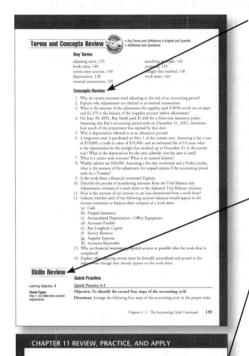

- **Concepts Review** questions at the end of each chapter cover the major topics and accounting theory introduced in the chapter.

> **Study Tip** To prepare for completing the chapter assessments, work through the additional questions that are available in the *Study Guide and Working Papers* supplement and on the Study Partner CD.

- The **Skills Review** section provides exercises that focus on specific chapter topics. The two groups of activities, "Quick Practice" and "Exercises," are keyed to the chapter-opening Learning Objectives.

- Two sets of **Case Problems** also appear at the end of each chapter: Groups A and B. The Case Problems cover the major topics of the chapter, and the specific topic covered is stated in the objective that introduces each problem. Select problems, identified with the logos (P) and (Q) can be solved using either Peachtree 2008 or QuickBooks 2008.

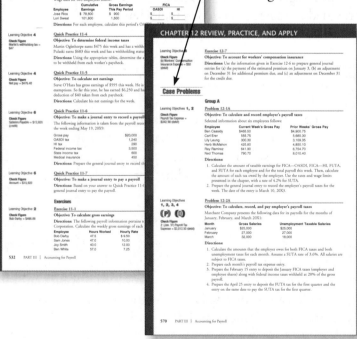

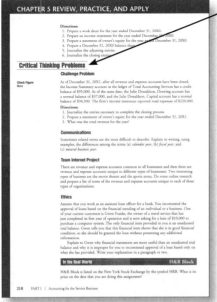

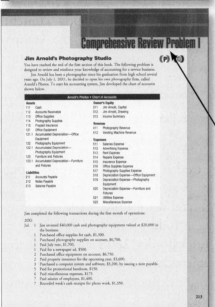

• Each chapter concludes with a set of five **Critical Thinking Problems** that assess your ability to apply what you have learned to a new situation. If you can accurately solve these problems, you can feel confident you have mastered the chapter concepts and skills.

➤ The **Challenge Problem** asks you to apply the major concepts in the chapter and requires more creative work than the other end-of-chapter activities.

➤ The **Communications** and **Ethics** problems ask you to write about or discuss your understanding of a concept presented in the chapter. These activities help you reflect on the reasons for the accounting procedures you have learned.

➤ The **Team Internet Project** presents a question or problem that you and one or more teammates will solve using the Internet. There may be more than one correct answer; the best answers will be complete and will include documentation of the sites referenced.

➤ The **In the Real World** exercise relates accounting concepts to the company featured in the Part introduction. These activities help you understand how H&R Block and other well-known companies use accounting concepts and accounting documents.

• A **Comprehensive Review Problem** follows each major segment of the book. These problems simulate a real accounting situation and require you to combine theory and procedures from several chapters. The *Study Guide and Working Papers* supplement includes forms to use in solving these problems. Work can also be completed using the Excel electronic working papers or Peachtree and QuickBooks templates, all provided as separate student supplements.

Additional Student Resources

The textbook is only one part of your set of tools for learning accounting. The following print-based and electronic supplements provide templates for completing exercises, self-tests to check your progress, extra content to expand and reinforce your knowledge, and online homework-checking with grading.

• **Study Partner CD.** The Study Partner CD study tool includes animated tutorials illustrating the complete service business accounting cycle. In addition, the CD provides several features to help you learn the accounting concepts taught in each chapter.

➤ Chapter-based glossary with English audio and Spanish translations of the key terms and definitions and flash cards

➤ Matching activities to reinforce chapter terms and concepts
➤ Interactive chapter summaries with English audio and Spanish translations
➤ Quizzing in Practice and Reported modes with feedback linked to learning objectives

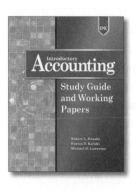

- *Study Guide and Working Papers.* In addition to providing forms to solve all of the end-of-chapter exercises and problems, the *Study Guide and Working Papers* includes a summary of each chapter as well as a practice test with answers. By completing the practice test, you can check your understanding of the chapter material and identify areas you should review. Each practice test contains true/false, matching, fill-in-the-blank, multiple choice, and short essay questions.

- **Internet Resource Center at www.emcp.net/accounting.** This companion Web site offers additional information and learning tools to help you succeed in your accounting course. The Study Notes documents available for download consist of chapter outlines, terms lists, and open-ended questions to guide the study of chapter content. Through the Web Links page, visit the Web sites for the companies highlighted in the In the Real World features as well as other informative accounting-related Web sites. And, if you ever leave your Study Partner CD at school, you can go online to review a tutorial, take a practice quiz, or complete an interactive matching activity.

- **Electronic Working Papers.** Excel 2007 spreadsheet files are available for working all of the end-of-chapter exercises and problems and comprehensive review problems. Files are designed with color coding for data entry and programmed with "Correct" and "Try Again" feedback on select cells.

- **Computerized Accounting with QuickBooks 2008 and Peachtree 2008.** Certain end-of-chapter Case Problems and all of the Comprehensive Review Problems are supported with QuickBooks and Peachtree templates. Look for icons next to the problems.

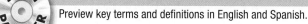

Introduction

Welcome to the exciting and challenging world of accounting. You are entering a system of recording and organizing data that keeps the entire Western Hemisphere *in balance*. Without accounting, our modern society, as we know it, could not operate.

Accounting is the *language of business*. Every firm and every individual needs accounting information to make good judgments and sensible business decisions. Only by using this information can owners or managers of businesses know if they are operating successfully.

Careers in Accounting

Accounting offers many job and career opportunities. Before learning about specific vocational opportunities in accounting, you should understand the difference between a job and a career.

A **job** is an activity that you perform for which you are paid. There are thousands of jobs in our country, ranging from actor to zookeeper. You will probably hold several different jobs in your lifetime, but you should consider whether these jobs will lead to a career. A **career** is a planned sequence of increasingly more challenging and better-paying positions, beginning with an entry-level job.

An **entry-level job** is a paid position that you can obtain because you have had certain educational training; you don't necessarily need previous work experience. Two specific entry-level accounting jobs are those of accounting clerk and bookkeeper, both obtainable with one year of accounting study.

An **accounting clerk** sorts, records, and files accounting data. The high volume of everyday financial events in

Every organization, regardless of size, needs accounting workers. Some small firms may employ only a single part-time bookkeeper, whereas companies such as Coca-Cola and IBM employ thousands of accounting and accounting support personnel.

many organizations requires full-time accounting clerks to maintain up-to-date records, both by hand and in computerized systems. In large organizations, an accounting clerk can specialize in areas such as accounts payable, accounts receivable, inventory, and payroll.

A **bookkeeper** performs general accounting tasks. Some bookkeepers also participate in the processes of summarizing and analyzing accounting

job an activity or task performed for pay

career a planned sequence of increasingly more challenging and better-paying positions that begin with an entry-level job

entry-level job a job requiring education but not necessarily work experience

> **Accounting Clerk**
> Local accounting firm is looking for an accounting clerk to assist in payroll and do bookkeeping tasks. Experience preferred but not required.

accounting clerk one who sorts, records, and files accounting data; usually considered an entry-level job

bookkeeper one whose primary job is to record financial information

1

data. The bookkeeper's duties vary depending on the organization's size and the extent to which the organization uses outside accounting services. A *full-charge bookkeeper* is responsible for the entire bookkeeping process and can supervise accounting clerks.

Accounting and bookkeeping are often thought of as being the same. Bookkeeping is, however, only one part of the accounting process; it is the recording part. While bookkeeping focuses on recording accounting data, accounting goes far beyond this and involves classifying, analyzing, and interpreting accounting data.

The pathway to a career can lead in many directions. A sound, fundamental knowledge of accounting allows you to navigate through the various paths to reach your career goal.

Advancement in Accounting Careers

accountant one who records, plans, summarizes, analyzes, and interprets financial information

An entry-level job is only the beginning of a career path. Many entry-level accounting jobs can lead to the job of accountant. An **accountant** records, plans, summarizes, analyzes, and interprets financial information. Accountants have practical experience and usually have college degrees.

Moving up the Career Ladder

career ladder a diagram showing the stages of advancement in a career field

A useful way to discuss a career path is by means of a **career ladder**, a diagram that shows how you can advance in a field. Figure I-1 shows the accounting career ladder of Katherine Spencer, as she envisions it.

Figure I-1
The Accounting Career Ladder

Certified Public Accountant
Education + Experience + CPA Exam

Professional Accountant
Education + Experience

Bookkeeper
Education + Experience

Accounting Clerk
Education

certified public accountant (CPA) an accountant who has met a state's education and experience requirement and has passed a comprehensive examination prepared by the American Institute of Certified Public Accountants (AICPA)

Katherine will start up the career ladder as an accounting clerk, based on her one year's study of accounting. She plans to move up the ladder after a year or two of work experience and become a bookkeeper. Katherine then plans to complete her bachelor's degree in the evenings and advance to the position of accountant. She must then acquire further experience and pass a comprehensive examination to reach her ultimate goal of becoming a **certified public accountant (CPA)**.

The requirements for becoming a CPA vary from state to state. In general, one must be a U.S. citizen, at least 21 years old, and a college graduate with a major concentration in accounting. Additionally, CPA candidates must pass a comprehensive two and one-half day examination in accounting and related subjects, such as law. Katherine plans to use both education and experience, the keys to a successful career, to advance in the profession of accounting.

Accounting as a Profession

accountancy the profession of accounting

The word *profession* usually brings to mind medicine, teaching, engineering, and law. These groups have certain common features that lead to their professional status: (1) required education, (2) a thorough and growing body of knowledge, (3) a code of professional ethics, and (4) professional organizations consisting of members of the group. Accounting also has these features, and it too is a profession. The profession of accounting is known as **accountancy**. All professions include fields within the profession. The accounting profession can be divided into four broad fields: (1) public accounting, (2) private accounting, (3) not-for-profit accounting, and (4) forensic accounting.

Public Accounting

public accountant an accountant who works on a fee basis for individuals and organizations

auditor an accountant who reviews a company's accounting systems, operations, and financial reports; also called an external auditor

A **public accountant** is a professional who, for a fee, performs services for individuals or for organizations. A public accountant does not work for any specific company, except as a member of a public accounting firm.

One of the principal services offered by public accountants is auditing. An **auditor** is an accountant who makes an independent review of a company's books to see if proper accounting procedures are being followed. Other services offered by public accountants include management advising, tax advising, and general accounting.

Private Accounting

private accountant an accountant who is employed by a specific company

controller the chief accountant or chief financial officer for an organization

A **private accountant** is employed by a specific company, such as a department store, a gas company, a manufacturing plant, or a restaurant. This category includes job titles such as *general accountant, industrial accountant, management accountant,* and *controller.* A **controller** is the chief accountant or chief financial officer for an organization.

Some accountants specialize in one aspect of accounting. *Tax accountant, cost accountant,* and *accounting instructor* are among the job titles of these professionals.

Not-for-Profit Accounting

A **not-for-profit accountant** works for a college or university, a public hospital, a public charity, a government (state, local, or federal) agency, or other organization that operates for an objective other than that of earning a profit.

In recent years, the not-for-profit sector of our economy has grown considerably. As a consequence, the demand for accounting workers in such organizations has grown.

Forensic Accounting

A **forensic accountant** works in most major accounting firms and is needed for investigating mergers and acquisitions, tax investigations, economic crime investigations, various types of civil litigation support, specialized audits, and even terrorist investigations. Forensic accountants work throughout the business world, including public accounting, corporations, and all branches of government (from the Federal Bureau of Investigation and Central Intelligence Agency to the offices of local authorities).

Accounting Concepts and Principles

The practice of accounting is guided by **generally accepted accounting principles (GAAP)**, which are rules that govern how accounting personnel measure, process, and report financial information. Table I-1 shows nine of these rules. Each will be discussed in greater detail in the book.

Organizations That Influence Accounting Practice

Many organizations directly or indirectly influence GAAP. The most important of these organizations are the American Institute of Certified Public Accountants, the Financial Accounting Standards Board, the Securities and Exchange Commission, and the Internal Revenue Service.

American Institute of Certified Public Accountants

The American Institute of Certified Public Accountants (AICPA) is a professional association whose membership is made up of CPAs in public practice, private business, education, and government. Over the years, the AICPA has had a very strong influence on the development of GAAP. From 1938 to 1958, the AICPA's Committee on Accounting Procedures issued a series of pronouncements dealing with the development of accounting standards, principles, and procedures. In 1959, the AICPA organized the Accounting Principles Board (APB) to replace the Committee on Accounting

Table I-1 Generally Accepted Accounting Principles (GAAP)

Principle	Definition
Adequate disclosure	Financial reports of a business contain all the information that is needed to determine the business's financial condition.
Business entity concept	The financial records of a business are kept separate from the personal financial records of the owners of the business.
Consistency	The same accounting procedures are followed from one accounting period to another unless there is valid reason to change.
Cost principle	All goods and services acquired by a business are recorded at their actual cost (also called *historical cost*).
Going concern concept	Financial reports of a business are prepared with the expectation that the business will remain in operation indefinitely.
Matching principle	Revenue (income) earned during an accounting period is recorded in the same period as the expenses associated with earning that revenue.
Materiality	Accounting records and reports are prepared according to the guidelines set by GAAP. However, accountants can handle very small amounts (such as the purchase of a screwdriver for $.69) in the easiest and quickest way.
Objective evidence	Financial events recorded in accounting records are supported by written source documents.
Realization principle	A business earns (realizes) revenue when goods or services are sold to customers, even though cash may not be collected until sometime in the future.

Procedures. From 1959 to 1973, the APB issued a number of opinions that had a strong influence on accounting practice.

Financial Accounting Standards Board

In 1973, the Financial Accounting Standards Board (FASB) was established to develop financial accounting standards for private business and not-for-profit organizations. The FASB is governed by a board of trustees that includes the president of the AICPA and other members who are elected by the AICPA.

Securities and Exchange Commission

The Securities and Exchange Commission (SEC) is an agency of the U.S. government that was established in 1934 to regulate the sale of stock to the public. Although the SEC was given the power to set and enforce accounting practices for companies whose securities are sold to the general public, it has generally relied on the accounting profession to perform these functions. In very few cases has the SEC exercised its legal authority by disagreeing with a position taken by the AICPA or the FASB.

Internal Revenue Service

The Internal Revenue Service (IRS) interprets and enforces the income tax laws and regulations that are passed by Congress. Through these functions, the IRS has a direct effect on accounting practice as it relates to taxes.

Professional Certifications in Accounting

As we have learned, there are many career opportunities in accounting and many career paths from which to choose. Regardless of the career path you may choose, you may want to pursue a professional certification. Professional certifications broaden your job opportunities, increase your chances for advancement and promotion, and increase your earnings potential. There are several professional certifications in accounting. In this section, we will discuss five common certifications.

Certified Public Accountant

The AICPA administers the Certified Public Accountant exam. Each state has its own requirements for sitting for the exam. Check with the Board of Accountancy in your state to obtain current information regarding educational requirements to sit for the CPA exam and the amount of job experience required before the CPA certificate will be issued. At the time of this writing, 46 states have passed legislation requiring CPA candidates to complete 150 semester hours (or 225 quarter hours) of college credit before becoming eligible to sit for the CPA exam. This translates into five years of college. Many CPA candidates continue their education to obtain a master's degree before sitting for the CPA exam.

Most CPAs work for CPA firms or are self-employed. The size of a CPA firm ranges from one person to firms with national operations and thousands of employees.

Certified Fraud Examiner

Generally, applicants for the Certified Fraud Examiner (CFE) certification have a minimum of a bachelor's degree (or equivalent) from an institution of higher learning. No specific field of study is required. If you do not have a bachelor's degree, you may substitute two years of fraud-related professional experience for each year of academic study. For example, if you successfully attended college full-time for only two years, you would need an additional four years of professional experience to satisfy the educational requirements. When you apply to take the exam, you will be awarded qualifying points for the amount of education you have.

At the time you are certified, you must have at least two years of professional experience in a field either directly or indirectly related to the detection or deterrence of fraud.

Certified Internal Auditor

The Certified Internal Auditor (CIA) designation is the only globally accepted certification for internal auditors. The CIA remains the standard by which individuals demonstrate their competency and professionalism in the internal auditing field.

An **internal auditor** works for a specific organization, as opposed to an **external auditor**, such as a CPA, who, for a fee, reviews the records of a business to provide written assurance to the general public that the business's financial reports are fairly presented and prepared in conformity with GAAP. For example, PepsiCo, makers of Pepsi Cola, employs internal auditors who continuously review various aspects of the company's operations and accounting functions. Once a year, PepsiCo also employs an independent CPA firm to review the company's financial reports to ensure that they are accurate and prepared according to the standards of the profession.

CIA candidates must hold a bachelor's degree or its equivalent from an accredited college or university. For this certification, work experience will not substitute for any part of the appropriate degree requirement. A copy of the candidate's diploma, transcripts, or other written proof of completion of a degree program must accompany the candidate's application.

To prepare for the CIA exam, self-study programs, such as Gleim's self-study CIA program, are available that provide educational experience, information, and business tools that can be applied immediately in any organization or business environment.

The Institute of Internal Auditors (IIA) will accept student candidates into the CIA program who (1) are in their senior year of college or enrolled as a graduate student, (2) have full-time student status as defined by the institution in which they are enrolled (a minimum of 12 semester hours or its equivalent is required for undergraduate students and nine semester hours for graduate students), and (3) register for and take the CIA exam while enrolled in school.

Certified Management Accountant

The Institute of Management Accountants (IMA) allows candidates to sit for the Certified Management Accountant (CMA) exam if either one of the two requirements is met:

- The candidate has a bachelor's degree from an accredited college or university.
- The candidate has been awarded a score in the 50th percentile or higher on either the Graduate Management Admission Test (GMAT) or Graduate Record Examination (GRE). If the candidate passes the CMA exam without a college degree, the candidate must earn a bachelor's degree from an accredited college or university within seven years of passing the CMA exam in order to receive the CMA certificate.

Once the CMA exam has been passed, the candidate must complete two continuous years of professional experience in management accounting or financial management. The experience requirement may be completed before applying to take the exam or within seven years of passing the exam.

Certified Bookkeeper

Most professional certifications require at least a four-year degree. An exception is the **certified bookkeeper (CB)**, which recognizes bookkeeping as a profession and bookkeepers as professionals. The following are the three requirements for becoming a certified bookkeeper:

- **Experience**   Have at least two years of full-time experience or the part-time or freelance equivalent.
- **Examination**   Pass a four-part examination administered by the American Institute of Professional Bookkeepers (AIPB).
- **Code of Ethics**   Sign a code of ethics.

To learn more about the AIPB and how to become a CB, go to *AIPB.org*.

Computers and Accounting

Creating both challenge and opportunity, the computer has dramatically influenced the way we process accounting data. The computer has taken over most of the time-consuming and mundane pencil-pushing tasks associated with manual accounting systems, thus freeing accounting workers to do more important tasks. With a click of a button, computers process data with incredible speed and accuracy and generate financial reports that at one time could take days to prepare. The information provided by computers offers managers a better basis for decision making and planning.

The availability of powerful and inexpensive computerized accounting software programs—such as Peachtree and QuickBooks—brought the power of the computer to the smallest of businesses. Other commercial software programs, such as Microsoft Dynamics GP (formerly Microsoft Great Plains), offer cost-effective solutions for managing and integrating finances, e-commerce, accounting, customer relationships, and human resource management. Some businesses hire software development firms to develop or customize a system tailored to the specific needs of the business operations.

Regardless of how automated and sophisticated accounting systems become, however, you need a firm foundation in basic accounting principles and procedures. Only by having such a foundation can you understand the accounting process and how information moves through various types of accounting systems. Study the early chapters of this text well; they will form the foundation on which all your further accounting knowledge will rest.

PART 1

Accounting for the Service Business

In the Real World

H&R Block is the world's largest tax service company, with over 12,500 offices in the United States and 1,300 among the countries of Canada, Australia, and the United Kingdom. In 2007, the company had over 20 million clients and filed nearly half of all the tax returns filed electronically with the Internal Revenue Service. The organization offers tax preparation services and guidance, financial advice in such areas as banking and investing, and other financial services such as mortgage assistance. A full list of services can be found on its home page, *www.hrblock.com*.

The corporation is an example of American entrepreneurship, as two brothers, Henry and Richard Bloch, founded the company in 1955 in Kansas City, Missouri, with the goal of helping individuals and the small business person. Today, its world headquarters is located in a 17-story building on Main Street in Kansas City. It is a major service company, one that might be a career choice for you when you complete your college degree.

Speaking of career opportunities, there are many with H&R Block. You may work in the call center, at the corporate headquarters, or at a tax office on a full-time or seasonal basis. There are also opportunities in buying or opening your own office as a franchise of H&R Block.

In Part I, you will have the chance to work with data from H&R Block and apply what you have learned to the first of several real-world businesses in this text. Two types of this service firm's financial statements are shown in Part I: the balance sheets at the end of Chapter 1 and the income statements at the end of Chapter 4. The end-of-chapter exercise titled "In the Real World" asks you to locate and report certain kinds of data and to compare H&R Block's financial statements with those presented in the chapters of Part I.

CHAPTER

1

The Nature of Accounting

Learning Objectives

1 Define *accounting* and related terms.
2 Explain who uses accounting information.
3 Identify four forms of business organizations and three types of business operations.
4 Define and describe the elements of accounting.
5 State the accounting equation.
6 Define *business transaction*.
7 Record business transactions in equation form.
8 Identify four types of transactions that affect owner's equity.
9 Prepare three basic financial statements.
10 Define *ethics* and explain the importance of ethical behavior in modern business.

On a farm in Maine, Drew Beedy is counting this year's crop of potatoes. At home in North Dakota, Janice Graham is trying to reach an agreement between her checkbook records and her bank statement for the month. In a clothing factory in southern California, Lynn Bennett is trying to keep accurate records of uniforms that are being produced for the armed forces. In an office in Maryland, Ray Clermont is calculating the amount of his take-home pay for the week so he can decide how much to set aside for a new car. All of these individuals, along with millions of other Americans and American organizations, are practicing accounting.

What Is Accounting and Who Uses It?

Learning Objective

1 Define *accounting* and related terms.

accounting the process of recording, summarizing, analyzing, and interpreting financial (money-related) activities to permit individuals and organizations to make informed judgments and decisions

Accounting is the process of recording, summarizing, analyzing, and interpreting financial (money-related) activities to permit individuals and organizations to make informed judgments and decisions. *Recording* means making written records of events. *Summarizing* is the process of combining these written records, at regular intervals, into reports. *Analyzing* means examining these reports by breaking them down in order to determine financial success or failure. *Interpreting* involves the use of financial data to make sound decisions and explain how well a company is meeting its objectives. Accounting combines these four activities—recording, summarizing, analyzing, and interpreting—into a single process and applies this process to financial activities.

Accounting goes beyond bookkeeping. Accountants also summarize, analyze, interpret, and report financial information.

A common impression is that accounting is a narrow, specialized field that serves only a part of our society. This impression is incorrect, for every individual and every organization in America needs accounting. As Table 1-1 shows, many individuals and groups use the accounting language in important, decisive ways.

Accounting has often been called the *language of business*. This title is appropriate, because a language allows people to communicate to others. In financial terms, accounting is used to communicate information about a business to those who have a need or legal right to know.

Learning Objective

2 Explain who uses accounting information.

business an organization that operates with the objective of earning a profit

sole proprietorship a business owned by one person

Learning Objective

3 Identify four forms of business organizations and three types of business operations.

Forms of Business Organization

A **business** is an organization that operates with the objective of earning a profit. The four major forms of business organization in this country are the sole proprietorship, the partnership, the corporation, and the limited liability company.

A **sole proprietorship** is a business owned by one person. This person, called the proprietor, receives all profits or losses and is personally liable for the

Table 1-1 Users of Accounting Information

Users	Use of Accounting Information
Individuals	Individuals, such as Janice Graham and Ray Clermont, must understand accounting to function personally within our society, which is very dependent on financial activities. They—and you—keep checkbooks and other bank records, receive paychecks, pay taxes, use charge cards, borrow money, and purchase a variety of products and services.
Owners	Business owners, such as Drew Beedy and Lynn Bennett, must understand accounting to achieve success in their organizations. Very often, the owners do not actually run the business. In such cases, the owners rely on accounting information to determine how well their businesses are being managed.
Managers	Managers use accounting data extensively in deciding on alternatives, such as what to sell, how to price, and when to expand the product line.
Investors	Investors use accounting data for insights on the financial condition of potential investments when deciding whether to invest in a business.
Banks and other lending institutions	Lenders, such as banks, use accounting data in deciding whether to approve a loan.
Governments	Governmental units (federal, state, and local) also record, summarize, analyze, and interpret financial events to operate with limited resources.
Tax authorities	Tax authorities use accounting data reported to the government in deciding whether a business is complying with tax rules and regulations. Since our country has an extensive taxing system, this is a major use of accounting data.

A sole proprietorship may have many employees, but there is only one owner—the sole proprietor.

Key Point ⊘

A partnership is similar to a proprietorship except that a partnership has two or more owners.

partnership a business co-owned by two or more people

corporation a form of business organization that is owned by stockholders

limited liability company (LLC) a type of business organization that combines features of a corporation and those of a partnership or sole proprietorship

Key Point ⊘

Businesses are usually organized as proprietorships, partnerships, corporations, or LLCs.

service business a business that performs services for customers to earn a profit

merchandising business a business that purchases goods produced by others and then sells them to customers to earn a profit

obligations of the business. Sole proprietorships represent about 70% of all businesses in the United States; however, most of them are small businesses.

A **partnership** is a form of business that is co-owned by two or more persons. The partners enter into a contract, written or oral, that sets forth how the business will be run and how profits and losses will be divided. Partnerships comprise about 10% of business organizations in the United States. Most are small- to medium-sized operations; however, some are huge, with 1,000 or more partners.

A **corporation** is a form of business that is owned by investors called stockholders. Unlike a proprietorship or a partnership, a corporation is legally separate from its owners. This means that the corporation itself, and not the owners, is responsible for its obligations. If a corporation goes bankrupt, lenders cannot take the personal possessions of the stockholders. Corporations comprise about 20% of all business organizations in the United States. However, they generate 90% of the total dollar volume of business. Most large companies are organized as corporations.

A **limited liability company (LLC)** is a relatively new form of business that combines features of a corporation and those of proprietorships and partnerships. Like stockholders of a corporation, owners of an LLC are not personally responsible for the debts of the business. Other features of LLCs are more like a partnership, or a proprietorship if there is only one owner. The LLC is becoming a popular form of ownership for small businesses because the owners are shielded from the company's debts.

Types of Business Operations

The most common types of business operations in this country are the service business, the merchandising business, and the manufacturing business. Table 1-2 shows some well-known businesses listed according to the type of operation.

A **service business** performs services for customers to earn a profit. Examples of service businesses include doctors, lawyers, engineers, barber shops, beauty salons, dry cleaners, and public accounting firms.

A **merchandising business** purchases goods produced by others and then sells these goods to customers. Examples of merchandising businesses include department stores, supermarkets, antique dealers, and music stores.

▌Take This Into Account

The world's largest retailer, Wal-Mart, is a merchandising business organized as a corporation.

Table 1-2 Examples of Business Operations

Service Businesses		Merchandising Businesses		Manufacturing Businesses	
Company Name	Service	Company Name	Product	Company Name	Product
Aflac	Insurance	Amazon.com	Books, music, and videos	Ben & Jerry's	Ice cream
AT&T	Telephone and wireless communication	Baskin-Robbins	Ice cream	Coca-Cola	Beverages
Gold's Gym	Fitness and personal training	Burger King	Food, restaurant	General Motors	Cars and trucks
Google	Internet search engine	The Gap	Apparel	Harley-Davidson	Motorcycles
H&R Block	Tax and financial services	Home Depot	Household and building materials	H.J. Heinz	Food
Hertz	Car rentals	Neiman Marcus	Clothing and accessories	IBM	Computers
Merrill Lynch	Financial services	Outback Steakhouse	Food, restaurant	Kellogg	Breakfast cereal
United Parcel Service (UPS)	Package delivery	Sears	General merchandise	Levi Strauss	Clothing
Viacom	Pay TV	Toys"R"Us	Toys and clothing	Microsoft	Computer software
Waste Management	Waste disposal	Wal-Mart	General merchandise	Sony	Stereo, TVs, games

manufacturing business a business that produces a product to sell to its customers to earn a profit

A **manufacturing business** produces a product to sell to its customers. Examples of manufacturing businesses include automobile manufacturers, toy manufacturers, and bakeries.

The Elements of Accounting

Learning Objective

4 Define and describe the elements of accounting.

Tutorial 1

Understanding the Accounting Equation

In 1494, an Italian monk named Luca Pacioli published a mathematics text entitled *Summa Mathematica*. For the first time, a complete description was given of a way of keeping business records that had gradually developed over many centuries. The double-entry system described by Pacioli was to become the basis of our modern accounting system. The double-entry system is a simple system based on three elements: *assets*, *liabilities*, and *owner's equity*.

Assets

asset an item with a money value owned by a business

An **asset** is an item with money value that is owned by a business. This definition contains two key phrases, the first of which is "with money value." An item must have a dollar value to be recorded in accounting records. Therefore, while good health is an asset to you, it is not an asset in accounting, because no definite dollar value can be placed on it.

The second key phrase is "owned by a business." An owner's personal car is not classified as a business asset, because the car is not used for business purposes.

cash an asset including currency (paper money), coins, checks, and money orders made payable to the business

A business has several types—or groupings—of assets, which normally include cash, accounts receivable, equipment, and supplies. The asset **cash** includes currency (paper money), coins, checks, and money orders made payable to the business. To calculate the value of cash, the amount of each item is totaled.

Businesses often sell goods or services on credit to customers. When goods and services are sold on credit, they are sold with the understanding that payment will be received at a later date. The asset arising from selling goods or services on credit to a customer is called **accounts receivable**. Stated another way, an account receivable is a dollar amount due from a credit customer.

The asset **equipment** includes the physical assets that a business needs in order to operate. Among these physical assets are office equipment (copiers and computers), office furniture (desks and chairs), store equipment (cash registers and display cases), and delivery equipment (vans and trucks). In addition to equipment, other physical assets include land, buildings, and machinery. These types of assets have several common features: (1) they are **tangible** (capable of being touched); (2) they are expected to be used in the operation of the business, not sold to customers; and (3) they are expected to last for at least one year.

The asset **supplies**, like equipment, includes physical items needed to operate a business. Unlike equipment, however, supplies are usually used up within a year. Common examples of supplies are office supplies (pens, stamps, paper, and printer toner), store supplies (string, bags, and wrapping paper), and delivery supplies (boxes, tape, and mailing labels).

Liabilities

A **liability** is a debt owed by the business. In our economy, it is not always possible or convenient to pay cash for everything that is obtained. Thus, it is common for businesses—even very large and profitable businesses—to regularly purchase goods and services on credit. The liability that results from purchasing goods and services on credit is called **accounts payable**. The person or business to whom an account payable is owed is called a **creditor**.

Another form of liability is the **note payable**, which is a formal written promise to pay a specified amount at a definite future date. A note payable is commonly issued when money is borrowed or when property is mortgaged. We will discuss other forms of liabilities in later chapters. Regardless of the form, however, a liability represents a creditor's claim against the assets of a business.

Owner's Equity

Assets are owned, and liabilities are owed. The difference between the two is the part of the business that the owner can claim—the owner's equity. **Owner's equity** is the excess of assets over liabilities. For example, if a business has assets of $30,000 and liabilities of $10,000, the owner's equity is $20,000, the difference between the two. Owner's equity is also called capital, proprietorship, and net worth.

accounts receivable the asset arising from selling goods or services on credit to customers

equipment a physical asset used by a business in its operations

tangible capable of being touched; the quality of a physical asset

supplies short-term physical assets needed in the operation of a business

liability a debt owed to a creditor, a party outside of the business

accounts payable the liability that results from purchasing goods or services on credit

creditor a business or person to whom a debt is owed

note payable a formal written promise to pay a specified amount at a definite future date

owner's equity the difference between assets and liabilities; also referred to as capital, proprietorship, and net worth

accounting equation
the equation that expresses the relationship between the accounting elements in a simple mathematical form: assets = liabilities + owner's equity; also referred to as the basic accounting equation

Key Point ⊘

Assets | Liabilities + Owner's Equity

The Accounting Equation

The relationship among the accounting elements can be expressed in a simple mathematical form known as the **accounting equation** or the *basic accounting equation:*

Assets = Liabilities + Owner's Equity

or, in symbolic form:

A = L + OE

For example, on December 31, 20X2, Jeanette Deese has business assets of $30,000, business liabilities of $10,000, and owner's equity of $20,000. Her accounting equation is:

Assets	=	Liabilities	+	Owner's Equity
$30,000	=	$10,000	+	$20,000

or

$30,000	=	$30,000

Note that the left side of the accounting equation (the asset side) balances with the right side of the equation (the liabilities and owner's equity side). Also note that in the accounting equation, liabilities are placed before owner's equity. This is done because the creditors' claim to assets (liabilities) takes legal priority over the owner's claim to assets (owner's equity).

If two elements of the accounting equation are known, the third can always be found. For example, if assets total $10,000 and liabilities total $6,000, what is the owner's equity? The accounting equation can be rewritten as follows:

Assets	−	Liabilities	=	Owner's Equity

then,

A	−	L	=	OE
$10,000	−	$6,000	=	$4,000

Review Quiz 1-1   Find the missing element in each of the following.

	A	=	L	+	OE
(a)	$40,000		$25,000		$_____
(b)	$_____		$38,000		$52,000
(c)	$70,000		$_____		$48,000
(d)	$75,000		$ 0		$_____

Check your answers on page 52.

Business Transactions and the Accounting Equation

Learning Objective

6 Define *business transaction.*

transaction any activity that changes the value of a firm's assets, liabilities, or owner's equity

The value of a firm's assets, liabilities, and owner's equity changes constantly as everyday business occurs. Any activity that changes the value of a firm's assets, liabilities, or owner's equity is called a **transaction**. Any event that does not cause such a change is not a transaction. For example, firing an employee does not change the value of any asset, liability, or owner's equity item, so it is not a transaction. Table 1-3 shows some examples of business transactions.

The last business transaction in Table 1-3 leads to an important accounting concept. For accounting purposes, the owner of a business and the business itself are considered to be two separate units. The **business entity concept**, one of the many concepts that guide how accounting is done, states that for accounting purposes, a business is a distinct economic entity or unit that is separate from its owner and from any other business. For example, in addition to personal items, Ginger Dennis owns a Ben & Jerry's ice cream parlor, a Subway restaurant franchise, and a Roni Deutch Tax Center franchise. Ginger's personal items and each of her three businesses are separate accounting units.

Table 1-3 Examples of Business Transactions

Purchase of equipment on credit
Cash payment to a creditor
Receipt of cash for services rendered to a customer
Purchase of supplies for cash
Payment of rent for the month
Payment of utility bill
Receipt of a bill to be paid later
Payment to employees for the payroll
Owner investment of cash in the business

Understanding the Dual Effect of Business Transactions

As stated earlier, total assets must always equal liabilities plus owner's equity. In other words, the accounting equation—A = L + OE—must always balance. To maintain this balance, transactions are recorded as having a **dual effect** on the basic accounting elements. For example, assume that the O'Malley Company purchased equipment for $3,000 on credit. This transaction has two effects on the accounting elements: (1) since an asset was acquired, assets increase; and (2) since the asset was purchased on credit, liabilities also increase.

Assets	=	Liabilities	+	Owner's Equity
+$3,000		+$3,000		

Assets (on one side of the equation) increased by $3,000, while liabilities (on the other side of the equation) also increased by $3,000, thus maintaining the equation in balance.

Summing Up

> Every business transaction has at least two effects on the accounting equation. This is a rule that will always hold true.

Recording the Effect of Transactions on the Accounting Equation

As we just saw, the effect of business transactions can be stated in terms of changes in the basic elements of the accounting equation. To determine exactly how the equation is affected, each transaction must be *analyzed*, that is, broken down to determine how it affects the accounting elements. After analysis, the changes that result can be recorded. To illustrate, let's look at the transactions completed by Marilyn Johnson during July 20X3. Marilyn is an attorney who decided to open her own law practice. The following transactions took place during her first month of operation. Each transaction is analyzed and recorded in an *expanded accounting equation*.

Transaction (a): Marilyn Invested $20,000 Cash to Start Her Business

An owner's investment is a contribution of assets to the business. Marilyn's investment of $20,000 increased the assets of her firm from $0 to $20,000. It also increased her equity in the firm by the same amount because the $20,000 came from Marilyn, not from a creditor. Thus, both assets and owner's equity increased by $20,000. After this transaction, Marilyn's accounting equation appears as follows:

	Assets	=	Liabilities	+	Owner's Equity	
	Cash	=		+	Marilyn Johnson, Capital	*Description*
(a)	+$20,000				+$20,000	Investment

Note that the asset Cash is individually named. Also note that Marilyn's equity in the business is shown as Marilyn Johnson, Capital. If Marilyn had invested another asset at the same time, such as equipment, each asset would have been increased, and Marilyn Johnson, Capital would have been increased by the total amount of both assets.

Transaction (b): Purchased Equipment for $30,000 on Credit

This transaction caused an increase in an asset and a corresponding increase in a liability. Specifically, the asset Equipment and the liability Accounts Payable were increased by $30,000. The effect on the equation is as follows.

	Assets			=	Liabilities	+	Owner's Equity
	Cash	+	Equipment	=	Accounts Payable	+	Marilyn Johnson, Capital
(a)	$20,000						+$20,000
(b)			+$30,000		+$30,000		
Bal.	$20,000	+	$30,000	=	$30,000	+	$20,000
		$50,000				$50,000	

Note that we subtotaled the items after the second transaction. The subtotals (called *balances*) allow a quick check to see if the equation is still in balance.

Transaction (c): Purchased Supplies for Cash, $2,000

As a result of this transaction, the firm's supplies increased by $2,000, but the firm's cash decreased by the same $2,000. This is called a **shift in assets**; that is, the individual assets changed, but the total dollar value of assets remained the same. The effect on the equation is as follows.

	Assets			=	Liabilities	+	Owner's Equity
	Cash	+ Supplies +	Equipment	=	Accounts Payable	+	Marilyn Johnson, Capital
Bal.	$20,000		$30,000		$30,000		$20,000
(c)	−2,000	+$2,000					
Bal.	$18,000 +	$2,000 +	$30,000	=	$30,000	+	$20,000

$50,000 — $50,000

As you study this recording, note that dollar signs are used only in two circumstances: (1) next to the first entry in a column and (2) next to the balance. Also note that when a shift in assets occurs, only the asset side of the equation changes.

The assets purchased in Transactions (b) and (c) were recorded at cost, which leads to another fundamental concept of accounting—the cost principle. The **cost principle** states that when purchased, all assets are recorded at their actual cost regardless of market value. The actual value of the equipment purchased in Transaction (b) may have been more or less than $30,000. This, however, is not considered when the transaction is recorded. The firm paid $30,000 for the equipment; thus, $30,000 is recorded.

Transaction (d): Performed Legal Services for Clients and Collected $900 Cash

Marilyn operates a service business, the practice of law. Her major activity is service to clients, for which she receives cash. In this transaction, Marilyn has earned **revenue**—income from carrying out the major activity of a firm—which increases the value of her business. Thus, both the asset Cash and Marilyn Johnson, Capital increased by $900. The effect on the equation is as follows:

	Assets			=	Liabilities	+	Owner's Equity		
					Accounts		Marilyn Johnson,		
	Cash	+ Supplies +	Equipment	=	Payable	+	Capital	+ Revenue	Description
Bal.	$18,000	$2,000	$30,000		$30,000		$20,000		
(d)	+900							+$900	Legal fees
Bal.	$18,900 +	$2,000 +	$30,000	=	$30,000	+	$20,000	+ $900	

$50,900 — $50,900

Notice that we set up a separate column for recording revenue under the Owner's Equity heading. We did this so that the amount of revenue could easily be determined at any time. Another way to record the revenue would have been simply to add it to the balance of Marilyn Johnson, Capital. Regardless of how we record revenue, however, keep in mind that revenue *always* increases owner's equity.

> ! Take This Into Account
>
> Other terms may be used to describe certain kinds of revenue, such as *fees earned* for amounts charged by a physician, *fares earned* for amounts received by a taxi service, *sales* for the sale of merchandise by a merchandising business, and *rent income* for amounts received on property that is rented to others.

Transaction (e): Paid Salaries of Employees, $1,500

expenses the costs of operating a business; does not provide a future benefit to the business and is thus a reduction in owner's equity

Expenses are costs related to operating a business. Unlike the cost of an asset, however, the cost of an expense does not provide a future benefit to the business. Therefore, expenses *decrease* the value of the business. In this transaction, salaries of $1,500 were paid. As shown below, the effect on the equation is a decrease in the asset Cash and a decrease in Marilyn Johnson, Capital.

	Assets			=	Liabilities	+		Owner's Equity			
					Accounts		Marilyn Johnson,				
	Cash	+ Supplies +	Equipment	=	Payable	+	Capital	+ Revenue	– Expenses	*Description*
Bal.	$18,900	$2,000	$30,000		$30,000		$20,000	$900		
(e)	–1,500								+$1,500	Salaries expense
Bal.	$17,400 +	$2,000 +	$30,000	=	$30,000	+	$20,000	+ $900	– $1,500	
		$49,400					$49,400			

Key Point ⊙

An increase in an expense decreases owner's equity. An expense decreases the value of a business.

Notice that, as with revenue, we set up a separate column for recording expenses under the Owner's Equity heading. Notice also that the decrease in owner's equity caused by the expense is shown by increasing an expense entitled Salaries Expense. *An increase in an expense decreases owner's equity.* Another way to record the expense would have been to subtract it directly from the balance of Marilyn Johnson, Capital.

> **CAUTION**
>
> Expenses decrease owner's equity. The decrease is recorded by increasing individual expenses. By increasing expenses, we are simply accumulating the total of expenses incurred during the month so that the total can be subtracted from owner's equity at the end of the month.

Transaction (f): Paid $5,000 of the Amount Owed on Equipment

A liability is a debt that must be paid. When all or part of a debt is paid, less is owed to creditors. Therefore, Marilyn's $5,000 payment decreased her liabilities. Since the payment was made in cash, the asset Cash also decreased. The effect on the equation is shown below.

	Assets			=	Liabilities	+		Owner's Equity			
					Accounts		Marilyn Johnson,				
	Cash	+ Supplies +	Equipment	=	Payable	+	Capital	+ Revenue	– Expenses	*Description*
Bal.	$17,400	$2,000	$30,000		$30,000		$20,000	$900	$1,500	
(f)	–5,000				–5,000					
Bal.	$12,400 +	$2,000 +	$30,000	=	$25,000	+	$20,000	+ $900	– $1,500	
		$44,400					$44,400			

Transaction (g): Marilyn Withdrew $700 Cash from the Business for Her Personal Use

withdrawal the removal of business assets for the owner's personal use

Unlike employees, the owner of a business does not receive a salary. Consequently, it is common for the owner to withdraw cash or other assets for personal use. An owner's **withdrawal**—the removal of business assets for personal use—has the dual effect of decreasing both the asset taken and the value of the business.

In this case, Marilyn withdrew cash. The effect on the equation is a decrease in the asset Cash and a decrease in Marilyn Johnson, Capital.

	Assets			=	Liabilities	+	Owner's Equity			
	Cash +	Supplies +	Equipment	=	Accounts Payable	+	Marilyn Johnson, Capital	+ Revenue	– Expenses	Description
Bal.	$12,400	$2,000	$30,000		$25,000		$20,000	$900	$1,500	
(g)	– 700						– 700			Withdrawal
Bal.	$11,700 +	$2,000 +	$30,000	=	$25,000	+	$19,300	+ $900	– $1,500	
		$43,700						$43,700		

Key Point

Withdrawals *always* decrease owner's equity.

Notice that, unlike revenue and expenses, we did not provide a separate column for recording owner withdrawals. As a rule, withdrawals don't occur as frequently as revenue and expenses. As a result, we recorded Marilyn's withdrawal by subtracting it directly from the balance of Marilyn Johnson, Capital. Remember that withdrawals *always* decrease owner's equity.

Transaction (h): Performed Additional Services for Clients, Receiving $2,600 Cash

As stated in the analysis of Transaction (d), cash received for services performed increases Cash and Owner's Equity. The effect on the equation is as follows.

	Assets			=	Liabilities	+	Owner's Equity			
	Cash +	Supplies +	Equipment	=	Accounts Payable	+	Marilyn Johnson, Capital	+ Revenue	– Expenses	Description
Bal.	$11,700	$2,000	$30,000		$25,000		$19,300	$ 900	$1,500	
(h)	+2,600							+2,600		Legal fees
Bal.	$14,300 +	$2,000 +	$30,000	=	$25,000	+	$19,300	+ $3,500	– $1,500	
		$46,300						$46,300		

Transaction (i): Paid Two Additional Expenses: Utilities, $250, and Office Rent, $600

As stated in the analysis of Transaction (e), expenses decrease owner's equity. And since cash was paid, assets also decrease. Marilyn's equation now appears as follows.

	Assets			=	Liabilities	+	Owner's Equity			
	Cash +	Supplies +	Equipment	=	Accounts Payable	+	Marilyn Johnson, Capital	+ Revenue	– Expenses	Description
Bal.	$14,300	$2,000	$30,000		$25,000		$19,300	$3,500	$1,500	
(i)	–250								+250	Utilities expense
	–600								+600	Rent expense
Bal.	$13,450 +	$2,000 +	$30,000	=	$25,000	+	$19,300	+ $3,500	– $2,350	
		$45,450						$45,450		

Summing Up

- Revenue always increases owner's equity.
- Expenses always decrease owner's equity.
- Owner withdrawals always decrease owner's equity.

Transaction (j): Performed Legal Services for a Client on Credit, $500

In this transaction, Marilyn performed legal services and expects to receive payment in the future. As we discussed earlier, selling goods or services on credit increases the asset Accounts Receivable, which is the measure of cash to be received from credit customers. Selling goods or services on credit also increases owner's equity because revenue is earned. According to the **realization principle**, revenue is recorded when it is earned, even though cash may not be received until later. After recording this transaction, Marilyn's equation appears as follows:

	Assets				=	Liabilities	+	Owner's Equity			
		Accounts				Accounts		Marilyn Johnson,			
	Cash	+ Receivable	+ Supplies	+ Equipment	=	Payable	+	Capital	+ Revenue	– Expenses	Description
Bal.	$13,450		$2,000	$30,000		$25,000		$19,300	$3,500	$2,350	
(j)		+$500							+500		Legal fees
Bal.	$13,450 +	$500	+ $2,000	+ $30,000	=	$25,000	+	$19,300	+ $4,000	– $2,350	
	└─────────────── $45,950 ───────────────┘					└──────────────────── $45,950 ────────────────────┘					

Transaction (k): Received $300 Cash as Partial Payment for Services Performed on Account

In this transaction, Marilyn received cash for services that she had performed on account earlier, in Transaction (j). The effect on her equation is an increase in the asset Cash and a decrease in another asset, Accounts Receivable.

	Assets				=	Liabilities	+	Owner's Equity			
		Accounts				Accounts		Marilyn Johnson,			
	Cash	+ Receivable	+ Supplies	+ Equipment	=	Payable	+	Capital	+ Revenue	– Expenses	Description
Bal.	$13,450	$500	$2,000	$30,000		$25,000		$19,300	$4,000	$2,350	
(k)	+300	–300									
Bal.	$13,750 +	$200	+ $2,000	+ $30,000	=	$25,000	+	$19,300	+ $4,000	– $2,350	
	└─────────────── $45,950 ───────────────┘					└──────────────────── $45,950 ────────────────────┘					

CAUTION

When recording the collection of an account receivable, you always increase the asset Cash, and you always decrease the asset Accounts Receivable. No revenue is recorded, because the revenue was recorded when it was earned. *Do not record the same revenue twice.*

After all transactions have been recorded, Marilyn's equation is still in balance. The total assets ($45,950) equal the total liabilities plus owner's equity ($45,950). With accurate recording, the accounting equation will always balance.

Marilyn's transactions are those of a service business. However, certain conclusions can be drawn that apply to all forms of business:

- The effect of every business transaction can be stated in terms of increases or decreases (or both) in the basic elements of the accounting equation.
- The effect of recording a business transaction must always leave the two sides of the accounting equation in balance.

Summarizing the Transactions

The business transactions of Marilyn Johnson, Attorney at Law, are summarized in tabular form in Figure 1-1.

Learning Objective

8 Identify four types of transactions that affect owner's equity.

It should be stressed that the accounting equation includes only business assets and liabilities. The owner's personal assets and liabilities are excluded (as part of the business entity concept we discussed earlier).

As you study the summary of Marilyn's transactions, note that owner's equity was only *increased* by owner investment and revenue [Transactions (a), (d), (h), and (j)]. Also note that owner's equity was only *decreased* by owner withdrawals and expenses [Transactions (e), (g), and (i)]. We can illustrate the effect of these four types of transactions on owner's equity as shown in Figure 1-2.

Figure 1-1 Business Transaction Summary

	Cash	+ Accounts Receivable	+ Supplies	+ Equipment	= Accounts Payable	+ Marilyn Johnson, Capital	+ Revenue	– Expenses	Description
(a)	+$20,000					+$20,000			Investment
(b)				+$30,000	+$30,000				Equipment purchase
Bal.	$20,000			$30,000	$30,000	$20,000			
(c)	−2,000		+$2,000						Supplies purchase
Bal.	$18,000		$2,000	$30,000	$30,000	$20,000			
(d)	+900						+$ 900		Legal fees
Bal.	$18,900		$2,000	$30,000	$30,000	$20,000	$ 900		
(e)	−1,500							+$1,500	Salaries expense
Bal.	$17,400		$2,000	$30,000	$30,000	$20,000	$ 900	$1,500	
(f)	−5,000				−5,000				Paid on account
Bal.	$12,400		$2,000	$30,000	$25,000	$20,000	$ 900	$1,500	
(g)	−700					−700			Withdrawal
Bal.	$11,700		$2,000	$30,000	$25,000	$19,300	$ 900	$1,500	
(h)	+2,600						+2,600		Legal fees
Bal.	$14,300		$2,000	$30,000	$25,000	$19,300	$3,500	$1,500	
(i)	−250							+250	Utilities expense
	−600							+600	Rent expense
Bal.	$13,450		$2,000	$30,000	$25,000	$19,300	$3,500	$2,350	
(j)		+$500					+500		Legal fees
Bal.	$13,450	$500	$2,000	$30,000	$25,000	$19,300	$4,000	$2,350	
(k)	+300	−300							Recieved payment on account
Bal.	$13,750 +	$200	+ $2,000 +	$30,000	= $25,000 +	$19,300	+ $4,000 –	$2,350	

———————— $45,950 ———————— ———————— $45,950 ————————

The last row shows the totals of each column, and each column total is double-ruled. This formatting is an example of standard accounting practice.

Figure 1-2

Transactions that
Affect Owner's Equity

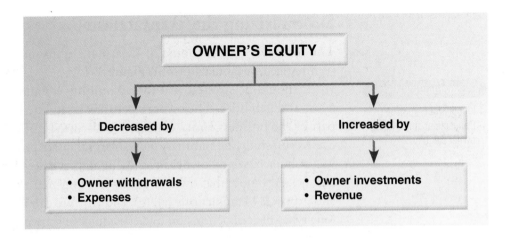

OWNER'S EQUITY

Decreased by

- **Owner withdrawals**
- **Expenses**

Increased by

- **Owner investments**
- **Revenue**

Review Quiz **1-2**

Record the following transactions for Susan Wright in an expanded accounting equation with these headings: Cash + Accounts Receivable + Supplies = Accounts Payable + Susan Wright, Capital + Revenue − Expenses. Include a Description column. After recording the last transaction, prove that the equation is in balance.

(a) Susan invested $10,000 cash in the business.
(b) Invested supplies valued at $2,000 in the business.
(c) Paid rent for the month, $600.
(d) Performed services and received cash, $800.
(e) Purchased supplies on credit, $200.
(f) Performed services on credit, $625.
(g) Withdrew cash for personal use, $500.
(h) Received $250 cash as partial payment for services performed on account.

Check your answers on page 52.

financial statements
summaries of financial
activities

accounting period a
period for which ac-
counting records are
maintained, typically a
year but can be as short
as a month

Financial Statements

Learning Objective

9 Prepare three basic
financial statements.

We have concentrated on the recording function of accounting for most of this chapter. The chapter concludes with three summaries prepared by the accountant. **Financial statements** are summaries of financial activities. Financial statements are prepared on a regular basis at the end of an accounting period and are used to communicate important accounting information.

An **accounting period** is typically one year; however, it can be any length of time for which accounting records are maintained. Usually, the minimum length of an accounting period is one month, and the maximum length is one year. Marilyn Johnson is using an accounting period of one month, as she is interested in what has happened by July 31, 20X3, the end of her first month of operation.

Financial statements report the results of a business's operations and its financial condition to managers inside the business, as well as to users outside the business—such as banks and other lenders, taxing authorities, and owners.

The three basic financial statements are the income statement, the statement of owner's equity, and the balance sheet:

- *Income statement.* A summary of a business's revenue and expenses for a specific period of time, such as a month or a year.
- *Statement of owner's equity.* A summary of the changes that have occurred in owner's equity during a specific period of time, such as a month or a year.
- *Balance sheet.* A listing of a firm's assets, liabilities, and owner's equity at a specific point in time, such as the last day of a month or the last day of a year.

Marilyn's financial statements for her first month of operation are shown in Figure 1-3. The statements were prepared directly from the information shown on the tabular summary of Marilyn's July transactions (Figure 1-1).

The Income Statement

As stated above, an **income statement** shows a summary of a business's revenue and expenses for a specific period of time. When revenue exceeds expenses, there is a **net income**. On the other hand, when expenses exceed revenue, there is a **net loss**. Marilyn's income statement shows a net income of $1,650 because her revenue for the period exceeded her expenses for the same period.

Observe these points about Marilyn's income statement:

- The heading consists of three lines answering the questions *who*, *what*, and *when*. *Who* is the name of the firm, not that of the owner (business entity concept). *What* is an income statement. *When* is for the accounting period just ended.
- *Only* revenue and expenses are placed on the income statement. An owner investment is a contribution of assets to the firm, not revenue. An owner withdrawal is the removal of assets from the firm, not a business expense. Thus, both owner investments and owner withdrawals are stated in terms of changes in owner's equity, not in terms of revenue and expenses. That is why they *do not* appear on the income statement.
- Net income is the difference between total revenue and total expenses. Marilyn's revenue is $4,000, and her expenses are $2,350. The difference between the two ($4,000 − $2,350 = $1,650) is the net income for the period. Had expenses exceeded revenue, the words net loss would have been substituted for net income.
- Expenses are listed in order of size, beginning with the largest; this is a common arrangement.

Other terms used to describe the income statement are *earnings statement*, *operating statement*, and *statement of operations*. Another term less frequently used is *profit and loss statement*, or *P & L statement*.

The Statement of Owner's Equity

The **statement of owner's equity** is a summary of the changes that have taken place in owner's equity during the accounting period. As you have already

income statement a summary of a business's revenue and expenses for a specific period of time, such as a month or a year; also called earnings statement, operating statement, statement of operations, and profit and loss (P & L) statement

net income excess of revenue over total expenses; also referred to as net profit or net earnings; the opposite of net loss

net loss excess of total expenses over revenue; the opposite of net income

Key Point ⊙

Income Statement
    Revenue
  − *Expenses*
  Net Income
  (or Net Loss)

statement of owner's equity a summary of the changes that have occurred in owner's equity during a specific period of time, such as a month or year; also referred to as a capital statement

Figure 1-3
Financial Statements

Income Statement

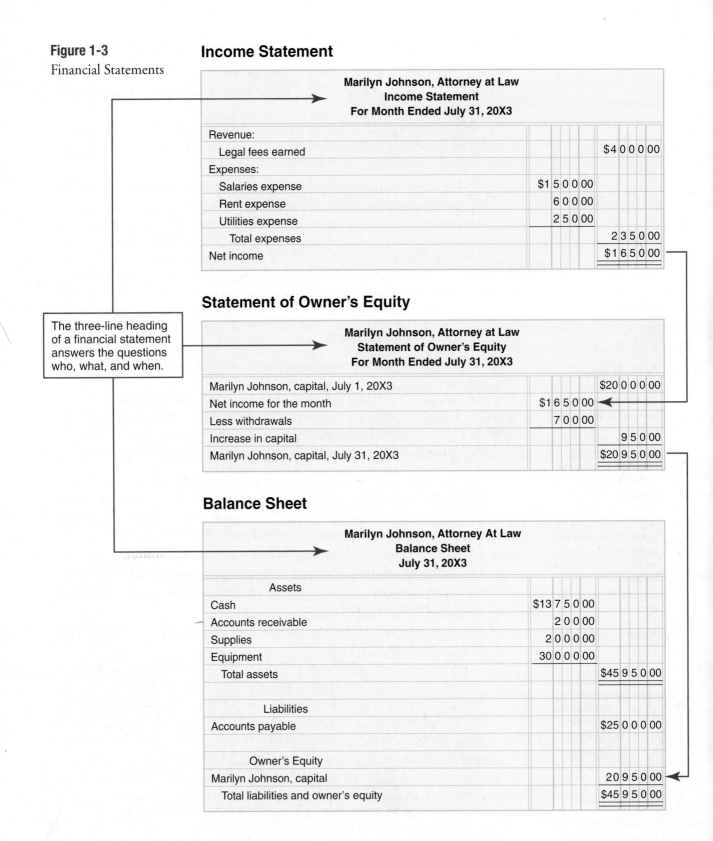

Marilyn Johnson, Attorney at Law
Income Statement
For Month Ended July 31, 20X3

Revenue:		
Legal fees earned		$4 0 0 0 00
Expenses:		
Salaries expense	$1 5 0 0 00	
Rent expense	6 0 0 00	
Utilities expense	2 5 0 00	
Total expenses		2 3 5 0 00
Net income		$1 6 5 0 00

The three-line heading of a financial statement answers the questions who, what, and when.

Statement of Owner's Equity

Marilyn Johnson, Attorney at Law
Statement of Owner's Equity
For Month Ended July 31, 20X3

Marilyn Johnson, capital, July 1, 20X3		$20 0 0 0 00
Net income for the month	$1 6 5 0 00	
Less withdrawals	7 0 0 00	
Increase in capital		9 5 0 00
Marilyn Johnson, capital, July 31, 20X3		$20 9 5 0 00

Balance Sheet

Marilyn Johnson, Attorney At Law
Balance Sheet
July 31, 20X3

Assets		
Cash	$13 7 5 0 00	
Accounts receivable	2 0 0 00	
Supplies	2 0 0 0 00	
Equipment	30 0 0 0 00	
Total assets		$45 9 5 0 00
Liabilities		
Accounts payable		$25 0 0 0 00
Owner's Equity		
Marilyn Johnson, capital		20 9 5 0 00
Total liabilities and owner's equity		$45 9 5 0 00

learned, four types of transactions affect owner's equity: (1) revenue and (2) owner investments, which increase it; and (3) expenses and (4) withdrawals, which decrease it. All of these items are reflected in a statement of owner's equity, except that two of them (revenue and expenses) are combined into the net income or net loss figure.

Observe these points about Marilyn's statement of owner's equity:

- The three-line heading is similar to that of the income statement in that both the income statement and the statement of owner's equity cover a specific period of time.
- Since this was Marilyn's first month of operation, her beginning capital balance was her initial investment of $20,000. Next month, she will begin with a balance of $20,950.
- The net income figure is obtained from the income statement. Therefore, the income statement should be prepared first.
- The increase in capital is the difference between Marilyn's net income for the period and her withdrawals for the period. Had Marilyn shown a net loss for the period, or if her withdrawals had exceeded her net income, there would have been a decrease in capital, which would have been *subtracted* from the opening capital balance.

The statement of owner's equity is also called the *capital statement*.

The Balance Sheet

balance sheet a listing of the firm's assets, liabilities, and owner's equity at a specific point in time; also referred to as statement of financial position and position statement

As stated earlier, the **balance sheet** shows a firm's assets, liabilities, and owner's equity at a specific point in time, the end of the accounting period. It is an expanded statement of the accounting equation showing that A = L + OE.

Note these points about Marilyn's balance sheet, shown in Figure 1-3:

- It has a three-line heading that differs significantly on the *when* line. While an income statement and a statement of owner's equity describe what happened over a period of time, a balance sheet tells "what is" on a given date. The first two statements have been described as motion pictures. The balance sheet has been described as a snapshot.
- The figure for Marilyn Johnson, Capital ($20,950) was taken from the statement of owner's equity. Thus, the statement of owner's equity is prepared before the balance sheet.
- The final, double-ruled totals show balance or equality. A balance sheet shows that A = L + OE.
- If there had been additional liabilities, the format for the liabilities section would have been the same as that for the assets section.
- This form of balance sheet, with the liabilities and owner's equity sections presented directly below the assets section, is called the *report form*. Another common arrangement lists the assets on the left and the liabilities and owner's equity on the right. This arrangement is called the *account form of balance sheet* because of its similarity to the account. (The account is a basic accounting record we will study in Chapter 2.) Let's look at Marilyn's balance sheet in account form. (See Figure 1-4.)

Other terms used to describe the balance sheet are *statement of financial position* and *position statement*.

Figure 1-4

Account Form of the Balance Sheet

Marilyn Johnson, Attorney at Law Balance Sheet July 31, 20X3		
Assets		**Liabilities**
Cash	$13 7 5 0 00	Accounts payable $25 0 0 0 00
Accounts receivable	2 0 0 00	
Supplies	2 0 0 0 00	**Owner's Equity**
Equipment	30 0 0 0 00	Marilyn Johnson, capital 20 9 5 0 00
		Total liabilities
Total assets	$45 9 5 0 00	and owner's equity $45 9 5 0 00

Review Quiz 1-3

Tim Emery started Emery's Delivery Service on August 1, 20X1. His August transactions are recorded in equation form below. Using these data, prepare: (1) an income statement, (2) a statement of owner's equity, and (3) a balance sheet in report form.

	Cash	+	Supplies	+	Equipment	=	Accounts Payable	+	Tim Emery, Capital	+	Revenue	–	Expenses	Description
	Assets					=	**Liabilities** +		**Owner's Equity**					
(a)	+$10,000								+$10,000					Investment
(b)	−1,000		+$1,000											Supplies purchase
Bal.	$ 9,000		$1,000						$10,000					
(c)					+$18,000		+$18,000							Equipment purchase
Bal.	$ 9,000		$1,000		$18,000		$18,000		$10,000					
(d)	−500												+$ 500	Rent expense
Bal.	$ 8,500		$1,000		$18,000		$18,000		$10,000				$ 500	
(e)	−300												+300	Utilities expense
Bal.	$ 8,200		$1,000		$18,000		$18,000		$10,000				$ 800	
(f)	+1,200										+$1,200			Delivery revenue
Bal.	$ 9,400		$1,000		$18,000		$18,000		$10,000		$1,200		$ 800	
(g)	−200												+200	Salaries expense
Bal.	$ 9,200	+	$1,000	+	$18,000	=	$18,000	+	$10,000	+	$1,200	–	$1,000	

Check your answers on page 53.

Ethics in Accounting

Learning Objective

10 Define *ethics* and explain the importance of ethical behavior in modern business.

Nevada, New Jersey, and Mississippi are three states that have benefited enormously from legalized gambling. Casinos in each of these states provide thousands of jobs and generate millions in tourism dollars for the local economy. Additionally, license fees and taxes on casino profits generate millions of dollars in tax revenue for state coffers. Why are casinos so successful, and why are so many people so eager to "take the gamble"? One explanation is that gamblers trust that casinos are highly regulated, and they have confidence that dealers are honest and professional and that machines and tables are not rigged. Casual or professional gamblers would not take a chance in a casino they thought was rigged. Just as gamblers will not make a bet in a rigged establishment, investors will not invest in companies if they think the stock prices are rigged.

In recent years, the financial news has been filled with stories of business scandal, corporate greed, and illegal activity. Enron, WorldCom, Tyco International, Adelphia Communications, and HealthSouth are five highly publicized examples of companies with questionable business practices, or whose financial statements were not reliable and did not present a fair picture of the company profits and financial condition.

Soon after its bankruptcy in December 2001, Enron became the poster child for corporate scandal. Enron was an energy company with over 21,000 employees in 40 countries and was one of the world's leading electricity, natural gas, pulp and paper, and communications companies. Unfortunately, the firm's success was based on massive fraud. Enron overstated its profits and concealed debts that were not reported on its balance sheet. In an investigation by the U.S. Department of Justice, internal documents surfaced detailing sham transactions that kept billions of dollars of debt off Enron's balance sheet and created the illusion of increasing profits. As Enron's house of cards collapsed, the company's stock price fell from $90 a share to less than a dollar, costing investors and employees hundreds of millions of dollars.

The Enron scandal played a major role in shaking investor confidence in the reliability of financial statements because the firm was able to hide its losses for nearly five years. The resulting public outcry from the Enron scandal, and other scandals of the early 2000s, led Congress to pass the **Sarbanes-Oxley Act of 2002**. The purpose of this Act, often referred to as simply Sarbanes-Oxley or SOX, is to restore public confidence and trust in the financial statements of companies. Top management must now certify the accuracy of financial information. Additionally, the act imposes much harsher penalties on top management for fraudulent financial activity.

The standards of conduct that lead to honest, reliable, and fair behavior are referred to as **ethics**. The success of the entire American economy depends, in large part, on sound ethical behavior. Imagine the difficulty of starting a business, investing for retirement, or funding a child's college fund if you couldn't trust financial statements to be honestly prepared.

The benefit of sound ethical behavior extends beyond top management to all levels of a company. Each year, companies suffer billions of dollars in lost productivity as a result of employees taking excessive breaks, surfing the Web on company time, conducting personal business while on the job, and so on. Imagine an employee making $12 an hour who surfs the Web for 30 minutes a day on company time. That amounts to $6 a day paid to the employee who produced no product or service in return. This amount may not sound like much, but when you consider that $6 a day is $30 a week, and when multiplied by the number of work weeks in a year, the amount is substantial. And when thousands of employees are engaging in similar behavior, the amount of loss is staggering.

As you reach the end of your first chapter in accounting, you should now be able to identify the accounting elements, record business transactions in equation form, and prepare the basic financial statements. In other words, you are forming the foundation for the study of accounting. You will use this accounting foundation throughout this course and in all other accounting courses and practices.

Sarbanes-Oxley Act of 2002 a law, passed by Congress, requiring companies to certify the accuracy of their financial information and intended to restore the public's confidence in the financial statements of companies; often referred to as Sarbanes-Oxley or SOX

ethics principles of moral conduct that guide the behavior of individuals and businesses

The U.S. Mortgage Industry Hit by Fraud and Decline

The Federal National Mortgage Association (Fannie Mae) and the Federal Home Mortgage Corporation (Freddie Mac) are the largest sources of money for the home mortgage industry. Prior to September 8, 2008, both companies operated as government-sponsored enterprises (GSEs). This means that the two companies, although stockholder owned and privately operated, were protected financially by the federal government. The government protections included exemption from state and local income taxes and exemption from U.S. Securities and Exchange Commission (SEC) oversight. Further, Fannie Mae and Freddie Mac were the only two Fortune 500 companies that were not required to inform the public of financial difficulties the company might be experiencing. This lack of oversight led some in Congress and the private sector to worry that a financial collapse within either company could make taxpayers responsible for billions of dollars in outstanding debt. This possibility became reality on September 8, 2008, when, in the face of a declining real estate market and a record rate of home foreclosures, the federal government took control of both companies.

The government takeover came as a shock to a few but was anticipated by many. As early as 2003, investigations by the Justice Department revealed signs of trouble in the home mortgage industry. In 2004, Fannie Mae fired Chief Executive Officer Franklin Raines and Chief Financial Officer J. Timothy Howard five weeks after saying it might need to restate profit by $9 million and after 18 months of assuring investors and testifying to Congress that their accounting was sound.

Federal regulators stated that Fannie Mae engaged in "extensive financial fraud" and manipulated earnings in a way to make it appear the company had reached its earnings target, triggering maximum executive bonuses for top management, including Raines and Howard.

In 2004, the Bush Administration proposed reforming Fannie Mae and Freddie Mac but opponents countered that reform would result in thousands of Americans being unable to qualify for home loans. During the first half of 2004, Fannie

Franklin Raines, left, and Tim Howard prepare to testify about Fannie Mae's accounting practices.

and Freddie spent $11.7 million lobbying against increased oversight. The result was a continuation of questionable lending practices that granted thousands of mortgages to people who could not afford the monthly payments. By early September 2008, government action seemed necessary to prevent the financial collapse of the home mortgage industry. Fannie Mae and Freddie Mac owned or guaranteed just under half the country's $12 trillion in mortgage debt, and their failure could devastate the national economy.

On September 8, the federal government seized control of both Fannie Mae and Freddie Mac. The Treasury Department pledged up to $200 billion to help the companies deal with heavy losses on mortgage defaults, with both companies being placed under the umbrella of the Federal Housing Finance Agency.

Sources: James Tyson, "Fannie Mae Fires Raines, Howard Over Accounting Flaws," www.Bloomberg.com, December 24, 2004; Kathleen Day, "Study Finds 'Extensive' Fraud at Fannie Mae," www.Washingtonpost.com, May 24, 2006.

For Discussion

1. What motivated Raines to manipulate the accounting books so that it appeared Fannie Mae's earnings targets were reached?
2. What was the massive fraud that was perpetrated at Fannie Mae?
3. What led to the government bailout of Fannie Mae and Freddie Mac?

Joining the Pieces

The Expanded Accounting Equation

Assets =	Liabilities +	Owner's Equity +	Revenue −	Expenses
Anything of value that is owned by the business in order to operate	Debts owed by the business	The difference between assets and liabilities	Inflow of assets (cash and accounts receivable) from operating during the accounting period	Costs necessary to operate the business
Examples:	**Examples:**	**Also called:**	**Examples:**	**Examples:**
Cash	Accounts Payable	Capital	Service Revenue	Rent Expense
Accounts Receivable	Notes Payable	Net Worth	Accounting Fees	Salaries Expense
Supplies	Taxes Payable	Proprietorship	Fares Earned	Repairs Expense
Equipment			Rent Income	Utilities Expense
Buildings			Medical Fees Earned	
Land				

Owner's Withdrawals

The removal of assets from the business for the personal use of the owner

Dual Effect of Withdrawal:

1. Decrease in the asset taken
2. Decrease in owner's equity

Guide for Financial Statement Preparation

Income Statement
Summarizes revenue and expenses to determine the amount of net income (or net loss) to be carried to the statement of owner's equity.

Newcomb Company
Income Statement
For Year Ended December 31, 20XX

Revenue:		
Service revenue		$10 0 0 0 00
Expenses:		
Salaries expense	$3 0 0 0 00	
Rent expense	2 0 0 0 00	
Utilities expense	1 0 0 0 00	
Total expenses		6 0 0 0 00
Net income		$ 4 0 0 0 00

Statement of Owner's Equity
Summarizes the changes that have taken place in owner's equity and provides an updated capital figure to be carried to the balance sheet.

Newcomb Company
Statement of Owner's Equity
For Year Ended December 31, 20XX

Todd Newcomb, capital, January 1, 20XX		$ 9 0 0 0 00
Net income for period	$4 0 0 0 00	
Less withdrawals	2 0 0 0 00	
Increase in capital		2 0 0 0 00
Todd Newcomb, capital, December 31, 20XX		$11 0 0 0 00

Balance Sheet
A listing of assets, liabilities, and owner's equity as of a certain date.

Newcomb Company
Balance Sheet
December 31, 20XX

Assets		
Cash	$3 0 0 0 00	
Accounts receivable	2 0 0 0 00	
Supplies	1 0 0 0 00	
Equipment	6 0 0 0 00	
Total assets		$12 0 0 0 00
Liabilities		
Accounts payable		$ 1 0 0 0 00
Owner's Equity		
Todd Newcomb, capital		11 0 0 0 00
Total liabilities and owner's equity		$12 0 0 0 00

1 Define *accounting* and related terms.

Accounting is the process of recording, summarizing, analyzing, and interpreting financial (money-related) activities to permit individuals and organizations to make informed judgments and decisions. Recording means making written records of transactions and events that have a financial effect on the business. Summarizing is the process of combining these written records, at regular intervals, into reports that owners and managers can use in the decision-making process. Analyzing means examining these reports by breaking them down in order to determine financial success or failure. Interpreting involves the use of financial data to make sound decisions and determine if a company is meeting its plans and objectives.

2 Explain who uses accounting information.

All members of our society use accounting information. Individuals use accounting information to function in a society that is dependent on financial activities. For example, we use accounting information when we analyze our paychecks to determine if the correct amount of taxes has been withheld, when we take out loans, when we buy goods and services, and when we use charge and credit cards.

Owners of businesses use accounting information to help control expenses, monitor revenue, and protect assets. Managers use accounting information to make better business decisions. Investors use accounting information to help them decide if an investment in a particular company would be profitable. Lenders use accounting information to decide if a company has sufficient financial strength to qualify for a loan. Government agencies and taxing authorities use accounting information to operate and to determine how well private businesses are complying with tax rules and regulations.

3 Identify four forms of business organizations and three types of business operations.

The four most popular forms of business in this country are the sole proprietorship, the partnership, the corporation, and the limited liability company. A **sole proprietorship** is a business owned by one person only. A **partnership** is a business that is co-owned by two or more persons. A **corporation** is a form of business owned by stockholders. A **limited liability company (LLC)** is a form of business that combines features of a corporation and those of partnerships and proprietorships.

The three most common types of business operations are the service business, the merchandising business, and the manufacturing business. A **service business** sells a service to its customers—such as tax assistance provided by H&R Block. A **merchandising business** buys goods produced by others and then sells these goods to customers. Examples of merchandising businesses include Sears, Wal-Mart, and Macy's. A **manufacturing business** actually produces the goods it sells—such as Ford Motor Company, Coca-Cola, and IBM.

4 Define and describe the elements of accounting.

An **asset** is an item with money value that is owned by a business. This element includes Cash, Accounts Receivable, Equipment, and Supplies. Assets are the money and material with which a business has to work.

A **liability** is a debt owed to a **creditor**. Creditors are individuals or organizations from which a purchase on credit has been made or a loan of money has been obtained. The most common type of liability is Accounts Payable.

Owner's equity is the dollar value of the claim of the owner to the assets of a business. It is the interest of the owner in the business.

5 State the accounting equation.

The **accounting equation** is:

Assets = Liabilities + Owner's Equity

or, expressed in symbols,

A = L + OE

6 Define *business transaction.*

A **business transaction** is any activity that changes the value of a firm's assets, liabilities, or owner's equity.

7 Record business transactions in equation form.

Several different business transactions follow for Cody Gray, architect, during June 20XX, recorded in equation form. For simplicity, we have chosen to put the balances only at the end of June 20XX.

(a) Cody Gray invested $25,000 in an architectural firm.
(b) Purchased supplies for cash, $750.
(c) Purchased equipment for $2,700, paying $500 cash and owing the balance.
(d) Paid rent for the month, $700.
(e) Performed design services for cash, $1,700.
(f) Paid $1,000 of the amount owed for equipment.
(g) Performed design services on account, $400.
(h) Paid salaries for the month, $600.
(i) Cody withdrew $300 cash for personal use.
(j) Received $250 as partial payment from services performed on account in

	Assets				=	Liabilities +		Owner's Equity				
	Cash	+ Receivable +	Supplies +	Equipment =		Accounts Payable +		Cody Gray, Capital	+ Revenue –	Expenses	Description
(a)	+$25,000							+$25,000			Investment
(b)	−750		+$750								Supplies purchase
(c)	−500			+$2,700		+$2,200					Equipment purchase
(d)	−700									+$ 700	Rent expense
(e)	+1,700								+$1,700		Design fees
(f)	−1,000					−1,000					Paid on account
(g)		+$400							+400		Design fees
(h)	−600									+600	Salaries expense
(i)	−300							−300			Withdrawal
(j)	+250	−250									Received on account
Bal.	$23,100 +	$150 +	$750 +	$2,700 =		$1,200 +		$24,700	+ $2,100 –	$1,300	
		——— $26,700 ———						——— $26,700 ———			

Transaction (g).

8 Identify four types of transactions that affect owner's equity.

Owner's equity is affected by four types of transactions: (1) owner investments and (2) revenue, which increase it; and (3) expenses and (4) owner withdrawals, which decrease it.

9 Prepare three basic financial statements.

The **income statement**, the **statement of owner's equity**, and the **balance sheet** in Figure 1-5 are prepared from the information used in Objective 7.

Figure 1-5

Three Basic Financial Statements

Cody Gray, Architect Income Statement For Month Ended June 30, 20XX		
Revenue:		
Design fees earned		$2 1 0 0 00
Expenses:		
Rent expense	$7 0 0 00	
Salaries expense	6 0 0 00	
Total expenses		1 3 0 0 00
Net income		$ 8 0 0 00

Cody Gray, Architect Statement of Owner's Equity For Month Ended June 30, 20XX		
Cody Gray, capital, June 1, 20XX		$25 0 0 0 00
Net income for the month	$8 0 0 00	
Less withdrawals	3 0 0 00	
Increase in capital		5 0 0 00
Cody Gray, capital, June 30, 20XX		$25 5 0 0 00

Cody Gray, Architect Balance Sheet June 30, 20XX		
Assets		
Cash	$23 1 0 0 00	
Accounts receivable	1 5 0 00	
Supplies	7 5 0 00	
Equipment	2 7 0 0 00	
Total assets		$26 7 0 0 00
Liabilities		
Accounts payable		$ 1 2 0 0 00
Owner's Equity		
Cody Gray, capital		25 5 0 0 00
Total liabilities and owner's equity		$26 7 0 0 00

10 Define *ethics* and explain the importance of ethical behavior in modern business.

Ethics are the principles of moral conduct that guide the behavior of individuals and businesses. A strong ethical framework is essential to the success of individual businesses, and the economy as a whole, because effective and accurate financial reporting depend on sound ethical behavior. For example, a bank must be able to rely on the accuracy of financial statements presented by someone seeking a loan. Likewise, an investor must be able to rely on the accuracy of the profit reported by a company when deciding whether or not to invest in that company.

Terms and Concepts Review

- Key Terms and Definitions in English and Spanish
- Additional Quiz Questions

Key Terms

accounting, 13
accounting equation, 18
accounting period, 26
accounts payable, 17
accounts receivable, 17
asset, 16
balance sheet, 29
business, 14
business entity concept, 19
cash, 16
corporation, 15
cost principle, 21
creditor, 17
dual effect, 19
equipment, 17
ethics, 31
expenses, 22
financial statements, 26
income statement, 27
liability, 17

limited liability company (LLC), 15
manufacturing business, 16
merchandising business, 15
net income, 27
net loss, 27
note payable, 17
owner's equity, 17
partnership, 15
realization principle, 24
revenue, 21
Sarbanes-Oxley Act of 2002, 31
service business, 15
shift in assets, 20
sole proprietorship, 14
statement of owner's equity, 27
supplies, 17
tangible, 17
transaction, 18
withdrawal, 22

Concepts Review

1. Phil Watson records and summarizes financial data. Is he doing accounting? Explain your answer.
2. Identify some of the users of accounting information.
3. Classify the following businesses as service, merchandising, or manufacturing: (a) car dealer, (b) supermarket, (c) dental office, (d) computer factory, (e) e-mail network provider.
4. Identify and explain each of the basic accounting elements.
5. Why is good health not an asset in accounting?
6. What is the major difference between the assets Equipment and Supplies?
7. Why is firing an employee not considered to be a transaction?

8. Bill Taylor has two businesses. Does the business entity concept state that Bill should combine both businesses into a single entity for accounting purposes? Explain your answer.
9. Which of the following are business transactions? (a) paid salaries, (b) hired an employee, (c) received cash for services performed, (d) the owner paid her home electric bill from her personal checking account.
10. Explain the dual effect in accounting.
11. What four types of transactions affect owner's equity?
12. How does buying an asset for cash differ from paying an expense?
13. Martha DeBice performed legal services for a client today but agreed to let the client pay her in four equal installments, starting in 30 days. Has Martha earned revenue today, or will she earn it when the installments are received? Explain your answer.
14. Why is the balance sheet referred to as a snapshot, while the income statement and the statement of owner's equity are referred to as motion pictures?
15. How does the account form of the balance sheet differ from the report form?
16. What is the Sarbanes-Oxley Act of 2002, and why was it passed?
17. What are ethics, and why are they so important in American business?

Skills Review

Learning Objective **5**

Check Figure
(a) $130,000

Quick Practice

Quick Practice 1-1

Objective: To compute the missing value in the accounting equation

Directions: In each of these examples, find the missing value.

	Assets	Liabilities	Owner's Equity
(a)	$ 198,000	$ 68,000	$_____
(b)	$_____	$ 55,000	$ 72,000
(c)	$ 94,500	$_____	$ 28,000

Learning Objective **5**

Check Figure
Three are correct.

Quick Practice 1-2

Objective: To state the accounting equation

Directions: Indicate which of the following statements of the accounting equation are correct or incorrect.

(a) Assets = Liabilities + Owner's Equity
(b) Liabilities = Assets + Owner's Equity
(c) Owner's Equity = Liabilities – Assets
(d) Liabilities + Owner's Equity = Assets
(e) Assets = Liabilities – Owner's Equity
(f) Assets – Liabilities = Owner's Equity

Learning Objective **7**

Check Figure
(a) + asset, + liabilities

Quick Practice 1-3

Objective: To indicate the effect of business transactions on the accounting elements

Directions: Using check marks, indicate the effect on the accounting elements for each of the business transactions presented.

Transaction	Assets	=	Liabilities	+	Owner's Equity
	+ −		− +		− +
Example: Owner invested cash	✓				✓
(a) Purchased supplies on credit					
(b) Performed services for cash					
(c) Paid operating expenses					
(d) Owner withdrew cash					

Learning Objective 9

Check Figure
Net income = $6

Quick Practice 1-4

Objective: To prepare an income statement

Directions: From the following data, prepare an income statement in good form for the Premier RV Park for the year ended December 31, 20XX. Please note that you will not need all information provided for the income statement.

Item	Amount
Cash	$ 20
Accounts Receivable	30
Supplies	5
Building	80
Land	16
Accounts Payable	15
John Boyd, Capital, January 1	133
John Boyd, Capital, December 31	?
John Boyd, Drawing	3
Revenue from Services	52
Salary Expense	33
Utilities Expense	7
Maintenance Expense	4
Miscellaneous Expense	2

Learning Objective 9

Check Figure
Ending capital = $136

Quick Practice 1-5

Objective: To prepare a statement of owner's equity

Directions: Using the data in Quick Practice 1-4, prepare a statement of owner's equity in good form for the Premier RV Park for the year ended December 31, 20XX.

Learning Objective 9

Check Figure
Total assets = $151

Quick Practice 1-6

Objective: To prepare a balance sheet in report form

Directions: Using the data in Quick Practice 1-4, prepare a balance sheet in report form for the Premier RV Park as of December 31, 20XX.

Learning Objective 5

Check Figure
Ending equity = $181,500

Quick Practice 1-7

Objective: To determine the amount of owner's equity at the end of the accounting year

Directions: Blake DeBice, owner of DeBice Software Solutions, started 20X9 with owner's equity of $125,000. Blake's income statement shows a profit of $92,500 for the year, and he withdrew $3,000 *per month* for personal use. Compute the amount of Blake's equity at the end of 20X9.

Quick Practice 1-8

Objective: To identify balance sheet items

Directions: From the following list of items, identify those that would appear on the balance sheet.

(a) Accounts receivable
(b) Equipment
(c) Revenue from services
(d) Cash
(e) Accounts payable
(f) Steve Nix, capital
(g) Salary expense
(h) Utilities expense
(i) Steve Nix, drawing
(j) Land

Quick Practice 1-9

Objective: To identify accounts on financial statements

Directions: From the following list of items, identify each as an asset (A), liability (L), owner's equity (OE), revenue (R), or expense (E). Indicate the financial statement on which the account is reported: Income Statement (IS), Statement of Owner's Equity (SOE), or Balance Sheet (BS).

Item	Classification	Financial Statement
1. Cash		
2. Jeff Gordan, Capital		
3. Jeff Gordan, Drawing*		
4. Revenue from Services		
5. Accounts Payable		
6. Salaries Expense		
7. Equipment		
8. Rent Expense		

* This account appears on two finished statements.

Exercises

Exercise 1-1

Objective: To calculate the value of the missing element in the accounting equation

Directions: In each of these examples, find the missing value.

	A	=	L	+	OE
(a)	$85,800		$34,900		$_____
(b)	$92,655		$_____		$48,395
(c)	$_____		$66,000		$34,500
(d)	$45,952		$_____		$30,044
(e)	$_____		$44,558		$27,934
(f)	$_____		$44,300		($16,300)

Exercise 1-2

Objective: To indicate the effect of business transactions on the accounting elements

Directions: Using check marks, indicate the effects on the accounting elements for each of the business transactions presented.

	A		=	L		+	OE	
	+	–		–	+		–	+
Example: Owner invested cash	✓							✓
(a) Purchased equipment on credit								
(b) Bought supplies for cash								
(c) Paid liability for equipment								
(d) Performed services for cash								
(e) Paid operating expenses								
(f) Performed services on credit								
(g) Owner withdrew cash								
(h) Collected on services from (f)								

Exercise 1-3

Objective: To record business transactions in equation form

Directions: Use the transactions from Exercise 1-2 and record them by using plus and minus signs in the expanded equation: Cash + Accounts Receivable + Supplies + Equipment = Accounts Payable + Tracy Corrigen, Capital + Revenue – Expenses.

Exercise 1-4

Objective: To prepare an income statement

Directions: From the following data, prepare an income statement in good form for the Twin City Barber Shop for the year ended December 31, 20XX. Use only those items that are needed.

Item	Amount
Salaries Expense	$ 23,800
Rent Expense	18,000
Supplies	3,500
Utilities Expense	9,600
Revenue from Services	138,250
Cash	19,400
Repairs Expense	900
Miscellaneous Expense	700

Exercise 1-5

Objective: To prepare a statement of owner's equity

Directions: Robert Downie is a financial planner. Prepare his statement of owner's equity for the year ended December 31, 20XX, if he began the year with a capital balance of $43,600, earned a net income of $36,400 during the year, and withdrew $2,000 per month.

Learning Objective **9**

Check Figure
Four items would not appear
on the balance sheet.

Exercise 1-6

Objective: To identify balance sheet items

Directions: From the following list of items from the records of Ace Plumbing Company, identify those items that would appear on the balance sheet.

(a) Revenue from Services
(b) Cash
(c) Land
(d) Equipment
(e) Miscellaneous Expense
(f) Accounts Payable

(g) Repairs Expense
(h) Notes Payable
(i) Supplies
(j) Bill Rese, Capital
(k) Rent Expense
(l) Accounts Receivable

Learning Objective **9**

Check Figure
Total assets = $84,300

Exercise 1-7

Objective: To prepare a balance sheet in report form

Directions: From the following information, prepare a balance sheet in report form for Tidy Maid, a professional maid and janitorial service. The date is December 31, 20XX, and the owner is Katy Kwan.

Item Amount	
Accounts Payable	$17,800
Accounts Receivable	14,000
Cash	14,600
Katy Kwan, Capital, January 1, 20XX	35,200
Katy Kwan, Capital, December 31, 20XX	?
Withdrawals	12,800
Equipment	42,000
Supplies	13,700
Net income for the year	44,100

Learning Objective **9**

Check Figure
One error is that the date
should be December 31,
20XX, not "For Year Ended
December 31, 20XX."

Exercise 1-8

Objective: To prepare a corrected balance sheet

Directions: The following balance sheet was prepared by an inexperienced bookkeeper. Several errors were made. Find and list the errors.

Speedy Repair Shop **Balance Sheet** **For Year Ended December 31, 20XX**	
Assets	
Cash	$17 3 0 0 00
Supplies	7 5 0 00
Equipment	21 7 0 0 00
Total assets	$38 7 5 0 00
Liabilities	
Accounts payable	$ 8 4 6 0 00
Owner's Equity	
Speedy Repair Shop, capital	$29 2 9 0 00
Total liabilities and owner's equity	38 7 5 0 00

Case Problems

Group A

Problem 1-1A

Objective: To record business transactions in an expanded accounting equation

Sheryl Rogers opened a tutoring service on January 2, 20XX. During January, the following transactions occurred:

(a) Sheryl invested $8,000 cash in the firm.
(b) Purchased office supplies on credit, $1,950.
(c) Purchased office equipment on credit, $7,000.
(d) Invested a personal computer, valued at $2,500, into the firm.
(e) Paid rent, $500.
(f) Received cash for tutoring fees, $700.
(g) Paid salary of receptionist, $400.
(h) Paid $1,000 of the liability for office equipment.
(i) Received cash for tutoring fees, $1,200.
(j) Paid utility bill, $390.
(k) Sheryl withdrew $900 cash for personal use.

Directions: Record each of these transactions in an expanded accounting equation with the following headings:

Assets			=	Liabilities	+	Owner's Equity		
Cash +	Office Supplies +	Office Equipment =		Accounts Payable +		Sheryl Rogers, Capital +	Revenue –	Expenses

Calculate balances after recording each transaction.

Problem 1-2A

Objective: To record business transactions in an expanded accounting equation

Philip Seder opened a shoe repair business on April 1, 20XX. During April, he completed the following transactions:

(a) Philip invested $10,000 cash in the firm.
(b) Purchased supplies on credit, $1,450.
(c) Purchased equipment on credit, $4,800.
(d) Paid rent for the month of April, $700.
(e) Received cash for services performed, $425.
(f) Performed shoe repair services on credit, $650.
(g) Paid half of the liability for supplies, $725.
(h) Paid $1,500 on the liability for equipment.
(i) Received cash for services performed, $390.
(j) Philip withdrew $500 cash for personal use.
(k) Paid utilities expense for April, $350.
(l) Collected $200 of the revenue earned in Transaction (f).

Directions: Record these transactions in an expanded accounting equation with the following headings:

Assets				=	Liabilities	+	Owner's Equity		
Cash +	Accounts Receivable +	Supplies +	Equipment =		Accounts Payable +		Phillip Seder, Capital +	Revenue –	Expenses

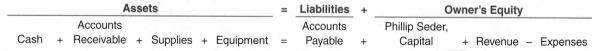

Calculate balances after recording each transaction.

Problem 1-3A

Objective: To record business transactions in an expanded accounting equation

Laura Scallion opened a printer and computer repair shop this month. During the month, she completed the following transactions:

(a) Laura invested $8,000 cash and $11,000 worth of equipment in the firm.
(b) Paid cash for office supplies, $425.
(c) Purchased wrapping paper, string, and cash register tape for cash, $395.
(d) Purchased equipment for $1,900, paying $500 down and owing the balance.
(e) Paid rent for the month, $675.
(f) Performed repair services for cash, $450.
(g) Performed repair services on credit, $775.
(h) Returned $40 of defective supplies purchased in Transaction (c), receiving a cash refund.
(i) Received $200 cash for the services performed in Transaction (g).
(j) Paid utilities expense for the month, $380.
(k) Paid half of the amount due on Transaction (d), $700.

Directions: Record Laura's transactions for the month in an expanded accounting equation with the following headings:

Assets					=	Liabilities	+	Owner's Equity			
Cash	+ Accounts Receivable	+ Office Supplies	+ Store Supplies	+ Equipment	=	Accounts Payable	+	Laura Scallion, Capital	+ Revenue	– Expenses	

Calculate balances after each transaction.

Problem 1-4A

Objective: To prepare three financial statements

The data presented below are for Drug-a-Bug, an insect exterminator, on April 30, 20XX.

Item	Amount
Accounts Payable	$6,310
Accounts Receivable	1,000
Cash	2,700
Chemical Supplies	445
William Bloom, Capital, April 1	4,850
Miscellaneous Expense	150
Office Equipment	4,200
Office Supplies	375
Rent Expense	510
Revenue from Services	3,150
Salaries Expense	780
Truck	3,500
Utilities Expense	350
Withdrawals	300

Directions:

1. Prepare an income statement for the month ended April 30, 20XX.
2. Prepare a statement of owner's equity for the month ended April 30, 20XX.
3. Prepare a balance sheet in report form as of April 30, 20XX.

Problem 1-5A

Objective: To record business transactions and prepare financial statements

Jeff Edwards, CPA, started his practice on September 1, 20X1. He completed the following transactions during his first month of operations:

(a) Jeff invested the following in the firm: cash, $12,400; office supplies, $700; office equipment, $4,500.
(b) Paid rent for the month, $550.
(c) Purchased a computer for $3,700 on credit.
(d) Purchased a copier for $8,000, paying $500 down and agreeing to pay the balance in three equal installments.
(e) Performed services for cash, $1,025.
(f) Jeff wrote business checks for personal bills, $500.
(g) Purchased a printer for cash, $600.
(h) Purchased printer ink for cash, $110.
(i) Performed services on credit, $1,200.
(j) Paid utilities for the month, $315.
(k) Paid cash for a new desk for Jeff's office, $850.
(l) Collected $750 for the services performed in Transaction (i).
(m) Paid for the computer purchased in Transaction (c), $3,700.
(n) Paid salary of part-time employee, $600.
(o) Paid first installment due on the copier purchased in Transaction (d), $2,500.

Directions:

1. Record Jeff's September transactions in an expanded accounting equation with the following headings. Use the Description column to provide a brief explanation of each transaction involving owner's equity, such as rent expense, fees earned, or withdrawal. [Calculate balances only after Transaction (o).]

Assets				=	Liabilities	+	Owner's Equity			
Cash	+ Accounts Receivable	+ Office Supplies	+ Office Equipment	=	Accounts Payable	+	Jeff Edwards, Capital	+ Revenue	– Expenses	*Description*

2. Prepare an income statement for September.
3. Prepare a statement of owner's equity for September.
4. Prepare a September 30 balance sheet in *account* form.

Group B

Problem 1-1B

Objective: To record business transactions in an expanded accounting equation

Tom Atchinson opened a software design service on January 8, 20XX. During January, the following transactions occurred:

(a) Tom invested $14,000 cash in the business to get it started.
(b) Purchased office supplies on credit, $755.
(c) Purchased office equipment on credit, $3,500.
(d) Invested office equipment, valued at $11,000, in the firm.
(e) Paid rent, $600.
(f) Received cash for services performed, $800.
(g) Paid salary of assistant, $600.
(h) Paid half of the liability for the equipment purchased in Transaction (c), $1,750.
(i) Received cash for services performed, $500.

(j) Paid telephone bill, $200.

(k) Tom withdrew $1,000 cash for personal use.

Directions: Record each of these transactions in an expanded accounting equation with the following headings:

Assets			=	Liabilities	+	Owner's Equity		
				Accounts		Tom Atchinson,		
Cash +	Office Supplies +	Office Equipment	=	Payable	+	Capital	+ Revenue −	Expenses

Calculate balances after recording each transaction.

Learning Objective **7**

Check Figure
Ending capital balance =
$7,800

Problem 1-2B

Objective: To record business transactions in an expanded accounting equation

Bill Bruno opened a shoe repair business on May 1, 20XX. During May, he completed the following transactions:

(a) Bill invested $8,500 cash in the firm.

(b) Purchased supplies on credit, $1,150.

(c) Purchased equipment on credit, $4,400.

(d) Paid rent for the month of May, $900.

(e) Received cash for services performed, $525.

(f) Performed shoe repair services on credit, $750.

(g) Paid half of the liability for supplies, $575.

(h) Paid $1,600 on the liability for equipment.

(i) Received cash for services performed, $490.

(j) Bill withdrew cash for personal use, $700.

(k) Paid utilities expense for May, $450.

(l) Collected $300 of the revenue earned in Transaction (f).

Directions: Record these transactions in an expanded accounting equation with the following headings:

Assets				=	Liabilities	+	Owner's Equity		
	Accounts				Accounts		Bill Bruno,		
Cash +	Receivable +	Supplies +	Equipment	=	Payable	+	Capital	+ Revenue −	Expenses

Calculate balances after recording each transaction.

Learning Objective **7**

Check Figure
Ending cash balance =
$6,105

Problem 1-3B

Objective: To record business transactions in an expanded accounting equation

Sherril Shaw opened a printer and computer repair shop this month. During the month, she completed the following transactions:

(a) Sherril invested $9,000 cash and $12,000 worth of equipment in the firm.

(b) Paid cash for office supplies, $525.

(c) Purchased wrapping paper, string, and cash register tape for cash, $355.

(d) Purchased equipment for $2,900, paying $700 down and owing the balance.

(e) Paid rent for the month, $775.

(f) Performed repair services for cash, $550.

(g) Performed repair services on credit, $875.

(h) Returned $50 of defective supplies purchased in Transaction (c), receiving a cash refund.

(i) Received $300 cash for the services performed in Transaction (g).

(j)   Paid utilities expense for the month, $340.

(k)   Paid half of the amount due on Transaction (d), $1,100.

Directions: Record Sherril's transactions for the month in an expanded accounting equation with the following headings:

		Assets			=	Liabilities	+		Owner's Equity		
Cash	+ Accounts Receivable	+ Office Supplies	+ Store Supplies	+ Equipment	=	Accounts Payable	+	Sherril Shaw, Capital	+ Revenue	− Expenses	

Calculate balances after each transaction.

Learning Objective **9**

Check Figure
Net income = $2,120; balance sheet totals = $12,820

Problem 1-4B

Objective: To prepare three financial statements

The data presented below are for Raise the Roof, a roof repair firm, on May 31, 20XX.

Item	Amount
Accounts Payable	$6,810
Accounts Receivable	1,100
Cash	2,850
Bob Daoust, Capital, May 1	4,690
Miscellaneous Expense	190
Truck	4,200
Office Supplies	375
Repair Supplies	445
Rent Expense	710
Revenue from Services	4,350
Salaries Expense	880
Office Equipment	3,850
Utilities Expense	450
Withdrawals	800

Directions:
1. Prepare an income statement for the month ended May 31, 20XX.
2. Prepare a statement of owner's equity for the month ended May 31, 20XX.
3. Prepare a balance sheet in report form as of May 31, 20XX.

Learning Objectives
7, 8, 9

Check Figure
Net income = $1,605; balance sheet totals = $22,605

Problem 1-5B

Objective: To record business transactions and prepare financial statements

Cynthia Killingsworth is a CPA who started her own practice on October 1, 20X1. During October, she completed the following transactions:

(a)   Cynthia invested the following in the firm: cash, $9,800; office supplies, $600; office equipment, $5,200.

(b)   Paid rent for the month, $650.

(c)   Purchased a computer for $2,400 on credit.

(d)   Purchased a copier for $10,000, paying $1,000 down and agreeing to pay the balance in three equal installments.

(e)   Performed services for cash, $1,350.

(f)   Wrote business checks for personal bills, $600.

(g)   Purchased a printer for cash, $595.

(h)   Purchased printer ink for cash, $90.

(i)   Performed services on credit, $1,800.

(j)   Paid utilities for the month, $295.

(k)   Paid cash for a new office desk, $900.

(l)   Collected $750 for the services performed in Transaction (i).

(m) Paid for the computer purchased in Transaction (c).

(n) Paid salary of part-time employee, $600.

(o) Paid first installment due on the copier purchased in Transaction (d).

Directions:

1. Record Cynthia's October transactions in an expanded accounting equation with the following headings. Use the Description column to provide a brief explanation of each transaction involving owner's equity, such as rent expense, fees earned, or withdrawal. [Calculate balances only after Transaction (o).]

Assets				=	Liabilities	+	Owner's Equity				
Cash +	Accounts Receivable +	Office Supplies +	Office Equipment =		Accounts Payable +		Cynthia Killingsworth, Capital	+ Revenue	– Expenses		Description

2. Prepare an income statement for October.

3. Prepare a statement of owner's equity for October.

4. Prepare an October 31 balance sheet in account form.

Critical Thinking Problems

Challenge Problem

Andi McWhorter is the owner of McWhorter's Bookkeeping and Tax Service, a sole proprietorship that has operated successfully for several years. On January 1, 20X1, the firm had balances as follows:

Item	Balance
Cash	$ 7,600
Accounts Receivable	2,100
Office Supplies	880
Office Furniture	6,500
Office Equipment	11,600
Accounts Payable	2,800
Notes Payable	7,000
Andi McWhorter, Capital	18,880

The following transactions occurred during January and February 20X1:

January transactions:

(a) Paid rent for the month, $550.

(b) Purchased office supplies on credit, $700.

(c) Paid for repairs to copier, $275.

(d) Purchased a used computer for cash, $575.

(e) Paid Simmons Company, a creditor, $600 on an account payable.

(f) Received cash from various clients for services performed, $1,725.

(g) Performed services on account for a client, $325.

(h) Purchased two boxes of printer ink for cash, $75.

(i) Paid for the office supplies purchased in Transaction (b), $700.

(j) Received cash on account from credit clients, $1,300.

(k) Paid utility bill for the month, $490.

(l) Paid salaries of employees, $2,580.

(m) Received cash from various clients for services performed, $1,840.

(n) Purchased office supplies for cash, $228.

(o) Returned a defective paper cutter purchased in Transaction (n), receiving a cash refund, $40.

(p) Performed services on account for a client, $150.

(q) Andi withdrew cash for personal use, $1,600.
(r) Received cash from various clients for services performed, $800.
(s) Paid the telephone bill, $165.
(t) Paid $1,100 on a note payable, which was issued when equipment was purchased on credit months earlier.
(u) Received cash from various clients for services performed, $1,000.

February transactions:
(a) Paid rent for the month, $550.
(b) Paid $700 for advertising on a local radio station.
(c) Paid $225 to have advertising leaflets printed.
(d) Received cash from various clients for services performed, $1,760.
(e) Received cash on account from credit clients, $600.
(f) Purchased a desk for use in the reception area, $525.
(g) Andi withdrew cash for personal use, $1,600.
(h) Paid a personal dental bill using the firm's bank account, $200.
(i) Purchased three filing cabinets for cash, $470.
(j) Received cash from various clients for services performed, $1,980.
(k) Paid $1,100 on a note payable for equipment purchased earlier.
(l) Paid utility bill, $472.
(m) Paid telephone bill, $171.
(n) Paid salaries of employees, $2,500.
(o) Received cash from various clients for services performed, $1,350.
(p) Performed services on account for a client, $400.
(q) Withdrew cash for personal use, $300.
(r) Purchased land for $6,000 as a future building site, paying $1,000 down and giving a note payable due in two years for the difference.
(s) Received cash on account from credit clients, $330.

Directions:
1. List the following headings at the top of a sheet of paper turned sideways: Cash + Accounts Receivable + Office Supplies + Office Furniture + Office Equipment + Land = Accounts Payable + Notes Payable + Andi McWhorter, Capital + Revenue – Expenses. Place the heading *Description* next to Expenses. Enter the beginning balance of each item on the first line under the headings.
2. Record the firm's January transactions. Use the *Description* column to provide a brief explanation of each transaction involving owner's equity, such as rent, fees earned, or withdrawal. Calculate balances only after the last transaction for the month.
3. Prepare financial statements at the end of January.
4. Record the firm's February transactions. Enter balances only after the last transaction.
5. Prepare financial statements at the end of February.

Communications

As you learned in this chapter, a major reason why companies keep good accounting records is to comply with tax rules and regulations. This, however, is only one reason to keep accurate and complete accounting records. Before 1913, there was no Internal Revenue Service. (Congress was given the power to tax our income in 1913 with the Sixteenth Amendment to the Constitution.) Yet, companies have always maintained accounting records.

Write a paragraph offering at least two different reasons why a firm should keep accounting records even if no taxing authority requires these records.

Team Internet Project

Forensic accounting is an emerging field. Search the Internet, and prepare a list of common job duties of the forensic accountant.

Ethics

Gregory Charles owns two different businesses—a roof repair firm and a painting company. During the current year, the roofing business made a net income of $75,000 while the painting company lost $50,000. In order to show himself in a less profitable way, Gregory combined the two businesses under a single name—Roof 'n Paint Company. He then reported to all interested parties a $25,000 net income for the year.

Write a brief statement indicating which accounting principle Gregory is violating. Explain why his method of reporting violates this principle.

In the Real World	H&R Block

Figure 1-6 shows the partial balance sheets for H&R Block as of April 30 for the years 2005, 2006, and 2007. Note: All amounts are in thousands; dates are end of period.

Based on your study of Chapter 1, identify as of April 30, 2007 (a) total assets and (b) total liabilities. (c) How does the liabilities and owner's equity section of this balance sheet differ from the ones you studied earlier in this chapter?

Figure 1-6
Balance Sheet

H&R Block Comparative Balance Sheet			
	April 30, 2007	April 30, 2006	April 30, 2005
Assets			
Cash	$1 2 5 4 4 8 4 00	$1 0 8 8 4 2 7 00	$1 6 1 7 1 2 2 00
Receivables	9 6 6 7 7 7 00	9 9 9 7 6 5 00	1 0 0 9 0 1 4 00
Property, plant, and equipment	3 7 9 0 6 6 00	4 4 3 7 8 5 00	3 3 0 1 5 0 00
Other assets	4 8 9 9 1 6 6 00	3 4 5 7 1 5 8 00	2 5 8 1 7 7 0 00
Total assets	$7 4 9 9 4 9 3 00	$5 9 8 9 1 3 5 00	$5 5 3 8 0 5 6 00
Liabilities			
Accounts payable	$1 8 5 5 3 3 0 00	$2 3 8 6 4 4 4 00	$2 2 0 9 2 5 1 00
Other liabilities	4 2 2 9 2 6 4 00	1 4 5 4 8 9 2 00	1 3 7 9 5 3 7 00
Total liabilities	$6 0 8 4 5 9 4 00	$3 8 4 1 3 3 6 00	$3 5 8 8 7 8 8 00
Stockholders' equity			
Stockholders' equity	$1 4 1 4 8 9 9 00	$2 1 4 7 7 9 9 00	$1 9 4 9 2 6 8 00

CHAPTER 1 REVIEW, PRACTICE, AND APPLY

Answers to Review Quizzes

Review Quiz 1-1

(a) $15,000
(b) $90,000
(c) $22,000
(d) $75,000

Review Quiz 1-2

	Cash	+	Accounts Receivable	+	Supplies	=	Accounts Payable	+	Susan Wright, Capital	+	Revenue	–	Expenses	Description
(a)	+$10,000								+$10,000					Investment
(b)					+$2,000				+2,000					Investment
Bal.	$10,000				$2,000				$12,000					
(c)	−600												+$600	Rent expense
Bal.	$9,400				$2,000				$12,000				$600	
(d)	+800										+$800			Revenue
Bal.	$10,200				$2,000				$12,000		$800		$600	
(e)					+200		+$200							Supplies
Bal.	$10,200				$2,200		$200		$12,000		$800		$600	
(f)			+$625								+625			Revenue
Bal.	$10,200		$625		$2,200		$200		$12,000		$1,425		$600	
(g)	−500								−500					Withdrawal
Bal.	$9,700		$625		$2,200		$200		$11,500		$1,425		$600	
(h)	+250		−250											Received Payment
Bal.	$9,950	+	$375	+	$2,200	=	$200	+	$11,500	+	$1,425	–	$600	
			$12,525							$12,525					

1.

Emery's Delivery Service Income Statement For Month Ended August 31, 20X1			
Revenue:			
Delivery revenue			$1 2 0 0 00
Expenses:			
Rent expense	$ 5 0 0 00		
Utilities expense	3 0 0 00		
Salaries expense	2 0 0 00		
Total expenses		1 0 0 0 00	
Net income		$ 2 0 0 00	

2.

Emery's Delivery Service Statement of Owner's Equity For Month Ended August 31, 20X1		
Tim Emery, capital, August 1, 20X1		$10 0 0 0 00
Net income for the month	$ 2 0 0 00	
Less withdrawals	—	
Increase in capital		2 0 0 00
Tim Emery, capital, August 31, 20X1		$10 2 0 0 00

3.

Emery's Delivery Service Balance Sheet August 31, 20X1		
Assets		
Cash	$ 9 2 0 0 00	
Supplies	1 0 0 0 00	
Equipment	18 0 0 0 00	
Total assets		$28 2 0 0 00
Liabilities		
Accounts payable		$18 0 0 0 00
Owner's Equity		
Tim Emery, capital		10 2 0 0 00
Total liabilities and owner's equity		$28 2 0 0 00

Recording Business Transactions

Learning Objectives

1 Explain the double-entry accounting framework.
2 Describe the standard form of account.
3 Describe the T account.
4 Explain the rules of debit and credit as applied to asset, liability, and owner's equity accounts.
5 Explain the need for temporary owner's equity accounts.
6 Explain the rules of debit and credit as applied to temporary owner's equity accounts.
7 Record business transactions in T accounts and prepare a trial balance.

Learning Objective

1 Explain the double-entry accounting framework.

double-entry accounting a system in which each transaction is recorded as having at least two effects on the accounting elements; the sum of all debits must equal the sum of all credits

In Chapter 1, we learned that the elements of accounting are assets, liabilities, and owner's equity. We also learned that every business transaction has at least two effects on the accounting elements. For example, the purchase of equipment for cash causes: (1) an increase in the asset *Equipment*, and (2) a decrease in the asset *Cash*. This dual effect provides the basis for what is commonly called double-entry accounting. **Double-entry accounting** means that each business transaction has at least two effects, both of which are recorded in the accounting records. *It does not mean that business transactions are recorded twice.*

We also learned in Chapter 1 that business transactions can be recorded in terms of their effect on the basic elements of the accounting equation. To review, a $500 purchase of supplies on account can be recorded as follows:

Assets	=	Liabilities	+	Owner's Equity
Supplies	=	**Accounts Payable**		
+$500		+$500		

Recording transactions in terms of their effect on the accounting equation is easy to understand, and it clearly shows the dual effect. The volume of daily transactions, however, makes this form of recording impractical for an actual accounting system, because all transactions are recorded on a single sheet. To prepare reports and statements, accountants must have day-to-day information available for *each* accounting element. Therefore, separate records are needed to show increases and decreases in each asset, each liability, and each aspect of owner's equity. Such a record is called an *account*, which we will discuss next.

Accounts are the basic storage units for accounting data. A separate account is maintained for each asset, liability, and owner's equity item.

The Account

An **account** is an individual record or form used to record and summarize information related to each asset, each liability, and each aspect of owner's equity. An account can be thought of as a storage bin. As business transactions occur, financial information is recorded and stored in various asset, liability, and owner's equity accounts. In this way, financial information is easily and quickly available for preparing financial statements and reports.

The exact form of an account varies, depending on its use. Some accounts may be bound in book form, others may be in loose-leaf binders, and others may be part of a computer system. Figure 2-1 shows the **standard form of account**, which has three major parts:

- The account title and number.
- The left side, which is called the debit side.
- The right side, which is called the credit side.

Learning Objective

2 Describe the standard form of account.

Figure 2-1

The Standard Form of Account

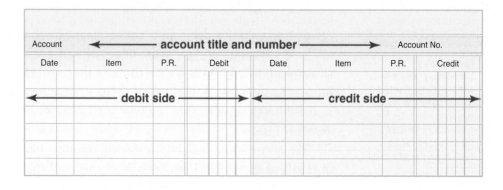

Each account is given an appropriate title to identify it as asset, liability, or owner's equity. Accounts are also assigned numbers to aid in locating and recording. The account title and account number are written on the first horizontal line of the form.

The *Date* column of an account is used to record the date on which a transaction occurs. The *Item* column is used to record a brief description of the entry, if needed. The *P.R.* (Posting Reference) column is discussed in Chapter 3. The *Debit* and *Credit* columns are money columns used to record the dollar amounts of transactions. Soon we will look at how to record transactions using debits and credits.

Accounts are often grouped together in book form; such a grouping of accounts is called a **ledger**. Thus, accounts are frequently referred to as *ledger accounts*.

account an individual form used to record increases and decreases in a specific asset, liability, or owner's equity item

standard form of account a form of account with separate debit and credit sides

ledger a grouping of all accounts a company uses

The T Account

Learning Objective

3 Describe the T account.

T account skeleton version of the standard form of an account

The **T account**, so named because it looks like a capital letter T, is a skeleton version of the standard form of account. The T account provides the same basic data as the standard form of account: (1) the account title, (2) the debit side, and (3) the credit side. Because they can be drawn quickly and easily, T accounts are useful for learning purposes. The T account is illustrated as follows:

Title of Account	
Debit Side	Credit Side

Debits and Credits

to debit to enter an amount on the left, or debit, side of the account; abbreviated as Dr.

to credit to enter an amount on the right, or credit, side of the account; abbreviated as Cr.

The left side of *any* account is the debit side. **To debit** an account means to enter an amount on the left, or debit, side. The right side of *any* account is the credit side. **To credit** an account means to enter an amount on the right, or credit, side. To save time, the abbreviation *Dr.* is commonly used for debit, and the abbreviation *Cr.* is commonly used for credit. These abbreviations come from the Latin terms *debe̲re̲* and *crede̲re̲*.

The word *charge* is sometimes used as a synonym for debit. Thus, *to charge* an account means the same as *to debit* an account.

Rules of Debit and Credit

Learning Objective

4 Explain the rules of debit and credit as applied to asset, liability, and owner's equity accounts.

Key Point ⊙

Debit = left
Credit = right

Let us stress that to debit an account means to enter an amount on the left side of the account, and to credit an account means to enter an amount on the right side of the account. *Do not* think of the terms *debit* and *credit* as meaning increase or decrease; only think of them as meaning left and right.

Debit can signify *either* increase or decrease, depending on the type of account. Likewise, credit can signify *either* increase or decrease, depending on the type of account. The rules for debiting and crediting are best understood by relating the left and right sides of the accounting equation to the debit and credit sides of the T account, as follows:

Left Side of Equation		**Right Side of Equation**
Assets	=	Liabilities + Owner's Equity

Title of Account	
Left, or Debit Side	Right, or Credit Side

Assets are on the left side of the equation; debit is on the left side of the account. Therefore, asset accounts are increased on the debit side. Liabilities and owner's equity are on the right side of the equation; credit is on the right side of the account. Therefore, liability accounts and the owner's capital account (the name given to the main account for owner's equity) are increased on the credit side.

An account has only two sides; thus, the decrease side is always opposite the increase side. Because asset accounts are increased on the debit side, they are decreased on the credit side. On the other hand, liability and owner's equity accounts are decreased on the debit side because they are increased on the credit side.

The rules of debit and credit can be shown as follows:

Assets	=	Liabilities	+	Owner's Equity
Asset Accounts		Liability Accounts		Owner's Capital Account

Debit	Credit		Debit	Credit		Debit	Credit
+	−		−	+		−	+

The rules of debit and credit are based on logic and tradition. Since assets are on the left side of the equation and debit is on the left side of the account, it is logical to increase assets on the debit side. The same logic is applied to increasing liability and owner's equity accounts on the credit (right) side, since liabilities and owner's equity are on the right side of the equation. It is possible that the rules of debit and credit could be reversed had the accounting equation developed in reverse order.

Review Quiz **2-1**

Do the terms *debit* and *credit* mean increase or decrease, or may they mean either? Explain.

Check your answer on page 86.

Recording Transactions in Asset, Liability, and Owner's Equity Accounts

Remember

As you learned in Chapter 1, a transaction is an event that changes a firm's financial position.

As we just learned, the account is an accounting record used to record increases and decreases in the various asset, liability, and owner's equity items. We stressed that to debit an account simply means to enter an amount on the left side of the account, and to credit an account means to enter an amount on the right side. To illustrate how this works, we will look at the first month's transactions of a new business started by Stanley Walker. For several years, Stanley worked for a large talent and booking agency. In November 20X1, he started his own firm, which he named Walker and Associates. Several transactions occurred and were recorded during November. In order to make a proper entry for each transaction, a careful analysis is made to determine:

Tutorial 3

Recording Transactions in T Accounts

- The titles of the accounts affected by the transaction.
- Whether the accounts affected were increased or decreased.
- How to increase or decrease (debit or credit) the accounts affected.

For illustration purposes, the following recorded transactions are identified by letters instead of the date on which they occurred.

Transaction (a): Stanley Invested $10,000 Cash into His Business to Get It Started

Analysis: Cash was received by the business. Therefore, the Cash account must be increased. The Cash account—an asset account—is increased on the debit side.

Owner investments increase the equity of the business. Therefore, the owner's capital account—in this case, called the Stanley Walker, Capital account—must be increased. The owner's capital account is increased on the credit side.

Key Point ▷

Amounts entered on the left side of an account are debits; amounts entered on the right side are credits.

Entry:

Cash		Stanley Walker, Capital	
Debit	Credit	Debit	Credit
+	–	–	+
(a) 10,000			(a) 10,000

Transaction (b): Purchased Office Equipment for $3,000 on Account

Analysis: The business acquired an asset, office equipment. Therefore, an asset account entitled Office Equipment must be increased. Asset accounts are increased on the debit side.

The business incurred a liability as a result of purchasing office equipment on account. Therefore, a liability account called Accounts Payable is increased. Liability accounts are increased on the credit side.

Key Point ▷

The amount entered on the left side of the account *must* equal the amount entered on the right side of another account.

Entry:

Office Equipment		Accounts Payable	
Debit	Credit	Debit	Credit
+	–	–	+
(b) 3,000			(b) 3,000

Transaction (c): Purchased Office Supplies for Cash, $125

Analysis: The business acquired an asset—office supplies. Therefore, the Office Supplies account must be increased. Office Supplies—an asset account—is increased on the debit side.

Cash was paid. Therefore, the Cash account must be decreased. Cash—an asset account—is decreased on the credit side.

Entry:

Office Supplies		Cash	
Debit	Credit	Debit	Credit
+	–	+	–
(c) 125		(a) 10,000	(c) 125

Transaction (d): Paid $500 on Equipment Purchased in Transaction (b)

Analysis: Cash was paid. Therefore, the Cash account must be decreased. Cash—an asset account—is decreased on the credit side.

Part of an account payable was paid. Therefore, the Accounts Payable account must be decreased by the amount of the payment. Accounts Payable—a liability account—is decreased on the debit side.

Entry:

Cash				Accounts Payable			
Debit		Credit		Debit		Credit	
+		–		–		+	
(a) 10,000		(c) 125		**(d) 500**		(b) 3,000	
		(d) 500					

Key Point ⊛

For each ledger entry, the debit part of the entry equals the credit part of the entry.

Note that in each of the preceding ledger entries, the debit part of the entry equals the credit part of the entry. This is an accounting rule that must always hold true. In the double-entry system, a debit recorded in one account must be accompanied by an equal credit recorded in another account. Making equal debits and credits maintains the accounting equation in balance and provides a means of verifying the mathematical accuracy of recorded transactions.

CAUTION

It is the dollar amounts of the debits and credits that must be equal; the actual count of debit transactions and credit transactions does not matter.

Review Quiz 2-2

On plain paper, draw T accounts and record the following transactions, and identify each transaction by letter.

(a) Greg Calloway invested $8,000 in a new business to be called Calloway Electronics.
(b) Purchased equipment on account, $1,200.
(c) Purchased office supplies for cash, $500.
(d) Purchased shop supplies on account, $300.
(e) Paid $600 on equipment purchased in Transaction (b).

Check your answers on page 87.

Temporary Owner's Equity Accounts

In Chapter 1, you learned that there are two ways to increase owner's equity: (1) investments of cash or other assets into the business by the owner and (2) revenue from various sources. You also learned that there are two ways to decrease owner's equity: (1) withdrawals of cash or other assets by the owner and (2) expenses of operating the business.

It is possible to record all changes in owner's equity directly in the owner's capital account. Expenses and withdrawals reduce owner's equity. Thus, expenses and withdrawals would be recorded on the debit side (the decrease side) of the owner's capital account. Investments and revenue increase owner's equity. Thus, investments and revenue would be recorded on the credit side (the increase side) of the owner's capital account. The owner's capital account would then appear as follows:

Owner's Capital Account

Debit	Credit
–	+
Expenses	Owner investments
Owner withdrawals	Revenue

Learning Objective

5 Explain the need for temporary owner's equity accounts.

temporary owner's equity accounts accounts whose balances will be transferred to the owner's capital account at the end of the accounting period; examples include expense accounts, revenue accounts, and the owner's drawing account

The procedure just described is not practical, however. In most businesses, expense and revenue transactions occur constantly, and the owner frequently withdraws assets for personal use. Recording these transactions in the owner's capital account clutters the account and does not yield a separate record for expense items, revenue items, and owner withdrawals. To determine the net income or net loss for an accounting period, the owner's capital account would have to be analyzed very carefully to determine the amount of revenue and expenses.

It is generally considered a better accounting practice to have a separate ledger account for each type of expense, each type of revenue, and withdrawals. These accounts are subdivisions of the owner's capital account and are used to show changes that occur in owner's equity during an accounting period. When the period is over, these accounts will have served their purpose, and their balances will be transferred to the owner's capital account. Thus, expense accounts, revenue accounts, and the owner's drawing account are said to be **temporary owner's equity accounts**.

Rules of Debit and Credit as Applied to Revenue and Expense Accounts

Learning Objective

6 Explain the rules of debit and credit as applied to temporary owner's equity accounts.

Since revenue and expense accounts are subdivisions of the owner's capital account, the rules of debit and credit are applied to these accounts based on their relationship to owner's equity. Revenue increases owner's equity. Thus, the rules of debit and credit are the *same* for revenue accounts as they are for the owner's capital account. The owner's capital account is increased on the credit side; revenue accounts are likewise increased on the credit side. The owner's capital account is decreased on the debit side; revenue accounts are likewise decreased on the debit side.

Expenses are the opposite of revenue; they decrease owner's equity. Thus, the increase and decrease sides of expense accounts are *opposite* the increase and decrease sides of the owner's capital account. The owner's capital account is decreased on the debit side; expense accounts are increased on the debit side. The owner's capital account is increased on the credit side; expense accounts are decreased on the credit side.

The relationship of revenue and expense accounts to the owner's capital account is illustrated in Figure 2-2.

Figure 2-2 The Owner's Capital Account and Its Relationship to Expense and Revenue Accounts

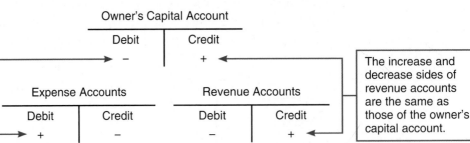

Recording Transactions in Revenue and Expense Accounts

To illustrate recording expense and revenue transactions, let's continue looking at the first month's transactions of Walker and Associates.

Transaction (e): Paid First Month's Rent, $400

Analysis: Rent was paid for November. Therefore, an expense account entitled Rent Expense must be increased. Expense accounts are increased on the debit side.

Cash was paid. Therefore, the Cash account must be decreased by the amount of the payment. Cash—an asset account—is decreased on the credit side.

Entry:

Rent Expense		Cash	
Debit	Credit	Debit	Credit
+	–	+	–
(e) 400		(a) 10,000	(c) 125
			(d) 500
			(e) 400

Transaction (f): Paid for Repairs to Equipment, $50

Analysis: Repairs were made to equipment. Therefore, the Repairs Expense account must be increased. Expense accounts are increased on the debit side.

Cash was paid. Therefore, the Cash account must be decreased. Cash—an asset account—is decreased on the credit side.

Entry:

Repairs Expense		Cash	
Debit	Credit	Debit	Credit
+	–	+	–
(f) 50		(a) 10,000	(c) 125
			(d) 500
			(e) 400
			(f) 50

Transaction (g): Received Cash from Customers for Services, $1,800

Analysis: Cash was received from customers. Therefore, the Cash account must be increased. Cash—an asset account—is increased on the debit side.

Cash received from services yields revenue to the business. Therefore, a revenue account must be increased. Revenue accounts are increased on the credit side. We will use a revenue account entitled Service Revenue.

Entry:

Cash			Service Revenue	
Debit	**Credit**		**Debit**	**Credit**
+	–		–	+
(a) 10,000	(c) 125			(g) 1,800
(g) 1,800	(d) 500			
	(e) 400			
	(f) 50			

Transaction (h): Performed Services on Account, $400

Analysis: Services were performed on credit for customers. Therefore, the Accounts Receivable account must be increased. Accounts Receivable—an asset account—is increased on the debit side.

Services performed, whether for cash or on account, yield revenue to the business. Therefore, a revenue account must be increased. Revenue accounts are increased on the credit side.

Entry:

Accounts Receivable			Service Revenue	
Debit	**Credit**		**Debit**	**Credit**
+	–		–	+
(h) 400				(g) 1,800
				(h) 400

Let's pause for a minute to look at Figure 2-3, which shows a summary of the debit and credit rules we have learned so far.

Figure 2-3
Debit and Credit Rule Summary

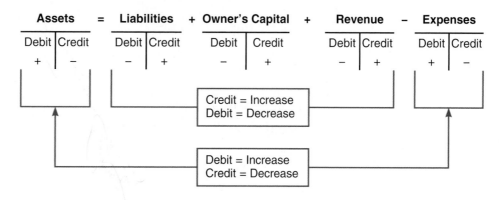

To help remember the rules of debit and credit, think of the position of the accounts within the accounting equation. Assets (to the far left of the equation) and expenses (to the far right of the equation) are handled the same: they are both increased with debits and decreased with credits. On the other hand, the three account classifications in the middle of the equation—liabilities, owner's capital, and revenue—are just the opposite: they are increased with credits and decreased with debits.

Take This Into Account

Investments by the owner usually occur infrequently. Therefore, a separate ledger account is not maintained for owner investments. Instead, investments are recorded directly in the owner's capital account.

Owner's Drawing Account

drawing account a temporary owner's equity account used to record a business owner's withdrawals of cash or other assets from the business for personal use

Owners of businesses frequently withdraw cash or other assets from the business for their personal use. As stated earlier, it is possible to record withdrawals directly in the owner's capital account; however, it is usually considered better practice to have a separate **drawing account**. Since withdrawals decrease owner's equity, the drawing account is increased on the debit side (the decrease side of owner's equity). As shown in Figure 2-4, the increase and decrease sides of the owner's drawing account are opposite those of the owner's capital account.

Figure 2-4

The Owner's Capital Account and Its Relationship to the Owner's Drawing Account

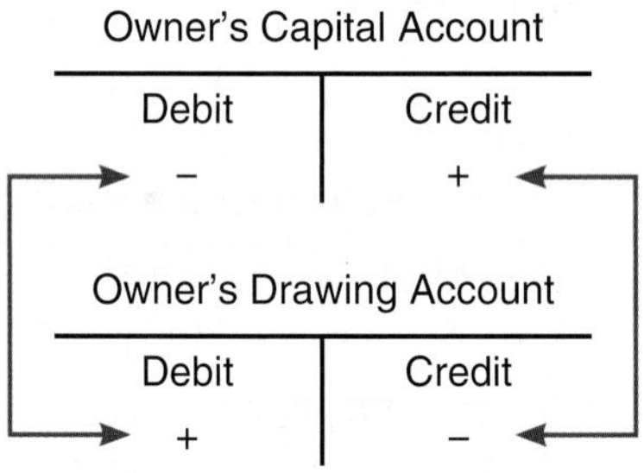

To illustrate the recording of an owner withdrawal, let's look at the next transaction completed by Stanley during his first month of operations.

Transaction (i): Stanley Withdrew $800 Cash from the Business for Personal Use

Analysis: Cash was withdrawn from the business. Therefore, the Cash account must be decreased by the amount of the withdrawal. Cash—an asset account—is decreased on the credit side.

Owner withdrawals result in an increase in the owner's drawing account, representing a decrease in owner's equity. The owner's drawing account is increased on the debit side.

Entry:

Cash				Stanley Walker, Drawing			
Debit		Credit		Debit		Credit	
+		−		+		−	
(a)	10,000	(c)	125	(i)	800		
(g)	1,800	(d)	500				
		(e)	400				
		(f)	50				
		(i)	800				

Transaction (j): Collected $100 Cash on Account from Credit Customers in Transaction (h)

Analysis: Cash was received from credit customers. Therefore, the Cash account must be increased. Cash—an asset account—is increased on the debit side.

Collections on account from credit customers result in a decrease in the Accounts Receivable account. Accounts Receivable—an asset account—is decreased on the credit side.

Entry:

Cash				Accounts Receivable			
Debit		Credit		Debit		Credit	
+		−		+		−	
(a)	10,000	(c)	125	(h)	400	(j)	100
(g)	1,800	(d)	500				
(j)	100	(e)	400				
		(f)	50				
		(i)	800				

Now that we have analyzed and recorded all of Stanley's November transactions, let's review the steps involved in analyzing a transaction.

Before recording each transaction, you should decide:

1. Which accounts are affected by the transaction.
2. Whether there is an increase or decrease in the accounts.
3. How to increase or decrease (debit or credit) the accounts involved.

These decisions are so important that you should firmly entrench them in your mind. A careful analysis of a transaction will yield a correct entry. Take Transaction (g), for example, in which Stanley received $1,800 in cash for services performed. The thought quickly comes to mind, "We have cash." And what is cash? It is an asset. How do you increase an asset account? Assets are increased on the debit side. Now we have the debit part of our entry, and you know that we must also have an equal credit. Cash received from services is revenue to the business. Thus, we need to increase a revenue account. How are revenue accounts increased? They are increased on the credit side. By following these steps, we obtain a debit to the Cash account for $1,800 and a credit to the Service Revenue account for $1,800.

After each entry, *check to make sure that the debit part of your entry equals the credit part.* When all the transactions have been recorded in the accounts, the total of all the debits should be equal to the total of all the credits.

Total debits must always equal total credits.

Debit | Credit

Debits are used to record:	Credits are used to record:
• increases in asset accounts	• increases in liability accounts
• increases in expense accounts	• increases in the owner's capital account
• increases in the owner's drawing account	• increases in revenue accounts
• decreases in liability accounts	• decreases in asset accounts
• decreases in the owner's capital account	• decreases in expense accounts
• decreases in revenue accounts	• decreases in the owner's drawing account

Review Quiz 2-3

On plain paper, draw T accounts and record the following transactions made by Lynn Dowdy. Label each debit and credit with the transaction's letter.

(a) Received cash for services performed, $5,000.
(b) Paid rent for the month, $600.
(c) Paid utility bill, $540.
(d) Paid salaries of employees, $1,800.
(e) Paid for repairs to equipment, $200.
(f) Lynn withdrew cash for personal use, $500.

Check your answers on page 87.

The Trial Balance

Learning Objective

7 Record business transactions in T accounts and prepare a trial balance.

trial balance a listing of all ledger accounts and their balances to test the equality of debits and credits in the ledger at the end of an accounting period, usually at the end of each month

balance the difference between total debits and total credits to an account; determined by footing (adding) the debit side, footing the credit side, and subtracting the smaller total from the larger

footing the total of the debit column or credit column of an account

As we have stressed, total debits must always equal total credits in a double-entry accounting system. To test the equality of debits and credits in the ledger, a trial balance is prepared periodically. A **trial balance** is a listing, as of a certain date, of all ledger accounts with their balances. A trial balance is typically prepared at the end of each month. However, a trial balance can be prepared any time it is felt that the equality of debits and credits should be checked.

The first step in preparing a trial balance is to find the balance of each ledger account. The **balance** of any account is the difference between the total debits and the total credits in that account. Balances are arrived at by **footing** (adding) the debit and credit columns of each account and calculating the difference between the two columns. As an example, the balance of the Cash account of Walker and Associates is found as follows:

Cash

Debit		Credit	
+		−	
(a)	10,000	(c)	125
(g)	1,800	(d)	500
(j)	100	(e)	400
10,025	11,900	(f)	50
		(i)	800
			1,875

debit balance   footings ⟶

The debit column footing is $11,900. The credit column footing is $1,875. The balance of the account, $10,025, is determined by subtracting the lesser footing from the greater footing. The balance is written on the same line as the greater footing. When the debit footing is greater, as in this case, the account has a **debit balance**; thus, the balance is written on the debit side. On the other hand, when the credit footing is greater, the account has a **credit balance**; thus, the balance is written on the credit side.

Manual accounting records are done in ink. However, footings are customarily done in pencil (in case of an arithmetic error). Therefore, footings are also called *pencil footings*.

The ledger accounts of Walker and Associates are reproduced in Figure 2-5. To show their relationship to the accounting equation, accounts are listed under the headings Assets = Liabilities + Owner's Equity. Note that when an account has both debit and credit amounts—as does the Cash account—it is necessary to foot and balance the account. When an account has only one debit amount and one credit amount—as does the Accounts Payable account—it is not necessary to foot the sides, because there is only one amount on each side. In this situation, it is only necessary to balance the account. When an account has entries only on one side—as does the Service Revenue account—it is only necessary to foot the account. And when an account has only one entry—as do Stanley Walker, Drawing; Rent Expense; and Repairs Expense—it is not necessary to calculate a balance, as there is only one amount (which is the balance).

Figure 2-5

Ledger Accounts of Walker and Associates

Assets		=	Liabilities		+	Owner's Equity	

Cash

Debit	Credit
+	–
(a) 10,000	(c) 125
(g) 1,800	(d) 500
(j) 100	(e) 400
10,025 11,900	(f) 50
	(i) 800
	1,875

Accounts Payable

Debit	Credit
–	+
(d) 500	(b) 3,000
	2,500

Stanley Walker, Capital

Debit	Credit
–	+
	(a) 10,000

Accounts Receivable

Debit	Credit
+	–
(h) 400	(j) 100
300	

Stanley Walker, Drawing

Debit	Credit
+	–
(i) 800	

Office Supplies

Debit	Credit
+	–
(c) 125	

Service Revenue

Debit	Credit
–	+
	(g) 1,800
	(h) 400
	2,200

Continues

Figure 2-5

Continued

Assets	=	Liabilities	+	Owner's Equity

Office Equipment

Debit	Credit
+	–
(b) 3,000	

Rent Expense

Debit	Credit
+	–
(e) 400	

Repairs Expense

Debit	Credit
+	–
(f) 50	

A trial balance is prepared to prove the equality of debits and credits in the ledger. The trial balance can be prepared manually using a calculator, as we did here, or prepared automatically using computer software.

After each account has been balanced, each account balance is carefully transferred to a two-column sheet, with the debit balances in one column and the credit balances in the other. Each column is then totaled, and the totals are compared.

The trial balance of Walker and Associates is shown in Figure 2-6. The trial balance was prepared on November 30, 20X1, and this date is entered in the heading.

It should be stressed that a trial balance shows only that total debits equal total credits. A trial balance is not a formal financial statement or report. However, information to prepare formal statements can come directly from the trial balance. A trial balance can be prepared on analysis paper, as we did for Walker and Associates, or simply by totaling debit and credit balances on an adding machine tape or using computer software.

Figure 2-6

A Trial Balance

Walker and Associates
Trial Balance
November 30, 20X1

Account Title	Debit	Credit
Cash	10 0 2 5 00	
Accounts Receivable	3 0 0 00	
Office Supplies	1 2 5 00	
Office Equipment	3 0 0 0 00	
Accounts Payable		2 5 0 0 00
Stanley Walker, Capital		10 0 0 0 00
Stanley Walker, Drawing	8 0 0 00	
Service Revenue		2 2 0 0 00
Rent Expense	4 0 0 00	
Repairs Expense	5 0 00	
Totals	14 7 0 0 00	14 7 0 0 00

Since the trial balance is not a formal financial statement, no dollar signs are needed.

Don't confuse the trial balance with the balance sheet. A balance sheet is a listing of a company's assets, liabilities, and owner's equity at a certain point in time. It is a formal financial statement that is used by managers inside the business, and by users outside the business—such as banks and other lenders. A trial balance is an informal test of the equality of debits and credits in the ledger. No one outside the accounting department sees the trial balance.

Normal Balance of Accounts

normal balance the increase side of an account or where you would expect to find the balance of that account

An account usually has more increases than decreases. Consequently, the **normal balance** side of an account is always the same as the increase side. Asset, expense, and drawing accounts are increased on the debit side; therefore, they normally have debit balances. Liability, owner's capital, and revenue accounts, on the other hand, are increased on the credit side; thus, they normally have credit balances. Table 2-1 shows where account balances would normally be listed on a trial balance.

Table 2-1 Normal Balances on the Trial Balance

Account	Normal Debit Balance	Normal Credit Balance
Asset	✓	
Liability		✓
Owner's Capital		✓
Owner's Drawing	✓	
Revenue		✓
Expense	✓	
Equal Totals	✓	✓

Review Quiz 2-4

The ledger of Coastal Realty appears as follows on July 31, 20XX. Determine the balance of each account and prepare a trial balance.

Assets		=	**Liabilities**	+	**Owner's Equity**

Cash			Accounts Payable		George Lawson, Capital
(a) 18,000	(b) 500		(c) 900		(a) 18,000
(h) 850	(f) 800		(d) 300		
(j) 1,200	(g) 400		(e) 2,000		
	(i) 800				
	(k) 960				

Office Supplies					George Lawson, Drawing
(b) 500					(i) 800

Continues

Assets	=	Liabilities	+	Owner's Equity

Store Supplies

(c) 900
(d) 300

Store Equipment

(e) 2,000

Commission Revenue

(h)   850
(j) 1,200

Rent Expense

(f) 800

Utilities Expense

(g) 400

Travel Expense

(k) 960

Check your answers on page 87.

Summary of Debit and Credit Rules

At this point, you may still feel a little unsure about when to debit and when to credit. If you are feeling uncertainty, don't worry; it will pass. When you drive your car, don't you automatically pull onto the right side of the road without having to stop and think? You do this because you have practiced it so much. In accounting, like anything else, you improve when you practice. Study the debit and credit rules closely and continue practicing. You will soon find debits and credits as natural as driving on the right side of the road.

We have studied several rules of debit and credit. These rules can be summarized as shown in the chart in Table 2-2. Notice that the increase side and the normal balance are the same color. This emphasizes that an account's normal balance is always on the increase side.

Table 2-2 Summary of Debit and Credit Rules

Account	Increase Side	Decrease Side	Normal Balance
Asset	Debit	Credit	Debit
Liability	Credit	Debit	Credit
Owner's Capital	Credit	Debit	Credit
Owner's Drawing	Debit	Credit	Debit
Revenue	Credit	Debit	Credit
Expense	Debit	Credit	Debit

Figure 2-7

Expanded Basic Accounting Equation

Let's now tie our rules together and look at an expanded statement of the basic accounting equation, as illustrated in Figure 2-7.

Assets	=	Liabilities	+	Owner's Capital	+	Revenue	−	Expenses	−	Owner's Drawing
+ | −		− | +		− | +		− | +		+ | −		+ | −
Left | Right		Left | Right		Left | Right		Left | Right		Left | Right		Left | Right
Debit | Credit		Debit | Credit		Debit | Credit		Debit | Credit		Debit | Credit		Debit | Credit

Review Quiz **2-5** Why do expense accounts and the owner's drawing account have debit balances?

Check your answer on page 88.

Focus on ETHICS

Tyco Fraud

Tyco is a conglomerate manufacturing corporation that manufactures anything from electronic components to health care products. Their 240,000 employees are located in more than a hundred countries. The Securities and Exchange Commission (SEC) began investigating Tyco's top executives in January 2002. As a result, they discovered that Dennis Kozlowski, Tyco's former chief executive officer; Mark Swartz, Tyco's former chief financial officer; and Mark Belnick, the company's chief legal officer, were taking out loans from the company without obtaining permission from the shareholders or the Board of Directors' compensation committee. The loans, which amounted to $170 million, were taken with small to zero interest. Several of the loans were claimed as unapproved bonuses. It was further determined that Kozlowski and Swartz sold 7.5 million shares of Tyco stock for $430 million. Investors were never notified.

The estimated loss to Tyco was $600 million. Kozlowski and Swartz were both convicted on charges of conspiracy, securities fraud, and grand larceny. Both are currently appealing their convictions. As a result of the scandal, one half of the members of the Board of Directors were replaced, even though there was no evidence that they were involved in the fraud.

Chairman Dennis Kozlowski was one of Tyco's top executives convicted of conspiracy, securities fraud, and grand larceny.

Sources: Staff, "Einstein Law, Inc.," www.securitiesfraudfyi.com; Staff, "Tyco Agrees to $50 Million Settlement," *National Legal News*, April 17, 2006.

For Discussion

1. What were the reasons that the SEC began investigating Tyco?
2. What internal control was violated in this example?
3. Why do you believe that one half of the Board of Directors was replaced even though there was no evidence that they were involved in the fraud?
4. Is it even legal or a violation of ethics for top management to sell shares of their own stock in the corporation in which they manage?

Joining the Pieces

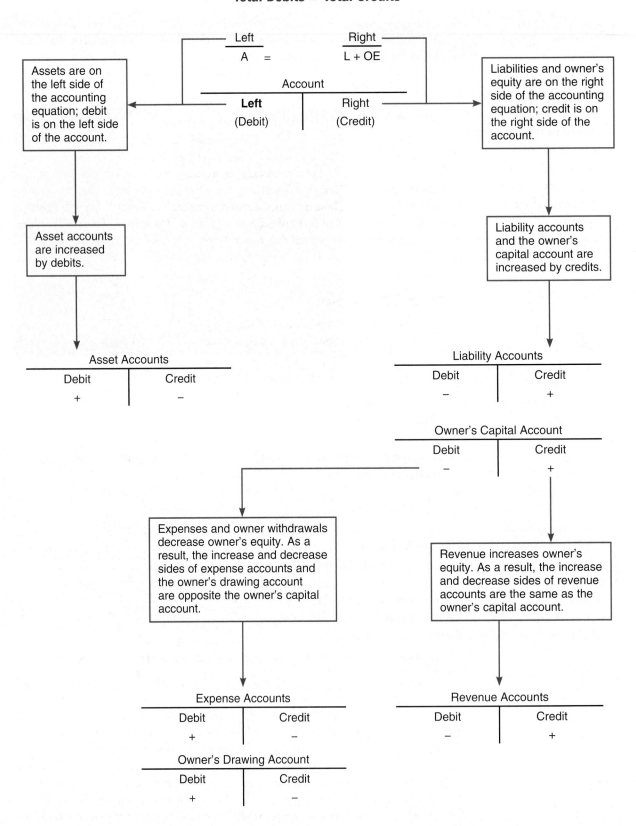

Total Debits = Total Credits

Assets are on the left side of the accounting equation; debit is on the left side of the account.

Liabilities and owner's equity are on the right side of the accounting equation; credit is on the right side of the account.

Asset accounts are increased by debits.

Liability accounts and the owner's capital account are increased by credits.

Expenses and owner withdrawals decrease owner's equity. As a result, the increase and decrease sides of expense accounts and the owner's drawing account are opposite the owner's capital account.

Revenue increases owner's equity. As a result, the increase and decrease sides of revenue accounts are the same as the owner's capital account.

Summary — Interactive Summary in English and Spanish

1 Explain the double-entry accounting framework.

Each business transaction affects the accounting elements in at least two ways. Recording both effects of a transaction is called **double-entry accounting**. The double-entry system provides a means of verifying the mathematical accuracy of recorded transactions. When both effects of a transaction have been recorded, assets equal liabilities plus owner's equity.

2 Describe the standard form of account.

An **account** is an individual record or form used to record increases and decreases in each asset, each liability, and owner's equity. The exact form of account can vary, depending on the use. The **standard form of account** is a basic account form with two amount (or money) columns. The left column is the *Debit* column. The right column is the *Credit* column. These columns are used to record the dollar value of business transactions. The standard form of account also has a *Date* column for recording the date on which transactions occur; an *Item* column for recording a brief description of an entry, if needed; and a *P.R. (Posting Reference)* column, which will be discussed in Chapter 3.

3 Describe the T account.

The **T account** is a skeleton version of the standard form of account. The T account is used mainly for illustrations, since it can be drawn quickly and easily. The T account, so named because it looks like the letter T, has a space for the account title, a left, or debit, side, and a right, or credit, side. The T account is shown here:

Account Title	
Debit Side	Credit Side

4 Explain the rules of debit and credit as applied to asset, liability, and owner's equity accounts.

Transactions are recorded in accounts using the rules of debit and credit. Asset accounts are increased by entering an amount on the debit side. Asset accounts are decreased by entering an amount on the credit side. The reverse is true of liability and the owner's capital accounts. These accounts are increased by entering an amount on the credit side and decreased by entering an amount on the debit side. These rules evolved from the accounting equation Assets = Liabilities + Owner's Equity. By having opposite increase and decrease sides for accounts on the left side of the equation (assets) and accounts on the right side of the equation (liabilities and owner's equity), the equation is maintained in balance.

5 Explain the need for temporary owner's equity accounts.

Owner's equity can be increased in two ways: (1) investments of cash or other assets by the owner and (2) revenue. Conversely, owner's equity can be decreased in two ways: (1) owner withdrawals of cash or other assets from the business and (2) expenses of operating the business. These changes could be recorded directly in the owner's capital account. However, this would clutter the account and complicate the determination of net income or net loss. Therefore, it is considered a better practice to maintain separate ledger accounts for revenue, expenses, and owner withdrawals. When the accounting period is over, the balances of these accounts are transferred to the owner's capital account. Thus, these accounts are referred to as **temporary owner's equity accounts**.

6 Explain the rules of debit and credit as applied to temporary owner's equity accounts.

The rules of debit and credit are applied to temporary owner's equity accounts based on their relationship to owner's equity. Revenue increases owner's equity. Consequently, the rules of debit and credit are the same for revenue accounts as they are for the owner's capital account. Revenue accounts are increased on the credit side and decreased on the debit side (the same as the owner's capital account). Expenses and owner withdrawals decrease owner's equity. Thus, the increase and decrease sides of these accounts are opposite the increase and decrease sides of the owner's capital account. Expense accounts and the owner's drawing account are increased on the debit side and decreased on the credit side (the opposite of the owner's capital account).

7 Record business transactions in T accounts and prepare a trial balance.

The Lawson Company incurred the following transactions during June 20X2:

(a) Stan Lawson invested $6,000 in his new cement finishing service.
(b) Purchased supplies for cash, $800.
(c) Invested a used truck, valued at $5,200, in the business.
(d) Purchased office equipment on account, $800.
(e) Received cash for services rendered, $125.
(f) Received cash for services rendered, $250.
(g) Purchased gasoline and truck parts for cash, $68.
(h) Paid salary of assistant, $350.
(i) Received cash for services rendered, $300.
(j) Paid utility bill, $292.
(k) Paid salary of assistant, $350.

Transactions are recorded, T accounts are footed and balanced, and a trial balance is prepared, as shown in Figure 2-8.

Figure 2-8

Preparation of a Trial Balance

Cash					Accounts Payable			Stan Lawson, Capital	
(a)	6,000	(b)	800			(d)	800	(a)	6,000
(e)	125	(g)	68					(c)	5,200
(f)	250	(h)	350						11,200
(i)	300	(j)	292						
4,815	6,675	(k)	350						
			1,860						

Supplies			Service Revenue	
(b)	800		(e)	125
			(f)	250
			(i)	300
				675

Office Equipment			Salaries Expense	
(d)	800		(h)	350
			(k)	350
				700

Continues

Figure 2-8
Continued

Truck	
(c) 5,200	

Truck Expense	
(g) 68	

Utilities Expense	
(j) 292	

Lawson Company
Trial Balance
June 30, 20X2

Account Title	Debit	Credit
Cash	4 8 1 5 00	
Supplies	8 0 0 00	
Office Equipment	8 0 0 00	
Truck	5 2 0 0 00	
Accounts Payable		8 0 0 00
Stan Lawson, Capital		11 2 0 0 00
Service Revenue		6 7 5 00
Salaries Expense	7 0 0 00	
Truck Expense	6 8 00	
Utilities Expense	2 9 2 00	
Totals	12 6 7 5 00	12 6 7 5 00

Terms and Concepts Review

- Key Terms and Definitions in English and Spanish
- Additional Quiz Questions

Key Terms

account, 56
balance, 66
to credit, 57
credit balance, 67
to debit, 57
debit balance, 67
double-entry accounting, 55
drawing account, 64

footing, 66
ledger, 56
normal balance, 69
standard form of account, 56
T account, 57
temporary owner's equity accounts, 61
trial balance, 66

Concepts Review

1. What is meant by double-entry accounting?
2. What is an account?
3. Why is it better to record business transactions in accounts rather than in equation form?
4. A ledger is sometimes called a book of accounts. Is this always a good description of a ledger? Explain.
5. What is the meaning of the word *debit*? The word *credit*?
6. Explain the rules of debit and credit as applied to asset, liability, and owner's capital accounts.
7. List three reasons for using temporary owner's equity accounts.
8. Explain the rules of debit and credit as applied to temporary owner's equity accounts.

9. How are account balances calculated?
10. What is a footing?
11. Is it possible for an account to have a zero balance if there are entries on both the debit and credit sides of that account? Explain.
12. What is a trial balance?
13. What does a trial balance prove?
14. What is meant by the normal balance of an account?

Skills Review

Quick Practice

Learning Objective **4**

Check Figure
(a) debit

Quick Practice 2-1

Objective: To identify the rules of debit and credit

Directions: Complete the following statements using either "debit" or "credit."

(a) The Cash account is increased with a _____.
(b) The liability account, Accounts Payable, is increased with a _____.
(c) The revenue account, Fees Earned, is increased with a _____.
(d) The Salary Expense account is increased with a _____.
(e) The owner's capital account is increased with a _____.
(f) The asset account, Supplies, is increased with a _____.
(g) The Cash account is decreased with a _____.
(h) The owner's drawing account is increased with a _____.

Learning Objective **4**

Check Figure
(1) debit

Quick Practice 2-2

Objective: Normal balance of an account

Directions: Indicate the normal balance (debit or credit) for each of the following accounts.

1. Cash _____
2. Equipment _____
3. Owner's Capital _____
4. Accounts Payable _____
5. Wages Expense _____
6. Supplies _____
7. Owner's Drawing _____
8. Accounts Receivable _____

Learning Objective **4**

Check Figure
(See first item)

Quick Practice 2-3

Objective: To apply the rules of debit and credit

Directions: Complete the following chart concerning increases and decreases in the accounting elements, and indicate the normal balance. The first item is done as an example.

Account	Increase Side	Decrease Side	Normal Balance
Asset	Debit	Credit	Debit
Liability	_____	_____	_____
Owner's Capital	_____	_____	_____
Revenue	_____	_____	_____
Owner's Drawing	_____	_____	_____
Expense	_____	_____	_____

Quick Practice 2-4

Objective: To analyze a set of transactions

Directions: Read each of the following transactions and write an analysis of how each would be recorded. Use the examples found in this chapter as a guide.

(a) Owner invested cash in the business.
(b) Performed services for cash.
(c) Bought equipment on account.
(d) Performed services on credit.
(e) Paid creditors on account.
(f) Collected cash from credit customers.
(g) Owner withdrew cash from the business for personal use.

Quick Practice 2-5

Objective: Balancing T accounts

Directions: Foot and balance the two T accounts shown below.

Cash		Accounts Payable	
300	100	100	400
700	400	300	100
200			500

Quick Practice 2-6

Objective: To record business transactions in T accounts

Directions: Use a set of T accounts to record each of the following transactions, and identify each transaction by letter. Use the following account titles: Cash; Accounts Receivable; Supplies; Accounts Payable; Jeff Stuart, Capital; Jeff Stuart, Drawing; Revenue from Services; and Wages Expense.

(a) Owner invested cash in the business, $800.
(b) Received cash for services performed, $70.
(c) Bought supplies on account, $100.
(d) Performed services on account, $600.
(e) Paid for supplies purchased on account, $50.
(f) Received cash from customers on account, $150.
(g) Paid wages, $400.
(h) Jeff withdrew $250 for personal use.

Quick Practice 2-7

Objective: To prepare a trial balance

Directions: Using your solution to Quick Practice 2-6, foot and balance the accounts and prepare a trial balance for Jeff Stuart Service Co. as of June 30, 20XX.

Exercises

Learning Objectives **4, 6**

Check Figure
Five normal debit balances;
five normal credit balances

Exercise 2-1

Objective: To identify the rules of debit and credit

Directions: Fill in the blanks in the following chart. The first one is done as an example.

	Type of Account	Increase Side	Decrease Side	Normal Balance
Cash	Asset	Debit	Credit	Debit
Equipment				
Gene Hopkins, Drawing				
Accounts Payable				
Service Revenue				
Accounts Receivable				
Gene Hopkins, Capital				
Taxes Payable				
Fees Earned				
Rent Expense				

Learning Objectives **4, 6**

Check Figure
Five debits; two credits

Exercise 2-2

Objective: To apply the rules of debit and credit

Directions: Complete the following chart concerning increases and decreases in the accounting elements. The first item is done as an example.

	Recorded on Debit Side	Recorded on Credit Side
(a) Increase in Cash account	✓	
(b) Decrease in Accounts Payable account		
(c) Increase in owner's drawing account		
(d) Increase in owner's capital account		
(e) Increase in expense account		
(f) Decrease in owner's capital account		
(g) Increase in revenue account		

Learning Objective **7**

Check Figure
The Cash account has one
debit and three credits.

Exercise 2-3

Objective: To record business transactions in T accounts

Directions: Use a set of T accounts to record each of the following transactions. Identify each transaction by letter.

(a) Bought equipment on account, $600.
(b) Received cash for services performed, $900.
(c) Paid rent for the month, $350.
(d) Paid creditors on account, $400.
(e) Bought equipment for cash, $300.

Learning Objective **4**

Check Figure
None

Exercise 2-4

Objective: To analyze a set of transactions

Directions: Read each of the following transactions and write an analysis of how each would be recorded. Use the examples found in this chapter as a guide.

(a) Bought supplies on account.
(b) Performed services for cash.
(c) Paid a creditor on account.
(d) Bought equipment on account.
(e) Performed services on credit.
(f) Paid rent for the month.

(g) Paid salaries of employees.

(h) Owner withdrew cash for personal use.

(i) Purchased equipment for cash.

(j) Owner made an additional investment of cash in the firm.

Learning Objective **7**

Check Figure
The Cash account has two debits and six credits.

Exercise 2-5

Objective: To record business transactions in T accounts

Directions: Set up T accounts with the following titles: Cash; Accounts Receivable; Supplies; Equipment; Accounts Payable; Ray Ingram, Capital; Ray Ingram, Drawing; Revenue from Commissions; Rent Expense; and Utilities Expense. Record the following transactions in your accounts, identifying each transaction by letter.

(a) Ray invested $11,000 cash in his real estate firm.

(b) Purchased supplies for cash, $250.

(c) Purchased equipment on account, $950.

(d) Paid rent for the month, $600.

(e) Sold a house and received a commission of $3,900.

(f) Paid $600 on the equipment purchased in Transaction (c).

(g) Sold a house and earned a commission of $4,000 to be received next month.

(h) Ray withdrew $600 cash for personal use.

(i) Purchased supplies for cash, $355.

(j) Paid utility bill for the month, $320.

(k) Ray invested a personal computer, valued at $1,200, into the business.

Learning Objective **7**

Check Figure
Trial balance totals = $20,450

Exercise 2-6

Objective: To prepare a trial balance

Directions: Using your solution to Exercise 2-5, foot the accounts and prepare a trial balance for Ray Ingram Realty as of June 30, 20X1.

Case Problems

Group A

Learning Objectives
4, 5, 6, 7

Check Figure
Trial balance totals = $28,050

Problem 2-1A

Objective: To record business transactions in T accounts and prepare a trial balance

On May 5, 20X1, Michael Ditch started a carpet cleaning business called Best Way Carpet Cleaners. He completed the following transactions during the month:

(a) Michael transferred $15,500 from his personal savings account to a bank account for the business.

(b) Michael invested a small truck, which he had owned personally, in the business. The value of the truck was $8,000.

(c) Paid rent on a small office, $625.

(d) Purchased office supplies for cash, $575.

(e) Purchased equipment on account, $4,000.

(f) Received cash for services performed, $150.

(g) Performed services on credit, $350.

(h) Purchased truck supplies on account, $125.

(i) Paid salary of employee, $550.

(j) Paid for repairs to truck, $225.

(k) Received $200 for the services performed in Transaction (g).

(l) Paid utilities, $315.

(m) Paid creditor $75 on the purchase in Transaction (h).

(n) Michael withdrew cash for personal use, $625.

(o) Paid salary of employee, $575.

Directions: (1) Draw a set of T accounts with the following titles: Cash; Accounts Receivable; Office Supplies; Truck Supplies; Equipment; Truck; Accounts Payable; Michael Ditch, Capital; Michael Ditch, Drawing; Cleaning Fees; Rent Expense; Salaries Expense; Truck Expense; and Utilities Expense. (2) Record each of the transactions in the T accounts. (3) Foot and calculate the balance of each account and then prepare a trial balance as of May 31, 20X1.

Learning Objectives
4, 5, 6

Check Figure
None

Problem 2-2A

Objective: To describe transactions recorded in T accounts

Directions: For each entry in the following T accounts, describe the transaction (both debit and credit parts) that created the entry.

Cash	
(a)4,000	(b) 200
(f) 225	(c) 800
(k) 600	(g) 280
	(h) 500
	(i) 200

Equipment	
(c) 800	

Peggy Wilson, Drawing	
(h) 500	

Accounts Receivable	
(d) 900	(f) 225

Accounts Payable	
(i) 200	(e) 400
	(j) 300

Service Revenue	
	(d) 900
	(k) 600

Office Supplies	
(b) 200	
(e) 400	

Peggy Wilson, Capital	
	(a) 4,000

Delivery Expense	
(g) 280	

Store Supplies	
(j) 300	

Learning Objectives
4, 5, 6, 7

Check Figure
Trial balance totals = $23,425

Problem 2-3A

Objective: To record business transactions in T accounts and prepare a trial balance

On June 1, 20X1, David Mack established a small business, Century Bookkeeping Service, to keep records for small businesses and to provide tax assistance to businesses and individuals. During June, David completed the following transactions:

(a) David began the business by placing $15,000 into a business checking account.

(b) Purchased office supplies for cash, $450.

(c) Purchased office equipment on account, $3,900.

(d) Purchased a computer system (office equipment) for $4,200, paying $1,100 down and agreeing to pay the balance in 90 days.

(e) Paid first month's rent, $600.

(f) Paid for an advertisement in the local newspaper, $170.

(g) Received cash for services performed, $400.

(h) Purchased a laser printer (office equipment) on account, $600.

(i) Performed services on credit, $425.

(j) Paid salary of part-time employee, $350.

(k) Purchased a case of CDs for use with the computer, $160.

(l) Paid utility bill for the month, $299.

(m) Paid telephone bill, $180.

(n) Collected $200 from the services performed in Transaction (i).

(o) David withdrew cash for personal use, $700.

(p) Paid to have the carpet cleaned, $75.

(q) Paid salary of part-time employee, $350.

Directions: (1) Draw a set of T accounts with the following titles: Cash; Accounts Receivable; Office Supplies; Office Equipment; Accounts Payable; David Mack, Capital; David Mack, Drawing; Revenue from Fees; Rent Expense; Salaries Expense; Advertising Expense; Telephone Expense; Utilities Expense; and Miscellaneous Expense. (2) Record the transactions in the T accounts, using the transaction letters to identify the debits and credits. (3) Foot and find the balance of each account and then prepare a trial balance dated June 30, 20X1.

Learning Objectives
4, 5, 6, 7

Check Figure
Trial balance totals = $51,895

Problem 2-4A

Objective: To record business transactions in T accounts and prepare a trial balance

Randy Minton started an air-conditioning and heating repair business on March 1, 20X1, and completed the following transactions during his first month of operations:

(a) Randy invested $30,000 in his new business known as Minton Service Company.

(b) Purchased office supplies for cash, $375.

(c) Purchased office equipment on account, $3,200.

(d) Purchased a used automobile for cash, $8,500.

(e) Purchased two light-duty utility trucks, $24,600, paying $6,000 down with the balance on account.

(f) Paid $90 for gasoline and oil.

(g) Paid rent for the month, $800.

(h) Received $110 for repairing an air-conditioning unit at Cody Motel.

(i) Earned $450 for repairs to a heating unit at Cody Motel. Will receive cash later this month.

(j) Paid for repairs to automobile, $75.

(k) Earned $610 for repairing the air-conditioning unit at Central Hospital. Cash is to be received next month.

(l) Paid salaries of employees, $925.

(m) Paid telephone bill, $125.

(n) Paid utility bill, $205.

(o) Randy withdrew $800 for personal use.

(p) Randy paid a personal bill using a company check, $75.

(q) Made first payment on the trucks, $575.

(r) Paid $500 on the equipment purchased in Transaction (c).

(s) Received the cash due from Transaction (i), $450.

Directions: (1) Draw a set of T accounts with the following titles: Cash; Accounts Receivable; Office Supplies; Office Equipment; Automobile; Trucks; Accounts Payable; Randy Minton, Capital; Randy Minton, Drawing; Service Revenue; Rent Expense; Salaries Expense; Gasoline and Oil Expense; Telephone Expense; Utilities Expense; and Miscellaneous Expense. (2) Record Randy's transactions in the T accounts. (3) Foot and find the balance of each account and then prepare a trial balance dated March 31, 20X1.

Learning Objectives **7**

Check Figure
Capital balance = $67,750

Problem 2-5A

Objective: To prepare a trial balance from a group of alphabetized accounts

Directions: Following is an alphabetized list of the accounts and their balances for Curry Company on July 31, 20X2. Prepare a trial balance in correct order and form.

Account	Amount
Accounts Payable	$ 9,000
Accounts Receivable	3,000
Building	43,000
Cash	11,500
Equipment	30,500
Robert Curry, Capital	?
Robert Curry, Drawing	13,500
Rent Expense	7,000
Revenue from Services	39,900
Salaries Expense	2,850
Telephone Expense	1,000
Utilities Expense	4,300

Group B

Learning Objectives
4, 5, 6, 7

Check Figure
Trial balance totals = $27,615

Problem 2-1B

Objective: To record business transactions in T accounts and prepare a trial balance

On August 1, 20X1, Melody Tawzer started a food catering service called Al La Foods. She completed the following transactions during the month:

(a) Melody transferred $15,500 from her personal savings account to a bank account for the business.

(b) Invested a small truck, which she had owned personally, in the business. The value of the truck was $7,800.

(c) Paid rent on a small office, $475.

(d) Purchased office supplies for cash, $550.

(e) Purchased equipment on account, $3,700.

(f) Received cash for services performed, $190.

(g) Performed services on credit, $330.

(h) Purchased truck supplies on account, $180.

(i) Paid salary of employee, $575.

(j) Paid for repairs to truck, $220.

(k) Received $250 for the services performed in Transaction (g).

(l) Paid utilities, $330.

(m) Paid creditor $85 on the purchase in Transaction (h).

(n) Melody withdrew cash for personal use, $650.

(o) Paid salary of employee, $600.

Directions: (1) Draw a set of T accounts with the following titles: Cash; Accounts Receivable; Office Supplies; Truck Supplies; Equipment; Truck; Accounts Payable; Melody Tawzer, Capital; Melody Tawzer, Drawing; Catering Fees; Rent Expense; Salaries Expense; Truck Expense; and Utilities Expense. (2) Record each of the transactions in the T accounts. (3) Foot and calculate the balance of each account and then prepare a trial balance as of August 31, 20X1.

Problem 2-2B

Objective: To describe transactions recorded in T accounts

Directions: For each entry in the following T accounts, describe the transaction (both debit and credit parts) that created the entry.

Cash			
(a) 7,000		(c)	135
(h) 710		(e)	115
(k) 630		(f)	295
		(g)	700
		(i)	250

Equipment	
(b) 475	

Lynn Whiddon, Drawing	
(g) 700	

Accounts Receivable	
(d) 835	(h) 710

Accounts Payable			
(i) 250		(b)	475
		(j)	365

Fees Earned		
	(d)	835
	(k)	630

Office Supplies	
(c) 135	
(j) 365	

Lynn Whiddon, Capital	
	(a) 7,000

Delivery Expense	
(e) 115	

Store Supplies	
(f) 295	

Problem 2-3B

Objective: To record business transactions in T accounts and prepare a trial balance

On May 1, 20X1, Joelyn Bell established a word processing service called Bell Business Services. During May, Joelyn completed the following transactions:

(a) Joelyn began the business by placing $14,000 into a business checking account.
(b) Purchased office supplies for cash, $425.
(c) Purchased office equipment on account, $4,300.
(d) Purchased a computer system (office equipment) for $4,700, paying $1,400 down and agreeing to pay the balance in 90 days.
(e) Paid first month's rent, $550.
(f) Paid for an advertisement in the local newspaper, $175.
(g) Received cash for services performed, $325.
(h) Purchased a laser printer (office equipment) on account, $800.
(i) Performed services on credit, $350.
(j) Paid salary of part-time employee, $375.
(k) Purchased a case of CDs for use with the computer, $180.
(l) Paid utility bill for the month, $277.
(m) Paid telephone bill, $226.
(n) Collected $250 from the services performed in Transaction (i).
(o) Joelyn withdrew cash for personal use, $800.
(p) Paid to have the company name painted on the door, $90.
(q) Paid salary of part-time employee, $375.

Directions: (1) Draw a set of T accounts with the following titles: Cash; Accounts Receivable; Office Supplies; Office Equipment; Accounts Payable; Joelyn Bell, Capital; Joelyn Bell, Drawing; Revenue from Fees; Rent Expense; Salaries Expense; Advertising Expense; Telephone Expense; Utilities Expense; and Miscellaneous Expense. (2) Record the transactions in the T accounts, using the transaction letters to identify the debits and credits. (3) Foot and find the balance of each account and then prepare a trial balance dated May 31, 20X1.

Problem 2-4B

Objective: To record business transactions in T accounts and prepare a trial balance

Learning Objectives
4, 5, 6, 7

Check Figure
Trial balance totals = $44,025

On April 1, 20X1, Brenda Boone started a DVD and CD player repair business called Boone Video Repair, and completed the following transactions during her first month of operations:

(a) Brenda invested $22,000 in her new business.
(b) Purchased office supplies for cash, $390.
(c) Purchased office equipment on account, $2,700.
(d) Purchased a used automobile for cash, $7,400.
(e) Purchased two light-duty utility trucks, $25,600, paying $6,500 down with the balance on account.
(f) Paid $85 for gasoline and oil.
(g) Paid rent for the month, $775.
(h) Received $75 for repairing a DVD player at Mid-Town Motel.
(i) Earned $750 for repairs to several items at the Mid-Town Motel. Will receive cash later this month.
(j) Paid for repairs to automobile, $70.
(k) Earned $600 for repairing and cleaning DVD and CD players at Ochee School District. Cash is to be received next month.
(l) Paid salaries of employees, $875.
(m) Paid telephone bill, $108.
(n) Paid utility bill, $150.
(o) Brenda withdrew $825 for personal use.
(p) Brenda paid a personal bill using a company check, $85.
(q) Made first payment on the trucks, $625.
(r) Paid $575 on the equipment purchased in Transaction (c).
(s) Received the cash due from Transaction (i), $750.

Directions: (1) Draw a set of T accounts with the following titles: Cash; Accounts Receivable; Office Supplies; Office Equipment; Automobile; Trucks; Accounts Payable; Brenda Boone, Capital; Brenda Boone, Drawing; Service Revenue; Rent Expense; Salaries Expense; Gasoline and Oil Expense; Telephone Expense; Utilities Expense; and Miscellaneous Expense. (2) Record Brenda's transactions in the T accounts. (3) Foot and find the balance of each account and then prepare a trial balance dated April 30, 20X1.

Learning Objective **7**

Check Figure
Capital balance = $16,160

Problem 2-5B

Objective: To prepare a trial balance from a group of alphabetized accounts

Directions: Following is an alphabetized list of the accounts and their balances for Jenkins Company on June 30, 20X2. From this alphabetized list, prepare a trial balance in correct order and form.

Account	Amount
Accounts Payable	$3,900
Accounts Receivable	1,000
Cash	7,200
Delivery Expense	95
Equipment	3,900
Daniel Jenkins, Capital	?
Daniel Jenkins, Drawing	800
Rent Expense	650
Revenue from Services	4,750
Salaries Expense	2,590
Truck	8,200
Utilities Expense	375

Critical Thinking Problems

Challenge Problem

On August 1, 20X1, David Payne started Fast Track Delivery Company, a local pickup and delivery service. David incurred the following transactions during his first month of operations:

(a) David invested the following assets in the business: cash, $12,000; office supplies, $60; truck supplies, $32; and equipment, $5,000.

(b) Purchased additional office supplies and paid cash, $125.

(c) Purchased a new delivery truck for $19,400, paying $2,500 down and signing a note payable for the balance.

(d) Paid for gasoline and oil, $70.

(e) Made deliveries to charge customers, $335.

(f) Paid rent for the month, $550.

(g) Made deliveries to cash customers, $228.

(h) Collected the amount due from the customers in Transaction (e), $335.

(i) Paid for repairs to truck, $90.

(j) Purchased truck supplies on account, $75.

(k) Paid salaries of employees, $900.

(l) Made deliveries to credit customers, $345.

(m) Purchased a computer system for cash, $2,300.

(n) Purchased printer ink, CDs, and paper for cash, $425.

(o) As a favor, David sold an ink cartridge at cost, $20, to the owner of the business next door.

(p) Paid cash for gasoline and oil, $135.

(q) Discovered that a $40 box of CDs had been stored too close to the heating vent and was ruined.

(r) Collected $150 of the amount due from Transaction (l).

(s) Paid $15 to have a flat tire repaired.

(t) Paid the telephone bill, $148.

(u) Paid utility bill, $399.

(v) Paid salaries of employees, $900.

(w) Made deliveries to cash customers, $665.

(x) David withdrew cash for personal use, $900.

Directions: (1) Set up T accounts with the following titles: Cash; Accounts Receivable; Office Supplies; Truck Supplies; Equipment; Truck; Accounts Payable; Notes Payable; David Payne, Capital; David Payne, Drawing; Delivery Revenue; Rent Expense; Salaries Expense; Gasoline and Oil Expense; Utilities Expense; Telephone Expense; Repair

Expense; and Miscellaneous Expense. (2) Record the transactions in the T accounts. (3) Foot and find the balance of the accounts and then prepare a trial balance as of August 31, 20X1. (4) Prepare an income statement for the month ended August 31, 20X1. (5) Prepare a statement of owner's equity for the month ended August 31, 20X1. (6) Prepare a balance sheet in report form as of August 31, 20X1.

Communications

Pennie Eddy just completed the second chapter in her college accounting course. After being introduced to debits and credits, Pennie wondered why some accounts are increased by debits while others are decreased by debits. She asks "Why can't all accounts be increased by debits and decreased by credits?"

Write a brief paragraph providing an answer to Pennie's question.

Team Internet Project

Look into a variation on the way that the accounting recording process has been presented in this chapter. You have learned double-entry accounting, a system in which each transaction is recorded as having at least two effects on the accounting equation. There is another system used by some—the single-entry system. Search the Internet to find out about the single-entry system and then prepare a comparison of the two systems.

Ethics

John Dark owns a small appliance repair shop. This month, his business's electric bill was $375, and his home electric bill was $125. John wrote a single check to the utility company and debited the Utilities Expense account for the total.

Explain (a) what John has done wrong and (b) why what he did violates proper accounting principles, and identify the particular principle he violated.

In the Real World	H&R Block

Based on the partial balance sheet of H&R Block shown on page 52 in Chapter 1, indicate whether or not total assets have increased or decreased and by how much (a) from 2005 to 2006 and (b) from 2006 to 2007.

Answers to Review Quizzes

Review Quiz 2-1

Either. To asset accounts, debit means increase and credit means decrease. To liability accounts and the owner's capital account, debit means decrease and credit means increase.

Review Quiz 2-2

Cash				Accounts Payable			
(a)	8,000	(c)	500	(e)	600	(b)	1,200
		(e)	600			(d)	300

Office Supplies		Greg Calloway, Capital	
(c) 500		(a)	8,000

Shop Supplies	
(d) 300	

Equipment	
(b) 1,200	

Review Quiz 2-3

Cash				Lynn Dowdy, Drawing	
(a) 5,000		(b)	600	(f) 500	
		(c)	540		
		(d)	1,800		
		(e)	200		
		(f)	500		

Service Revenue		Salaries Expense		Rent Expense	
	(a) 5,000	(d) 1,800		(b) 600	

Utilities Expense		Repairs Expense	
(c) 540		(e) 200	

Review Quiz 2-4

Coastal Realty
Trial Balance
July 31, 20XX

Account Title	Debit	Credit
Cash	16 5 9 0 00	
Office Supplies	5 0 0 00	
Store Supplies	1 2 0 0 00	
Store Equipment	2 0 0 0 00	
Accounts Payable		3 2 0 0 00
George Lawson, Capital		18 0 0 0 00
George Lawson, Drawing	8 0 0 00	
Commission Revenue		2 0 5 0 00
Rent Expense	8 0 0 00	
Utilities Expense	4 0 0 00	
Travel Expense	9 6 0 00	
Totals	23 2 5 0 00	23 2 5 0 00

Review Quiz 2-5

Expense accounts and the owner's drawing account are used to record decreases in the owner's capital account. Therefore, the increase and decrease sides of these accounts are opposite those of the owner's capital account. Since the owner's capital account is increased with a credit and decreased with a debit, the expense and drawing accounts are increased with a debit and decreased with a credit.

CHAPTER

3

Starting the Accounting Cycle for a Service Business

Learning Objectives

1 Describe the standard form of a two-column journal.
2 Record business transactions in a two-column journal.
3 Prepare a chart of accounts.
4 Describe the balance form of account.
5 Post from a two-column journal to ledger accounts.
6 Prepare a trial balance from a ledger after posting.
7 Describe the procedures for locating and correcting errors in the accounting process.
8 Make entries to correct errors in the ledger.

In Chapter 2, you learned the basic rules of debit and credit as you recorded business transactions in T accounts. You also learned that, because of the dual effect, at least two accounts are affected by each business transaction. In addition, you learned how to check the equality of debits and credits in the ledger by preparing a trial balance.

The Accounting Cycle

Having successfully mastered the objectives of Chapter 2, you are now ready to begin studying the series of steps that businesses use to process accounting data. The sequence of steps and procedures used by a business to record and summarize accounting data is known as the **accounting cycle**. In Chapter 3, we will study the first four steps in the accounting cycle for a service business. We will then study the next four steps in the accounting cycle in Chapter 4 and conclude our study in Chapter 5. The first four steps in the accounting cycle are:

accounting cycle the sequence of steps and procedures used to record and summarize accounting data during an accounting period

Step **1** Analyze transactions from source documents.
Step **2** Record transactions in a journal.
Step **3** Post from the journal to the ledger.
Step **4** Prepare a trial balance of the ledger.

A source document is any business paper that shows that a transaction occurred. Providing objective evidence, source documents are the basis for recording business transactions.

Step 1: Analyze Transactions from Source Documents

When business transactions occur, business papers are prepared as evidence of those transactions. Business papers can take the form of check stubs, receipts, sales slips, cash register tapes, invoices, bills, or any other document that serves as proof that a business transaction has taken place. These business papers, called **source documents**, are used by the accountant to analyze a transaction. The accounting **principle of objective evidence** states that source documents should form the foundation for recording business transactions.

Step 2: Record Transactions in a Journal

The objective of double-entry accounting is to make equal (and accurate) debit and credit entries in the proper ledger accounts. Recording business transactions in T accounts accomplishes this. However, recording transactions directly in T accounts breaks up the debit and credit parts of an entry since the debit is recorded in one account and the credit is recorded in another. The likelihood of errors is greater when the debit and credit parts of an entry are recorded on separate pages of the ledger. To overcome this problem, an important step in the accounting cycle occurs before recording transactions in T accounts. The first formal record of business transactions is made in a form known as the journal. The **journal** provides a complete record of each transaction in chronological order (by order of date).

Since the journal is the first place transactions are formally recorded, it is referred to as the **book of original entry**. Various types of journals are used today. The basic form of journal is a two-column journal called the general journal. The **general journal** is an all-purpose journal in which any business transaction can be recorded in chronological sequence from the first transaction of the accounting period to the last. The general journal is shown in Figure 3-1.

Figure 3-1
The General Journal

		General Journal			**1** Page 1
	2 Date	**3** Account Title	**4** P.R.	Debit	**5** Credit
1					1
2					2
3					3
4					4

After transactions are analyzed from source documents, they are recorded in a journal—the book of original entry.

Note the following features of the general journal:

1 Numbered pages, beginning with page 1.

2 A *Date* column used to record the date on which a transaction occurs.

3 An *Account Title* column, used to record the accounts affected by a transaction, as well as a brief explanation of the transaction.

4 A posting reference (*P.R.*) column, which has a special use and is described on page 99.

5 Two money (or amount) columns, labeled *Debit* and *Credit*, respectively. Each is used to record the dollar amount of transactions.

 Tutorial 4

Recording Transactions in General Journal Form

Learning Objective

2 Record business transactions in a two-column journal.

journalizing the process of recording transactions in a journal

Remember

As you learned in Chapter 2, to record a transaction, it must be analyzed into its debit and credit parts. For each transaction, you must decide:

- Which accounts are affected by the transaction
- Whether the accounts affected were increased or decreased
- How to increase or decrease (debit or credit) the accounts affected

Take This Into Account

The actual first recording of a business transaction is on however, source documents are not formal accounting re

Making Journal Entries

The process of recording transactions in a journal Journalizing differs from recording in T accounts in fo the transactions and the accounts used are identical. To journal entries, we will again look at Stanley Walker's and Associates during November 20X1. (Remember Chapter 2.) This time, however, we will record the journal format by the date the transactions occurred,

Transaction, November 1, 20X1: Stanley Invested $10,000 Cash in His Business

Analysis: Cash was received in the business. Therefore, the Cash account, an asset, must be increased. Increases in asset accounts are recorded as debits, so the Cash account is debited for $10,000. Owner investments increase the equity of the business. Therefore, the owner's capital account must be increased. The owner's capital account is increased by a credit, so Stanley Walker, Capital is credited for $10,000.

Entry:

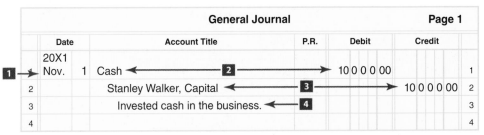

	General Journal				Page 1	
Date	Account Title	P.R.	Debit	Credit	
20X1						
Nov. 1	Cash ◄————**2**————►		10 0 0 0 00		1
2	Stanley Walker, Capital ◄——**3**——►			10 0 0 0 00	2
3	Invested cash in the business. ◄—**4**				3
4					4

Note the following features of Stanley's first general journal entry:

1 The date of the entry consists of the year (20X1), the month (Nov.), and the day of the month (1).

2 The title of the account to be debited (Cash) is written on the first line at the extreme left margin of the Account Title column. The amount of the debit ($10,000.00) is written in the Debit column on the same line. Debits are *always* written before credits. Dollar signs *are not* used in the journal.

3 The title of the account to be credited (Stanley Walker, Capital) is written on the second line of the Account Title column and indented one-fourth to one-half inch. The amount of the credit ($10,000.00) is written in the Credit column on the same line.

Key Point ⊙

As you learn accounting, it's a good idea to provide a brief explanation for your journal entries. Think of them as telling someone not trained in accounting what occurred in a transaction. This will help reinforce your understanding of transactions.

4 The explanation of the entry (Invested cash in the business) is written on the third line and indented an additional one-fourth to one-half inch. Some accountants prefer to omit the explanation if the nature of the entry is self-explanatory.

Transaction, November 6: Purchased Office Equipment for $3,000 on Account

Analysis: The business acquired an asset, office equipment. Increases in asset accounts are recorded as debits. The Office Equipment account is therefore debited for $3,000. The business incurred a liability as a result of purchasing an asset on credit. Therefore, the liability account Accounts Payable must be increased. Increases in liability accounts are recorded as credits, so the Accounts Payable account is credited for $3,000.

Entry:

5		6	Office Equipment		3 0 0 0 00			5
6			Accounts Payable			3 0 0 0 00		6
7			Purchased equipment on account.					7
8								8

Note that the date is simply listed as 6. It is not necessary to repeat the year or the month until either one changes or a new page in the journal is started.

Transaction, November 9: Purchased Office Supplies for Cash, $125

Analysis: The business acquired an asset, office supplies. Increases in asset accounts are recorded as debits. The Office Supplies account is therefore debited for $125. Cash, an asset, was paid. Decreases in asset accounts are recorded as credits. The Cash account is therefore credited for $125.

Entry:

9		9	Office Supplies		1 2 5 00			9
10			Cash			1 2 5 00		10
11			Purchased office supplies for cash.					11
12								12

Transaction, November 12: Paid $500 on the Equipment Purchased on November 6

Analysis: Part of an account payable was paid. Therefore, the liability account, Accounts Payable, must be decreased by the amount of the payment. Decreases in liability accounts are recorded as debits, so the Accounts Payable account is debited for $500. The payment decreased cash, so the Cash account is decreased by a credit of $500.

Entry:

13	12	Accounts Payable	5 0 0 00		13
14		Cash		5 0 0 00	14
15		Made payment on account—Nov. 6.			15
16					16

Review Quiz **3-1**

The following transactions are those of Becky McAfee during March 20XX. Record each transaction in a general journal. Omit the explanations.

Mar. 1 Becky invested $7,000 cash in her business.
     4 Purchased supplies on credit, $750.
     6 Purchased equipment for cash, $475.
     9 Paid half of the amount owed for supplies, $375.

Check your answers on page 131.

Transaction, November 15: Paid First Month's Rent, $400

Analysis: Rent, an expense, was paid. Therefore, the Rent Expense account must be increased. Increases in expense accounts are recorded as debits, so the Rent Expense account is debited for $400. The payment decreased cash, so the Cash account is decreased by a credit of $400.

Entry:

17	15	Rent Expense	4 0 0 00		17
18		Cash		4 0 0 00	18
19		Paid first month's rent.			19
20					20

Transaction, November 17: Paid for Repairs to Equipment, $50

Analysis: Equipment was repaired. Therefore, the Repairs Expense account must be increased. Increases in expense accounts are recorded as debits, so the Repairs Expense account is debited for $50. Cash was decreased by the payment, so the Cash account is credited for $50.

Entry:

21	17	Repairs Expense	5 0 00		21
22		Cash		5 0 00	22
23		Paid for equipment repairs.			23
24					24

Transaction, November 18: Received Cash from Customers for Services Performed, $1,800

Analysis: Cash, an asset, was received from customers. Therefore, the Cash account must be increased. Increases in asset accounts are recorded as debits, so the Cash account is debited for $1,800. Cash received for services performed yields revenue to the business. Therefore, a revenue account must be increased. Revenue accounts are increased by credits, so the Service Revenue account is credited for $1,800.

Entry:

25		18	Cash		1 8 0 0 00		25
26			Service Revenue			1 8 0 0 00	26
27			Performed services for cash.				27
28							28

Transaction, November 20: Performed Services on Account, $400

Analysis: Services were performed on credit for customers. Therefore, the Accounts Receivable account, an asset, must be increased. Increases in asset accounts are recorded as debits, so the Accounts Receivable account is debited for $400. Performing services, whether for cash or on account, increases revenue. Revenue accounts are increased by credits, so the Service Revenue account is credited for $400.

Entry:

29		20	Accounts Receivable		4 0 0 00		29
30			Service Revenue			4 0 0 00	30
31			Performed services on account.				31
32							32

Transaction, November 27: Stanley Withdrew $800 from the Business for Personal Use

Analysis: Owner withdrawals result in an increase in the owner's drawing account. The owner's drawing account is increased by a debit, so Stanley Walker, Drawing is debited for $800. The withdrawal also decreased cash, so the Cash account is credited for $800 to show the decrease.

Entry:

33		27	Stanley Walker, Drawing		8 0 0 00		33
34			Cash			8 0 0 00	34
35			Withdrew cash for personal use.				35
36							36

Transaction, November 29: Collected $100 on Account

Analysis: Cash was collected from a credit customer. Therefore, the Cash account, an asset, must be increased. Increases in asset accounts are recorded as debits, so the Cash account is debited for $100. Part of an account receivable was collected. Therefore, the Accounts Receivable account, an asset, must be decreased. Decreases in assets are recorded as credits, so the Accounts Receivable account is credited for $100. Assume that this transaction is recorded on page 2 of the journal, so the year and month are listed.

Remember

As you learned in Chapter 1, revenue is recorded when it is earned, no matter when the actual receipt of cash takes place (realization principle).

Entry:

	Date		Account Title	P.R.	Debit	Credit	
			General Journal			**Page 2**	
1	20X1 Nov.	29	Cash		1 0 0 00		1
2			Accounts Receivable			1 0 0 00	2
3			Collected cash on account.				3
4							4

Compound Journal Entry

We have now journalized all of the transactions we introduced for Walker and Associates in Chapter 2. Each transaction had only one debit and one credit. When only two accounts are affected by the transaction (a debit and a credit), it is often referred to as a simple entry. To record some transactions, however, you will have to use more than one debit or credit. An entry requiring three or more accounts is called a **compound entry**. The following entry shows how to record a compound entry.

Transaction, November 30: Purchased Office Furniture for $2,000, Paying $500 Down, with the Balance Owed on Account

Analysis: The business acquired an asset, office furniture. Increases in asset accounts are recorded as debits, so the Office Furniture account is debited for $2,000. Cash was paid. The Cash account is therefore decreased by a credit of $500. The business also incurred a liability as a result of purchasing an asset on credit. Increases in liability accounts are recorded as credits, so the Accounts Payable account is credited for $1,500.

Entry:

5		30	Office Furniture		2 0 0 0 00		5
6			Cash			5 0 0 00	6
7			Accounts Payable			1 5 0 0 00	7
8			Purchase, paying part cash.				8
9							9

Key Point ⊘

Regardless of the number of accounts used in a compound entry, the total of the debit amounts must equal the total of the credit amounts.

Note how the two credits are simply listed, one under the other. A compound entry with two debits would list both debits at the left margin of the account title column, followed by an indented credit. When making compound entries, the total of the debits must *always* equal the total of the credits—the same as in a simple entry.

The completed journal of Walker and Associates for the month of November 20X1 is shown in Figure 3-2. To help you remember debits and credits, we have placed callouts next to each journal entry in Figure 3-2. Each callout has a plus or minus sign indicating the effect on the related account. Thus, + *asset* indicates an increase in an asset account, – *asset* indicates a decrease in an asset account, and so on.

Figure 3-2

General Journal for Walker and Associates, November 20X1

General Journal Page 1

		Date		Account Title	P.R.	Debit	Credit	
+ asset →	1	20X1 Nov.	1	Cash		10 0 0 0 00		1
+ owner's capital →	2			Stanley Walker, Capital			10 0 0 0 00	2
	3			Invested cash in the business.				3
	4							4
+ asset →	5		6	Office Equipment		3 0 0 0 00		5
+ liability →	6			Accounts Payable			3 0 0 0 00	6
	7			Purchased equipment on account.				7
	8							8
+ asset →	9		9	Office Supplies		1 2 5 00		9
− asset →	10			Cash			1 2 5 00	10
	11			Purchased office supplies for cash.				11
	12							12
− liability →	13		12	Accounts Payable		5 0 0 00		13
− asset →	14			Cash			5 0 0 00	14
	15			Made payment on account—Nov. 6.				15
	16							16
+ expense →	17		15	Rent Expense		4 0 0 00		17
− asset →	18			Cash			4 0 0 00	18
	19			Paid first month's rent.				19
	20							20
+ expense →	21		17	Repairs Expense		5 0 00		21
− asset →	22			Cash			5 0 00	22
	23			Paid for equipment repairs.				23
	24							24
+ asset →	25		18	Cash		1 8 0 0 00		25
+ revenue →	26			Service Revenue			1 8 0 0 00	26
	27			Performed services for cash.				27
	28							28
+ asset →	29		20	Accounts Receivable		4 0 0 00		29
+ revenue →	30			Service Revenue			4 0 0 00	30
	31			Performed services on account.				31
	32							32
+ owner's drawing →	33		27	Stanley Walker, Drawing		8 0 0 00		33
− asset →	34			Cash			8 0 0 00	34
	35			Withdrew cash for personal use.				35

It is customary to skip a line after each journal entry.

General Journal Page 2

		Date		Account Title	P.R.	Debit	Credit	
+ asset →	1	20X1 Nov.	29	Cash		1 0 0 00		1
− asset →	2			Accounts Receivable			1 0 0 00	2
	3			Collected cash on account.				3
	4							4
+ asset →	5		30	Office Furniture		2 0 0 0 00		5
− asset →	6			Cash			5 0 0 00	6
+ liability →	7			Accounts Payable			1 5 0 0 00	7
	8			Purchase, paying part cash.				8

The year and the month are rewritten if the page changes.

Advantages of Using a Journal

Now that we have introduced the journal and discussed how transactions are recorded in this type of record, let's review the advantages of using a journal as the book of original entry. Four major advantages of using a journal are:

- The journal provides a chronological (by order of date) record of transactions. In effect, it is a complete diary of a firm's transactions. Should it become necessary to check an entry, the entire entry can be found by referring to the date the transaction was recorded. When entries are recorded directly in T accounts, it is not possible to find the complete entry in this way.
- The journal provides a place to make an explanation of an entry if an explanation is needed.
- Use of the journal lessens the possibility of a recording error, because both the debit and credit parts of an entry are recorded together. When entries are recorded directly in T accounts, the debit and credit parts of the entry are recorded in separate accounts. This increases the likelihood of omitting the debit part of an entry, omitting the credit part of an entry, or making duplicate debits and credits.
- Because the journal shows both the debit and credit parts of an entry in one place, it is easier to locate recording errors.

Review Quiz   **3-2**   John Dark's business had the following transactions in June 20X1. Record each transaction in a general journal. Omit explanations.

Jun.   12   Paid utilities expense, $145.
      17   John withdrew cash for personal use, $175.
      22   Received cash for services performed, $950.
      25   John made the following additional investments in his business: office supplies, $75; and a truck, $4,000.

Check your answers on page 132.

Step 3: Post from the Journal to the Ledger

As we have emphasized, use of the journal offers the strong advantage of a complete record of transactions in chronological order. The journal, however, does not provide a summary of financial information about each account. If, for example, you were asked to find the balance of the Cash account from the general journal, you would have to go through the entire journal and write down all debits to Cash (the increases) and all credits to Cash (the decreases) and then find the difference between the two. This, obviously, is not practical. So, to provide a summary, we need to transfer the information from the journal to the individual ledger accounts. The process of transferring entries from the journal to the ledger is called **posting**, which is the third step in the accounting cycle. Before we discuss how to post, however, let's look at a system used to organize and identify accounts in the ledger.

posting the process of transferring entries from the journal to the ledger

The Chart of Accounts

Learning Objective

3 Prepare a chart of accounts.

In making journal entries and transferring them to the ledger, the accountant needs a directory of accounts available. A directory of accounts available in the ledger is called a **chart of accounts**. The chart of accounts for Walker and Associates is shown in Table 3-1.

Table 3-1 Chart of Accounts for Walker and Associates

Account Category	Account Number	Account Title
Assets (100–199)	111	Cash
	112	Accounts Receivable
	113	Office Supplies
	116	Office Equipment
	117	Office Furniture
Liabilities (200–299)	211	Accounts Payable
Owner's Equity (300–399)	311	Stanley Walker, Capital
	312	Stanley Walker, Drawing
Revenue (400–499)	411	Service Revenue
Expenses (500–599)	511	Rent Expense
	512	Repairs Expense

The numbering scheme used by Walker and Associates is a three-digit, five-category plan, with the first digit indicating the category of account (1 = asset, 2 = liability, 3 = owner's equity, 4 = revenue, 5 = expenses) and the second and third digits indicating the position of the individual accounts within their particular classifications. Often, a gap is left between account numbers so that new accounts can be added in the future at the appropriate place in the ledger.

Large business firms may use a four-digit or five-digit numbering plan. Additionally, the ledger may be divided into other categories of accounts.

The number of accounts needed by a business depends on the size of the business and the nature of its operations. Small businesses, such as Walker and Associates, may need relatively few accounts. Large businesses, particularly manufacturing firms, could need hundreds (or thousands) of ledger accounts to provide a summary of operations.

The order of accounts in the ledger usually follows the order of accounts listed on the financial statements, with balance sheet accounts being shown first, followed by income statement accounts. Thus, the usual sequence of accounts in the ledger is assets, liabilities, owner's equity, revenue, and expenses.

The Balance Form of Account

To this point, the ledger accounts we have worked with have consisted of T accounts and the standard form of account. The T account is a good tool for emphasizing the contrast between debit and credit entries, and some businesses use the standard form of account. However, most businesses use a more practical form of ledger account. This is the **balance form of account**, also referred to as the four-column account form. Look closely at the balance form of account illustrated in Figure 3-3. Notice that there are four amount columns: (1) a *Debit* column, (2) a *Credit* column, (3) a *Debit Balance* column, and (4) a *Credit Balance* column. The debit and credit columns are used to

Figure 3-3

The Balance Form of
Account

General Ledger						
Account					Account No.	
Date	Item	P.R.	Debit	Credit	Balance	
					Debit	Credit

enter debits and credits from the journal. The balance columns are used to enter the balance of the account after each posting.

The advantages of the balance form of account include:

- Only one Date column is needed.
- You can easily see whether the balance of an account is a debit or a credit.
- Since the four-column account form shows the balance of the account after each posting, the detail involved in footing and balancing the standard form of account is reduced. As a result, there is less chance of confusion and error when determining account balances.

Now, let's look at how the November transactions of Walker and Associates are posted to the ledger.

Posting Illustrated

We will first show the five-step process of posting the debit part of an entry and then the five-step process of posting the credit part of an entry. The five steps for posting the debit part of an entry (shown in Figure 3-4) are as follows:

Step **1** Record the date of the journal entry (Nov. 1, 20X1) in the Date column of the account.

Step **2** Record the amount of the journal entry ($10,000.00), without a dollar sign or decimal point, in the Debit column of the account.

Step **3** Record the code GJ (for general journal) and the page number (1) of the journal in the P.R. (for posting reference) column of the account. The purpose of this step is to be able to trace the entry back to the journal.

Step **4** Record the number of the Cash account (111) in the P.R. column of the journal. This step has two purposes: (1) it indicates that posting has been done, and (2) it indicates the account to which posting has been made. After steps 3 and 4 have been completed, a **cross-reference**, which connects a journal entry to the ledger accounts to which it was posted, will be established. A cross-reference exists because the page number of the journal appears in the P.R. column of the Cash account, and the number of the Cash account appears in the P.R. column of the journal.

Step **5** Calculate the new balance of the account. You keep a running balance of the account. Since the account had no previous balance, the $10,000 posting becomes the balance. Had there been a previous balance, the

Learning Objective

5 Post from a two-column journal to ledger accounts.

cross-reference a ledger account number in the posting reference (P.R.) column of the journal and the journal page number in the P.R. column of the ledger account posting would have been added to obtain the new balance. A credit posting would be subtracted because the Cash account normally has a debit balance.

Figure 3-4

Posting the Debit Part
of an Entry

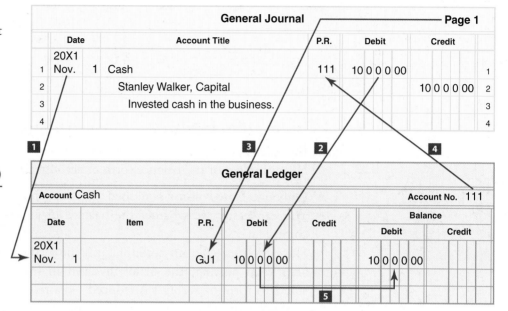

Key Point ⊘

The Item column is left
blank. Its use will be discussed in future chapters.

Posting the credit part of an entry is a similar five-step process, shown in Figure 3-5. The five steps for posting the credit part of an entry are as follows:

Step **1** Record the date of the journal entry (Nov. 1, 20X1) in the Date column of the account.

Step **2** Record the amount ($10,000.00) in the Credit column of the account.

Step **3** Record the code GJ1 in the P.R. column of the account.

Step **4** Record the number of the account (311) in the P.R. column of the journal.

Step **5** Calculate the new balance of the account.

Figure 3-5

Posting the Credit Part
of an Entry

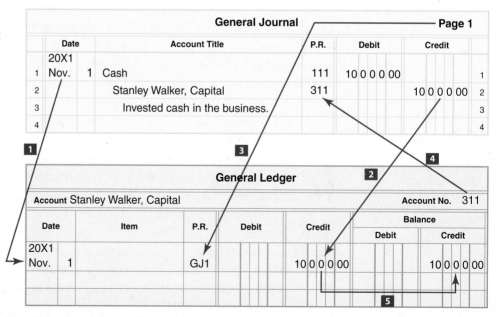

A similar procedure is followed in posting all entries to the ledger. The fully posted ledger of Walker and Associates is shown in Figure 3-6.

Figure 3-6
Fully Posted Ledger of Walker and Associates

Footings are not needed with the four-column account form.

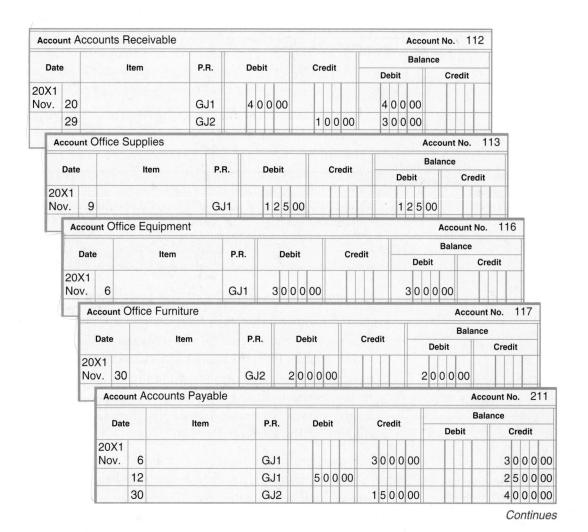

General Ledger

Account Cash   Account No. 111

Date	Item	P.R.	Debit	Credit	Balance Debit	Balance Credit
20X1 Nov. 1		GJ1	10 0 0 0 00		10 0 0 0 00	
9		GJ1		1 2 5 00	9 8 7 5 00	
12		GJ1		5 0 0 00	9 3 7 5 00	
15		GJ1		4 0 0 00	8 9 7 5 00	
17		GJ1		5 0 00	8 9 2 5 00	
18		GJ1	1 8 0 0 00		10 7 2 5 00	
27		GJ1		8 0 0 00	9 9 2 5 00	
29		GJ2	1 0 0 00		10 0 2 5 00	
30		GJ2		5 0 0 00	9 5 2 5 00	

Account Accounts Receivable   Account No. 112

Date	Item	P.R.	Debit	Credit	Balance Debit	Balance Credit
20X1 Nov. 20		GJ1	4 0 0 00		4 0 0 00	
29		GJ2		1 0 0 00	3 0 0 00	

Account Office Supplies   Account No. 113

Date	Item	P.R.	Debit	Credit	Balance Debit	Balance Credit
20X1 Nov. 9		GJ1	1 2 5 00		1 2 5 00	

Account Office Equipment   Account No. 116

Date	Item	P.R.	Debit	Credit	Balance Debit	Balance Credit
20X1 Nov. 6		GJ1	3 0 0 0 00		3 0 0 0 00	

Account Office Furniture   Account No. 117

Date	Item	P.R.	Debit	Credit	Balance Debit	Balance Credit
20X1 Nov. 30		GJ2	2 0 0 0 00		2 0 0 0 00	

Account Accounts Payable   Account No. 211

Date	Item	P.R.	Debit	Credit	Balance Debit	Balance Credit
20X1 Nov. 6		GJ1		3 0 0 0 00		3 0 0 0 00
12		GJ1	5 0 0 00			2 5 0 0 00
30		GJ2		1 5 0 0 00		4 0 0 0 00

Continues

Figure 3-6

Continued

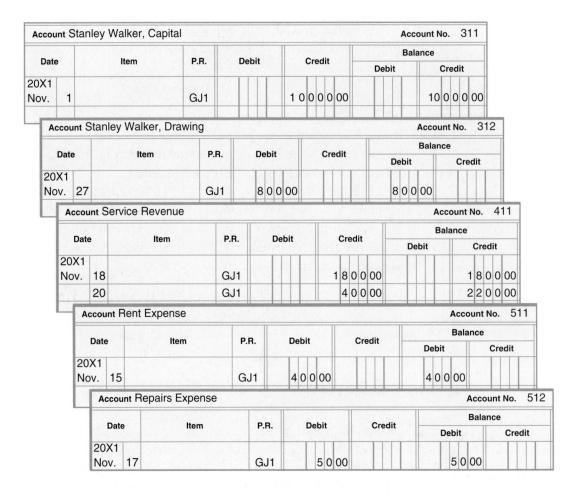

Account Stanley Walker, Capital					Account No. 311		
Date	Item	P.R.	Debit	Credit	Balance		
					Debit	Credit	
20X1 Nov. 1		GJ1		1 0 0 0 0 00		10 0 0 0 00	

Account Stanley Walker, Drawing					Account No. 312		
Date	Item	P.R.	Debit	Credit	Balance		
					Debit	Credit	
20X1 Nov. 27		GJ1	8 0 0 00		8 0 0 00		

Account Service Revenue					Account No. 411		
Date	Item	P.R.	Debit	Credit	Balance		
					Debit	Credit	
20X1 Nov. 18		GJ1		1 8 0 0 00		1 8 0 0 00	
20		GJ1		4 0 0 00		2 2 0 0 00	

Account Rent Expense					Account No. 511		
Date	Item	P.R.	Debit	Credit	Balance		
					Debit	Credit	
20X1 Nov. 15		GJ1	4 0 0 00		4 0 0 00		

Account Repairs Expense					Account No. 512		
Date	Item	P.R.	Debit	Credit	Balance		
					Debit	Credit	
20X1 Nov. 17		GJ1	5 0 00		5 0 00		

Summing Up

When calculating a new account balance, add debit postings to debit balances and subtract credit postings from debit balances. Likewise, add credit postings to and subtract debit postings from credit balances.

Note two matters of form in the fully posted ledger:

- As in the journal, the year (20X1) is written only at the top of the Date column, and the month (Nov.) is written only with the first posting of the month to an account. Entries after that are dated with just the number of the day, as on the second line of the Cash account.
- It was assumed that a second journal page was used to record the transactions of November 29 and 30. Thus, GJ2 was written in the P.R. columns of the accounts affected.

Since transactions are recorded first in the journal (the book of original entry) and then transferred to the ledger, the ledger is often referred to as the **book of final entry**. After the ledger is fully posted, the next step in the accounting cycle is to prepare a trial balance to check the equality of debits and credits in the ledger.

book of final entry the ledger to which amounts are transferred (posted) from the journal

Step 4: Prepare a Trial Balance of the Ledger

In Chapter 2, you learned how to test the equality of debits and credits in the ledger by preparing a trial balance. Using a journal for original entries and then posting to the ledger increases the importance of this test because two records, the journal and the ledger, are now involved. Preparing a trial balance is the fourth step in the accounting cycle.

As we explained in Chapter 2, the first step in preparing a trial balance is to find the balance of each account in the ledger. Since Walker and Associates is using the balance form of account, all accounts were balanced at the time of posting. So, we just need to very carefully transfer the balances to the trial balance form, entering debit balances in one column and credit balances in the other. The November 30, 20X1, trial balance of Walker and Associates is illustrated in Figure 3-7.

Figure 3-7

Trial Balance of Walker and Associates

Walker and Associates
Trial Balance
November 30, 20X1

Account Title	Debit	Credit
Cash	9 5 2 5 00	
Accounts Receivable	3 0 0 00	
Office Supplies	1 2 5 00	
Office Equipment	3 0 0 0 00	
Office Furniture	2 0 0 0 00	
Accounts Payable		4 0 0 0 00
Stanley Walker, Capital		10 0 0 0 00
Stanley Walker, Drawing	8 0 0 00	
Service Revenue		2 2 0 0 00
Rent Expense	4 0 0 00	
Repairs Expense	5 0 00	
Totals	16 2 0 0 00	16 2 0 0 00

Key Point ⊙

Notice how the order of accounts on the trial balance is consistent with the order on the financial statements and chart of accounts.

Review Quiz 3-3

From the following list of account balances, use your knowledge of normal balances to prepare a trial balance for LeAnn's TV Repair Shop on December 31, 20XX. Place accounts in proper order.

Account	Balance
Accounts Payable	$ 7,210
Cash	1,400
Equipment	16,400
LeAnn Lovering, Capital	14,600
LeAnn Lovering, Drawing	700
Rent Expense	3,000
Repairs Expense	450
Revenue from Services	16,380
Salaries Expense	2,510
Supplies	3,860
Truck	9,400
Utilities Expense	470

Check your answer on page 132.

Summary of the First Four Steps in the Accounting Cycle

Now that we have discussed the trial balance, let's take a moment to review the first four steps in the accounting cycle, as shown in Figure 3-8.

Figure 3-8
The First Four Steps in the Accounting Cycle

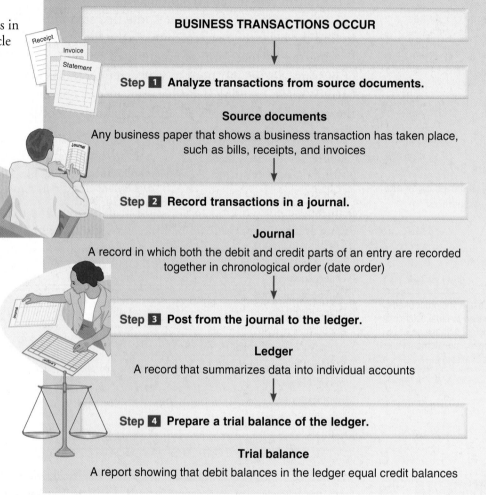

BUSINESS TRANSACTIONS OCCUR

Step 1 Analyze transactions from source documents.

Source documents
Any business paper that shows a business transaction has taken place, such as bills, receipts, and invoices

Step 2 Record transactions in a journal.

Journal
A record in which both the debit and credit parts of an entry are recorded together in chronological order (date order)

Step 3 Post from the journal to the ledger.

Ledger
A record that summarizes data into individual accounts

Step 4 Prepare a trial balance of the ledger.

Trial balance
A report showing that debit balances in the ledger equal credit balances

Locating and Correcting Errors

Learning Objective

7 Describe the procedures for locating and correcting errors in the accounting process.

Accountants and accounting students are all too familiar with the old saying, "To err is human," because without a doubt, errors will occasionally be made in recording journal entries and posting to the ledger. A good accounting system contains a built-in warning that certain types of errors have been made. That warning is an unbalanced trial balance. If the trial balance does not have equal debit and credit totals, there is an error somewhere in the records. That error can be a math error, a recording error, or a posting error. Each of these is discussed next.

Types of Errors

math error an addition or subtraction mistake

A **math error** is simply an error in adding or subtracting. A math error is made when balancing accounts or when adding the columns of a trial balance. Math

recording error a mistake made in a journal entry

posting error an incorrect transfer from the journal to an account or from the ledger to the trial balance

transposition a type of posting error caused by the reversal of digits, such as entering 240 for 420

slide a type of posting error caused by an incorrectly placed decimal point, such as entering 100 for 1,000 or 24.50 for 245

errors are so common that the first thing you should do if your trial balance does not balance is add the columns again.

A **recording error** is an error made in journalizing, such as not recording equal debits and credits or making debits or credits to the wrong account or for an incorrect amount.

A **posting error** is an error made in the process of transferring figures from the journal to the ledger. Examples include the following:

- Posting a debit or a credit more than once
- Posting a debit to the credit side of an account, or vice versa
- Leaving out the posting of a debit or a credit
- Posting the wrong amount

The last type of posting error is common and includes transpositions and slides. A **transposition** is a reversal of digits, such as recording 87 for 78, or 123 for 132. A **slide** is the entry of a number with an incorrectly placed decimal point, such as recording 2,170 for 21,700, or 4,500 for 450. A quick way to check for either a transposition or a slide is to find the difference between the debit and credit column totals of the trial balance and divide this amount by 9. An answer without a remainder indicates that either a transposition or a slide *may* have been made. To find these types of errors, you carefully check all amounts on the trial balance against the ledger account balances to make sure that all balances were correctly copied, and you may need to check the ledger back to the journal.

It is important to determine what type of error has been made, for the method of correcting an error depends on its type.

Correcting Errors

Some errors are corrected by erasure, others by lining out the incorrect information and writing in the correct information, and still others by making a journal entry. Some errors are so small in amount that they are not worth the time and effort involved in correcting them. Each method of correction is described in this section as it relates to the type of error made.

Math Errors

Math errors, if made in pencil, are corrected by erasing the wrong figure and writing the correct figure. If made in ink, math errors are corrected by lining out the wrong figure, initialing the correction (for future reference), and entering the correct figure in ink.

Recording Errors

How you correct a recording error depends on *when* you find the error. Recording errors discovered *before* posting can be corrected by lining out the incorrect information

The first step in error correction is to determine what type of error occurred. The effect of the error is then determined, and a proper correction is made.

and entering the correct information. In the following entry, for example, the Utilities Expense account was incorrectly debited for the payment of salaries to employees. We can correct the error as follows.

		General Journal						Page 1	
	Date	Account Title	P.R.	Debit		Credit		
1	20XX Jun. 10	*Salaries Expense* ~~Utilities Expense~~ *BSK*		4 0 0 00				1
2		Cash				4 0 0 00		2
3		Paid salaries of employees.						3

When an error has been made in recording an amount, draw a line through the incorrect amount and write the correct amount immediately above it. In the following entry, for example, a $225 purchase of store supplies was incorrectly recorded as $252.

		General Journal						Page 1	
	Date	Account Title	P.R.	Debit		Credit		
1	20X1 Apr. 8	Store Supplies		*B.D.* *2 2 5 00* ~~2 5 2 00~~				1
2		Cash				*B.D.* *2 2 5 00* ~~2 5 2 00~~		2
3		Purchased store supplies.						3

Some recording errors may not be discovered until after the error has been posted to the ledger. For example, assume that on June 9, 20X2, a $700 cash purchase of office supplies was incorrectly journalized as a debit to the Office Equipment account (instead of a debit to the Office Supplies account) and a credit to the Cash account. The entry was then posted. The error was then discovered on June 30 as a result of routine tracing of journal entries to the ledger. Since the error now appears in *both* the journal and the ledger, it should not be corrected by lining out the incorrect information and entering the correct information. Instead, you should make a **correcting entry**, which is an entry used to correct certain types of errors in the ledger.

A good way to make a correcting entry is to set up T accounts both for the incorrect entry that was made and for the correct entry that should have been made. The two sets of T accounts can then be compared, and a proper correcting entry can be prepared. For example, for the recording error stated above, T accounts can be prepared as follows.

Transaction, June 9, 20X2: Purchased Office Supplies for Cash, $700
Incorrect entry that was made:

Office Equipment		Cash	
+	−	+	−
700			700

Entry that should have been made:

Office Supplies		Cash	
+	−	+	−
700			700

correcting entry an entry used to correct certain types of errors in the ledger

Learning Objective

8 Make entries to correct errors in the ledger.

Now, by looking at the two sets of T accounts, we can see that only part of the entry is incorrect. The credit to the Cash account is correct. Therefore, an entry is needed to transfer $700 from the Office Equipment account to the Office Supplies account. The correcting entry follows.

	20X2					
1	Jun.	30	Office Supplies	7 0 0 00		1
2			Office Equipment		7 0 0 00	2
3			To correct error of June 9, in which			3
4			a purchase of office supplies was			4
5			debited to Office Equipment.			5
6						6

Posting Errors

An amount that is correctly entered in the journal but posted incorrectly to the ledger can be corrected by drawing a line through the error and writing the correct figure above it. For example, on May 4, 20X1, a $600 receipt of cash for services performed was correctly journalized as a debit to Cash and a credit to Service Revenue. However, it was posted to the ledger as a debit to Cash for $600 and a credit to Service Revenue for $6,000. We can correct the Service Revenue account as follows.

Account Service Revenue						Account No. 411		
Date		Item	P.R.	Debit	Credit	Balance		
							Debit	Credit
20X1					*ML* 6 0 0 00 ~~6 0 0 0 00~~		*ML* 6 0 0 00 ~~6 0 0 0 00~~	
May	4		GJ1					

As we just saw, you can line out an incorrect amount that has been posted to the correct account. But when a posting is made to the wrong account, you should make a correcting entry. For example, a $75 payment for a repair bill was journalized correctly as a debit to Repairs Expense and a credit to Cash. But the entry was posted as a debit to Rent Expense and a credit to Cash. The error can be corrected by the following entry.

	20X1					
1	Jan.	5	Repairs Expense	7 5 00		1
2			Rent Expense		7 5 00	2
3			To correct error in which Rent			3
4			Expense was debited for a repair.			4
5						5

Suppose the amount of the above error had been only $2. Would such a small correction be worth the time involved in making it? Probably not, but the answer is not a clear yes or no. If the amount of an error is deemed to be small and insignificant, a correction may not be made. On the other hand, if not making the correction would result in a misstatement of net income or financial position, a correction must be made. The accounting **principle of materiality** states that proper procedures must be strictly followed only for items and transactions whose values are significant enough to affect the business's financial statements.

principle of materiality
the principle that proper accounting procedures have to be strictly followed only for events and transactions that would have an effect on a business's financial statements

Summary of Error Correction Procedures

We have discussed quite a few ways to correct the various types of errors. Let's pause and look at the summary shown in Table 3-2.

Table 3-2 Summary of Correction Procedures

Type of Error	Method of Correction
Math error made in pencil	Erasure
Math error made in pen	Line out the incorrect figure, initial, and enter the correct figure
Recording error discovered before posting	Line out incorrect information, initial, and enter correct information
Recording error that has been posted	Correcting entry
An incorrect amount posted to the correct account	Line out, initial, and enter the correct amount
A correct amount posted to the incorrect account	Correcting entry

Errors That Do Not Cause the Trial Balance to Be Out of Balance

Certain errors cause the trial balance to be out of balance. However, many types of errors will not result in the trial balance being out of balance. Examples of such errors include:

- Failure to record a transaction
- Failure to post an entire entry to the ledger
- Posting the wrong amount to the debit *and* credit sides of the correct accounts
- Posting the debit (or credit) part of an entry to the wrong account but to the correct side
- Recording a transaction twice
- Posting a transaction twice

The point to remember is that a trial balance shows equality of debits and credits. It does not give you absolute certainty that no errors have been made—so work carefully.

Review Quiz **3-4**

Indicate how each of the following errors should be corrected:

1. A cash purchase of equipment was recorded as a cash purchase of supplies. The entry has not been posted to the ledger.
2. A journal entry for $470 was posted as $47 in one of the accounts involved.
3. A cash payment of $50 for repairs expense was journalized as a debit to Rent Expense and a credit to Cash. The entry was then posted.
4. In a company with over $6,000,000 in annual sales, it was discovered that the purchase of a $6.40 book of stamps was debited to Advertising Expense, instead of to Postage Expense.

Check your answers on page 132.

Plastic Surgeon Involved in Skimming

Brian Lee is a plastic surgeon from the Southwest who earned between $300,000 and $800,000 a year performing cosmetic surgery. He was employed by a prominent physician-owned clinic and was renowned for nose jobs, liposuction, face lifts, and breast enhancements.

He must have had a lifestyle that required more than his salary, because he began skimming money from the clinic by asking patients to pay him personally. He would therefore bypass the billing system in the clinic.

It was by accident that his crime was detected. After performing a rhinoplasty on a patient, she

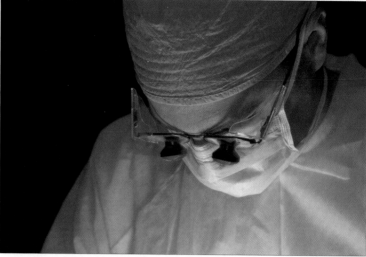

To protect themselves from the possibility of physicians skimming funds, clinics should not allow surgeons to be paid directly for services performed.

later called the clinic in an effort to see if her insurance would pay for the surgery. There was no bill on file at the clinic.

When confronted with the crime, Brian confessed and helped the fraud examiner unravel the case, revealing that he had stolen hundreds of thousands of dollars from the clinic. He admitted that his motive for the crime was to try and outdo his brother and father financially.

Since he was such an excellent doctor, the clinic let him remain as long as he repaid all the stolen money. His only punishment was to be removed from any possibility of receiving cash in the future. He admitted that given the opportunity, he would likely repeat the crime!

"Skimming" is when cash is stolen or embezzled before it has been recorded on the books. It can be done either in its entirety, where the employer never sees the transaction,

or it can be partial, when the company receives a report of a transaction that is smaller than the amount of the actual sale.

Source: Joseph T. Wells, CPA, CFE, "An Unholy Trinity: The Three Ways Employees Embezzle Cash," *ACFE* (April 1998).

For Discussion

1. How was the plastic surgeon able to steal several hundred thousands of dollars from his clinic?
2. What is the term that describes this type of fraudulent activity?
3. How can this type of fraud be prevented in the future?
4. Why do you believe the plastic surgeon kept his job at the clinic even though he admitted that he had stolen several hundred thousands of dollars?

Joining the Pieces

The First Four Steps in the Accounting Cycle

Source document: Any business paper that proves a transaction occurred.

Journal: The first place transactions are formally recorded; the book of original entry.

Ledger: A grouping of all accounts used by a business; the book of final entry.

Trial balance: A listing of the debit and credit balances in the ledger—typically prepared at the end of a month to prove the equality of debits and credits.

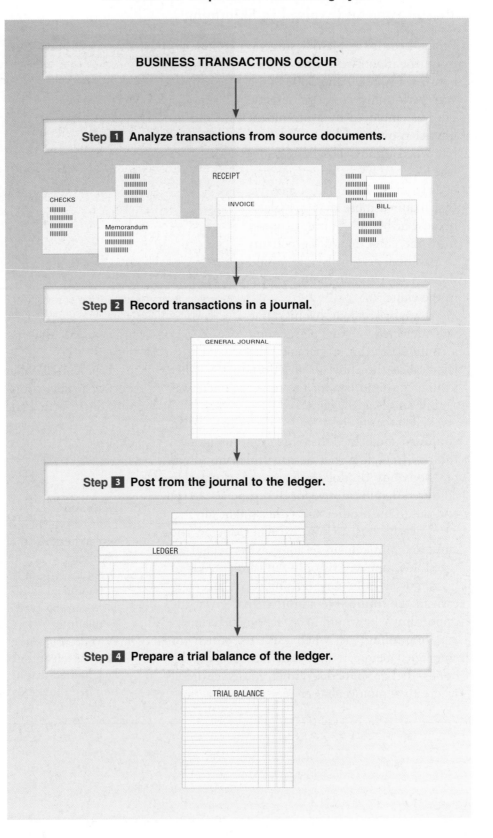

BUSINESS TRANSACTIONS OCCUR

Step 1 Analyze transactions from source documents.

CHECKS · RECEIPT · INVOICE · Memorandum · BILL

Step 2 Record transactions in a journal.

GENERAL JOURNAL

Step 3 Post from the journal to the ledger.

LEDGER

Step 4 Prepare a trial balance of the ledger.

TRIAL BALANCE

1 Describe the standard form of a two-column journal.

The standard form of a two-column journal, or **general journal**, has numbered pages, beginning with page number 1. It contains a *Date* column, used to record the date on which a transaction occurs; an *Account Title* column, used to record the accounts affected by a transaction as well as a brief description of the transaction; and a P.R. column, used to record the numbers of the accounts to which a posting has been made. It also contains two money columns, labeled *Debit* and *Credit*, used to record the dollar amounts of transactions.

2 Record business transactions in a two-column journal.

Several business transactions and their journal recordings (shown in Figure 3-9) follow. Remember that the callouts in the margin are to help you remember the rules of debits and credits.

20XX

May 1 Keith Hendrick started Keith's Furniture Repair, a furniture repair and refinishing business, by investing the following assets into the firm: cash, $5,000; supplies, $2,000; and equipment, $9,000.

    3 Paid rent for the month, $425.

    5 Purchased additional supplies on credit, $480.

    7 Performed services for cash, $990.

    9 Purchased a used pick-up truck for $8,500 by paying $1,000 down and signing a note payable for the difference.

  28 Paid for the supplies purchased on May 5, $480.

  29 Keith withdrew $600 cash for personal use.

  29 Performed services for cash, $1,075.

  30 Paid utility bill, $360.

  31 Paid telephone bill, $125.

  31 Paid salary of part-time employee, $450.

  31 Paid for repairs to truck, $30.

  31 Performed services for cash, $300.

Figure 3-9
General Journal
Recordings

		Date		Account Title	P.R.	Debit	Credit	
		20XX						
+ asset →	1	May	1	Cash		5 0 0 0 00		1
+ asset →	2			Supplies		2 0 0 0 00		2
+ asset →	3			Equipment		9 0 0 0 00		3
+ owner's capital →	4			Keith Hendrick, Capital			16 0 0 0 00	4
	5			Invested assets in the business.				5
	6							6
+ expense →	7		3	Rent Expense		4 2 5 00		7
− asset →	8			Cash			4 2 5 00	8
	9			Paid first month's rent.				9
	10							10
+ asset →	11		5	Supplies		4 8 0 00		11
+ liability →	12			Accounts Payable			4 8 0 00	12
	13			Purchased supplies on credit.				13

General Journal   **Page 1**

Continues

Figure 3-9

Continued

		Date	Account Title		Debit	Credit	
	14						14
+ asset →15	15	7	Cash		9 90 00		15
+ revenue →16	16		Service Revenue			9 90 00	16
	17		Performed services for cash.				17
	18						18
+ asset →19	19	9	Truck		8 500 00		19
− asset →20	20		Cash			1 000 00	20
+ liability →21	21		Notes Payable			7 500 00	21
	22		Purchased a truck, paying				22
	23		$1,000 down.				23
	24						24
− liability →25	25	28	Accounts Payable		4 80 00		25
− asset →26	26		Cash			4 80 00	26
	27		Paid an account—May 5.				27
	28						28
+ owner's drawing →29	29	29	Keith Hendrick, Drawing		6 00 00		29
− asset →30	30		Cash			6 00 00	30
	31		Withdrew cash for personal use.				31
	32						32
+ asset →33	33	29	Cash		1 0 75 00		33
+ revenue →34	34		Service Revenue			1 0 75 00	34
	35		Performed services for cash.				35
	36						36
	37						37
	38						38

		Date		Account Title	P.R.	Debit	Credit	
				General Journal			**Page 2**	
		20XX						
+ expense → 1	1	May	30	Utilities Expense		3 60 00		1
− asset → 2	2			Cash			3 60 00	2
	3			Paid utility bill.				3
	4							4
+ expense → 5	5		31	Telephone Expense		1 25 00		5
− asset → 6	6			Cash			1 25 00	6
	7			Paid telephone bill.				7
	8							8
+ expense → 9	9		31	Salaries Expense		4 50 00		9
− asset →10	10			Cash			4 50 00	10
	11			Paid salary of employee.				11
	12							12
+ expense →13	13		31	Repairs Expense		3 0 00		13
− asset →14	14			Cash			3 0 00	14
	15			Paid for repairs to truck.				15
	16							16
+ asset →17	17		31	Cash		3 00 00		17
+ revenue →18	18			Service Revenue			3 00 00	18
	19			Performed services for cash.				19

3 Prepare a chart of accounts.

A chart of accounts for Keith's Furniture Repair is shown in Table 3-3. The numbering scheme is the three-digit, five-category plan illustrated in the chapter.

Table 3-3 Chart of Accounts for Keith's Furniture Repair

Account Category	Account Number	Account Title
Assets (100–199)	111	Cash
	112	Supplies
	115	Equipment
	116	Truck
Liabilities (200–299)	211	Accounts Payable
	212	Notes Payable
Owner's Equity (300–399)	311	Keith Hendrick, Capital
	312	Keith Hendrick, Drawing
Revenue (400–499)	411	Service Revenue
Expenses (500–599)	511	Rent Expense
	512	Salaries Expense
	513	Utilities Expense
	514	Telephone Expense
	515	Repairs Expense

4 Describe the balance form of account.

The **balance form of account**, like the standard form of account, has a debit and a credit column. However, the balance form of account also has *debit and credit balance columns* to maintain a continuous or running balance of the account. The balance form of account is widely used in practice.

5 Post from a two-column journal to ledger accounts.

The journal entries recorded in Figure 3-9 by Keith Hendrick are posted to the ledger as shown in Figure 3-10 on the next page. Missing are P.R. marks in the journal, since there is little value in showing the journal again. Look closely at the Accounts Payable account, which shows how you should handle an account with a zero balance.

Figure 3-10

Ledger Posting
Example

General Ledger

Account Cash   **Account No.** 111

Date		Item	P.R.	Debit	Credit	Balance Debit	Balance Credit
20XX May	1		GJ1	5 000 00		5 000 00	
	3		GJ1		4 25 00	4 575 00	
	7		GJ1	9 90 00		5 565 00	
	9		GJ1		1 000 00	4 565 00	
	28		GJ1		4 80 00	4 085 00	
	29		GJ1		6 00 00	3 485 00	
	29		GJ1	1 075 00		4 560 00	
	30		GJ2		3 60 00	4 200 00	
	31		GJ2		1 25 00	4 075 00	
	31		GJ2		4 50 00	3 625 00	
	31		GJ2		30 00	3 595 00	
	31		GJ2	3 00 00		3 895 00	

Account Supplies   **Account No.** 112

Date		Item	P.R.	Debit	Credit	Balance Debit	Balance Credit
20XX May	1		GJ1	2 000 00		2 000 00	
	5		GJ1	4 80 00		2 480 00	

Account Equipment   **Account No.** 115

Date		Item	P.R.	Debit	Credit	Balance Debit	Balance Credit
20XX May	1		GJ1	9 000 00		9 000 00	

Account Truck   **Account No.** 116

Date		Item	P.R.	Debit	Credit	Balance Debit	Balance Credit
20XX May	9		GJ1	8 500 00		8 500 00	

Account Accounts Payable   **Account No.** 211

Date		Item	P.R.	Debit	Credit	Balance Debit	Balance Credit
20XX May	5		GJ1		4 80 00		4 80 00
	28		GJ1	4 80 00		—	—

Account Notes Payable   **Account No.** 212

Date		Item	P.R.	Debit	Credit	Balance Debit	Balance Credit
20XX May	9		GJ1		7 500 00		7 500 00

Account Keith Hendrick, Capital   **Account No.** 311

Date		Item	P.R.	Debit	Credit	Balance Debit	Balance Credit
20XX May	1		GJ1		16 000 00		16 000 00

Account Keith Hendrick, Drawing   **Account No.** 312

Date		Item	P.R.	Debit	Credit	Balance Debit	Balance Credit
20XX May	29		GJ1	6 00 00		6 00 00	

Continues

Figure 3-10
Continued

Account Service Revenue   **Account No.** 411

Date	Item	P.R.	Debit	Credit	Balance Debit	Balance Credit
20XX May 7		GJ1		9 90 00		9 90 00
29		GJ1		10 75 00		20 65 00
31		GJ2		3 00 00		23 65 00

Account Rent Expense   **Account No.** 511

Date	Item	P.R.	Debit	Credit	Balance Debit	Balance Credit
20XX May 3		GJ1	4 25 00		4 25 00	

Account Salaries Expense   **Account No.** 512

Date	Item	P.R.	Debit	Credit	Balance Debit	Balance Credit
20XX May 31		GJ2	4 50 00		4 50 00	

Account Utilities Expense   **Account No.** 513

Date	Item	P.R.	Debit	Credit	Balance Debit	Balance Credit
20XX May 30		GJ2	3 60 00		3 60 00	

Account Telephone Expense   **Account No.** 514

Date	Item	P.R.	Debit	Credit	Balance Debit	Balance Credit
20XX May 31		GJ2	1 25 00		1 25 00	

Account Repairs Expense   **Account No.** 515

Date	Item	P.R.	Debit	Credit	Balance Debit	Balance Credit
20XX May 31		GJ2	30 00		30 00	

6 Prepare a trial balance from a ledger after posting.

The trial balance for Keith's Furniture Repair is shown in Figure 3-11. It is taken from the ledger shown in Figure 3-10. Note that the Accounts Payable account, with a zero balance, is omitted.

Figure 3-11
Trial Balance Example

Keith's Furniture Repair
Trial Balance
May 31, 20XX

Account Title	Debit	Credit
Cash	3 8 9 5 00	
Supplies	2 4 8 0 00	
Equipment	9 0 0 0 00	
Truck	8 5 0 0 00	
Notes Payable		7 5 0 0 00
Keith Hendrick, Capital		16 0 0 0 00
Keith Hendrick, Drawing	6 0 0 00	
Service Revenue		2 3 6 5 00
Rent Expense	4 2 5 00	
Salaries Expense	4 5 0 00	
Utilities Expense	3 6 0 00	
Telephone Expense	1 2 5 00	
Repairs Expense	3 0 00	
Totals	25 8 6 5 00	25 8 6 5 00

7 Describe the procedures for locating and correcting errors in the accounting process.

The initial step in locating errors is to be aware that an error exists. The built-in warning that an error is present is an unbalanced trial balance. It is then necessary to determine the type of error that has been made.

A **math error** results from incorrect adding or subtracting. Thus, the first way to look for a math error is to add an unbalanced trial balance again. A **recording error** is an error made in the journal. A **posting error** results from incorrect transfers of amounts from the journal to the ledger, or from the ledger to the trial balance. Typical posting errors include the **transposition** and **slide**, each of which can be detected by dividing the difference in trial balance totals by the number 9. If the division is without a remainder, either type of error is likely (but not definite).

Only errors made in pencil can be corrected by erasure. Math errors made in ink, recording errors that have not been posted, and errors made by posting an incorrect amount to the right account can be corrected by lining out the incorrect information, initialing, and entering the correct information. Recording errors that have been posted to the ledger and errors made by posting an amount to the wrong account are corrected by making **correcting entries**. We will review correcting entries next.

8 Make entries to correct errors in the ledger.

The following two examples illustrate when correcting entries are needed.

Example 1: A $500 payment for a newspaper ad was correctly journalized as a debit to Advertising Expense and a credit to Cash. But when the entry was posted, the debit part of the entry was incorrectly posted to the Advertising Supplies account. We can correct this error as follows:

		20X1					
+ expense →	1	May	12	Advertising Expense	5 0 0 00		1
– asset →	2			Advertising Supplies		5 0 0 00	2
	3			To correct error in which a payment			3
	4			for a newspaper ad had been			4
	5			debited to Advertising Supplies.			5
	6						6
	7						7
	8						8

Example 2: A $60 purchase of office supplies was journalized as a debit to Store Supplies and a credit to Cash. The entry was then posted. The error can be corrected by the following entry:

		20X4					
+ asset →	1	Jun.	25	Office Supplies	6 0 00		1
– asset →	2			Store Supplies		6 0 00	2
	3			To correct error in which a purchase			3
	4			of office supplies had been debited			4
	5			to Store Supplies.			5
	6						6
	7						7
	8						8

Terms and Concepts Review

- Key Terms and Definitions in English and Spanish
- Additional Quiz Questions

Key Terms

accounting cycle, 89
balance form of account, 98
book of final entry, 102
book of original entry, 90
chart of accounts, 98
compound entry, 95
correcting entry, 106
cross-reference, 99
general journal, 90
journal, 90

journalizing, 91
math error, 104
posting, 97
posting error, 105
principle of materiality, 107
principle of objective evidence, 90
recording error, 105
slide, 105
source documents, 90
transposition, 105

Concepts Review

1. Why can it be difficult to determine the order in which transactions occurred using only a set of T accounts?
2. What are the first two steps in the accounting cycle?
3. Why is a journal referred to as a book of original entry?
4. Describe the procedure for recording a compound entry in the journal.
5. What purpose is served by a chart of accounts?
6. What is the usual sequence of accounts in the ledger?
7. Using the five-category numbering plan shown in this chapter, indicate the first digit for each of the following accounts: (a) Accounts Payable; (b) Service Revenue; (c) William Brown, Drawing; (d) Store Equipment; and (e) Utilities Expense.
8. What is the third step in the accounting cycle?
9. What is the fourth step in posting either a debit or a credit from the journal to the ledger?
10. What is the fourth step in the accounting cycle?
11. Indicate whether each of the following errors is a math error, a recording error, or a posting error.
    a. A purchase of supplies for cash was entered in the journal as a debit to Equipment and a credit to Cash.
    b. A debit to Accounts Payable was correctly journalized for $950 but was posted as $590.
    c. A $500 debit to the Cash account was correctly posted, but the balance of the account was calculated incorrectly.
12. How would you correct each of the errors described in Question 11?
13. Give examples of a transposition and a slide. Prove that the difference, in each, is evenly divisible by 9.
14. Give three examples of errors that *will not* prevent a trial balance from balancing.

Skills Review

Learning Objectives **2, 5, 6**

Check Figure
Step 1. (d) Analyze transactions from source documents.

Quick Practice

Quick Practice 3-1

Objective: To identify the first four steps of the accounting cycle

Directions: List the following four steps of the accounting cycle in the proper order.

(a) Post from the journal to the ledger.
(b) Prepare a trial balance of the ledger.
(c) Record transactions in a journal.
(d) Analyze transactions from source documents.

Quick Practice 3-2

Objective: To record transactions in a general journal

Directions: The following transactions were incurred by Shaw Service Company during September 20XX, its first month of operations. Journalize these transactions using the following account titles: Cash; Accounts Receivable; Supplies; Equipment; Accounts Payable; Sherril Shaw, Capital; Sherril Shaw, Drawing; Service Revenue; Salaries Expense; and Rent Expense.

20XX

Sep. 1 Sherril invested $10,000 in cash to start the business.
  2 Paid rent for the month, $500.
  4 Purchased supplies for cash, $280.
  9 Purchased equipment on credit, $2,200.
  10 Performed services for customers and received cash, $1,600.
  12 Purchased supplies on account, $230.
  13 Performed services for customers on account, $7,000.
  18 Paid $1,000 on the equipment purchased on September 9.
  30 Paid salaries for the month, $1,200.
  30 Customers paid on account, $1,500.
  30 Sherril withdrew cash for personal use, $2,000.

Quick Practice 3-3

Objective: To post to a balance form of account

Directions: Open a balance form of account for Cash, account number 111, and post to this account the cash-related transactions in Quick Practice 3-2.

Quick Practice 3-4

Objective: To record compound journal entries

Directions: Each of the two situations presented in this exercise requires a compound journal entry. Record each in a general journal.

1. Susan Wright invested $20,000 cash and $42,000 worth of equipment in her business.
2. Purchased $17,000 worth of equipment, paying $2,000 down and owing the balance.

Quick Practice 3-5

Objective: To record compound journal entries

Directions: Record a compound journal entry for Dan Nixon, who invested the following assets into his consulting business on May 1, 20XX: Cash $18,000, Supplies $1,300, Equipment $20,300, Building $40,000, and Land $20,000.

Quick Practice 3-6

Objective: To correct errors in the Cash account

Directions: Correct the postings to the Cash account from page 6 of Cascade Realty's general journal.

General Ledger

Account Cash   **Account No.** 111

Date		Item	P.R.	Debit	Credit	Balance Debit	Balance Credit
20XX Oct.	1		GJ6	30 0 0 0 00		30 0 0 0 00	
	2		GJ6		1 5 0 0 00		1 5 0 0 00
	4		GJ6	1 8 0 0 00		1 8 0 0 00	
	5		GJ6	1 9 0 0 00		1 9 0 0 00	
	5		GJ6		7 1 0 0 00		7 1 0 0 00

Learning Objective 4

Check Figure
Accounts Payable; credit, credit

Quick Practice 3-7

Objective: To determine normal balances and the increase side of accounts

Directions: A list of 10 accounts follows. For each, use check marks to indicate the normal balance and the increase side.

	Increase Side		Normal Balance	
Account Title	**Debit**	**Credit**	**Debit**	**Credit**
1. Accounts Payable				
2. Accounts Receivable				
3. Cash				
4. Owner, Capital				
5. Owner, Drawing				
6. Rent Expense				
7. Rental Revenue				
8. Service Revenue				
9. Supplies				
10. Utilities Expense				

Learning Objective 6

Check Figure
Trial balance totals $145,600

Quick Practice 3-8

Objective: To prepare a trial balance from account balances

Directions: A list of alphabetized accounts and their balances follows. Prepare a trial balance in proper form for Killingsworth Electronics as of December 31, 20XX.

Account	Balance
Accounts Payable	$ 1,300
Accounts Receivable	1,600
Building	50,000
Cash	7,500
Equipment	14,500
Cynthia Killingsworth, Capital	66,300
Cynthia Killingsworth, Drawing	27,000
Rent Expense	12,000
Revenue from Services	78,000
Salaries Expense	24,000
Supplies	1,800
Utilities Expense	7,200

Learning Objective 7

Check Figure
(1) Trial balance is in balance

Quick Practice 3-9

Objective: To determine the effect of errors on the trial balance

Directions: Several errors are listed below. Considering each error individually, state whether the trial balance will balance or not.

P/2

1. A $400 debit to Rent Expense was posted to the debit side of Salaries Expense. The credit part of the entry was posted correctly.
2. A $600 payment for utilities was journalized correctly but never posted.
3. A $500 cash receipt from a customer on account was correctly journalized but was posted as a debit and a credit for $50.
4. A $200 payment for advertising was posted as a debit to Advertising Expense and a debit to Cash.
5. A $300 payment on account was posted twice to both accounts affected.

Learning Objective 8

Check Figure
(1) Debit Rent Expense $500; credit Office Supplies $500

Quick Practice 3-10

Objective: To record correcting entries

Directions: In two-column form, journalize a correcting entry for each of the following errors.

1. A $500 payment of rent expense was recorded as a purchase of office supplies for cash.
2. A collection of $800 from credit customers was recorded as a debit to the Cash account and a credit to the Fees Earned account.

Exercises

Learning Objective 2

Check Figure
None

Tutorial 4

Recording Transactions in General Journal Form

Exercise 3-1

Objective: To record transactions in a general journal

Directions: The following transactions were incurred by Bowick Service Company during October 20X1, its first month of operation. Record each of the transactions in a general journal. Use the following account titles: Cash; Accounts Receivable; Supplies; Equipment; Accounts Payable; Leslie Bowick, Capital; Leslie Bowick, Drawing; Service Revenue; Salaries Expense; and Rent Expense.

20X1

Oct. 1 Leslie invested $15,000 in cash to start the business.
     2 Paid rent for the month, $850.
     4 Purchased supplies for cash, $575.
     8 Purchased equipment on credit, $3,100.
   10 Performed services for customers and received cash, $800.
   12 Purchased supplies on account, $400.
   15 Performed services for customers on account, $1,800.
   21 Leslie withdrew cash for personal use, $900.
   27 Paid salaries for the month, $950.
   31 Paid $200 on the equipment purchased on October 8.

Learning Objective 2

Check Figure
None

Exercise 3-2

Objective: To record compound journal entries

Directions: Each of the three situations presented in this exercise requires a compound journal entry. Record each in a general journal.

1. Delyse Totter invested $10,000 cash and $18,000 worth of equipment in her business.
2. Purchased office supplies, $800, and store supplies, $900, on credit.
3. Purchased $18,500 worth of equipment, paying $4,000 down and owing the balance.

Exercise 3-3

Objective: To determine normal balances and the increase sides of accounts

Directions: A list of 15 accounts follows. For each, use check marks to indicate the normal balance and the increase side.

		Increase Side		Normal Balance	
	Account Title	**Debit**	**Credit**	**Debit**	**Credit**
1.	Supplies				
2.	Tim Green, Drawing				
3.	Accounts Receivable				
4.	Truck				
5.	Service Revenue				
6.	Payroll Taxes Payable				
7.	Tim Green, Capital				
8.	Accounts Payable				
9.	Miscellaneous Expense				
10.	Office Equipment				
11.	Rent Expense				
12.	Fees Earned				
13.	Cash				
14.	Rental Revenue				
15.	Utilities Expense				

Exercise 3-4

Objective: To post to the four-column account form

Directions: Open balance form of ledger accounts for the following accounts: Cash, 111; Supplies, 112; Equipment, 115; Accounts Payable, 211; and D.D. Payne, Capital, 311. Post the following entries:

	Date		Account Title	P.R.	Debit	Credit	
	General Journal					Page 1	
1	20X1 Jul.	6	Cash		14 0 0 0 00		1
2			Supplies		1 8 0 0 00		2
3			Equipment		7 0 0 0 00		3
4			D.D. Payne, Capital			22 8 0 0 00	4
5			Invested assets to start the				5
6			business.				6
7							7
8		8	Equipment		12 0 0 0 00		8
9			Accounts Payable			12 0 0 0 00	9
10			Purchased additional equipment				10
11			on account.				11
12							12
13		9	Supplies		3 2 5 00		13
14			Cash			3 2 5 00	14
15			Purchased additional supplies				15
16			for cash.				16
17							17

Exercise 3-5

Objective: To prepare a trial balance from account balances

Directions: A list of alphabetized accounts and their balances follows. Prepare a trial balance in proper form for Paseur Electronics as of June 30, 20X2.

Account	Balance
Accounts Payable	$ 6,390
Accounts Receivable	2,455
Building	62,000
Cash	10,300
Delivery Truck	9,700
Equipment	15,700
Henry Paseur, Capital	?
Henry Paseur, Drawing	1,600
Mortgage Note Payable	56,000
Rent Expense	5,600
Repairs Expense	2,210
Revenue from Services	32,745
Salaries Expense	17,500
Supplies	5,110
Utilities Expense	2,600

Exercise 3-6

Objective: To make correcting entries

Directions: The following three situations require correcting entries. In each situation, record the correcting entry in a general journal.

1. A $700 purchase of office equipment for cash was recorded in the journal as a $700 purchase of store equipment for cash. The entry had already been posted when the error was discovered.
2. A $560 purchase of supplies on credit was recorded in the journal as a $650 purchase of supplies on credit. The entry was then posted.
3. A payment of $600 for the owner's home mortgage was debited to the Rent Expense account, and the entry was posted.

Exercise 3-7

Objective: To determine the effect of errors on the trial balance

Directions: Several errors are listed below. Considering each error individually, state whether the trial balance will balance or not.

1. A $500 debit to Rent Expense was posted to the debit side of Telephone Expense. The credit part of the entry was posted correctly.
2. A $700 payment for utilities was journalized correctly but never posted.
3. A $60 payment for advertising was posted as a debit to Advertising Expense and a debit to Cash.
4. A $400 payment on account was posted twice to both accounts affected.
5. A $450 cash receipt from a customer on account was correctly journalized but was posted as a debit and a credit of $540.

Group A

Problem 3-1A

Objective: To record transactions in a general journal

Domingo Cantoria's electronics repair shop opened on March 1, 20X2. During March, the following transactions occurred:

20X2
Mar. 1 Domingo invested $7,000 cash in his business.
      1 Paid rent for the month, $450.
      3 Purchased supplies for cash, $650.
      5 Purchased equipment on credit, $3,800.
      6 Made repairs and received cash, $210.
      7 Made repairs on credit, $250.
     15 Hired an assistant at a monthly salary of $900.
     17 Invested an additional $2,000 in the business.
     20 Purchased supplies on credit, $450.
     22 Paid for advertising in a local newspaper, $95.
     25 Made repairs and received cash, $775.
     28 Paid gas and electric bills for the month, $350.
     30 Collected the amount due from March 7, $250.
     31 Paid the two-week salary due to the assistant hired on March 15, $450.
     31 Made repairs on credit, $295.
     31 Paid telephone bill, $105.

Directions: Record the transactions in a general journal. Use the following account titles: Cash; Accounts Receivable; Supplies; Equipment; Accounts Payable; Domingo Cantoria, Capital; Repair Revenue; Rent Expense; Salaries Expense; Advertising Expense; Utilities Expense; and Telephone Expense.

Problem 3-2A

Objective: To make entries, including compound entries, in a general journal

John Costic's new business, Effective Career Planning, opened on April 1, 20X1. The following transactions occurred during the first month of operations:

20X1
Apr. 1 John invested the following assets in the business: cash, $4,200; office supplies, $400; and a computer valued at $2,100.
      1 Paid rent for April, $550.
      3 Purchased additional office supplies, $500, and office equipment, $1,200, paying $600 down with the balance on account.
      7 Paid for repairs to equipment, $230.
     12 Invested an additional $1,600 cash and a car valued at $9,000 in the business.
     16 Paid utility bill for the month, $518.
     19 Paid salary of administrative assistant, $560.
     24 Hired a cleaning service to maintain the property, starting in May, at $750 a month.
     28 John withdrew office supplies for personal use, $175.
     30 Recorded fees earned and received for the month, $2,025.

Directions: Record the transactions in a general journal, using the following account titles: Cash; Office Supplies; Office Equipment; Automobile; Accounts Payable; John Costic, Capital; John Costic, Drawing; Professional Fees; Rent Expense; Salaries Expense; Repairs Expense; and Utilities Expense.

Learning Objectives
2, 5, 6

Check Figure
Trial balance totals = $26,100

Problem 3-3A

Objective: To record transactions, post, and prepare a trial balance

On June 1, 20X2, Julie Boyles began an accounting practice called Boyles and Associates. During the first month of operations, the firm completed the following transactions:

20X2

Jun. 1 Julie invested the following assets in the firm: cash, $3,700; office supplies, $600; and office equipment, $16,500.

   1 Paid rent for the month, $775.

   3 Purchased office supplies for cash, $225.

   5 Purchased an executive desk and chair set, $2,700, paying $600 down and owing the balance.

   8 Received cash for accounting services performed, $3,200.

   11 Julie withdrew $200 cash for personal use.

   14 Performed accounting services on credit, $2,100.

   17 Paid the liability of June 5, $2,100.

   20 Paid utilities for the month, $550.

   22 Paid $75 for repairs to equipment.

   25 Purchased additional office supplies for cash, $375.

   27 Discovered that $35 worth of the office supplies purchased on June 25 were of poor quality. The supplies were returned for a cash refund.

   29 Collected $1,300 of the amount due from June 14.

   30 Paid salaries for the month, $1,050.

   30 Paid telephone bill, $195.

   30 Paid miscellaneous expenses, $175.

Directions:

1. Open a ledger of four-column accounts for Boyles and Associates using the following account titles and numbers: Cash, 111; Accounts Receivable, 112; Office Supplies, 113; Office Equipment, 118; Accounts Payable, 211; Julie Boyles, Capital, 311; Julie Boyles, Drawing, 312; Accounting Fees Earned, 411; Rent Expense, 511; Salaries Expense, 512; Utilities Expense, 513; Telephone Expense, 514; Repairs Expense, 515; and Miscellaneous Expense, 516.
2. Record the transactions in a general journal.
3. Post the journal entries to the ledger.
4. Prepare a trial balance of the ledger as of June 30, 20X2.

Learning Objective **8**

Check Figure
(1) Debit store supplies $800; credit office supplies $800

Problem 3-4A

Objective: To record correcting entries

During a routine audit, the following errors were discovered in the ledger of Capital Company:

1. A $800 purchase of store supplies for cash was recorded as a purchase of office supplies for cash.
2. A $1,000 credit purchase of store supplies was recorded as a cash purchase.
3. The owner of the business, Susan Long, used a company check to pay a personal utility bill of $95. The payment had been recorded and posted as a debit to Utilities Expense.
4. A $1,500 purchase of equipment on credit was recorded as $15,000 in both accounts affected.
5. A collection of $500 from credit customers was recorded as a debit to the Cash account and a credit to the Fees Earned account.

Directions: In two-column form, journalize a correcting entry for each of the five errors.

Problem 3-5A

Objective: To record transactions, post, and prepare a trial balance for an established business

Following is the August 31, 20X1, trial balance of Ken Leibham, MD:

	Ken Leibham, MD Trial Balance August 31, 20X1		
	Account Title	Debit	Credit
111	Cash	11 0 0 0 00	
112	Accounts Receivable	3 0 0 0 00	
113	Office Supplies	2 0 0 0 00	
114	Medical Supplies	3 0 0 0 00	
117	Office Equipment	9 0 0 0 00	
118	Medical Equipment	10 7 0 0 00	
211	Accounts Payable		1 5 0 0 00
311	Ken Leibham, Capital		26 5 0 0 00
312	Ken Leibham, Drawing	35 9 0 0 00	
411	Medical Fees Earned		80 8 0 0 00
511	Salaries Expense	23 5 0 0 00	
512	Rent Expense	6 0 0 0 00	
513	Utilities Expense	3 5 0 0 00	
514	Laboratory Fees Expense	1 0 0 0 00	
515	Miscellaneous Expense	2 0 0 00	
	Totals	108 8 0 0 00	108 8 0 0 00

Ken completed the following transactions during September. Note: Read directions for this problem before journalizing.

20X1

Sep. 1 Paid office rent for the month, $1,050.
2 Purchased office equipment on account, $7,000.
3 Collected $2,000 of the amount due from credit patients.
4 Purchased office supplies on account, $700.
6 Paid cash for medical supplies, $1,300.
7 Paid cash for laboratory analysis (laboratory fees expense), $365.
9 Paid salaries of employees, $1,600.
11 Paid cash to creditors on account, $2,100.
12 Paid miscellaneous expenses, $400.
13 Recorded amount received from cash patients, $5,250.
15 Purchased medical equipment on account, $10,000.
17 Discovered that part of the equipment purchased on the September 15 had dents and scratches. The seller of the equipment agreed to a price reduction of $1,000.
21 Recorded charges to credit patients, $4,750.
25 Paid cash from the business bank account for a personal bill, $445.
28 Paid electric bill, $2,300.
29 Paid water bill, $65.
29 Paid to have carpet cleaned in the reception room, $190.
30 Paid salaries of employees, $1,600.
30 Paid cash for laboratory analysis (laboratory fees expense), $290.

Directions:

1. Open a balance form of account for each account listed in Ken's trial balance. Enter the balances in his accounts, dating them September 1, 20X1, writing the word *Balance* in the Item column, and placing a check mark (✓) in the P.R. column, as illustrated here for the Cash account.

Account Cash							Account No. 111	
Date	Item	P.R.	Debit	Credit	Balance			
					Debit		Credit	
20X1 Sep. 1	Balance	✓			11 0 0 0 00			

2. Record the September transactions in a two-column journal beginning on page 17.
3. Post the journal entries to the ledger.
4. Prepare a trial balance as of September 30, 20X1.

Group B

Problem 3-1B

Learning Objective **2**

(P) (Q)

Check Figure
No entry needed on May 15

Objective: To record transactions in a general journal

Jeannie Beckman's watch and jewelry repair shop opened on May 1, 20X2. During May, the following transactions occurred:

20X2

May	1	Jeannie invested $7,500 cash in her business.
	1	Paid rent for the month, $500.
	3	Purchased supplies for cash, $600.
	5	Purchased equipment on credit, $4,100.
	6	Made repairs and received cash, $335.
	7	Made repairs on credit, $390.
	15	Hired an assistant at a monthly salary of $850.
	17	Invested an additional $2,200 in the business.
	20	Purchased supplies on credit, $475.
	22	Paid for advertising in a local newspaper, $105.
	25	Made repairs and received cash, $400.
	28	Paid gas and electric bills for the month, $480.
	30	Collected the amount due from May 7, $390.
	31	Paid the salary due to the assistant hired on May 15, $425.
	31	Made repairs on credit, $305.
	31	Paid telephone bill, $108.

Directions: Record the transactions in a general journal. Use the following account titles: Cash; Accounts Receivable; Supplies; Equipment; Accounts Payable; Jeannie Beckman, Capital; Repair Revenue; Rent Expense; Salaries Expense; Advertising Expense; Utilities Expense; and Telephone Expense.

Problem 3-2B

Learning Objective **2**

Check Figure
Three compound entries; no entry on November 24

Objective: To make entries, including compound entries, in a general journal

Cassandra Smith's new business, Best Exterminators, opened on November 1, 20X1. The following transactions occurred during the first month of operations:

20X1

Nov. 1 Cassandra invested the following assets in the business: cash, $5,200; office supplies, $450; and a computer valued at $2,200.

   1 Paid rent for November, $600.

   3 Purchased additional office supplies, $600, and office equipment, $1,300, paying $800 down with the balance on account.

   7 Paid for repairs to equipment, $245.

   12 Invested an additional $1,700 cash and a car valued at $11,000 in the business.

   16 Paid utility bill for the month, $427.

   19 Paid salary of administrative assistant, $580.

   24 Hired a cleaning service to maintain the property, starting in December, at $650 a month.

   28 Cassandra withdrew office supplies for personal use, $180.

   30 Recorded fees earned and received for the month, $2,725.

Directions: Record the transactions in a general journal using the following account titles: Cash; Office Supplies; Office Equipment; Automobile; Accounts Payable; Cassandra Smith, Capital; Cassandra Smith, Drawing; Professional Fees; Rent Expense; Salaries Expense; Repairs Expense; and Utilities Expense.

Learning Objectives
2, 5, 6

Check Figure
Trial balance totals = $25,500

Problem 3-3B

Objective: To record transactions, post, and prepare a trial balance

On January 2, 20X1, Yuliana Auld began an income tax preparation firm called Auld and Associates. During the first month of operations, the firm completed the following transactions:

20X1

Jan. 2 Yuliana invested the following assets in the firm: cash, $3,900; office supplies, $550; and office equipment, $15,500.

   2 Paid rent for the month, $675.

   3 Purchased office supplies for cash, $230.

   5 Purchased an executive desk and chair set, $3,200, paying $800 down and owing the balance.

   8 Received cash for accounting services performed, $3,300.

   11 Yuliana withdrew $250 cash for personal use.

   14 Performed accounting services on credit, $2,250.

   17 Paid the liability of January 5, $2,400.

   20 Paid utilities for the month, $600.

   22 Paid $65 for repairs to equipment.

   25 Purchased additional office supplies for cash, $400.

   27 Discovered that $45 worth of the office supplies purchased on January 25 were of poor quality. The supplies were returned for a cash refund.

   29 Collected $1,200 of the amount due from January 14.

   30 Paid salaries for the month, $1,100.

   31 Paid telephone bill, $224.

   31 Paid miscellaneous expenses, $185.

Directions:

1. Open a ledger of balance form of accounts for Auld and Associates using the following account titles and numbers: Cash, 111; Accounts Receivable, 112; Office Supplies, 113; Office Equipment, 118; Accounts Payable, 211; Yuliana Auld, Capital, 311; Yuliana Auld, Drawing, 312; Accounting Fees Earned, 411; Rent Expense, 511; Salaries Expense, 512; Utilities Expense, 513; Telephone Expense, 514; Repairs Expense, 515; and Miscellaneous Expense, 516.

2. Record the transactions in a general journal.
3. Post the journal entries to the ledger.
4. Prepare a trial balance of the ledger as of January 31, 20X1.

Learning Objective **8**

Check Figure
(1) Debit store supplies $950;
    credit office supplies $950

Problem 3-4B

Objective: To record correcting entries

During a routine audit, the following errors were discovered in the ledger of the Martin Company:

1. A $950 purchase of store supplies for cash was recorded as a purchase of office supplies for cash.
2. A $1,300 credit purchase of store supplies was recorded as a cash purchase.
3. The owner of the business, Lorelei Martin, used a company check to pay a personal utility bill of $180. The payment had been recorded and posted as a debit to Utilities Expense.
4. A $1,600 purchase of equipment on credit was recorded as $16,000 in both accounts affected.
5. A collection of $700 from credit customers was recorded as a debit to the Cash account and a credit to the Fees Earned account.

Directions: In two-column form, journalize a correcting entry for each of the five errors.

Learning Objectives
2, 5, 6

Check Figure
Trial balance totals =
$143,805

Problem 3-5B

Objective: To record transactions, post, and prepare a trial balance for an established business

Following is the October 31, 20X1, trial balance of Linda Bruss, MD. Note: Read directions for this problem before journalizing.

Linda Bruss, MD — Trial Balance — October 31, 20X1		
Account Title	**Debit**	**Credit**
111 Cash	13 0 0 0 00	
112 Accounts Receivable	3 0 0 0 00	
113 Office Supplies	3 0 0 0 00	
114 Medical Supplies	4 0 0 0 00	
117 Office Equipment	8 5 0 0 00	
118 Medical Equipment	20 0 0 0 00	
211 Accounts Payable		2 5 0 0 00
311 Linda Bruss, Capital		29 0 0 0 00
312 Linda Bruss, Drawing	32 6 0 0 00	
411 Medical Fees Earned		88 6 0 0 00
511 Salaries Expense	24 3 0 0 00	
512 Rent Expense	5 5 0 0 00	
513 Utilities Expense	4 0 0 0 00	
514 Laboratory Fees Expense	1 4 0 0 00	
515 Miscellaneous Expense	8 0 0 00	
Totals	120 1 0 0 00	120 1 0 0 00

Linda completed the following transactions during November:

20X1

Nov. 1 Paid office rent for the month, $1,075.

2 Purchased office equipment on account, $7,800.

3 Collected $2,500 of the amount due from credit patients.

4 Purchased office supplies on account, $650.

6 Paid cash for medical supplies, $1,350.

7 Paid cash for laboratory analysis (laboratory fees expense), $400.

9 Paid salaries of employees, $1,900.

11 Paid cash to creditors on account, $2,600.

12 Paid miscellaneous expenses, $390.

15 Recorded amount received from cash patients, $9,000.

15 Purchased medical equipment on account, $5,205.

17 Discovered that part of the equipment purchased on the November 15 had scratches and dents. The seller of the equipment agreed to a price reduction of $900.

21 Recorded charges to credit patients, $4,550.

25 Paid cash from the business bank account for a personal bill, $450.

28 Paid electric bill, $2,500.

29 Paid water bill, $75.

29 Paid to have carpet cleaned in the reception room, $290.

30 Paid salaries of employees, $1,900.

30 Paid cash for laboratory analysis (laboratory fees expense), $305.

Directions:

1. Open a balance form of account for each account listed in Linda's trial balance. Enter the balances in her accounts, dating them November 1, 20X1, writing the word *Balance* in the Item column, and placing a check mark (✓) in the P.R. column, as illustrated below for the Cash account.

Account Cash					Account No. 111		
					Balance		
Date	Item	P.R.	Debit	Credit	Debit		Credit
20X1 Nov. 1	Balance	✓			13 0 0 0 00		

2. Record the November transactions in a two-column journal beginning on page 17.
3. Post the journal entries to the ledger.
4. Prepare a trial balance as of November 30, 20X1.

Critical Thinking Problems

Challenge Problem

The Georgian Theater is a Victorian-style theater that operated profitably for many years. In recent years, however, it had started to lose money due to intense competition from several multiscreen theaters that had opened in the area. The original owner made several unsuccessful attempts to sell the theater while it was still in operation. Finally, it was closed on January 14, 20X0, and has been vacant since. On April 2, 20X2, Kamiar Jackson entered into a contract with the owner to purchase and restore the theater. He completed the following transactions during April:

20X2

Apr. 2 Kamiar transferred the balance of his savings account, $15,000, to a bank account for the business.

3 Using the value of his home as security, Kamiar borrowed $45,000 from a local bank by signing a five-year note payable.

4 Purchased the Georgian Theater for $175,000, paying $30,000 down with the balance on a 30-year mortgage note payable. Assets of the purchase are allocated as follows: building, $100,000; land, $40,000; projection equipment, $20,000; concession equipment, $15,000.

5 Purchased office equipment on account, $6,000.

5 Entered into a contract with a food-vending company to run the concession stand. The contract calls for the concessionaire to pay rent of 10% of the monthly concession sales, with a minimum of $500, which was collected in advance.

5 Purchased office supplies for cash, $245.

6 Paid $2,000 to have all seats and carpets steam cleaned.

6 Paid for a full-page ad in a local newspaper, $900.

7 Opened the theater to the public by offering a free showing.

9 Paid for advertising leaflets, $300.

10 Paid miscellaneous expenses, $225.

12 Cash received from admissions for the week totaled $4,500.

15 Paid semimonthly wages, $2,540.

17 Purchased office supplies on account, $75.

19 Cash received from admissions for the week totaled $6,500.

21 Returned a defective printer cartridge (from the April 17 purchase) and received a credit of $12.

21 Purchased six video machines for use in the lobby, $24,500, paying $5,000 down with the balance on account.

23 Paid a personal bill using the business bank account, $40.

27 Cash received from admissions for the week totaled $8,200.

28 Paid water bill, $120.

29 Paid electric bill, $2,500.

29 Paid telephone bill, $95.

30 Paid film rental expense for the month, $5,500.

30 Cash received from video machines totaled $590.

30 Paid creditors on account, $1,000.

30 Cash received from admissions for the last three days in the month totaled $3,600.

30 Made first payment to the bank for the loan of April 3, $475.

30 The concessionaire reported sales for the month of $10,500.

Directions: On May 1, you were hired as bookkeeper for the theater. By carefully going through each April transaction, you are to complete the following:

1. Develop a complete chart of accounts using a three-digit, five-category plan.
2. Develop a ledger by opening an account for each account title you listed in the chart of accounts.
3. Record the April transactions in a general journal.
4. Post the journal entries to the ledger.
5. Prepare a trial balance as of April 30, 20X2.
6. Prepare an income statement for the month ended April 30, as Kamiar is eager to see how well the business did during its first month of operations.

Communications

Robert Downie, who owns a small business, is taking an accounting course to help him manage his business. After studying the general journal, Robert is wondering if he should set up his books using a journal and a ledger. He reasons that since his business is small, he can just set up ledger accounts and enter his transactions directly into the ledger.

In writing, explain why a better accounting system uses both a journal and a ledger.

Team Internet Project

Luca Pacioli is reported to be the creator of the double-entry accounting system that we use today. Search the Internet for information about him, and prepare a brief report of his life and contributions.

Ethics

David DeMarkey runs a computer repair service. He has not been thorough in keeping records of transactions to use as the basis for journal entries, but he is interested in trying to be accurate in what he records. Thus, he asks you, a current student of accounting, to look over his records and give your opinion about the system he is using.

You immediately find an entry in his journal for the receipt of cash for services performed in the amount of $250, but you find no document to support the entry. When you ask David about it, he replies, "That's how I remember it."

Write a brief explanation of what David is doing wrong. What accounting principle is he violating, and why is he violating it?

In the Real World	H&R Block

Based on the April 30, 2007, balance sheet for H&R Block shown in Chapter 1, why do you think the dollar value of the Property, Plant, and Equipment account is so low in comparison to the Cash account?

Answers to Review Quizzes

Review Quiz 3-1

	Date		Account Title	P.R.	Debit	Credit	
	General Journal					**Page 1**	
1	20XX Mar.	1	Cash		7 0 0 0 00		1
2			Becky McAfee, Capital			7 0 0 0 00	2
3							3
4		4	Supplies		7 5 0 00		4
5			Accounts Payable			7 5 0 00	5
6							6
7		6	Equipment		4 7 5 00		7
8			Cash			4 7 5 00	8
9							9
10		9	Accounts Payable		3 7 5 00		10
11			Cash			3 7 5 00	11
12							12
13							13

Review Quiz 3-2

	20X1					
1	Jun.	12	Utilities Expense	1 4 5 00		1
2			Cash		1 4 5 00	2
3						3
4		17	John Dark, Drawing	1 7 5 00		4
5			Cash		1 7 5 00	5
6						6
7		22	Cash	9 5 0 00		7
8			Service Revenue		9 5 0 00	8
9						9
10		25	Office Supplies	7 5 00		10
11			Truck	4 0 0 0 00		11
12			John Dark, Capital		4 0 7 5 00	12
13						13
14						14

Review Quiz 3-3

LeAnn's TV Repair Shop
Trial Balance
December 31, 20XX

Account Title	Debit	Credit
Cash	1 4 0 0 00	
Supplies	3 8 6 0 00	
Equipment	16 4 0 0 00	
Truck	9 4 0 0 00	
Accounts Payable		7 2 1 0 00
LeAnn Lovering, Capital		14 6 0 0 00
LeAnn Lovering, Drawing	7 0 0 00	
Revenue from Services		16 3 8 0 00
Rent Expense	3 0 0 0 00	
Salaries Expense	2 5 1 0 00	
Utilities Expense	4 7 0 00	
Repairs Expense	4 5 0 00	
Totals	38 1 9 0 00	38 1 9 0 00

Review Quiz 3-4

1. Line out the title Supplies in the journal and write the title Equipment above it.
2. Line out $47 in the ledger account and write $470 above it.
3. Make the following correcting entry:

1		Repairs Expense	5 0 00		1
2		Rent Expense		5 0 00	2

4. The error could be corrected by the following correcting entry:

1		Postage Expense	6 40		1
2		Advertising Expense		6 40	2

Due to the small amount of this error, however, it may not be corrected, since it would not significantly affect the company's net income figure.

CHAPTER

4

The Accounting Cycle Continued
Work Sheet, Financial Statements, and Adjusting Entries

Learning Objectives

1 Explain the need for adjusting entries.
2 Make adjusting entries for supplies used, expired insurance, depreciation, and unpaid wages.
3 Complete a work sheet for a service business.
4 Prepare financial statements from a work sheet.
5 Journalize and post adjusting entries.

Having met the objectives of the first three chapters, you can now (1) use source documents as a basis for recording business transactions, (2) record business transactions in a general journal, (3) post journal entries to a ledger, and (4) take a trial balance of the ledger. In other words, you have learned the first four steps in the accounting cycle. As you will recall, the accounting cycle represents the steps involved in the recording and summarizing processes of accounting.

In Chapter 4, we will study the next four steps in the accounting cycle for a service business:

Step 5 Determine needed adjustments.
Step 6 Prepare a work sheet.
Step 7 Prepare financial statements from a completed work sheet.
Step 8 Journalize and post adjusting entries.

In Chapter 3, we recorded the November 20X1 transactions of Walker and Associates in a two-column general journal. After the journal was posted, we took a trial balance of the ledger on November 30. We now look again at the books of Walker and Associates. It is now December 31, one month later. Many of Walker and Associates' November transactions (such as the payment of rent and utilities) occurred again in December. Several new transactions also took place in December. One of the December transactions, on December 1, involved payment of cash for a one-year insurance policy, which Stanley felt he needed to protect his assets. A **premium**, which is a fee paid for insurance coverage, of $240 was paid for this policy, to run from December 1, 20X1, to November 30, 20X2.

premium a fee paid for insurance coverage that will benefit the business in the future

133

Prepaid Insurance	
Debit	Credit
+	−

Insurance paid in advance can be debited to an asset account entitled Prepaid Insurance, which Stanley added to his chart of accounts and ledger as account number 114. The following journal entry was made to record the prepayment. It was then posted to the ledger.

	Date		Account Title	P.R.	Debit	Credit	
	20X1						
1	Dec.	1	Prepaid Insurance	114	2 40 00		1
2			Cash	111		2 40 00	2
3			Paid insurance premium for one year.				3

General Journal — **Page 2**

+ asset → (row 1)
− asset → (row 2)

Remember from Chapter 1 that an asset is any item with money value that the business owns. Insurance paid in advance represents a service that will benefit the business in the future. It is owned and has monetary value; thus, it is considered an asset.

Another December event was the hiring of an assistant, Carol Ogden, at a weekly salary of $350. Carol started work on Monday, December 8, and is paid every Friday. Carol's salary will be recorded in an expense account entitled Salaries Expense, which was added to the chart of accounts and ledger as account number 513. This account was debited for $350 on December 12, 19, and 26 for a total of $1,050. On December 31, after all December transactions were recorded and posted, the trial balance shown in Figure 4-1 was prepared.

Now that we know where Walker and Associates stands at the end of December, it is time for us to look at the next step in the accounting cycle.

Prepaid insurance is considered an asset because it provides something of value—monetary protection of assets—that benefits the business in the current and future periods.

Step 5: Determine Needed Adjustments

As we have seen, much of the accounting process involves recording the day-to-day business transactions. Some transactions, however, are not recorded by routine accounting entries. This is not due to error or lack of attention but is a result of changes in the nature of certain accounts brought about by the passage of time.

For example, the Office Supplies account shows the value of office supplies purchased for use in the business. But office supplies are used constantly in the daily operation of most businesses. Practically every minute, office workers

Figure 4-1

Trial Balance for
Walker and Associates

Walker and Associates Trial Balance December 31, 20X1		
Account Title	Debit	Credit
Cash	8 4 8 5 00	
Accounts Receivable	3 0 0 00	
Office Supplies	2 7 5 00	
Prepaid Insurance	2 4 0 00	
Office Equipment	3 0 0 0 00	
Office Furniture	2 0 0 0 00	
Accounts Payable		3 0 0 0 00
Stanley Walker, Capital		10 0 0 0 00
Stanley Walker, Drawing	1 5 0 0 00	
Service Revenue		4 7 0 0 00
Rent Expense	8 0 0 00	
Repairs Expense	5 0 00	
Salaries Expense	1 0 5 0 00	
Totals	17 7 0 0 00	17 7 0 0 00

use such items as postage stamps, computer paper, pens, stationery, and paper clips. It would be totally impractical to try to keep up with these items as they are used. Consequently, no regular journal entry is made to record the value of office supplies consumed on a daily basis. Thus, as time passes, the balance of the Office Supplies account does not show the true value of office supplies still on hand.

To illustrate this, let's look again at the December 31 trial balance of Walker and Associates in Figure 4-1. The Office Supplies account shows a balance of $275, which is the result of purchases of office supplies during November and December. On December 31, this balance does not represent the value of office supplies on hand, because some supplies have been used during the past two months. Thus, the Office Supplies account needs to be *adjusted* to reflect the value of supplies used.

An **adjusting entry** is an entry made at the end of an accounting period to bring up to date the balance of an account that has become out of date. Adjusting entries are referred to as **internal transactions** because they do not involve parties outside the business. And since no outside parties are involved, adjusting

Adjusting entries are *internal transactions* because they update certain ledger account balances without involving any party outside the business. Since no outside parties are involved, the Cash account is never used in an adjusting entry.

adjusting entry an entry made at the end of an accounting period to bring the balance of an account up to date

internal transactions adjusting entries that update the ledger without involving parties outside the business

entries *never* involve the Cash account. Walker and Associates determined that adjustments for the following items were needed as of December 31, 20X1: (1) supplies used, (2) insurance expired, (3) depreciation of office equipment and office furniture, and (4) unpaid salaries.

In practice, adjusting entries are recorded in the journal and posted to the ledger. For illustration purposes, however, we will first record them in T accounts. Later in the chapter, we will see how they are journalized and posted.

Supplies Used

Learning Objective

2 Make adjusting entries for supplies used, expired insurance, depreciation, and unpaid wages.

As we stated earlier, the Office Supplies account of Walker and Associates shows a $275 balance as of December 31. On December 31, Stanley took an inventory and found $230 worth of office supplies actually left on hand. The amount that should be shown in the Office Supplies account is thus $230; the difference ($275 – $230 = $45) has been used, as shown here:

	Amount had	$275	(balance of account)
–	Amount left	– 230	(inventory count on December 31)
	Amount used	$ 45	(amount used during the period)

The portion of an asset that has been used no longer provides a future benefit to the business; *it becomes an expense*. As a result, we need to take the amount of office supplies used, $45, out of the Office Supplies account and put it into an expense account entitled Office Supplies Expense. Stanley added this account to the chart of accounts and ledger as account number 514.

Increases in expense accounts are recorded as *debits*, and decreases in asset accounts are recorded as *credits*. Therefore, the entry to adjust the Office Supplies account involves a debit to the Office Supplies Expense account and a credit to the Office Supplies account, as shown below.

Office Supplies Expense	514	Office Supplies	113
+	–	+	–
Adjusting 45		Balance 275	Adjusting 45
		New Balance 230	

Notice that Office Supplies now has a balance of $230, which is equal to the amount of office supplies on hand as of December 31. Thus, this account is up to date.

In this adjusting entry, we made a debit to Office Supplies Expense (an income statement account) and made a credit to Office Supplies (a balance sheet account). Thus, both the income statement and the balance sheet were affected by the adjusting entry. Every adjusting entry involves at least one income statement account and at least one balance sheet account.

Remember

Balance Sheet
    Assets
    Liabilities
    Owner's Equity

Income Statement
    Revenue
– Expenses
    Net income (or loss)

We can summarize the adjustment for supplies as follows:

Adjusting Entry for Supplies Used

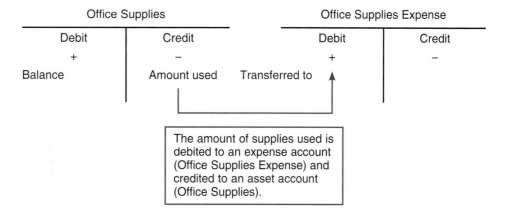

Office Supplies		Office Supplies Expense	
Debit	Credit	Debit	Credit
+	–	+	–
Balance	Amount used	Transferred to	

The amount of supplies used is debited to an expense account (Office Supplies Expense) and credited to an asset account (Office Supplies).

Insurance Expired

As we said earlier, insurance paid in advance is considered to be an asset. As time passes, however, the prepayment gradually expires, and the asset becomes an expense.

On December 31, Stanley's Prepaid Insurance account shows a balance of $240, which represents a one-year premium paid in advance on December 1. At December 31, one month of the premium has expired, which amounts to $20, as shown below:

$$\frac{\text{Amount of prepayment}}{\text{Number of months prepaid}} = \frac{\$240}{12} = \$20 \text{ per month}$$

The adjusting entry for expired insurance involves transferring the amount that has expired, $20, from the Prepaid Insurance account to the Insurance Expense account, as we see below:

Insurance Expense		515	Prepaid Insurance		114
+	–		+	–	
Adjusting 20			Balance 240	Adjusting 20	
			New Balance 220		

The Prepaid Insurance account now has a balance of $220, which is the unexpired portion of the premium—the portion that is still an asset. We can summarize the adjustment for insurance expired as follows:

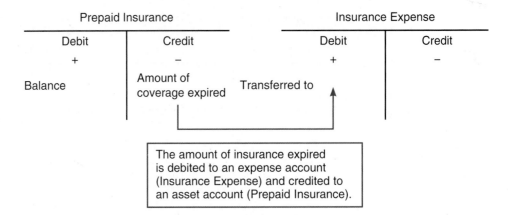

Depreciation of Office Equipment and Office Furniture

In addition to the Office Supplies and Prepaid Insurance accounts, Stanley's trial balance shows two other asset accounts that need adjusting: Office Equipment and Office Furniture. These assets are referred to as *long-term assets* because they are expected to remain useful for several years. As time passes, however, the usefulness of the assets will decline, and eventually they will no longer serve their original purpose. The accounting system must, therefore, reflect the fact that the equipment and furniture will gradually wear out or become obsolete and will have to be replaced.

Depreciation is the term used to describe the expense that results from the loss in usefulness of an asset due to age, wear and tear, and obsolescence. The purpose of depreciation accounting is to spread the cost of an asset over its useful life rather than treating the asset's cost as an expense in the year it was purchased. In other words, part of the cost of a depreciable asset should be transferred to an expense account during each period the asset is used in producing revenue.

Since it is difficult to determine exactly how long an asset will last, the amount calculated for depreciation is an estimate. On December 31, Stanley has used his office equipment for two months and his office furniture for one month. Depreciation for the time each was used should be estimated and recorded. There are several acceptable ways to calculate depreciation. Stanley uses the **straight-line method**, which is a very popular method that yields the same amount of depreciation for each full period an asset is used. Under the straight-line method, the cost of an asset, less any estimated trade-in value, is divided by the number of years the asset is estimated to remain useful, as shown here:

$$\frac{\text{Cost of asset} - \text{Trade-in value}}{\text{Estimated years of usefulness}} = \text{Annual depreciation expense}$$

Stanley estimates that his $3,000 of office equipment will last for 10 years and his $2,000 of office furniture will last for 5 years. Further, he estimates

---

depreciation an allocation process in which the cost of a long-term asset (except land) is divided over the periods in which the asset is used in the production of the business's revenue; always recorded by debiting the Depreciation Expense account and crediting the Accumulated Depreciation account

straight-line method a popular method of calculating depreciation that yields the same amount of depreciation for each full period an asset is used

Key Point ⊚

Trade-in value is also referred to as salvage value and residual value.

that the office equipment will not have a trade-in value at the end of its useful life, but that the office furniture will be worth $200. Using these factors, we can calculate Stanley's estimated depreciation expense for 20X1 as follows:

Step **1** Office equipment (used for two months in 20X1):

$$\frac{\text{Cost of asset – Trade-in value}}{\text{Estimated years of usefulness}} = \frac{\$3,000 - \$0}{10 \text{ years}} = \frac{\$3,000}{10 \text{ years}} = \$300 \text{ per year}$$

Since the office equipment was used for only two months in 20X1, we further calculate the depreciation as follows:

$$\frac{\$300}{12 \text{ months}} = \$25 \text{ depreciation per month}$$

$$\$25 \times 2 \text{ months} = \$50$$

Step **2** Office furniture (used for one month in 20X1):

$$\frac{\text{Cost of asset – Trade-in value}}{\text{Estimated years of usefulness}} = \frac{\$2,000 - \$200}{5 \text{ years}} = \frac{\$1,800}{5 \text{ years}} = \$360 \text{ per year}$$

Since the office furniture was used for only one month in 20X1, we further calculate depreciation as follows:

$$\frac{\$360}{12 \text{ months}} = \$30 \text{ depreciation per month}$$

Depreciation is *always* recorded by debiting an expense account entitled *Depreciation Expense* and crediting an account entitled *Accumulated Depreciation*. When depreciation is recorded for more than one type of asset, it is common to have a depreciation expense account and an accumulated depreciation account for each type of asset. Depreciation on Stanley's long-term assets is recorded as follows:

Office Equipment

Depr. Expense—Office Equipment	516		Accum. Depr.—Office Equipment	116.1
+	−		−	+
Adjusting 50				Adjusting 50

Office Furniture

Depr. Expense—Office Furniture	517		Accum. Depr.—Office Furniture	117.1
+	−		−	+
Adjusting 30				Adjusting 30

You may be wondering why Accumulated Depreciation is credited instead of the asset itself. Recording the credit in the separate Accumulated Depreciation account allows the original cost of the asset to be shown in the asset account and the related depreciation *accumulated* or summarized in a separate account. This way, the business has a record of the asset's original cost and a separate record of the total amount the asset is estimated to have depreciated.

On the balance sheet, the balance of Accumulated Depreciation is subtracted from the balance of the related asset account, as illustrated in Figure 4-2, which shows the partial balance sheet of Walker and Associates. The difference between an asset's cost and its accumulated depreciation is referred to as the asset's **book value**.

book value the difference between an asset's cost and its accumulated depreciation

Figure 4-2
Partial
Balance
Sheet

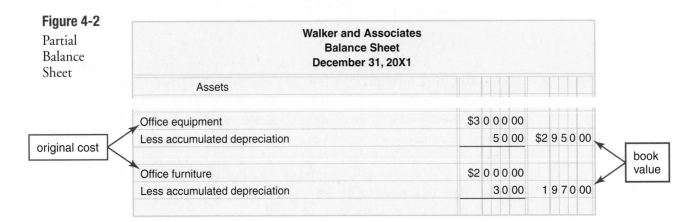

Accumulated Depreciation is an example of a **contra asset account**. Contra means opposite or offsetting. Thus, the balance of an Accumulated Depreciation account is the opposite of the asset account to which it relates. Since asset accounts normally have debit balances, Accumulated Depreciation will have a credit balance. The following T account illustrates this relationship.

contra asset account an account whose balance is opposite the asset to which it relates; an account with a credit balance, because it is opposite to an asset account having a debit balance

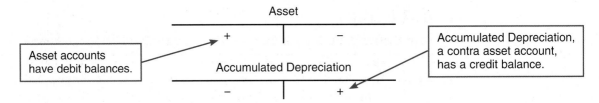

Stanley assigned account number 116.1 to Accumulated Depreciation—Office Equipment. It is opposite (contra) account number 116, the Office Equipment account. Likewise, account number 117.1 was assigned to Accumulated Depreciation—Office Furniture, to indicate its contra relationship to account number 117, the Office Furniture account. These accounts, along with account number 516 (Depreciation Expense—Office Equipment) and account number 517 (Depreciation Expense—Office Furniture), were added to the chart of accounts and ledger of Walker and Associates. The adjustment for estimated depreciation is summarized as follows:

Adjusting Entry for Estimated Depreciation

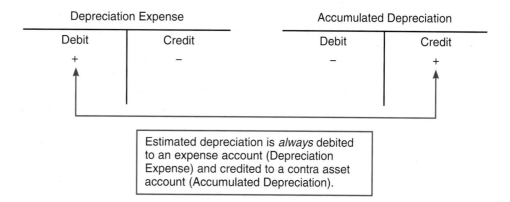

We should stress that only physical, long-lasting assets are depreciated. For Walker and Associates, this includes only two types of assets. Other depreciable assets include trucks and automobiles, buildings, machinery, fixtures on a building, parking lots, carpeting, cash registers, display cases, computers, and so on. There is, however, one long-term asset that we do not depreciate—land. Land has an unlimited useful life. Consequently, generally accepted accounting principles (GAAP) and tax laws do not allow depreciation to be taken on land.

Unpaid Salaries

When Carol Ogden was hired as an assistant on December 8, it was agreed that she would receive a weekly salary of $350, payable every Friday. On December 31, the Salaries Expense account shows a $1,050 balance, representing payments as follows:

Payroll Period	Paid On
Dec. 8–12	Dec. 12
Dec. 15–19	Dec. 19
Dec. 22–26	Dec. 26

The next payroll period is for the week starting on Monday, December 29, 20X1, and ending on Friday, January 2, 20X2. However, this payroll period is different than the previous three payroll periods in December. To see how it is different, let's look at a calendar for December 20X1 (Figure 4-3).

Figure 4-3

Payroll Periods

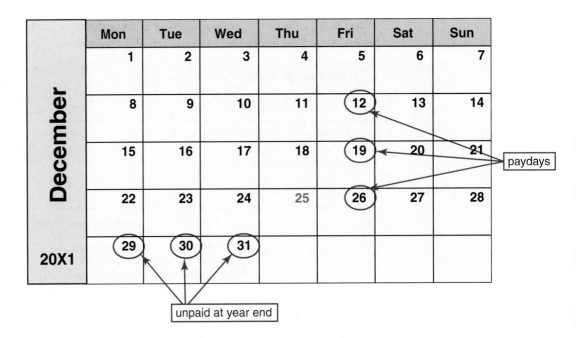

The end of the accounting period, December 31, falls in the middle of the payroll period. By stating Carol's salary on a daily basis ($350 ÷ 5 = $70), we determine that she is paid $70 a day. We can illustrate the situation as follows:

	20X1				20X2		
Dec.	29	30	31	Jan.	1	2	
	Monday	Tuesday	Wednesday		Thursday	Friday	Total
	$70	$70	$70		$70	$70	$350
		$210 (20X1)				$140 (20X2)	

As you can see, the first three days (Monday, Tuesday, and Wednesday) of this payroll period are in 20X1, and the remaining two days are in 20X2. When 20X1 ends, three days of salary expense will not have been paid. These days will not be paid until the next regular payday, which is Friday, January 2, 20X2. However, all expenses of an accounting period should be recorded in that period, even though payment may not have been made. Therefore, on December 31, an adjusting entry is needed to record three days' salary at $70 per day ($70 × 3 = $210).

As illustrated below, the adjusting entry for unpaid salaries involves a debit to the Salaries Expense account and a credit to a liability account entitled Salaries Payable, which Stanley added to his chart of accounts and ledger as account number 212.

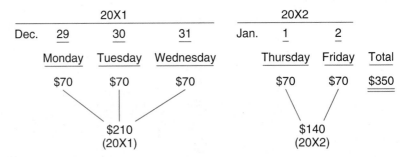

Salaries Expense		513			Salaries Payable		212
+		−			−		+
Balance	1,050					Adjusting	210
Adjusting	210						
New Balance	1,260						

Salaries Expense now shows a balance of $1,260, which is the correct amount of salaries expense for the period. Unpaid salaries always occur when the last day of the accounting period is not the same as the last day of the payroll period.

We can summarize the adjustment for unpaid salaries as follows:

Adjusting Entry for Unpaid Salaries

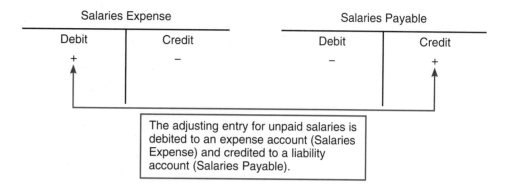

The adjusting entry for unpaid salaries is debited to an expense account (Salaries Expense) and credited to a liability account (Salaries Payable).

Take This Into Account

Adjusting entries are not caused by errors; they are a planned part of the accounting cycle. For practical reasons, the accounting for internal transactions is postponed until the end of the accounting period.

The Matching Principle of Accounting

matching principle a rule of accounting that requires that revenue and expenses be recorded in the accounting period in which they occur; a rule stating that an accurate net income or net loss for an accounting period be reported by offsetting revenue earned by the expenses that were necessary to produce that revenue

The five adjusting entries for Walker and Associates are based on the matching principle of accounting. The **matching principle** requires that revenue and expenses be recorded in the accounting period in which they occurred. Stated another way, the matching principle states that expenses incurred during an accounting period should be matched with the revenue that was earned during the same period. To match expenses with revenue means to subtract the expenses from revenue to calculate the net income or net loss for the period.

Adjusting entries are needed to properly match expenses and revenue. Had Stanley not made his adjustments, several expenses would have gone unrecorded for 20X1. Unrecorded expenses result in an understatement of expenses on the income statement. This, in turn, results in an overstatement of net income and owner's equity. Also, assets would be overvalued, as no recognition would have been given to the value of assets used up or expired (supplies and prepaid insurance) or assets depreciated (office equipment and office furniture). Finally, liabilities would be understated, because unpaid salaries at the end of the accounting period would not have been recorded. Table 4-1 summarizes the effects on Stanley's financial statements had he not made adjusting entries.

Although accounts can be adjusted at any time, they are normally adjusted at the end of a month or the end of the year. In relation to the total accounts of a business, only a few generally need adjusting, and after you have been

Table 4-1 Effects of *Not* Recording Adjusting Entries

Adjustment	Entry		Effect of *Not* Recording on:				
	Debit	Credit	Income Statement		Balance Sheet		
			Expenses	Net Income	Assets	Liabilities	Owner's Equity
Office supplies used	Supplies Expense	Supplies	Understated	Overstated	Overstated	No effect	Overstated
Expired insurance	Insurance Expense	Prepaid Insurance	Understated	Overstated	Overstated	No effect	Overstated
Depreciation	Depreciation Expense	Accumulated Depreciation	Understated	Overstated	Overstated	No effect	Overstated
Unpaid salaries	Salaries Expense	Salaries Payable	Understated	Overstated	No effect	Understated	Overstated

through the adjusting process even once, these accounts become easy to recognize.

Now that we have determined the necessary adjustments, we are ready for the next step in the accounting cycle.

Review Quiz **4-1** Using T accounts, record adjusting entries for the following: (1) the Office Supplies account shows a $900 balance; however, a current count reveals that $750 worth remain on hand; (2) insurance expired, $50; (3) depreciation of trucks, $1,000; and (4) unpaid salaries, $150.

Check your answers on page 174.

Step 6: Prepare a Work Sheet

Learning Objective

3 Complete a work sheet for a service business.

work sheet an informal working paper used by the accountant to organize data for the financial statements and lessen the possibility of overlooking an adjustment

The **work sheet** is an informal working paper that the accountant uses in preparing the financial statements and completing the work of the accounting cycle. The work sheet has been described as the accountant's scratch pad, and it is used to (1) organize data, (2) lessen the possibility of overlooking an adjustment, (3) provide an arithmetical check on the accuracy of work, and (4) arrange data in logical form for the preparation of financial statements. The work sheet is typically prepared in pencil, and usually only the accountant sees it.

The form of the work sheet varies with the needs of the business using it. In completing the accounting cycle for Walker and Associates, we will use a 10-column work sheet, which is shown in Figure 4-4 on page 146.

Steps in Completing the Work Sheet

The following eight steps are used to complete the work sheet:

1. **Enter the heading**. The heading consists of the name of the business, the title Work Sheet, and the period of time covered.
2. **Enter the current trial balance in the Trial Balance columns.** The current trial balance, including accounts without balances—such as those accounts used for adjusting entries—is entered in the Trial Balance

columns. The trial balance can be prepared on a separate sheet and copied onto the work sheet, or it can be prepared directly on the work sheet.

3 **Enter the adjustments in the Adjustments Debit and Credit columns.** We now enter the adjustments in the Adjustments columns of the work sheet. Make certain that each adjustment has an equal debit and credit. Each adjustment is labeled as (a), (b), (c), and so on. For example, the first adjustment is a debit to Office Supplies Expense and a credit to Office Supplies. Both the debit and credit are labeled as (a). After all adjustments have been entered, the Adjustments columns are totaled and ruled.

4 **Complete the Adjusted Trial Balance columns.** Amounts in the Adjustments columns are now combined with account balances in the Trial Balance columns, and the updated amounts are extended to the Adjusted Trial Balance columns. Amounts are extended as follows:

   a. If an account balance *has not* been adjusted, it is simply extended to the same column in the Adjusted Trial Balance section. For example, Cash has a debit balance of $8,485, *and there was no adjustment to this account*. So, the $8,485 balance in the Trial Balance section is extended directly to the Adjusted Trial Balance Debit column.

   b. If an account has a debit balance and the adjustment is a credit, the *difference* between the two amounts is extended to the Adjusted Trial Balance Debit column. For example, Office Supplies has a debit balance of $275 and a credit adjustment of $45. The difference between the two amounts, $230, is extended to the Adjusted Trial Balance Debit column.

   c. If an account has a debit balance and the adjustment is also a debit, the two figures are *added*, and the total is extended to the Adjusted Trial Balance Debit column. For example, the Salaries Expense account has a debit balance of $1,050 and a $210 debit adjustment. The two debits are added, and the total, $1,260, is extended to the Adjusted Trial Balance Debit column.

   d. After all amounts have been extended to the Adjusted Trial Balance columns, total and rule the columns.

5 **Complete the Income Statement columns.** An income statement summarizes revenue and expenses for an accounting period. Therefore, the balance of the Service Revenue account and the balance of each of the expense accounts are extended from the Adjusted Trial Balance columns to the Income Statement columns by following these rules:

   a. **A credit remains a credit.** Thus, the $4,700 credit balance of the Service Revenue account is extended to the Income Statement Credit column.

   b. **A debit remains a debit.** Thus, the debit balance of each expense account is extended to the Income Statement Debit column.

6 **Complete the Balance Sheet columns.** The remaining account balances—assets, liabilities, owner's capital, and drawing—are extended to the Balance Sheet columns, following these rules:

   a. **A debit remains a debit.** Thus, the debit balance of each asset account is extended to the Balance Sheet Debit column.

Figure 4-4
Ten-Column Work Sheet

Account Title	Trial Balance		Adjustments		Adjusted Trial Balance		Income Statement		Balance Sheet		
	Debit	Credit	Debit	Credit	Debit	Credit	Debit	Credit	Debit	Credit	
1											1
2											2
3											3
4											4
5											5
6											6
7											7
8											8
9											9
10											10
11											11
12											12
13											13
14											14
15											15
16											16
17											17
18											18
19											19
20											20
21											21
22											22
23											23

b. **A credit remains a credit.** Thus, the credit balance of each accumulated depreciation account and each liability account and the $10,000 credit balance of the owner's capital account are extended to the Balance Sheet Credit column.

c. The $1,500 debit balance of the owner's drawing account is extended to the Balance Sheet Debit column. Notice that the drawing account is not an asset. It is extended to the Balance Sheet Debit column so that it will be opposite the owner's capital account, which was extended to the Balance Sheet Credit column.

7 **Total the Income Statement and Balance Sheet columns.** The Income Statement Debit and Credit columns and the Balance Sheet Debit and Credit columns are totaled, and each column total is entered directly below the column.

8 **Determine the amount of net income or net loss, and balance the statement columns.** Since the Income Statement Credit column contains the amount of revenue and the Income Statement Debit column contains the amount of expenses, the net income or net loss can be determined by calculating the difference between the two column totals as follows:

Income Statement Credit column (revenue)	$4,700.00
Income Statement Debit column (expenses)	− 2,255.00
Net income	$2,445.00

Since revenue exceeded expenses, we have a net income for the period. The term *Net Income* is written in the Account Title column, and the amount of net income is entered under the Income Statement Debit column and the Balance Sheet Credit column. The columns are totaled again, as an arithmetic check, and ruled. Had there been a net loss, the amount of the loss would have been entered under the Income Statement Credit column and the Balance Sheet Debit column and described as *Net Loss* in the Account Title column.

It should be stressed that the work sheet is not a formal financial statement but an aid to the accountant. Figure 4-5, which shows the proper placement of items on the work sheet, can be used as a guide when preparing work sheets.

Figure 4-5

Placement of Items on a Work Sheet

Account Classification	Trial Balance		Adjustments		Adjusted Trial Balance		Income Statement		Balance Sheet	
	Debit	Credit	Debit	Credit	Debit	Credit	Debit	Credit	Debit	Credit
Assets	X				X				X	
Liabilities		X				X				X
Capital		X				X				X
Drawing	X				X				X	
Revenue		X				X		X		
Expenses	X				X		X			

Review Quiz **4-2**

On a completed work sheet, can the amount of net income (or net loss) be obtained by finding the difference between the total of the Balance Sheet Debit column and the total of the Balance Sheet Credit column? If so, why?

Check your answer on page 175.

Step 7: Prepare Financial Statements from a Completed Work Sheet

Financial statements are usually prepared as soon as possible after the work sheet has been completed in order to get the statements to those who need them. The amounts used to prepare the financial statements are taken directly from the work sheet. An income statement, a statement of owner's equity, and a balance sheet for Walker and Associates are illustrated in Figure 4-6.

The Income Statement

The income statement is a summary of revenue and expenses showing net income or net loss for an accounting period. It is prepared directly from data in the Income Statement columns of the work sheet. An income statement is typically prepared at the end of each month, quarter, or year; however, it can be prepared for any period of time.

The Statement of Owner's Equity

The statement of owner's equity summarizes the changes that have occurred in owner's equity during an accounting period, such as a month or a year. It is prepared from the following three pieces of information on the work sheet:

- The owner's capital account balance in the Balance Sheet Credit column
- The owner's drawing account balance in the Balance Sheet Debit column
- The amount of net income or net loss, which is shown at the bottom of the Income Statement section

The Balance Sheet

The balance sheet shows that assets = liabilities + owner's equity. Balance sheet data come from the Balance Sheet columns of the work sheet. The up-to-date amount for owner's equity on the balance sheet is taken from the statement of owner's equity.

Notice that Stanley's balance sheet is simply dated December 31, 20X1. As you recall from Chapter 1, the balance sheet—unlike the income statement or the statement of owner's equity—does not show what happened over a period of time. Instead, it shows the financial position of the business at a particular point in time.

Also notice that the accumulated depreciation accounts are subtracted from the related asset accounts. (Remember that depreciation of a long-term asset is not recorded directly in the asset account but in an accumulated depreciation contra asset account.)

Figure 4-6

Financial Statements

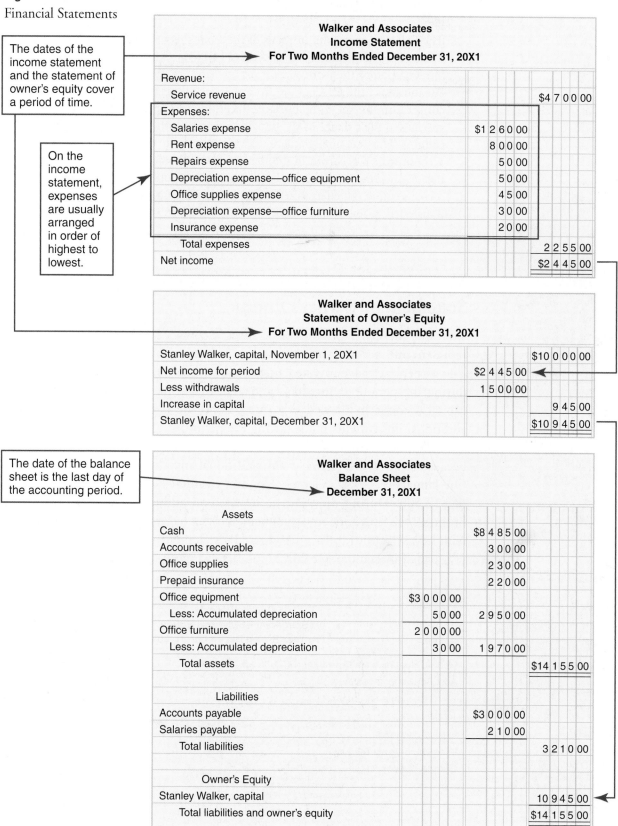

The dates of the income statement and the statement of owner's equity cover a period of time.

On the income statement, expenses are usually arranged in order of highest to lowest.

Walker and Associates
Income Statement
For Two Months Ended December 31, 20X1

Revenue:			
Service revenue			$4 7 0 0 00
Expenses:			
Salaries expense	$1 2 6 0 00		
Rent expense	8 0 0 00		
Repairs expense	5 0 00		
Depreciation expense—office equipment	5 0 00		
Office supplies expense	4 5 00		
Depreciation expense—office furniture	3 0 00		
Insurance expense	2 0 00		
Total expenses			2 2 5 5 00
Net income			$2 4 4 5 00

Walker and Associates
Statement of Owner's Equity
For Two Months Ended December 31, 20X1

Stanley Walker, capital, November 1, 20X1			$10 0 0 0 00
Net income for period		$2 4 4 5 00	
Less withdrawals		1 5 0 0 00	
Increase in capital			9 4 5 00
Stanley Walker, capital, December 31, 20X1			$10 9 4 5 00

The date of the balance sheet is the last day of the accounting period.

Walker and Associates
Balance Sheet
December 31, 20X1

Assets				
Cash			$8 4 8 5 00	
Accounts receivable			3 0 0 00	
Office supplies			2 3 0 00	
Prepaid insurance			2 2 0 00	
Office equipment	$3 0 0 0 00			
Less: Accumulated depreciation		5 0 00	2 9 5 0 00	
Office furniture	2 0 0 0 00			
Less: Accumulated depreciation		3 0 00	1 9 7 0 00	
Total assets				$14 1 5 5 00
Liabilities				
Accounts payable			$3 0 0 0 00	
Salaries payable			2 1 0 00	
Total liabilities				3 2 1 0 00
Owner's Equity				
Stanley Walker, capital				10 9 4 5 00
Total liabilities and owner's equity				$14 1 5 5 00

CAUTION

The Balance Sheet column totals of the work sheet ($15,735) *do not* match the totals of the formal balance sheet ($14,155). This is because the Balance Sheet section of the work sheet *is not* a balance sheet; *it is balance sheet data.* We must take the information from the work sheet and arrange it into the correct form for the formal balance sheet. For example, on the work sheet we showed the balance of the drawing account in the Balance Sheet Debit column. This was done because drawing is opposite the owner's capital account, which is shown in the Balance Sheet Credit column. Drawing is not reported on the formal balance sheet; it is reported on the statement of owner's equity. Its effect is reflected in an updated capital figure, which is transferred to the formal balance sheet.

Showing Additional Investments on the Statement of Owner's Equity

The amount listed on the work sheet as owner's capital does not always represent the account balance at the beginning of the accounting period. The owner may have invested additional cash (or other assets) in the business during the period. If this has happened, it will be necessary to refer to the capital account in the ledger to determine the beginning balance and any additional investments made during the period.

To illustrate this, we will use a company other than Walker and Associates, because Stanley didn't make any additional investments during the period. On January 1, 20X2, George Hendrix's capital account showed a balance of $12,500. During the year, he invested an additional $6,000 cash in the business. His 20X2 income statement shows a net income of $22,600, and he withdrew $15,000 during the year. His statement of owner's equity for the year ended December 31, 20X2, appears in Figure 4-7.

Figure 4-7
Statement of Owner's Equity

George Hendrix
Statement of Owner's Equity
For Year Ended December 31, 20X2

George Hendrix, capital, January 1, 20X2		$12 500 00
Add: Additional investment	$ 6 000 00	
Net income for the year	22 600 00	
Total increases	$28 600 00	
Less withdrawals	15 000 00	
Increase in owner's equity		13 600 00
George Hendrix, capital, December 31, 20X2		$26 100 00

The financial statement columns of Sether Company's work sheet are shown below. Prepare (1) an income statement, (2) a statement of owner's equity, and (3) a balance sheet.

Sether Company
Work Sheet
For Year Ended December 31, 20X2

	Account Title	Income Statement Debit	Income Statement Credit	Balance Sheet Debit	Balance Sheet Credit	
1	Cash			6 2 0 0 00		1
2	Accounts Receivable			9 2 0 00		2
3	Supplies			6 0 0 00		3
4	Equipment			22 0 0 0 00		4
5	Accumulated Depreciation—Equipment				2 0 0 00	5
6	Accounts Payable				1 8 0 0 00	6
7	Tim Sether, Capital				15 9 1 5 00	7
8	Tim Sether, Drawing			18 0 0 0 00		8
9	Service Revenue		52 0 0 0 00			9
10	Salaries Expense	14 3 0 0 00				10
11	Rent Expense	4 2 0 0 00				11
12	Telephone Expense	1 5 7 0 00				12
13	Utilities Expense	2 9 0 0 00				13
14	Depreciation Expense	8 0 0 00				14
15	Office Supplies Expense	2 2 5 00				15
16		23 9 9 5 00	52 0 0 0 00	47 7 2 0 00	19 7 1 5 00	16
17	Net Income	28 0 0 5 00			28 0 0 5 00	17
18		52 0 0 0 00	52 0 0 0 00	47 7 2 0 00	47 7 2 0 00	18

Check your answers on pages 175–176.

Step 8: Journalize and Post Adjusting Entries

Learning Objective

5 Journalize and post adjusting entries.

Key Point

The work sheet is not a journal. Thus, the adjustments must be taken from the work sheet and entered in the journal.

Earlier in the chapter, we recorded adjusting entries in T accounts. This was done to introduce adjustments and to show you how they affect the ledger. In actual practice, adjustments are first recorded on the work sheet. However, the work sheet is not a journal, and it cannot be used as a basis for posting adjusting entries to the ledger. Consequently, adjustments must be formally journalized and posted to the ledger so that ledger account balances will be up to date and will agree with the balances reported on the financial statements. Remember that accounting information is not officially a part of the accounting cycle until it is recorded in the general journal—the book of original entry.

The accountant simply copies the adjusting entries from the work sheet to the journal. The heading *Adjusting Entries* is written in the Account Title column above the adjusting entries. No further explanation is needed. Adjusting entries for Walker and Associates are shown in Figure 4-8. Notice that each adjusting entry is dated as of the last day of the accounting period.

Figure 4-8

Journalizing Adjusting Entries

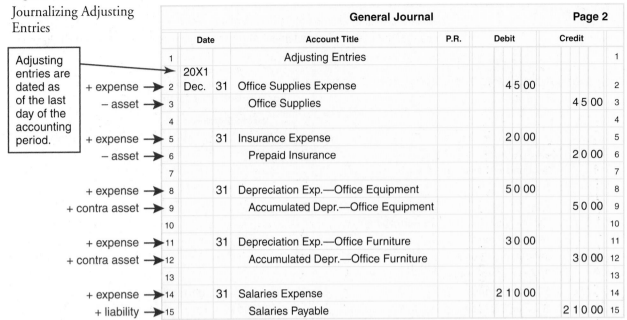

Adjusting entries are dated as of the last day of the accounting period.

	Date		Account Title	P.R.	Debit	Credit	
1			Adjusting Entries				1
2	20X1 Dec.	31	Office Supplies Expense		45 00		2
3			Office Supplies			45 00	3
4							4
5		31	Insurance Expense		20 00		5
6			Prepaid Insurance			20 00	6
7							7
8		31	Depreciation Exp.—Office Equipment		50 00		8
9			Accumulated Depr.—Office Equipment			50 00	9
10							10
11		31	Depreciation Exp.—Office Furniture		30 00		11
12			Accumulated Depr.—Office Furniture			30 00	12
13							13
14		31	Salaries Expense		2 10 00		14
15			Salaries Payable			2 10 00	15

General Journal — Page 2

+ expense → 2
− asset → 3
+ expense → 5
− asset → 6
+ expense → 8
+ contra asset → 9
+ expense → 11
+ contra asset → 12
+ expense → 14
+ liability → 15

Summing Up

The source of the information for the adjusting entries is the Adjustments columns of the work sheet. Each adjustment shown on the work sheet affects at least two general ledger accounts. The debit and credit parts of each adjusting entry are found by matching the letters of the adjustments recorded on the work sheet.

After the adjusting entries have been journalized, the next step is to post them to the ledger, thereby bringing the ledger up to date. When posting adjusting entries, you should write the word *Adjusting* in the Item column of the respective ledger account. Figure 4-9 shows the Office Supplies account and the Office Supplies Expense account after the above adjusting entries are posted.

Figure 4-9

Office Supplies and Office Supplies Expense Accounts after Adjusting Entries Are Posted

General Ledger

Account Office Supplies — Account No. 113

Date		Item	P.R.	Debit	Credit	Balance Debit	Balance Credit
20X1 Dec.	1	Balance	✓			1 25 00	
	5		GJ2	1 50 00		2 75 00	
	31	Adjusting	GJ2		45 00	2 30 00	

Account Office Supplies Expense — Account No. 514

Date		Item	P.R.	Debit	Credit	Balance Debit	Balance Credit
20X1 Dec.	31	Adjusting	GJ2	45 00		45 00	

Review Quiz **4-4** If adjusting entries are entered on the work sheet, why is it necessary to formally journalize them and post to the ledger?

Check your answer on page 176.

Focus on ETHICS

Executives at Computer Associates Accused of Fraud

Sanjay Kumar was convicted of backdating $2.2 billion of revenue of Computer Associates, where he was chief executive officer.

Computer Associates (CA) is a large manufacturer of computer components and products based in Islandia, New York. The chief executive officer, Sanjay Kumar, and vice president, Stephen Woghin, were charged with "perpetrating a massive accounting fraud that cost public investors hundreds of millions of dollars when it collapsed." After being caught, the executives lied to cover up the fraud.

Kumar and Woghin kept the company books open at the end of a fiscal year and then told their sales managers to finalize and then backdate all license agreements. The Securities and Exchange Commission found that $2.2 billion of revenue was backdated.

CA had to pay $225 million and agreed to help investigators recover compensation from current or former employees who had been involved in fraudulent behavior. Both Kumar and Woghin were indicted on fraud charges.

Source: Matt Hamblin, "Former CA Chief Sanjay Kumar Indicted on Fraud Charges," *Computer World* (September 22, 2004).

For Discussion
1. How does "backdating" license agreements violate the matching principle in accounting?
2. What would motivate Kumar and Woghin to keep the company books open at the end of the fiscal year and engage in manipulation of accounting data?
3. What might happen when investigators begin recovering compensation from current or former employees who were involved in fraudulent behavior?

Joining the Pieces

Adjusting Entries

Supplies Used

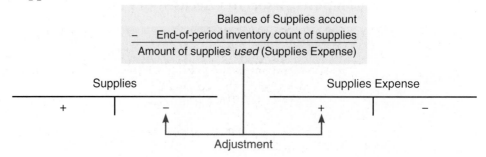

Insurance Expired

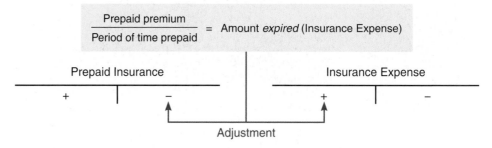

Depreciation of Long-Term Assets

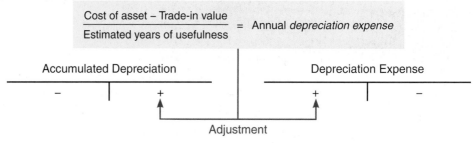

Unpaid Salaries

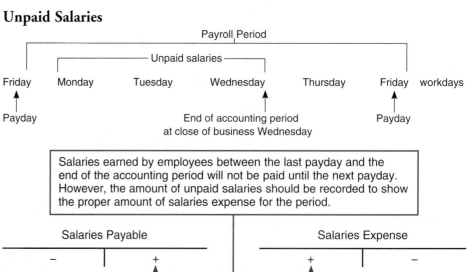

Summary

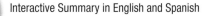 Interactive Summary in English and Spanish

1 Explain the need for adjusting entries.

Adjusting entries are made to:
*   Bring the ledger up to date.
*   Better match expenses and revenue to more accurately determine the net income (or loss) for the accounting period.
*   More accurately state the amount of assets, liabilities, and owner's equity.

2 Make adjusting entries for supplies used, expired insurance, depreciation, and unpaid wages.

M & K Shoe Repair shows the following account balances as of December 31, 20XX:

Account	Balance
Cash	$ 7,755
Supplies	965
Prepaid Insurance	1,800
Equipment	20,000
Accumulated Depreciation—Equipment	4,000
Accounts Payable	7,600
Michael Knebel, Capital	19,780
Michael Knebel, Drawing	2,500
Revenue from Services	62,240
Rent Expense	7,200
Salaries Expense	51,000
Utilities Expense	2,400

Adjustment data are as follows:
(a) Supplies on hand, $750.
(b) Insurance expired, one year of a three-year premium.
(c) Depreciation of equipment. (Equipment has an estimated life of 10 years and no trade-in value.)
(d) Salaries unpaid for five days at $200 per day.

Adjustments are prepared as shown below.

(a) Supplies used:

Balance of account	$965
Amount on hand	– 750
Value of supplies used	$215

Adjusting entry:

Supplies Expense				Supplies			
+		–		+		–	
(a) 215				Balance 965		(a) 215	

(b) Insurance expired: $1,800 ÷ 3 years = $600 per year

Adjusting entry:

Insurance Expense				Prepaid Insurance			
+		–		+		–	
(b) 600				Balance 1,800		(b) 600	

(c) Depreciation: $20,000 \div 10$ years $= $2,000 per year

   Adjusting entry:

Depreciation Expense—Equipment		Accumulated Depreciation—Equipment	
+	−	−	+
(c) 2,000			Balance 4,000
			(c) 2,000

(d) Salaries unpaid: 5 days $\times$ $200 = $1,000

   Adjusting entry:

Salaries Expense		Salaries Payable	
+	−	−	+
Balance 51,000			(d) 1,000
(d) 1,000			

3 Complete a work sheet for a service business.

The information for M & K Shoe Repair is summarized on the work sheet in Figure 4-10 on page 157. Additional accounts needed for adjusting entries have been added at the appropriate places. Note that M & K incurred a net loss for the year.

4 Prepare financial statements from a work sheet.

M & K's income statement, statement of owner's equity, and balance sheet for 20XX are shown in Figure 4-11 on page 158. Each was prepared from the information supplied by M & K's completed work sheet. Notice how the net loss is shown on the first two statements. Also notice that on a statement of owner's equity, withdrawals are *added* to the net loss.

5 Journalize and post adjusting entries.

Using the Adjustments columns of M & K's work sheet, adjusting entries are journalized as shown below.

		General Journal			Page 1	
	Date	Account Title	P.R.	Debit	Credit	
		Adjusting Entries				
	20XX					
1	Dec. 31	Supplies Expense		2 1 5 00		1
2		Supplies			2 1 5 00	2
3						3
4	31	Insurance Expense		6 0 0 00		4
5		Prepaid Insurance			6 0 0 00	5
6						6
7	31	Depreciation Expense—Equipment		2 0 0 0 00		7
8		Accumulated Depreciation—Equipment			2 0 0 0 00	8
9						9
10	31	Salaries Expense		1 0 0 0 00		10
11		Salaries Payable			1 0 0 0 00	11
12						12
13						13

+ expense → 1
− asset → 2
+ expense → 4
− asset → 5
+ expense → 7
+ contra asset → 8
+ expense → 10
+ liability → 11

Figure 4-10
Work Sheet for M & K Shoe Repair

M & K Shoe Repair
Work Sheet
For Year Ended December 31, 20XX

	Account Title	Trial Balance Debit	Trial Balance Credit	Adjustments Debit	Adjustments Credit	Adjusted Trial Balance Debit	Adjusted Trial Balance Credit	Income Statement Debit	Income Statement Credit	Balance Sheet Debit	Balance Sheet Credit	
1	Cash	7 7 5 5 00				7 7 5 5 00				7 7 5 5 00		1
2	Supplies	9 6 5 00			(a) 2 1 5 00	7 5 0 00				7 5 0 00		2
3	Prepaid Insurance	1 8 0 0 00			(b) 6 0 0 00	1 2 0 0 00				1 2 0 0 00		3
4	Equipment	20 0 0 0 00				20 0 0 0 00				20 0 0 0 00		4
5	Accum. Depr.—Equip.		4 0 0 0 00		(c) 2 0 0 0 00		6 0 0 0 00				6 0 0 0 00	5
6	Accounts Payable		7 6 0 00				7 6 0 00				7 6 0 00	6
7	Salaries Payable				(d) 1 0 0 0 00		1 0 0 0 00				1 0 0 0 00	7
8	Michael Knebel, Capital		19 7 8 0 00				19 7 8 0 00				19 7 8 0 00	8
9	Michael Knebel, Drawing	2 5 0 0 00				2 5 0 0 00				2 5 0 0 00		9
10	Revenue from Services		62 2 4 0 00				62 2 4 0 00		62 2 4 0 00			10
11	Rent Expense	7 2 0 0 00				7 2 0 0 00		7 2 0 0 00				11
12	Salaries Expense	51 0 0 0 00		(d) 1 0 0 0 00		52 0 0 0 00		52 0 0 0 00				12
13	Utilities Expense	2 4 0 0 00				2 4 0 0 00		2 4 0 0 00				13
14	Supplies Expense			(a) 2 1 5 00		2 1 5 00		2 1 5 00				14
15	Insurance Expense			(b) 6 0 0 00		6 0 0 00		6 0 0 00				15
16	Depr. Expense—Equip.			(c) 2 0 0 0 00		2 0 0 0 00		2 0 0 0 00				16
17		93 6 2 0 00	93 6 2 0 00	3 8 1 5 00	3 8 1 5 00	96 6 2 0 00	96 6 2 0 00	64 4 1 5 00	62 2 4 0 00	32 2 0 5 00	34 3 8 0 00	17
18	Net Loss								2 1 7 5 00	2 1 7 5 00		18
19								64 4 1 5 00	64 4 1 5 00	34 3 8 0 00	34 3 8 0 00	19

Figure 4-11

Financial Statements for M & K Shoe Repair

M & K Shoe Repair
Income Statement
For Year Ended December 31, 20XX

Revenue:		
Revenue from services		$62 2 4 0 00
Expenses:		
Salaries expense	$52 0 0 0 00	
Rent expense	7 2 0 0 00	
Utilities expense	2 4 0 0 00	
Depreciation expense—equipment	2 0 0 0 00	
Insurance expense	6 0 0 00	
Supplies expense	2 1 5 00	
Total expenses		64 4 1 5 00
Net loss		($ 2 1 7 5 00)

M & K Shoe Repair
Statement of Owner's Equity
For Year Ended December 31, 20XX

Michael Knebel, capital, January 1, 20XX		$19 7 8 0 00
Net loss for the year	$2 1 7 5 00	
Add: Withdrawals	2 5 0 0 00	
Decrease in capital		4 6 7 5 00
Michael Knebel, capital, December 31, 20XX		$15 1 0 5 00

M & K Shoe Repair
Balance Sheet
December 31, 20XX

Assets			
Cash		$ 7 7 5 5 00	
Supplies		7 5 0 00	
Prepaid insurance		1 2 0 0 00	
Equipment	$20 0 0 0 00		
Less: Accumulated depreciation	6 0 0 0 00	14 0 0 0 00	
Total assets			$23 7 0 5 00
Liabilities			
Accounts payable		$ 7 6 0 0 00	
Salaries payable		1 0 0 0 00	
Total liabilities			$ 8 6 0 0 00
Owner's Equity			
Michael Knebel, capital			15 1 0 5 00
Total liabilities and owner's equity			$23 7 0 5 00

Terms and Concepts Review

- Key Terms and Definitions in English and Spanish
- Additional Quiz Questions

Key Terms

adjusting entry, 135
book value, 140
contra asset account, 140
depreciation, 138
internal transactions, 135

matching principle, 143
premium, 133
straight-line method, 138
work sheet, 144

Concepts Review

1. Why do certain accounts need adjusting at the end of an accounting period?
2. Explain why adjustments are referred to as internal transactions.
3. What is the amount of the adjustment for supplies used if $950 worth are on hand and $1,375 is the balance of the Supplies account before adjustment?
4. On June 30, 20X1, Ray Smith paid $1,440 for a three-year insurance policy. Assuming that Ray's accounting period ends on December 31, 20X1, determine how much of the prepayment has expired by that date.
5. Why is depreciation referred to as an allocation process?
6. A long-term asset is purchased on May 1 of the current year. Assuming it has a cost of $70,000, a trade-in value of $10,000, and an estimated life of 10 years, what is the depreciation by the straight-line method up to December 31 in the current year? What is the depreciation for the next calendar year the asset is used?
7. What is a contra asset account? What is its normal balance?
8. Weekly salaries are $30,000. Assuming a five-day workweek and a Friday payday, what is the amount of the adjustment for unpaid salaries if the accounting period ends on a Tuesday?
9. Is the work sheet a financial statement? Explain.
10. Describe the process of transferring amounts from the Trial Balance and Adjustments columns of a work sheet to the Adjusted Trial Balance columns.
11. How is the amount of net income or net loss determined from a work sheet?
12. Indicate whether each of the following account balances would appear in the income statement or balance sheet columns of a work sheet.
    (a) Cash
    (b) Prepaid Insurance
    (c) Accumulated Depreciation—Office Equipment
    (d) Accounts Payable
    (e) Ray Langford, Capital
    (f) Service Revenue
    (g) Supplies Expense
    (h) Accounts Receivable
13. Why are financial statements prepared as soon as possible after the work sheet is completed?
14. Explain why adjusting entries must be formally journalized and posted to the ledger, even though they already appear on the work sheet.

Skills Review

Learning Objective 1

Check Figure
Step 1. (b) Determine needed adjustments.

Quick Practice

<u>Quick Practice 4-1</u>

Objective: To identify the second four steps of the accounting cycle

Directions: Arrange the following four steps of the accounting cycle in the proper order.

(a) Journalize and post adjusting entries.
(b) Determine needed adjustments.
(c) Prepare financial statements from a completed work sheet.
(d) Prepare a work sheet.

Learning Objectives **2, 5**

Check Figure
Supplies used = $1,160

Quick Practice 4-2

Objective: To determine the amount of adjustment for supplies used and record the adjusting entry in general journal form

The Supplies account had a balance of $830 on January 1, 20X7. Additional supplies were purchased on March 1, 20X7, for $380 and September 9, 20X7, for $560. A year-end inventory shows that $610 worth are on hand.

Directions: Determine the amount of the supplies used as of December 31, 20X7, and prepare the adjusting entry.

Learning Objectives **2, 5**

Check Figure
Insurance expired = $2,700

Quick Practice 4-3

Objective: To determine the amount of adjustment for expired insurance and record the adjusting entry

Before adjustment, the Prepaid Insurance account has a balance of $10,800 on December 31, 20X7, representing premiums paid for a three-year policy on April 1, 20X7.

Directions: Determine the amount of adjustment for insurance expired during the year, and prepare the adjusting entry.

Learning Objectives **2, 5**

Check Figure
Depreciation expense = $5,000

Quick Practice 4-4

Objective: To determine the amount of adjustment for depreciation for the year and record the adjusting entry

Equipment was purchased for $60,000 on January 2, 20X5. The equipment has an estimated useful life of 10 years and an estimated trade-in value of $10,000.

Directions: Determine the amount of adjustment for depreciation expense for the year ended December 31, 20X5, and prepare the adjusting entry.

Learning Objectives **2, 5**

Check Figure
Unpaid salaries = $28,000

Quick Practice 4-5

Objective: To determine the amount of unpaid salaries at the end of the year and record the adjusting entry

Salaries of $35,000 are paid weekly on Fridays. December 31, 20X3, falls on a Thursday.

Directions: Determine the amount of unpaid salaries at December 31, 20X7, and prepare the adjusting entry.

Learning Objective **2**

Check Figure
(a) $415

Quick Practice 4-6

Objective: To determine the amount of adjustment for supplies used

Directions: Analyze the following T-accounts and determine the amount of the adjusting entry.

(Balance Sheet)

Supplies

Bal.	640		
		Adj.	_____
New Bal.	225		

(b) Amount of supplies used is $280.

(Income Statement)

Supplies Expense

Adj. _____ |

Quick Practice 4-7

Objective: To determine the amount of adjustment for insurance expired

Directions: Analyze the following T-accounts and determine the amount of the adjusting entry.

(Balance Sheet)

Prepaid Insurance

Bal.	2,800		
		Adj.	_____
New Bal.	1,600		

(Income Statement)

Insurance Expense

Adj. _____ |

Quick Practice 4-8

Objective: To calculate depreciation

Directions: On March 1, 20X7, office equipment was purchased for $18,000. The office equipment has an estimated useful life of five years, and the estimated trade-in value is $6,000. Using the straight-line method of depreciation, calculate the depreciation as of December 31, 20X7.

Quick Practice 4-9

Objective: To show the financial statement presentation of a long-term asset

On January 3, 20X1, Boice Company purchased equipment for $90,000. The estimated trade-in value at the end of its useful life is $6,000, and the equipment is estimated to have a useful life of 10 years.

Directions: Show how the equipment would be reported seven years after purchase on a December 31, 20X8, balance sheet.

Quick Practice 4-10

Objective: To show the extension of accounts on the work sheet from the Adjusted Trial Balance columns to the Income Statement Debit or Credit columns or to the Balance Sheet Debit or Credit columns

Directions: Indicate with a check mark where each amount from the Adjusted Trial Balance columns should be extended. The amounts will be extended to either the Income Statement Debit or Credit columns or the Balance Sheet Debit or Credit columns.

Work Sheet

Adjusted Trial Balance Account Title	Income Statement Debit	Credit	Balance Sheet Debit	Credit
Cash				
Accounts Receivable				
Office Supplies				
Prepaid Insurance				
Office Equipment				
Accumulated Depreciation— Office Equipment				
Accounts Payable				
Salaries Payable				
Shunda Ware, Capital				
Shunda Ware, Drawing				
Service Revenue				
Rent Expense				
Salaries Expense				
Depreciation Expense— Office Equipment				
Office Supplies Expense				
Insurance Expense				

Learning Objective 3

Check Figure
Net Income: Income Statement Debit, Balance Sheet Credit

Quick Practice 4-11

Objective: To show how a net income or net loss is entered onto the work sheet

Directions: Indicate with a check mark where the amount of net income or net loss will appear in the Income Statement Debit or Credit columns and the Balance Sheet Debit or Credit columns on the work sheet.

Work Sheet

Account Title	Income Statement Debit	Credit	Balance Sheet Debit	Credit
Net Income				

Work Sheet

Account Title	Income Statement Debit	Credit	Balance Sheet Debit	Credit
Net Loss				

Exercises

Learning Objective 2

Check Figure
(b) Insurance expired = $900
(c) Depreciation expense = $3,000

Exercise 4-1

Objective: To record adjusting entries in T accounts

Directions: Five situations follow, each requiring an adjusting entry. Prepare the appropriate entry in T-account form. The last day of the accounting period is December 31 of the current year.

(a) The Supplies account has a balance of $2,650 before adjustment. A count of supplies on hand shows $1,850.

(b) A one-year insurance policy was purchased on October 1 at a $3,600 premium, which was debited to the Prepaid Insurance account.

(c) Equipment for the office was purchased on January 2 for $36,000. It is estimated to have no trade-in value and a useful life of 12 years.

(d) A truck was purchased on July 1 for $30,000. It is expected to be used for six years and have a trade-in value of $6,000.

(e) Salaries for three days are unpaid. Salaries are $50,000 for a five-day week.

Learning Objective **3**

Check Figure
Net Income = $70; totals of
Balance Sheet columns =
$270

Exercise 4-2

Objective: To prepare a work sheet

Directions: From the information that follows, prepare a work sheet for Ragan Financial Services for the year ended December 31, 20X2. Notice that the amounts in this exercise may seem unrealistically small. Our objective is to allow you to do a work sheet without arithmetic getting in the way.

Account	Balance
Cash	$ 60
Accounts Receivable	30
Supplies	40
Prepaid Insurance	30
Equipment	100
Accumulated Depreciation—Equipment	20
Accounts Payable	60
Salaries Payable	—
Donna Ragan, Capital	100
Donna Ragan, Drawing	30
Fees Earned	161
Salaries Expense	11
Rent Expense	40
Supplies Expense	—
Insurance Expense	—
Depreciation Expense—Equipment	—

Adjustment data:
(a) Supplies on hand, $30.
(b) Insurance expired, $10.
(c) Depreciation of equipment, $10.
(d) Unpaid salaries, $10.

Learning Objective **2**

Check Figure
(a) Unpaid salaries = $9,600

Exercise 4-3

Objective: To record adjusting entries for unpaid salaries

Directions: The Redeker Company has a weekly payroll of $48,000, payable every Friday. Journalize the adjusting entry for unpaid salaries, assuming that the last day of the accounting period is on a (a) Monday; (b) Thursday; (c) Wednesday.

Learning Objective **5**

Check Figure
None

Exercise 4-4

Objective: To journalize adjusting entries

Directions: Journalize adjusting entries for the following:

(a) The Prepaid Insurance account shows a balance of $1,200. Of this amount, $690 has expired.

(b) The Repair Supplies account shows a balance of $525. A current inventory count reveals that $95 worth remains on hand.

(c) Office equipment is estimated to have depreciated $1,975.

(d) Unpaid and unrecorded salaries total $230.

Learning Objective **5**

Check Figure
None

Exercise 4-5

Objective: To journalize adjusting entries using the Adjustments columns of a work sheet

Directions: Following are the Adjustments columns of Patil Company's work sheet for the year ended December 31, 20X1. Journalize the company's adjusting entries.

Patil Company
Work Sheet
For Year Ended December 31, 20X1

	Account Title	Adjustments Debit	Adjustments Credit	Adjusted Trial Balance Debit	Adjusted Trial Balance Credit	
1	Cash					1
2	Supplies		(a) 3 0 0 00			2
3	Prepaid Insurance		(b) 6 7 5 00			3
4	Equipment					4
5	Accumulated Depreciation—Equipment		(c) 8 0 0 00			5
6	Accounts Payable					6
7	Salaries Payable		(d) 3 2 5 00			7
8	Geeta Patil, Capital					8
9	Geeta Patil, Drawing					9
10	Professional Fees					10
11	Rent Expense					11
12	Salaries Expense	(d) 3 2 5 00				12
13	Utilities Expense					13
14	Supplies Expense	(a) 3 0 0 00				14
15	Insurance Expense	(b) 6 7 5 00				15
16	Depreciation Expense—Equipment	(c) 8 0 0 00				16

Learning Objective **4**

Check Figure
1. $32,800; 4. $5,000 net
increase

Exercise 4-6

Objective: To calculate financial statement figures

Directions: A list of several account titles and balances follows. Answer the questions that relate to this list.

Account	Balance
Accounts Payable	$12,000
Accounts Receivable	7,000
Accumulated Depreciation	6,000
Cash	8,000
Depreciation Expense	3,000
Equipment	22,000
Fees Earned	35,110
Insurance Expense	200
Prepaid Insurance	600
Rent Expense	3,200
Kim Bishop-Nelson, Capital	15,300
Kim Bishop-Nelson, Drawing	8,000
Salaries Payable	500
Salaries Expense	15,310
Supplies	1,200
Supplies Expense	400

1. What are the total assets?
2. What are the total liabilities?
3. What is the net income or net loss?

4. What is the net increase or net decrease in capital?

5. What is Kim Bishop-Nelson's end-of-year capital balance?

Learning Objective **4**

Check Figure
Total assets = $39,110

Exercise 4-7

Objective: To prepare financial statements from the financial statement columns of a work sheet

Directions: From the following partial work sheet of the Dave Rodriguez Company, prepare (1) an income statement, (2) a statement of owner's equity, and (3) a balance sheet.

The Dave Rodriguez Company
Work Sheet
For Year Ended June 30, 20XX

	Account Title	Income Statement Debit	Income Statement Credit	Balance Sheet Debit	Balance Sheet Credit	
1	Cash			2 8 0 0 00		1
2	Accounts Receivable			3 0 0 00		2
3	Office Supplies			9 0 0 00		3
4	Prepaid Insurance			8 0 0 00		4
5	Office Equipment			35 5 1 0 00		5
6	Accumulated Depreciation—Office Equipment				1 2 0 0 00	6
7	Accounts Payable				9 0 0 00	7
8	Salaries Payable				8 0 00	8
9	Dave Rodriguez, Capital				14 1 2 0 00	9
10	Dave Rodriguez, Drawing			10 8 0 0 00		10
11	Service Revenue		59 0 0 0 00			11
12	Rent Expense	6 0 0 0 00				12
13	Salaries Expense	9 8 7 0 00				13
14	Utilities Expense	6 2 0 0 00				14
15	Depreciation Expense—Office Equipment	8 0 0 00				15
16	Telephone Expense	5 6 0 00				16
17	Office Supplies Expense	4 0 0 00				17
18	Insurance Expense	3 6 0 00				18
19		24 1 9 0 00	59 0 0 0 00	51 1 1 0 00	16 3 0 0 00	19
20	Net Income	34 8 1 0 00			34 8 1 0 00	20
21		59 0 0 0 00	59 0 0 0 00	51 1 1 0 00	51 1 1 0 00	21

Case Problems

Group A

Problem 4-1A

Learning Objective **2**

Check Figure
(a) Supplies used = $3,530;
(d) Unpaid salaries = $22,800

Objective: To determine the amount of adjustments and record the adjustments in general journal form

Mestemaker Service Company has the following adjustment data on December 31, 20X2:

(a) The Supplies account had a balance of $3,300 on January 1, 20X2. Supplies were purchased on May 1, 20X2, ($575) and August 6, 20X2, ($1,600). A year-end inventory shows $1,945 on hand.

(b) The Prepaid Insurance account has a balance of $23,400, representing premiums paid for a three-year policy on March 1, 20X2.

(c) Equipment was purchased for $90,000 in January 20X1. The equipment has an estimated useful life of 10 years and an estimated trade-in value of $10,000.

(d) Salaries of $38,000 are paid weekly on Fridays. December 31, 20X2, falls on a Wednesday.

Directions: Record each adjusting entry in general journal form.

Problem 4-2A

Learning Objective **3**

Check Figure
Net income = $780

Objective: To prepare a work sheet

The following are the account balances of Taylor Enterprises on December 31, 20X2:

Account	Balance
Cash	$ 4,500
Accounts Receivable	3,000
Supplies	1,700
Prepaid Insurance	1,850
Equipment	38,000
Accumulated Depreciation—Equipment	12,000
Accounts Payable	10,600
Salaries Payable	—
Paul Taylor, Capital	35,770
Paul Taylor, Drawing	15,000
Fees Earned	91,000
Salaries Expense	75,400
Rent Expense	7,200
Utilities Expense	2,175
Repairs Expense	545
Supplies Expense	—
Insurance Expense	—
Depreciation Expense—Equipment	—

Adjustment data:
(a) Supplies on hand, $800.
(b) Insurance expired, $600.
(c) Depreciation of equipment, $2,600.
(d) Salaries unpaid, $800.

Directions: Prepare a work sheet for Taylor Enterprises for the year ended December 31, 20X2.

Problem 4-3A

Objective: To prepare financial statements from a completed work sheet

Directions: Using the work sheet that you completed for Taylor Enterprises in Problem 4-2A, prepare (1) an income statement for the year ended December 31, 20X2; (2) a statement of owner's equity for the year ended December 31, 20X2; and (3) a balance sheet dated December 31, 20X2.

Problem 4-4A

Objective: To prepare financial statements from adjusted account balances

Following is a list of accounts and their adjusted balances from the work sheet of The Shannon Group, a management consulting firm, for the six months ended June 30, 20X2:

Account	Adjusted Balance
Accounts Payable	$ 16,650
Accounts Receivable	10,000
Accumulated Depreciation—Automobiles	13,500
Accumulated Depreciation—Office Equipment	4,500
Automobiles	35,000
Auto Supplies	2,575
Auto Supplies Expense	1,620
Cash	13,750
Depreciation Expense—Automobiles	6,200
Depreciation Expense—Office Equipment	1,200
Fees Earned	154,000
Insurance Expense	3,200
Office Equipment	15,000
Office Supplies	8,500
Office Supplies Expense	9,210
Dana Shannon, Capital	60,580
Dana Shannon, Drawing	26,000
Prepaid Insurance	9,600
Rent Expense	4,800
Repairs Expense	575
Salaries Payable	2,000
Salaries Expense	104,000

Directions:
1. Prepare an income statement for the six months ended June 30, 20X2.
2. Prepare a statement of owner's equity for the six months ended June 30, 20X2.
3. Prepare a balance sheet as of June 30, 20X2.

Problem 4-5A

Objective: To prepare a work sheet and financial statements and journalize adjusting entries

Abbas Mottaghi, owner of Mottaghi Photography, prepared the following trial balance on December 31, 20X2:

Mottaghi Photography
Trial Balance
December 31, 20X2

Account Title	Debit	Credit
Cash	6 1 1 0 00	
Accounts Receivable	2 0 0 0 00	
Office Supplies	6 3 7 5 00	
Photo Supplies	11 6 3 0 00	
Prepaid Insurance	3 7 2 0 00	
Office Equipment	25 0 0 0 00	
Accumulated Depreciation—Office Equipment		5 0 0 0 00
Photo Equipment	40 0 0 0 00	
Accumulated Depreciation—Photo Equipment		12 0 0 0 00
Accounts Payable		25 5 0 0 00
Salaries Payable		
Abbas Mottaghi, Capital		52 5 8 5 00
Abbas Mottaghi, Drawing	17 0 0 0 00	
Photography Revenue		127 2 5 0 00
Rent Expense	6 0 0 0 00	
Office Supplies Expense		
Photo Supplies Expense		
Insurance Expense		
Salaries Expense	102 0 0 0 00	
Depreciation Expense—Office Equipment		
Depreciation Expense—Photo Equipment		
Utilities Expense	2 5 0 0 00	
Totals	222 3 3 5 00	222 3 3 5 00

Adjustment data:
- (a) Office supplies on hand, $5,010.
- (b) Photo supplies on hand, $2,610.
- (c) Insurance expired during the year, $2,440.
- (d) Depreciation of office equipment during the year, $2,500.
- (e) Depreciation of photo equipment during the year, $4,000.
- (f) Salaries unpaid at the end of the year, $2,000.

Directions:
1. Record the trial balance on a 10-column work sheet, and complete the work sheet.
2. Prepare an income statement for the year ended December 31, 20X2.
3. Prepare a statement of owner's equity for the year ended December 31, 20X2.
4. Prepare a balance sheet as of December 31, 20X2.
5. Journalize the December 31, 20X2, adjusting entries.

Group B

Learning Objective **2**

Check Figure
(a) Supplies used = $3,290;
(d) Unpaid salaries = $18,000

Problem 4-1B

Objective: To determine the amount of adjustments and record the adjustments in general journal form

Mueller Service Company has the following adjustment data on December 31, 20X2:

(a) The Supplies account had a balance of $3,800 on January 1, 20X2. Supplies were purchased on June 1, 20X2, ($585) and September 7, 20X2, ($1,350). A year-end inventory shows $2,445 on hand.

(b) The Prepaid Insurance account has a balance of $23,760, representing premiums paid for a three-year policy on May 1, 20X2.

(c) Equipment was purchased for $130,000 in January 20X1. The equipment has an estimated useful life of 10 years and an estimated trade-in value of $10,000.

(d) Salaries of $45,000 are paid weekly on Fridays. December 31, 20X2, falls on a Tuesday.

Directions: Record each adjusting entry in general journal form.

Learning Objective **3**

Check Figure
Net income = $13,025

Problem 4-2B

Objective: To prepare a work sheet

The following are the account balances of Tujo Enterprises on December 31, 20X2:

Account	Balance
Cash	$ 5,500
Accounts Receivable	2,500
Supplies	2,100
Prepaid Insurance	1,760
Equipment	42,000
Accumulated Depreciation—Equipment	10,500
Accounts Payable	8,600
Salaries Payable	—
John Tujo, Capital	30,970
John Tujo, Drawing	16,500
Fees Earned	97,000
Salaries Expense	62,800
Rent Expense	8,000
Utilities Expense	5,500
Repairs Expense	410
Supplies Expense	—
Insurance Expense	—
Depreciation Expense—Equipment	—

Adjustment data:
(a) Supplies on hand, $860.
(b) Insurance expired, $750.
(c) Depreciation of equipment, $4,200.
(d) Salaries unpaid, $1,075.

Directions: Prepare a work sheet for Tujo Enterprises for the year ended December 31, 20X2.

Learning Objective **4**

Check Figure
Total assets = $37,170

Problem 4-3B

Objective: To prepare financial statements from a completed work sheet

Directions: Using the work sheet that you completed for Tujo Enterprises in Problem 4-2B, prepare (1) an income statement for the year ended December 31, 20X2; (2) a statement of owner's equity for the year ended December 31, 20X2; and (3) a balance sheet dated December 31, 20X2.

Learning Objective **4**

Check Figure
Net income = $39,020;
balance sheet totals =
$80,700

Problem 4-4B

Objective: To prepare financial statements from adjusted account balances

Following is a list of accounts and their adjusted balances from the work sheet of The Stat Team, a consumer research firm, for the six months ended June 30, 20X2:

Account	Adjusted Balance
Accounts Payable	$ 15,600
Accounts Receivable	8,000
Accumulated Depreciation—Office Equipment	5,000
Accumulated Depreciation—Research Equipment	12,400
Cash	22,300
Depreciation Expense—Office Equipment	2,000
Depreciation Expense—Research Equipment	4,200
Fees Earned	141,900
Insurance Expense	3,800
Office Equipment	18,000
Office Supplies	7,200
Office Supplies Expense	6,450
Prepaid Insurance	8,500
Rent Expense	9,600
Repairs Expense	640
Research Equipment	30,600
Research Supplies	3,500
Research Supplies Expense	1,890
Salaries Expense	74,300
Salaries Payable	2,250
Maureen Wright, Capital	47,830
Maureen Wright, Drawing	24,000

Directions:

1. Prepare an income statement for the six months ended June 30, 20X2.
2. Prepare a statement of owner's equity for the six months ended June 30, 20X2.
3. Prepare a balance sheet as of June 30, 20X2.

Learning Objectives
2, 3, 4, 5

Check Figure
Net income = $40,315;
balance sheet totals =
$49,000

Problem 4-5B

Objective: To prepare a work sheet and financial statements and journalize adjusting entries

Greg Westby, owner of Westby Delivery Service, prepared the following trial balance on December 31, 20X2:

Westby Delivery Service
Trial Balance
December 31, 20X2

Account Title	Debit	Credit
Cash	6 1 0 0 00	
Accounts Receivable	2 1 0 0 00	
Office Supplies	6 2 3 5 00	
Truck Supplies	6 5 0 0 00	
Prepaid Insurance	4 3 5 0 00	
Office Equipment	21 0 0 0 00	
Accumulated Depreciation—Office Equipment		4 0 0 0 00
Trucks	32 0 0 0 00	
Accumulated Depreciation—Trucks		8 4 0 0 00
Accounts Payable		6 0 0 0 00
Salaries Payable		—
Greg Westby, Capital		16 4 8 5 00
Greg Westby, Drawing	15 0 0 0 00	
Service Revenue		98 8 0 0 00
Rent Expense	4 8 0 0 00	
Office Supplies Expense	—	
Truck Supplies Expense	—	
Insurance Expense	—	
Salaries Expense	33 0 0 0 00	
Depreciation Expense—Office Equipment	—	
Depreciation Expense—Trucks	—	
Utilities Expense	2 6 0 0 00	
Totals	133 6 8 5 00	133 6 8 5 00

Adjustment data:
(a) Office supplies on hand, $2,000.
(b) Truck supplies on hand, $2,650.
(c) Insurance expired during the year, $1,800.
(d) Depreciation of office equipment during the year, $2,800.
(e) Depreciation of trucks during the year, $4,200.
(f) Salaries unpaid at the end of the year, $1,200.

Directions:
1. Record the trial balance on a 10-column work sheet, and complete the work sheet.
2. Prepare an income statement for the year ended December 31, 20X2.
3. Prepare a statement of owner's equity for the year ended December 31, 20X2.
4. Prepare a balance sheet as of December 31, 20X2.
5. Journalize the December 31, 20X2, adjusting entries.

Critical Thinking Problems

Check Figure
Net income = $46,657;
balance sheet totals =
$45,357

Challenge Problem

John Wrigley, owner of Wrigley Engineering Services, prepared the following trial balance on November 30, 20X2, reflecting activity beginning November 1, 20X2:

	Wrigley Engineering Services Trial Balance November 30, 20X2		
	Account Title	**Debit**	**Credit**
111	Cash	9 6 0 0 00	
112	Accounts Receivable	6 5 0 0 00	
113	Office Supplies	3 4 0 0 00	
114	Engineering Supplies	6 3 3 0 00	
115	Prepaid Insurance	1 2 0 0 00	
117	Office Equipment	12 4 0 0 00	
117.1	Accumulated Depreciation—Office Equipment		2 8 0 0 00
118	Drafting Equipment	17 5 0 0 00	
118.1	Accumulated Depreciation—Drafting Equipment		3 4 5 0 00
119	Tools	7 2 0 0 00	
119.1	Accumulated Depreciation—Tools		2 2 0 0 00
211	Accounts Payable		1 5 9 0 00
212	Salaries Payable		—
311	John Wrigley, Capital		33 6 3 0 00
312	John Wrigley, Drawing	38 0 0 0 00	
411	Professional Fees		118 4 0 0 00
511	Salaries Expense	45 7 0 0 00	
512	Rent Expense	7 2 0 0 00	
513	Depreciation Expense—Office Equipment	—	
514	Depreciation Expense—Drafting Equipment	—	
515	Depreciation Expense—Tools	—	
516	Utilities Expense	3 8 0 0 00	
517	Telephone Expense	2 4 0 0 00	
518	Office Supplies Expense	—	
519	Engineering Supplies Expense	—	
520	Insurance Expense	—	
521	Miscellaneous Expense	8 4 0 00	
	Totals	162 0 7 0 00	162 0 7 0 00

(Note: Enter the above balances in the ledger accounts before journalizing and posting the December transactions.)

The firm incurred the following transactions during December:

20X2

Dec. 1 Paid rent, $700.

1 Performed services for cash, $2,500.

1 Completed plans for a new office building for Eastway Company. The contract price of the plans was $6,000, with $2,000 to be received when the plans were completed and the balance in 30 days.

4 Purchased office supplies for cash, $500.

5 Purchased engineering supplies on account, $625.

7 Paid salaries of employees, $2,500.

9 Performed services for cash, $800.

10 Performed services for cash, $1,800.

12 Paid telephone bill, $128.

15 Paid salaries of employees, $2,200.

18 Roger Hobbs, a client, paid $500 for blueprints that the firm had done for him on a credit basis in November.

Dec. 20   Paid cash for a new drafting table, $1,800.
     21   Purchased drawing pads, pens, and drafting paper on account, $225.
     22   Paid cash for two electric pencil sharpeners, $15 each. (Record this as an office supplies expense, because the accountant decided that under the materiality concept, the value is insignificant and thus can be expensed directly.)
     22   Paid salaries of employees, $2,340.
     24   Discovered that one of the pencil sharpeners purchased on December 22 was defective. Returned it for a more expensive model, $25, paying the difference in cash.
     26   Paid utility bill, $380.
     27   Performed services for cash, $590.
     28   Performed services for a client on credit, $350.
     29   Paid miscellaneous expenses, $80.
     29   Paid salaries of employees, $2,050.
     30   Paid cash for engineering supplies, $325.
     31   Paid cash for office supplies, $200.
     31   Received the amount due from Eastway Company, $4,000.
     31   Prepaid a six-month insurance premium, $1,400.

Directions:
1. Open a ledger account for each account that is listed on Wrigley's November 30 trial balance. Use December 1 as the date, and, for each account that has a balance, enter the balance in the appropriate column.
2. Record Wrigley's December transactions in a general journal.
3. Post from the journal to the ledger.
4. Prepare a trial balance directly on a 10-column work sheet.
5. Complete the work sheet using the following adjustment data:
   (a) Office supplies on hand, $1,860.
   (b) Engineering supplies on hand, $1,450.
   (c) Insurance expired, $950.
   (d) Depreciation of office equipment, $1,200.
   (e) Depreciation of drafting equipment, $1,450.
   (f) Depreciation of tools, $900.
   (g) Unpaid salaries, $630.
6. Prepare an income statement for the year ended December 31, 20X2.
7. Prepare a statement of owner's equity for the year ended December 31, 20X2.
8. Prepare a balance sheet as of December 31, 20X2.
9. Journalize and post the adjusting entries.

Communications

Cameron Wilson just completed a test on adjusting entries. Even though he did very well on the test, he believes that recording depreciation in a separate contra asset account is redundant and unnecessary. He asks, "Why can't we just record the depreciation as a credit to the asset itself and be done with it?"

   Write a note to Cameron explaining the benefit of recording depreciation in a contra account.

Team Internet Project

While many expense accounts are common to all businesses, a farmer has some expense accounts that are unique to a farming operation. Search the Internet, and prepare a list of some of the expense accounts that you might find in the ledger of a farmer.

Ethics

Brian Wornath is the owner of a delivery service. Since he has an associate's degree in accounting, he keeps his own records. As you look them over for him, you come to the shocking discovery that there are no adjusting entries. As you explore further, you notice that all prepaid expenses, such as prepaid insurance, are recorded as expenses in their full amounts on payment. In addition, items such as unpaid salaries are simply not recorded until they are paid in the next accounting period.

When you ask Brian why he does not use adjusting entries, he replies "They are a pain. Besides, we get to the same place after a few days anyway."

Write a brief memo to Brian stating why what he is doing is not appropriate accounting procedure.

| In the Real World | | | | | | H&R Block |

Following are partial income statements for H&R Block for the periods ended April 30, 2005, 2006, and 2007. All amounts are in thousands.

PERIOD ENDING	30-Apr-07	30-Apr-06	30-Apr-05
Total Revenue	$4 0 2 1 2 7 4 00	$4 8 7 2 8 0 1 00	$4 4 2 0 0 1 9 00
Total Expenses	4 4 5 4 9 2 7 00	4 3 8 2 3 9 3 00	3 7 9 6 1 0 9 00
Net Income	(4 3 3 6 5 3 00)	4 9 0 4 0 8 00	6 2 3 9 1 0 00

From the statements presented, identify (a) the amount of net income or loss for each time period. (b) Why is the amount for 2007 a negative number?

Review Quiz 4-1

Answers to Review Quizzes

1.

Office Supplies Expense				Office Supplies	
+	−		+	−	
Adjusting 150			Balance 900	Adjusting 150	

2.

Insurance Expense			Prepaid Insurance	
+	−		+	−
Adjusting 50				Adjusting 50

3.

Depreciation Expense—Trucks			Accumulated Depreciation—Trucks	
+	−		−	+
Adjusting 1,000				Adjusting 1,000

4.

Salaries Expense			Salaries Payable	
+	−		−	+
Adjusting 150				Adjusting 150

Review Quiz 4-2

Yes, because differences between revenue and expenses will either increase or decrease capital. The difference between the totals of the Balance Sheet Debit and Credit columns of the work sheet reflects the net income or net loss that has not yet been transferred to the owner's capital account.

Review Quiz 4-3

1.

Sether Company Income Statement For Year Ended December 31, 20X2		
Revenue:		
Service revenue		$52 0 0 0 00
Expenses:		
Salaries expense	$14 3 0 0 00	
Rent expense	4 2 0 0 00	
Utilities expense	2 9 0 0 00	
Telephone expense	1 5 7 0 00	
Depreciation expense	8 0 0 00	
Office supplies expense	2 2 5 00	
Total expenses		23 9 9 5 00
Net income		$28 0 0 5 00

2.

Sether Company Statement of Owner's Equity For Year Ended December 31, 20X2		
Capital, January 1, 20X2		$15 9 1 5 00
Net income for period	$28 0 0 5 00	
Less withdrawals	18 0 0 0 00	
Increase in capital		10 0 0 5 00
Capital, December 31, 20X2		$25 9 2 0 00

3.

Sether Company Balance Sheet December 31, 20X2				
Assets				
Cash			$ 6 2 0 0 00	
Accounts receivable			9 2 0 00	
Supplies			6 0 0 00	
Equipment	$22 0 0 0 00			
Less: Accumulated depreciation	2 0 0 0 00	20 0 0 0 00		
Total assets				$27 7 2 0 00
Liabilities				
Accounts payable				$ 1 8 0 0 00
Owner's Equity				
Tim Sether, capital				25 9 2 0 00
Total liabilities and owner's equity				$27 7 2 0 00

Review Quiz 4-4

It is necessary to make journal entries for adjustments because the work sheet is not a journal. It is an informal document used to organize data and facilitate the work at the end of an accounting period. However, no posting is made from the work sheet. After adjustments have been journalized and posted, the ledger will be up to date and will agree with the data presented on the financial statements.

C H A P T E R

5

Completing the Accounting Cycle for a Service Business
Closing Entries and the Post-Closing Trial Balance

Learning Objectives

1 Explain the purpose of the closing process.
2 Journalize and post closing entries.
3 Prepare a post-closing trial balance.

In Chapter 4, we learned that at the end of an accounting period, some accounts normally need adjusting to bring them up to date. We also learned how to prepare a work sheet as an aid in completing the work at the end of the accounting cycle. We used a completed work sheet to prepare financial statements and journalize adjusting entries. In Chapter 5, we will complete our study of the accounting cycle for a service business. Two steps remain to be covered:

Step **9** Journalize and post closing entries.
Step **10** Prepare a post-closing trial balance.

Purpose of Closing Entries

Revenue and expense accounts and the owner's drawing account are **temporary accounts** (also called nominal accounts) used to show changes in owner's equity during a single accounting period. When an accounting period is over, the temporary accounts will have served their purpose for that period. Therefore, their balances are summarized and transferred to the owner's capital account.

The process of transferring the balances of the temporary accounts to the owner's capital account is called the **closing process**. Entries necessary to accomplish the closing process are called **closing entries**.

The closing process has two objectives:

---

temporary accounts accounts whose balances are not carried over from one accounting period to another but instead are closed to the owner's capital account at period-end; revenue, expense, and drawing accounts; also referred to as nominal accounts

Learning Objective

1 Explain the purpose of the closing process.

closing process the process of transferring the balances of temporary accounts to the owner's capital account

closing entries entries made at the end of an accounting period to transfer the balances of the temporary accounts to the owner's capital account

---

Closing entries eliminate the balances of the temporary accounts, update the balance of the owner's capital account, and make the ledger ready for entries in the next accounting period.

- To reduce the balances of temporary owner's equity accounts to zero and thus make the accounts ready for entries in the next accounting period. Otherwise, amounts for the next accounting period would be added to amounts from previous accounting periods, which would violate the matching principle.
- To update the balance of the owner's capital account.

Step 9: Journalize and Post Closing Entries

Learning Objective

2 Journalize and post closing entries.

Income Summary account a clearing account used to summarize the balances of revenue and expense accounts that is used only at the end of an accounting period and is opened and closed during the closing process

clearing account an account used to summarize the balances of other accounts

Remember

The complete work sheet was shown in Chapter 4 on page 146.

 **Tutorial 6**

Preparing Closing Entries

In the closing process, we will use a new account called Income Summary. The **Income Summary account** is a **clearing account** used to summarize the balances of revenue and expense accounts. Use of the Income Summary account avoids the unnecessary detail of closing the balance of each revenue account and each expense account directly into the owner's capital account. The Income Summary account is used only at the end of an accounting period and is opened and closed during the closing process.

Steps in the Closing Process

The closing process consists of four steps:

Step **1** Close the balance of each revenue account to the Income Summary account.

Step **2** Close the balance of each expense account to Income Summary.

Step **3** Close the balance of Income Summary to the owner's capital account.

Step **4** Close the balance of the owner's drawing account directly to the owner's capital account.

Let's now return to the end-of-period activities of Walker and Associates and look again at the financial statement columns of Stanley Walker's December 31 work sheet, as illustrated in Figure 5-1. The work sheet is very useful when preparing closing entries, because up-to-date balances of all temporary accounts are clearly shown together in one place.

To illustrate closing entries, we will record Stanley's closing entries in T-account form. Later in the chapter, we will see how closing entries are formally journalized and posted to the ledger.

Figure 5-1
Financial Statement Columns
of the Work Sheet

Walker and Associates
Work Sheet
For Two Months Ended December 31, 20X1

	Account Title	Income Statement Debit	Income Statement Credit	Balance Sheet Debit	Balance Sheet Credit	
1	Cash			8 4 8 5 00		1
2	Accounts Receivable			3 0 0 00		2
3	Office Supplies			2 3 0 00		3
4	Prepaid Insurance			2 2 0 00		4
5	Office Equipment			3 0 0 0 00		5
6	Accumulated Depreciation—Office Equipment				5 0 00	6
7	Office Furniture			2 0 0 0 00		7
8	Accumulated Depreciation—Office Furniture				3 0 00	8
9	Accounts Payable				3 0 0 0 00	9
10	Salaries Payable				2 1 0 00	10
11	Stanley Walker, Capital				10 0 0 0 00	11
12	Stanley Walker, Drawing			1 5 0 0 00		12
13	Service Revenue		4 7 0 0 00			13
14	Rent Expense	8 0 0 00				14
15	Repairs Expense	5 0 00				15
16	Salaries Expense	1 2 6 0 00				16
17	Office Supplies Expense	4 5 00				17
18	Insurance Expense	2 0 00				18
19	Depreciation Expense—Office Equipment	5 0 00				19
20	Depreciation Expense—Office Furniture	3 0 00				20
21		2 2 5 5 00	4 7 0 0 00	15 7 3 5 00	13 2 9 0 00	21
22	Net Income	2 4 4 5 00			2 4 4 5 00	22
23		4 7 0 0 00	4 7 0 0 00	15 7 3 5 00	15 7 3 5 00	23

Key Point ⊘

Income Summary is a clearing account that serves as a temporary "holding tank" into which revenue and expense account balances are transferred prior to their final transfer to the owner's capital account.

Step 1: Close the Balance of Each Revenue Account to Income Summary

As we have seen, all revenue accounts appear in the Income Statement Credit column of the work sheet. Walker and Associates' work sheet shows only one revenue account, Service Revenue, with a credit balance of $4,700. To close an account, we must make an entry that will reduce the balance of the account to zero. Thus, the Service Revenue account must be *debited* for its $4,700 *credit* balance. Our credit is to the Income Summary account.

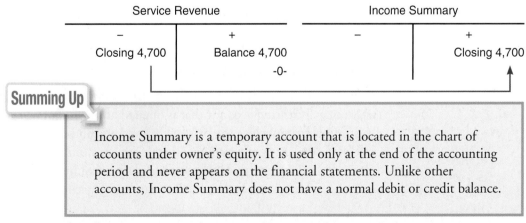

Service Revenue
−	+
Closing 4,700	Balance 4,700
	-0-

Income Summary
−	+
	Closing 4,700

Summing Up

Income Summary is a temporary account that is located in the chart of accounts under owner's equity. It is used only at the end of the accounting period and never appears on the financial statements. Unlike other accounts, Income Summary does not have a normal debit or credit balance.

Step 2: Close the Balance of Each Expense Account to Income Summary

Expense accounts are shown in the Income Statement Debit column of the work sheet. Walker and Associates has seven expense accounts, each with a debit balance. Thus, each must be credited to close it. The Income Summary account could be debited seven times; or, more realistically, there could be one compound debit. This step is shown in Figure 5-2.

Figure 5-2

Closing the Balance of Each Expense Account to Income Summary

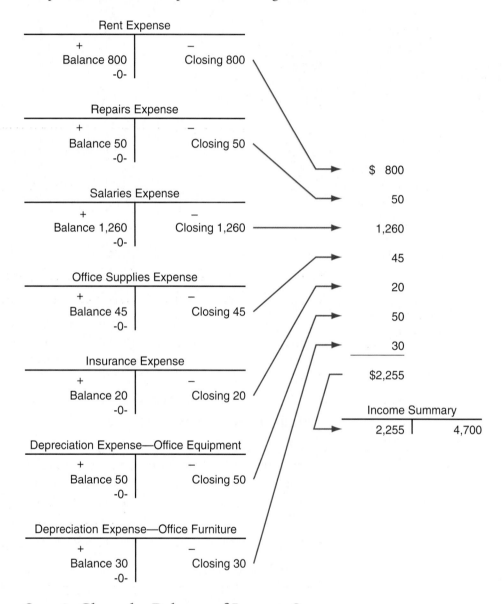

Step 3: Close the Balance of Income Summary to the Owner's Capital Account

We mentioned at the start of our discussion that the Income Summary account is a clearing account that is opened at the end of an accounting period to summarize and close the balances of revenue and expense accounts. Having closed the balances of revenue and expense accounts in steps 1 and 2, we now close the balance of the Income Summary account into the owner's capital account. The balance of the Income Summary account is found as follows:

Credit	$4,700
Debit	− 2,255
Balance	$2,445 ◄──── balance is a credit

This balance should be a familiar one—it is the net income figure. The balance is as it should be, since both revenue and expense accounts have been closed into the Income Summary account. Because this balance is a credit, it is closed by making a debit for the same amount, as shown below:

Income Summary		Stanley Walker, Capital	
(Expenses) 2,255	(Revenue) 4,700	−	+
Closing 2,445	-0-		Balance 10,000
			2,445

At this stage of the closing process, the Income Summary account will always reflect the amount of net income or net loss. In this case, there is a net income. It is, therefore, transferred to the credit side (the increase side) of the owner's capital account. Had there been a net loss for the period, the entries would have been reversed and the net loss would be transferred to the debit side (the decrease side) of the owner's capital account.

Step 4: Close the Balance of the Owner's Drawing Account Directly to the Owner's Capital Account

Key Point ⊙

The owner's drawing account is not closed to Income Summary.

The balance of the owner's drawing account does not enter into the determination of net income or net loss. Therefore, the drawing account *is not* closed to the Income Summary account. Its balance, instead, is closed directly into the owner's capital account. The drawing account has a debit balance; thus, it is closed by making an equal credit. The amount of drawing is found in the Balance Sheet Debit column of the work sheet.

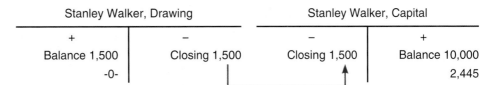

Stanley Walker, Drawing		Stanley Walker, Capital	
+	−	−	+
Balance 1,500	Closing 1,500	Closing 1,500	Balance 10,000
-0-			2,445

If we now balance the Stanley Walker, Capital account, we will find that it has a credit balance of $10,945.

Stanley Walker, Capital		
−	+	
1,500	Balance 10,000	To balance a T account, find the difference between the two sides: $12,445 − $1,500 = $10,945.
	2,445	
	12,445	
	New Balance 10,945	

The capital account is now up to date because its balance agrees with the total capital as reported on Stanley's statement of owner's equity, which was illustrated in Chapter 4 on page 149. All revenue, expenses, and owner's drawing accounts have zero balances, as does the Income Summary account. Therefore, the closing process is complete.

Incidentally, the accounts that remain open—assets, contra assets, liabilities, and the owner's capital account—are referred to as **permanent** (or real) **accounts**. They are permanent in the sense that their balances will be carried into the next accounting period. Table 5-1 summarizes the difference between temporary and permanent accounts.

Table 5-1 Temporary versus Permanent Accounts

	Temporary Accounts	Permanent Accounts
Examples	All revenue accounts	All asset and contra-asset accounts
	All expense accounts	All liability accounts
	Owner's drawing account	Owner's capital account
Balance	Reduced to zero at the end of each accounting period	Remain open and carried over to the next accounting period
Alternative Name	Nominal accounts	Real accounts

Journalizing Closing Entries

We recorded Stanley's closing entries in T accounts to illustrate the closing process. In reality, closing entries must be formally journalized and posted to the ledger. The next free line in the journal is used for writing the heading *Closing Entries*. No further explanation is necessary. To illustrate, the closing entries of Walker and Associates are journalized in Figure 5-3. As with adjusting entries, closing entries are dated as of the last day of the accounting period.

Figure 5-3

Closing Entries in the General Journal

Revenue

Expenses

Income Summary

Drawing

	Date		Account Title	P.R.	Debit	Credit	
1	20X1		Closing Entries				1
2	Dec.	31	Service Revenue		4 7 0 0 00		2
3			Income Summary			4 7 0 0 00	3
4							4
5		31	Income Summary		2 2 5 5 00		5
6			Rent Expense			8 0 0 00	6
7			Repairs Expense			5 0 00	7
8			Salaries Expense			1 2 6 0 00	8
9			Office Supplies Expense			4 5 00	9
10			Insurance Expense			2 0 00	10
11			Depr. Expense—Office Equipment			5 0 00	11
12			Depr. Expense—Office Furniture			3 0 00	12
13							13
14		31	Income Summary		2 4 4 5 00		14
15			Stanley Walker, Capital			2 4 4 5 00	15
16							16
17		31	Stanley Walker, Capital		1 5 0 0 00		17
18			Stanley Walker, Drawing			1 5 0 0 00	18

General Journal — Page 3

The closing process is often referred to as closing the books. This expression, however, is not completely accurate, because we are not actually closing the books, just the temporary accounts.

Diagram of the Closing Process

Now that we have illustrated the closing process, let's summarize the steps in diagram form, as shown in Figure 5-4.

Step **1** Close the balance of revenue accounts to Income Summary.

Step **2** Close the balance of expense accounts to Income Summary.

Step **3** Close the balance of Income Summary to the owner's capital account. After steps 1 and 2, the Income Summary account will show the amount of net income or net loss for the period.

Step **4** Close the balance of the owner's drawing account to the owner's capital account.

In Figure 5-4, it is assumed that there is a net income for the period; that is, the Income Summary account has a credit balance after expense and revenue accounts are closed. Should a net loss occur, it will appear as a debit balance in the Income Summary account and will be closed to the debit side (the decrease side) of the owner's capital account.

Figure 5-4

The Four Steps of the Closing Process

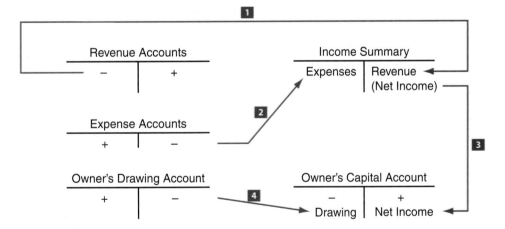

The financial statement columns from the work sheet of Wright Realty Co. are shown below. Journalize the entries necessary to close the temporary accounts.

Wright Realty Co.
Work Sheet
For Year Ended June 30, 20XX

	Account Title	Income Statement Debit	Income Statement Credit	Balance Sheet Debit	Balance Sheet Credit	
1	Cash			3 000 00		1
2	Accounts Receivable			1 000 00		2
3	Office Supplies			8 00 00		3
4	Prepaid Insurance			4 00 00		4
5	Office Equipment			12 000 00		5
6	Accumulated Depreciation—Office Equipment				3 000 00	6
7	Automobiles			26 000 00		7
8	Accumulated Depreciation—Automobiles				6 000 00	8
9	Accounts Payable				2 000 00	9
10	Salaries Payable				4 00 00	10
11	Susan Wright, Capital				35 500 00	11
12	Susan Wright, Drawing			19 000 00		12
13	Service Revenue		89 600 00			13
14	Rent Expense	6 000 00				14
15	Salaries Expense	57 400 00				15
16	Office Supplies Expense	1 00 00				16
17	Telephone Expense	6 00 00				17
18	Insurance Expense	2 00 00				18
19	Depreciation Expense—Office Equipment	1 000 00				19
20	Depreciation Expense—Automobiles	2 000 00				20
21	Utilities Expense	6 30 00				21
22	Miscellaneous Expense	7 00 00				22
23		74 300 00	89 600 00	62 200 00	46 900 00	23
24	Net Income	15 300 00			15 300 00	24
25		89 600 00	89 600 00	62 200 00	62 200 00	25

Check your answers on page 211.

Posting Closing Entries

After closing entries have been journalized, the next step in the accounting cycle is to post these entries from the general journal to the ledger. After posting has occurred, the permanent accounts will have up-to-date balances, and the temporary accounts will have zero balances. To illustrate, the complete ledger of Walker and Associates is shown in Figure 5-5. Notice that the balances of the permanent accounts (assets, liabilities, and owner's equity) agree with the amounts reported on the financial statements we prepared for Stanley in Chapter 4. Also notice that we indicate that the temporary accounts are closed by writing the word *Closing* in the Item column of each account and by drawing a line in both the Debit Balance and Credit Balance columns.

Figure 5-5

Complete Ledger for
Walker and Associates

General Ledger

Account Cash   **Account No.** 111

Date		Item	P.R.	Debit	Credit	Balance Debit	Balance Credit
20X1 Dec.	1	Balance	✓			9 4 2 5 00	
	1		GJ2		2 4 0 00	9 1 8 5 00	
	5		GJ2		1 5 0 00	9 0 3 5 00	
	12		GJ2		3 5 0 00	8 6 8 5 00	
	15		GJ2		4 0 0 00	8 2 8 5 00	
	19		GJ2		1 0 0 0 00	7 2 8 5 00	
	19		GJ2		3 5 0 00	6 9 3 5 00	
	20		GJ2	1 0 0 00		7 0 3 5 00	
	22		GJ2		7 0 0 00	6 3 3 5 00	
	23		GJ2	2 5 0 0 00		8 8 3 5 00	
	26		GJ2		3 5 0 00	8 4 8 5 00	

Account Accounts Receivable   **Account No.** 112

Date		Item	P.R.	Debit	Credit	Balance Debit	Balance Credit
20X1 Dec.	1	Balance	✓			3 0 0 00	

Account Office Supplies   **Account No.** 113

Date		Item	P.R.	Debit	Credit	Balance Debit	Balance Credit
20X1 Dec.	1	Balance	✓			1 2 5 00	
	5		GJ2	1 5 0 00		2 7 5 00	
	31	Adjusting	GJ2		4 5 00	2 3 0 00	

Account Prepaid Insurance   **Account No.** 114

Date		Item	P.R.	Debit	Credit	Balance Debit	Balance Credit
20X1 Dec.	1		GJ2	2 4 0 00		2 4 0 00	
	31	Adjusting	GJ2		2 0 00	2 2 0 00	

Account Office Equipment   **Account No.** 116

Date		Item	P.R.	Debit	Credit	Balance Debit	Balance Credit
20X1 Dec.	1	Balance	✓			3 0 0 0 00	

Account Accumulated Depreciation—Office Equipment   **Account No.** 116.1

Date		Item	P.R.	Debit	Credit	Balance Debit	Balance Credit
20X1 Dec.	31	Adjusting	GJ2		5 0 00		5 0 00

Continues

Figure 5-5

Continued

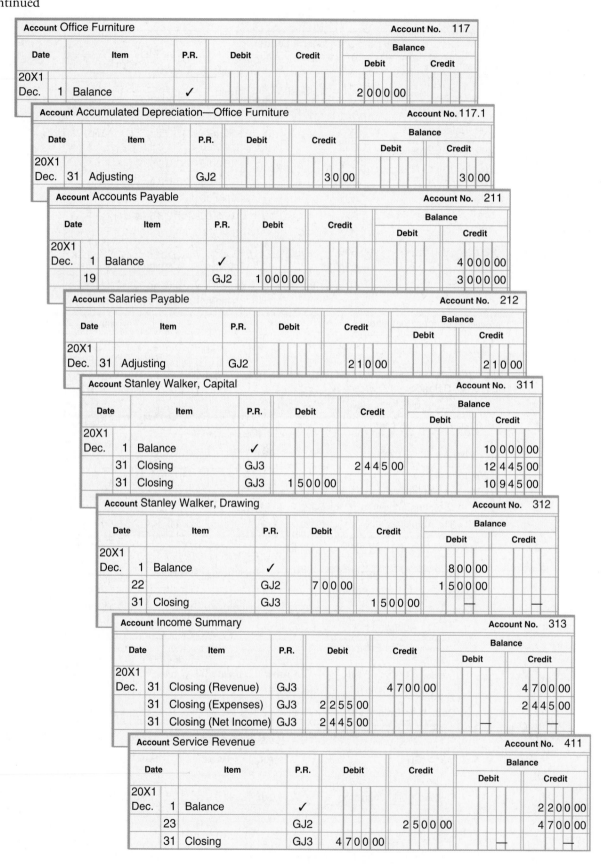

Account Office Furniture   **Account No.** 117

Date		Item	P.R.	Debit	Credit	Balance Debit	Balance Credit
20X1 Dec.	1	Balance	✓			2 0 0 0 00	

Account Accumulated Depreciation—Office Furniture   **Account No.** 117.1

Date		Item	P.R.	Debit	Credit	Balance Debit	Balance Credit
20X1 Dec.	31	Adjusting	GJ2		3 0 00		3 0 00

Account Accounts Payable   **Account No.** 211

Date		Item	P.R.	Debit	Credit	Balance Debit	Balance Credit
20X1 Dec.	1	Balance	✓				4 0 0 0 00
	19		GJ2	1 0 0 0 00			3 0 0 0 00

Account Salaries Payable   **Account No.** 212

Date		Item	P.R.	Debit	Credit	Balance Debit	Balance Credit
20X1 Dec.	31	Adjusting	GJ2		2 1 0 00		2 1 0 00

Account Stanley Walker, Capital   **Account No.** 311

Date		Item	P.R.	Debit	Credit	Balance Debit	Balance Credit
20X1 Dec.	1	Balance	✓				10 0 0 0 00
	31	Closing	GJ3		2 4 4 5 00		12 4 4 5 00
	31	Closing	GJ3	1 5 0 0 00			10 9 4 5 00

Account Stanley Walker, Drawing   **Account No.** 312

Date		Item	P.R.	Debit	Credit	Balance Debit	Balance Credit
20X1 Dec.	1	Balance	✓			8 0 0 00	
	22		GJ2	7 0 0 00		1 5 0 0 00	
	31	Closing	GJ3		1 5 0 0 00	—	

Account Income Summary   **Account No.** 313

Date		Item	P.R.	Debit	Credit	Balance Debit	Balance Credit
20X1 Dec.	31	Closing (Revenue)	GJ3		4 7 0 0 00		4 7 0 0 00
	31	Closing (Expenses)	GJ3	2 2 5 5 00			2 4 4 5 00
	31	Closing (Net Income)	GJ3	2 4 4 5 00		—	—

Account Service Revenue   **Account No.** 411

Date		Item	P.R.	Debit	Credit	Balance Debit	Balance Credit
20X1 Dec.	1	Balance	✓				2 2 0 0 00
	23		GJ2		2 5 0 0 00		4 7 0 0 00
	31	Closing	GJ3	4 7 0 0 00		—	—

Continues

Figure 5-5
Continued

Account Rent Expense   **Account No.** 511

Date		Item	P.R.	Debit	Credit	Balance Debit	Balance Credit
20X1 Dec.	1	Balance	✓			4 0 0 00	
	15		GJ2	4 0 0 00		8 0 0 00	
	31	Closing	GJ3		8 0 0 00	—	—

Account Repairs Expense   **Account No.** 512

Date		Item	P.R.	Debit	Credit	Balance Debit	Balance Credit
20X1 Dec.	1	Balance	✓			5 0 00	
	31	Closing	GJ3		5 0 00	—	—

Account Salaries Expense   **Account No.** 513

Date		Item	P.R.	Debit	Credit	Balance Debit	Balance Credit
20X1 Dec.	12		GJ2	3 5 0 00		3 5 0 00	
	19		GJ2	3 5 0 00		7 0 0 00	
	26		GJ2	3 5 0 00		1 0 5 0 00	
	31	Adjusting	GJ2	2 1 0 00		1 2 6 0 00	
	31	Closing	GJ3		1 2 6 0 00	—	—

Account Office Supplies Expense   **Account No.** 514

Date		Item	P.R.	Debit	Credit	Balance Debit	Balance Credit
20X1 Dec.	31	Adjusting	GJ2	4 5 00		4 5 00	
	31	Closing	GJ3		4 5 00	—	—

Account Insurance Expense   **Account No.** 515

Date		Item	P.R.	Debit	Credit	Balance Debit	Balance Credit
20X1 Dec.	31	Adjusting	GJ2	2 0 00		2 0 00	
	31	Closing	GJ3		2 0 00	—	—

Account Depreciation Expense—Office Equipment   **Account No.** 516

Date		Item	P.R.	Debit	Credit	Balance Debit	Balance Credit
20X1 Dec.	31	Adjusting	GJ2	5 0 00		5 0 00	
	31	Closing	GJ3		5 0 00	—	—

Account Depreciation Expense—Office Furniture   **Account No.** 517

Date		Item	P.R.	Debit	Credit	Balance Debit	Balance Credit
20X1 Dec.	31	Adjusting	GJ2	3 0 00		3 0 00	
	31	Closing	GJ3		3 0 00	—	—

T-account balances of Tamatha Hoyez, as of December 31, 20X1, are shown below. Prepare, in general journal form, entries necessary to close the balances of the temporary accounts.

Cash			Tamatha Hoyez, Capital			Depr. Expense—Equipment	
4,000				17,850		2,000	

Accounts Receivable			Tamatha Hoyez, Drawing			Utilities Expense	
2,000			9,000			4,000	

Supplies			Fees Earned			Income Summary	
2,000				52,000			

Equipment			Salaries Expense	
18,000			26,000	

Accum. Depr.—Equipment			Supplies Expense	
	4,000		650	

Accounts Payable			Rent Expense	
	800		7,000	

Check your answers on page 211.

Step 10: Prepare a Post-Closing Trial Balance

3 Prepare a post-closing trial balance.

post-closing trial balance a trial balance prepared after closing entries have been posted and consisting only of permanent accounts; also called an after-closing trial balance

After closing entries have been posted, you should verify the equality of debits and credits in the accounts that remain open. To do this, you prepare a post-closing trial balance, which is the final step in the accounting cycle. The purpose of the **post-closing trial balance** (also called the after-closing trial balance) is to make sure that the ledger will be in balance at the start of the next accounting period. The only accounts appearing on the post-closing trial balance are the permanent accounts, since the balances of all temporary accounts have been reduced to zero. The post-closing trial balance of Walker and Associates is shown in Figure 5-6.

Figure 5-6

The Post-Closing Trial Balance

Key Point ⊚

Only permanent account balances appear on the post-closing trial balance, because the temporary accounts have been closed.

Walker and Associates Post-Closing Trial Balance December 31, 20X1		
Account Title	**Debit**	**Credit**
Cash	8 4 8 5 00	
Accounts Receivable	3 0 0 00	
Office Supplies	2 3 0 00	
Prepaid Insurance	2 2 0 00	
Office Equipment	3 0 0 0 00	
Accumulated Depreciation—Office Equipment		5 0 00
Office Furniture	2 0 0 0 00	
Accumulated Depreciation—Office Furniture		3 0 00
Accounts Payable		3 0 0 0 00
Salaries Payable		2 1 0 00
Stanley Walker, Capital		10 9 4 5 00
Totals	14 2 3 5 00	14 2 3 5 00

Summary of the Steps in the Accounting Cycle

We have now completed all the steps in the accounting cycle for a service business, from analyzing source documents to the post-closing trial balance. Let's pause and look at a listing of all the steps we have studied:

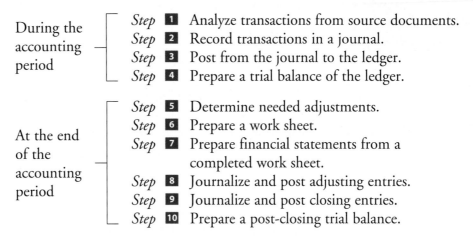

During the accounting period
- *Step* **1** Analyze transactions from source documents.
- *Step* **2** Record transactions in a journal.
- *Step* **3** Post from the journal to the ledger.
- *Step* **4** Prepare a trial balance of the ledger.

At the end of the accounting period
- *Step* **5** Determine needed adjustments.
- *Step* **6** Prepare a work sheet.
- *Step* **7** Prepare financial statements from a completed work sheet.
- *Step* **8** Journalize and post adjusting entries.
- *Step* **9** Journalize and post closing entries.
- *Step* **10** Prepare a post-closing trial balance.

Notice that we divided the accounting cycle into work that is performed *during* the accounting period (steps 1–4) and work that is performed *at the end* of the accounting period (steps 5–10). The greater number of steps to be done at the end of the period may suggest that most of the work of the accounting cycle comes at the end of the accounting period. This, however, is not the case. The routine journalizing and posting that is done during the accounting period takes far more time than the end-of-period work.

Let us stress that most businesses prepare adjusting entries, closing entries, and the post-closing trial balance *only* at the end of a 12-month accounting period. We used a two-month accounting period for Walker and Associates—November and December, 20X1. These were the first two months Stanley was open for business. The next time Stanley performs the work at the end of the accounting cycle it will be for the year ended December 31, 20X2.

We should also emphasize that steps 5 through 10 of the accounting cycle are performed *as of* the last day of the accounting period, not *on* the last day of the accounting period. The accountant will need some time in the new accounting period to assemble the data necessary to complete the work at the end of the preceding period. Thus, it could take several days (or weeks) to complete the work of the previous accounting cycle. Nonetheless, the work sheet, financial statements, adjusting entries, closing entries, and post-closing trial balance are prepared as of the last day of the accounting period.

Fiscal Period

fiscal period the period of time that covers a complete accounting cycle

fiscal year a fiscal period covering 12 months but not necessarily coinciding with the calendar year

A **fiscal period** is any period of time covering the complete accounting cycle, from the analysis of transactions to the post-closing trial balance. A fiscal period consisting of 12 consecutive months is a **fiscal year**. A fiscal year does not necessarily coincide with the calendar year (from January 1 to December 31). Many businesses have seasonal peaks. For them, it is logical to

A business can use any 365-day period as its fiscal year.

end the accounting period at the point in the operating cycle in which activity is at its lowest. A fiscal year can thus cover any 12-month period, starting on the first day of a month and ending 12 months later.

For example, the fiscal year of a ski lodge that is operated only during the snow season may be from July 1 of one year to June 30 of the next year. This way, the ledger would be adjusted and closed as of June 30, which would be the period in which the least amount of business activity is being conducted. A fiscal year ending at a business's lowest point of activity is referred to as a **natural business year**.

The Bases of Accounting

In Chapter 4, we discussed the matching principle, which states that revenue earned during an accounting period should be offset by the expenses that were necessary to generate that revenue. In other words, revenue earned and expenses incurred during any accounting period should be reported (matched) on the income statement for that period.

To apply the matching principle, most accounting systems operate on the accrual basis of accounting. As we have already learned, sometimes a transaction occurs in one accounting period, but the cash involved is not received or paid out until a later period. Under the **accrual basis of accounting**, revenue is recorded when it is earned, no matter when cash is received, and expenses are recorded when they are incurred, no matter when cash is paid. For example, if goods or services are sold on account, in the accrual basis one records revenue at the point of sale, even though the receipt of cash may be in a later period. Likewise, an expense is recorded when it is incurred, even though payment may not be made until a later accounting period. According to generally accepted accounting principles (GAAP), the accrual basis *must* be used by businesses in which the major activity is the production or trading of goods.

Another basis of accounting is the cash basis. With the **cash basis of accounting**, revenue is recorded only when cash is received, and expenses are recorded only when cash is paid. The cash basis is used mostly by individual taxpayers when filing their personal income tax returns. Here, personal income (wages, salaries, interest, etc.) is reported only when cash has been received, and expenses are reported as personal deductions only when cash has been paid.

Businesses rarely use a strictly cash basis because most companies have some type of equipment, and the Internal Revenue Service requires that equipment be depreciated over a period of years—which results in an expense (depreciation expense) that does not involve cash. As a result, many

modified cash basis of accounting a basis of accounting where revenue is recorded only when cash is received and expenses are recorded only when cash is paid; however, adjustments are made for expenditures for items having an economic life of more than one year—such as equipment, prepaid insurance, and large purchases of supplies

professional firms and service businesses use the modified cash basis, which is a mixed or hybrid of the accrual basis and the cash basis. Under the **modified cash basis of accounting**, revenue is recorded only when cash is received, and expenses are recorded only when cash is paid. However, adjustments must be made for the depreciation of long-term assets. Adjustments must also be made for insurance premiums paid in advance and for purchases of large amounts of supplies. Table 5-2 summarizes the differences between the accrual basis and the cash basis.

Table 5-2 Accrual Basis of Accounting versus Cash Basis of Accounting

	Accrual Basis of Accounting	Cash Basis of Accounting
When revenue is recorded	When earned, no matter when received	When received, no matter when earned
When expenses are recorded	When incurred, regardless of when paid	When paid, no matter when incurred
Who uses	Most medium- and large-sized businesses	Individuals and small-sized businesses with few receivables and payables

Focus on ETHICS

Rite Aid Executives Charged with Criminal Fraud

Chief Financial Officer Frank Bergonzi was accused of manipulating Rite Aid's financial statements, which resulted in an increase in the bonuses paid to executives.

Three former Rite Aid officers and one current employee were indicted by a grand jury on charges of securities fraud, obstruction of justice, and witness tampering. Their actions resulted in a restatement of earnings by $1.6 billion by the second largest drugstore chain in the United States.

The former Rite Aid chief executive officer, Martin Grass; the former chief financial officer, Frank Bergonzi; and former vice chairman, Franklin Brown, were accused of manipulating the company's accounting records for personal gain. Bergonzi was accused of telling bookkeepers to adjust their records by millions, which inflated Rite Aid's financial performance and therefore increased the executives' bonuses.

All defendants denied any deliberate crime, and Bergonzi's attorney claimed he was simply confused by the current accounting laws.

Sources: *Ethics Newsline*, a publication of the Institute for Global Ethics, July 1, 2002; Staff, "Cash-and-Apothecary," *BNET* (June 2002); "SEC Announces Fraud Charges against Former Rite Aid Senior Management," Securities and Exchange Commission, 2002.

For Discussion

1. What was the motivation of the former Rite Aid executives to falsify the accounting records?
2. Why would it be difficult for the company bookkeepers to refuse to manipulate the accounting records when requested?
3. Why do you believe that a certified public accounting (CPA) firm finds it very difficult to catch accounting fraud when top management is involved in the crime?
4. Not mentioned in this article, one of the nation's largest accounting firms actually withdrew from their audit engagement with Rite Aid before the alleged crimes became public knowledge. Why didn't the CPA firm go directly to the government and report any knowledge of crime or accounting irregularities?

Joining the Pieces

Steps in the Accounting Cycle for a Service Business

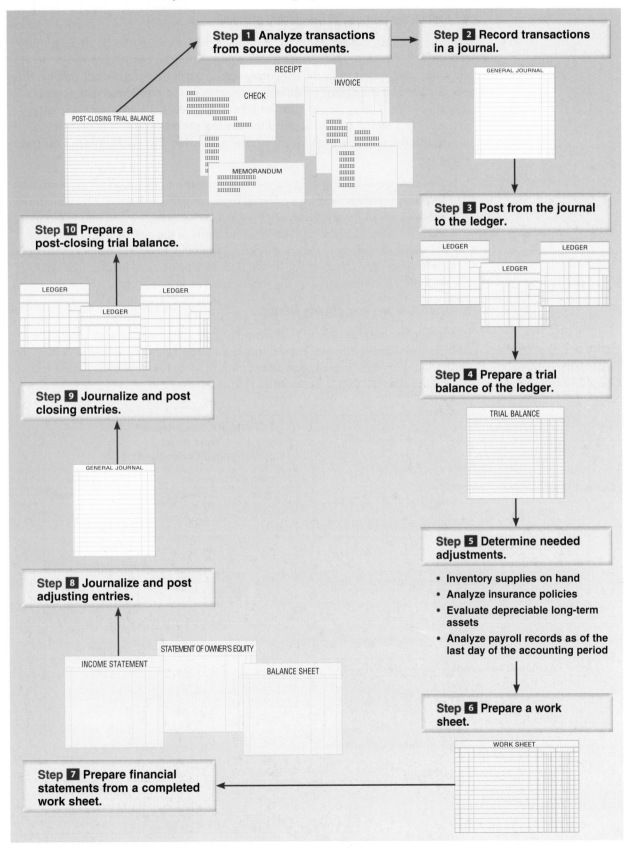

Step 1 Analyze transactions from source documents.

RECEIPT

CHECK

INVOICE

MEMORANDUM

POST-CLOSING TRIAL BALANCE

Step 2 Record transactions in a journal.

GENERAL JOURNAL

Step 3 Post from the journal to the ledger.

LEDGER

LEDGER

LEDGER

Step 10 Prepare a post-closing trial balance.

LEDGER

LEDGER

LEDGER

Step 4 Prepare a trial balance of the ledger.

TRIAL BALANCE

Step 9 Journalize and post closing entries.

GENERAL JOURNAL

Step 5 Determine needed adjustments.

- Inventory supplies on hand
- Analyze insurance policies
- Evaluate depreciable long-term assets
- Analyze payroll records as of the last day of the accounting period

Step 8 Journalize and post adjusting entries.

STATEMENT OF OWNER'S EQUITY

INCOME STATEMENT

BALANCE SHEET

Step 6 Prepare a work sheet.

WORK SHEET

Step 7 Prepare financial statements from a completed work sheet.

Summary  Interactive Summary in English and Spanish

1 Explain the purpose of the closing process.

Revenue accounts, expense accounts, and the owner's drawing account are **temporary accounts** used to show changes in owner's equity during an accounting period. When the accounting period ends, the temporary accounts will have served their purpose for that period. Therefore, their balances are summarized and transferred to the owner's capital account. The process of transferring the balances of the temporary accounts to the owner's capital account is called the **closing process**. Entries necessary to accomplish the closing process are called **closing entries**. The closing process has two objectives:

- *To reduce the balances of temporary accounts to zero and thus make the accounts ready for entries in the next accounting period.* By starting the new accounting period with zero balances in the temporary accounts, we can accumulate new information about revenue, expenses, and owner withdrawals in the new period.
- *To update the balance of the owner's capital account.* Closing the temporary accounts summarizes their effect on capital and leads to a new capital balance that agrees with the amount reported on the statement of owner's equity.

2 Journalize and post closing entries.

In restating the learning objectives of Chapter 4, we illustrated the work sheet of M & K Shoe Repair. For our review of the closing process, we again use M & K as our illustration. Let's look at the statement columns of M & K's work sheet for the year ended December 31, 20XX, as shown in Figure 5-7.

Figure 5-7

Financial Statement Columns of the Work Sheet

M & K Shoe Repair
Work Sheet
For Year Ended December 31, 20XX

	Account Title	Income Statement Debit	Income Statement Credit	Balance Sheet Debit	Balance Sheet Credit	
1	Cash			7 7 5 5 00		1
2	Supplies			7 5 0 00		2
3	Prepaid Insurance			1 2 0 0 00		3
4	Equipment			20 0 0 0 00		4
5	Accumulated Depreciation—Equipment				6 0 0 0 00	5
6	Accounts Payable				7 6 0 0 00	6
7	Salaries Payable				1 0 0 0 00	7
8	Michael Knebel, Capital				19 7 8 0 00	8
9	Michael Knebel, Drawing			2 5 0 0 00		9
10	Revenue from Services		62 2 4 0 00			10
11	Rent Expense	7 2 0 0 00				11
12	Salaries Expense	52 0 0 0 00				12
13	Utilities Expense	2 4 0 0 00				13
14	Supplies Expense	2 1 5 00				14
15	Insurance Expense	6 0 0 00				15
16	Depreciation Expense—Equipment	2 0 0 0 00				16
17		64 4 1 5 00	62 2 4 0 00	32 2 0 5 00	34 3 8 0 00	17
18	Net Loss		2 1 7 5 00	2 1 7 5 00		18
19		64 4 1 5 00	64 4 1 5 00	34 3 8 0 00	34 3 8 0 00	19

The work sheet is the source of all information needed to prepare the closing entries. Current balances of expense and revenue accounts are found in the Income Statement Debit and Credit columns, and the balance of the owner's drawing account is found in the Balance Sheet Debit column.

Four separate journal entries are needed to close the temporary accounts of M & K:

- The balance of the revenue account is transferred to the credit side of the Income Summary account.
- The balances of the expense accounts are transferred to the debit side of the Income Summary account.
- The balance of the Income Summary account is transferred to the owner's capital account.
- The balance of the owner's drawing account is transferred to the debit side of the owner's capital account.

M & K's closing entries are journalized in Figure 5-8.

Figure 5-8

Closing Entries in the General Journal

	Date		Account Title	P.R.	Debit	Credit	
1			Closing Entries				1
2	20XX Dec.	31	Revenue from Services		62 2 4 0 00		2
3			Income Summary			62 2 4 0 00	3
4							4
5		31	Income Summary		64 4 1 5 00		5
6			Rent Expense			7 2 0 0 00	6
7			Salaries Expense			52 0 0 0 00	7
8			Utilities Expense			2 4 0 0 00	8
9			Supplies Expense			2 1 5 00	9
10			Insurance Expense			6 0 0 00	10
11			Depreciation Expense—Equipment			2 0 0 0 00	11
12							12
13		31	Michael Knebel, Capital		2 1 7 5 00		13
14			Income Summary			2 1 7 5 00	14
15							15
16		31	Michael Knebel, Capital		2 5 0 0 00		16
17			Michael Knebel, Drawing			2 5 0 0 00	17

General Journal — Page 2

Once closing entries have been journalized, the next step is to post the closing entries to the ledger. Since this is a mechanical step, the posting of M & K's closing entries will not be illustrated here.

3 Prepare a post-closing trial balance.

After closing entries have been posted, the accountant should prepare a **post-closing trial balance** (also called an after-closing trial balance) to make sure that the ledger is still in balance. As we stated above, M & K's ledger is not illustrated; however, its post-closing trial balance, taken as of December 31, 20XX, appears in Figure 5-9. Notice that only the permanent accounts are shown with balances, as all temporary accounts have been closed.

Figure 5-9

The Post-Closing Trial Balance

Account Title	Debit	Credit
M & K Shoe Repair		
Post-Closing Trial Balance		
December 31, 20XX		
Cash	7 7 5 5 00	
Supplies	7 5 0 00	
Prepaid Insurance	1 2 0 0 00	
Equipment	20 0 0 0 00	
Accumulated Depreciation—Equipment		6 0 0 0 00
Accounts Payable		7 6 0 0 00
Salaries Payable		1 0 0 0 00
Michael Knebel, Capital		15 1 0 5 00
Totals	29 7 0 5 00	29 7 0 5 00

Terms and Concepts Review

- Key Terms and Definitions in English and Spanish
- Additional Quiz Questions

Key Terms

accrual basis of accounting, 190
cash basis of accounting, 190
clearing account, 178
closing entries, 177
closing process, 177
fiscal period, 189
fiscal year, 189

Income Summary account, 178
modified cash basis of accounting, 191
natural business year, 190
permanent accounts, 182
post-closing trial balance, 188
temporary accounts, 177

Concepts Review

1. Why are the balances of certain accounts transferred to the owner's capital account?
2. What are the two objectives of the closing process?
3. What purpose is served by the Income Summary account?
4. Which accounts are closed to the Income Summary account?
5. Identify the steps involved in the closing process.
6. How does the work sheet aid in the closing process?
7. What purpose is served by the post-closing trial balance?
8. Which account balances appear on the post-closing trial balance?
9. The closing process is sometimes referred to as "closing the books." Is this statement totally accurate? Explain.
10. What is meant by a fiscal period?
11. Differentiate between a calendar year and a fiscal year.
12. Why have some businesses adopted a natural business year for fiscal purposes?
13. Differentiate between the accrual basis of accounting and the cash basis of accounting.
14. Why do many professional firms and service businesses use a modified cash basis of accounting?

Learning Objective **2**

Check Figure
1. (d) Close the balance of each revenue account to Income Summary.

Quick Practice

Quick Practice 5-1

Objective: To identify the four steps in the closing process

Directions: List the following four steps in the closing process in the normal order in which they are performed.

a. Close the balance of Income Summary to the owner's capital account.
b. Close the balance of the owner's drawing account directly to the owner's capital account.
c. Close the balance of each expense account to Income Summary.
d. Close the balance of each revenue account to Income Summary.

Quick Practice 5-2

Objective: To journalize closing entries from account balances

Directions: Prepare closing entries for the year ended December 31, 20X2, in general journal form from the following list of adjusted account balances of Mottaghi Photography.

Account	Balance
Photography Revenue	$96,000
Rent Expense	7,200
Supplies Expense	1,240
Salaries Expense	15,000
Depreciation Expense—Equipment	3,100
Utilities Expense	750
Abbas Mottaghi, Drawing	50,000
Abbas Mottaghi, Capital	42,800

Quick Practice 5-3

Objective: To journalize closing entries from account balances

Directions: Prepare closing entries in general journal form for the following accounts of Linda Bruss, MD. Linda's fiscal year ends on June 30, 20X1.

Account	Balance
Linda Bruss, Capital	$84,320.25
Linda Bruss, Drawing	75,000.00
Medical Fees	160,000.00
Rent Expense	30,000.00
Medical Supplies Expense	7,980.30
Office Supplies Expense	1,396.45
Depreciation Expense—Equipment	2,500.00
Utilities Expense	13,689.75
Miscellaneous Expense	814.60

Quick Practice 5-4

Objective: To analyze and close the Income Summary account

Directions: Prepare a journal entry to close the Income Summary account for Robert H. Lee, owner of Lee Training Institute, and answer the three questions on the next page.

General Ledger							
Account Income Summary						Account No.	313
Date	Item	P.R.	Debit	Credit	Balance		
					Debit	Credit	
20X8 Dec. 31	Closing	GJ9		59 000 00		59 000 00	
31	Closing	GJ9	51 000 00			8 000 00	

1. What is the total revenue?
2. What are the total expenses?
3. What is the net income (or the net loss)?

Learning Objective **2**

Check Figure
Income Summary balance
$2,000 (debit) after second
closing entry

Quick Practice 5-5

Objective: To prepare closing entries from a set of T accounts

Directions: Using the T accounts below, journalize the necessary closing entries as of December 31, 20XX.

Cash

| 1,580 | |

Supplies

| 870 | |

Jerry Lasselle, Capital

| | 51,800 |

Jerry Lasselle, Drawing

| 8,000 | |

Revenue from Services

| | 22,000 |

Salaries Expense

| 12,000 | |

Rent Expense

| 10,000 | |

Utilities Expense

| 2,000 | |

Learning Objective **2**

Check Figure
Income Summary balance
$90,500 (credit) after second
closing entry

Quick Practice 5-6

Objective: To journalize closing entries from the Income Statement columns of a work sheet

Directions: Journalize the closing entries from the information in the Income Statement columns of Marilyn Johnson's work sheet for the fiscal year ended June 30, 20XX. Marilyn is an attorney who withdrew $80,000 during the year.

	Income Statement	
	Debit	Credit
Legal Fees Earned		130,000
Salaries Expense	21,000	
Rent Expense	15,000	
Depreciation Expense—Equipment	2,200	
Utilities Expense	900	
Miscellaneous Expense	400	

Learning Objective **3**

Check Figure
Nine accounts will appear on
post-closing trial balance.

Quick Practice 5-7

Objective: To identify the accounts that appear on the post-closing trial balance

Directions: Indicate with a check mark the accounts that will appear on a post-closing trial balance. The first one is done as an example.

	Appear on Post-Closing Trial Balance?	
	Yes	No
1. Accounts Payable	✓	
2. Accounts Receivable		
3. Building		
4. Cash		
5. Delivery Truck		
6. Equipment		
7. Pam Knight, Capital		
8. Pam Knight, Drawing		
9. Mortgage Note Payable		
10. Rent Expense		
11. Repairs Expense		
12. Revenue from Services		
13. Supplies		
14. Utilities Expense		

Learning Objective **3**

Check Figure
Net income $110,800

Quick Practice 5-8

Objective: To prepare an income statement from a partial work sheet

Directions: Prepare an income statement for the year ended December 31, 20XX, from the following partial work sheet of Usha Ramanujam, CPA.

Usha Ramanujam, CPA
Work Sheet (Partial)
For Year Ended December 31, 20XX

	Account Title	Income Statement Debit	Income Statement Credit	Balance Sheet Debit	Balance Sheet Credit	
1	Cash			27 6 6 0 00		1
2	Accounts Receivable			9 2 0 0 00		2
3	Office Supplies			1 1 3 0 00		3
4	Prepaid Insurance			1 2 0 0 00		4
5	Office Equipment			15 7 1 0 00		5
6	Accumulated Depreciation—Office Equipment				1 5 0 0 00	6
7	Accounts Payable				1 7 0 0 00	7
8	Salaries Payable				9 0 0 00	8
9	Usha Ramanujam, Capital				20 0 0 0 00	9
10	Usha Ramanujam, Drawing			80 0 0 0 00		10
11	Fees Earned		150 0 0 0 00			11
12	Rent Expense	12 0 0 0 00				12
13	Salaries Expense	20 0 0 0 00				13
14	Depreciation Expense—Office Equipment	8 0 0 00				14
15	Office Supplies Expense	1 9 0 0 00				15
16	Insurance Expense	4 5 0 0 00				16
17		39 2 0 0 00	150 0 0 0 00	134 9 0 0 00	24 1 0 0 00	17
18	Net Income	110 8 0 0 00			110 8 0 0 00	18
19		150 0 0 0 00	150 0 0 0 00	134 9 0 0 00	134 9 0 0 00	19

Learning Objective 3

Check Figure
Ending capital $50,800

Quick Practice 5-9

Objective: To prepare a statement of owner's equity from a work sheet

Directions: Prepare a statement of owner's equity for Usha Ramanujam, CPA, for the year ended December 31, 20XX, from the partial work sheet in Quick Practice 5-8.

Learning Objective 3

Check Figure
Total assets $53,400

Quick Practice 5-10

Objective: To prepare a balance sheet from a work sheet

Directions: Prepare a balance sheet as of December 31, 20XX, for Usha Ramanujam, CPA, from the work sheet in Quick Practice 5-8.

Exercises

Learning Objective 1

Check Figure
Eight accounts are permanent.

Exercise 5-1

Objective: To classify accounts as permanent or temporary and to indicate the financial statement classification

Directions: Complete the following form. Each line should have two check marks and the word *Yes* or *No*. The first one is done as an example.

Account Title	Permanent	Temporary	Closed?	Reported On Balance Sheet	Reported On Income Statement
Cash	✓		No	✓	
Salaries Payable					
Accumulated Depr.					
Fees Earned					
Accounts Receivable					
Supplies Expense					
Owner, Capital					
Accounts Payable					
Rent Expense					
Supplies					
Equipment					

Learning Objective 2

Check Figure
Net income (in third entry) is
$8,642.

Tutorial 6

Preparing Closing
Entries

Exercise 5-2

Objective: To journalize closing entries from account balances

The following are adjusted account balances from the work sheet of Smallwood Service Company for the year ended December 31, 20X1:

Account	Balance
Service Revenue	$ 52,000
Rent Expense	8,200
Supplies Expense	1,750
Salaries Expense	27,358
Depreciation Expense—Equipment	4,000
Utilities Expense	2,050
Mary Merrill, Drawing	15,000
Mary Merrill, Capital	39,900

Directions: Prepare closing entries in general journal form.

Learning Objective 2

Check Figure
Net income is $55,342.15.

Exercise 5-3

Objective: To journalize closing entries from account balances

As of December 31, 20X1, the ledger of Verna Reardon, MD, contained the following adjusted balances:

Account	Balance
Verna Reardon, Capital	$57,304.25
Verna Reardon, Drawing	36,000.00
Medical Fees	80,205.00
Rent Expense	12,000.00
Medical Supplies Expense	2,455.80
Office Supplies Expense	1,235.90
Depreciation Expense—Equipment	3,000.00
Utilities Expense	5,445.35
Miscellaneous Expense	725.80

Directions: Prepare closing entries in general journal form.

Learning Objective 2

Check Figure
4. Net income is $64,000.

Exercise 5-4

Objective: To analyze and close the Income Summary account

After all revenue and expense accounts of Mike DeMott and Associates have been closed, the Income Summary account appears as shown on the next page.

General Ledger

Account Income Summary						Account No.	313

Date	Item	P.R.	Debit	Credit	Balance Debit	Balance Credit
20X2 Dec. 31	Closing	GJ8		153 000 00		153 000 00
31	Closing	GJ8	89 000 00			64 000 00

Directions:

1. Make a journal entry to close the Income Summary account.
2. Total revenue is _____.
3. Total expenses are _____.
4. Net income (or net loss) is _____.

Learning Objective **2**

Check Figure
Net income is $22,200.

Exercise 5-5

Objective: To make closing entries from a set of T accounts

Directions: Using the T accounts shown below, journalize necessary closing entries as of July 31, 20X0.

Cash			Accounts Payable			Gary Moser, Capital	
4,000				1,850			14,550

Supplies		Gary Moser, Drawing	
1,800		18,000	

Equipment		Fees Earned	
17,000			45,000

Accum. Depr.—Equipment		Salaries Expense	
	3,200	15,200	

Rent Expense	
4,500	

Utilities Expense	
2,800	

Supplies Expense	
300	

Learning Objective **2**

Check Figure
Net income is $30,760.

Exercise 5-6

Objective: To journalize closing entries from the Income Statement columns of a work sheet

The following items appear in the Income Statement columns of Karen Jolly's work sheet for the fiscal year ended July 31, 20X2. Karen is an attorney who withdrew $32,000 during the year.

	Income Statement	
	Debit	**Credit**
Legal Fees Earned		66,000
Salaries Expense	24,000	
Rent Expense	6,000	
Office Supplies Expense	1,350	
Depreciation Expense—Equipment	1,500	
Utilities Expense	1,490	
Miscellaneous Expense	900	
	35,240	66,000

Directions: Journalize Karen's closing entries.

Learning Objective **3**

Check Figure
Seven accounts will appear on the post-closing trial balance.

Exercise 5-7

Objective: To indicate which accounts will appear on a post-closing trial balance

Directions: Indicate which of the following accounts will appear on a post-closing trial balance by listing the numbers of those accounts.

1. Cash
2. Accounts Payable
3. Randy Brush, Drawing
4. Randy Brush, Capital
5. Insurance Expense

6. Fees Earned
7. Accumulated Depreciation
8. Prepaid Insurance
9. Accounts Receivable
10. Salaries Payable

Learning Objective **1**

Check Figure
None

Exercise 5-8

Objective: To arrange the steps in the accounting cycle in proper sequence

Directions: List the following steps of the accounting cycle in the proper sequence.

1. Journalize and post closing entries.
2. Record transactions in a journal.
3. Prepare a post-closing trial balance.
4. Analyze transactions from source documents.
5. Journalize and post adjusting entries.
6. Post from the journal to the ledger.
7. Prepare financial statements from a completed work sheet.
8. Determine needed adjustments.
9. Prepare a work sheet.
10. Prepare a trial balance of the ledger.

Case Problems

Group A

Learning Objective **2**

Check Figure
Net income is $27,500.

Problem 5-1A

Objective: To journalize closing entries from account balances

After the adjusting entries for Greg Rapp, CPA, were posted, his ledger contained the account balances on the following page as of April 30, 20X1.

Account	Balance
Cash	$22,600
Accounts Receivable	3,000
Office Supplies	1,850
Equipment	32,800
Accumulated Depreciation—Equipment	4,000
Accounts Payable	7,800
Salaries Payable	900
Greg Rapp, Capital	39,050
Greg Rapp, Drawing	18,000
Income Summary	—
Accounting Fees Earned	61,500
Salaries Expense	22,600
Rent Expense	5,200
Depreciation Expense—Equipment	1,200
Utilities Expense	3,600
Telephone Expense	900
Office Supplies Expense	500

Directions: Journalize the closing entries.

Learning Objective **2**

Check Figure
2. Balance of the capital account after closing is $18,160.

Problem 5-2A

Objective: To journalize closing entries from a partial work sheet

The financial statement columns of the work sheet for Dave's Carpet Service are shown below.

Dave's Carpet Service
Work Sheet
For Year Ended December 31, 20XX

	Account Title	Income Statement Debit	Income Statement Credit	Balance Sheet Debit	Balance Sheet Credit	
1	Cash			2 680 00		1
2	Office Supplies			980 00		2
3	Delivery Supplies			500 00		3
4	Office Equipment			9 000 00		4
5	Accumulated Depreciation—Office Equipment				3 000 00	5
6	Delivery Equipment			13 000 00		6
7	Accumulated Depreciation—Delivery Equipment				2 000 00	7
8	Accounts Payable				2 200 00	8
9	Salaries Payable				800 00	9
10	Dave Garlington, Capital				2 320 00	10
11	Dave Garlington, Drawing			15 000 00		11
12	Income Summary					12
13	Service Revenue		60 000 00			13
14	Salaries Expense	19 000 00				14
15	Rent Expense	6 000 00				15
16	Depreciation Expense—Office Equipment	1 000 00				16
17	Depreciation Expense—Delivery Equipment	1 200 00				17
18	Office Supplies Expense	300 00				18
19	Delivery Supplies Expense	430 00				19
20	Utilities Expense	900 00				20
21	Miscellaneous Expense	330 00				21
22		29 160 00	60 000 00	41 160 00	10 320 00	22
23	Net Income	30 840 00			30 840 00	23
24		60 000 00	60 000 00	41 160 00	41 160 00	24

Directions:

1. Prepare journal entries to close the temporary accounts.
2. What is the balance of the owner's capital account after closing?

Learning Objective **2**

Check Figure
Net income = $34,185

Problem 5-3A

Objective: To prepare a work sheet and journalize adjusting and closing entries

Brenda Houcher, owner of Houcher Software Services, prepared the following trial balance on December 31, 20X2:

Houcher Software Services Trial Balance December 31, 20X2		
Account Title	**Debit**	**Credit**
Cash	10 000 00	
Accounts Receivable	2 000 00	
Office Supplies	2 500 00	
Prepaid Insurance	1 200 00	
Office Equipment	18 000 00	
Accumulated Depreciation—Office Equipment		3 000 00
Accounts Payable		2 000 00
Salaries Payable		
Brenda Houcher, Capital		15 760 00
Brenda Houcher, Drawing	25 700 00	
Service Revenue		77 600 00
Salaries Expense	22 500 00	
Rent Expense	12 600 00	
Advertising Expense	2 400 00	
Telephone Expense	9 00 00	
Office Supplies Expense		
Insurance Expense		
Depreciation Expense—Office Equipment		
Miscellaneous Expense	5 60 00	
Totals	98 360 00	98 360 00

Adjustment data:

(a) Office supplies on hand, $300.
(b) Insurance expired during the year, $1,000.
(c) Depreciation of office equipment, $1,000.
(d) Unpaid salaries at year end, $255.

Directions:

1. Prepare a work sheet for the year ended December 31, 20X2.
2. Journalize adjusting and closing entries.

Learning Objectives **2, 3**

Check Figure
Ending balance of the capital account is $20,500.

Problem 5-4A

Objective: To journalize and post adjusting and closing entries and prepare a post-closing trial balance

The completed work sheet of Comprehensive Management Services is presented in the *Study Guide/Working Papers*.

Directions:

1. Using the Trial Balance section of the work sheet, record all beginning balances in the ledger accounts provided. The Income Summary account, which does not appear on the work sheet, has no balance.
2. Journalize and post the adjusting entries.
3. Journalize and post the closing entries.
4. Prepare a post-closing trial balance.

Problem 5-5A

Objective: To complete a work sheet and the work of the accounting cycle

Account balances of Kholer Enterprises appear as follows on December 31, 20X0:

Number	Account Title	Balance
111	Cash	$ 37,350
112	Accounts Receivable	5,000
113	Office Supplies	19,640
114	Store Supplies	16,110
115	Delivery Supplies	27,500
116	Prepaid Insurance	36,000
117	Office Equipment	90,000
117.1	Accumulated Depreciation—Office Equipment	45,000
118	Store Equipment	75,000
118.1	Accumulated Depreciation—Store Equipment	30,000
119	Truck	40,000
119.1	Accumulated Depreciation—Truck	20,000
211	Accounts Payable	47,500
212	Salaries Payable	—
311	Jerry Kholer, Capital	85,800
312	Jerry Kholer, Drawing	21,200
411	Fees Earned	351,500
511	Rent Expense	12,000
512	Salaries Expense	200,000
513	Office Supplies Expense	—
514	Store Supplies Expense	—
515	Delivery Supplies Expense	—
516	Insurance Expense	—
517	Depreciation Expense—Office Equipment	—
518	Depreciation Expense—Store Equipment	—
519	Depreciation Expense—Truck	—

Adjustment data:

(a) Office supplies on hand, $3,510.
(b) Store supplies on hand, $10,140.
(c) Delivery supplies on hand, $21,900.
(d) Depreciation of office equipment, $9,000.
(e) Depreciation of store equipment, $10,000.
(f) Depreciation of truck, $10,000.
(g) Insurance expired, $6,000.
(h) Salaries unpaid, $5,000.

Directions:

1. Prepare a work sheet for the year ended December 31, 20X0.
2. Prepare an income statement for the year ended December 31, 20X0.
3. Prepare a statement of owner's equity for the year ended December 31, 20X0.
4. Prepare a December 31, 20X0, balance sheet.
5. Journalize the adjusting entries.
6. Journalize the closing entries.

Group B

Problem 5-1B

Objective: To journalize closing entries from account balances

After the adjusting entries for Hugo Grimaldi, MD, were posted, his ledger contained the following account balances as of May 31, 20X1:

Account	Balance
Cash	$25,500
Accounts Receivable	2,500
Office Supplies	2,000
Equipment	34,500
Accumulated Depreciation—Equipment	4,200
Accounts Payable	8,000
Salaries Payable	1,200
Hugo Grimaldi, Capital	44,755
Hugo Grimaldi, Drawing	27,000
Income Summary	—
Medical Fees Earned	75,500
Salaries Expense	28,300
Rent Expense	6,000
Depreciation Expense—Equipment	1,500
Utilities Expense	3,800
Telephone Expense	980
Office Supplies Expense	575

Directions: Journalize the closing entries.

Learning Objective **2**

Check Figure
Balance of the capital account
after closing entries is $18,975.

Problem 5-2B

Objective: To journalize closing entries from a partial work sheet

The financial statement columns of the work sheet for Joan's Plumbing Company are shown below.

Joan's Plumbing Company
Work Sheet
For Year Ended December 31, 20XX

	Account Title	Income Statement Debit	Income Statement Credit	Balance Sheet Debit	Balance Sheet Credit	
1	Cash			3 0 6 5 00		1
2	Office Supplies			1 6 3 0 00		2
3	Plumbing Supplies			9 8 0 00		3
4	Prepaid Insurance			1 8 0 0 00		4
5	Office Equipment			17 0 0 0 00		5
6	Accumulated Depreciation—Office Equipment				6 0 0 0 00	6
7	Plumbing Equipment			7 5 0 0 00		7
8	Accumulated Depreciation—Plumbing Equipment				4 0 0 0 00	8
9	Accounts Payable				2 7 5 0 00	9
10	Salaries Payable				2 5 0 00	10
11	Joan Ryan, Capital				20 8 6 0 00	11
12	Joan Ryan, Drawing			1 7 0 0 00		12
13	Revenue from Services		23 6 5 0 00			13
14	Rent Expense	4 0 0 0 00				14
15	Salaries Expense	11 0 0 0 00				15
16	Office Supplies Expense	1 3 7 5 00				16

Continues

#	Account Title	Col 1	Col 2	Col 3	Col 4	#
17	Plumbing Supplies Expense	2 6 1 0 00				17
18	Insurance Expense	9 0 0 00				18
19	Depreciation Expense—Office Equipment	2 0 0 0 00				19
20	Depreciation Expense—Store Equipment	1 0 0 0 00				20
21	Utilities Expense	9 5 0 00				21
22		23 8 3 5 00	23 6 5 0 00	33 6 7 5 00	33 8 6 0 00	22
23	Net Loss		1 8 5 00	1 8 5 00		23
24		23 8 3 5 00	23 8 3 5 00	33 8 6 0 00	33 8 6 0 00	24

Directions:
1. Prepare journal entries to close the temporary accounts.
2. What is the balance of the owner's capital account after closing entries are posted?

Learning Objective **2**

Check Figure
Net income = $34,755

Problem 5-3B

Objective: To prepare a work sheet and journalize adjusting and closing entries

Scott Wallace, owner of Wallace Consulting Group, prepared the following trial balance on December 31, 20X1:

Wallace Consulting Group
Trial Balance
December 31, 20X1

Account Title	Debit	Credit
Cash	10 5 0 0 00	
Accounts Receivable	2 8 0 0 00	
Office Supplies	1 5 0 0 00	
Prepaid Insurance	1 2 0 0 00	
Office Equipment	21 0 0 0 00	
Accumulated Depreciation—Office Equipment		3 8 0 0 00
Accounts Payable		2 2 0 0 00
Salaries Payable		
Scott Wallace, Capital		19 4 4 0 00
Scott Wallace, Drawing	26 7 0 0 00	
Service Revenue		82 9 0 0 00
Salaries Expense	24 6 0 0 00	
Rent Expense	14 8 0 0 00	
Advertising Expense	2 5 0 0 00	
Telephone Expense	1 8 9 0 00	
Office Supplies Expense		
Insurance Expense		
Depreciation Expense—Office Equipment		
Miscellaneous Expense	8 5 0 00	
Totals	108 3 4 0 00	108 3 4 0 00

Adjustment data:
(a) Office supplies on hand, $450.
(b) Insurance expired during the year, $1,025.
(c) Depreciation of office equipment, $1,150.
(d) Unpaid salaries at year end, $280.

Directions:
1. Prepare a work sheet for the year ended December 31, 20X1.
2. Journalize adjusting and closing entries.

Learning Objectives **2, 3**

Check Figure
Ending balance of the capital account is $23,700.

Problem 5-4B

Objective: To journalize and post adjusting and closing entries and prepare a post-closing trial balance

The completed work sheet of DataPlus Bookkeeping Service is presented in the *Study Guide/Working Papers*.

Directions:
1. Using the Trial Balance section of the work sheet, record all beginning balances in the ledger accounts provided. The Income Summary account, which does not appear on the work sheet, has no balance.
2. Journalize and post the adjusting entries.
3. Journalize and post the closing entries.
4. Prepare a post-closing trial balance.

Learning Objectives
1, 2, 3

Check Figure
Balance sheet totals = $145,900

Problem 5-5B

Objective: To complete a work sheet and the work of the accounting cycle

Account balances of Shields Enterprises appear as follows on December 31, 20X0:

Number	Account Title	Balance
111	Cash	$ 30,350
112	Accounts Receivable	4,000
113	Office Supplies	17,640
114	Store Supplies	15,110
115	Delivery Supplies	26,500
116	Prepaid Insurance	24,000
117	Office Equipment	45,000
117.1	Accumulated Depreciation—Office Equipment	22,500
118	Store Equipment	65,000
118.1	Accumulated Depreciation—Store Equipment	26,000
119	Truck	30,000
119.1	Accumulated Depreciation—Truck	15,000
211	Accounts Payable	37,500
212	Salaries Payable	—
311	Pam Shields, Capital	38,200
312	Pam Shields, Drawing	21,100
411	Fees Earned	351,500
511	Rent Expense	12,000
512	Salaries Expense	200,000
513	Office Supplies Expense	—
514	Store Supplies Expense	—
515	Delivery Supplies Expense	—
516	Insurance Expense	—
517	Depreciation Expense—Office Equipment	—
518	Depreciation Expense—Store Equipment	—
519	Depreciation Expense—Truck	—

Adjustment data:
(a) Office supplies on hand, $2,510.
(b) Store supplies on hand, $10,140.
(c) Delivery supplies on hand, $20,900.
(d) Depreciation of office equipment, $4,500.
(e) Depreciation of store equipment, $6,500.
(f) Depreciation of truck, $7,500.
(g) Insurance expired, $4,000.
(h) Salaries unpaid, $5,000.

Directions:
1. Prepare a work sheet for the year ended December 31, 20X0.
2. Prepare an income statement for the year ended December 31, 20X0.
3. Prepare a statement of owner's equity for the year ended December 31, 20X0.
4. Prepare a December 31, 20X0 balance sheet.
5. Journalize the adjusting entries.
6. Journalize the closing entries.

Critical Thinking Problems

Challenge Problem

As of December 31, 20X1, after all revenue and expense accounts have been closed, the Income Summary account in the ledger of Total Accounting Services has a credit balance of $95,000. As of the same date, the Julie Donaldson, Drawing account has a normal balance of $37,000, and the Julie Donaldson, Capital account has a normal balance of $94,500. The firm's income statement reported total expenses of $220,000.

Directions:
1. Journalize the entries necessary to complete the closing process.
2. Prepare a statement of owner's equity for the year ended December 31, 20X1.
3. What was the total revenue for the year?

Communications

Sometimes related terms are the most difficult to describe. Explain in writing, using examples, the differences among the terms (a) *calendar year*, (b) *fiscal year*, and (c) *natural business year*.

Team Internet Project

There are revenue and expense accounts common to all businesses and then there are revenue and expense accounts unique to different types of businesses. Two interesting types of business are the movie theater and the sports arena. Do some online research and prepare a list of some of the revenue and expense accounts unique to each of these types of organizations.

Ethics

Assume that you work as an assistant loan officer for a bank. You recommend the approval of loans based on the financial standing of an individual or a business. One of your current customers is Gwen Franks, the owner of a travel service that has just completed its first year of operation and is now asking for a loan of $10,000 to purchase a computer system. The only financial item provided to you is an unadjusted trial balance. Gwen tells you that this financial item shows that she is in good financial condition, so she should be granted the loan without presenting any additional information.

   Explain to Gwen why financial statements are more useful than an unadjusted trial balance and why it is improper for you to recommend approval of a loan based only on what she has provided. Write your explanation in a paragraph or two.

In the Real World   H&R Block

H&R Block is listed on the New York Stock Exchange by the symbol HRB. What is its price on the date that you are doing this assignment?

Answers to Review Quizzes

Review Quiz 5-1

	Date		Account Title	P.R.	Debit	Credit	
1			Closing Entries				1
2	20XX Jun.	30	Service Revenue		89 6 0 0 00		2
3			Income Summary			89 6 0 0 00	3
4							4
5		30	Income Summary		74 3 0 0 00		5
6			Rent Expense			6 0 0 0 00	6
7			Salaries Expense			57 4 0 0 00	7
8			Office Supplies Expense			1 0 0 00	8
9			Telephone Expense			6 0 0 00	9
10			Insurance Expense			2 0 0 00	10
11			Depr. Expense—Office Equipment			1 0 0 0 00	11
12			Depr. Expense—Automobiles			2 0 0 0 00	12
13			Utilities Expense			6 3 0 0 00	13
14			Miscellaneous Expense			7 0 0 00	14
15							15
16		30	Income Summary		15 3 0 0 00		16
17			Susan Wright, Capital			15 3 0 0 00	17
18							18
19		30	Susan Wright, Capital		19 0 0 0 00		19
20			Susan Wright, Drawing			19 0 0 0 00	20

General Journal   **Page 3**

Review Quiz 5-2

	Date		Account Title	P.R.	Debit	Credit	
1			Closing Entries				1
2	20X1 Dec.	31	Fees Earned		52 0 0 0 00		2
3			Income Summary			52 0 0 0 00	3
4							4
5		31	Income Summary		39 6 5 0 00		5
6			Salaries Expense			26 0 0 0 00	6
7			Supplies Expense			6 5 0 00	7
8			Rent Expense			7 0 0 0 00	8
9			Depreciation Expense—Equipment			2 0 0 0 00	9
10			Utilities Expense			4 0 0 0 00	10
11							11
12		31	Income Summary		12 3 5 0 00		12
13			Tamatha Hoyez, Capital			12 3 5 0 00	13
14							14
15		31	Tamatha Hoyez, Capital		9 0 0 0 00		15
16			Tamatha Hoyez, Drawing			9 0 0 0 00	16

General Journal   **Page 3**

Comprehensive Review Problem I

Jim Arnold's Photography Studio Ⓟ Ⓠ

You have reached the end of the first section of this book. The following problem is designed to review and reinforce your knowledge of accounting for a service business.

Jim Arnold has been a photographer since his graduation from high school several years ago. On July 1, 20X1, he decided to open his own photography firm, called Arnold's Photos. To start his accounting system, Jim developed the chart of accounts shown below.

Arnold's Photos • Chart of Accounts	
Assets	**Owner's Equity**
111 Cash	311 Jim Arnold, Capital
112 Accounts Receivable	312 Jim Arnold, Drawing
113 Office Supplies	313 Income Summary
114 Photography Supplies	
115 Prepaid Insurance	**Revenue**
121 Office Equipment	411 Photography Revenue
121.1 Accumulated Depreciation—Office Equipment	412 Vending Machine Revenue
122 Photography Equipment	**Expenses**
122.1 Accumulated Depreciation—Photography Equipment	511 Salaries Expense
123 Furniture and Fixtures	512 Advertising Expense
123.1 Accumulated Depreciation—Furniture and Fixtures	513 Rent Expense
	514 Repairs Expense
	515 Insurance Expense
Liabilities	516 Office Supplies Expense
211 Accounts Payable	517 Photography Supplies Expense
212 Notes Payable	518 Depreciation Expense—Office Equipment
213 Salaries Payable	519 Depreciation Expense—Photography Equipment
	520 Depreciation Expense—Furniture and Fixtures
	521 Utilities Expense
	522 Miscellaneous Expense

Jim completed the following transactions during the first month of operations:

20X1

Jul. 1 Jim invested $40,000 cash and photography equipment valued at $20,000 in the business.
   1 Purchased office supplies for cash, $1,300.
   1 Purchased photography supplies on account, $6,700.
   1 Paid July rent, $1,700.
   1 Paid for a newspaper ad, $500.
   2 Purchased office equipment on account, $6,750.
   2 Paid property insurance for the upcoming year, $3,600.
   3 Purchased a computer system and software, $3,200, by issuing a note payable.
   5 Paid for promotional handouts, $150.
   6 Paid miscellaneous expenses, $175.
   7 Paid salaries of employees, $1,400.
   7 Recorded week's cash receipts for photo work, $1,350.

Jul. 8 Paid for carpet cleaning (a miscellaneous expense), $75.
9 Recorded photo work done for a customer on account, $855.
9 Purchased additional photography supplies on account, $3,200.
10 Purchased additional photography equipment for cash, $3,500.
10 Entered into a contract with Southside Food Vendors to place vending machines in the waiting room. Jim is to receive 10% of all sales, with a minimum of $200 monthly. Received $200 as an advance payment.
11 Purchased furniture for the lobby area, $1,700. Paid cash in full.
12 Paid cash for the installation of overhead lighting fixtures, $900.
15 Recorded second week's cash receipts for photo work, $2,170.
15 Paid weekly salaries, $1,400.
17 Jim withdrew cash for personal use, $800.
18 Paid for TV ad, $710.
19 Paid for repair to equipment, $80.
19 Collected $500 for the photo work done on account on July 9.
22 Recorded third week's cash receipts for photo work, $2,045.
22 Paid weekly salaries, $1,400.
23 Did a special wedding photo session for a customer on credit, $550.
28 Recorded fourth week's cash receipts for photo work, $1,995.
29 Paid salaries of employees, $1,400.
30 Paid water bill for July, $75.
30 Paid electric bill for July, $1,095.
31 Made a $500 payment on the note for the computer purchased on July 3.
31 Made a payment for the office equipment purchased on account, $2,000.
31 Made a payment on the photography supplies purchased on account, $1,000.
31 Wrote a business check to pay for Jim's home phone bill, $310.
31 Southside Food Vendors reported a total of $2,800 of vending machine sales for July. Ten percent of these sales is $280. Since $200 had already been received and recorded in July, Jim was owed $80. Received the $80 check.

Directions:
1. Open an account in the ledger for each account shown in the chart of accounts.
2. Journalize each of the transactions for July, beginning on page 1 of the general journal.
3. Post the journal entries to the ledger.
4. Prepare a trial balance of the ledger in the first two columns of a 10-column work sheet.
5. Complete the 10-column work sheet. Assume for the purposes of this problem that Jim has a one-month accounting period. Data for adjustments are as follows:
   (a) Office supplies on hand, $850.
   (b) Photography supplies on hand, $5,550.
   (c) Insurance expired, $300.
   (d) Salaries unpaid, two days of a five-day week; weekly salaries are $1,400.
   (e) Depreciation of office equipment, $190.
   (f) Depreciation of photography equipment, $275.
   (g) Depreciation of furniture and fixtures, $75.
6. Prepare an income statement for the month ended July 31.
7. Prepare a statement of owner's equity for the month ended July 31.
8. Prepare a balance sheet as of July 31.
9. Journalize adjusting entries from the completed work sheet.
10. Journalize closing entries.
11. Post adjusting and closing entries to the ledger.
12. Prepare a post-closing trial balance.

PART II

Accounting for Cash and the Merchandising Business

Target Corporation is one of America's largest full-service retail stores. Identified by its distinctive bulls-eye logo, the organization has focused on moving from its department store roots to a discount store approach to retailing.

In 1902, its founder, George Dayton, opened his first retail store, Goodfellows, in Minneapolis. The first Target Store opened in 1962, followed by the first SuperTarget store in 1995 and online retailing via target.com in 1999. In 2008, the organization has over 1,300 stores in 47 states (all except Alaska, Hawaii, and Vermont) and employs over 300,000 team members. Target Corporation is expanding outside the boundaries of the United States with the opening of an office in Bangalore, India, in 2008. Additional data about Target can be found at *www.target.com*.

Students with an undergraduate degree in business have a choice of many careers with the organization. Opportunities exist in the areas of product design and development, advertising and marketing, merchandise planning, merchandise presentation, finance and accounting, human resources, and information technology, among others.

In Part II of this book, you will have the chance to work with data from the company and apply what you learn in Chapters 6 through 10. Two sets of this merchandising firm's financial information are shown in Part II: balance sheet data follow Chapter 6 and income statement data follow Chapter 8.

CHAPTER 6

Internal Control and Accounting for Cash

Learning Objectives

1. Define *internal control* and identify and describe its objectives.
2. Define *cash* as it is used in accounting.
3. Describe internal control procedures related to cash.
4. Describe the purpose of and need for a petty cash fund.
5. Record the establishment of a petty cash fund.
6. Record the replenishment of a petty cash fund.
7. Record the establishment of a change fund.
8. Record cash shortages and overages.
9. Prepare a bank reconciliation.

In Chapters 1 through 5, we covered the complete accounting cycle for a service business, from analyzing source documents to the post-closing trial balance. Throughout the accounting cycle, certain measures are necessary to protect a company's assets from theft, loss, and misuse. Cash is an asset that is particularly vulnerable to such factors. In this chapter, we will study those procedures that are necessary to protect and control cash and other assets.

The Sarbanes-Oxley Act of 2002

Public Company Accounting Oversight Board (PCAOB) a not-for-profit corporation created by the Sarbanes-Oxley Act of 2002 to oversee the auditors of public companies in order to protect the interest of investors and further the public's interest in the preparation of fair and reliable financial reports

In Chapter 1, we mentioned that accounting scandals at Enron and WorldCom shook the public's confidence in the reliability of financial statements. Enron overstated profits and hid debt. WorldCom reported expenses as assets, thereby overstating both profit and total assets. Further, both companies were able to hide their fraud for several years. Many in the public asked "How could this have happened? How did auditors miss such large-scale fraud?" Congress responded by passing the Sarbanes-Oxley Act of 2002. As we stated in Chapter 1, the purpose of this act, abbreviated as SOX, is to restore public confidence and trust in the financial statements of companies. To accomplish this, SOX created a new body, the **Public Company Accounting Oversight Board (PCAOB)**, to oversee the work of auditors of public companies. Other provisions of SOX are:

- Harsh penalties for violators—25 years in prison for securities fraud and 20 years imprisonment for an executive making false statements under oath.
- Public accounting firms may not audit a client's books and also provide certain consulting services for the same client.
- Increased responsibility of the boards of directors.
- Companies are required to maintain strong and effective internal controls over recording business transactions and preparing financial statements.

As we just stated, SOX requires companies to maintain strong internal controls when recording business transactions and preparing financial statements. Maintaining control over transactions and financial statements is a part of a company's overall system of internal control, which we discuss next.

The Need for Internal Control

Learning Objective

1 Define *internal control* and identify and describe its objectives.

The highly publicized frauds at Enron and WorldCom involved members of management whose fraudulent activity cost employees, investors, and lenders millions, and sometime billions, of dollars. And while it is true that managers are usually responsible for the worst cases of fraud, American businesses lose billions of dollars every year to employee fraud and theft. When you open your daily newspaper on just about any given day, there is a very good chance you will see an article about an employee who was charged with some form of theft from his or her place of employment. The financial news recently reported the following:

Employee scan cards are one way to protect assets and trade secrets, because they limit access to only designated persons.

Over a two-year period, a computer operator embezzled $21 million from Wells Fargo Bank.

A woman who claimed her ailing boyfriend as her husband in order for him to receive medical treatments cost her employer over $100,000 in out-of-pocket costs.

Two employees at a retail establishment supposedly stole and sold store merchandise for profit on eBay. Thus far but still counting, stolen merchandise is already valued at over $50,000.

A 24-year-old software engineer at AOL, LLC was arrested on federal charges that he hacked into the company's computers to steal 92 million e-mail addresses that were later sold and used to bombard AOL members with spam.

Woman charged in connection with the theft of $559,810.58 of funds from Thoroughbred Aviation, LTD, a company that owns and charters airplanes, over a period of seven years while she was employed there.

Businesses also lose billions each year to shoplifting and other nonemployee theft. So, what can a company do to protect its assets from theft and fraud? The answer is to have a strong and effective system of internal control.

Internal control refers to the methods and procedures a business uses to internally protect its assets. As we stated in the previous section, internal controls are required by SOX. But aside from the law, good internal controls help companies guide their operations and protect assets from theft and other abuses. Let's look at the objectives of internal control.

A good system of internal control is designed to do the following:

Accurate and up-to-date records are a vital part of a good system of internal control.

- *Safeguard assets.* A company must have procedures in place to protect its assets from theft, loss, improper use, and unauthorized use. The safeguards a company uses will depend on its size, the nature of its operations, and the type of assets owned. Employee identification systems, alarm systems, cameras, and other monitoring devices are common safeguards. Accurate and up-to-date records of assets owned, where they are located, and who is responsible for them are also common safeguards.

- *Ensure the accuracy and reliability of accounting records.* Good financial records are necessary to determine profit or loss, prepare accurate financial statements, and protect assets. Accurate records and safeguarding assets go hand in hand. How can a company protect its assets unless it has complete information on the number, whereabouts, and operating condition of all assets owned? For example, regularly changing the oil in a delivery truck safeguards the vehicle's engine from excessive wear. Having accurate and up-to-date maintenance records alerts the company when service is due.

- *Promote operational efficiency.* The more efficient a company is, the lower its expenses and the greater its profit. Well-trained, motivated, reliable, and ethical employees increase a company's operating efficiency. Having the right assets for the operation of the company also increases efficiency. For example, what if the owner of a retail florist really likes Mack trucks? Would it be efficient to buy a heavy-duty Mack truck to make local deliveries? Obviously not; it would be way too much truck needed to deliver flowers. Instead, what if the owner bought a van with a refrigerated body? This would be the correct type of vehicle, but would one van be enough to make timely deliveries? It would hurt a company's efficiency if business was consistently good enough to justify two vans but only one was in use. While comparing a van to a Mack truck to deliver flowers may seem like an extreme example, it makes its point. Have the right assets for your operation. Don't overbuy or underbuy. Either situation can hurt your operating efficiency.

- *Ensure compliance with laws and regulations.* Businesses must comply with all applicable laws and regulations. Examples include filing proper tax forms, meeting safety regulations, and complying with various laws—such as the Americans with Disabilities Act.

Figure 6-1 summarizes the objectives of internal control.

Figure 6-1

Objectives of Internal
Control

Safeguard
assets

Keep accurate
records

Comply with laws
and regulations

Operate
efficiently

Internal Control of Cash

Learning Objectives

2 Define *cash* as it is used
in accounting.

3 Describe internal control
procedures related to
cash.

Remember

Recall from Chapter 1,
cash is defined as an
asset including currency
(paper money), coins,
checks, and money orders
made payable to the
business.

Cash includes currency (paper money), coins, checks made payable to the business, money orders, and amounts on deposit in banks and other financial institutions. Normally, we consider cash as anything we can deposit in our bank accounts. Thus, currency, coins, and checks made payable to you can be deposited in your bank account. As a result, these items are all considered to be cash.

Cash is generally considered the most precious of all assets. Without adequate cash, a business cannot survive. Cash is needed not only to pay employees, creditors, expenses, and taxes, but cash is also needed for the business to grow and expand.

Special controls are needed to protect cash, because almost everyone wants it, and it is easily taken if not protected. Further, by altering accounting records, it is often easy to conceal the theft or misuse of cash. Some common steps that are used to control and protect cash include the following:

- *Establish responsibility.* Only a few properly designated persons should be involved in the receipt, payment, and accounting for cash.
- *Separation of duties.* Those who physically handle cash (cashiers, clerks, etc.) should not be the same as those who account for cash (bookkeepers, accountants).
- *Physical protection.* All cash received should be kept in a secure place and deposited in a bank daily.

- *Documentation.* Documents, such as cash register tapes and summaries of checks received in the mail, should be maintained to show total cash receipts. Checks should be prenumbered so that it is easy to see what checks have been written and when.
- *Independent verification.* Supervisors should count cash and review cash register summaries (register checks) prepared by cashiers. The company treasurer should compare total cash receipts to daily bank deposits.
- *Keep only a small amount of cash on hand.* Only a small amount of cash (called petty cash) should be kept on hand for making small expenditures. All other payments should be made by check.

Figure 6-2 summarizes internal control procedures for cash.

In this section, we studied internal control and procedures for controlling and protecting cash. Let's now turn to specific types of cash transactions. Petty cash is discussed next.

Figure 6-2

Internal Control
Procedures for Cash

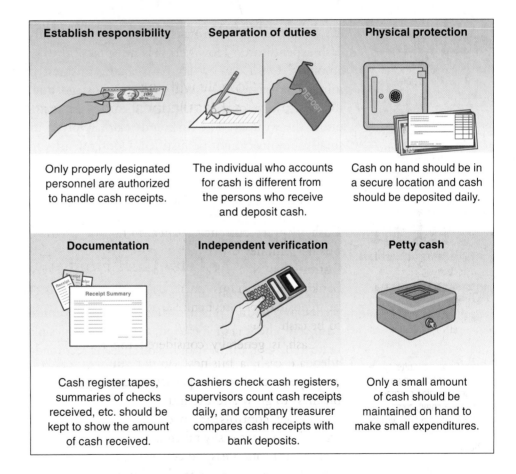

Establish responsibility	Separation of duties	Physical protection
Only properly designated personnel are authorized to handle cash receipts.	The individual who accounts for cash is different from the persons who receive and deposit cash.	Cash on hand should be in a secure location and cash should be deposited daily.
Documentation	**Independent verification**	**Petty cash**
Cash register tapes, summaries of checks received, etc. should be kept to show the amount of cash received.	Cashiers check cash registers, supervisors count cash receipts daily, and company treasurer compares cash receipts with bank deposits.	Only a small amount of cash should be maintained on hand to make small expenditures.

Below are cash procedures followed by the Jerry Larsen Company. Jerry Larsen, the company's owner, has asked you to review each procedure and state whether it is an example of a good internal control or a weak internal control. For each weak example you identify, explain why you think it is a weak internal control.

1. Jerry allows anyone who is free at the end of the day to carry the cash deposit to the bank.
2. No cash, except for the $200 change fund and $100 in petty cash, is kept on hand.
3. Jerry, being the only supervisor at his business, does not always have time to verify the cashier's check of the register. He relies on the honor system.
4. The head cashier also does the bookkeeping.
5. All receipts, bills, cash register tapes and summaries, and other business papers are kept in a daily file.

Check your answers on page 258.

The Petty Cash Account

Learning Objective

4 Describe the purpose of and need for a petty cash fund.

petty cash fund a small amount of cash kept in the office for making small payments for items such as postage and office supplies; recorded in the Petty Cash account

To control cash, most businesses use bank checking accounts when making cash expenditures. However, it is not practical to write checks for very small amounts. On a day-by-day basis, many business firms need to make small immediate payments—such as $0.30 postage due on a delivery, a $12.00 toner cartridge, or a $2.00 get-well card for a customer who has been a little under the weather. The time and effort involved in writing a check for such small amounts cannot be justified. Consequently, most businesses maintain a **petty cash fund**—*petty* meaning small—which is a small amount of money kept in the office for making small expenditures.

The amount of the petty cash fund depends on the needs of the individual business. It can be $25, $50, $100, or any amount considered necessary.

Establishing the Petty Cash Fund

Petty Cash account an asset account in which the amount of the petty cash fund is recorded

The first step in establishing a petty cash fund is to estimate the amount of cash needed in the fund. Then, a check for this amount is written payable to Petty Cash. The check is then cashed, and the money is placed in a box, a drawer, or a safe to be used for the fund. The check is recorded in the journal by debiting the **Petty Cash account** (an asset) and crediting the Cash account.

For example, Cathy Nash is a financial planner. On July 2, 20XX, she wrote a check for $75 to establish a petty cash fund. Cathy recorded this transaction as follows:

	General Journal			Page 6	
Date	Account Title	P.R.	Debit	Credit	
20XX					
Jul. 2	Petty Cash		75 00		1
	Cash			75 00	2
	Established petty cash fund.				3

+ asset → 1
− asset → 2

Making Payments from the Petty Cash Fund

To maintain control over the petty cash fund, the disbursing of money from the fund is usually restricted to one person, the **petty cashier**. The petty cashier can be a bookkeeper, a secretary, an office manager, or anyone else who is properly designated.

When a petty cash payment is made, the petty cashier prepares a petty cash voucher. The **petty cash voucher** shows the details of the payment and serves as proof that a payment was made from the fund. A petty cash voucher is shown in Figure 6-3.

Figure 6-3

Petty Cash Voucher

Petty Cash Voucher

No. _2_   Date _July 5, 20XX_

Paid to: _U.S. Postal Service_

Purpose: _Postage due_   Amount

Account charged: _Postage Expense_   1 | 27

Payment received by:

Bill Winner   Approved by: _C.N._

A properly approved voucher is the petty cashier's authority to make payment out of the fund. The petty cashier should ask the person receiving payment to sign the petty cash voucher. If there is a receipt (as in the case of a retail purchase), it should be attached to the voucher.

Maintaining the Petty Cash Payments Record

Some firms prefer to record all petty cash payments on a single sheet called the **petty cash payments record**. A petty cash payments record is not a journal. Instead, it is an auxiliary record used as a basis for making a journal entry. An **auxiliary record** is a form that is not essential but is helpful in maintaining records that are essential. At some point in time, usually at the end of the month, the petty cash payments record is summarized, and the total is entered in the journal.

Cathy made the following expenditures from her petty cash fund during July 20XX. These expenditures are recorded in the petty cash payments record shown in Figure 6-4 on the next page.

20XX

Jul. 3 Issued Voucher 1 for small office supply items, $15.

5 Issued Voucher 2 for postage due on package received, $1.27.

7 Issued Voucher 3 for postage stamps, $3.

9 Issued Voucher 4 for the purchase of a first-aid package, $8.

12 Issued Voucher 5 for a personal cash withdrawal, $10.

Figure 6-4
Petty Cash Payments Record

Petty Cash Payments for Month of July, 20XX — **Page 1**

	Day	Description	Vou. No.	Total Amount	Distribution of Charges: Office Supplies Exp.	Miscellaneous Expense	Postage Expense	Other Accounts	Amount	
1	2	Established Fund	✓							1
2	3	Office Supplies	1	15 00	15 00					2
3	5	Postage Due	2	1 27			1 27			3
4	7	Stamps	3	3 00			3 00			4
5	9	First-Aid Package	4	8 00		8 00				5
6	12	Owner Withdrawal	5	10 00				Cathy Nash, Drawing	10 00	6
7	18	Stamps	6	6 00			6 00			7
8	25	Advertisement in School Annual	7	25 00				Advertising Expense	25 00	8
9	30	Postage Due	8	57			57			9
10				68 84	15 00	8 00	10 84		35 00	10
11										11
12	31	Balance in Fund $ 6.16								12
13		Replenish Fund 68.84								13
14		Total in Fund $75.00								14

July 18 Issued Voucher 6 for postage stamps, $6.
    25 Issued Voucher 7 for the purchase of a one-quarter page advertisement in a local high school annual, $25.
    30 Issued Voucher 8 for postage due on package received, $0.57.

The petty cash payments record shows that the fund was established on July 2, 20XX. The words *Established Fund* and the amount *$75* are written in the Description column. The formal journal entry to record the establishment of the fund was illustrated on page 224.

All payments made from the petty cash fund are recorded in the Total Amount column. The amount of each payment is then extended to a special column at the right, which identifies the specific type of expense that was paid. Special columns are provided for the expenses most often paid out of petty cash. Cathy has provided special columns for Office Supplies Expense, Miscellaneous Expense, and Postage Expense. When a transaction occurs that affects an account for which no special column is provided, the title of the account affected is written in the Other Accounts column, and the amount of the payment is entered in the Amount column.

Replenishing the Petty Cash Fund

To replenish the petty cash fund means to put back into the fund the amount that has been paid out of the fund. The petty cash fund is usually replenished at the end of the month. However, it can be replenished any time the fund begins to run low.

To replenish the fund, compare the amount left in the fund with the original amount of the fund. For example, if the original amount of the fund was $50, and there is $3 in the fund at the end of the month, you must put $47 into the fund to bring it back up to its original balance of $50.

The journal entry to record replenishing the petty cash fund involves a debit to *each item* listed in the petty cash payments record and a credit to the Cash account. To illustrate, refer again to Cathy's petty cash payments record in Figure 6-4. During July, Cathy paid the following items out of petty cash:

Expense	Amount
Office Supplies Expense	$15.00
Miscellaneous Expense	8.00
Postage Expense	10.84
Cathy Nash, Drawing	10.00
Advertising Expense	25.00
Total	$68.84

Since $68.84 was paid out of the fund during July, it is necessary to put this amount back into the fund. The entry to record replenishment of the fund is shown in the general journal on page 228.

Let us stress that the journal entry to record the replenishment of the petty cash fund involves a debit to each item listed in the petty cash payments record and a credit to Cash. The petty cash fund is a continuous or revolving fund that when depleted is brought back up to its original balance. Thus, the Petty Cash account itself *is not debited* when the fund is replenished. The Petty

General Journal — Page 1

	Date		Account Title	P.R.	Debit	Credit	
	20XX						
+ expense → 1	Jul.	31	Office Supplies Expense		15 00		1
+ expense → 2			Miscellaneous Expense		8 00		2
+ expense → 3			Postage Expense		10 84		3
+ drawing → 4			Cathy Nash, Drawing		10 00		4
+ expense → 5			Advertising Expense		25 00		5
– asset → 6			Cash			68 84	6
7			Replenished petty cash fund.				7
8							8

Cash account is debited *only* when the fund is being established or when the amount in the fund is increased. The Petty Cash account is credited *only* when the amount of the fund is decreased or eliminated completely.

Review Quiz 6-2

On January 2, 20XX, Nancy Herbert established a petty cash fund in the amount of $75. During January, she made the following payments from the fund: office supplies, $10; postage stamps, $18; window cleaning (Miscellaneous Expense), $35; and postage due on package received, $1.25.

1. In general journal form, record the establishment of the fund on January 2.
2. In general journal form, record the replenishment of the fund on January 31.

Check your answers on page 259.

Summing Up

> The Petty Cash account is not debited when the fund is replenished. The Petty Cash account is debited only when the fund is established or when the original amount in the fund is increased. The Petty Cash account is credited only when the amount in the fund is decreased or when the fund is eliminated.

Learning Objective

7 Record the establishment of a change fund.

change fund an amount of money that is maintained in the cash register for making change for cash customers; recorded in the Change Fund account

Change Fund account an asset account in which the amount of the change fund is recorded

The Change Fund Account

Businesses that have many cash transactions usually establish a **change fund**, which is an amount of money that is placed in the cash register drawer and is used to make change for customers who pay in cash. To establish a change fund, two factors must be considered: (1) the amount of money that needs to be in the fund and (2) the various denominations of bills and coins that are needed.

The establishment of a change fund is recorded by debiting the **Change Fund account** (an asset) and crediting the Cash account. To illustrate, we will use a business other than the one belonging to Cathy Nash, because Cathy is a financial planner and does not have many cash transactions. Let's assume that on March 23, 20X1, Don Hefner, owner of The Snack Shop, decides to put $125 in a change fund. Don's entry to record the change fund is as follows.

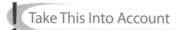

	20X1				
+ asset → 1	Mar.	23	Change Fund	1 2 5 00		1
– asset → 2			Cash		1 2 5 00	2
3			Established a change fund.			3

At the close of business each day, Don will take $125 (in the appropriate denominations) out of the cash register and put it in a safe place so that it can be put back in the register the next morning. The remaining cash is then deposited in the bank.

> **Take This Into Account**
>
> The Change Fund account, like the Petty Cash account, is debited only once—when the fund is established. It is left at the initial amount unless the amount in the fund is increased or decreased.

Let's now look at how to record errors that are made when making change to customers.

The Cash Short and Over Account

Learning Objective

8 Record cash shortages and overages.

cash shortage an amount of cash in the cash register that is less than the amount indicated by the cash sales; recorded in the Cash Short and Over account

cash overage an amount of cash in the cash register that is more than the amount indicated by the cash sales; recorded in the Cash Short and Over account

Cash Short and Over account an account used to bring the Cash account into agreement with the actual amount of cash on hand and can be used by businesses that have many cash transactions and thus often have small amounts of cash over or under what the cash register shows

In many businesses, such as grocery stores and drugstores, cash is exchanged constantly. In such situations, it is hard to avoid errors in receiving cash from customers and making change to customers. Thus, at the end of a business day, it is not uncommon for the amount of cash in the cash register to differ from the cash sales that were rung up on the register. When this happens, there is a cash shortage or a cash overage, either of which should be investigated—and corrected if possible. A **cash shortage** results when the amount of cash in the cash register that is less than the amount of cash sales rung up on the register. A **cash overage** results when the amount of cash in the cash register is more than the cash sales rung up on the register.

If the source of the shortage or overage cannot be determined, the **Cash Short and Over account** can be used to bring the cash on hand into agreement with the cash sales. The Cash Short and Over account is used to record *both* shortages and overages. (The Cash Short and Over account can also be used to record shortages and overages in the petty cash fund.) To illustrate, let's look at two different situations. In the first, which we will call Situation A, sales for the day totaled $600. After the change fund was removed, however, there was only $598 in the cash register—a $2 shortage. In the second situation, Situation B, sales for the day totaled $769. But after the change fund was removed, the amount of cash in the register totaled $774—a $5 overage. Journal entries to record these situations follow.

Situation A: Recording a $2.00 Shortage

+ asset →	1	X	X	Cash	5 9 8 00		1
no normal balance →	2			Cash Short and Over	2 00		2
+ revenue →	3			Sales Revenue		6 0 0 00	3
	4			To record sales revenue and			4
	5			a cash shortage.			5

Situation B: Recording a $5.00 Overage

+ asset →	1	X	X	Cash	7 7 4 00		1
+ revenue →	2			Sales Revenue		7 6 9 00	2
no normal balance →	3			Cash Short and Over		5 00	3
	4			To record sales revenue and			4
	5			a cash overage.			5

Key Point ⊘

Cash Short and Over

Debit	Credit
Cash shortage	Cash overage

In Situation A, the Cash Short and Over account is *debited* for the amount of the shortage. In Situation B, the Cash Short and Over account is *credited* for the amount of the overage. After the journal entries are posted, the Cash Short and Over account appears as follows.

Account Cash Short and Over						Account No.	530
Date	Item	P.R.	Debit	Credit	Balance Debit	Balance Credit	
X X		GJ3	2 00		2 00		
X		GJ3		5 00		3 00	

Since the cash overage of $5 (the credit side) exceeded the cash shortage of $2 (the debit side), there is a net overage of $3 (a credit balance in the account). Shortages and overages tend to balance each other out over the course of the accounting period. Therefore, there should only be a small balance in the Cash Short and Over account at the end of the period. How you account for any end-of-period balance in the Cash Short and Over account depends on whether that balance is a debit or a credit. Should the account end up with a debit balance (net shortage), it is reported on the income statement as a miscellaneous expense. On the other hand, an end-of-period credit balance (net overage) is reported on the income statement as miscellaneous income. In either case, the balance of the Cash Short and Over account is closed to Income Summary during the closing process.

Summing Up

The Cash Short and Over account does not have a normal balance, because it is a summarizing account. At the end of the month, if it has a debit balance, it is considered an expense; if it has a credit balance, it is considered revenue.

At the close of business on Tuesday, John Olds, owner of Olds' Great Subs, totaled and cleared his cash register. According to the register, his total sales for the day amounted to $957. However, when he counted the amount of money in the register and subtracted his $100 change fund, he found only $954. Record the sales revenue and the cash shortage in general journal form.

Check your answer on page 259.

Bank Checking Accounts

Earlier in the chapter, we stressed that a very important feature of any good system of internal control is the efficient management of cash. For a business of any size, all cash received during operating hours should be deposited in a bank account at the end of the day. And all payments made by the business—except those made out of petty cash—should be made by check.

Offering convenience as well as protection, the use of a bank checking account has become a near universal business practice. A **bank checking account** holds deposited amounts of cash that the bank must pay at the written order of the depositor. Cash that is deposited in a bank is physically protected. And since only authorized persons can write checks, control over cash payments is also provided.

For identification purposes, banks are assigned numbers by the American Bankers Association. An **American Bankers Association (ABA) transit number** is a number that identifies the bank, the area in which the bank is located, and other information. The ABA number appears on bank documents such as checks and deposit slips which we will discuss shortly. For instance, the ABA number of Citizens Bank & Trust Company is $\frac{64\text{-}60}{601}$. This number contains three pieces of information:

1. 64 is the number assigned to all banks located in the Atlanta, Georgia, area.
2. 60 is the number specifically assigned to Citizens Bank & Trust Company.
3. 601 is a number used for check routing. This number aids the banking system in routing checks first to the area in which a bank is located and then to the specific bank on which the check is drawn.

You are probably familiar with how to open a checking account, make deposits, and write checks. In this section, we will discuss the importance of signature cards, the use of deposit slips and endorsements, and the process of writing checks, and we will also explain the value of electronic funds transfers.

The Signature Card

A checking account is opened by filling out a short application with the bank, making a deposit, and signing a signature card. A **signature card** lists personal information and contains the signature of the person or persons who are authorized to write checks on the account. The bank keeps the signature card on file as an aid in identifying possible forgeries. When Cathy Nash opened a checking account with Citizens Bank & Trust Company, she signed

bank checking account an amount of cash on deposit with a bank that the bank must pay at the written order of the depositor

American Bankers Association (ABA) transit number a number printed on checks and deposit slips that identifies the bank and the area in which the bank is located as well as other information

signature card a form kept by a bank documenting personal information and the signature of the person(s) authorized to write checks on a bank account the signature card. Later, she authorized her assistant, Akiah Smith, to write checks as well. Therefore, Akiah also signed the card. The signature card showing both signatures is illustrated in Figure 6-5.

Date _5-1-20XX_   Account Number _12 17 860_

Depositor _Cathy Nash_

Citizens Bank & Trust Company will recognize payment of funds, or other business on this account, only as authorized by the signatures below.

Signature _Cathy Nash_

Signature _Akiah Smith_

deposit slip a form that is prepared when coin, currency, or checks are deposited in a bank account indicating the depositor's name and account number and summarizes the amount deposited; also referred to as a deposit ticket

depositor the business or person under whose name a checking account is opened

Making Deposits

A **deposit slip** or *deposit ticket* is prepared when coin, currency, or checks are deposited in a bank account; it indicates the name of the **depositor**, which is the person or business who opened the account, and the account number, and summarizes the amount deposited. The deposit slip prepared by Cathy on July 15, 20XX, is shown in Figure 6-6.

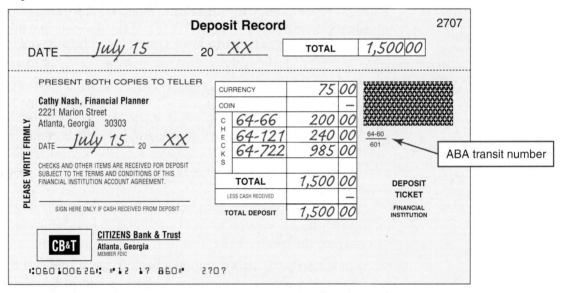

The name, address, and account number of the depositor are usually preprinted on the deposit slip. When making a deposit, the depositor enters both coin and currency on the lines provided. Checks being deposited should also be listed on the lines provided. Each check should be listed according to its ABA transit number, located in the upper right corners of checks.

endorsement a signature or stamp on the back of a check that transfers ownership of the check to the bank or to another person

Endorsements

Checks and money orders must be endorsed before a bank will accept them for deposit. An **endorsement** is a signature or stamp on the back of the check that transfers ownership of the check to the bank (or to another business or to

Figure 6-7
Types of Check
Endorsements

Cathy Nash	Pay to the order of Robert Sterling Cathy Nash	For Deposit Only Cathy Nash
(a) blank endorsement	(b) full endorsement	(c) restrictive endorsement

an individual) and authorizes payment of the check. There are three common forms of endorsement: (1) the blank endorsement, (2) the full endorsement, and (3) the restrictive endorsement.

The Blank Endorsement

An endorsement consisting only of the depositor's name signed or stamped on the back of a check is called a **blank endorsement**. Figure 6.7(a) shows an example of this type of endorsement. A lost or stolen check with this type of endorsement can be cashed by anyone who has possession of it. Therefore, a blank endorsement should be used only when a depositor is in a bank ready to cash the check or make a deposit.

The Full Endorsement

A **full endorsement**, shown in Figure 6.7(b), specifies the party to whom a check is being transferred. The phrase *Pay to the order of* is written before the name of the person (or business) to whom the check is being transferred. A full endorsement is safer than a blank endorsement because only the person or business named in the endorsement can transfer the check to someone else.

The Restrictive Endorsement

A **restrictive endorsement**, shown in Figure 6.7(c), specifies the purpose for which the money is to be used. For example, a check endorsed *For Deposit Only* cannot be cashed; it can only be deposited. The restrictive endorsement is popular among businesses because of the protection provided by the restriction of funds.

Writing Checks

A **check** is a written order directing a bank to pay a specified sum of money to a designated person or business. A check is said to be drawn against the account of the person who wrote it. Thus, the person (or business) who writes a check is called the **drawer**. The bank on which a check is drawn is called the **drawee**. The person (or business) to whom a check is made payable is called the **payee**.

A complete description of all checks written should be made in a **checkbook**, which is the depositor's record of the checking account. A checkbook is a bound book of checks, and each check has a related **check stub**. Checks are perforated for easy removal, and the stub remains in the checkbook as a permanent record of the check.

Two checks written by Cathy during June 20XX are shown in Figure 6-8. Notice that the check number appears on both the check and the stub. Both

blank endorsement an endorsement consisting only of a depositor's signature allowing anyone who possesses a check to cash it

full endorsement an endorsement using the phrase "Pay to the order of," followed by the name of the business or person to whom the check is being transferred, thus allowing only the specified business or person to cash the check

restrictive endorsement an endorsement using a phrase "For deposit only," which limits or restricts any further transfer of the check

check a written order directing a bank to pay a specified sum of money to a designated person or business

drawer a person or business who writes a check

drawee the bank on which a check is drawn

payee the business or person to whom a check is made payable

checkbook a bound book of checks with stubs; the depositor's record of the checking account

check stub part of a check that remains in the checkbook as a permanent record of the check; often referred to as a stub

Figure 6-8

Checks and Stubs

Check 132 stub:

	BALANCE BROUGHT FORWARD		
NO. 132	3,148	00	
June 29, 20XX			
PAY TO Georgia Power Co.			
FOR Utilities Expense			
DEPOSIT		—	
DEPOSIT		—	
BALANCE	3,148	00	
AMOUNT THIS CHECK	380	00	
BALANCE	2,768	00	

Check 132:

Cathy Nash, Financial Planner
2221 Marion Street
Atlanta, Georgia 30303

June 29 20 XX

64-60 / 601

PAY TO THE ORDER OF Georgia Power Company $ 380.00

Three hundred eighty and no/100 —————— DOLLARS

CB&T CITIZENS Bank & Trust
Atlanta, Georgia
MEMBER FDIC

Utilities Expense   Cathy Nash

⑆000133⑆ ⑆060100626⑆ 12 17 860

ABA transit number

Check 133 stub:

NO. 133	2,768	00	
June 30, 20XX			
PAY TO Roger Hommer			
FOR Salaries Expense			
DEPOSIT			
DEPOSIT June 30, 20XX	750	00	
BALANCE	3,518	00	
AMOUNT THIS CHECK	325	00	
BALANCE	3,193	00	

Check 133:

Cathy Nash, Financial Planner
2221 Marion Street
Atlanta, Georgia 30303

June 30 20 XX

64-60 / 601

PAY TO THE ORDER OF Roger Hommer $ 325.00

Three hundred twenty-five and no/100 —————— DOLLARS

CB&T CITIZENS Bank & Trust
Atlanta, Georgia
MEMBER FDIC

Salaries Expense   Cathy Nash

⑆000134⑆ ⑆060100626⑆ 12 17 860

the stub and the check also contain the date of the check, the amount of the check, the party to whom the check was written (the payee), and the purpose of the expenditure. Since the check stub often serves as a source document for a journal entry, all information on the stub should be filled in *before* the check is written. Otherwise, the record of the check could be overlooked if one is working under pressure or in a hurry.

Look at how the amount of a check is written. It is written first in figures. The amount is then restated in words on the line below the name of the payee. The amount of cents is shown as a fraction of a dollar. Thus, 20 cents is written as 20/100. If there are no cents, *00/100* or *no/100* is written. After the amount of the check has been written out in words, a line is drawn to fill in any empty space remaining—to avoid the possibility of the amount being altered.

Some businesses prepare checks mechanically on small machines called checkwriters (or check protectors). Checkwriters are used to write and perforate the amount of a check, making it impossible to alter the dollar amount for which the check is written. Computer-generated checks are also commonly used.

A properly filled-in check stub provides valuable information about a transaction and can serve as a source document to record the transaction.

Transferring Funds Electronically

electronic funds transfer (EFT) the movement of cash by electronic communication rather than by paper documents (money, checks, money orders, etc.)

An increasingly popular way to handle a cash transaction is through an **electronic funds transfer (EFT)**, which is the movement of cash by electronic communication. Electronic transfers offer safety, convenience, reliability, and cost savings in both the receipt and payment of cash.

Cash Received by Electronic Funds Transfer

Today, many businesses encourage customers to pay bills by EFTs. For example, members of a health club may authorize EFTs from their checking accounts to pay monthly membership dues. When this happens, the health club has members sign a form that is sent to the member's bank authorizing the monthly transfers of money from the member's bank account directly into the club's bank account. Each month, the club electronically notifies the member's bank of the amount of the transfer and the date it should take place.

Companies encourage automatic electronic transfers by customers for several reasons.

- EFTs are less costly than receiving payment by mail or face-to-face because money goes directly into the company's bank account and thus eliminates the need for employees to process and handle cash receipts.
- EFTs eliminate the possibility of theft because no one physically handles the cash.
- EFTs are more timely and reliable. Businesses do not have to worry about a customer forgetting to make a payment, as the payment is automatic.

Cash Paid by Electronic Funds Transfer

Businesses and individuals also frequently pay cash through EFT systems. A common example is payment of employee wages through EFT. First, employees authorize the direct deposit of their payroll checks into their checking accounts. Then, each pay period, payroll funds are electronically transferred from the company's checking account into the checking accounts of individual employees. The resulting cost savings can be substantial because checks do not have to be prepared and mailed.

Since it is less expensive to pay a bill without having to mail a check, many individuals are also paying mortgage, rent, insurance, utility, cable, and other bills by EFT. With the affordability of computers and increased access to the Internet, this practice is almost certain to increase.

The Bank Statement

bank statement the bank's summary of checking account transactions, usually prepared monthly and mailed to the depositor (or made available online)

Once a month, the bank sends each depositor a **bank statement**, which is a report showing the bank's record of the checking account. The bank statement shows the balance of the account at the beginning of the month, the amount of deposits received by the bank during the month, the checks paid by the bank during the month, the service charge or other bank fees, any

canceled check a check that has been paid by the bank out of the depositor's account

other additions to or subtractions from the account, and the balance of the account at the end of the month. A **canceled check** is a check that has been written against the depositor's account and has been paid by the bank out of the account. For some bank customers, canceled checks are returned along with the corresponding bank statement.

The bank statement received by Cathy Nash on September 3, 20XX, is shown in Figure 6-9.

Figure 6-9
Bank Statement

To: Cathy Nash, Financial Planner
2221 Marion Street
Atlanta, Georgia   30303
Account No. 12 17 860

CB&T

CITIZENS Bank & Trust
Atlanta, Georgia
MEMBER FDIC

CHECKS		DEPOSITS	DATE	BEGINNING BALANCE: $6,200
#168	$ 400		8-01-XX	$5,800
#169	225		8-02-XX	5,575
#170	120		8-05-XX	5,455
#171	80		8-10-XX	5,375
#172	300		8-12-XX	5,075
#174	50	$1,500	8-15-XX	6,525
#175	70		8-16-XX	6,455
#176	80		8-16-XX	6,375
#178	325		8-18-XX	6,050
#179	450		8-23-XX	5,600
#182	25		8-25-XX	5,575
#183	1,825		8-27-XX	3,750
		750	8-29-XX	4,500
#184	150		8-30-XX	4,350
SC	12		8-30-XX	4,338
#185	528		8-30-XX	3,810

ENDING BALANCE: $3,810

Reconciling the Bank Statement

Learning Objective

9 Prepare a bank reconciliation.

The bank statement and the checkbook are both records of a depositor's checking account transactions. However, the balance shown on the bank statement and the balance in the checkbook normally do not agree at the end of the month. This lack of agreement is usually not due to errors but is the result of time lags between the depositor making an entry in the checkbook and the bank making the same entry. Also, the bank often makes deductions from (or additions to) an account that the depositor is unaware of until the statement arrives. Let's look at some common reasons why the bank statement balance may not agree with the checkbook balance:

- *Outstanding checks.* When a depositor writes a check, the check is immediately entered in the checkbook. However, it may take several days before the check reaches the depositor's bank for payment. If the outstanding check a check that was recorded in the checkbook but does not appear on the bank statement because it did not reach the bank's accounting department in time to be included on the statement

deposit in transit a deposit made and appearing in the checkbook but not appearing on the bank statement; also referred to as an outstanding deposit

service charge an account maintenance fee charged by the bank and deducted directly from the depositor's balance; also referred to as a bank fee

NSF (Not Sufficient Funds) check a check drawn against an account in which there are not sufficient funds; also referred to as an uncollectible, or bad, check

bank reconciliation the process of bringing the cash balance reported on the bank statement into agreement with the balance in the depositor's checkbook; also referred to as reconciling the bank statement

check appears in the checkbook but not on the statement, it is referred to as an **outstanding check**.

- *Deposits in transit.* Certain deposits such as deposits made late in the day, night deposits, deposits by mail, and deposits made to automated teller machines (ATMs) may not reach the bank's accounting department in time to be added to the depositor's account when the statement is being prepared. A deposit made (and appearing in the checkbook) but not appearing on the bank statement is called a **deposit in transit**. A deposit in transit is also called an outstanding deposit.

- *Service charges and other bank fees.* In most cases, banks charge a fee for providing checking accounts. The fee, called a **service charge**, is subtracted directly from the depositor's account. The service charge, along with other charges, is shown on the bank statement. Other charges that the bank may make include fees for imprinting checks, fees for collecting money for the depositor, and fees for the use of ATMs.

- *Errors.* It is not uncommon for depositors to make (1) arithmetic errors when making entries in a checkbook and (2) errors due to transpositions and slides. On occasion, the bank will also make errors. Due to the use of electronic processing equipment, however, the bank is less likely to make errors.

- *Bank collections.* As a convenience to customers, some banks collect notes or other securities for the depositor and enter these amounts directly in the depositor's account. Such collections appear on the bank statement but not in the checkbook. Also, some checking accounts pay interest, which is calculated by the bank and entered directly into the depositor's account.

- *NSF (Not Sufficient Funds) checks.* When a check is deposited, it is counted as cash. On occasion, however, some checks that have been deposited turn out to be bad. In a **NSF (Not Sufficient Funds) check**, the issuer of the check does not have sufficient funds in the account to pay the check. The bank will notify the depositor of any bad checks. The depositor must in turn make a deduction from the Cash account and the checkbook.

When the bank statement balance and the checkbook balance do not agree, the two must be brought into agreement. The process of making the bank statement balance agree with the checkbook balance is called **bank reconciliation**, or reconciling the bank statement. The bank statement is reconciled by the following steps:

Step **1** Add the amount of deposits in transit to the bank statement balance.

Step **2** Subtract the amount of outstanding checks from the bank statement balance.

Step **3** Add to the checkbook balance the amount of any interest earned on the account or any collection made by the bank for the depositor.

Step **4** Subtract any charges appearing on the bank statement from the checkbook balance.

After making the necessary adjustments, the adjusted balance of the bank statement should agree with the adjusted balance of the checkbook.

To illustrate the adjustment process, let's look again at Cathy Nash's bank statement in Figure 6-9. According to the statement, Cathy's ending bank balance is $3,810. On the same date, however, Cathy's checkbook balance is $2,940. The two records are reconciled as follows:

Step **1** Cathy compares each deposit recorded in the checkbook with that appearing on the bank statement. She discovers that a deposit of $800, made on August 31, has not reached the bank in time to be entered on the bank statement. Thus, the deposit is outstanding.

Step **2** Cathy arranges her canceled checks in numerical order and compares the amount of each check appearing on the bank statement with the amount recorded on her check stubs. A check mark (✓) is placed by each check that appears on both records. Those checks recorded on stubs that have not been checked off are outstanding. Using this process, Cathy finds that the following checks are outstanding:

Check Number	Amount
173	$1,200
177	212
180	160
181	140

Step **3** Cathy examines the bank statement for charges made against her account. She finds a $12 service charge.

Step **4** By comparing the amounts of the canceled checks with the amounts recorded on the check stubs, Cathy finds that she wrote a check for $150 but recorded it in the checkbook as $120. This caused her checkbook balance to be overstated by $30.

Based on this analysis, Cathy prepared the bank reconciliation statement shown in Figure 6-10. Note that every bank reconciliation begins with two known factors: the balance per bank statement and the balance per checkbook. Our goal is to get the two balances to agree (reconcile). Compare Figure 6-10 to Figure 6-11, which presents an overview of the steps to follow when reconciling a bank statement and a checkbook.

Figure 6-10

Bank Reconciliation Statement

Cathy Nash, Financial Planner Bank Reconciliation Statement August 31, 20XX		
Balance per bank statement		$ 3 8 1 0 00
Add: Deposit in transit		8 0 0 00
		$ 4 6 1 0 00
Deduct: Outstanding checks		
#173	$ 1 2 0 0 00	
#177	2 1 2 00	
#180	1 6 0 00	
#181	1 4 0 00	1 7 1 2 00
Adjusted bank statement balance		$ 2 8 9 8 00
Balance per checkbook		$ 2 9 4 0 00
Deduct:		
Service charge	$ 1 2 00	
Error in checkbook	3 0 00	4 2 00
Adjusted checkbook balance		$ 2 8 9 8 00

Figure 6-11

Steps for Reconciling a Bank Statement and a Checkbook

Bank Statement			Checkbook		
Starting balance		$XXX	Starting balance		$XXX
Step 1 Add					
Deposits in transit	$XXX		Bank collections	$XXX	
Bank errors that understate statement balance	XX	XXX	Interest earned	XXX	
			Recording errors that understate balance	XXX	XXX
Step 2 Deduct					
Outstanding checks	$XXX		Recording errors that overstate balance	$XXX	
Bank errors that overstate statement balance	XXX	XXX	Service charges	XXX	
			Imprinting check charges	XXX	
			NSF checks	XXX	
			Other bank charges	XXX	XXX
Step 3 Determine Adjusted Balances					
Adjusted (reconciled) bank statement balance		$XXX	Adjusted (reconciled) checkbook balance		$XXX

Review Quiz 6-4

Stacy Christenson received her bank statement on October 1, 20XX. According to her statement, Stacy has a bank balance of $922. However, Stacy's checkbook shows a balance of $870. Closer observation revealed the following:

1. A deposit of $40 was in transit.
2. Check #34 for $41 and Check #38 for $56 were outstanding.
3. A service charge of $4 had been made against Stacy's account.
4. Stacy wrote Check #36 for $31; however, she entered only $30 in her checkbook.

Prepare a bank reconciliation statement for Stacy.

Check your answer on page 259.

Updating Cash Records

All the checkbook adjustments appearing on the bank reconciliation statement should be entered in the checkbook to bring the checkbook balance into agreement with the cash in the bank. Cathy's bank reconciliation statement shows two checkbook adjustments: (1) a $12 deduction for a bank service charge and (2) a $30 deduction due to incorrectly recording a $150 check as $120. The service charge should be entered in the checkbook as a deduction on the next unused check stub. The words *August S.C.* are written on the check stub to identify the amount. The $30 error adjustment should also be entered in the checkbook as a deduction because the checkbook balance is overstated due to recording only $120 for a check that was written for $150.

A journal entry is needed for the $12 service charge because it is a cash payment, even though no check was written. (It was taken directly from the account by the bank.) No journal entry is needed for the $30 error adjustment, because the effect of the error was confined solely to the checkbook. (The check had been written for the correct amount and journalized correctly but

Key Point ▶

Journal entries are needed for checkbook adjustments appearing on the bank reconciliation statement.

entered incorrectly on the check stub.) The entry to record the service charge is journalized as follows:

	20XX										
+ expense → 1	Aug.	31	Miscellaneous Expense			1 2 00					1
− asset → 2			Cash						1 2 00		2
3			Recorded service charge for								3
4			the month.								4

Note that an account entitled Bank Service Charge could have been used instead of the Miscellaneous Expense account.

Journal entries *are not* needed for adjustments to the bank statement balance because these amounts relate to the bank's records. However, if the bank has made an error, the bank's accounting department should be notified so that the necessary corrections can be made.

Completing a More Detailed Bank Reconciliation

We were able to reconcile Cathy's bank statement by following the steps that are somewhat standard in the reconciliation process. Let's take a moment to look at an example that is a little more involved. The accountant for McGreggor Company assembled the following data as of April 30, 20X1:

1. Bank statement balance, $12,900.
2. Checkbook balance, $8,130.
3. Deposit in transit, $950.
4. Checks outstanding (total), $3,160.
5. Bank had charged a $75 check written by McGreggor Lawn Service to the account of McGreggor Company.
6. Bank collected a $3,000 note for McGreggor, charging a $15 collection fee.
7. A $300 check that McGreggor had deposited was returned by the bank because it is a bad (NSF) check.
8. Bill McGreggor made a personal withdrawal at an ATM, $50.

Based on this data, we can prepare McGreggor's bank reconciliation as shown in Figure 6-12.

Figure 6-12

Bank Reconciliation Statement

McGreggor Company Bank Reconciliation Statement April 30, 20X1			
Balance per bank statement			$12 9 0 0 00
Add: Deposit in transit	$ 9 5 0 00		
Error made by bank	7 5 00	1 0 2 5 00	
		$13 9 2 5 00	
Deduct: Outstanding checks		3 1 6 0 00	
Adjusted bank statement balance		$10 7 6 5 00	
Balance per checkbook		$ 8 1 3 0 00	
Add: Note collected		3 0 0 0 00	
		$11 1 3 0 00	
Deduct:			
Collection fee	$ 1 5 00		
NSF check	3 0 0 00		
Cash withdrawal	5 0 00	3 6 5 00	
Adjusted checkbook balance		$10 7 6 5 00	

Remember that when an adjustment is made *to the checkbook balance* in the reconciliation process, a journal entry is needed. The following entries are thus needed to update McGreggor's books. Notice that the $300 NSF check is debited to the Accounts Receivable account. This is because the amount is still owed by the customer, even though the check bounced. The $300 will remain in Accounts Receivable until it is collected, at which time it will be debited to Cash and credited to Accounts Receivable.

		20X1					
+ asset →	1	Apr.	30	Cash	3 0 0 0 00		1
– asset →	2			Notes Receivable		3 0 0 0 00	2
	3			Note collected by bank.			3
	4						4
+ expense →	5		30	Miscellaneous Expense	1 5 00		5
– asset →	6			Cash		1 5 00	6
	7			Bank collection fee.			7
	8						8
+ asset →	9		30	Accounts Receivable	3 0 0 00		9
– asset →	10			Cash		3 0 0 00	10
	11			NSF check returned by bank.			11
	12						12
+ drawing →	13		30	Bill McGreggor, Drawing	5 0 00		13
– asset →	14			Cash		5 0 00	14
	15			Owner withdrew cash using ATM.			15

Church Fraud and Tax Evasion

Cletus William was hired by First Church to handle all accounting for the congregation. He was authorized to write and approve all checks, except his own paycheck. After a church member noticed a theft of $60,000, Charles Counter, another church member, was hired to perform an internal audit on the books.

Counter found a number of internal control problems. He cited a lack of accounting and internal control knowledge and a quickness to trust without questioning on the part of the church leadership.

William was accused of recording salary advances in the books without reimbursing the church. In violation of good internal control, he wrote his own paychecks. Further, he wrote extra paychecks and, to avoid suspicion, had them approved by different people. He wrote checks for amounts greater than the actual expenses. In total, the fraud amounted to $61,238.

As if that weren't enough, he understated the church payroll tax records, so the money he received went untaxed. Following Counter's research of the fraud, William owed over $9,000 in taxes to the Internal Revenue Service.

Each of these issues could have been resolved long before William embezzled over $60,000 if the very simple accounting procedure of separation of duties had been followed. Neither a nonprofit organization or any other organization should ever trust one person to handle all cash receipts without proper checks and balances.

Source: J. E. McEldowney, T. L. Barton, and David Ray, "Look Out for Cletus William," *CPA Journal,* Vol. 63, No. 12 (1993) 44–47 .

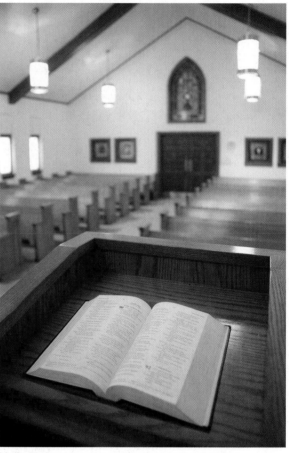
Unlimited trust can result in temptation that is irresistible.

For Discussion
1. Why do you believe that churches are vulnerable to accounting fraud?
2. What internal controls could have prevented this fraud from taking place?
3. What lessons can be learned from this case?

Joining the Pieces

The Bank Reconciliation Procedure

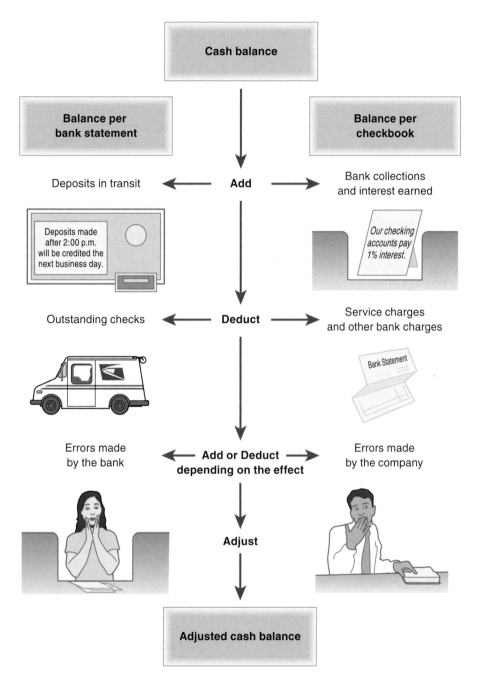

Summary  Interactive Summary in English and Spanish

1 Define *internal control* and identify and describe its objectives.

Internal control refers to the methods and procedures a business uses to internally protect its assets. The objectives of a good system of internal control include the following:

- *Safeguard assets.* All companies must protect their assets from theft, loss, and misuse. The safeguards a company uses depend on the size of the business and the nature of its operations.
- *Ensure the accuracy and reliability of accounting records.* Accurate accounting records are necessary to determine the amount of net income; accurately state the amount of assets, liabilities, and owner's equity; file correct tax forms; and provide managers with reliable information needed to make valid decisions.
- *Promote operational efficiency.* Inefficiency hurts a company's profits, hinders growth, and wastes resources. If a company reduces waste and increases efficiency, the company increases profits.
- *Ensure compliance with laws and regulations.* Good records are necessary to comply with laws and regulations.

2 Define *cash* as it is used in accounting.

In a narrow sense, cash refers to the amount of currency and coins owned by a business or individual. However, items such as traveler's checks, money orders, and checks made payable to the business are also included in cash.

3 Describe internal control procedures related to cash.

Internal control describes the procedures and measures used by a business to protect its assets from theft, loss, and misuse. Typical measures taken to protect and control cash include the following:

- Cashiers, clerks, and others who actually handle cash (i.e., by operating cash registers, maintaining cash drawers, receiving payments from customers, etc.) should not make journal entries to record the receipt and payment of cash.
- All cash receipts should be deposited daily in a bank account.
- Only a small amount of cash (called a **petty cash fund**) should be kept on hand.
- All cash payments, except for petty cash, should be made by check.
- Checks should be prenumbered so that it is easy to see what checks have been written and when.
- Only a few properly designated persons should be involved in the receipt, payment, and recording of cash.
- Receipt and payment of cash should be recorded efficiently and accurately.

4 Describe the purpose of and need for a petty cash fund.

To aid in the control of cash, most businesses use a **bank checking account**. Making all payments by check, however, would mean that someone authorized to write checks must always be available. This is not always practical. Nor is it practical to write checks for very small amounts. Each working day, business firms are confronted with transactions that involve the immediate payment of cash, such as postage due on packages, overnight deliveries, coffee and doughnuts, a birthday card for a customer, small items of office supply, and the like. Making these payments by check would be costly and time-consuming. Consequently, an office fund known as the petty cash fund (*petty* means small) is usually maintained for making small expenditures.

5 Record the establishment of a petty cash fund.

The first step in establishing a petty cash fund is to estimate how much cash is needed in the fund. An entry is then made debiting the **Petty Cash account** and crediting the Cash account. For example, on March 2, 201X, Robert Herndon, owner of Herndon's Pawn Shop, estimated that his business needed $75 in a petty cash fund. Robert's entry to record the establishment of the fund is shown in general journal form as follows:

		201X				
+ asset →	1	Mar.	2	Petty Cash	7 5 00	1
– asset →	2			Cash	7 5 00	2
	3			Established petty cash fund.		3

6 Record the replenishment of a petty cash fund.

On March 31, 20X1, the following expenses had been paid from the petty cash fund of Herndon's Pawn Shop:

Expense	Amount
Postage Expense	$10.00
Office Supplies Expense	15.00
Window Cleaning (Miscellaneous Expense)	25.00
Contributions Expense	12.50
Total	$62.50

Since $62.50 has been paid out of the fund, this amount must be placed back in the fund to bring it back to its balance on March 2. The entry to record the replenishment of the fund is shown next in general journal form.

		201X				
+ expense →	1	Mar.	31	Postage Expense	1 0 00	1
+ expense →	2			Office Supplies Expense	1 5 00	2
+ expense →	3			Miscellaneous Expense	2 5 00	3
+ expense →	4			Contributions Expense	1 2 50	4
– cash →	5			Cash	6 2 50	5
	6			Replenished petty cash fund.		6

7 Record the establishment of a change fund.

Businesses that have frequent cash transactions usually establish a **change fund** in order to make change for customers. The change fund is established by first determining how much is needed in the fund and then deciding what denominations of currency and coin are needed. A journal entry is then made debiting the **Change Fund account** (an asset) and crediting the Cash account. For example, Shelley Ledbetter is getting ready to open a gift shop. On July 2, 20X2, Shelley established a change fund in the amount of $100. Her general journal entry to record the fund is shown as follows:

		20X2				
+ asset →	1	Jul.	2	Change Fund	1 0 0 00	1
– asset →	2			Cash	1 0 0 00	2
	3			Established a change fund.		3

8 Record cash shortages and overages.

Example 1. A **cash shortage**: A cash register reading indicated that sales for the day totaled $600. However, there was only $596 cash in the register after the change fund was removed. The entry to record the sales revenue and the $4 cash shortage is shown below in general journal form.

+ asset →	1	X	X	Cash		5 9 6 00		1
no normal balance →	2			Cash Short and Over		4 00		2
+ revenue →	3			Sales Revenue			6 0 0 00	3
	4			Recorded sales revenue and				4
	5			a cash shortage.				5

The shortage is considered an expense.

Example 2. A **cash overage**: A cash register reading indicated that sales for the day totaled $525. However, the cash in the register totaled $528 after the change fund was removed. The entry to record the sales revenue and the $3 overage is shown below in general journal form.

+ asset →	1	X	X	Cash		5 2 8 00		1
+ revenue →	2			Sales Revenue			5 2 5 00	2
no normal balance →	3			Cash Short and Over			3 00	3
	4			Recorded sales revenue and				4
	5			a cash overage.				5

The overage is considered a revenue.

9 Prepare a bank reconciliation.

Regularly, usually once a month, the bank will send each **depositor** a **bank statement**, which is a copy of the bank's record of the checking account. Although the bank statement and the **checkbook** are both records of the depositor's account transactions, their balances rarely agree at the time the statement is prepared. This difference is usually due to time lags between the same entry being recorded in both records. A **bank reconciliation** is needed when the bank statement and the checkbook do not agree. Their balances must be reconciled (brought into agreement). For example, Ron Neely is a plumbing contractor. His October bank statement shows a balance of $1,600. However, Ron's checkbook shows a balance of $1,301. Further investigation revealed the following:

1. The bank had not yet recorded an October 31 deposit, $400.
2. The following list shows each **outstanding check**:

Check Number	Amount
143	$200
151	30
153	120

3. The bank had collected a note receivable of $300 plus interest of $35 and had credited Ron's account.
4. A bank service charge of $13 was made against Ron's account.
5. Ron had written a check for $225 but had entered $252 in his checkbook.

Ron's bank reconciliation is shown on the next page.

Ron Neely Bank Reconciliation Statement October 31, 20XX					
Balance per bank statement				$ 1 6 0 0 00	
Add: Deposit in transit				4 0 0 00	
				$ 2 0 0 0 00	
Deduct: Outstanding checks					
#143	$ 2 0 0 00				
#151	3 0 00				
#153	1 2 0 00		3 5 0 00		
Adjusted bank statement balance				$ 1 6 5 0 00	
Balance per checkbook				$ 1 3 0 1 00	
Add: Note and interest collected	$ 3 3 5 00				
Error in checkbook	2 7 00		3 6 2 00		
				1 6 6 3 00	
Deduct: Service charge				1 3 00	
Adjusted checkbook balance				$ 1 6 5 0 00	

Terms and Concepts Review

- Key Terms and Definitions in English and Spanish
- Additional Quiz Questions

Key Terms

American Bankers Association (ABA) transit number, 231
auxiliary record, 225
bank checking account, 231
bank reconciliation, 237
bank statement, 235
blank endorsement, 233
canceled check, 236
cash overage, 229
Cash Short and Over account, 229
cash shortage, 229
change fund, 228
Change Fund account, 228
check, 233
check stub, 233
checkbook, 233
deposit in transit, 237
deposit slip, 232
depositor, 232
drawee, 233

drawer, 233
electronic funds transfer (EFT), 235
endorsement, 232
full endorsement, 233
internal control, 221
NSF (Not Sufficient Funds) check, 237
outstanding check, 237
payee, 233
Petty Cash account, 224
petty cash fund, 224
petty cash payments record, 225
petty cash voucher, 225
petty cashier, 225
Public Company Accounting Oversight Board (PCAOB), 219
to replenish the petty cash fund, 227
restrictive endorsement, 233
service charge, 237
signature card, 231

Concepts Review

1. What is internal control, and why is it important to a business?
2. Why are special controls necessary to protect cash?
3. Identify three methods of internal control for cash that you think are important.
4. Why should cash transactions be handled by more than one person?

5. Cash in a petty cash fund is not subjected to the same measures of control as cash in a bank account. How is this practice justified?
6. What is meant by *establishing* a petty cash fund?
7. What information should be shown on a petty cash voucher?
8. Is a petty cash payments record a type of journal? Explain your answer.
9. What is meant by an *auxiliary* record?
10. How often is a petty cash fund replenished?
11. What is a change fund?
12. What is the purpose of the Cash Short and Over account?
13. What is the normal balance of the Cash Short and Over account? Explain your answer.
14. How does a bank checking account provide both physical and internal protection of cash?
15. Why do banks require a new depositor to fill out a signature card?
16. What information is shown on the bank statement?
17. The bank statement and the checkbook are both records of a depositor's checking account transactions. Why, then, do they rarely agree at the end of the month?
18. What is an electronic funds transfer (EFT), and why does it provide cost savings?

Skills Review

Quick Practice

Learning Objective 5

Check Figure
April 1 increase = $300

Quick Practice 6-1

Objective: To record the establishment and increase in a petty cash fund

On February 1, 20X3, Samantha Hopf, owner of Cascade Accounting Services, established a petty cash fund in the amount of $100. On April 1, Samantha increased the fund to $400.

Directions: Record these transactions in a general journal.

Learning Objective 6

Check Figure
Credit to the Cash
account = $119

Quick Practice 6-2

Objective: To record replenishment of a petty cash fund

During November 20X3, Bob Daoust paid the following expenses from his petty cash fund:

Postage Expense	$39.00
Supplies Expense	
Bob Daoust, Drawing	50.00

Directions: In general journal form, record the replenishment of the fund on November 30.

Learning Objectives 5, 6

Check Figure
May 31 credit to the Cash
account = $84.15

Quick Practice 6-3

Objective: To record petty cash transactions

Janna Bakker owns an art studio. During May and June 20XX, Janna incurred the following petty cash transactions:

May 1   Established a petty cash fund in the amount of $100.
     31   Replenished the fund for expenditures as follows: postage expense, $30; art supplies expense, $40.35; and miscellaneous expense, $13.80.

Directions: Record these transactions in general journal form.

Quick Practice 6-4

Objective: To record cash shortages and overages

Directions: Record the following transactions in a general journal, page 5.

Jun. 1, 20XX Cash in cash register totaled $358. Sales for the day totaled $363.
Jun. 2, 20XX Cash in cash register totaled $620. Sales for the day totaled $619.
Jun. 3, 20XX Cash in cash register totaled $184. Sales for the day totaled $187.

Quick Practice 6-5

Objective: To post cash shortages and overages to the ledger

Directions: Post the cash shortages and overages from Quick Practice 6-4 to the Cash Short and Over account, number 530.

Quick Practice 6-6

Objective: To determine the adjusted bank statement balance

Nika Hall owns a janitorial service. Her ending cash balance is $3,580 as of April 30, 20X4. The balance shown on the bank statement of the same date is $4,457. The bookkeeper found the following:

Deposit in transit, $1,400
Outstanding checks, $1,545
Note collected by bank for Nika, $750
Service charge, $18

Directions: Compute Nika's adjusted bank statement balance.

Quick Practice 6-7

Objective: To prepare a bank reconciliation statement

Yuliana Auld, CPA, received her bank statement dated July 31, 20XX. According to the bank statement, Yuliana has a bank balance of $3,872. On the same date, Yuliana's checkbook indicates a balance of $3,261. Yuliana discovered the following:

(a) A $200 deposit made on July 31 was not on the bank statement.
(b) Outstanding checks amounted to $365.
(c) The bank had collected a note for $463 from a customer of Yuliana's and entered it directly in her account.
(d) The bank charged $17 for a service charge and deducted it from Yuliana's account.

Directions: Prepare a bank reconciliation statement.

Quick Practice 6-8

Objective: To prepare journal entries from a bank reconciliation statement

Directions: Using the bank reconciliation statement prepared for Quick Practice 6-7, journalize the entries needed to update the Cash account.

Exercises

Exercise 6-1

Objective: To determine which items are classified as cash

Directions: For each item listed, place a check mark in the Yes column if the item is classified as cash or a check mark in the No column if it is not classified as cash.

Classified as Cash

Item	Yes	No
(a) Checks made payable to the business		
(b) Money orders		
(c) Postage stamps		
(d) Savings bonds due to mature in 10 years		
(e) Currency		
(f) Cashier's check		
(g) Coin		
(h) Traveler's check		
(i) Petty cash		
(j) Change fund		
(k) Amount on deposit in a bank checking account		

Learning Objective 5

Check Figure
July 1 amount = $50

Exercise 6-2

Objective: To record the establishment of and an increase in a petty cash fund

On May 1, 20XX, Lola Lackey established a petty cash fund in the amount of $200. On July 1, she increased the fund to $250.

Directions: Record both transactions in general journal form.

Learning Objective 6

Check Figure
Credit to the Cash account = $148

Exercise 6-3

Objective: To record replenishment of a petty cash fund

During May 20X0, Brent Leong paid the following expenses from his petty cash fund:

Postage Expense	$50
Miscellaneous Expense	23
Supplies Expense	25
Advertising Expense	15
Brent Leong, Drawing	35

Directions: In general journal form, record the replenishment of the fund on May 31.

Learning Objectives 5, 6

Check Figure
(b) Credit to Cash Account = $66.50

Exercise 6-4

Objective: To record petty cash transactions in a general journal

Dawna Martin is a design engineer. During June 20X1, she incurred the following petty cash transactions:

(a) Established a petty cash fund in the amount of $75.
(b) Replenished the fund for expenditures as follows: postage expense, $17; office supplies expense, $14; design supplies expense, $20; and miscellaneous expense, $15.50.
(c) Increased the fund by an additional $50.

Directions: Record the above transactions in general journal form.

Learning Objective 7

Check Figure
July 5 credit to Change Fund = $25

Exercise 6-5

Objective: To record the establishment of and a decrease in a change fund

On June 15, 20X1, Carol Landers established a change fund in the amount of $150 for her new catering service. On July 5, she decreased the fund to $125. (Hint: A reverse of the first entry.)

Directions: Record both transactions in general journal form.

Learning Objective 8

Check Figure
May 2 debit to Cash Short and Over = $6

Exercise 6-6

Objective: To record cash shortages and overages

Directions: Record the following cash sales and cash shortages and overages in general journal form.

May 1, 20X1: Cash in cash register totaled $672. Sales for the day totaled $672.
May 2, 20X1: Cash in cash register totaled $455. Sales for the day totaled $461.
May 3, 20X1: Sales for the day totaled $789. Cash in cash register totaled $798.

Learning Objective **9**

Check Figure
None

Exercise 6-7

Objective: To classify items for a bank reconciliation

Directions: Identify each item in the following list as (a) added to the bank statement balance, (b) subtracted from the bank statement balance, (c) added to the checkbook balance, or (d) subtracted from the checkbook balance.

1. Deposits in transit
2. Outstanding checks
3. Service charge
4. NSF check charge
5. Deposit on bank statement but not in checkbook
6. Charge for printing checks

Learning Objective **9**

Check Figure
True balance = $6,499

Exercise 6-8

Objective: To determine the true balance of cash

The Hartman Company's Cash account shows a balance of $5,250 as of March 31, 20XX. The balance shown on the bank statement of the same date is $7,114. The bookkeeper found the following:

Deposit in transit, $1,200
Outstanding checks, $1,815
Note collected by bank for Hartman, $1,270
Service charge, $21

Directions: Calculate the adjusted bank statement balance and the true cash balance as of March 31.

Learning Objective **9**

Check Figure
Adjusted balance = $2,407

Exercise 6-9

Objective: To prepare a bank reconciliation statement

David Dona received his bank statement dated September 1, 20XX. According to the statement, David has a bank balance of $2,450. On the same date, however, David's checkbook indicates a balance of $2,282. Closer observation revealed the following facts:

(a) A $60 deposit made on August 31 was not on the bank statement.
(b) Checks 76 ($25) and 79 ($78) were outstanding.
(c) The bank had collected $140 from a customer of David's and entered it directly in his account.
(d) The bank charged $15 for service and deducted it from David's account.

Directions: Prepare a bank reconciliation statement.

Learning Objective **9**

Check Figure
Two journal entries are needed.

Exercise 6-10

Objective: To make journal entries from a bank reconciliation statement

Directions: From the following bank reconciliation statement of Janicki Company, prepare journal entries needed to update the Cash account.

Janicki Company Bank Reconciliation Statement June 30, 20X5					
Balance per bank statement				$10 2 0 0 00
Add: Deposit in transit				1 4 0 0 00
				$11 6 0 0 00
Deduct: Outstanding checks				
#122	$ 1 1 8 00			
#125	2 2 5 00			
#129	9 2 00		4 3 5 00
Adjusted bank statement balance				$11 1 6 5 00
Balance per checkbook				$ 9 6 9 0 00
Add: Collection of note				1 5 0 0 00
				$11 1 9 0 00
Deduct: Service charge				2 5 00
Adjusted checkbook balance				$11 1 6 5 00

Case Problems

Learning Objective **1**

Check Figure
Four good controls

Group A

Problem 6-1A

Objective: To identify strengths and weaknesses in internal control

The following procedures are followed by M. Ditch Company:

(a) Since the head cashier has had some accounting experience, her duties were expanded to include bookkeeping.

(b) Cash shortages are investigated, but cash overages are ignored.

(c) At the end of a shift, each cashier counts the amount of cash in the cash register and checks this amount against the total sales rung up for the day. A supervisor then reviews and verifies the cashier's check.

(d) No payment can be made from petty cash until approved in advance.

(e) The manager, who is not the owner, often takes lunch money directly from a cash register and tells the cashier, "Remind me later to put this back." He returns the cash most of the time—but occasionally never mentions it again, and the cashier must thus report it as a cash shortage.

(f) There is a company policy that no cashier can leave the register, even for a restroom break, without first calling the manager so that the register can be locked.

(g) If a cashier becomes ill or has an emergency during busy hours when all checking stations must be open, the manager assigns the bookkeeper to the register until the cashier can return. The register is not checked before the bookkeeper takes over or after the cashier returns.

(h) Cash receipts are deposited twice a day: morning receipts are deposited at noon, and the afternoon and evening receipts are placed in the bank's night depository.

Directions: Indicate whether each of the procedures represents (1) good internal control or (2) a weakness in internal control. For each weakness, state the reason.

Check Figure
Amount to replenish the petty cash fund is $146.20.

Problem 6-2A

Objective: To record cash transactions including petty cash, cash shortages, and cash overages

The following transactions were completed by Boone Company during October 200X:

Oct. 1 Established a petty cash fund in the amount of $150.

    8 Total cash sales rung up on the cash register amounted to $4,238. A count and recount of cash in the register totaled $4,235.

   20 Total cash sales rung up on the cash register amounted to $5,415. Cash in the register totaled $5,419.

   31 The amount of petty cash on hand was $3.80. Replenished the petty cash fund for the following disbursements, each evidenced by a properly prepared petty cash voucher:

      Oct. 5 File folders, $16.00 (Office Supplies Expense).

         9 Postage stamps, $15.20.

        11 Birthday card for a customer, $3.50 (Miscellaneous Expense).

        14 Pens for the office, $10.00 (Office Supplies Expense).

        18 Lock replaced on front door, $40.00 (Miscellaneous Expense).

        21 Paid $28.00 to UPS when a package was picked up for delivery (Delivery Expense).

        26 Postage due on special delivery letter, $21.50.

        30 Owner withdrawal, $12.00 (Brenda Boone, Drawing).

   31 Increased the amount in the petty cash fund to $200.

Directions: Journalize the transactions.

Check Figure
$52.14 is needed to replenish the fund.

Problem 6-3A

Objective: To record journal entries to establish and replenish a petty cash fund and to record petty cash payments in a petty cash record

On March 1, 20X3, Shannon Greene established a petty cash fund. The following petty cash transactions occurred during the month:

Mar. 1 Shannon established the petty cash fund in the amount of $60.

    2 Issued Voucher No. 1 for postage due on a package, $3.

    3 Issued Voucher No. 2 for postage due on a package, $3.50.

    8 Issued Voucher No. 3 to have a spot removed from the carpet, $15 (Miscellaneous Expense).

   15 Issued Voucher No. 4 for the purchase of pens for the office, $9.45.

   19 Issued Voucher No. 5 for the purchase of a box of staples, $2.95.

   20 Issued Voucher No. 6 for Shannon's personal use, $10.

   23 Issued Voucher No. 7 for the purchase of office supplies, $7.50.

   30 Issued Voucher No. 8 for postage due on a package, $0.74.

   31 Replenished the fund.

Directions:

1. Journalize the entry to establish the petty cash fund.
2. Record the disbursements from the fund in a petty cash payments record.
3. Complete the petty cash payments record—total, rule, and set up for the new month.
4. Journalize the entry to replenish the fund.

Problem 6-4A

Objective: To reconcile a bank statement and journalize necessary entries

The following data relate to the checking account of Cassie Stafford as of July 31, 20X1:

Balance per bank statement		$7,800
Balance per checkbook		6,200
Deposit in transit		75
Outstanding checks:		
#122	$400	
#126	50	
#129	125	
#130	200	775
Bank service charge		13
Imprinting check charge		18
Note receivable collected by bank		
and entered in Cassie's account		931

Directions:

1. Prepare a statement to reconcile Cassie's checkbook with her July bank statement.
2. Journalize any entries needed to bring the Cash account into agreement with the adjusted checkbook balance.

Group B

Problem 6-1B

Objective: To identify strengths and weaknesses in internal control

The following procedures are followed by S. Walker Company:

(a) No petty cash fund exists. When small expenditures are needed, the manager takes the money out of the cash register and makes only a mental note to replace it.
(b) Cash shortages and overages of small amounts are ignored.
(c) At the end of a shift, each cashier double counts the amount of cash in the cash register and checks this amount against the total sales rung up for the day. The cashier then prepares a summary showing the details of the register check (date and time, amount of cash, and shortage or overage, if any). The manager counts the cash a third time and reviews the cashier's summary.
(d) Cashiers can leave the assigned cash register for short periods of time as long as the adjacent cashier is notified.
(e) Cash receipts are deposited three times daily: at 12:00 PM, 3:00 PM, and at night.
(f) The bookkeeper pays all bills and reconciles the bank statement at month-end.
(g) An area supervisor periodically reviews the records of the manager.
(h) The manager has two children, ages 7 and 9 years, and he often leaves them unattended in his office.

Directions: Indicate whether each of the procedures represents (1) good internal control or (2) a weakness in internal control. For each weakness, state the reason.

Problem 6-2B

Objective: To record cash transactions including petty cash, cash shortages, and cash overages

The following transactions were completed by J. Bell Company during November 20X1:

20X1
Nov. 1 Established a petty cash fund in the amount of $200.
      7 Total cash sales rung up on the cash register amounted to $6,578. A count and recount of cash in the register totaled $6,580.
     30 Total cash sales rung up on the cash register amounted to $9,618. Cash in the register totaled $9,615.

Nov. 30 The amount of petty cash on hand was $5.40. Replenished the petty cash fund for the following disbursements, each evidenced by a properly prepared petty cash voucher:

Nov. 5 Toner cartridge, $31.00 (Office Supplies Expense).
       8 Postage stamps, $8.20.
      11 Happy wedding anniversary card for a customer, $3.50 (Miscellaneous Expense).
      15 File folders and box of pens, $18.00
      18 Carpet cleaned in reception area, $33.00 (Miscellaneous Expense).
      21 Purchased refreshments for meeting, $15.90 (Miscellaneous Expense).
      26 Postage due on special delivery letter, $12.60.
      30 Various small items of office supply, $22.40.
      30 Owner withdrew $50 (Joseph Bell, Drawing).

      30 Increased the amount in the petty cash fund to $250.

Directions: Journalize the transactions.

Learning Objectives **5, 6**

Check Figure
$84.97 is needed to replenish the fund.

Problem 6-3B

Objective: To record journal entries to establish and replenish a petty cash fund and to record petty cash payments in a petty cash record

On October 1, 20XX, Nancy Espinosa established a petty cash fund. The following petty cash transactions occurred during October:

Oct. 1 Nancy established a petty cash fund in the amount of $90.
       2 Issued Voucher No. 1 for postage due, $3.75.
       5 Issued Voucher No. 2 for cab fare, $15.
       9 Issued Voucher No. 3 for purchase of flowers for an employee's birthday, $15.
      14 Issued Voucher No. 4 for purchase of small items of office supply, $30.
      20 Issued Voucher No. 5 for postage due, $2.25.
      22 Issued Voucher No. 6 for Nancy's personal use, $17.
      29 Issued Voucher No. 7 for postage due, $1.97.
      31 Replenished the fund.

Directions:
1. Journalize the entry to establish the petty cash fund.
2. Record the disbursements from the fund in a petty cash payments record.
3. Complete the petty cash payments record—total, rule, and set up for the new month.
4. Journalize the entry to replenish the fund.

Learning Objective **9**

Check Figure
Adjusted balance = $7,811

Problem 6-4B

Objective: To reconcile a bank statement and journalize necessary entries

The following data relate to the checking account of Ali King as of August 31, 20X1:

Balance per bank statement		$7,555
Balance per checkbook		7,646
Deposit in transit		650
Outstanding checks:		
#103	$ 85	
#107	110	
#111	96	
#112	103	394
Bank service charge		15
Imprinting check charge		10
Collection of a note receivable		190

Directions:
1. Prepare a statement to reconcile Ali's checkbook with his August bank statement.
2. Journalize any entries needed to bring the Cash account into agreement with the adjusted checkbook balance.

Critical Thinking Problems

Challenge Problem

Check Figure
Adjusted balance = $5,463.61

Lakewood Realty Company's bank statement just arrived. To reconcile the statement, Lakewood's accounting clerk gathered the following data:

1. The statement, dated June 30, 20X1, shows a balance of $4,845.18.
2. The bank statement shows the following deposits:

Date		Amount
Jun.	7	$5,315.75
	10	1,345.69
	14	2,456.75
	25	3,456.80

3. Lakewood's checkbook shows the following deposits:

Date		Amount
Jun.	5	$5,315.75
	9	1,345.69
	12	2,456.75
	25	3,456.80
	29	1,500.00

4. The bank statement includes two charges for returned checks. One is a NSF check in the amount of $80 from Nancy Obymako, a client. The other is a $400 check from Tommie Redwine that was returned with the imprint "Account Closed."
5. The following checks are outstanding:

Number	Amount
418	$521.50
510	314.67
512	76.90
521	125.40
525	98.10

6. Jason Marshall, a client, owed Lakewood $595.65. He paid this amount directly to Lakewood's bank on June 15, and it was entered into Lakewood's account. The bank charged a $15 collection fee for this service.
7. The bank statement shows the following ATM withdrawals for the owner's personal use. None has been recorded by the owner.

Date		Amount
Jun.	14	$30.00
	18	25.00
	23	45.00
	30	10.00

8. The bank statement lists a $12.80 service charge.
9. The bank statement lists a $255 check drawn by Lakeside Rental Company. Lakewood notified the bank of this error.
10. Lakewood's Cash account shows a balance of $5,485.76 on June 30.

Directions:

1. Prepare a bank reconciliation statement for Lakewood as of June 30.
2. Journalize any entries needed in Lakewood's records to bring the balance of the Cash account into agreement with the adjusted checkbook balance.

Communications

Lowell Lumberton uses a checkbook for all payments, except for petty cash, in his lawn care business. However, Lowell does not take time to reconcile his bank statement. He figures that since his bank uses electronic equipment, its records must be correct. He thus accepts that the balance shown on his bank statement is his true balance of cash.

Write an explanation of why a bank reconciliation is always needed.

Team Internet Project

In the text, you have seen the word *cash* defined with an indication that it includes paper currency, coins, money orders, checks, and so forth. In accounting language, you often see the term *cash equivalents*. Search the Internet for the meaning of *cash equivalents* and report your findings.

Ethics

Ginny Larkins is the manager and bookkeeper of Sunderland's Appliance Company. Ginny also fills in as cashier when one of the regular cashiers is on break, out ill, or on vacation. In addition to keeping up with all cash transactions and funds, Ginny does the company's data entry, ordering, and inventory, as well as the monthly bank reconciliation.

Ginny is an honest, ethical person. However, the system at Sunderland's allows for all kinds of ethical violations. Discuss the potential for dishonesty at the firm. Indicate which internal controls are missing in its structure.

In the Real World   **Target Corporation**

The balance sheets for Target Corporation as of January 28, 2006, and February 3, 2007 are shown on the following page. All amounts are in millions.

Target Corporation Balance Sheet		
	February 3, 2007	January 28, 2006
Assets		
Cash	$ 8 1 3 00	$ 1 6 4 8 00
Accounts receivable	6 1 9 4 00	5 6 6 6 00
Inventory	6 2 5 4 00	5 8 3 8 00
Other current assets	1 4 4 5 00	1 2 5 3 00
Total current assets	$14 7 0 6 00	$14 4 0 5 00
Property, plant, equipment	21 4 3 1 00	19 0 3 8 00
Other noncurrent assets	1 2 1 2 00	1 5 5 2 00
Total assets	$37 3 4 9 00	$34 9 9 5 00
Liabilities and Shareholders' Investment		
Accounts payable	$ 6 5 7 5 00	$ 6 2 6 8 00
Other current liabilities	4 5 4 2 00	3 3 2 0 00
Total current liabilities	$11 1 1 7 00	$ 9 5 8 8 00
Long-term liabilities	10 5 9 9 00	11 2 0 2 00
Shareholders' investment	15 6 3 3 00	14 2 0 5 00
Total liabilities and shareholders' investment	$37 3 4 9 00	$34 9 9 5 00

Notice that this balance sheet looks different from the balance sheets you studied in Part I. In this balance sheet, both assets and liabilities are separated into current and noncurrent categories. In Chapter 10, you will learn the exact differences between these categories.

Based on the balance sheets, answer the following questions:

(a) What is the amount and direction of the change in the balance of the Cash account from 2006 to 2007?

(b) What is the amount and direction of the change in total assets from 2006 to 2007?

(c) How might you explain the large difference in both the amounts and the directions of the answers to questions (a) and (b)?

Answers to Review Quizzes

Review Quiz 6-1

1. Weak internal control: Only a few properly designated employees should be allowed to handle cash.
2. Good internal control.
3. Weak internal control: Independent verification should always exist in a good system of internal control.
4. Weak internal control: Allowing the head cashier to keep the books is a violation of separation of duties and puts the employee in the dual position of handling cash while, at the same time, accounting for it.
5. Good internal control.

Review Quiz 6-2

1.

	20XX					
1	Jan.	2	Petty Cash	7 5 00		1
2			Cash		7 5 00	2
3			Established petty cash fund.			3

2.

1		31	Office Supplies Expense	1 0 00		1
2			Postage Expense	1 9 25		2
3			Miscellaneous Expense	3 5 00		3
4			Cash		6 4 25	4
5			Replenished petty cash fund.			5

Review Quiz 6-3

1	X	X	Cash	9 5 4 00		1
2			Cash Short and Over	3 00		2
3			Sales Revenue		9 5 7 00	3

Review Quiz 6-4

Stacy Christenson Bank Reconciliation Statement October 1, 20XX			
Balance per bank statement			$9 2 2 00
Add: Deposit in transit			4 0 00
			$9 6 2 00
Deduct: Outstanding checks			
#34	$4 1 00		
#38	5 6 00		9 7 00
Adjusted bank statement balance			$8 6 5 00
Balance per checkbook			$8 7 0 00
Deduct:			
Service charge	$ 4 00		
Error in checkbook	1 00		5 00
Adjusted checkbook balance			$8 6 5 00

The Combined Journal

Learning Objectives

1 Record transactions in a combined journal.
2 Post the combined journal to the ledger and cross-reference the two records.

Learning Objective

1 Record transactions in a combined journal.

In many businesses, cash is the most active element, with receipts and payments occurring constantly. So far, we have recorded all receipts and payments of cash in a two-column general journal. The two-column journal is a basic journal in which any business transaction, no matter how complex, can be recorded. However, the use of a two-column journal can be extremely time-consuming. Let's look again at an entry in a two-column journal.

	Date		Account Title	P.R.	Debit	Credit	
	20XX						
1	May	1	Rent Expense	511	5 00 00		1
2			Cash	111		5 00 00	2
3			Paid rent for the month.				3

General Journal — Page 6

+ expense → 1
– asset → 2

In this entry, Rent Expense is debited for $500, and Cash is credited for $500. In addition to writing the amount of the transaction in the Debit and Credit columns, it is necessary to write both account titles in the Account Title column. Additionally, when the entry is posted to the ledger, it is necessary to post an individual debit to the Rent Expense account and an individual credit to the Cash account. If 40 business transactions were recorded in a two-column journal during the month, it would be necessary to make 40 individual debits, 40 individual credits, and 80 postings to the ledger. (Even more postings would be required if some of the entries were compound entries.)

A two-column journal may be all that is needed in a business that has few transactions. When there are many transactions, however, the detail of two-column entries and the numerous postings of debits and credits are very time-consuming. In this situation, errors are more likely to occur.

To save journalizing and posting time, a combined journal can be used. A **combined journal**, also called a combination journal, is a multicolumn journal that typically has two special columns for recording cash transactions, various other special columns for recording transactions that occur often, and two general columns for recording transactions that occur less often.

The combined journal is used mainly by small businesses with one bookkeeper. The top portion of the combined journal used by Diana Ellis, Interior Decorator, is shown in Figure A-1.

The use of a combined journal saves journalizing time because it is not necessary to write the titles of the accounts when entries are made in special columns. It also saves posting time because special columns are posted by totals rather than item by item.

combined journal a multicolumn journal used by small businesses to help save journalizing and posting time that has two special columns for recording debits and credits to Cash, various other special columns for recording transactions that occur often, and two general columns for recording transactions that occur less often; also referred to as a combination journal

Pr 6-1A - white

6-2A - green
flour

Figure A-1
Combined Journal

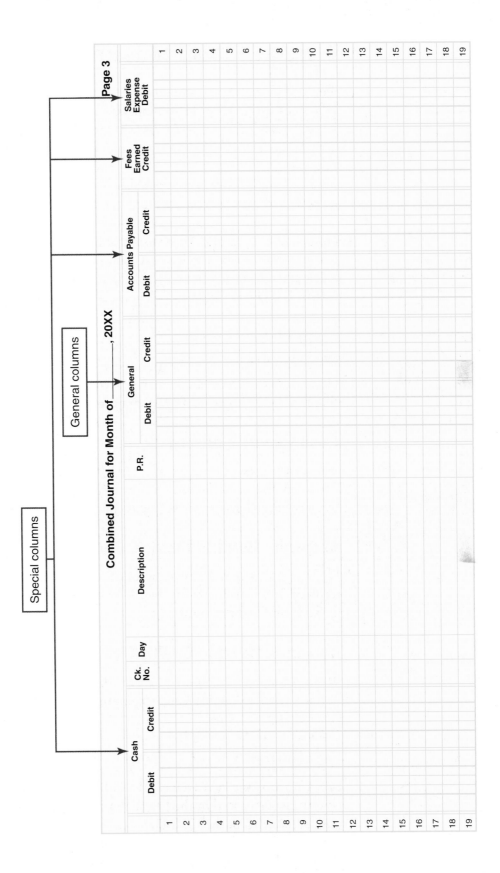

Designing a Combined Journal

The combined journal should be designed to fit the individual needs of the business using it. Special columns should be set up for those accounts that are most often affected by business transactions. Cash, for example, is usually active. Therefore, having special columns only for recording increases and decreases in Cash saves journalizing and posting time. For some businesses, the Accounts Payable account is also very active. For these businesses, special increase and decrease columns for Accounts Payable can be justified.

Within reason, the combined journal can have as many special columns as the business deems practical. Diana feels that her needs are met by having a combined journal with General Debit and Credit columns and special columns for Cash Debit and Credit, Accounts Payable Debit and Credit, Fees Earned Credit, and Salaries Expense Debit. Let's look at these column headings in a bit more detail.

Cash Debit Column

When cash is increased, the amount of the increase is recorded in the Cash Debit column. The related credit is recorded in the Accounts Payable Credit column, the Fees Earned Credit column, or the General Credit column.

Cash Credit Column

When cash is decreased, the amount of the decrease is recorded in the Cash Credit column. The related debit is recorded in the Accounts Payable Debit column, the Salaries Expense Debit column, or the General Debit column.

Accounts Payable Debit Column

When payment is made on an account payable, the amount of the payment is recorded in the Accounts Payable Debit column. The related credit is recorded in the Cash Credit column.

Accounts Payable Credit Column

When Accounts Payable is increased, the amount of the increase is recorded in the Accounts Payable Credit column. The related debit is entered in the General Debit column.

Fees Earned Credit Column

Fees Earned is the title Diana gave to her revenue account. When she earns revenue, it is recorded in the Fees Earned Credit column. The related debit to Cash is recorded in the Cash Debit column.

Salaries Expense Debit Column

Diana pays employees every week. When payment is made, the amount of the payment is recorded in the Salaries Expense Debit column. The related credit is to Cash, which is recorded in the Cash Credit column.

General Debit and Credit Columns

It is not practical to maintain special columns that will seldom be used. Therefore, the combined journal contains General Debit and Credit columns for recording entries in accounts for which no special column is provided. For example, the electric bill is usually paid only once a month. Thus, a special column entitled Utilities Expense Debit would have only one entry a month. This would not be an efficient use of space. So, when the electric bill is paid, the debit to Utilities Expense is made in the General Debit column.

Recording Business Transactions in a Combined Journal

Let's now turn our attention to how entries are recorded in the combined journal. To illustrate recording transactions in a combined journal, let's look at a narrative of the transactions completed by Diana during June 20XX. These transactions are recorded in the combined journal in Figure A-2. As with any journal, each transaction must be analyzed into its debit and credit parts before recording. To review how to analyze a transaction, the first three transactions are shown with an analysis.

Jun. 1 Issued Check No. 120 for June Rent, $600

The payment of rent causes an increase in Rent Expense and a decrease in Cash. A special column is provided only when it will be used frequently. Rent is paid only once a month. Thus, there is no special column for recording increases in Rent Expense. Instead, the debit is recorded in the General Debit column. The account title, Rent Expense, is written in the Description column. The decrease in Cash is recorded in the Cash Credit column. The number of the check, 120, is written in the Ck. No. (check number) column.

Rent Expense		Cash	
+	−	+	−
600			600

Jun. 1 Received cash for Services Performed, $400

The receipt of cash for services performed caused an increase in Cash and an increase in revenue. The increase in Cash is recorded in the Cash Debit column. The increase in revenue is recorded in the Fees Earned Credit column. Since both debit and credit amounts are recorded in special columns, it is not necessary to write the title of either account in the Description column. Therefore, a check mark is placed in the Description column to show that no account title needs to be written.

Cash		Fees Earned	
+	−	−	+
400			400

Figure A-2

The Combined Journal for Diana Ellis, June 20XX

Combined Journal for Month of June, 20XX

#	Cash Debit	Cash Credit	Ck. No.	Day	Description	P.R.	General Debit	General Credit	Accounts Payable Debit	Accounts Payable Credit	Fees Earned Credit	Salaries Expense Debit
1		600 00	120	1	Rent Expense		600 00					
2	400 00			1	✓						400 00	
3	200 00			2	Office Equipment			200 00				
4				3	Office Supplies		250 00			250 00		
5	800 00			5	✓						800 00	
6		500 00	121	5	✓				500 00			
7		325 00	122	7	Decorating Supplies		900 00			900 00		
8		75 00	123	8	✓							325 00
9		450 00	124	9	Miscellaneous Expense		75 00					
10		325 00	125	10	Office Equipment		1200 00			1200 00		
11		1000 00	126	12	Prepaid Insurance		450 00					
12		800 00	127	14	✓							325 00
13	2546 00	80 00	128	16	Automobile		12000 00					
14		325 00	129	18	Notes Payable			11000 00				
15		250 00	130		✓						2546 00	
16		40 00	131	20	Diana Ellis, Drawing		800 00					
17		380 00	132	21	Advertising Expense		80 00					
18		325 00	133	21	✓							325 00
19	750 00	900 00	134	23	✓				250 00			
20				27	Repairs Expense		40 00					
21				29	Utilities Expense		380 00					
22				30	✓							325 00
23				30	✓						750 00	
24				30	✓				900 00			
25	4696 00	6375 00					16775 00	11200 00	1650 00	2350 00	4496 00	1300 00

Jun. 2 Received Cash from the Sale of Old Office Equipment at Cost, $200

The receipt of cash from the sale of office equipment caused a *shift in assets*. One asset, cash, was increased while another asset, office equipment, was decreased. The increase in Cash is recorded in the Cash Debit column. The decrease in Office Equipment is recorded in the General Credit column because there is no special column entitled Office Equipment Credit.

Cash		Office Equipment	
+	−	+	−
200			200

Following are the remainder of the transactions that occurred in June.

Jun. 3 Purchased office supplies on account from Keith Office Supply Company, $250.

5 Received cash for services performed, $800.

5 Issued Check No. 121 for $500 to Timmers Company, a creditor.

7 Purchased decorating supplies on account from Engle Suppliers, $900.

8 Issued Check No. 122 for salary of employee, $325.

9 Issued Check No. 123 for miscellaneous expenses, $75.

10 Purchased office equipment on account, $1,200.

12 Issued Check No. 124 for a six-month prepayment of insurance premiums, $450.

14 Issued Check No. 125 for salary of employee, $325.

16 Purchased an automobile for use in the business, $12,000. Issued Check No. 126 for the down payment, $1,000, and issued a note payable for the balance.

18 Received cash for services performed, $2,546.

20 Diana withdrew $800 for personal use. Issued Check No. 127.

21 Issued Check No. 128 for an ad in a local newspaper, $80.

21 Issued Check No. 129 for salary of employee, $325.

23 Issued Check No. 130 for $250 to Keith Office Supply Company for the supplies purchased on June 3.

27 Issued Check No. 131 for repair to office equipment, $40.

29 Issued Check No. 132 for utility bill, $380.

30 Issued Check No. 133 for salary of employee, $325.

30 Received cash for services performed, $750.

30 Issued Check No. 134 for $900 to Engle Suppliers for payment of decorating supplies purchased on June 7.

Proving the Combined Journal

When the month's transactions have been journalized, each column of the combined journal should be totaled and the equality of debits and credits proved. We can do this as follows:

```
+    4,696
-    6,375
+   16,775
-   11,200
+    1,650
-    2,350
-    4,496
+    1,300
        -0-
```

Column Titles	Column Totals	
	Debit	Credit
Cash	$ 4,696	$ 6,375
General	16,775	11,200
Accounts Payable	1,650	2,350
Fees Earned		4,496
Salaries Expense	1,300	
Totals	$24,421	$24,421

zero proof test a test performed using the plus and minus bars of a calculator; passing this test indicates that equal columns have a zero difference

A less formal way to prove the combined journal is to use a calculator and enter each debit column total using the plus (+) bar and each credit column total using the minus (–) bar. After all column totals have been entered in this manner, press the Total key, and a zero (0) will appear on the display screen. This procedure is called the zero proof test. Passing the **zero proof test** means that equal columns have a zero difference.

Learning Objective

2 Post the combined journal to the ledger and cross-reference the two records.

Posting the Combined Journal

Like posting from the general journal, posting from the combined journal is usually done at the end of each month. Two types of postings are made from the combined journal: (1) individual postings of amounts in the General Debit and Credit columns, and (2) summary postings of amounts in special columns.

Posting the General Columns

The procedure for posting amounts in the General Debit and Credit columns is similar to posting from a two-column journal. Each entry is posted individually to the account identified in the Description column. To illustrate, let's look at Figure A-3, which shows how the June 1 debit to Rent Expense is posted. The five steps for posting the debit are as follows:

Step **1** Enter the date of the entry (Jun. 1) in the Date column of the Rent Expense account.

Step **2** Enter the amount of the entry ($600) in the Debit column of the Rent Expense account.

Step **3** Calculate the new balance of the Rent Expense account by adding the current posting to the previous balance: $600 + $3,000 = $3,600.

Step **4** Enter the reference "CJ" and the page number of the combined journal (6) in the P.R. column of the Rent Expense account.

Step **5** Enter the number of the Rent Expense account (516) in the P.R. column of the combined journal.

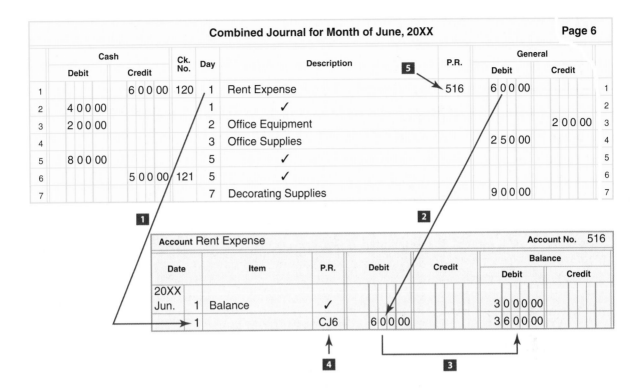

Figure A-3

Posting an Entry from the General Columns of a Combined Journal

Posting the Totals of Special Columns

Special columns are used only for recording debits or credits to specific accounts. For example, only increases in cash are recorded in the Cash Debit column, and only decreases in cash are recorded in the Cash Credit column. Thus, at the end of the month, the total of the Cash Debit column is posted to the debit side of the Cash account, and the total of the Cash Credit column is posted to the credit side of the Cash account. All other special columns are posted in the same way. To illustrate, Figure A-4 on pages 268-269 shows how the special column totals of Diana Ellis's combined journal are posted. Notice that the number of each account to which a posting was made is written in parentheses directly below the special column total. The check marks below the General Debit and Credit columns mean that amounts in these columns are posted individually, not by totals.

Figure A-4

Posting the Special
Columns of a
Combined Journal

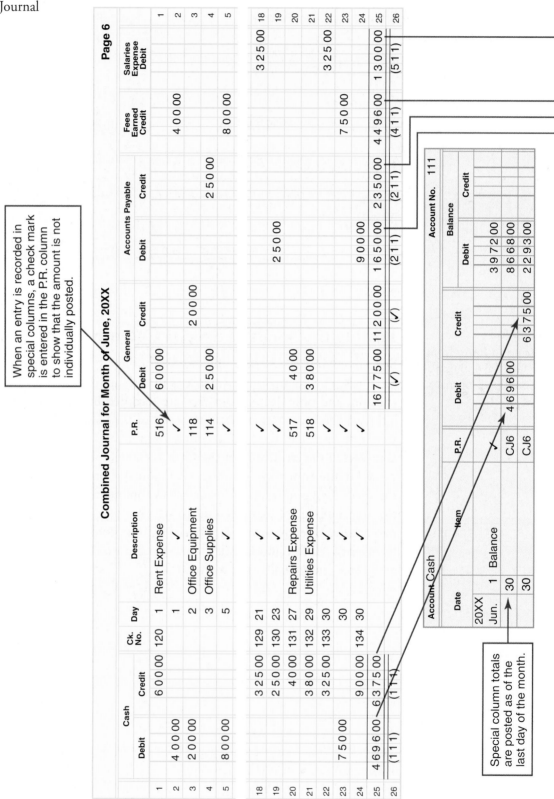

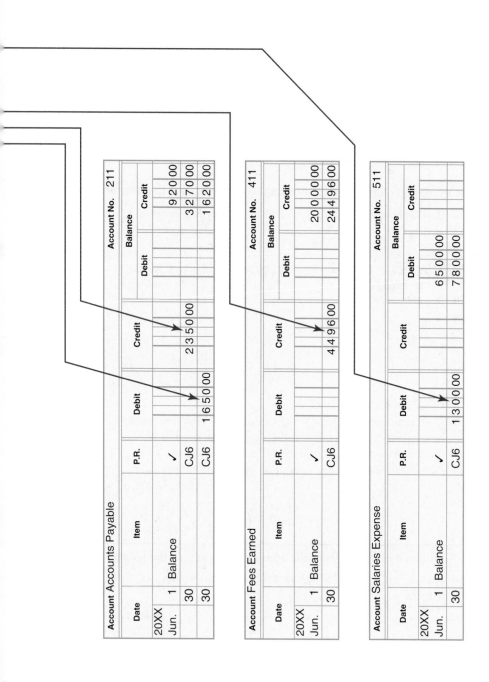

Account Accounts Payable   **Account No.** 211

Date		Item	P.R.	Debit	Credit	Balance Debit	Balance Credit
20XX Jun.	1	Balance	✓				9 2 0 00
	30		CJ6		2 3 5 0 00		3 2 7 0 00
	30		CJ6	1 6 5 0 00			1 6 2 0 00

Account Fees Earned   **Account No.** 411

Date		Item	P.R.	Debit	Credit	Balance Debit	Balance Credit
20XX Jun.	1	Balance	✓				20 0 0 0 00
	30		CJ6		4 4 9 6 00		24 4 9 6 00

Account Salaries Expense   **Account No.** 511

Date		Item	P.R.	Debit	Credit	Balance Debit	Balance Credit
20XX Jun.	1	Balance	✓			6 5 0 0 00	
	30		CJ6	1 3 0 0 00		7 8 0 0 00	

APPENDIX A REVIEW, PRACTICE, AND APPLY

Summary

Interactive Summary in English and Spanish

1 Record transactions in a combined journal.

A **combined journal** is a multicolumn journal designed to save journalizing and posting time. Typically, a combined journal has two special columns for recording increases and decreases in cash, various other special columns for recording transactions that occur often, and two general columns for recording transactions that are not recorded in special columns. The use of a combined journal saves journalizing time because it is not necessary to write account titles when making entries in special columns. The combined journal is illustrated in Figures A-1 and A-2.

2 Post the combined journal to the ledger and cross-reference the two records.

Posting from the combined journal is illustrated in Figures A-3 and A-4.

Terms and Concepts Review

Key Terms and Definitions in English and Spanish

Key Terms

combined journal, 260
zero proof test, 266

Concepts Review

1. What factors should be considered when designing a combined journal?
2. What is the purpose of special columns in a combined journal?
3. How are the special columns of a combined journal posted?
4. How are the general columns of a combined journal posted?

Skills Review

Learning Objective **2**

Check Figure
Six columns posted by totals

Exercise A-1

Objective: To post transactions from the combined journal to the ledger

Directions: Indicate with a check mark how columns in the combined journal are posted to the ledger.

	Posted by Total	Posted Individually
(a) Cash Debit column		
(b) Cash Credit column		
(c) General Debit colum		
(d) General Credit column		
(e) Accounts Payable Debit column		
(f) Accounts Payable Credit colum		
(g) Fees Earned Credit column		
(h) Salaries Expense Debit column		

Learning Objective **2**

Check Figure
Ending cash balance =
$16,500 (debit)

Exercise A-2

Objective: To post from the combined journal to the ledger

The beginning balance in the Cash account for January 1, 20XX, was $19,630. On January 31, page 9 of the combined journal showed that the Cash Debit column total was $30,280 and the Cash Credit column total was $33,410.

Directions: Post the Cash Debit and Credit column totals from the combined journal to the Cash account and update the account balance.

Account Cash							Account No.	111
Date	Item	P.R.	Debit	Credit	Balance			
					Debit		Credit	
20XX Jan. 1	Balance	✓			19 6 3 0 00			

Learning Objective **1**

Check Figure
Total debits = $13,740

Exercise A-3

Objective: To prove the combined journal

Mike Fritz, CPA, enters his transactions into a combined journal. On August 31, 20XX, the column totals are as follows: Cash Debit $7,320; Cash Credit, $3,450; General Debit, $1,710; General Credit, $1,420; Accounts Payable Debit, $1,250; Accounts Payable Credit, $1,380; Fees Earned Credit, $7,490; and Salaries Expense Debit, $3,460.

Directions: Prove the totals of the combined journal by showing total debits equal to total credits.

Case Problems

Learning Objective **1**

Check Figure
Total debits = $11,688

Problem A-1

Objective: To record business transactions in a combined journal

The following transactions were incurred by Regan Ertle Company during May 20X2:

20X2

May 1 Issued Check No. 41 for May rent, $1,200.
   1 Issued Check No. 42 for the purchase of office supplies, $180.
   2 Issued Check No. 43 for the purchase of a new printer, $550 (Office Equipment).
   4 Received cash for services performed, $550.
   5 Purchased office supplies on account from Gerald Blake, $110.
   6 Received cash for services performed, $910.
   7 Issued Check No. 44 for salaries of employees, $900.
   8 Received cash for services performed, $75.
   9 Issued Check No. 45 for phone bill, $121 (Utilities Expense).
   10 Issued Check No. 46 for repairs to office equipment, $140.
   12 Received cash for services performed, $780.
   14 Issued Check No. 47 for salaries of employees, $900.
   16 Received cash for services performed, $326.
   17 Issued Check No. 48 for office supplies, $175.
   21 Received cash for services performed, $750.
   21 Issued Check No. 49 for salaries of employees, $900.
   22 Purchased office supplies on account from Paul White, $420.
   23 Purchased a new calculator on account from Ace Suppliers, $159.
   25 Issued Check No. 50 for utility bill, $528.
   27 Received cash for services performed, $105.
   28 Issued Check No. 51 to Gerald Blake in payment of office supplies purchased on May 5, $110.
   29 Received cash for services performed, $340.

May 31   Issued Check No. 52 to Ace Suppliers in payment of the calculator purchased on May 23, $159.

     31   Issued Check No. 53 for salaries of employees, $900.

     31   Received cash for services performed, $400.

Directions:

1. Record these transactions in a combined journal similar to the one illustrated on page 261.
2. Total, prove, and rule the journal.

Learning Objective **1**

Check Figure
Total debits = $10,958

Problem A-2

Objective: To record business transactions in a combined journal

The following transactions were incurred by Graber Company during July 20X2:

20X2

Jul. 31   Issued Check No. 321 for July rent, $1,000.

     1   Issued Check No. 322 for office supplies, $95.

     3   Received cash for services performed, $190.

     5   Purchased office supplies on account from David Evans, $299.

     7   Received cash for services performed, $285.

     8   Issued Check No. 323 for salaries of employees, $900.

     9   Issued Check No. 324 for the purchase of a new computer, $2,800.

    11   Received cash for services performed, $400.

    13   Issued Check No. 325 for electric bill, $355.

    15   Purchased a calculator on account from Fox Supplies, $140.

    17   Received cash for services performed, $105.

    19   Issued Check No. 326 for equipment repairs, $60.

    20   Issued Check No. 327 to David Evans to pay for the purchase on July 5, $299.

    21   Received cash for services performed, $205.

    22   Issued Check No. 328 for automobile supplies, $75.

    23   Issued Check No. 329 for salaries of employees, $935.

    25   Received cash for services performed, $250.

    25   Issued Check No. 330 for telephone bill, $230.

    28   Received cash for services performed, $800.

    29   Purchased office equipment on account from Emery Foster, $325.

    30   Issued Check No. 331 to Fox Supplies to pay for the purchase of July 15, $140.

    31   Issued Check No. 332 for salaries of employees, $890.

    31   Received cash for services performed, $180.

Directions:

1. Record Graber's transactions in a combined journal similar to the one illustrated on page 261.
2. Total, prove, and rule the journal.

Learning Objectives **1, 2**

Check Figure
Trial balance totals = $16,239

Problem A-3

Objective: To open ledger accounts, journalize transactions in a combined journal, post to the ledger, and prepare a trial balance

The following is the May 31, 20X1, trial balance of the Platt Service Company.

Platt Service Company Trial Balance May 31, 20X1		
Account Title	**Debit**	**Credit**
111 Cash	3 0 5 0 00	
114 Office Supplies	4 0 0 00	
115 Advertising Supplies	6 0 0 00	
125 Office Equipment	1 8 0 0 00	
211 Accounts Payable		9 8 0 00
215 Notes Payable		2 5 0 0 00
311 Melinda Platt, Capital		3 3 9 0 00
312 Melinda Platt, Drawing	1 2 0 0 00	
411 Fees Earned		2 4 1 0 00
511 Rent Expense	8 0 0 00	
512 Salaries Expense	9 0 0 00	
513 Repairs Expense	5 0 00	
514 Utilities Expense	4 0 0 00	
518 Miscellaneous Expense	8 0 00	
Totals	9 2 8 0 00	9 2 8 0 00

Platt Service Company incurred the following transactions during June:

20X1

Jun. 1 Issued Check No. 14 for June rent, $500.
    1 Issued Check No. 15 to Jay Smith in partial payment of an account payable, $250.
    2 Received cash for services performed, $900.
    3 Received cash for services performed, $175.
    5 Purchased office supplies on account from Walsh Company, $420.
    6 Purchased a computer system for $5,000. Issued Check No. 16 for a $1,000 down payment and issued a note payable for the balance.
    7 Received cash for services performed, $189.
    8 Issued Check No. 17 for the monthly phone bill, $95 (Utilities Expense).
    10 Issued Check No. 18 for salaries of employees, $450.
    11 Received cash for services performed, $600.
    12 Issued Check No. 19 for an owner withdrawal, $600.
    15 Issued Check No. 20 for window cleaning, $75.
    18 Received cash for services performed, $600.
    19 Issued Check No. 21 in partial payment of a note payable, $185.
    21 Issued Check No. 22 for salaries of employees, $475.
    25 Received cash for services performed, $130.
    26 Received cash for services performed, $800.
    30 Issued Check No. 23 to Walsh Company in payment of the office supplies purchased on June 5, $420.
    30 Issued Check No. 24 for salaries of employees, $480.

Directions:

1. Open a ledger account and enter the balance, as of June 1, of each account on the trial balance. (Note: Enter the beginning balances from the May 31 trial balance before posting the June transactions to the general ledger.)
2. Record the transactions in a combined journal like the one illustrated on page 261.
3. Total, prove, and rule the combined journal, and post to the ledger.
4. Prepare a trial balance as of June 30.

Problem A-4

Objective: To open ledger accounts, journalize transactions in a combined journal, post to the ledger, and prepare a trial balance

The following is the June 30, 20X2, trial balance of the Hutchins Service Company.

	Account Title	Debit	Credit
	Hutchins Service Company		
	Trial Balance		
	June 30, 20X2		
111	Cash	1 2 5 0 00	
114	Office Supplies	6 4 0 00	
115	Advertising Supplies	6 0 0 00	
125	Office Equipment	4 8 0 0 00	
211	Accounts Payable		7 8 0 00
215	Notes Payable		1 2 9 0 00
311	Holly Hutchins, Capital		5 4 5 0 00
312	Holly Hutchins, Drawing	1 6 5 0 00	
411	Fees Earned		4 7 1 5 00
511	Rent Expense	1 0 5 0 00	
512	Salaries Expense	1 5 9 0 00	
513	Repairs Expense	5 0 00	
514	Utilities Expense	4 6 0 00	
518	Miscellaneous Expense	1 4 5 00	
	Totals	12 2 3 5 00	12 2 3 5 00

The following transactions were incurred during July.

20X2

Jul. 1 Received cash for services performed, $800.

3 Issued Check No. 24 for July rent, $750.

5 Issued Check No. 25 to Roger Sawyer in partial payment on an account payable, $300.

6 Received cash for services performed, $600.

8 Purchased office supplies, $275, and advertising supplies, $90, on account from Acme Company.

10 Issued Check No. 26 for a utility bill, $120.

11 Holly Hutchins, the owner, invested an additional $1,000 cash in the business.

12 Received cash for services performed, $1,400.

15 Issued Check No. 27 for salaries of employees, $575.

15 Issued Check No. 28 for office cleaning, $65 (Miscellaneous Expense).

17 Issued Check No. 29 for owner withdrawal, $400.

19 Received cash for services performed, $350.

22 Issued Check No. 30 for office equipment, $560.

26 Received cash for services performed, $900.

29 Issued Check No. 31 to Acme Company for the purchase of July 8, $365.

30 Issued Check No. 32 in partial payment of a note payable, $1,000.

31 Received cash for services performed, $400.

31 Issued Check No. 33 for salaries of employees, $595.

Directions:
1. Open a ledger account and enter the balance, as of July 1, of each account on the trial balance. (Note: Enter the beginning balances from the June 30 trial balance before posting the July transactions to the ledger.)
2. Record the transactions in a combined journal like the one illustrated on page 261.
3. Total, prove, and rule the combined journal, and post to the ledger.
4. Prepare a trial balance as of July 31.

B APPENDIX

The Voucher System

Learning Objectives

1 Describe the voucher system and identify its benefits.
2 Record vouchers issued in general journal form.
3 Record checks issued in general journal form.

Learning Objective

1 Describe the voucher system and identify its benefits.

voucher system a method of accounting for cash payments in which all payments are authorized in advance

voucher a receipt or document showing authorization of a payment; recorded in the Vouchers Payable account

In Appendix B, we will discuss the voucher system, which is another internal control system designed specifically to control cash payments. The **voucher system** is a method of accounting for cash payments in which all payments are approved when a transaction occurs, rather than when payment is actually made. The voucher system requires that no purchase of a good or service or payment of a liability happens without proper authorization. In effect, it is a system of checks and balances to prevent unauthorized or improper payments of cash.

The voucher system begins with a **voucher** (Figure B-1), which is a form authorizing a purchase or a payment. The voucher system ends with payment of the voucher. All payments a company makes, except those from petty cash, must be supported by a properly approved voucher. Even routine payments, such as rent and utilities, cannot be made without an approved voucher. For example, Dodge Company prepared the voucher in Figure B-1 to support payment of the company's rent on July 1, 20X2. The information on the front of the voucher and in the Distribution section on the back was entered when the voucher was prepared; the information in the Payment section was entered when the voucher was paid.

Figure B-1
A Voucher

Dodge Company
2000 River Road
Manchester, NH
Voucher No. 1

Date Issued 7-1-X2 Terms cash Pay To Carlson Realty

Date Due 7-1-X2

Invoice Date	Description	Amount
7-1-X2	Rent	1,200 00

Authorized by JD Prepared by RJ

(a) Front

Distribution

Debit	Amount
Rent Expense	1,200 00
Credit Vouchers Payable	1,200 00

Payment

Authorized by DR Date made 7-1-X2 By PR

(b) Back

unpaid vouchers file a
file of vouchers to be
paid, organized by date
due so vouchers can be
paid promptly

If the voucher is to be paid immediately, as in this case, it is passed on for payment authorization. Once authorized, the voucher can be paid. If payment will not be made until a future date, the voucher is filed by payment date in an **unpaid vouchers file.**

Recording Vouchers

Learning Objective

2 Record vouchers issued
in general journal form.

**Vouchers Payable
account** a liability
account in which unpaid
vouchers are recorded

When a voucher is prepared, its amount is immediately credited to the **Vouchers Payable account**, a liability account in which unpaid vouchers are recorded. The debit is to the account(s) affected by the transaction. To illustrate, Dodge Company made the following general journal entry to record Voucher 1 (Figure B-1) for the July rent:

	Date		Account Title	P.R.	Debit	Credit	
	General Journal					**Page 1**	
1	20X2 July	1	Rent Expense		1 2 0 0 00		1
2			Vouchers Payable			1 2 0 0 00	2
3			Prepared Voucher 1 for July rent.				3
4							4

Paying Vouchers

Learning Objective

3 Record checks issued in
general journal form.

As we stated earlier, a voucher cannot be paid until it is authorized for payment. Once authorized, the actual payment can only be made by a designated person. To illustrate, after Voucher 1 was authorized for payment, Dodge Company issued a check to Carlson Realty. The voucher was then stamped "paid" and sent to the accounting department for recording, and the following entry was made:

5		1	Vouchers Payable		1 2 0 0 00		5
6			Cash			1 2 0 0 00	6
7			Paid Voucher 1.				7
8							8

Now, let's look back at the steps that led to this payment. On July 1, Voucher 1 was prepared by RJ (lower front side of the voucher). The voucher was then authorized by JD and passed on for payment authorization. The voucher was authorized for payment by DR, and the actual payment was made by PR (lower back side of the voucher). Finally, the payment was recorded by the company's accountant. So, there were five different individuals involved in paying the July rent. This is the workings of the voucher system, a network of approvals and authorizations by different individuals acting independently with the overriding objective being to control cash payments.

Recording Purchases

Since Dodge Company prepared Voucher 1 for the routine payment of rent, the voucher was immediately authorized for payment. In cases where a credit purchase is made, or an expense is incurred on account, a voucher is prepared and, as we stated earlier, filed in an unpaid vouchers file. For example, on July 2, 20X2, Dodge Company made a $600 credit purchase of office supplies from Consolidated Products Company. Terms of the payment were 30 days. On July 2, Voucher 2 was prepared, approved, and filed in the unpaid vouchers file. The following entry was made to record the purchase:

9		2	Office Supplies		6 0 0 00		9
10			Vouchers Payable			6 0 0 00	10
11			Recorded Voucher 2 for office				11
12			supplies.				12
13							13

paid vouchers file a file of vouchers that have been paid, organized by payment date

The voucher is filed in the unpaid vouchers file under a payment date of August 1 (30 days after the purchase). On August 1, the voucher is pulled from the files, authorized for payment, and a check is issued. The accountant then makes an entry debiting Vouchers Payable and crediting Cash, and the voucher is filed in a **paid vouchers file.**

Summary

Interactive Summary in English and Spanish

1 Describe the voucher system and identify its benefits.

The **voucher system** is a system of checks and balances where all payments of cash must be approved in advance and supported by a properly approved **voucher**. The voucher system provides internal control over cash payments because no purchase of a good or a service, and no payment of a liability, can happen without authorization.

2 Record vouchers issued in general journal form.

When a purchase is made, or a payment is to be made, a voucher is immediately prepared and passed on for authorization. Once authorized, a voucher is recorded in the journal in the **Vouchers Payable account**. For example, on March 23, 20X8, R. Sterling Company purchased $800 in store supplies on account from Alexandra Supply Company. Terms of the purchase were 30 days. To record the purchase, Voucher 18 was prepared and approved, filed in the **unpaid vouchers file**, and recorded as follows:

	Date		Account Title	P.R.	Debit	Credit	
	20X8						
1	Mar.	23	Store Supplies		8 00 00		1
2			Vouchers Payable			8 00 00	2
3			Prepared Voucher 18 for store				3
4			supplies.				4
5							5

General Journal — Page 1

3 Record checks issued in general journal form.

When prepared, vouchers are filed in the unpaid vouchers file according to the due date of the payment. At the payment date, the voucher is pulled and authorized for payment. A journal entry is then made to record the cash payment. To illustrate, on April 22, 20X8, R. Sterling Company paid Voucher 18 for the purchase of store supplies on March 23. The following journal entry records the payment:

General Journal — Page 2

	Date		Account Title	P.R.	Debit	Credit	
	20X8						
1	April	22	Vouchers Payable		8 00 00		1
2			Cash			8 00 00	2
3			Paid Voucher 18.				3
4							4

Terms Review

Key Terms and Definitions in English and Spanish

Key Terms

paid vouchers file, 278
unpaid vouchers file, 277
voucher, 276

voucher system, 276
Vouchers Payable account, 277

Skills Review

Learning Objective **2**

Check Figure
None

Exercise B-1

Objective: To record vouchers issued

On July 26, 20X5, A.A. Coco Company prepared Voucher 21 for the immediate payment of a $2,345 utility bill. On the same date, Voucher 22 was prepared for the $500 purchase of office supplies on 30 days credit.

Directions: Record both vouchers in general journal form. Make a separate entry for each voucher.

Learning Objective **3**

Check Figure
None

Exercise B-2

Objective: To record payment of vouchers

On July 26, 20X5, A.A. Coco Company paid Voucher 21, and on August 25, 20X5, Voucher 22 was paid.

Directions: Using data from Exercise B-1, record payment of both vouchers.

Case Problems

Learning Objectives **2, 3**

Check Figure
Two unpaid vouchers at month-end

Problem B-1

Objective: To record vouchers issued and paid

During November 20X2, BGD Company prepared the following vouchers.

Date	Voucher No.	Amount	For	Payable
Nov. 1	1	$1,800	Utilities Expense	Immediately
2	2	1,200	Rent Expense	Immediately
8	3	600	Repairs Expense	Immediately
12	4	710	Office Supplies	30 days
18	5	1,125	Store Supplies	30 days
25	6	800	Notes Payable	Immediately
30	7	4,815	Salaries Expense	Immediately

Directions: Record the issuance and payment of these vouchers. Hint: For voucher 6, the debit is to Notes Payable.

Learning Objectives **2, 3**

Check Figure
One unpaid voucher at month-end

Problem B-2

Objective: To record vouchers issued and paid

The following vouchers were issued by Travers Company during June 20X4:

20X4

June 1 Voucher 1 for June rent, $1,150; payable immediately.
     2 Voucher 2 for utilities, $2,458; payable immediately.
     4 Voucher 3 for repairs expense, $250; payable immediately.
     8 Voucher 4 for office supplies, $560; payable in 10 days.
    12 Voucher 5 for store supplies, $800; payable in 30 days.
    18 Paid Voucher 4, $560.
    19 Voucher 6 for the purchase of equipment, $4,000; payable in 10 days.
    22 Voucher 7 for gas and oil expense, $400; payable immediately.
    29 Paid Voucher 6, $4,000.
    30 Voucher 8 for salaries, $4,815; payable immediately.

Directions: Record the issuance and payment of these vouchers.

CHAPTER

7

Accounting for a Merchandising Business

Purchases and Cash Payments

Learning Objectives

1. Describe the procedures and forms used in purchasing merchandise.
2. Record credit purchases in a general journal and a purchases journal, and post to the accounts payable ledger and the general ledger.
3. Record purchases returns and allowances.
4. Record purchases discounts.
5. Record cash payments in a cash payments journal and post to the accounts payable ledger and the general ledger.
6. Prepare a schedule of accounts payable.
7. Record freight charges on incoming merchandise.

In Chapters 1 through 6, we studied accounting procedures suitable to businesses that perform personal services for their customers, such as legal services and financial planning. We also learned how to record business transactions in a two-column general journal. In Chapter 7, your accounting horizons will expand in three directions: (1) you will move to a different form of business, merchandising; (2) you will use two additional journals; and (3) you will learn how to operate an accounting system with more than one ledger.

Merchandising Activity

merchandising business a business that buys goods from other companies and then sells those goods to customers; also referred to as a trading business

merchandise goods held for sale to customers; also referred to as merchandise inventory and stock in trade

retail business a business such as a grocery store, drugstore, or restaurant that sells directly to consumers

A **merchandising business**, also called a trading business, is a business that earns its revenue by buying goods and then reselling the goods to customers. Goods that are to be sold to customers are called **merchandise**. Other terms for merchandise include merchandise inventory and stock in trade. Wal-Mart, Target, Kmart, and Macy's are merchandising businesses because they buy merchandise from other companies and then sell the merchandise to their customers.

Merchandising can take place at two levels—retail and wholesale. A **retail business**, such as a grocery store, drugstore, or restaurant, sells directly to consumers. The original meaning of the word *retail* was "to cut." Early

wholesaler a business that purchases goods in bulk from manufacturers and sells the goods to retailers, other wholesalers, schools and other nonprofit institutions, and, at times, directly to consumers

Key Point ⊘

Walgreen's is a retail business that could buy merchandise from McKesson, a wholesaler.

Learning Objective

1 Describe the procedures and forms used in purchasing merchandise.

retailers would cut small amounts from large purchases—such as yards of cloth or bushels of grain—and sell the small portions to customers. A **wholesaler** purchases goods in bulk from manufacturers and then sells the goods to retailers, other wholesalers, schools and other nonprofit institutions, and, at times, directly to consumers. For our

A retail business buys merchandise from wholesalers, manufacturers, and other producers—such as farmers—and sells the merchandise directly to the consuming public, usually in small quantities.

study of merchandising, we will use the example of Lakeside Electronics, a wholesaler. However, the procedures we will cover are also used in retail businesses.

Purchasing Procedures

There are two sides to merchandising: (1) purchasing and (2) selling. Each requires formal documents and control procedures. In Chapter 7, we are concerned with purchasing procedures; in Chapter 8, we will deal with selling procedures.

The purchasing procedures used by a company depend on the size of the business and the nature of its operations. In a smaller merchandising business, one person could be responsible for all purchases, usually the store manager or the owner. In large retail and wholesale concerns, the purchasing function is usually performed by a *purchasing agent* who heads the purchasing department.

Let's take a moment to preview the steps in the purchasing procedure:

Step **1** Managers identify goods needed and request them by preparing a purchase requisition, which is sent to the purchasing department.

Step **2** The purchasing department chooses the seller (vendor) and sends an order.

Step **3** The seller receives the order and prepares an invoice (bill), which is shipped with the goods or a few days after the goods.

Step **4** When the merchandise is received by the buyer, it is checked against the invoice and payment is approved.

The purchasing process begins with a department head or manager identifying the goods needed and sending the firm's purchasing agent a purchase requisition. The **purchase requisition** is a written request for goods to be purchased; an example is shown in Figure 7-1.

purchase requisition a written request for goods to be purchased; usually prepared by a department head or manager and sent to a firm's purchasing department

Figure 7-1

Purchase Requisition

Purchase Requisition	
No.: __237__	Date: **October 25, 20X1**
To: __Purchasing__ Department	
From: __Electrical__ Department	
Order:	

Quantity	Description
1,000 feet	**Galvanized copper cable, #4443-6**

Date Needed: __November 15, 20X1__	
Requested by: __B.K.__	

The purchasing department has the responsibility of determining the best source of supply and the best possible price. Once the decision to buy has been made, the purchasing department prepares a purchase order. A **purchase order** is a written or online form sent from a buyer of goods to the seller that specifies the quantity and description of goods to be purchased. The purchase order is prepared with at least three copies and distributed as follows:

purchase order a written or online form sent from a buyer of goods to the seller specifying the quantity and description of the goods to be purchased

- The original is sent to the seller (vendor).
- One copy is kept in the purchasing department (for its records).
- One copy is sent to the firm's accounting department (for comparison with the seller's invoice, which will arrive later).
- One copy is sent to the receiving department. This copy is often a blind copy (one without quantities) to encourage the receiving department to make an independent count of the goods when they arrive.

The flow of the purchase order is shown in Figure 7-2. The purchase order form used by Lakeside Electronics appears in Figure 7-3.

Figure 7-2

The Flow of the
Purchase Order

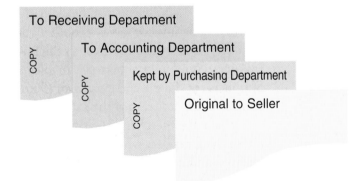

invoice the bill the seller of goods sends to the buyer of the goods that identifies and describes the goods and how they will be delivered; to the seller, referred to as the sales invoice; to the buyer, referred to as a purchase invoice

On receipt of the purchase order, the seller prepares an invoice to send with the goods (or a few days after the goods). An **invoice** is a business document that shows the names and addresses of the buyer and the seller, the date and terms of the sale, a description of the goods, the price of the goods and total owed, and the mode of transportation for delivery.

Figure 7-3

Purchase Order

Lakeside Electronics			Purchase Order	
1200 San Palo Road			No.: 199	
Los Angeles, CA 90099				

To: **Key Suppliers**   Date: **October 25, 20X1**
  Redville, CA 90362

Enter our order for:

Quantity	Description	Unit Price	Total	
1,000 feet	**Galvanized copper cable #4443-6**	**.575**	**575**	**00**

Fill by: _____   Ship via: **Truck**
Ordered by: **M.L.**   Requisition No.: **237**

Figure 7-4

Purchase Invoice

K KEY SUPPLIERS
Redville, CA 90362   *Invoice Control No. 101*

Invoice No.: **3329**

Sold to: **Lakeside Electronics**   Date: **November 2, 20X1**
  1200 San Palo Road   Ship Via: **Truck**
  Los Angeles, CA 90099   Your Order No.: **199**

Terms: **2/10,n/30**

Quantity	Description	Unit Price	Total	
1,000 feet	**Galvanized copper cable #4443-6**	**.575**	**575**	**00**

The same invoice serves as both a sales invoice and a purchase invoice. To the seller, it is a **sales invoice**; to the buyer, who gets a copy, it is a **purchase invoice**. Figure 7-4 shows the invoice sent to Lakeside Electronics by Key Suppliers for the purchase order of October 25. Lakeside has assigned its own control number (101) to the invoice.

When the merchandise arrives, the firm's receiving department prepares a **receiving report**, which is a form prepared to verify that goods have been received and accepted.

Our discussion of merchandising has now taken us from the decision to purchase goods to the actual receipt and verification of those goods. Our next step is to make a journal entry to record the cost of merchandise purchased. Before discussing accounting procedures for merchandise, however, we need to discuss merchandise discounts. Discounts are important in merchandising because they result in a decrease in the cost of merchandise purchased. Often, the decision to buy from a particular supplier will depend on what discounts

sales invoice the seller's copy of the bill that identifies and describes the goods sold and how they will be delivered

purchase invoice the buyer's copy of the bill that identifies and describes the goods sold and how they will be delivered

receiving report a form prepared by a buyer to verify that goods have been received and accepted are available. There are two common types of discounts on merchandise: (1) trade discounts and (2) cash discounts. Both are discussed next.

Trade Discounts

Sellers usually print catalogs that show the **list price**, or catalog price, of their merchandise. The actual price charged for identical items, however, may vary because of the class of the buyer (schools, hospitals, retailers, wholesalers, etc.), the quantity of the items sold, and general price changes. For example, a processor of food products may sell to schools and public hospitals at one price but to restaurants and motels at a higher price.

It would be expensive for sellers to print a new catalog each time there was a price change. To permit price changes without having to print new catalogs, many businesses offer **trade discounts**—percentage reductions from the list price of merchandise. For example, merchandise could be listed in a seller's catalog at $800 but offered for sale less a 10% trade discount. Trade discounts are often printed on separate sheets and made available (or not made available) to buyers. When there is an overall price increase on merchandise, the increase can be shown by reducing the discounts or eliminating them altogether.

Trade discounts *are not* recorded in the accounting records of the buyer or the seller. The buyer always records goods at their actual cost. (Remember the *cost principle* from Chapter 1.) The seller records items sold at their actual selling price. For example, Hollis & Sons had merchandise listed for sale at $2,000 less a 10% trade discount. Hise Company purchased the merchandise subject to these terms. The amount of the trade discount is $200 ($2,000 × 10%). Therefore, the amount recorded for the sale by Hollis & Sons is $1,800 ($2,000 – $200), and the amount recorded for the purchase by Hise Company is $1,800. The fact that the goods were listed for $2,000 is immaterial. The actual contract price was $1,800; thus, $1,800 is recorded by both the buyer and the seller.

Cash Discounts

Manufacturers and wholesalers often offer a cash discount to their credit customers. A **cash discount** is a discount offered to encourage prompt and early payment by a buyer. Unlike trade discounts, cash discounts *are recorded* in the accounting records of both the seller and the buyer. The seller refers to cash discounts as **sales discounts**; the buyer refers to them as **purchases discounts**.

A common expression of a cash discount is 2/10,n/30 (read *two ten, net thirty*). This means that a 2% discount can be taken from the invoice price of merchandise if the invoice is paid within 10 days of the date on the invoice. If payment is not made within 10 days, the total amount of the invoice is due within 30 days of the invoice date. If no cash discount is offered, the terms are often stated as n/30. (Net amount is due within 30 days.)

For example, let's assume that on January 1, merchandise with a cost of $600 is purchased subject to terms of 2/10,n/30. If the buyer pays for the goods within 10 days of January 1 (by January 11), a discount of $12 can be taken, as we see on the next page:

Invoice total	$600	Invoice total	$600
Discount rate	× .02	Discount amount	− 12
Discount amount	$ 12	Amount to be paid	$588

The buyer would thus pay $588 in full settlement of the invoice. If payment is not made within 10 days, the full $600 invoice price must be paid within 30 days (by January 31).

Key Point ⊘

The discount period starts with the date of the invoice, not with the date goods are received.

In Chapter 8, we will see how the seller accounts for a cash discount. Later in this chapter, we will record a cash discount for the buyer. For now, let's turn our attention to recording the cost of merchandise purchased.

Review Quiz **7-1**

What is the net amount due on each of the following invoices?

	Invoice Price	Date of Invoice	Terms	Date Paid
(a)	$1,400	June 10	2/10,n/30	June 19
(b)	800	August 28	2/10,n/30	September 5
(c)	900	July 6	1/10,n/30	July 31
(d)	980	December 2	3/10,2/20,n/30	December 18
(e)	400	July 8	n/30	August 7

Check your answers on page 330.

Recording Purchases of Merchandise

Learning Objective

2 Record credit purchases in a general journal and a purchases journal, and post to the accounts payable ledger and the general ledger.

In general use, the word *purchase* refers to the act of buying any product or service. In merchandising, however, the term *purchases*, unless stated otherwise, refers *only* to the purchase of merchandise intended for resale to customers. In this section, we will look at how the purchase of merchandise is recorded and work with a new account entitled Purchases.

The Purchases Account

The cost of all merchandise purchased during an accounting period is debited to a temporary owner's equity account entitled Purchases. (More exact titles, such as Merchandise Purchases or Purchases of Merchandise can be used; however, the briefer title is customary.)

Purchases account a temporary owner's equity account used to record the cost of merchandise purchased for resale; also referred to as the Merchandise Purchases account or the Purchases of Merchandise account

The *sole* purpose of the **Purchases account** is to keep a record of the cost of merchandise purchased for resale during an accounting period. The cost of assets that are not stock in trade, such as equipment and supplies, is recorded in the appropriate asset account, *not* in Purchases. In the final analysis, there are only two classes of buying that a merchandising firm enters into: (1) assets for operating the business and (2) purchases of merchandise for resale.

To better understand the function of the Purchases account, let's look at its placement in the expanded accounting equation.

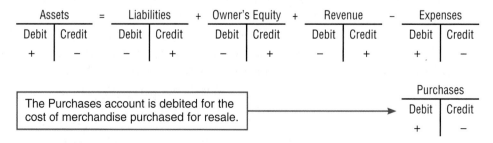

Assets		=	Liabilities		+	Owner's Equity		+	Revenue		−	Expenses	
Debit	Credit		Debit	Credit		Debit	Credit		Debit	Credit		Debit	Credit
+	−		−	+		−	+		−	+		+	−

	Purchases	
The Purchases account is debited for the cost of merchandise purchased for resale.	Debit	Credit
	+	−

The Purchases account falls under the category of cost accounts. **Cost accounts** are like expense accounts; both are presented on the income statement and enter into the calculation of net income (or net loss). They differ, however, in that expense accounts are used to record the cost of items necessary to operate the business (salaries of employees, rent, utilities, repairs, etc.), and cost accounts are used *only* to determine the cost of merchandise sold to customers. We will discuss how to determine the cost of merchandise sold in Chapter 10. Our task now is to record a purchase of merchandise.

Recording Purchases

Recall from Chapter 3 that source documents are used as a basis for making journal entries because they provide written evidence that a transaction has taken place. The source document for recording a purchase of merchandise is the purchase invoice. No journal entry is made from the purchase requisition or the purchase order because at the time they are prepared, no goods have changed hands. To illustrate recording a purchase of merchandise, let's look again at the invoice sent to Lakeside Electronics by Key Suppliers (Figure 7-4). The debit portion of Lakeside's entry is to Purchases, since merchandise was purchased. The credit portion of the entry is to Accounts Payable, since the merchandise was purchased on credit.

	20X1						
+ cost → 1	Nov.	2	Purchases		5 7 5 00		1
+ liability → 2			Accounts Payable—Key Suppliers	/		5 7 5 00	2
3			Purchased merchandise on account.				3

Had the merchandise in this transaction been purchased with cash, the credit would have been to the Cash account. Most merchandise, however, is bought on credit. Buying goods on credit often gives a business time to sell the goods and generate revenue before actually paying for the goods.

Summing Up

> The Purchases account is used only to record the cost of merchandise intended for resale. If the firm buys anything else, it is recorded in the appropriate asset account, not the Purchases account.

Review Quiz **7-2**   Record the following transactions in a general journal.

20X2
Mar.   1   Purchased supplies for cash, $400.
         5   Purchased equipment on account from E & H Co., $900.
         8   Purchased merchandise on account from C. Medlin Co., $1,200.
        18   Purchased merchandise for cash, $300.
        25   Purchased supplies for cash, $250.

Check your answers on page 330.

Special Journals

So far, we have journalized transactions in a two-column general journal. Every general journal entry has at least one debit and at least one credit—and each part of the entry must be individually posted to the ledger. Thus, when the volume of transactions is large, use of a general journal can be time-consuming. To expedite journalizing and posting, many companies use special journals in addition to the general journal. A **special journal** is a journal used to record transactions that are similar in nature. Special journals not only save time in recording specialized transactions but also allow for a delegation of work because individual accountants or bookkeepers can be assigned to specific journals.

In this section, we will start our discussion of special journals. The purchases journal is discussed first.

The Purchases Journal

A business that makes frequent credit purchases can save journalizing and posting time by using a purchases journal. The **purchases journal** is a journal used to record only credit purchases, since most purchases are made on credit. The actual design of a purchases journal is tailored to the needs of the business. Some businesses design their purchases journal to record only credit purchases of merchandise. Other businesses design their purchases journal to record all credit purchases. The purchases journal we will be working with is that of John Graham, owner of Lakeside Electronics—a wholesale distributor of TVs, radios, stereo equipment, electrical supplies, and electronic toys. John's purchases journal is shown in Figure 7-5.

special journal a journal used by businesses to record transactions that are similar in nature; examples are the purchases journal and the cash payments journal; also referred to as a special-purpose journal

purchases journal a special journal used only to record credit purchases of merchandise; sometimes a multicolumn journal used to record all credit purchases, not just merchandise

Lakeside Electronics is a wholesale distributor whose main customers are retail stores, motels, schools, and electrical contractors.

Figure 7-5
Purchases Journal

Key Point ⊙

Only credit purchases of merchandise are recorded in the one-column purchases journal.

	Purchases Journal				Page 1	
	Date	Invoice No.	Account Credited	P.R.	Purchases Dr. Accts. Pay. Cr.	
1	20X1 Nov. 2	101	Key Suppliers		5 7 5 00	1
2	5	102	Master Aerials		2 8 5 0 00	2
3	12	103	Pantech Corporation		6 3 0 0 00	3
4	19	104	Key Suppliers		4 1 0 00	4
5	26	105	Pantech Corporation		3 7 5 00	5
6	28	106	Master Aerials		2 8 0 00	6
7	29	107	Wilks Company		2 4 0 0 00	7
8	29	108	Williams Electrical Company		4 0 0 0 00	8
9	30		Total		17 1 9 0 00	9

Lakeside's purchases journal is designed to record only credit purchases of merchandise. Notice that it has only one money column, entitled Purchases Dr./Accts. Pay. Cr. One money column is enough, because *all* credit purchases of merchandise involve a debit to the Purchases account and a credit to the Accounts Payable account.

The standard Date and P.R. columns are included in Lakeside's purchases journal. Two additional nonmoney columns are also included: (1) an Invoice No. column for writing the number of the invoice for each purchase and (2) an Account Credited column for recording the names of suppliers from whom credit purchases are made.

To illustrate the use of a purchases journal, let's look at the credit purchases of merchandise made by Lakeside Electronics during November 20X1:

20X1
Nov. 2 Purchased copper cable from Key Suppliers, $575; terms, 2/10,n/30.
    5 Purchased antennas from Master Aerials, $2,850; terms, 2/10,n/30.
    12 Purchased TV sets from Pantech Corporation, $6,300; terms, 2/10,n/30.
    19 Purchased TV stands from Key Suppliers, $410; terms, n/30.
    26 Purchased receivers from Pantech Corporation, $375; terms, 2/10,n/30.
    28 Purchased aerials from Master Aerials, $280; terms, n/30.
    29 Purchased electronic toys from Wilks Company, $2,400; terms, 2/10,n/30.
    29 Purchased various items from Williams Electrical Company, $4,000; terms, 2/10,n/30.

Starting with Invoice No. 101, these purchases are recorded in the purchases journal in Figure 7-5. Notice that each entry is recorded on one horizontal line. Also notice that the name of each supplier is written in the Account Credited column, and the number of the invoice related to each purchase is entered in the Invoice No. column. After the last entry on November 29, the journal is totaled.

Take This Into Account

For control purposes, Lakeside Electronics consecutively numbers each purchase invoice when it is received. Some firms use the number assigned to the invoice by the supplier.

Review Quiz 7-3 The following credit purchases were made by Knight Used Cars during May 20X8:

20X8
May 2 Purchased office supplies from Ace Suppliers, $200.
    8 Purchased office equipment from Ace Suppliers, $800.
    12 Purchased automobiles for resale from Tower Auction, $12,400. Invoice No. 48.
    18 Purchased a microcomputer for use in the office from King Co., $4,500.

Continues

May 20 Purchased automobiles for resale from Tower Auction, $57,300. Invoice No. 49.
28 Purchased automobiles for resale from Tower Auction, $60,000. Invoice No. 50.
30 Purchased automobiles for resale from Burr Motors, $45,000. Invoice No. 51.
30 Purchased a van for resale from Clyde Wright, $11,200. Invoice No. 52.

Record these credit purchases using a one-column purchases journal and a two-column general journal. Total the purchases journal.

Check your answers on page 331.

The Accounts Payable Subsidiary Ledger

The Accounts Payable account, as we have seen, is a liability account that represents debts owed to the creditors of a business. When a business has only a few creditors, it is possible to maintain a separate Accounts Payable account for each creditor. If a business has many creditors, which is often the case, having an individual ledger account for each creditor could result in a very large and unwieldy ledger. Imagine, for example, that a business makes credit purchases from 200 different creditors. Then, envision the size of its ledger if, in addition to all other accounts, a separate account were maintained for each creditor. A single ledger would be too large to handle efficiently and would make it difficult to prepare a trial balance or the financial statements.

To overcome these problems, accounts for creditors are often set up in a *separate* ledger. A separate ledger containing only one type of account is called a **subsidiary ledger**. A subsidiary ledger containing only creditors' accounts is called an **accounts payable ledger** or a creditors' ledger. When subsidiary ledgers are used, the main ledger, containing the accounts needed to prepare financial statements, is called the **general ledger**.

Accounts in the accounts payable ledger are designed to show the balance owed to each creditor. The three-column account form, as shown in Figure 7-6, is usually used.

subsidiary ledger a ledger that contains only one type of account, such as the accounts payable ledger

accounts payable ledger a subsidiary ledger that lists the individual accounts of creditors; also referred to as the creditors' ledger

general ledger the main ledger; the ledger containing the accounts needed to prepare the financial statements

Figure 7-6
The Three-Column Account Form

Accounts Payable Ledger						
Name						
Address						
Date	Item	P.R.	Debit	Credit	Balance	

Liability accounts normally have credit balances. Therefore, with rare exceptions, creditors' accounts will have credit balances. Thus, the three-column account form shown above is more suited for creditors' accounts than the four-column account form commonly used in the general ledger.

Accounts in the accounts payable ledger are usually not assigned numbers. Instead, they are arranged in alphabetical order to make it easy to add new accounts and remove inactive accounts.

The balances of creditors' accounts in the accounts payable ledger are summarized by the Accounts Payable account in the general ledger. That is, when all posting is complete, the balance of the Accounts Payable account will equal the sum of the balances of the creditors' accounts. Thus, the Accounts Payable account is said to *control* the accounts payable ledger. A **controlling account** is an account in the general ledger that summarizes accounts in a related subsidiary ledger.

To illustrate the controlling account/subsidiary ledger relationship, let's look at the amounts owed by Judy Bowman, a health and beauty supplies distributor, on March 31, 20X9.

Creditor	Balance Owed
Bibb Cosmetics	$ 250
Davis Office Supply	200
Superior Natural Foods	400
Twin City Beauty Supplies	800
Total	$1,650

Figure 7-7

Relationship Between the Accounts Payable Ledger and the Controlling Account in the General Ledger

Judy maintains an accounts payable subsidiary ledger, which is summarized by an Accounts Payable controlling account in her general ledger. Figure 7-7 shows the relationship between the two.

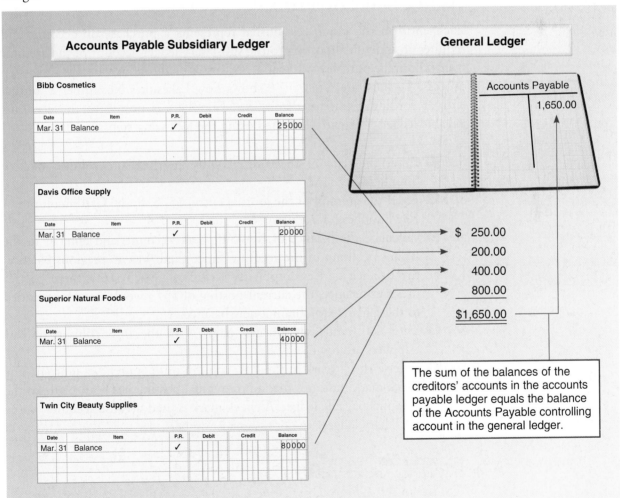

Posting the Purchases Journal

The process of posting from the purchases journal, or any special journal, requires extra care compared to the posting we did in earlier chapters because postings are made to *both* the subsidiary ledger and the general ledger. To illustrate, let's look again at Lakeside Electronics' purchases journal (shown in Figure 7-5). Two types of postings are made from Lakeside's purchases journal:

1. Posting of individual credits to creditors' accounts in the accounts payable ledger. To keep the accounts payable ledger current, posting is usually done on a daily basis.
2. Posting the total of the money column to the general ledger as a debit to the Purchases account and a credit to the Accounts Payable account. Since this total represents total credit purchases for the month, it is posted at the end of the month.

Posting to the Accounts Payable Ledger

Each entry in the purchases journal represents a purchase on account and requires an individual posting to the subsidiary ledger account of the creditor from whom the purchase was made. Posting to creditors' accounts is a five-step process. To illustrate, Figure 7-8 shows how Lakeside's November 2 journal entry recording a purchase from Key Suppliers is posted to the accounts payable ledger. The entry is posted using the following steps:

Step **1** Enter the date of the journal entry in the Date column of Key Suppliers' account.

Step **2** Enter the amount of the journal entry, $575, in the Credit column of Key Suppliers' account.

Step **3** Calculate the balance of Key Suppliers' account, and enter it in the Balance column of the account. Since there was no previous balance, the balance of Key Suppliers' account is $575. Had there been a previous balance, the current posting of $575 would have been added to that balance to obtain a new balance.

Step **4** Enter P1 (*purchases journal, page 1*) in the P.R. column of Key Suppliers' account.

Step **5** Enter a check mark in the P.R. column of the purchases journal. The check mark indicates that an individual posting has been made to the accounts payable ledger. A check mark is used because accounts in the subsidiary ledger are not assigned numbers.

Figure 7-8

Posting from the Purchases Journal to the Accounts Payable Ledger

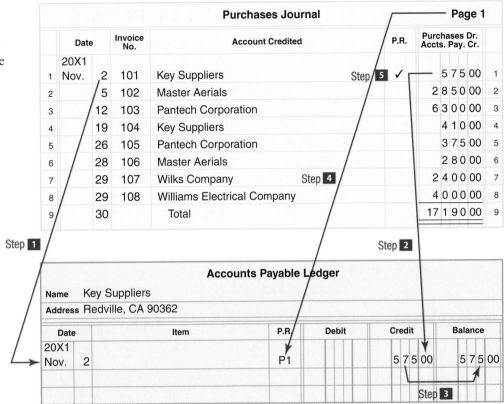

Posting to the General Ledger

Although the purchases journal has only one money column, the total of the column is posted *twice* to the general ledger; once as a debit to the Purchases account and once as a credit to the Accounts Payable account. This, too, is a five-step process. Let's look at Figure 7-9 to see how it is done for Lakeside Electronics on November 30, 20X1.

Step **1** Enter the last day of the month, November 30, in the Date columns of the Purchases and Accounts Payable accounts.

Step **2** Enter the total of the money column, $17,190, on the debit side of the Purchases account and the credit side of the Accounts Payable account.

Step **3** Calculate the new balance of the accounts by adding the current posting to the previous balance.

Step **4** Enter P1 in the P.R. columns of the accounts.

Step **5** Enter the numbers of the accounts, 211 and 511, directly below the column total in the purchases journal to indicate that the amounts have been posted.

We should note two other points concerning the posting of the purchases journal:

• The Purchases account is numbered 511. Purchases and related accounts are numbered in the 500 series, which we will use for cost accounts.

• Even though individual postings were made to each creditor's account in the accounts payable ledger, the total of the money column is still

Figure 7-9

Posting from the Purchases Journal to the General Ledger

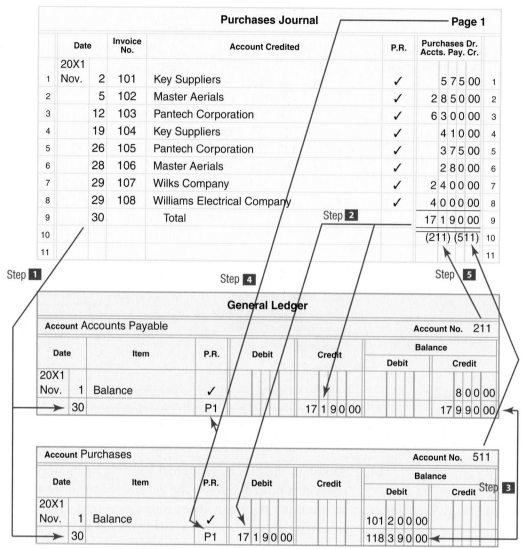

posted to the Accounts Payable controlling account in the general ledger. Remember that the balance of the Accounts Payable controlling account at the end of the month must equal the total of the balances of the creditors' accounts in the accounts payable subsidiary ledger.

CAUTION

Never record the same transaction in two journals. If a purchase recorded in the purchases journal is also recorded in the general journal, the result would be double recording and thus double posting.

Merchandise Returns and Allowances

In merchandising, a *return* occurs when a customer returns to the seller part (or all) of the items purchased. An *allowance* occurs when the seller grants a customer a price reduction on items due to some factor, such as damaged or defective goods.

purchases returns and allowances returns of merchandise purchased or price reductions received for damaged or irregular merchandise

Almost all merchandising concerns encounter the problem of merchandise returns and allowances. Goods may have been damaged while in shipment, may have been shipped in the wrong size or color, or may not suit the specific needs of the customer. Items purchased as gifts may be the wrong size and thus returned for a refund.

The seller refers to merchandise returns or allowances as sales returns and allowances; the purchaser refers to merchandise returns or allowances as **purchases returns and allowances**. In this chapter, we are concerned with purchases returns and allowances. In Chapter 8, we will learn the proper accounting treatment for sales returns and allowances.

Purchases Returns and Allowances

The effect of a purchase return or allowance is a decrease in the cost of merchandise purchased. The amount of returns and allowances could be *credited* directly to the Purchases account. (Recall that Purchases is *debited* when merchandise is purchased.) This practice, however, would not provide a separate record of purchases returns and allowances. To provide for better control, the amount of returns and allowances is usually recorded in a contra account entitled the **Purchases Returns and Allowances account**.

Purchases Returns and Allowances account a contra purchases account used to record returns and allowances on merchandise purchases

The Purchases Returns and Allowances account is contra to the Purchases account. Thus, the Purchases Returns and Allowances account has a normal credit balance, which is opposite the debit balance of the Purchases account. This is illustrated by the following T accounts.

Purchases 511		Purchases Returns and Allowances 511.1	
Debit	Credit	Debit	Credit
+	–	–	+
To record the cost of merchandise purchased for resale.			To record the cost of merchandise returned and allowances received.

Purchases Returns and Allowances is a deduction from Purchases. Its balance is thus opposite the balance of Purchases.

The balance of the Purchases Returns and Allowances account is shown on the income statement as a reduction in the balance of the Purchases account. The account number, 511.1, assigned to Purchases Returns and Allowances indicates that it is contra to account number 511, the Purchases account.

Recording Purchases Returns and Allowances

Learning Objective

3 Record purchases returns and allowances.

When a return or allowance on merchandise is needed, the buyer must inform the seller of the details surrounding the return or allowance. The buyer often does this by sending a debit memorandum. A **debit memorandum** is the buyer's written request to the seller for credit for a merchandise return or allowance. The buyer maintains an accounts payable ledger account for each creditor. Creditors' accounts in the accounts payable ledger have normal *credit* balances. When a return or allowance is made, part (or all) of the balance in the creditor's account will not be paid. Consequently, the buyer *debits* (decreases) the creditor's account for the amount of the return or allowance; thus, the term *debit memorandum*. The debit memorandum in Figure 7-10 was issued to Master Aerials by Lakeside Electronics on December 2, 20X1.

Figure 7-10

Debit Memorandum

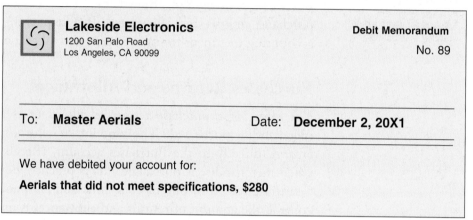

After receiving the buyer's debit memorandum, the seller usually issues a **credit memorandum**, or written statement that indicates a seller's willingness to reduce the amount owed by the buyer. (Credit memorandums will be discussed further in Chapter 8.) The buyer can use a copy of the debit memorandum as a source document for recording the return or wait for confirmation from the seller and use the credit memorandum as a source document. Lakeside uses debit memorandums as source documents to record purchases returns. The entry, with posting, that was made to record the above debit memorandum is shown in Figure 7-11.

Notice that the debit part of this entry involved Accounts Payable (a controlling account) and Master Aerials (a creditor's account). Debits or credits to the controlling account require a posting to *both* the controlling account in the general ledger and the creditor's account in the accounts payable ledger. To indicate that this dual posting is necessary, a diagonal line is drawn in the P.R. column of the journal at the time of journalizing. In the journal entry in Figure 7-11, the diagonal line signifies that a $280 debit posting needs to be made to *both* the Accounts Payable controlling account in the general ledger and the Master Aerials account in the accounts payable subsidiary ledger.

Posting is usually made to the general ledger at the end of the month, but it is usually made daily to the subsidiary ledger. When the entry in Figure 7-11 was posted to the subsidiary ledger, a small check mark (✓) was made to the right of the diagonal line. When posting was made to the Accounts Payable controlling account, the account number of Accounts Payable (211) was written to the left of the diagonal line.

Figure 7-11

Entry and Dual Posting to General and Subsidiary Ledgers

General Journal   Page 8

Date		Account Title	P.R.	Debit	Credit	
20X1						1
Dec.	2	Accounts Payable—Master Aerials	211/✓	2 8 0 00		1
		Purchases Returns and Allowances	511.1		2 8 0 00	2
						3

Accounts Payable Ledger

Name   Master Aerials

Address

Date		Item	P.R.	Debit	Credit	Balance
20X1						
Dec.	1	Balance	✓			2 8 0 00
	2		GJ8	2 8 0 00		-0-

General Ledger

Account   Accounts Payable   Account No.   211

Date		Item	P.R.	Debit	Credit	Balance Debit	Balance Credit
20X1							
Dec.	1	Balance	✓				8 2 6 5 00
	2		GJ8	2 8 0 00			7 9 8 5 00

Account   Purchases Returns and Allowances   Account No. 511.1

Date		Item	P.R.	Debit	Credit	Balance Debit	Balance Credit
20X1							
Dec.	1	Balance	✓				6 4 1 2 00
	2		GJ8		2 8 0 00		6 6 9 2 00

Review Quiz   7-4

The following selected transactions were completed by Scott Hayes, owner of the Hayes Company, during June 20X9. Record each transaction in a general journal.

20X9
Jun.   5   Purchased office supplies on account from B. Spence Suppliers, $300.
      9   Purchased merchandise for cash, $800.
    15   Purchased merchandise on account from Wilks Co., $1,200.
    16   Returned $30 of office supplies for credit to B. Spence Suppliers.
    21   Returned $200 of merchandise for credit to Wilks Co.

Check your answer on page 331.

Recording Cash Payments

As stated previously, most purchases are made on credit. Eventually, however, we must make cash payments for those purchases. We also commonly make cash payments for expenses of operating the business and for cash purchases of merchandise and other assets.

While cash payments can be recorded in a general journal, most businesses use a special journal called the *cash payments journal* or the *cash disbursements journal* to more efficiently record and post cash payments. Before looking at how cash payments are recorded in a cash payments journal, however, we need to take a minute to discuss how cash payments are handled when payment is made in time to take advantage of a purchases discount.

The Purchases Discounts Account

Learning Objective

4 Record purchases discounts.

Earlier in this chapter we learned that some sellers offer a cash discount to the buyer if payment for merchandise is made promptly. The effect of a purchases discount is a reduction in the cost of merchandise purchased. As such, purchases discounts could be recorded on the credit side (the reduction side) of the Purchases account. It is considered a better practice, however, to use a separate account that is contra to the Purchases account. This account is the **Purchases Discounts account**. The nature of the Purchases Discounts account can be illustrated as shown below.

Purchases Discounts	511.2
Debit	Credit
−	+
	To record discounts received for prompt payment of merchandise.

To illustrate how to record a purchases discount, let's look at one of Lakeside's November cash payments. On November 12, 20X1, Lakeside issued a check for $563.50 to Key Suppliers in payment of a November 2 invoice for $575 less a 2% discount ($575 × .02 = $11.50; $575 − $11.50 = $563.50). In general journal form, this entry appears as shown below.

− liability → 1	20X1 Nov.	12	Accounts Payable—Key Suppliers	211/✓	5 7 5 00		1
+ contra purchases → 2			Purchases Discounts	511.2		1 1 50	2
− asset → 3			Cash	111		5 6 3 50	3
4			Paid for November 2 purchase.				4

Now, let's look at how cash payments are recorded in a cash payments journal.

Cash Payments Journal

A **cash payments journal** (or cash disbursements journal) is a special journal used for recording all disbursements of cash. The source document for entries in the cash payments journal is a completed check stub, which you studied in Chapter 6. As with all special journals, the cash payments journal is designed to meet the needs of the business using it. For Lakeside Electronics, John Graham uses a standard cash payments journal (shown in Figure 7-12) with four money columns entitled Cash Cr., Purchases Discounts Cr., Accounts Payable Dr., and General Dr.

A Cash Credit column is always necessary in a cash payments journal because all cash payments involve a credit to the Cash account. The Purchases Discounts Credit column is used to record discounts received for paying invoices within the discount period. The Accounts Payable Debit column is used for recording payments to creditors. And the General Debit column is used for recording debits to accounts other than Accounts Payable. Firms with many frequently occurring expenses or many cash purchases may have other special debit columns.

John's cash payments journal also has a Date column, an Account Debited column, and a P.R. column. John also uses a Ck. No. column for recording the numbers of the source documents. To illustrate the use of the cash payments journal, let's look at Lakeside's cash payments for the month of November 20X1:

20X1

Nov. 2 Issued Ck. No. 126 for November rent, $675.

12 Issued Ck. No. 127 for $563.50 to Key Suppliers in payment of November 2 invoice, less 2% discount.

15 Issued Ck. No. 128 for $2,793 to Master Aerials in payment of November 5 invoice, less 2% discount.

22 Issued Ck. No. 129 for $6,174 to Pantech Corporation in payment of November 12 invoice, less 2% discount.

25 Issued Ck. No. 130 for the cash purchase of merchandise, $800.

27 Issued Ck. No. 131 for payment of the November power bill, $620.

28 Issued Ck. No. 132 for payment of employee salaries for the month, $2,250.

30 Issued Ck. No. 133 for payment of telephone bill, $240.

30 John issued Ck. No. 134 to himself for personal use, $1,500.

Starting with Ck. No. 126, John's November cash payments are recorded in his cash payments journal, as shown in Figure 7-12.

Figure 7-12

Cash Payments Journal

		Ck. No.	Account Debited	P.R.	General Dr.	Accounts Payable Dr.	Purchases Discounts Cr.	Cash Cr.	
	Date								
1	20X1 Nov. 2	126	Rent Expense		675 00			675 00	1
2	12	127	Key Suppliers			575 00	11 50	563 50	2
3	15	128	Master Aerials			2850 00	57 00	2793 00	3
4	22	129	Pantech Corporation			6300 00	126 00	6174 00	4
5	25	130	Purchases		800 00			800 00	5
6	27	131	Utilities Expense		620 00			620 00	6
7	28	132	Salaries Expense		2250 00			2250 00	7
8	30	133	Telephone Expense		240 00			240 00	8
9	30	134	John Graham, Drawing		1500 00			1500 00	9
10	30		Totals		6085 00	9725 00	194 50	15615 50	10

Cash Payments Journal   Page 3

The cash payments journal must be in balance before posting to the general ledger. The proof is shown in Table 7-1.

Table 7-1 Proof

	Debit Columns	Credit Columns
General	$ 6,085.00	
Accounts Payable	9,725.00	
Purchases Discounts		$ 194.50
Cash		15,615.50
Totals	$15,810.00	$15,810.00

Posting the Cash Payments Journal

Posting the cash payments journal follows some of the same procedures you learned for posting the purchases journal. To illustrate, let's look again at Lakeside's November cash payments journal. Three different types of postings are made:

- Posting of individual debits to creditors' accounts in the accounts payable ledger. As stated previously, posting to the accounts payable ledger is usually done on a daily basis.
- Posting of individual debits to appropriate general ledger accounts from the General Debit column. Amounts in this column can be posted on a daily, weekly, or monthly basis.
- Posting of special column totals to the appropriate general ledger accounts. Summary posting of special column totals is done at the end of the month.

Each type of posting is discussed and illustrated next.

Posting to the Accounts Payable Ledger

Each amount in the Accounts Payable Debit column is posted daily to the specific creditor's account in the accounts payable ledger, as shown in Figure 7-13 on pages 302–303.

To indicate that a posting has been made to the accounts payable ledger, a check mark is entered in the P.R. column of the cash payments journal next to the name of the creditor. To complete the cross-reference, the code CP and the page number of the cash payments journal are entered in the P.R. column of the creditor's account to which a posting was made. Notice that the debit postings from the cash payments journal reduce the balances of the creditors' accounts. Remember that creditors' accounts represent liabilities; thus, they normally have credit balances. Consequently, a debit posting results in a reduction in the account.

Posting Individual Entries in the General Debit Column to the General Ledger

Each amount appearing in the General Debit column is posted individually to the general ledger account named in the Account Debited column, as shown in Figure 7-13. The notation CP with a page number is entered in the P.R. column of each general ledger account to which a posting was made, and the appropriate account number is entered in the P.R. column of the cash payments journal. A check mark is entered under the General Debit column total to indicate that a summary posting is not made; the amounts have already been posted individually. Notice that the date used for posting is the *date of the journal entry*, even if posting is made at the end of the month.

Posting Special Column Totals to the General Ledger

Special column totals are posted to the general ledger at the end of the month, as shown in Figure 7-13.

As you have already learned, account numbers are entered below special column totals to indicate summary postings. To complete the cross-reference, the code CP with a page number is entered in the P.R. column of the ledger accounts affected. Notice that the date used for summary posting is November 30, the last day of the month.

Proving the Accounts Payable Ledger

Learning Objective

6 Prepare a schedule of accounts payable.

schedule of accounts payable a listing of the individual creditor account balances in the accounts payable ledger

Let's now look at Figure 7-14 on page 304 to see the complete accounts payable ledger of Lakeside Electronics, as it appears on November 30.

From the accounts payable ledger, we can prepare a **schedule of accounts payable**, which is simply a listing of the balances in the accounts payable ledger. Figure 7-15 on page 304 shows Lakeside's schedule of accounts payable as of November 30, 20X1.

The accounts payable ledger shows the amounts owed to individual creditors, and the Accounts Payable controlling account shows the total amount owed to *all* creditors. Thus, when all posting has been completed, the total of the schedule of accounts payable should agree with the balance of the Accounts Payable account. This is easy to check by comparing the schedule of accounts payable with the balance of the Accounts Payable account, which is shown in Figure 7-16 on page 305, fully posted.

Freight Charges on Incoming Merchandise

Learning Objective

7 Record freight charges on incoming merchandise.

FOB (free on board) shipping point a shipping term that means that the buyer is responsible for all freight costs while the goods are in transit

FOB (free on board) destination a shipping term that means that the seller is responsible for all freight costs until the goods reach their destination

Freight In account a cost account in which charges for freight on incoming merchandise are recorded; also referred to as Transportation In

The terms of a sale should always specify who—the buyer or the seller—bears the costs of transporting the goods to the buyer. If the terms are **FOB (free on board) shipping point**, the buyer is responsible for all freight costs while the goods are in transit. Under these terms, the seller pays the freight only to the shipping point; the buyer must pay the freight costs from the shipping point to the point of destination. On the other hand, if the goods are shipped **FOB (free on board) destination**, the seller is responsible for all freight costs until the goods reach their destination.

When the buyer is responsible for freight costs (FOB shipping point), the entire invoice price of goods, including freight, can be debited to the Purchases account. Or, the charges for freight can be debited to a separate account entitled Freight In. The **Freight In account**, also called Transportation In, is a cost account in which charges for freight on incoming merchandise are recorded. For example, on December 2, 20X1, Lakeside purchased merchandise costing $700 on account from Pantech Corporation. The goods were shipped *FOB*

Figure 7-13

Posting the Cash
Payments Journal to
the General Ledger
and the Accounts
Payable Ledger

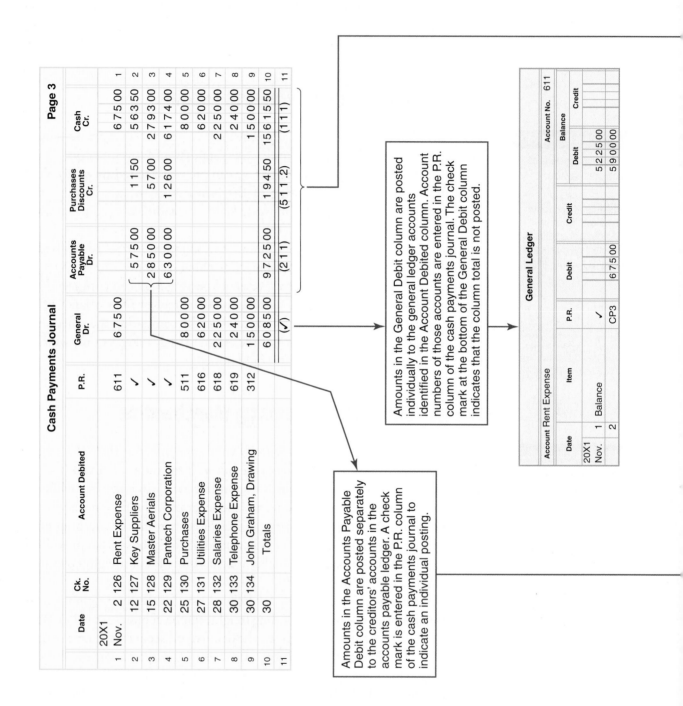

Cash Payments Journal   Page 3

Date		Ck. No.	Account Debited	P.R.	General Dr.	Accounts Payable Dr.	Purchases Discounts Cr.	Cash Cr.	
20X1									
Nov.	2	126	Rent Expense	611	675 00			675 00	1
	12	127	Key Suppliers	✓		575 00	11 50	563 50	2
	15	128	Master Aerials	✓		2850 00	57 00	2793 00	3
	22	129	Pantech Corporation	✓		6300 00	126 00	6174 00	4
	25	130	Purchases	511	800 00			800 00	5
	27	131	Utilities Expense	616	620 00			620 00	6
	28	132	Salaries Expense	618	2250 00			2250 00	7
	30	133	Telephone Expense	619	240 00			240 00	8
	30	134	John Graham, Drawing	312	1500 00			1500 00	9
	30		Totals		6085 00	9725 00	194 50	15615 50	10
					(✓)	(211)	(511.2)	(111)	11

Amounts in the Accounts Payable Debit column are posted separately to the creditors' accounts in the accounts payable ledger. A check mark is entered in the P.R. column of the cash payments journal to indicate an individual posting.

Amounts in the General Debit column are posted individually to the general ledger accounts identified in the Account Debited column. Account numbers of those accounts are entered in the P.R. column of the cash payments journal. The check mark at the bottom of the General Debit column indicates that the column total is not posted.

General Ledger

Account Rent Expense   Account No. 611

Date		Item	P.R.	Debit	Credit	Balance Debit	Balance Credit
20X1							
Nov.	1	Balance	✓			5225 00	
	2		CP3	675 00		5900 00	

The totals of special columns are posted to the general ledger accounts identified in the headings of the columns. Account numbers are entered under the column totals to indicate that a summary posting has been made.

General Ledger

Account Cash   **Account No.** 111

Date	Item	P.R.	Debit	Credit	Balance Debit	Balance Credit
20X1						
Nov. 1	Balance	✓			21400 00	
30		CP3		15615 50	5784 50	

Account Accounts Payable   **Account No.** 211

Date	Item	P.R.	Debit	Credit	Balance Debit	Balance Credit
20X1						
Nov. 1	Balance	✓				8000 00
30		P1		17190 00		17990 00
30		CP3	9725 00			8265 00

Account Purchases Discounts   **Account No.** 511.2

Date	Item	P.R.	Debit	Credit	Balance Debit	Balance Credit
20X1						
Nov. 1	Balance	✓				2321 00
30		CP3		194 50		2515 50

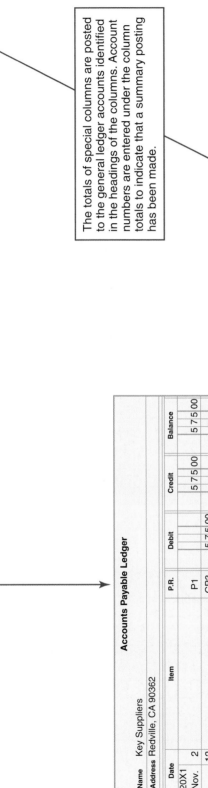

Accounts Payable Ledger

Name Key Suppliers
Address Redville, CA 90362

Date	Item	P.R.	Debit	Credit	Balance
20X1					
Nov. 2		P1		575 00	575 00
12		CP3	575 00		—

Name Master Aerials
Address 17 Tulane Way, Sacramento, CA 95816

Date	Item	P.R.	Debit	Credit	Balance
20X1					
Nov. 5		P1		2850 00	2850 00
15		CP3	2850 00		—

Name Pantech Corporation
Address 4460 Riverfront Dr., Columbus, OH 43206

Date	Item	P.R.	Debit	Credit	Balance
20X1					
Nov. 12		P1		6300 00	6300 00
22		CP3	6300 00		—

Figure 7-14

Complete
Accounts
Payable
Ledger

Accounts Payable Ledger

Name Key Suppliers
Address Redville, CA 90362

Date		Item	P.R.	Debit	Credit	Balance
20X1 Nov.	2		P1		5 7 5 00	5 7 5 00
	12		CP3	5 7 5 00		—
	19		P1		4 1 0 00	4 1 0 00

Name Master Aerials
Address 17 Tulane Way, Sacramento, CA 95816

Date		Item	P.R.	Debit	Credit	Balance
20X1 Nov.	5		P1		2 8 5 0 00	2 8 5 0 00
	15		CP3	2 8 5 0 00		—
	28		P1		2 8 0 00	2 8 0 00

Name Pantech Corporation
Address 4460 Riverfront Dr., Columbus, OH 43206

Date		Item	P.R.	Debit	Credit	Balance
20X1 Nov.	12		P1		6 3 0 0 00	6 3 0 0 00
	22		CP3	6 3 0 0 00		—
	26		P1		3 7 5 00	3 7 5 00

Name Wilks Company
Address 1211 12th Ave. West, Los Angeles, CA 90012

Date		Item	P.R.	Debit	Credit	Balance
20X1 Nov.	29		P1		2 4 0 0 00	2 4 0 0 00

Name Williams Electrical Company
Address 1718 54th St., Los Angeles, CA 90038

Date		Item	P.R.	Debit	Credit	Balance
20X1 Nov.	1	Balance	✓			8 0 0 00
	29		P1		4 0 0 0 00	4 8 0 0 00

Figure 7-15

Schedule of Accounts
Payable

Lakeside Electronics
Schedule of Accounts Payable
November 30, 20X1

Key Suppliers	4 1 0 00
Master Aerials	2 8 0 00
Pantech Corporation	3 7 5 00
Wilks Company	2 4 0 0 00
Williams Electrical Company	4 8 0 0 00
Total	8 2 6 5 00

Only accounts with open balances are included on the schedule of accounts payable.

Figure 7-16

Accounts Payable After
End-of-Month Posting

Account Accounts Payable						Account No. 211			
Date	Item	P.R.	Debit	Credit	Balance				
					Debit		Credit		
20X1 Nov. 1	Balance	✓						8 0 0	00
30		P1		17 1 9 0 00				17 9 9 0	00
30		CP3	9 7 2 5 00					8 2 6 5	00

shipping point, and there was a $30 transportation charge. The general journal entry to record the purchase is shown below.

		20X1					
+ cost →	1	Dec. 2	Purchases		7 0 0 00		1
+ cost →	2		Freight In		3 0 00		2
+ liability →	3		Accounts Payable—Pantech Corp.	/		7 3 0 00	3
	4		Purchased merchandise on account.				4

Since most of Lakeside's purchases are shipped FOB destination (seller pays the freight), Lakeside records such freight charges in a general journal. However, if a firm frequently buys merchandise FOB shipping point, the purchases journal can be expanded to three columns to record the freight charge. Let's assume for a moment that Lakeside uses such a purchases journal. The above entry would then be recorded as shown below.

	Purchases Journal						Page 2	
Date	Account Credited	Invoice No.	Terms	P.R.	Accts. Pay. Cr.	Freight In Dr.	Purchases Dr.	
20X1 1 Dec. 2	Pantech Corporation	113	2/10,n/30	✓	7 3 0 00	3 0 00	7 0 0 00	1

The balance of the Freight In account is not treated as an operating expense. Rather, its balance is shown on the income statement as an addition to the Purchases account, to obtain the delivered cost of purchases. We will discuss this further in Chapter 10 when we look at the income statement for a merchandising business.

We should stress that the Freight In account is used *only* to record freight on incoming merchandise. Freight paid on assets purchased for use in the business is debited to the asset account itself, *not* Freight In.

Summing Up

In this chapter, we have added the Purchases account and three purchases-related account titles to the chart of accounts and general ledger: Freight In, Purchases Returns and Allowances, and Purchases Discounts. Notice how each affects the Purchases account.

Key Point ⊗

Purchases
− Purchases Discount
− Purchases Returns and Allowances
+ Freight In
_____
Net Purchases

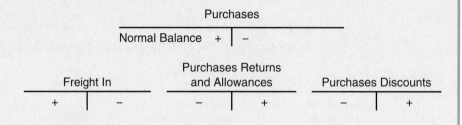

Purchases		
Normal Balance +	−	

Freight In		Purchases Returns and Allowances		Purchases Discounts	
+	−	−	+	−	+

Purchase Invoices as a Journal

We have stressed that the actual design of a special journal is tailored to the needs of the business using it. Thus, it naturally follows that there are many variations in the appearance and use of special journals. One variation involves using purchase invoices as a purchases journal. Using this method, posting is made to the accounts payable ledger directly from individual invoices. As a posting reference, invoice numbers are entered in the P.R. columns of creditors' accounts.

At the end of the month, the invoices are totaled, and a summarizing entry is made in the general journal. To illustrate this method, let's use the example of SaveWay Market, a small independent grocery store. At the end of August 20X3, SaveWay's bookkeeper sorts the month's invoices and finds that the totals are as follows: purchases of merchandise, $12,400; freight in, $288; store supplies, $212; office supplies, $190; and office equipment, $495. The bookkeeper then makes a summarizing entry, as shown below.

		20X3				
+ cost →	1	Aug.	31	Purchases	12 4 0 0 00		1
+ cost →	2			Freight In	2 8 8 00		2
+ asset →	3			Store Supplies	2 1 2 00		3
+ asset →	4			Office Supplies	1 9 0 00		4
+ asset →	5			Office Equipment	4 9 5 00		5
+ liability →	6			Accounts Payable		13 5 8 5 00	6
	7			Recorded purchases for August.			7

Inventory Fraud

To fulfill his dream of opening a hardware store in another state, the purchasing manager for a large company decided he could "borrow" from his employer. He started approving purchases of merchandise for his employer and then moving the inventory to a rented warehouse. He used this as his base to ship the merchandise to the new state. His limit for merchandise purchase approval was only $5,000, so all of his transactions were under that amount.

Internal auditors should examine *all* merchandise transactions.

One accounts payable clerk started noticing that large purchases frequently were being broken into smaller amounts. He wisely alerted the in-house fraud examiners, who quickly discovered hundreds of thousands of inventory purchases that were nonexistent. Had the auditors regularly conducted detailed reviews of purchases under $5,000, this crime could have been averted or prevented much earlier.

Source: Joseph T. Wells, CPA, CFE, "Occupational Fraud: The Audit as Deterrent," *AICPA* (April 2002).

For Discussion

1. What violation of internal controls has occurred?
2. How was this accounting fraud discovered?
3. Why should auditors be sure to audit smaller purchases of merchandise rather than audit only larger dollar amounts?

Joining the Pieces

Procedures for Posting the Purchases Journal

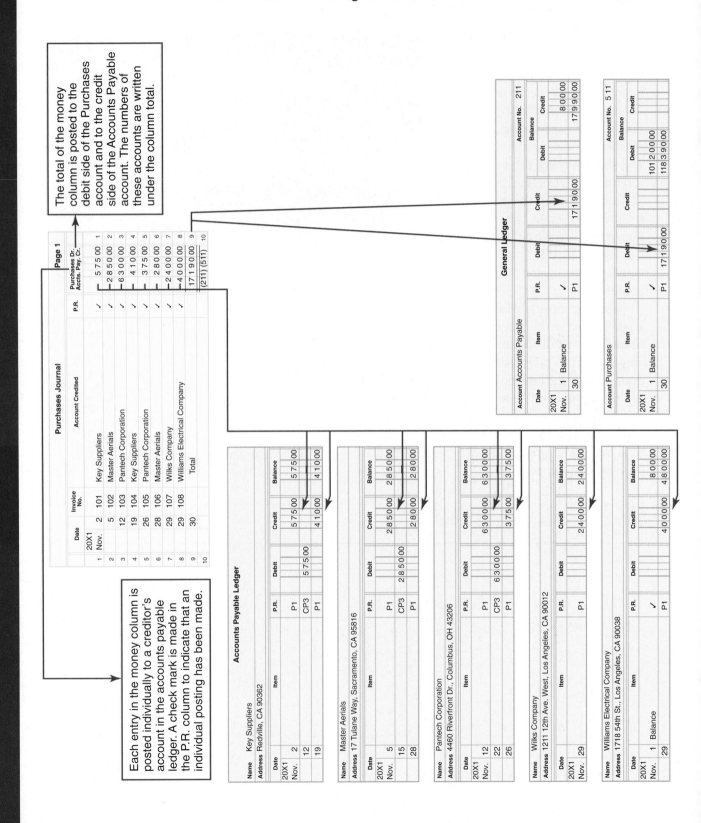

The total of the money column is posted to the debit side of the Purchases account and to the credit side of the Accounts Payable account. The numbers of these accounts are written under the column total.

Each entry in the money column is posted individually to a creditor's account in the accounts payable ledger. A check mark is made in the P.R. column to indicate that an individual posting has been made.

Procedures for Posting the Cash Payments Journal

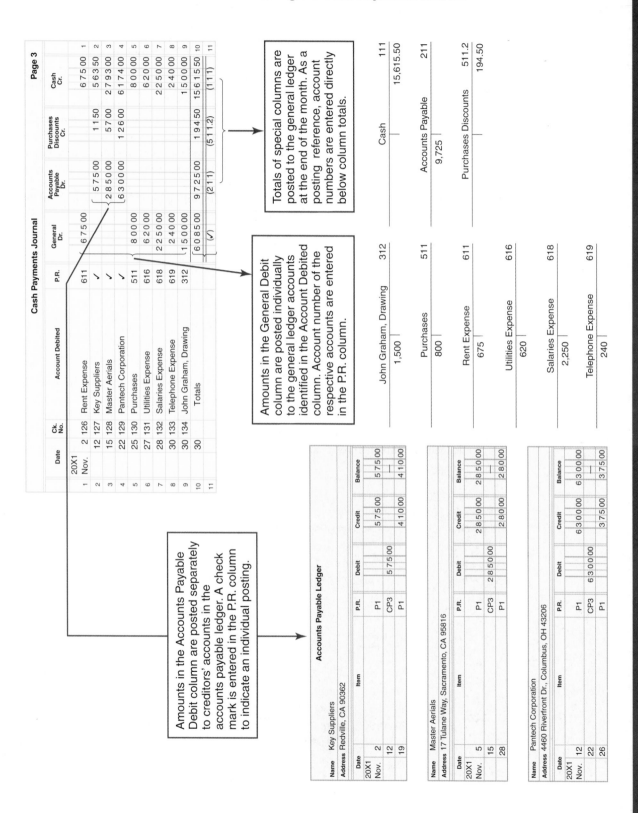

Summary

Interactive Summary in English and Spanish

1 Describe the procedures and forms used in purchasing merchandise.

Just as there is a great variety in the types and sizes of merchandising firms, there is also a great variety in the procedures used to buy goods to be resold. In a small retail firm, the owner may do all the buying. In large retail and wholesale concerns, purchasing begins with the preparation of a **purchase requisition** by any department in the firm. This form is sent to the purchasing department, where a **purchase order** is prepared and sent to a supplier. On receipt and acceptance of the purchase order, the supplier prepares an **invoice**, which is a form that describes the goods and the details of the purchase. The invoice is sent to the buyer with the goods or a few days later. When the buyer receives the goods, a **receiving report** is prepared by the receiving department.

2 Record credit purchases in a general journal and a purchases journal, and post to the accounts payable ledger and the general ledger.

The Yogurt Shoppe made the following credit purchases during July 20XX:

20XX
Jul.   1   Merchandise from Alder Company, $750; terms, 2/10,n/30.
        7   Merchandise from Beeler Company, $900; terms, 2/10,n/30.
       16   Equipment from Caldwell Company, $2,500; terms, n/30.
       22   Supplies from Lamont Suppliers, $400; terms, n/30.
       28   Merchandise from Beeler Company, $500; terms, 2/10,n/30.
       29   Merchandise from Alder Company, $400; terms, 2/10,n/30.

These transactions are recorded in the general journal and **purchases journal** that follow. Remember that only credit purchases of merchandise are recorded in a one-column purchases journal. Credit purchases of nonmerchandise items are recorded in the general journal. Posting references are shown in the purchase journal; however, the ledger accounts themselves are not shown since numerous examples are shown in the chapter.

		20XX						
+ asset →	1	Jul.	16	Equipment		2 5 0 0 00		1
+ liability →	2			Accounts Payable—Caldwell Company	/		2 5 0 0 00	2
	3							3
+ asset →	4		22	Supplies		4 00 00		4
+ liability →	5			Accounts Payable—Lamont Suppliers	/		4 00 00	5

			Purchases Journal			Page 1
	Date	Invoice No.	Account Credited	P.R.	Purchases Dr. Accts. Pay. Cr.	
	20XX					
1	Jul. 1	1	Alder Company	✓	7 5 0 00	1
2	7	2	Beeler Company	✓	9 0 0 00	2
3	28	5	Beeler Company	✓	5 0 0 00	3
4	29	6	Alder Company	✓	4 0 0 00	4
5	31		Total		2 5 5 0 00	5
6					(211) (511)	6

3 Record purchases returns and allowances.

On December 14, 20XX, Turner's Imported World purchased merchandise costing $5,800 on account from North American Importers. On December 19, on receipt of the merchandise, Turner discovered that an oriental rug costing $500 was not the one ordered. The item was returned for credit. In general journal form, entries to record the purchase and the return are shown below.

+ cost →	1	20XX Dec.	14	Purchases		5 80 0 00			1
+ liability →	2			Accts. Payable—No. American Importers	/		5 80 0 00		2
	3			Purchased merchandise on account.					3
	4								4
– liability →	5		19	Accts. Payable—No. American Importers	/	5 0 0 00			5
+ contra purchases →	6			Purchases Returns and Allowances			5 0 0 00		6
	7			Returned merchandise for credit.					7

4 Record purchases discounts.

A **cash discount** is a discount offered by a seller to encourage prompt payment by a buyer. To the seller, the cash discount is a **sales discount**; to the buyer, it is a **purchases discount**. A common expression of a cash discount is 2/10,n/30, which means that a 2% discount can be deducted if merchandise is paid for within 10 days of the date of the invoice.

To review how to record purchases discounts (sales discounts are discussed in Chapter 8), assume that on June 12, 20X3, Jeanette Register purchased $500 worth of merchandise, with terms of 2/10,n/30, from Joe Lewis Company. The following entry was made to record Jeanette's payment for the goods on June 22.

– liability →	1	20X3 Jun.	22	Accounts Payable—Joe Lewis Co.	/	5 0 0 00			1
+ contra purchases →	2			Purchases Discounts ($500 × .02)			1 0 00		2
– asset →	3			Cash			4 9 0 00		3
	4			Paid for June 12 purchase.					4

5 Record cash payments in a cash payments journal and post to the accounts payable ledger and the general ledger.

The Yogurt Shoppe made the following cash expenditures during July 20XX:

20XX
Jul.   1   Paid rent, $450.
       5   Purchased merchandise for cash, $820.
       9   Paid Alder Company amount owed, $750, less 2% discount.
     17   Paid Beeler Company amount owed, $900, less 2% discount.
     25   Paid Caldwell Company amount owed, $2,500, no discount.
     30   Paid utility bill for the month, $625.
     31   Paid salaries for the month, $1,200.

These payments are recorded in the **cash payments journal**. Posting references are shown in the P.R. column and below the money column totals; however, the ledgers are not shown since they are illustrated in the chapter.

	Date		Ck. No.	Account Debited	P.R.	General Dr.	Accounts Payable Dr.	Purchases Discounts Cr.	Cash Cr.	
						Cash Payments Journal			Page 2	
1	20XX Jul.	1	1	Rent Expense	611	4 50 00			4 50 00	1
2		5	2	Purchases	511	8 20 00			8 20 00	2
3		9	3	Alder Company	✓		7 50 00	15 00	7 35 00	3
4		17	4	Beeler Company	✓		9 00 00	18 00	8 82 00	4
5		25	5	Caldwell Company	✓		25 00 00		25 00 00	5
6		30	6	Utilities Expense	614	6 25 00			6 25 00	6
7		31	7	Salaries Expense	618	12 00 00			12 00 00	7
8		31		Totals		30 95 00	41 50 00	33 00	72 12 00	8
9						(✓)	(211)	(511.2)	(111)	9

6 Prepare a schedule of accounts payable.

A **schedule of accounts payable** is a listing of all account balances in the **accounts payable ledger**. The total of the schedule is compared with the balance of the Accounts Payable controlling account (in the general ledger) to verify the posting accuracy of the subsidiary ledger. After all postings are complete, the total of the schedule of accounts payable should agree with the balance of the Accounts Payable account.

7 Record freight charges on incoming merchandise.

When merchandise is shipped **FOB (free on board) shipping point**, the buyer is responsible for paying freight (to destination) charges. There are two ways of accounting for freight charges on incoming merchandise: (1) the freight charge can be debited to the Purchases account along with the cost of the merchandise purchased, or (2) the freight charge can be debited to a separate account entitled the **Freight In account**. To illustrate the use of the Freight In account, assume that on March 18, 20X4, Lee Drug Company purchased merchandise costing $800 on account from Central Supply Company. Terms of shipment were FOB shipping point, and there was a $40 freight charge. The purchase is recorded in general journal form as follows:

		20X4						
+ cost →	1	Mar.	18	Purchases		8 00 00		1
+ cost →	2			Freight In		40 00		2
+ liability →	3			Accts. Payable—Central Supply Co.	/		8 40 00	3
	4			Purchased merchandise on account.				4

Terms and Concepts Review

- Key Terms and Definitions in English and Spanish
- Additional Quiz Questions

Key Terms

accounts payable ledger, 290
cash discount, 285
cash payments journal, 298
controlling account, 291
cost accounts, 287
credit memorandum, 296
debit memorandum, 296
FOB (free on board) destination, 301

FOB (free on board) shipping point, 301
Freight In account, 301
general ledger, 290
invoice, 283
list price, 285
merchandise, 281
merchandising business, 281
purchase invoice, 284

purchase order, 283

purchase requisition, 282

Purchases account, 286

purchases discounts, 285

Purchases Discounts account, 298

purchases journal, 288

purchases returns and allowances, 295

Purchases Returns and Allowances
  account, 295

receiving report, 284

retail business, 281

sales discounts, 285

sales invoice, 284

schedule of accounts payable, 301

special journal, 288

subsidiary ledger, 290

trade discounts, 285

wholesaler, 282

Concepts Review

1. How can a computer be classified as equipment in one business but as merchandise in another?
2. What is the difference between merchandising activity on the retail level and that on the wholesale level?
3. How are trade discounts shown in the accounting records?
4. How does a cash discount differ from a trade discount?
5. How can one discount be both a sales discount and a purchases discount?
6. State the meaning of the following credit terms: (a) n/30; (b) 2/10,n/30; and (c) 3/10,2/20,n/30.
7. Why is the Purchases account an owner's equity account?
8. What form is used as a source document to record a purchase?
9. How does a special journal save time in both recording and posting?
10. Are all purchases recorded in the purchases journal? Explain your answer.
11. Why is a subsidiary ledger considered to be a secondary ledger?
12. Explain why posting an entry both to an individual creditor's account and to the Accounts Payable account does not cause an imbalance in the general ledger.
13. How does a merchandise allowance differ from a merchandise return?
14. Compare a debit memorandum with a credit memorandum by stating (a) who prepares each form and (b) what the debit memorandum's purpose is.
15. How does the purchaser of goods account for a cash discount?
16. What is the function of the General Debit column in the cash payments journal?
17. What three types of postings are made from the cash payments journal?
18. How is the accuracy of posting to a subsidiary ledger checked?
19. a. What is meant by transportation terms?
    b. Identify two common transportation terms.
20. Identify two ways to account for freight on incoming merchandise.
21. How can purchase invoices be used in place of a purchases journal?

Skills Review

Learning Objective **1**

Check Figure
None

Quick Practice

Quick Practice 7-1

Objective: To arrange purchasing procedures in correct order

Directions: Arrange the following purchasing procedures in the correct order.
  a. The purchasing department chooses the seller (vendor) and sends an order.
  b. When the merchandise is received by the buyer, it is checked against the invoice and payment is approved.
  c. Managers identify goods needed and request them by preparing a purchase requisition, which is sent to the purchasing department.
  d. The seller receives the order and prepares an invoice (bill), which is shipped with the goods or a few days after the goods are shipped.

Learning Objective 2

Check Figure
(a) $420

Quick Practice 7-2

Objective: To calculate net prices when trade discounts are used

Directions: For each letter, calculate the price to be recorded in the accounting records.

	List Price	Trade Discount Rate
(a)	$ 600	30%
(b)	1,350	20%
(c)	1,640	45%
(d)	8,000	14½%

Learning Objective 2

Check Figure
(a) $1,960

Quick Practice 7-3

Objective: To calculate amounts to be paid

Directions: Calculate the amount due on each of the following invoices:

	Invoice Price	Date of Invoice	Terms	Date Paid
(a)	$2,000	February 10	2/10,n/30	February 19
(b)	700	May 2	2/10,n/30	May 31
(c)	1,000	June 9	3/10,2/20,n/30	June 28
(d)	1,380	November 5	n/60	December 30

Learning Objective 2

Check Figure
(1) $2,550

Quick Practice 7-4

Objective: To calculate amounts to be paid

On August 13, 20XX, merchandise was purchased on account from Brunno Studios. The purchase price was $3,000, subject to a 15% trade discount and credit terms of 2/10,n/30.

Directions:
(1). Calculate the net amount to record the invoice, subject to the 15% trade discount.
(2). Calculate the amount to be paid on this invoice within the discount period.

Learning Objective 2

Check Figure
Purchases $2,210 (debit)

Quick Practice 7-5

Objective: To record a purchase of merchandise in a general journal

On January 3, 20XX, Lawrence Scott General Store purchased merchandise on account from Chatterton Company for $2,600 less a trade discount of 15%.

Directions: Record the purchase in a two-column general journal.

Learning Objective 2

Check Figure
Jul. 3 Purchases $7,200 (debit)

Quick Practice 7-6

Objective: To record purchases in a general journal

Redeker Pharmacy made the following credit purchases during July 20XX:

20XX
Jul. 3 Pharmaceutical products from Bruneau Supplies, $7,200
       8 A desk for use in the office from Wrigley Office Supply, $1,100
      24 Candies and gums from Miolla Distributers, $650

Directions: Record each purchase in a two-column general journal.

Learning Objective 2

Check Figure
Jul. 8 Office Equipment $1,100 (debit) in general journal

Quick Practice 7-7

Objective: To record purchases in the appropriate journal

Directions: Record the transactions from Quick Practice 7-6 in a general journal (page 1) and a purchases journal (page 4). Number invoices starting with 101.

Quick Practice 7-8

Objective: To record purchases, returns, and allowances in general journal form

Directions: Record each of the following transactions in general journal form:
(a) Purchased merchandise on credit from Daraee Company, $800.
(b) Returned $30 of the merchandise purchased in Transaction (a), receiving credit.
(c) Purchased merchandise for cash, $120.
(d) Discovered $40 of merchandise purchased in Transaction (c) was defective and received a cash refund.
(e) Purchased office supplies on credit from Zafiris Liquidators, $890.
(f) Discovered some stamp pads purchased in Transaction (e) were defective. An allowance of $20 was granted.

Quick Practice 7-9

Objective: To record cash payments in general journal form

Directions: Cantoria Cash and Carry made the following cash disbursements during May 20XX. Record each cash payment in general journal form.

20XX
May 1 Paid rent for the month, $900.
5 Paid Rapp Corp. for an invoice of April 28, $600 less a 2% discount.
11 Purchased merchandise for cash, $400.
17 Paid Ellis Associates for a $1,300 purchase of merchandise on May 7. The purchase carried terms of 2/10,n/30.
30 Paid monthly salaries, $3,220.

Quick Practice 7-10

Objective: To record cash payments in a cash payments journal

Directions: Record the cash payments from Quick Practice 7-9 in a cash payments journal. Number checks starting with 53. Total and rule the cash payments journal.

Quick Practice 7-11

Objective: To record journal entries to correct errors

Directions: Prepare entries in general journal form to correct each of the following errors:
(a) A $300 return of office supplies was credited to the Purchases Returns and Allowance account.
(b) An invoice for $100 for freight charges on a copy machine purchased for use in the office was debited to the Freight In account
(c) A $1,000 purchase of office calculators intended for resale was debited to the Office Equipment account.

Quick Practice 7-12

Objective: To indicate in which journals various transactions involving the purchase and return of items for a business should be recorded

Directions: Indicate with a check mark where the following transactions should be recorded. The first item is done as an example.

	Purchases Journal	General Journal	Cash Payments Journal
(a) Purchased store supplies on account		✓	
(b) Purchased merchandise on account			
(c) Purchased merchandise for cash			
(d) Purchased store equipment on account			
(e) Returned store supplies purchased on account			
(f) Returned merchandise purchased for cash			
(g) Returned merchandise purchased on account			

Exercises

Learning Objective **1**

Check Figure
(a) $720

Exercise 7-1

Objective: To calculate net prices when trade discounts are used

Directions: For each letter, calculate the price to be recorded in the accounting records.

	List Price	Trade Discount Rate
(a)	$ 900	20%
(b)	1,650	35%
(c)	3,375	18%
(d)	9,860	30%
(e)	1,980	12½%

Learning Objective **1**

Check Figure
(a) $1,960

Exercise 7-2

Objective: To calculate amounts to be paid

Directions: Calculate the amount due on each of the following invoices:

	Invoice Price	Date of Invoice	Terms	Date Paid
(a)	$2,000	July 6	2/10,n/30	July 14
(b)	800	October 30	2/10,n/30	November 9
(c)	880	May 12	1/10,n/30	May 27
(d)	925	June 27	3/10,2/20,n/30	July 13
(e)	1,450	August 24	n/60	October 12

Learning Objective **2**

Check Figure
Three debits to the Purchases account

Exercise 7-3

Objective: To record purchases in general journal form

Directions: Peoples Drugstore made the following credit purchases during March 20X1. Record each in a two-column general journal.

20X1

Mar. 3 Assorted medicines from Central Laboratories, $9,500.

7 Filing cabinets for use in the office from Allied Office Equipment Company, $195.

12 Hair care appliances from Ace Products, $4,000.

16 Candies and gums from Wholesale Distributors, $4,250.

22 Office supplies from Office Stationers, $355.

27 A used delivery truck from Acme Auto, $12,500.

Learning Objective **2**

Check Figure
Three entries in the purchases journal

Exercise 7-4

Objective: To record purchases in the appropriate journal

Directions: Record the transactions from Exercise 7-3 in a general journal (page 1) and a purchases journal (page 1). Number invoices starting with 1.

Learning Objectives **2, 3**

Check Figure
(f) Store Supplies = $45 (credit)

Exercise 7-5

Objective: To record purchases, returns, and allowances in general journal form

Directions: Record each of the following transactions in general journal form:
(a) Purchased merchandise on credit from Allard Corporation, $800.
(b) Returned $60 of the merchandise purchased in Transaction (a), receiving credit.
(c) Purchased merchandise for cash, $1,850.
(d) Discovered that a $50 item purchased in Transaction (c) was defective. It was returned, and a cash refund was received.
(e) Purchased store supplies on credit from Krystal Suppliers, $950.
(f) Discovered that some wrapping paper purchased in Transaction (e) was water stained. An allowance of $45 was granted.
(g) Purchased office equipment on credit, $9,000, from Stallard Equipment Company.
(h) An item of the equipment purchased in Transaction (g) was found to not work properly. It was returned, and credit was granted for $2,000.

Learning Objective **5**

Check Figure
Apr. 15 cash = $857.50 (credit)

Exercise 7-6

Objective: To record cash payments in general journal form

Directions: Stark's Variety Store made the following cash disbursements during April 20XX. Record each cash payment in general journal form.

20XX
Apr. 1   Paid rent for the month, $950.
     4   Paid Weaver Co. for an invoice for merchandise of March 26, $475, less a 2% discount.
     9   Purchased merchandise for cash, $2,500.
    15   Paid Reed Co. for an $875 purchase of merchandise on April 5. The purchase carried terms of 2/10,n/30.
    22   Purchased office equipment for cash, $1,850.
    27   Paid utility bill, $870.
    30   Paid monthly salaries, $2,560.

Learning Objective **5**

Check Figure
Cash Cr. column total = $10,053

Exercise 7-7

Objective: To record cash payments in a cash payments journal

Directions: Record the cash payments from Exercise 7-6 in a cash payments journal. Number checks starting with 94. Total and rule the cash payments journal.

Learning Objective **2**

Check Figure
None

Exercise 7-8

Objective: To record a summary entry from purchases invoices

Directions: At the end of October 20X1, the bookkeeper for The Sandwich Shoppe sorted the firm's invoices for the month and found that the totals are as follows: merchandise, $5,600; freight in, $145; store supplies, $165; office supplies, $120; and store equipment, $750. Record these purchases in general journal form.

Learning Objectives
2, 3, 7

Check Figure
(b) Freight in = $95 (credit)

Exercise 7-9

Objective: To make journal entries to correct errors

Directions: Make entries in general journal form to correct each of the following errors:

(a) A $150 return of store supplies was credited to the Purchases Returns and Allowances account.

(b) A bill of $95 for freight charges on a cash register purchased for use in the store was debited to the Freight In account.

(c) A $725 purchase of computer ribbons intended for resale was debited to the Office Supplies account.

Case Problems

Group A

Learning Objectives **2, 3**

Check Figure
Three entries in the purchases journal

Problem 7-1A

Objective: To record purchases and returns

The following transactions were completed by Kress Company during May 20X2:

20X2

Remember

Never record the same transaction in two separate journals.

May	1	Purchased merchandise on account from Clark Co., $1,295, Invoice No. 1.
	6	Purchased office supplies on account from Ellis Co., $240, Invoice No. 2.
	7	Purchased merchandise on account from Puan Co., $780, Invoice No. 3.
	11	Returned merchandise to Puan Co., receiving a $45 credit.
	12	Received a credit memorandum from Ellis Co. for a shortage on the purchase of May 6, $30.
	18	Purchased merchandise for cash, $875.
	22	Returned defective merchandise purchased on May 18, receiving a $50 cash refund.
	25	Purchased store equipment for $1,000, paying $400 down and owing Astor Co. the balance, Invoice No. 4.
	27	Purchased merchandise on account from Wilson Co., $850, Invoice No. 5.
	29	Received an allowance of $85 on the purchase of May 25 because the equipment was damaged during shipment.

Directions: Record these transactions in the appropriate journal, either a two-column general journal or a one-column purchases journal.

Learning Objectives
1, 2, 3, 6

Check Figure
Ending balance of Accounts Payable account = $41,600.80

Problem 7-2A

Objective: To record purchases and returns, post to two ledgers, and prepare a schedule of accounts payable

Credit purchases and related returns and allowances completed by College Bookstore during September 20X2 are as follows (Note: Read all directions before journalizing and posting the September transactions.):

20X2

Sep.	1	Purchased merchandise on account from Lang Co., $2,550.
	4	Purchased merchandise on account from MidWest Publishing Co., $6,890.
	7	Purchased merchandise on account from Clothing Wholesalers, $1,256.25, less a 20% trade discount.
	10	Purchased merchandise on account from Lang Co., $975.
	11	Purchased office supplies on account from Regents Supply Co., $245.80.
	14	Purchased office equipment on account from Hamer Equipment Co., $13,500.
	15	Purchased merchandise on account from Addington Co., $700.
	16	Received a credit memorandum from Regents Supply Co. for office supplies returned, $60.
	18	Purchased merchandise on account from MidWest Publishing Co., $4,700.

Sep. 21 Purchased store supplies on account from Hamer Equipment Co., $530.

25 Received a credit memorandum from MidWest Publishing Co. as an allowance for damaged goods, $110.

28 Purchased merchandise on account from Addington Co., $950.

30 Purchased office supplies on account from Regents Supply Co., $125.

Directions:

1. Open the following accounts in the general ledger, and enter the balances as of September 1:

Account		Balance
113	Store Supplies	$ 675.90
114	Office Supplies	345.75
121	Office Equipment	12,956.00
211	Accounts Payable	9,600.00
511	Purchases	98,568.35
511.1	Purchases Returns and Allowances	1,450.00

2. Open the following accounts in the accounts payable ledger, and enter the balances as of September 1:

Account	Balance
Addington Co.	$1,400.00
Clothing Wholesalers	1,250.00
Hamer Equipment Co.	2,500.00
Lang Co.	1,810.00
MidWest Publishing Co.	960.00
Regents Supply Co.	1,680.00

3. Record the September transactions in the appropriate journal, either a two-column general journal or a one-column purchases journal, posting to the accounts payable ledger after each entry. Number invoices starting with 126.

4. Total the purchases journal. Make all postings from the general journal to the general ledger at the end of the month. Then, post the column total from the purchases journal.

5. Prepare a schedule of accounts payable as of September 30.

6. Compare the balance of the Accounts Payable controlling account as of September 30 with the total of the schedule of accounts payable. The two amounts should be the same.

Learning Objectives
2, 6, 7

Check Figure
Balance of Accounts Payable account = $58,378.50

Problem 7-3A

Objective: To record and post purchases and freight charges

McMillan Appliance and Supply Company is located in Albuquerque, New Mexico. The following credit purchases were made by the firm during June 20XX (Note: Read all directions before journalizing and posting the June transactions.):

20XX

Jun. 1 Refrigerators from Allard Co., $7,790, Invoice No. 211; freight, $425, FOB Albuquerque.

5 Microwave ovens and toasters from Technical Products Co., $8,800, Invoice No. 212; freight, $510, FOB Birmingham, Alabama.

8 Ceiling fans from Buena Vista Co., $1,900, Invoice No. 213; freight, $88, FOB Las Cruces, New Mexico.

10 Space heaters from Alamogordo Co., $1,050, Invoice No. 214; freight, $77.50, FOB Alamogordo, New Mexico.

12 Office equipment from Thompson Suppliers, $5,500, Invoice No. 215; freight, $212, FOB Albuquerque.

Jun. 18   Store equipment from Carlsbad Co., $4,800, Invoice No. 216; freight, $228, FOB Carlsbad, New Mexico.

24   Freezers from Allard Co., $6,980, Invoice No. 217; freight, $418, FOB Albuquerque.

30   Blenders and mixers from Technical Products Co., $4,600, Invoice No. 218; freight, $100, FOB Birmingham.

Directions:

1. Open the following accounts in the general ledger, and record the balances as of June 1:

	Account	Balance
118	Office Equipment	$ 12,900
119	Store Equipment	25,900
211	Accounts Payable	15,955
511	Purchases	125,800
512	Freight In	2,410

2. Open the following accounts in the accounts payable ledger, and enter the balances as of June 1:

Account	Balance
Alamogordo Co.	$4,355
Allard Co.	2,510
Buena Vista Co.	875
Carlsbad Co.	2,590
Technical Products Co.	5,625
Thompson Suppliers	-0-

3. Record the June purchases in the appropriate journal, either a two-column general journal or a three-column purchases journal. Post to the accounts payable ledger after each entry.

4. Total the purchases journal. Make all postings from the general journal to the general ledger at the end of the month. Then, post the column totals from the purchases journal.

5. Prepare a schedule of accounts payable, and compare its total to the balance of the Accounts Payable controlling account.

Learning Objectives
2, 4, 5, 6, 7

Check Figure
Balance of Accounts Payable account = $6,870

Problem 7-4A

Objective: To record purchases and cash payments, post them, and prepare a schedule of accounts payable

The following selected transactions were completed by Svendsen's Sports Shop during February 20X1 (Note: Read all directions before journalizing and posting the February transactions.):

20X1

Feb.   1   Issued Check No. 113 for February rent, $900.

2   Issued Check No. 114 to All-American Co. for the balance of the account, less a 2% discount.

3   Issued Check No. 115 to Best Equipment Co. for the balance of the account, with no discount.

3   Purchased merchandise from All-American Co., $1,550; terms, 2/10,n/30; Invoice No. 109.

4   Purchased merchandise from Al's Sports Wholesalers, $2,850; terms, 2/10,n/30; Invoice No. 110.

7   Issued Check No. 116 for the cash purchase of merchandise, $745.

9   Issued Check No. 117 in payment of a three-year insurance policy, $850.

Feb. 11 Olaf Svendsen, the owner, issued Check No. 118 for his home phone bill, $275.

13 Issued Check No. 119 in full payment of the purchase of February 3.

15 Issued Check No. 120 for the cash purchase of office supplies, $325.

17 Purchased display cases from Best Equipment Co., $1,650; terms, n/30; Invoice No. 111.

22 Purchased office supplies from Office Suppliers, $920; terms, n/30; Invoice No. 112.

25 Issued Check No. 121 to Al's Sports Wholesalers for payment on account, $1,000.

27 Issued Check No. 122 for the purchase of February 17.

28 Issued Check No. 123 for monthly salaries, $1,500.

28 Issued Check No. 124 for freight charges on merchandise, $295.

Directions:

1. Open the following accounts in the general ledger, and enter the balances as of February 1:

	Account	Balance
111	Cash	$16,000
112	Office Supplies	980
113	Prepaid Insurance	75
116	Store Equipment	15,600
211	Accounts Payable	10,810
312	Olaf Svendsen, Drawing	1,200
511	Purchases	9,500
511.2	Purchases Discounts	345
512	Freight In	128
612	Salaries Expense	1,500
613	Rent Expense	900

2. Open the following accounts in the accounts payable ledger, and record the balances as of February 1:

Account	Balance
All-American Co.	$3,710
Al's Sports Wholesalers	2,350
Best Equipment Co.	3,000
Office Suppliers	1,750

3. Record the February transactions in the appropriate journal, either a two-column general journal, a one-column purchases journal, or a cash payments journal (like the ones illustrated in the chapter). Post to the accounts payable ledger after each entry.

4. Total the special journals. Make all individual postings from the cash payments journal and the general journal to the general ledger at the end of the month. Then, post the column totals from the special journals.

5. Prepare a schedule of accounts payable.

6. Compare the balance of the Accounts Payable controlling account with the total of the schedule of accounts payable.

Problem 7-5A

Objective: To record purchases, returns, and cash payments, and prepare a schedule of accounts payable

Diamond Jewelers, owned by Linda McCullough, has been in business for several years. On July 1, 20X1, the firm's accounts payable ledger contains the following accounts and balances:

Account	Balance
Best Diamond Co.	$1,540.00
Carter's Supplies	720.15
Modern Equipment Co.	2,675.00
Nash Jewelers	1,355.00
Wilson's Gems	725.60

The following transactions were completed during July. (Note: Read all directions before journalizing and posting the July transactions.)

20X1

Jul. 1 Issued Check No. 796 for July rent, $1,100.

5 Issued Check No. 797 to Wilson's Gems for the balance of the account, less a 2% discount.

7 Purchased merchandise from Best Diamond Co., $2,650; terms, 2/10,n/30; Invoice No. 621.

8 Returned merchandise to Best Diamond Co., receiving a $75 credit memorandum.

9 Issued Check No. 798 to Carter's Supplies for the balance of the account, with no discount.

12 Purchased $2,100 worth of merchandise from Wilson's Gems by issuing Check No. 799 for $700, with the balance of $1,400 owed on account, Invoice No. 622. (Hint: You need to use two journals to record this entry.)

15 Purchased display cases from Modern Equipment Co., $875.50; terms, n/30; Invoice No. 623.

17 Issued Check No. 800 to Best Diamond Co. for the purchase of July 7 less the credit of July 8. (Hint: No discount is allowed on returned merchandise.)

18 Issued Check No. 801 for a three-year insurance premium, $2,220.

25 Purchased office supplies, $675, and store supplies, $920, from Carter's Supplies; terms, n/30; Invoice No. 624.

27 Returned damaged office supplies to and received credit from Carter's Supplies, $85.

28 Issued Check No. 802 to Nash Jewelers as a payment on account, $200.

29 Issued Check No. 803 to Modern Equipment Co. for the July 1 balance of the account, with no discount.

30 Issued Check No. 804 to Carter's Supplies for a cash purchase of store supplies, $95.

30 Issued Check No. 805 to Wall Company for the purchase of a new cash register, $3,782.

30 Issued Check No. 806 to Beal Supply Co. for a cash purchase of merchandise, $3,900.

31 Issued Check No. 807 to Northern Transport Co. for freight charges on the July 30 delivery of merchandise, $210.

Directions:

1. Open an account in the accounts payable ledger for each creditor listed at the beginning of the problem. Enter balances as of July 1.
2. Open general ledger accounts, and enter the July 1 balances:

	Account	Balance
111	Cash	$19,267.75
115	Office Supplies	475.30
116	Store Supplies	946.20
117	Prepaid Insurance	320.00
121	Office Equipment	3,750.00
122	Store Equipment	11,500.00
211	Accounts Payable	7,015.75
511	Purchases	60,000.00
511.1	Purchases Returns and Allowances	4,000.00
511.2	Purchases Discounts	1,200.00
512	Freight In	800.00
613	Rent Expense	6,600.00

3. Record the July transactions in the appropriate journal, either a one-column purchases journal, a cash payments journal, or a general journal. Post to the accounts payable ledger after each entry.

4. Total the special journals. Make all individual postings from the cash payments journal and the general journal to the general ledger. Then, post the column totals from the special journals.

5. Prepare a schedule of accounts payable and compare the total with the balance of the Accounts Payable controlling account.

Group B

Learning Objectives **2, 3**

Check Figure
Three entries in the purchases journal

Problem 7-1B

Objective: To record purchases and returns

The following transactions were completed by Gusdorf Company during May 20X1:

20X1

May 1 Purchased merchandise on account from Hicks Co., $950, Invoice No. 1.
6 Purchased office supplies on account from Reese Co., $290, Invoice No. 2.
7 Purchased merchandise on account from Kane Co., $585, Invoice No. 3.
11 Returned merchandise to Kane Co., receiving a $50 credit.
12 Received a credit memorandum from Reese Co. for a shortage on the purchase of May 6, $38.
18 Purchased merchandise for cash, $930.
22 Returned defective merchandise purchased on May 18, receiving a $55 cash refund.
25 Purchased store equipment for $1,300, paying $500 down and owing King Co. the balance, Invoice No. 4.
27 Purchased merchandise on account from Lincoln Co., $1,075, Invoice No. 5.
29 Received an allowance of $90 on the purchase of May 25 because the equipment was damaged during shipment.

Directions: Record these transactions in the appropriate journal, either a two-column general journal or a one-column purchases journal.

Learning Objectives
1, 2, 3, 6

Check Figure
Ending balance of Accounts Payable account = $39,855.15

Problem 7-2B

Objective: To record purchases and returns, post to two ledgers, and prepare a schedule of accounts payable

Credit purchases and related returns and allowances completed by The Gazo Shop during June 20X1 are as follows (Note: Read all directions before journalizing and posting the June transactions.):

20X1

Jun. 1 Purchased merchandise on account from Lesan Co., $3,550.

Jun. 5 Purchased merchandise on account from Tamms, Inc., $5,800.

7 Purchased merchandise on account from Southern Wholesalers, $1,692.73, less a 25% trade discount.

12 Purchased office supplies on account from Central Supply Co., $285.60.

13 Purchased office equipment on account from Drummer Equipment Co., $11,900.

16 Purchased merchandise on account from Arrington Co., $900.

17 Received a credit memorandum from Central Supply Co. for office supplies returned, $70.

18 Purchased merchandise on account from Southern Wholesalers, $1,500.

22 Purchased store supplies on account from Drummer Equipment Co., $600.

25 Received a credit memorandum from Southern Wholesalers as an allowance for damaged goods, $135.

28 Purchased merchandise on account from Arrington Co., $925.

30 Purchased office supplies on account from Central Supply Co., $175.

Directions:

1. Open the following accounts in the general ledger, and enter the balances as of June 1:

	Account	Balance
113	Store Supplies	$ 643.75
114	Office Supplies	435.68
121	Office Equipment	12,975.00
211	Accounts Payable	13,155.00
511	Purchases	89,568.15
511.1	Purchases Returns and Allowances	1,255.00

2. Open the following accounts in the accounts payable ledger, and enter the balances as of June 1:

Account	Balance
Arrington Co.	$1,845.00
Central Supply Co.	2,455.00
Drummer Equipment Co.	3,590.00
Lesan Co.	3,585.00
Southern Wholesalers	-0-
Tamms, Inc.	1,680.00

3. Record the June transactions in the appropriate journal, either a two-column general journal or a one-column purchases journal, posting to the accounts payable ledger after each entry. Number invoices starting with 224.

4. Total the purchases journal. Make all postings from the general journal to the general ledger at the end of the month. Then, post the column total from the purchases journal.

5. Prepare a schedule of accounts payable as of June 30.

6. Compare the balance of the Accounts Payable controlling account as of June 30 with the total of the schedule of accounts payable. The two amounts should be the same.

**Learning Objectives
2, 6, 7**

Check Figure
Balance of Accounts Payable
account = $68,600

Problem 7-3B

Objective: To record and post purchases and freight charges

Saben Appliance and Home Center is located in Waterloo, Iowa. The following credit purchases were made by the firm during May 20XX (Note: Read all directions before journalizing and posting the May transactions.):

20XX

May 1 Washers and dryers from Hanson Co., $6,975, Invoice No. 318; freight, $690, FOB Iowa Falls, Iowa.

May 5 Refrigerators from Schendel Co., $9,500, Invoice No. 319; freight, $540, FOB Webster City, Iowa.

7 Upright freezer units from Hurley Products Co., $7,595, Invoice No. 320; freight, $325, FOB Conway, South Carolina.

11 Window fans from Fort Dodge Products Co., $1,345, Invoice No. 321; freight, $100, FOB Waterloo.

19 Office equipment from Webster Supply, $3,800, Invoice No. 322; freight, $312, FOB Ottumwa, Iowa.

20 Store equipment from Ankeny Co., $2,800, Invoice No. 323; freight, $318, FOB Waterloo.

28 Freezers from Schendel Co., $9,675, Invoice No. 324; freight, $775, FOB Webster City.

31 Various small kitchen appliances from Lakeworth Co., $5,595, Invoice No. 325; freight, $175, FOB La Porte, Indiana.

Directions:

1. Open the following accounts in the general ledger, and record the balances as of May 1:

	Account	Balance
118	Office Equipment	$ 15,600
119	Store Equipment	26,500
211	Accounts Payable	18,498
511	Purchases	138,900
512	Freight In	3,518

2. Open the following accounts in the accounts payable ledger, and enter the balances as of May 1:

Account	Balance
Ankeny Co.	$5,450
Fort Dodge Products Co.	1,850
Hanson Co.	1,560
Hurley Products Co.	4,588
Lakeworth Co.	2,250
Schendel Co.	-0-
Webster Supply	2,800

3. Record the May purchases in the appropriate journal, either a two-column general journal or a three-column purchases journal (like the ones illustrated in the chapter). Post to the accounts payable ledger after each entry.

4. Total the purchases journal. Make all postings from the general journal to the general ledger at the end of the month. Then, post the column totals from the purchases journal.

5. Prepare a schedule of accounts payable, and compare its total to the balance of the Accounts Payable controlling account.

Learning Objectives
2, 4, 5, 6, 7

Check Figure
Balance of Accounts Payable
account = $5,340

Problem 7-4B

Objective: To record purchases and cash payments, post them, and prepare a schedule of accounts payable

The following selected transactions were completed by Four Seasons Natural Food Store during March 20X2 (Note: Read all directions before journalizing and posting the March transactions.):

20X2

Mar. 1 Issued Check No. 205 for March rent, $1,300.

1 Issued Check No. 206 to Peachtree Foods for the balance of the account, less a 2% discount.

Mar. 2 Issued Check No. 207 to Lumpkin Equipment Co. for the balance of the account, with no discount.

3 Purchased merchandise from Peachtree Foods, $3,600; terms, 2/10,n/30; Invoice No. 205.

4 Purchased merchandise from Aiken Food Co., $3,860; terms, 2/10,n/30; Invoice No. 206.

8 Issued Check No. 208 for the cash purchase of merchandise, $692.

11 Issued Check No. 209 in payment of a two-year insurance policy, $1,070.

12 Nancy Kinner, the owner, issued Check No. 210 for her home electric bill, $225.

13 Issued Check No. 211 in full payment of the purchase of March 3.

15 Issued Check No. 212 for the cash purchase of office supplies, $418.

17 Purchased display cases from Lumpkin Equipment Co., $1,900; terms, n/30; Invoice No. 207.

22 Purchased office supplies from Office Equipment Co., $580, terms, n/30; Invoice No. 208.

26 Issued Check No. 213 to Aiken Food Co. for payment on account, $2,000.

27 Issued Check No. 214 for the purchase of March 17.

29 Issued Check No. 215 for monthly salaries, $1,500.

30 Issued Check No. 216 for freight charges on merchandise, $325.

Directions:

1. Open the following accounts in the general ledger, and enter the balances as of March 1:

	Account	Balance
111	Cash	$20,900
112	Office Supplies	684
113	Prepaid Insurance	130
116	Store Equipment	12,900
211	Accounts Payable	10,180
312	Nancy Kinner, Drawing	1,500
511	Purchases	12,450
511.2	Purchases Discounts	392
512	Freight In	150
612	Salaries Expense	3,000
613	Rent Expense	2,600

2. Open the following accounts in the accounts payable ledger, and record the balances as of March 1:

Account	Balance
Aiken Food Co.	$ -0-
Lumpkin Equipment Co.	5,000
Office Equipment Co.	2,900
Peachtree Foods	2,280

3. Record the March transactions in the appropriate journal, either a two-column general journal, a one-column purchases journal, or a cash payments journal. Post to the accounts payable ledger after each entry.

4. Total the special journals. Make all individual postings from the cash payments journal and the general journal to the general ledger at the end of the month. Then, post the column totals from the special journals.

5. Prepare a schedule of accounts payable.

6. Compare the balance of the Accounts Payable controlling account with the total of the schedule of accounts payable.

Problem 7-5B

Objective: To record purchases, returns, and cash payments, and prepare a schedule of accounts payable

Diamond Jewelers, owned by Linda McCullough, has been in business for several years. On July 1, 20X1, the firm's accounts payable ledger contains the following accounts and balances:

Account	Balance
Best Diamond Co.	$4,090.00
Carter's Supplies	2,155.00
Modern Equipment Co.	1,275.50
Nash Jewelers	1,255.00
Wilson's Gems	1,700.00

The following transactions were completed during July (Note: Read all directions before journalizing and posting the July transactions.):

20X1

Jul. 1 Issued Check No. 801 for July rent, $1,200.

     5 Issued Check No. 802 to Wilson's Gems for the balance of the account, less a 2% discount.

     7 Purchased merchandise from Best Diamond Co., $3,600; terms, 2/10,n/30; Invoice No. 601.

     8 Returned merchandise to Best Diamond Co., receiving a $70 credit memorandum.

     9 Issued Check No. 803 to Carter's Supplies for the balance of the account, with no discount.

   12 Purchased $2,200 worth of merchandise from Wilson's Gems by issuing Check No. 804 for $700, with the balance of $1,500 owed on account, Invoice No. 602. (Hint: You need to use two journals to record this entry.)

   15 Purchased display cases from Modern Equipment Co., $779.50; terms, n/30; Invoice No. 603.

   17 Issued Check No. 805 to Best Diamond Co. for the purchase of July 7 less the credit of July 8. (Hint: No discount is allowed on returned merchandise.)

   18 Issued Check No. 806 for a three-year insurance premium, $2,520.

   25 Purchased office supplies, $700, and store supplies, $912, from Carter's Supplies; terms, n/30; Invoice No. 604.

   27 Returned damaged office supplies to and received credit from Carter's Supplies, $70.

   28 Issued Check No. 807 to Nash Jewelers as a payment on account, $250.

   29 Issued Check No. 808 to Modern Equipment Co. for the July 1 balance of the account, with no discount.

   30 Issued Check No. 809 to Carter's Supplies for a cash purchase of store supplies, $105.

   30 Issued Check No. 810 to Wall Company for the purchase of a new cash register, $3,982.

   30 Issued Check No. 811 to Beal Supply Co. for a cash purchase of merchandise, $4,300.

   31 Issued Check No. 812 to Northern Transport Co. for freight charges on the July 30 delivery of merchandise, $225.

Directions:

1. Open an account in the accounts payable ledger for each creditor listed at the beginning of the problem. Enter balances as of July 1.

2. Open general ledger accounts and enter the July 1 balances:

	Account	Balance
111	Cash	$22,737.00
115	Office Supplies	1,160.30
116	Store Supplies	1,666.20
117	Prepaid Insurance	2,240.00
121	Office Equipment	4,000.00
122	Store Equipment	12,275.50
211	Accounts Payable	10,475.50
511	Purchases	52,000.00
511.1	Purchases Returns and Allowances	4,100.00
511.2	Purchases Discounts	1,750.00
512	Freight In	1,490.00
613	Rent Expense	7,200.00

3. Record the July transactions in the appropriate journal, either a one-column purchases journal, a cash payments journal, or a general journal. Post to the accounts payable ledger after each entry.
4. Total the special journals. Make all individual postings from the cash payments journal and the general journal to the general ledger. Then, post the column totals from the special journals.
5. Prepare a schedule of accounts payable, and compare the total with the balance of the Accounts Payable controlling account.

Critical Thinking Problems

Challenge Problem

Check Figure
Apr. 15 Purchases Discount = $165 (debit)

Bryson Monson recently completed a course in college accounting and accepted a job as accounting clerk at Handy Hardware. During Bryson's first four weeks on the job, he worked under the careful supervision of the company's accountant. Bryson is now through his training period and has assumed the responsibility of recording all purchases, returns, and payments. He is also responsible for posting to the accounts payable ledger and to the general ledger.

During April 20X2, Bryson's first month of working independently, he had very little trouble with day-to-day purchases, returns, and payments. The following transactions, however, did require Bryson to consult the accountant for help:

20X2

Apr. 12 Paid an $8,000 invoice for office equipment that was purchased from the Lowe Company on April 2 with terms of 2/10,n/30.

15 Discovered that $5,500 worth of lumber purchased on April 4 was of the wrong grade. The purchase carried terms of 3/10, n/30, and payment had been made on April 14 in time to take advantage of the cash discount. The supplier was notified of the error and immediately issued a cash refund.

16 Received a credit memorandum from Lang Company for a defect in store equipment, $95.

18 Discovered that a $99 freight charge on office equipment had been recorded in the Freight In account.

21 Paid an invoice for merchandise that had been purchased on April 11 from the Todd Company. The merchandise was listed for $7,000, but carried a 20% trade discount and terms of 2/10,n/30.

25 Discovered that $4,000 worth of merchandise that had been fully paid for was of inferior quality. Returned the merchandise. Instead of giving a cash refund, the supplier, Tanglewood Products Company, gave Handy Hardware credit against future purchases.

Apr. 30   When preparing a schedule of accounts payable, Bryson discovered that a $700 credit purchase from B. Merrill Company had been posted in the accounts payable ledger to the account of Merrill Supply Company. The entry was journalized correctly and had been posted correctly to the general ledger.

Directions: Assume that you are the accountant. Prepare the general journal entries needed to record each of these situations.

Communications

In earlier chapters, you learned that the accuracy of posting is checked by preparing a trial balance. That rule seems to have changed in this chapter, as you have learned that the accuracy of posting is checked by preparing a schedule of accounts payable.

Write an explanation of this seeming contradiction. Discuss why it is not a contradiction at all.

Team Internet Project

Today, much shipping is international shipping. On an export of goods from the United States to another country, what are some of the key data that must be provided in order make a shipment? Search the Internet, and prepare a list of these data.

Ethics

Kristy's Department Store is a successful small retail firm. The company is well managed and seems to have a good accounting system. In fact, the head bookkeeper takes advantage of all cash discounts even when bills are paid after the last date for discount. Kristy Newton, the owner, has started to investigate the bill-paying practice after receiving complaints from two creditors that they had been paid a couple of days after the cash discount date. Kristy discovers that it has been common practice to take these discounts late.

Write a brief paragraph explaining what Kristy should say to the head bookkeeper about this practice.

In the Real World   Target Corporation

Based on the balance sheets for 2006 and 2007 for Target Corporation presented in Chapter 6, answer the following questions:

1. What is the amount and direction of the change in total current assets from 2006 to 2007?

2. What is the amount and direction of the change in total assets from 2006 to 2007?

3. What is the amount and direction of the change in total current liabilities from 2006 to 2007?

4. What is the amount and direction of the change in total liabilities from 2006 to 2007?

Target Corporation Balance Sheet				
	February 3, 2007		**January 28, 2006**	
Assets				
Cash	$	8 1 3 00	$ 1 6 4 8 00	
Accounts receivable		6 1 9 4 00	5 6 6 6 00	
Inventory		6 2 5 4 00	5 8 3 8 00	
Other current assets		1 4 4 5 00	1 2 5 3 00	
Total current assets	$14	7 0 6 00	$14 4 0 5 00	
Property, plant, equipment	21	4 3 1 00	19 0 3 8 00	
Other noncurrent assets		1 2 1 2 00	1 5 5 2 00	
Total assets	$37	3 4 9 00	$34 9 9 5 00	
Liabilities and Shareholders' Investment				
Accounts payable	$ 6	5 7 5 00	$ 6 2 6 8 00	
Other current liabilities		4 5 4 2 00	3 3 2 0 00	
Total current liabilities	$11	1 1 7 00	$ 9 5 8 8 00	
Long-term liabilities		10 5 9 9 00	11 2 0 2 00	
Shareholders' investment		15 6 3 3 00	14 2 0 5 00	
Total liabilities and shareholders' investment	$37	3 4 9 00	$34 9 9 5 00	

*Amounts are in millions.

Answers to Review Quizzes

Review Quiz 7-1

(a) $1,372.00
(b) $784.00
(c) $900.00
(d) $960.40
(e) $400.00

Review Quiz 7-2

	20X2						
1	Mar.	1	Supplies		4 0 0 00		1
2			Cash			4 0 0 00	2
3							3
4		5	Equipment		9 0 0 00		4
5			Accounts Payable—E & H Co.	/		9 0 0 00	5
6							6
7		8	Purchases		1 2 0 0 00		7
8			Accounts Payable—C. Medlin Co.	/		1 2 0 0 00	8
9							9
10		18	Purchases		3 0 0 00		10
11			Cash			3 0 0 00	11
12							12
13		25	Supplies		2 5 0 00		13
14			Cash			2 5 0 00	14

Review Quiz 7-3

	Date		Invoice No.	Account Credited	P.R.	Purchases Dr. Accts. Pay. Cr.	
	Purchases Journal					Page 1	
1	20X8 May	12	48	Tower Auction		12 4 0 0 00	1
2		20	49	Tower Auction		57 3 0 0 00	2
3		28	50	Tower Auction		60 0 0 0 00	3
4		30	51	Burr Motors		45 0 0 0 00	4
5		30	52	Clyde Wright		11 2 0 0 00	5
6		30		Total		185 9 0 0 00	6

General Journal   **Page 1**

						Dr		Cr	
1	20X8 May	2	Office Supplies			2 0 0 00			1
2			Accounts Payable—Ace Suppliers	/				2 0 0 00	2
3									3
4		8	Office Equipment			8 0 0 00			4
5			Accounts Payable—Ace Suppliers	/				8 0 0 00	5
6									6
7		18	Office Equipment			4 5 0 0 00			7
8			Accounts Payable—King Co.	/				4 5 0 0 00	8

Review Quiz 7-4

						Dr		Cr	
1	20X9 Jun.	5	Office Supplies			3 0 0 00			1
2			Accounts Payable—B. Spence Suppliers	/				3 0 0 00	2
3									3
4		9	Purchases			8 0 0 00			4
5			Cash					8 0 0 00	5
6									6
7		15	Purchases			1 2 0 0 00			7
8			Accounts Payable—Wilks Co.	/				1 2 0 0 00	8
9									9
10		16	Accounts Payable—B. Spence Suppliers	/		3 0 00			10
11			Office Supplies					3 0 00	11
12									12
13		21	Accounts Payable—Wilks Co.	/		2 0 0 00			13
14			Purchases Returns and Allowances					2 0 0 00	14

Accounting for a Merchandising Business

Sales and Cash Receipts

Learning Objectives

1 Describe procedures and forms used in selling merchandise.
2 Record sales of merchandise in a sales journal and post to the general ledger and the accounts receivable ledger.
3 Record sales returns and allowances.
4 Record sales discounts.
5 Record cash receipts in a cash receipts journal and post to the general ledger and the accounts receivable ledger.
6 Prepare a schedule of accounts receivable.
7 Record credit card sales.

In Chapter 7, we started our study of merchandising by examining purchases and cash payments. We learned how to use two special journals and how to post to two separate ledgers. In Chapter 8, our study of merchandising will continue as we look at sales of merchandise and cash receipts. We will work with two more special journals—one for credit sales of merchandise and one for cash receipts. Also, we will work with another subsidiary ledger, one designed for the accounts of credit customers.

Sales Activity

Just as merchandising businesses follow certain procedures to process and record purchases, they follow certain procedures to process and record sales. The exact forms and procedures used for sales transactions depend on the type and size of the business. A small retail business may only use cash register tapes as source documents for recording sales; large retail and wholesale businesses may use very precise forms and follow very precise steps to process and record merchandise sales. To explore further, let's look at some of the procedures used by many businesses to record and process sales of merchandise.

Terms of Payment

The buyer and the seller should always have a definite understanding concerning the terms of payment for merchandise. Some businesses sell only on a cash basis. In such cases, no credit is allowed, and the terms of the sale are *cash* or *net cash*. Other businesses offer **credit terms** that allow customers a certain period of time (the **credit period**) in which to make payment.

Many retailers sell goods on a **revolving charge plan**, which allows customers to pay a percentage of their account plus finance charges on a monthly basis. Many manufacturing businesses and wholesalers sell on 30 days' credit. As we learned in Chapter 7, such credit terms are said to be n/30 (net thirty), which means that the invoice price of goods must be paid within 30 days of the date on the invoice.

Another common credit term is *n/EOM*, which means that payment for goods must be made by the end of the month in which the credit purchase was made. As we discussed in Chapter 7, some businesses offer credit terms that allow cash discounts if goods are paid for well in advance of the final date for payment (such as 10 days from the date of the invoice). Look at Table 8-1 to review common payment terms.

Table 8-1 Common Payment Terms

Term	Definition
Net cash	No credit is allowed by the seller. Payment must be made by the buyer at the time of purchase.
n/30	The amount of an invoice must be paid within 30 days of the date of the invoice.
2/10,n/30	A discount of 2% is allowed if an invoice is paid within 10 days of the date of the invoice. If payment is not made within 10 days, the total must be paid within 30 days of the date of the invoice.
n/EOM	Payment for goods must be made by the end of the month in which the goods were purchased.
C.O.D.	Cash on delivery. Under these terms, payment for goods must be made when goods are delivered to the buyer.
FOB shipping point	Free on board shipping point. Under these terms, the buyer is responsible for all freight charges from the point of shipment to the point of destination.
FOB destination point	Free on board destination. Under these terms, the seller is responsible for freight charges to the point of destination.

Procedures for Credit Sales

The process for a sale on credit starts in one of two ways: (1) receipt of a purchase order from a customer or (2) preparation of a sales order by one of the firm's salespersons. Actually, it is a common practice to write up a sales order in all cases, even after receipt of a purchase order. A **sales order** is a document prepared when an order is received from a customer that serves as an additional record of the sale and identifies the salesperson who handled the sale. The sales order in Figure 8-1 was prepared by Lakeside Electronics on receipt of a purchase order for two TVs from Andy's Motel on November 2, 20X1.

Figure 8-1

Sales Order

Sales Order	
No.: ____710____	

Purchase Order No.: __199__	Date: __November 2, 20X1__
Ship to: **Andy's Motel**	Salesperson: **J. Diaz**
61 Front Street	Ship Via: **Truck**
Riverside, CA 92502	

Quantity	Description
1	**19-inch color TV, Model No. 12-24457**
1	**25-inch color TV, Model No. 12-28378**

By: ____**R.S.**____

Remember

In Chapter 7, you learned the definition of a sales invoice.

A copy of the sales order is sent to the credit department for approval. Once approved, it is sent to the billing department, where the sales invoice is prepared. Sales invoices are prepared with several copies. One copy is sent to the customer, and another copy is sent to the accounting department to use as a source document for recording the sale. Also, copies are usually sent to the credit department and the shipping department. Figure 8-2 shows how Lakeside Electronics distributes copies of the sales invoice.

Figure 8-2

Distribution of Sales Invoice Copies

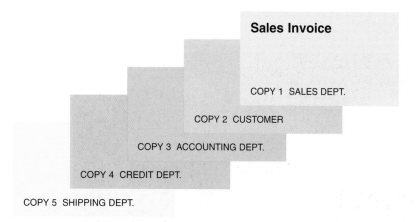

Now, let's look at an example of a sales invoice. The sales invoice prepared when Lakeside Electronics received the order from Andy's Motel on November 2 is shown in Figure 8-3 on the next page. Shortly, we will use a copy of this invoice to record the credit sale. But first, we need to discuss the procedures for cash sales.

Figure 8-3

Sales Invoice

	Lakeside Electronics 1200 San Palo Road Los Angeles, CA 90099			Invoice No.: __277__

Ship to: __Andy's Motel__   Date: __November 2, 20X1__

__61 Front Street__   Order No.: __199__

__Riverside, CA 92502__   Shipped by: __Truck__

Terms: __2/10,n/30__

Quantity	Description	Unit Price	Amount
1	19-inch color TV, Model No. 12-24457	$175.00	$175.00
1	25-inch color TV, Model No. 12-28378	275.00	275.00
	Total		$450.00

sales ticket a form prepared by the seller when a cash sale is made that describes the goods sold, identifies the customer, and serves as a source document for recording the sale; also referred to as the sales slip

cash register tape a variation of the sales ticket; the total of the tape serves as the source document for later journal entries

Procedures for Cash Sales

Cash sales are handled in a slightly different manner than credit sales. A commonly used form for cash sales is the **sales ticket** or sales slip. This is a form prepared by the seller at the time of sale that describes the goods sold, identifies the customer, and serves as a source document for recording the sale. A sample sales ticket is shown in Figure 8-4.

A copy of the sales ticket is given to the customer. Another copy is kept in the department that made the sale. And a third copy is sent to the accounting department as a source document for recording the sale.

A variation of the sales ticket is the **cash register tape**. A firm may ring up all cash sales on a cash register. At the end of each day, the register is totaled, and the total of the tape serves as the source document for later journal entries.

Businesses with many cash sales, such as grocery stores and department stores, often use electronic cash registers. Electronic cash registers are on-line with the firm's computer. That is, there is direct communication between the cash register and the firm's computer system. Sales rung up by sales clerks provide the information for the computer to update the firm's accounting records.

Retail businesses ring up sales on cash registers. Some wholesale firms also use cash registers, but many do not because they usually sell merchandise in bulk on a credit basis.

Figure 8-4

Sales Ticket

Recording Sales of Merchandise

MERRITT TV SALES

Manchester, NH 03104

Date: *1-21-XX*   No.: *1280*

Sold to: *C. Wilson*
114 West Street
Hartford, CT

Quantity	Description	Unit Price	Amount
2	*T.V. Stands*	*$15.00*	*$30.00*
1	*Aerial*	*40.00*	*40.00*
	Total		*$70.00*

Learning Objective

2 Record sales of merchandise in a sales journal and post to the general ledger and the accounts receivable ledger.

A sale of merchandise causes an increase in revenue, which increases owner's equity. In earlier chapters, you learned how to record revenue earned from services performed for cash. We used account titles such as Service Revenue and Fees Earned to make journal entries such as the following:

In this chapter, you will learn how to record sales of merchandise for cash and on credit, using a revenue account entitled Sales. The **Sales account**, like

	20XX					
+ asset → 1	May	1	Cash	111	8 0 0 00	1
+ revenue → 2			Sevice Revenue	411		8 0 0 00	2
3			Performed services for cash.			3

all revenue accounts, is a temporary account with a normal credit balance. The Sales account is used only to record the price of merchandise sold to customers and can be illustrated as follows:

Sales account a revenue account used to record the price of of merchandise sold to customers

Sales	411
Debit	Credit
–	+
	To record the price of merchandise sold to customers

Recording Sales in General Journal Form

Cash Sales

A cash sale of merchandise is recorded by debiting the Cash account and crediting the Sales account. For example, refer to the sales ticket for Merritt TV Sales (Figure 8-4). The following general journal entry can be made to record Merritt's cash sale.

+ asset →	1	20XX Jan.	21	Cash	70 00		1
+ revenue →	2			Sales		70 00	2
	3			Sold merchandise for cash.			3

Credit Sales

Accounts Receivable account an asset account that shows the total dollar amount due from credit customers

Credit sales of merchandise are recorded by debiting the Accounts Receivable account and crediting the Sales account. The **Accounts Receivable account** is an asset account that shows the total dollar amount due from credit customers. To illustrate, let's look again at the invoice in Figure 8-3 that Lakeside Electronics prepared when an order was received from Andy's Motel. Lakeside can record the sale in general journal form as follows:

+ asset →	1	20X1 Nov.	2	Accounts Receivable—Andy's Motel	/	4 50 00		1
+ revenue →	2			Sales			4 50 00	2
	3			Sold merchandise on credit.				3

Review Quiz   8-1

Record the following sales in general journal form:

(a) Sold merchandise for cash, $400.
(b) Sold merchandise on account, $1,200.
(c) Sold equipment (at cost) that was no longer needed by the business, $800.
(d) Sold supplies at cost to a competitor, $200.

Check your answers on page 386.

Recording Sales in a Sales Journal

To more efficiently record a large volume of credit sales, many businesses use a sales journal. The **sales journal** is a special journal used only to record credit sales of merchandise.

sales journal a special journal used only to record credit sales of merchandise

As with any special journal, the design of the sales journal is tailored to the needs of the business using it. Lakeside Electronics uses the sales journal shown in Figure 8-5, which is a common form.

Notice that the sales journal has only one money column, entitled *Accounts Receivable Debit* and *Sales Credit*. One money column is enough, as all credit sales of merchandise involve a debit to the Accounts Receivable account and a credit to the Sales account.

Lakeside's sales journal also has the standard Date and P.R. columns. Additionally, an Invoice Number column is included for writing the number of the sale, and a column entitled Customer's Name is used for identifying credit customers.

To illustrate the use of the sales journal, let's look at Lakeside's credit sales for the month of November 20X1:

20X1
Nov. 2 Sold two TVs to Andy's Motel, $450.
8 Sold 40 TVs to Champ's TV Sales, $7,290.
9 Sold four aerials to Larry's Pub, $160.
14 Sold 25 AM radios to Dawson's TV and Appliance Co., $261.
18 Sold various electronic toys to Toyland, $2,400.
24 Sold 14 AM/FM radios to Andy's Motel, $400.

Each of the above credit sales, starting with Invoice No. 277, is recorded in the sales journal in Figure 8-5. Notice the ease of recording compared to recording sales in general journal form.

Figure 8-5
Sales Journal

	Date		Invoice No.	Customer's Name	P.R.	Accts. Rec. Dr. Sales Cr.	
	20X1						
1	Nov.	2	277	Andy's Motel		4 5 0 00	1
2		8	278	Champ's TV Sales		7 2 9 0 00	2
3		9	279	Larry's Pub		1 6 0 00	3
4		14	280	Dawson's TV and Appliance Co.		2 6 1 00	4
5		18	281	Toyland		2 4 0 0 00	5
6		24	282	Andy's Motel		4 0 0 00	6
7		30		Total		10 9 6 1 00	7

Sales Journal · Page 14

The Accounts Receivable Ledger

In Chapter 7, you learned that businesses with many creditors often set up a separate account for each creditor in an accounts payable subsidiary ledger. Individual balances of creditors' accounts in the accounts payable ledger are summarized by the Accounts Payable controlling account, which remains in the general ledger. Along the same line of reasoning, businesses with many credit customers often set up an account for each customer in an **accounts receivable ledger**, also called a customers' ledger.

The accounts receivable ledger is a subsidiary ledger and has a controlling account—the Accounts Receivable account. Thus, the balance owed to a business by *each* credit customer is shown in the accounts receivable ledger, and the *total* amount owed by all credit customers is shown in the Accounts Receivable account.

As in the accounts payable ledger, accounts in the accounts receivable ledger are arranged in alphabetical order to make it easier to add new accounts and remove inactive accounts. Since the Accounts Receivable account is an asset with a normal debit balance, customers' accounts in the accounts receivable ledger will—with rare exceptions—have *debit* balances. Thus, accounts in the accounts receivable ledger will have three columns, rather than four that accounts in the general ledger usually have.

accounts receivable ledger a subsidiary ledger containing only accounts of credit customers; also referred to as the customers' ledger

Posting from the Sales Journal

The process of posting special journals is a familiar one to you. In Chapter 7, you learned how to post from the purchases journal and from the cash payments journal to both the accounts payable ledger and the general ledger. Posting the sales journal follows the same procedure. To review, let's look at how Lakeside's November sales journal is posted.

Posting to the Accounts Receivable Ledger

Each entry in the sales journal is posted separately to the accounts receivable ledger. To maintain current and up-to-date balances in customers' accounts, posting is usually done on a daily basis. Having current balances is helpful when answering customer inquiries, considering requests for additional credit, and sending out statements.

To illustrate posting to the accounts receivable ledger, the account of Andy's Motel is posted as shown in Figure 8-6.

Figure 8-6

Posting an Entry from the Sales Journal to the Accounts Receivable Ledger

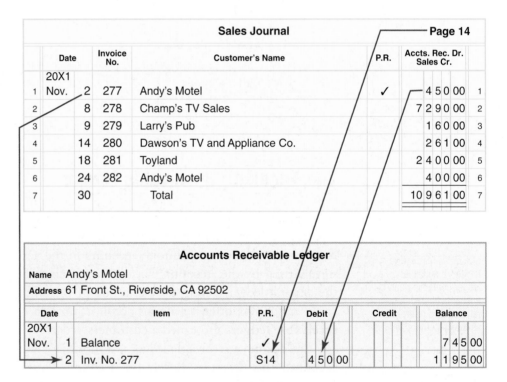

As you have already learned, a check mark is entered in the P.R. column of the sales journal to indicate that a separate posting has been made. To complete the cross-reference, the code S14 (*Sales journal, page 14*) is entered in the P.R. column of the Andy's Motel account. Other customers' accounts are posted in the same way.

Posting to the General Ledger

At the end of each month, the money column of the sales journal is totaled, and the total is posted twice: (1) as a debit to the Accounts Receivable account and (2) as a credit to the Sales account. The account numbers of these accounts are then written in parentheses directly below the column total. To complete the cross-reference, the code S14 is entered in the P.R. column of the respective accounts. Posting from the sales journal to the general ledger is shown in Figure 8-7.

Figure 8-7

Posting from the Sales Journal to the General Ledger

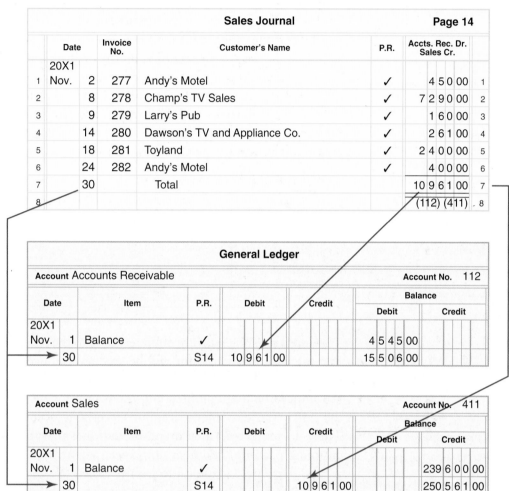

Check your answers on pages 386–387.

Review Quiz **8-2**

The following sales on account were made by Bob Hiller during May 20X5. Hint: Remember each transaction is recorded in only one journal.

20X5
May 1 Sold merchandise on account to Bill French, $300, Invoice No. 1.
    3 Sold merchandise for cash to David Mack, $500.
    8 Sold merchandise on account to Lee Smith, $800, Invoice No. 2.
    12 Sold merchandise for cash to Betty Carson, $670.
    18 Sold merchandise on account to Leah King, $590, Invoice No. 3.
    25 Sold store equipment for cash at cost, $4,000.
    30 Sold merchandise on account to Charles Swift, $500, Invoice No. 4.

Record these sales in a sales journal and a two-column general journal. Then, total the sales journal.

Recording Sales Returns and Allowances

Learning Objective

3 Record sales returns and allowances.

Sales Returns and Allowances account a contra revenue account with a normal debit balance used to record returns from and allowances to customers

In Chapter 7, we discussed merchandise returns and allowances from the standpoint of the purchaser. We learned that a *return* results when a buyer returns part, or all, of a purchase to the seller. An *allowance* results when a buyer decides to keep damaged or defective goods, but at a reduction from the original price.

On the books of the seller, a return or allowance is recorded as a reduction in sales revenue. Since the Sales account normally has a credit balance, returns and allowances could be recorded on the debit side (the reduction side) of the Sales account. To provide a better record, however, returns and allowances are often recorded in a separate account entitled Sales Returns and Allowances.

The **Sales Returns and Allowances account** is a contra revenue account. It thus has a debit balance that is opposite the credit balance of the Sales account. This can be illustrated as follows:

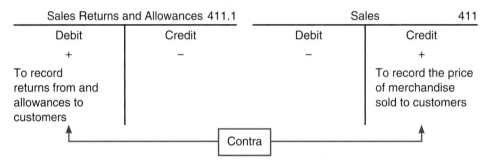

Goods sold on credit are often returned to the seller with the understanding that the customer's account will be credited (reduced) by the amount of the return. The seller usually issues the customer a credit memorandum that shows the amount of credit granted and the reason for the return. On the books of the seller, the customer's accounts receivable account has a *debit* balance. Thus, the term *credit* memorandum indicates that the seller has decreased the customer's account and does not expect payment.

To illustrate, Lakeside Electronics issued the credit memorandum shown in Figure 8-8 to Champ's TV Sales for the return of a 19-inch color TV that proved to be defective.

Remember

In Chapter 7, you learned the definitions of credit memorandum and debit memorandum.

Figure 8-8
Credit Memorandum

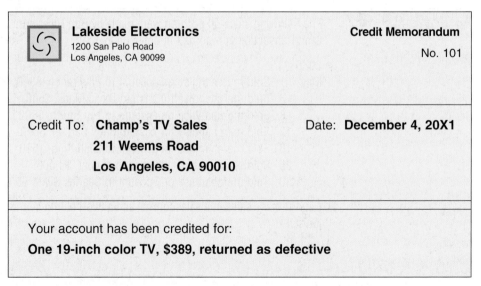

Lakeside used the credit memorandum in Figure 8-8 as a source document for the following general journal entry.

		20X1					
+ contra revenue →	1	Dec.	4 Sales Returns and Allowances	411.1	3 8 9 00		1
– asset →	2		Accounts Rec.—Champ's TV Sales	112/✓		3 8 9 00	2
	3		Granted credit to a customer.				3

The credit part of this entry involves both a controlling account (Accounts Receivable) in the general ledger and a customer's account (Champ's TV Sales) in the accounts receivable subsidiary ledger. As we have learned, debits or credits to a controlling account require a dual posting to the controlling account in the general ledger and to the customer's account in the accounts receivable ledger. To indicate that dual posting is necessary, a diagonal line is drawn in the P.R. column of the journal at the time the journal entry is made.

When the above entry was posted to the accounts receivable ledger, a small check mark was made to the right of the diagonal line. When posting was made to the Accounts Receivable controlling account, the account number of Accounts Receivable (112) was written to the left of the diagonal line.

If a cash refund is made because of a sales return or allowance, the Sales Returns and Allowances account is debited and the Cash account is credited. Cash refunds are recorded in the cash payments journal.

Review Quiz **8-3**

In general journal form, record the following transactions for Vivian Carney International:

(a) Sold merchandise on account to Camp Company, $800.
(b) Issued a credit memorandum for $200 to Camp Company for merchandise damaged while in transit.
(c) Issued a cash refund to Rossi and Sons, $400.
(d) Received the balance of Camp Company's account.

Check your answers on page 387.

Recording Sales Discounts

Learning Objective

4 Record sales discounts.

Sales Discounts account a contra revenue account with a normal debit balance used to record cash discounts granted to credit customers for prompt payment

We have learned that a cash discount is offered by a seller to encourage a buyer to make prompt payment for a credit purchase. We have also learned that a common form of cash discount is 2/10,n/30. In Chapter 7, we recorded cash discounts as purchases discounts on the books of the buyer. In this chapter, we are concerned with cash discounts as they affect the seller of merchandise.

For the seller, a cash discount is referred to as a sales discount and is recorded as a reduction in sales revenue. Sales discounts could thus be recorded on the debit side (the reduction side) of the Sales account. To provide a separate record, however, sales discounts are usually recorded in a contra revenue account entitled Sales Discounts. The **Sales Discounts account**, which is used to record cash discounts granted to credit customers for prompt payment, can be illustrated as follows:

		Sales Discounts	411.2

Debit	Credit
+	−
To record cash discounts granted to credit customers for prompt payment	

To illustrate recording a sales discount, let's look at one of Lakeside's credit sales during November 20X1. On November 2, Lakeside issued Invoice No. 277 to Andy's Motel for the sale of two TVs for $450, with terms of 2/10,n/30. If Andy's Motel pays the invoice within 10 days (by November 12), $9 of the invoice price (.02 × $450 = $9) can be deducted, and the difference, $441, can be remitted to Lakeside Electronics in full settlement of the debt. To record the cash receipt, Lakeside will debit the Cash account for the actual amount of cash received, $441; debit the Sales Discounts account for the amount of discount granted, $9; and credit Accounts Receivable and the customer's account for the full invoice amount of $450. This entry is illustrated below in general journal form.

		20X1						
+ asset →	1	Nov. 12	Cash		4 41 00			1
+ contra revenue →	2		Sales Discounts		9 00			2
− asset →	3		Accounts Receivable—Andy's Motel	/		4 50 00		3
	4		Received cash on account.					4

It should be stressed that even though the invoice price of the goods is $450, the receipt of a $441 payment within 10 days completely settles the debt because the customer complied with the terms of payment (2/10,n/30). Thus, the customer's account is credited for the full amount, $450.

Review Quiz **8-4**

On June 10, 20X2, Wachal Company purchased goods costing $9,000 from Entler Company. The terms of payment were 3/10,n/30. Wachal made payment on June 19, 20X2. In general journal form, record the following transactions:

(a) The purchase and cash payment by Wachal Company.
(b) The sale and cash receipt by Entler Company.

Check your answers on page 387.

Recording Cash Receipts

In a merchandising business, cash is received from cash sales, collections on account from credit customers, and various other sources. Lakeside Electronics' cash receipts for November 20X1 are as follows:

20X1
Nov. 4 Received $730.10 from Andy's Motel for the previous balance owed, $745, less 2% discount.
    5 Received $200 on account from Larry's Pub, no discount.

Nov. 8 As an accommodation, sold store supplies at cost to a competitor, $50.

9 Received $2,254 from Dawson's TV and Appliance for the balance owed, $2,300, less 2% discount.

12 Received $441 from Andy's Motel for the balance owed, $450, less 2% discount.

15 Recorded cash sales for the first half of the month, $4,910.

21 Received an $800 cash refund for the return of merchandise that proved to be defective.

24 Received $700 from Larry's Pub for the balance owed, no discount.

30 Recorded cash sales for the second half of the month, $5,140.

The Cash Receipts Journal

Learning Objective

5 Record cash receipts in a cash receipts journal and post to the general ledger and the accounts receivable ledger.

cash receipts journal a special journal used to record all receipts of cash, regardless of the source

All transactions that increase the amount of cash are recorded in a special journal called the **cash receipts journal**. The source documents for entries in the cash receipts journal are checks received, cash register tapes, and sales tickets.

Because the cash receipts journal is designed to record all receipts of cash, it must contain a *Cash Debit* column. The number and title of other special columns are determined by the accounts most often affected by cash receipts. Lakeside Electronics uses a cash receipts journal (Figure 8-9) that, in addition to a Cash Debit column, has special columns for *Sales Discounts Debit*, *Accounts Receivable Credit*, and *Sales Credit*. A *General Credit* column is also included for making credits to accounts for which no special column is provided.

To illustrate the use of a cash receipts journal, let's look again at Lakeside's November cash receipts (pages 344–345). The November receipts are recorded in the cash receipts journal shown in Figure 8-9.

Figure 8-9

Cash Receipts Journal

	Date		Account Credited	P.R.	General Cr.	Sales Cr.	Accounts Receivable Cr.	Sales Discounts Dr.	Cash Dr.	
				Cash Receipts Journal					**Page 18**	
1	20X1 Nov.	4	Andy's Motel				7 45 00	1 4 90	7 30 10	1
2		5	Larry's Pub				2 00 00		2 00 00	2
3		8	Store Supplies		50 00				50 00	3
4		9	Dawson's TV and Appl.				2 3 00 00	4 6 00	2 2 54 00	4
5		12	Andy's Motel				4 50 00	9 00	4 41 00	5
6		15	Cash Sales			4 9 1 0 00			4 9 1 0 00	6
7		21	Purch. Ret. and Allow.		8 00 00				8 00 00	7
8		24	Larry's Pub				7 00 00		7 00 00	8
9		30	Cash Sales			5 1 40 00			5 1 40 00	9
10		30	Totals		8 50 00	10 0 50 00	4 3 95 00	6 9 90	15 2 25 10	10

Figure 8-10

Posting the Cash
Receipts Journal

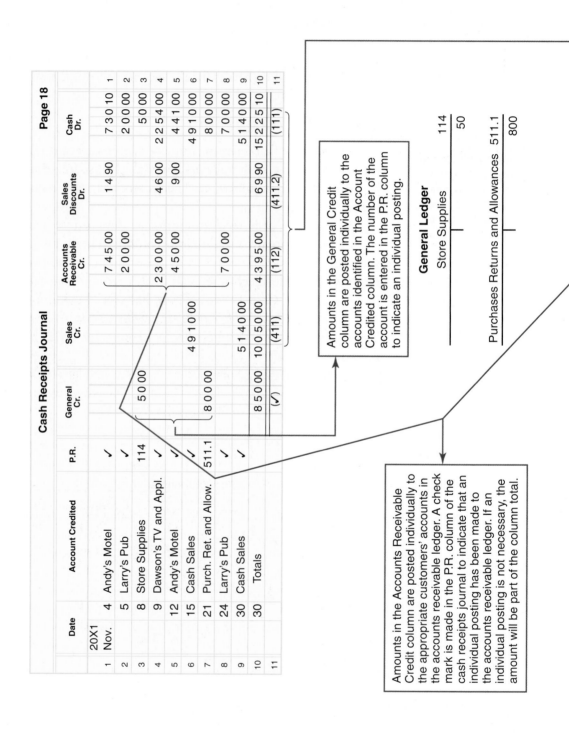

Cash Receipts Journal
Page 18

	Date	Account Credited	P.R.	General Cr.	Sales Cr.	Accounts Receivable Cr.	Sales Discounts Dr.	Cash Dr.	
	20X1								
1	Nov. 4	Andy's Motel	✓			7 45 00	14 90	7 30 10	1
2	5	Larry's Pub	✓			2 00 00		2 00 00	2
3	8	Store Supplies	114	50 00				50 00	3
4	9	Dawson's TV and Appl.	✓			2 3 00 00	46 00	2 2 54 00	4
5	12	Andy's Motel	✓			4 50 00	9 00	4 41 00	5
6	15	Cash Sales	✓		4 9 10 00			4 9 10 00	6
7	21	Purch. Ret. and Allow.	511.1	8 00 00				8 00 00	7
8	24	Larry's Pub	✓			7 00 00		7 00 00	8
9	30	Cash Sales	✓		5 1 40 00			5 1 40 00	9
10	30	Totals		8 50 00	10 0 50 00	4 3 95 00	69 90	15 2 25 10	10
11				(✓)	(411)	(112)	(411.2)	(111)	11

Amounts in the General Credit
column are posted individually to the
accounts identified in the Account
Credited column. The number of the
account is entered in the P.R. column
to indicate an individual posting.

Amounts in the Accounts Receivable
Credit column are posted individually to
the appropriate customers' accounts in
the accounts receivable ledger. A check
mark is made in the P.R. column of the
cash receipts journal to indicate that an
individual posting has been made to
the accounts receivable ledger. If an
individual posting is not necessary, the
amount will be part of the column total.

General Ledger

Store Supplies   114

                        50

Purchases Returns and Allowances   511.1

                        800

Special column totals are posted to the general ledger at the end of the month. The account number of the account is written directly under the column total. The check mark under the general credit column indicates the total of that column is not posted

General Ledger

Cash	111
15,225.10	

Sales Discounts	411.2
69.90	

Accounts Receivable	112
	4,395.00

Sales	411
	10,050.00

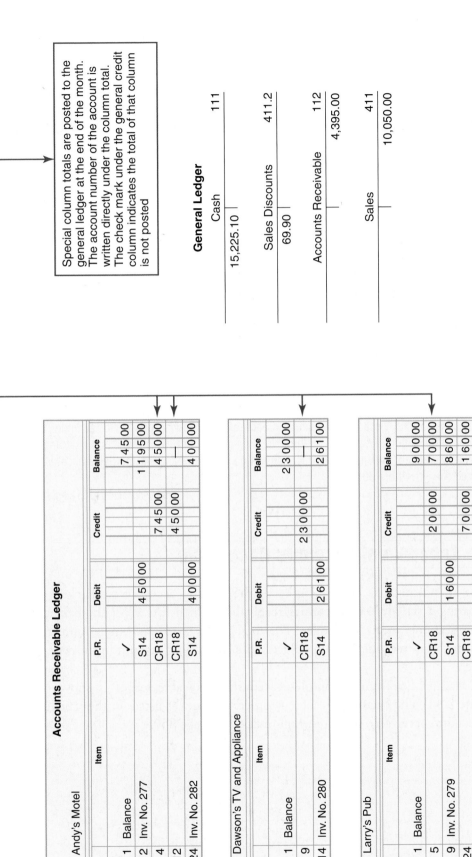

Accounts Receivable Ledger

Name Andy's Motel

Date		Item	P.R.	Debit	Credit	Balance
20X1						
Nov.	1	Balance	✓			7 4 5 00
	2	Inv. No. 277	S14	4 5 0 00		1 1 9 5 00
	4		CR18		7 4 5 00	4 5 0 00
	12		CR18		4 5 0 00	—
	24	Inv. No. 282	S14	4 0 0 00		4 0 0 00

Name Dawson's TV and Appliance

Date		Item	P.R.	Debit	Credit	Balance
20X1						
Nov.	1	Balance	✓			2 3 0 0 00
	9		CR18		2 3 0 0 00	—
	14	Inv. No. 280	S14	2 6 1 00		2 6 1 00

Name Larry's Pub

Date		Item	P.R.	Debit	Credit	Balance
20X1						
Nov.	1	Balance	✓			9 0 0 00
	5		CR18		2 0 0 00	7 0 0 00
	9	Inv. No. 279	S14	1 6 0 00		8 6 0 00
	24		CR18		7 0 0 00	1 6 0 00

Posting the Cash Receipts Journal

Three types of postings are made from the cash receipts journal:

1. Amounts appearing in the Accounts Receivable Credit column are posted separately to the subsidiary ledger accounts of the customers who made the payments. As we have seen, posting is usually made to the subsidiary ledger on a daily basis.
2. Amounts in the General Credit column are posted separately to the general ledger accounts identified in the Account Credited column. For example, on November 8, the Store Supplies account was credited for $50. Since there is no special column for credits to Store Supplies, the credit was entered in the General Credit column. Thus, a $50 credit posting must be made to the Store Supplies account. Such a posting can be made on a daily, weekly, or monthly basis.
3. Special column totals are posted to the general ledger at the end of the month.

Figure 8-10 on pages 346 and 347 shows how the cash receipts journal is posted.

Review Quiz   8-5

Referring to the cash receipts journal used by Lakeside Electronics in Figure 8-10, identify the meaning of the check marks located in each of the following positions: (a) under the General Credit column total; (b) in the P.R. column on the line on which a customer's account is credited; and (c) in the P.R. column on the line on which the Sales account is credited (on November 30).

Check your answers on page 388.

The Schedule of Accounts Receivable

Learning Objective

6 Prepare a schedule of accounts receivable.

schedule of accounts receivable a listing of the balances in the accounts receivable ledger

After all posting has been completed, the posting accuracy is checked by preparing a **schedule of accounts receivable**, which lists all of the balances in the accounts receivable ledger. The total of the schedule is then compared with the balance of the Accounts Receivable controlling account in the general ledger.

Lakeside Electronics' complete accounts receivable ledger is shown in Figure 8-11. The balance of each customer's account is listed on the schedule of accounts receivable shown in Figure 8-12 on page 350.

Figure 8-11

Complete Accounts Receivable Ledger

Name Andy's Motel

Address 61 Front St., Riverside, CA 92502

Date		Item	P.R.	Debit	Credit	Balance
20X1 Nov.	1	Balance	✓			7 4 5 00
	2	Inv. No. 277	S14	4 5 0 00		1 1 9 5 00
	4		CR18		7 4 5 00	4 5 0 00
	12		CR18		4 5 0 00	—
	24	Inv. No. 282	S14	4 0 0 00		4 0 0 00

Name Champ's TV Sales

Address 211 Weems Road, Los Angeles, CA 90010

Date		Item	P.R.	Debit	Credit	Balance
20X1 Nov.	8	Inv. No. 278	S14	7 2 9 0 00		7 2 9 0 00

Name Dawson's TV and Appliance

Address 6111 Nature Trail, Riverside, CA 92506

Date		Item	P.R.	Debit	Credit	Balance
20X1 Nov.	1	Balance	✓			2 3 0 0 00
	9		CR18		2 3 0 0 00	—
	14	Inv. No. 280	S14	2 6 1 00		2 6 1 00

Name Larry's Pub

Address 1136 West 8th, Los Angeles, CA 90017

Date		Item	P.R.	Debit	Credit	Balance
20X1 Nov.	1	Balance	✓			9 0 0 00
	5		CR18		2 0 0 00	7 0 0 00
	9	Inv. No. 279	S14	1 6 0 00		8 6 0 00
	24		CR18		7 0 0 00	1 6 0 00

Name Toyland

Address 2810 Glendale Dr., Los Angeles, CA 90018

Date		Item	P.R.	Debit	Credit	Balance
20X1 Nov.	1	Balance	✓			6 0 0 00
	18	Inv. No. 281	S14	2 4 0 0 00		3 0 0 0 00

Figure 8-12

Schedule of Accounts
Receivable

Lakeside Electronics Schedule of Accounts Receivable November 30, 20X1		
Andy's Motel		4 0 0 00
Champ's TV Sales		7 2 9 0 00
Dawson's TV and Appliance		2 6 1 00
Larry's Pub		1 6 0 00
Toyland		3 0 0 0 00
Total		11 1 1 1 00

After all posting is complete,
the total of the schedule of
accounts receivable should
agree with the balance of
the Accounts Receivable
controlling account in the
general ledger.

The total of the schedule agrees with the balance of the Accounts Receivable controlling account, which is shown fully posted in Figure 8-13.

Figure 8-13

Accounts Receivable
Controlling Account
with Totals Posted
from the Sales Journal
and the Cash Receipts
Journal at Month-End

Account Accounts Receivable					Account No. 112		
Date	Item	P.R.	Debit	Credit	Balance		
					Debit	Credit	
20X1 Nov. 1	Balance	✓			4 5 4 5 00		
30		S14	10 9 6 1 00		15 5 0 6 00		
30		CR18		4 3 9 5 00	11 1 1 1 00		

Accounting for Sales Taxes

sales tax a tax on the
retail price of goods
sold, collected by the
merchant and paid to the
governmental body that
levies the tax

**Sales Tax Payable
account** a liability
account used to record
sales taxes on retail
purchases

Most state governments and some county and city governments in our country levy a tax on the retail price of goods and services sold to the end user. The tax, called a **sales tax**, is collected from customers by the seller and later paid to the appropriate tax official in the state government.

Rates charged for sales taxes range from a low of 3% to a high of 11%, depending on the state. To illustrate how to account for sales taxes, we will use Angie Shaffer, who owns the Surf-N-Sand Shop, located on Tybee Island, Georgia. The sales tax rate on Tybee Island is 6%. Thus, when Angie recently sold a $200 surfboard, she collected a sales tax of $12 (.06 × $200). Accordingly, the customer paid Angie $212 for a $200 purchase. The following general journal entry records the sale. Notice that the amount of sales taxes is recorded in the **Sales Tax Payable account.**

+ asset →	1	X	X	Cash	2 1 2 00		1
+ liability →	2			Sales Tax Payable		1 2 00	2
+ revenue →	3			Sales		2 0 0 00	3
	4			Recorded cash sale.			4

Had the sale been on credit, the entry would be the same, except that the debit would have been to the Accounts Receivable account and the individual customer's account, instead of to the Cash account.

Reporting Sales Taxes Collected

Most states require that sales taxes collected during the month be sent to the appropriate state official by the middle of the following month. To record this, a debit is made to the Sales Tax Payable account (to decrease the merchant's liability for these taxes), and a credit is made to the Cash account.

To illustrate, we will continue with our example of the Surf-N-Sand Shop. During July 20X0, the store had total sales of $60,000. Since the sales tax rate in the area is 6%, $3,600 (.06 × $60,000) in sales taxes was collected on these sales. In Georgia, sales taxes collected one month must be sent to the State Department of Revenue by the 20th day of the next month. Angie thus prepared the sales tax report illustrated in Figure 8-14 on the next page and made the following entry to record payment of the taxes:

– liability →	1	20X0 Aug. 20	Sales Tax Payable		3 6 0 0 00		1
+ revenue →	2		Miscellaneous Income			3 7 5 00	2
– asset →	3		Cash			3 2 2 5 00	3
	4		Sent in sales taxes for July.				4

Notice that Angie was allowed to keep a small percentage of the sales taxes collected as her fee for collecting the taxes and sending them in. She records this fee ($375) as miscellaneous income. Had Angie been in a state that did not allow the merchant to keep a portion of the taxes as a fee, her entry would have been as follows:

– liability →	1	20X0 Aug. 20	Sales Tax Payable		3 6 0 0 00		1
– asset →	2		Cash			3 6 0 0 00	2
	3		Sent in sales taxes for July.				3

Recording Sales Tax in a Sales Journal

As we have seen, credit sales subject to a sales tax can be recorded in a general journal. If the volume of credit sales is large, however, a more efficient use of journalizing and posting time can be made by expanding a one-column sales journal to three columns: (1) Accounts Receivable Debit, (2) Sales Credit, and (3) Sales Tax Payable Credit. The total amount to be received from a sale (selling price plus sales tax) is entered in the Accounts Receivable Debit column. The amount of the sale is entered in the Sales Credit column. And the amount of sales tax charged on the sale is entered in the Sales Tax Payable Credit column.

To illustrate the use of a three-column sales journal, we will use the example of a company other than Lakeside Electronics because Lakeside is a wholesale firm and thus is not required to collect retail sales taxes. The March 20X5 sales journal of Jarvis Gift Shop, a retailer, is presented in Figure 8-15.

Figure 8-14
Monthly Sales Tax Report

GEORGIA DEPARTMENT OF REVENUE
SALES AND USE TAX DIVISION
P. O. BOX 105296
ATLANTA, GEORGIA 30348-5296

SEE INSTRUCTIONS FOR PREPARING
THIS REPORT, TAX BULLETIN AND
SALES TAX UPDATE INFORMATION.

0797030111

Surf-N-Sand Shop
1200 Beach Road
Tybee Island, GA

USE BLACK INK ONLY   COMMODITY CODE _____

SALES AND USE TAX REPORT FOR CALENDAR MONTH OR OTHER AUTHORIZED PERIOD OF *July 2020*

PART I.A.

☐ EFT Filer

☐ AMENDED RETURN (If Applicable)

		TAX RATE	PART I.B. TAX COLUMN
1. Total Sales	60 000 00		
2. Total Use	-0-		
3. Total Sales and Use	60 000 00		
COMPLETE EXEMPTION WORKSHEET AND ENTER TOTALS BELOW			
4. Taxable State Sales and Use (Line 3 minus Total State exemption Line A)	60 000 00	X .04 =	2 400 00
5. Taxable State Sales and Use on Motor Fuel (Line 3 minus Total 1% Motor Fuel exemption Line B)	-0-	X .01 =	
6. Taxable 2nd Motor Fuel Sales and Use (Line 3 minus Total 2nd Motor Fuel exemption Line C)	-0-	X .03 =	
7. Taxable MARTA Sales and Use (Fulton & Dekalb Only) (Line 3 minus Total MARTA exemption Line D)	-0-	X .01 =	
8. Taxable Local Option Sales and Use (Line 3 minus Total Local Option exemption Line E)	60 000 00	X .01 =	600 00
9. Taxable Towns County 2nd Local Option Sales and Use (Line 3 minus Total Towns County 2nd L.O. exemption Line F)	60 000 00	X .01 =	600 00
10. Taxable Special Purpose Sales and Use (Line 3 minus Total Special Purpose exemption Line G)	-0-	X .01 =	
11. Taxable Educational Sales and Use (Line 3 minus Total Educational exemption Line H)	-0-	X .01 =	
12. Taxable Homestead Sales and Use (Line 3 minus Total Homestead exemption Line I)	-0-	X .01 =	
13. Total Tax from Tax Column (Lines 4 - 12 of Part I.B.)	3 600 00	← TOTAL	3 600 00
14. Excess Tax: factor amount +			
15. Total Tax Due	3 600 00		
16. Vendor's Compensation. If timely filed and paid − (Use Vendor's Compensation Worksheet)	375 00		
17. Penalty (Use penalty worksheet) +			
18. Interest + (1% per month or fraction thereof)			
19. Estimated Tax Paid Last Month −			
20. Estimated Tax Due This Month +			
21. Credit Memo −			
22. Remit This Amount	3 225 00		

This return must be filed and paid by the 20th of the month following the period for which the tax is due to avoid loss of vendor's compensation and the payment of penalty and interest. DEALERS AND CONTRACTORS MUST FILE A TIMELY RETURN EVEN THOUGH NO TAX IS DUE. DO NOT SEND CASH BY MAIL.

Remittance by Electronic Funds Transfer (EFT) must be completed by 3:00 p.m. on the 19th. If the 20th is on a Saturday, Sunday, Monday or a Federal Holiday the EFT must be completed before 3:00 p.m., on the preceding Friday.

☐ IF THERE IS ANY CHANGE IN TRADE NAME, ADDRESS, OWNERSHIP OR TELEPHONE NUMBER, CHECK BOX AND INDICATE THE CHANGE IN THE SPACE ON BACK.

STATE USE ONLY
POSTMARK DATE

MONTH   DAY   YEAR

CORR. CODE   REFUND   AGENT CODE

PART II   SCHEDULE OF TOTAL SALES AND USE EXEMPTIONS FROM EXEMPTION WORKSHEET

A. Total State		F. Total Towns County 2nd L/O	
B. Total 1% Motor Fuel		G. Total Special Purpose	
C. Total 2nd Motor Fuel		H. Total Educational	
D. Total MARTA		I. Total Homestead	
E. Total Local Option			

PART III   I certify that this return, including the accompanying schedules or statements, has been examined by me and is, to the best of my knowledge and belief, a true and complete return made in good faith for the period stated. This *20th* day of *August*, 20 *20*.

Return Prepared By _____   Signature *Angie Shaffer* _____   *Owner*
Title (Owner, Partner, Corp. Officer)

Figure 8-15

Multicolumn Sales Journal

	Date	Invoice No.	Customer's Name	P.R.	Accounts Receivable Dr.	Sales Cr.	Sales Tax Payable Cr.	
	Sales Journal						**Page 1**	
1	20X5 Mar. 1	102	Clyde James	✓	3 1 8 00	3 0 0 00	1 8 00	1
2	3	103	Faye Jerrell	✓	7 9 50	7 5 00	4 50	2
3	5	104	Kyle Sharp	✓	1 3 2 50	1 2 5 00	7 50	3
4	9	105	Lisa Chadwick	✓	3 4 45	3 2 50	1 95	4
5	14	106	River Road School	✓	8 4 8 00	8 0 0 00	4 8 00	5
6	17	107	Bill Edwards	✓	1 0 6 00	1 0 0 00	6 00	6
7	25	108	Clyde James	✓	6 8 90	6 5 00	3 90	7
8	31	109	Beth Todd	✓	3 3 0 72	3 1 2 00	1 8 72	8
9	31		Totals		1 9 1 8 07	1 8 0 9 50	1 0 8 57	9
10					(112)	(411)	(212)	10

Notice the account numbers written in parentheses directly below the column totals in Figure 8-15. The account numbers, as you remember, show that the column totals were posted to the general ledger. The check marks in the P.R. column mean that the individual amounts were posted to customers' accounts in the accounts receivable ledger.

Sales Returns Involving a Sales Tax

If a customer returns merchandise on which a sales tax was charged, the amount of sales tax must also be returned to the customer. To illustrate this, look again at the sales journal of Jarvis Gift Shop. On March 12, Lisa Chadwick returned merchandise she bought on March 9 for $32.50 plus $1.95 sales tax. The following general journal entry was made to record the return.

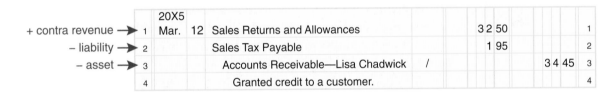

+ contra revenue → 1	20X5 Mar.	12	Sales Returns and Allowances	3 2 50		1
− liability → 2			Sales Tax Payable	1 95		2
− asset → 3			Accounts Receivable—Lisa Chadwick ✓		3 4 45	3
4			Granted credit to a customer.			4

Review Quiz 8-6

Willie Loeb is the owner of The Petite Boutique, which is located in a state with a 6% sales tax on the price of retail items. During the first two weeks in August 20X1, Willie had the following sales-related transactions. Record each transaction in general journal form.

20X1
Aug. 1 Sold merchandise for cash, $500.
   4 Sold merchandise on account to Eve Li, $200.
   6 Sold merchandise for cash, $600.
   10 Sold merchandise on account to Max Leatherwood, $1,400.
   12 Max Leatherwood returned $50 worth of merchandise and was given credit for the return.
   15 Paid sales taxes collected in July 20X1, $940.

Check your answer on page 388.

Credit cards are an enormous part of retailing, with over a billion credit cards in use in the United States. That's about three cards for each person (including children) in the country.

Credit Card Sales

Each day in this country millions of people use credit cards to purchase goods and services. There are three basic types of credit cards: (1) those issued by banks (referred to as *bank credit cards*), such as VISA and MasterCard; (2) those issued by private companies (referred to as *nonbank cards*), such as American Express and Diners Club; and (3) those issued by department stores and oil companies, such as Macy's and Exxon.

Bank Credit Card Sales

Learning Objective

7 Record credit card sales.

Most retail businesses accept bank credit cards, and there are a number of benefits to retailers who do so. First, the bank that issues the card takes the credit application from the user of the card, thus saving the merchant this task. Second, a merchant who accepts bank credit cards is able to make immediate bank deposits of credit card receipts, thereby receiving cash quickly. Third, the bank that issued the card is responsible for collection of the amount due. If a customer fails to make payment, the bank—not the merchant—absorbs the loss.

Recording Bank Credit Card Sales

Bank credit card sales are recorded as *cash sales* because credit card receipts can be deposited in a bank immediately. The bank deducts a discount (fee) that ranges from 3% to 7%. The difference between the receipt total and the discount is credited to the depositor's account.

To illustrate, assume that on June 5, 20XX, Jeans & Company sold merchandise for $100, plus $5 sales tax, to Jason Jones, who used his VISA card. The sale was written up by a sales clerk, and Jason was given a copy of the receipt.

This sale turned out to be the only bank credit card sale Jeans & Company made for the day. Therefore, the one receipt was taken to the bank for deposit at the end of the day. The bank that issued the card, National Bank and Trust, charges a discount rate of 4%, which is applied to the receipt total. A discount of $4.20 ($105 × .04) is thus computed by the bank. The difference between the credit card receipt and the discount ($105 – $4.20 = $100.80) is entered in the bank account of Jeans & Company. The discount is recorded in an expense account entitled **Credit Card Expense**. The entry to record the sale is made in general journal form as follows:

Credit Card Expense account an expense account that is used to record discounts paid when receipts for credit card sales are deposited with the bank that issued the card (such as VISA or MasterCard) or with the credit card company that issued the card (such as American Express)

		20XX									
+ asset →	1	Jun.	5	Cash			1 0 0	80			1
+ expense →	2			Credit Card Expense			4	20			2
+ revenue →	3			Sales					1 0 0	00	3
+ liability →	4			Sales Tax Payable					5	00	4
	5			Recorded bank credit card sale.							5

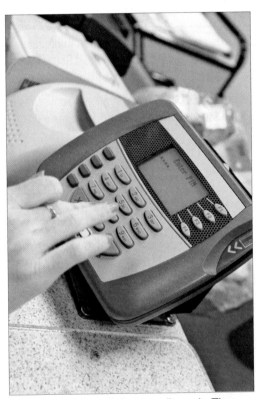

Retailers also benefit from credit cards. They don't have to take credit applications, check customers' credit ratings, keep accounts receivable records, or pursue collection if customers fail to pay.

Recording Private Company Credit Card Sales

A sales receipt from a nonbank credit card (such as American Express) generally cannot be deposited in a bank. Instead, the merchant summarizes sales receipts and submits them to the private card company for payment. The private card company, in turn, makes collection from the card user. This type of sale, unlike a bank credit card sale, is not treated as a cash sale; rather, it is recorded as a sale on account. However, the receivables generated by these sales should be kept separate from other receivables, since it is the credit card company—not the merchant—that is responsible for collection. An account entitled **Accounts Receivable—Credit Cards** can be used to record the amount due from nonbank credit card sales.

To illustrate recording nonbank credit card sales, let's assume that in addition to the bank credit card sale we recorded earlier, Jeans & Company sold $500 of merchandise (plus 5% sales tax) and accepted an American Express card in payment. Assuming that American Express charges a 6% discount rate ($525 × .06 = $31.50), the following general journal entry can be made to record the sale.

		20XX									
+ asset →	1	Jun.	5	Accounts Receivable—Credit Cards			4 9 3	50			1
+ expense →	2			Credit Card Expense			3 1	50			2
+ revenue →	3			Sales					5 0 0	00	3
+ liability →	4			Sales Tax Payable					2 5	00	4
	5			Recorded nonbank credit card sale.							5

Accounts Receivable—Credit Cards account an asset account used to record the amount due from nonbank credit card sales

If sales of this type are frequent, the sales journal can be designed so that such sales can be recorded more efficiently. Let's look at how this entry would be recorded in a specially designed sales journal.

Sales Journal									
	Date	Sale No.	Customer	P.R.	Accounts Receivable Dr.	Accounts Rec. Credit Cards Dr.	Credit Card Expense Dr.	Sales Cr.	Sales Tax Payable Cr.
1	20XX Jun. 5		American Express			4 9 3 50	3 1 50	5 0 0 00	2 5 00	1

Credit Cards Issued by Businesses

Many large department stores and oil companies—and some airlines—issue their own credit cards. This type of card usually can be used only in outlets of the company that issued the card. Sales from such cards are recorded as regular credit sales, since the company that issues the card does its own billing.

Review Quiz 8-7

Brad Tedrow accepts both bank credit cards and nonbank credit cards in his retail clothing business. The following credit card sales were made on April 8, 20X2. Record each sale in general journal form. Brad's business is located in an area with a 6% sales tax rate.

(a) Sold merchandise, $1,000, and accepted a VISA card (assume a discount rate of 4%).
(b) Sold merchandise, $400, and accepted a nonbank credit card (assume a discount rate of 5%).

Check your answers on page 388.

Review of Journals and Ledgers

In Chapters 7 and 8, you have added four special journals and two subsidiary ledgers to your accounting repertoire. Table 8-2 summarizes the uses of the four special journals and the general journal, which you learned about previously.

Table 8-2 Summary of Journals

Journal	Used for
Purchases	All credit purchases of merchandise
Cash Payments	All payments of cash
Sales	All credit sales of merchandise
Cash Receipts	All receipts of cash
General	All transactions not in a special journal

What kinds of transactions does this leave for the general journal? There are not many, but here is a list of some of them:

- Credit purchases of items other than merchandise
- Credit sales of assets other than merchandise
- Returns and allowances for credit
- Owner investments of assets other than cash
- Performance of services on credit
- Owner withdrawal of assets other than cash
- Correcting entries
- Adjusting entries
- Closing entries

There are now three ledgers—two subsidiary and one general. The uses of these ledgers are summarized in Table 8-3.

Table 8-3 Summary of Ledgers

Ledger	Used for
Accounts Payable (subsidiary)	Creditors' accounts
Accounts Receivable (subsidiary)	Customers' accounts
General	Financial statement accounts (asset, liability, owner's equity, revenue, cost, and expense) that are listed in the chart of accounts

The general ledger includes two controlling accounts—Accounts Payable and Accounts Receivable—which summarize the balances of the respective subsidiary ledgers. Figure 8-16 on the next page summarizes the controlling account/subsidiary ledger relationship. Here, we assume that a business has accounts receivable of $2,000—owed by three credit customers—and $1,500 in accounts payable, owed to three creditors.

CAUTION

Never record the same transaction in two separate journals. A transaction recorded in a special journal is never also recorded in the general journal.

Review Quiz **8-8** Identify the journal in which each of the following transactions would be recorded: (a) cash sale of merchandise; (b) credit purchase of equipment; (c) owner withdrawal of cash; (d) credit sale of merchandise; (e) receipt of cash from a customer; (f) adjusting entries; (g) cash sale of supplies; (h) closing entries; and (i) cash purchase of merchandise.

Check your answers on page 389.

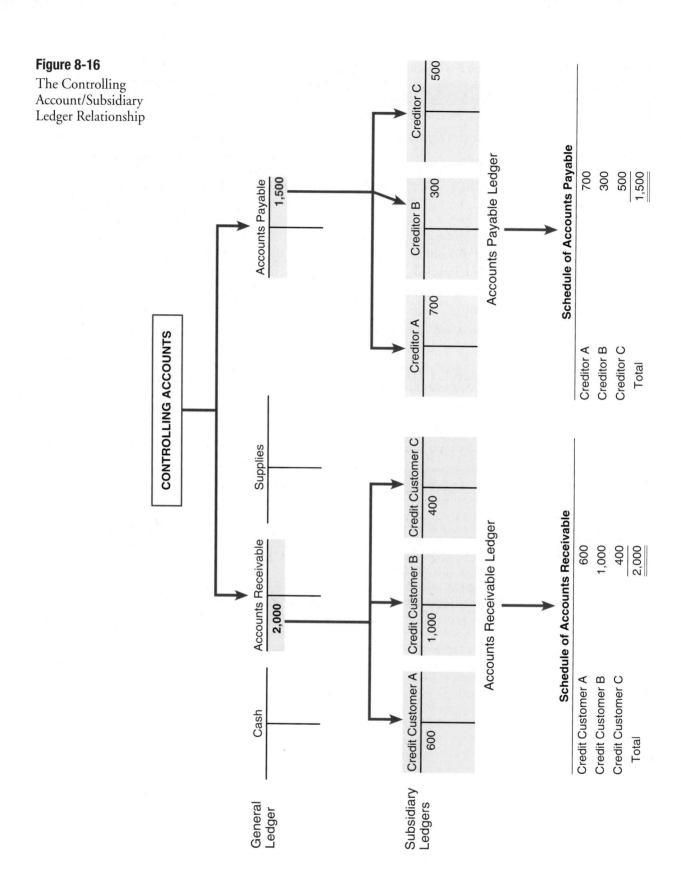

Figure 8-16
The Controlling
Account/Subsidiary
Ledger Relationship

CONTROLLING ACCOUNTS

General Ledger

Cash

Accounts Receivable
2,000

Supplies

Accounts Payable
1,500

Subsidiary Ledgers

Credit Customer A
600

Credit Customer B
1,000

Credit Customer C
400

Accounts Receivable Ledger

Creditor A
700

Creditor B
300

Creditor C
500

Accounts Payable Ledger

Schedule of Accounts Receivable

Credit Customer A	600
Credit Customer B	1,000
Credit Customer C	400
Total	2,000

Schedule of Accounts Payable

Creditor A	700
Creditor B	300
Creditor C	500
Total	1,500

Retail Store Larceny

A retail store hired a new manager who realized that out of seven check-out lines, one was not in use. He brought in his own personal cash register and placed it in the seventh line so that it appeared like all the other six lines. In this way, all money placed in that register was separate from the rest. Periodically, he would empty the register and take the money for himself.

The thefts went undetected for quite some time until a physical count of inventory showed huge shortages.

Source: Joseph T. Wells, CPA, CFE, "Enemies Within," *AICPA* (December 2001).

For Discussion
1. How was it possible that the new manager of the retail store was able to steal cash from the business?
2. How is this type of accounting fraud normally discovered?
3. Why was the manager able to get away with this kind of crime more easily than a lower-level employee?
4. Do business owners have reason to fear more from shoplifters or employee theft of merchandise? Why?

An ingenious and deceitful manager can cost a company more than a handful of shoplifters.

Joining the Pieces

Merchandising Transactions

Transaction: On April 3, 20X0, Daughtry Department Store purchased merchandise costing $3,000 on account from Ford Supply Company. Terms of the sale were 2/10,n/30, and payment was made within the discount period.

The Purchaser

On the books of Daughtry Department Store:

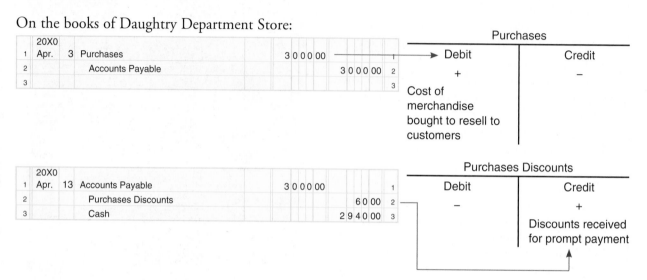

	20X0					
1	Apr.	3	Purchases	3 0 0 0 00		1
2			Accounts Payable		3 0 0 0 00	2
3						3

Purchases

Debit	Credit
+	−
Cost of merchandise bought to resell to customers	

	20X0					
1	Apr.	13	Accounts Payable	3 0 0 0 00		1
2			Purchases Discounts		6 0 00	2
3			Cash		2 9 4 0 00	3

Purchases Discounts

Debit	Credit
−	+
	Discounts received for prompt payment

The Seller

On the books of Ford Supply Company:

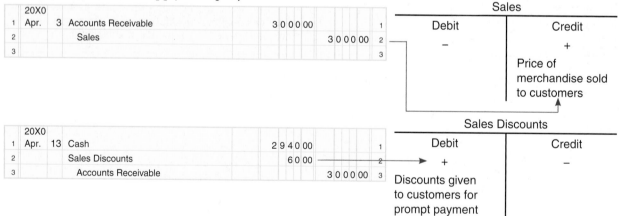

	20X0					
1	Apr.	3	Accounts Receivable	3 0 0 0 00		1
2			Sales		3 0 0 0 00	2
3						3

Sales

Debit	Credit
−	+
	Price of merchandise sold to customers

	20X0					
1	Apr.	13	Cash	2 9 4 0 00		1
2			Sales Discounts	6 0 00		2
3			Accounts Receivable		3 0 0 0 00	3

Sales Discounts

Debit	Credit
+	−
Discounts given to customers for prompt payment	

Types of Transactions

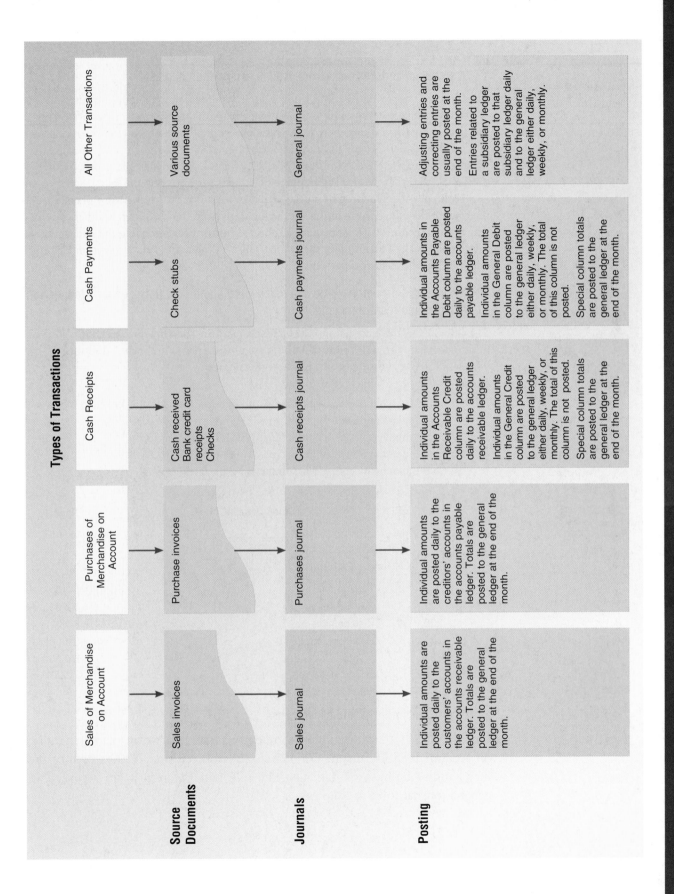

	Sales of Merchandise on Account	Purchases of Merchandise on Account	Cash Receipts	Cash Payments	All Other Transactions
Source Documents	Sales invoices	Purchase invoices	Cash received Bank credit card receipts Checks	Check stubs	Various source documents
Journals	Sales journal	Purchases journal	Cash receipts journal	Cash payments journal	General journal
Posting	Individual amounts are posted daily to the customers' accounts in the accounts receivable ledger. Totals are posted to the general ledger at the end of the month.	Individual amounts are posted daily to the creditors' accounts in the accounts payable ledger. Totals are posted to the general ledger at the end of the month.	Individual amounts in the Accounts Receivable Credit column are posted daily to the accounts receivable ledger. Individual amounts in the General Credit column are posted to the general ledger either daily, weekly, or monthly. The total of this column is not posted. Special column totals are posted to the general ledger at the end of the month.	Individual amounts in the Accounts Payable Debit column are posted daily to the accounts payable ledger. Individual amounts in the General Debit column are posted to the general ledger either daily, weekly, or monthly. The total of this column is not posted. Special column totals are posted to the general ledger at the end of the month.	Adjusting entries and correcting entries are usually posted at the end of the month. Entries related to a subsidiary ledger are posted to that subsidiary ledger daily and to the general ledger either daily, weekly, or monthly.

CHAPTER 8 REVIEW, PRACTICE, AND APPLY

Summary Interactive Summary in English and Spanish

1 Describe procedures and forms used in selling merchandise.

Sales on credit are initiated either when a purchase order is received from a customer or when a salesperson responds to a customer's request and prepares a **sales order**. In practice, many firms routinely write up sales orders in all cases, even after the receipt of a purchase order. A copy of the sales order often is used to prepare a sales invoice, which is sent to the buyer with the goods, a few days in advance of the goods, or after the goods. The sales invoice is the source document for recording the sale.

Cash sales are evidenced by a **sales ticket** or sales slip, which is a form prepared at the time of the sale. A copy of the sales ticket is given to the customer, another copy is sent to the accounting department as a source document for recording the sale, and a third copy usually remains with the salesperson who made the sale. A variation of the sales ticket is the **cash register tape**.

2 Record sales of merchandise in a sales journal and post to the general ledger and the accounts receivable ledger.

The July 20XX sales transactions of Hare Company are shown below. Each is recorded in the accompanying **sales journal**. Complete posting marks are included in the journal. However, posting is not shown at this point.

20XX
Jul. 5 Sold merchandise to West Company, $700; terms, 2/10,n/30.
7 Sold merchandise to Watson, Inc., $400; terms, 2/10,n/30.
12 Sold merchandise to Hall Company, $500; terms, n/30.
26 Sold merchandise to Watson, Inc., $600; terms, 2/10,n/30.
30 Sold merchandise to Hall Company, $250; terms, n/30.

	Date		Invoice No.	Customer's Name	P.R.	Accts. Rec. Dr. Sales Cr.	
	20XX						
1	Jul.	5	1	West Company	✓	7 00 00	1
2		7	2	Watson, Inc.	✓	4 00 00	2
3		12	3	Hall Company	✓	5 00 00	3
4		26	4	Watson, Inc.	✓	6 00 00	4
5		30	5	Hall Company	✓	2 50 00	5
6		31		Total		2 4 50 00	6
7						(112) (411)	7

Sales Journal — Page 1

3 Record sales returns and allowances.

On March 23, 20XX, Saunders Company sold $500 worth of merchandise on account to Bob Sutton. On March 26, Bob returned $200 worth of the merchandise because of damage. The sale and the return are recorded in general journal form as follows:

362 PART II | Accounting for Cash and the Merchandising Business

		20XX						
+ asset →	1	Mar.	23	Accounts Receivable—Bob Sutton	/	5 0 0 00		1
+ revenue →	2			Sales			5 0 0 00	2
	3			Recorded sale on account.				3
	4							4
+ contra revenue →	5		26	Sales Returns and Allowances		2 0 0 00		5
– asset →	6			Accounts Receivable—Bob Sutton	/		2 0 0 00	6
	7			Accepted return of merchandise				7
	8			from a customer.				8
	9							9

4 Record sales discounts.

A sales discount is a cash discount that is sometimes offered by a seller to encourage a buyer to make prompt payment for a credit purchase. To review, assume that on March 2, 20X4, Sigma Smith, owner of Sigma Products Company, sold merchandise with an invoice price of $800 to Lynn Sapp. The invoice carried terms of 2/10,n/30, and it was paid in full on March 12, 20X4. Sigma Products Company made the following entry to record the receipt of cash.

		20X4						
+ asset →	1	Mar.	12	Cash		7 8 4 00		1
+ contra revenue →	2			Sales Discounts		1 6 00		2
– asset →	3			Accounts Receivable—Lynn Sapp	/		8 0 0 00	3
	4			Received cash on account.				4
	5							5
	6							6

5 Record cash receipts in a cash receipts journal and post to the general ledger and the accounts receivable ledger.

The cash receipts of Hare Company for July 20XX are as follows:

20XX

Jul. 1 Nancy Hare invested $5,000 cash in the business.
     5 Sold merchandise for cash, $400.
     8 Sold office supplies at cost to a neighboring business, $90.
     8 Collected balance owed on Hall Company's account, $900, less 2% discount.
   10 Sold merchandise for cash, $1,400.
   14 Received payment on account from West Company, $700, less 2% discount.
   17 Received payment on account from Watson, Inc., $400, less 2% discount.
   31 Sold merchandise for cash, $1,080.

These transactions are recorded in the **cash receipts journal** shown in Figure 8-17. Complete posting marks are included in the journal. The **accounts receivable ledger** (Figure 8-18) and the **Accounts Receivable account**, a controlling account (Figure 8-19), are shown as well.

Figure 8-17

Cash Receipts Journal

	Date	Account Credited	P.R.	General Cr.	Sales Cr.	Accounts Receivable Cr.	Sales Discounts Dr.	Cash Dr.	
	20XX								
1	Jul. 1	Nancy Hare, Capital	311	5 0 0 0 00				5 0 0 0 00	1
2	5	Cash Sales	✓		4 0 0 00			4 0 0 00	2
3	8	Office Supplies	113	9 0 00				9 0 00	3
4	8	Hall Company	✓			9 0 0 00	1 8 00	8 8 2 00	4
5	10	Cash Sales	✓		1 4 0 0 00			1 4 0 0 00	5
6	14	West Company	✓			7 0 0 00	1 4 00	6 8 6 00	6
7	17	Watson, Inc.	✓			4 0 0 00	8 00	3 9 2 00	7
8	31	Cash Sales	✓		1 0 8 0 00			1 0 8 0 00	8
9	31	Totals		5 0 9 0 00	2 8 8 0 00	2 0 0 0 00	4 0 00	9 9 3 0 00	9
10				(✓)	(411)	(112)	(411.2)	(111)	10
11									11

Figure 8-18

Accounts Receivable Ledger

Accounts Receivable Ledger

Name Hall Company

Address 14 Greystoke Ln., Columbus, OH 43201

Date	Item	P.R.	Debit	Credit	Balance
20XX					
Jul. 1	Balance	✓			9 0 0 00
8		CR4		9 0 0 00	—
12	Inv. No. 3	S1	5 0 0 00		5 0 0 00
30	Inv. No. 5	S1	2 5 0 00		7 5 0 00

Name Watson, Inc.

Address 5000 Delmar Blvd., St. Louis, MO 63108

Date	Item	P.R.	Debit	Credit	Balance
20XX					
Jul. 7	Inv. No. 2	S1	4 0 0 00		4 0 0 00
17		CR4		4 0 0 00	—
26	Inv. No. 4	S1	6 0 0 00		6 0 0 00

Name West Company

Address 431 Highway South, Troy, AL 36081

Date	Item	P.R.	Debit	Credit	Balance
20XX					
Jul. 5	Inv. No. 1	S1	7 0 0 00		7 0 0 00
14		CR4		7 0 0 00	—

Figure 8-19
Accounts Receivable
Controlling Account

General Ledger

Account **Accounts Receivable**   Account No.   112

Date		Item	P.R.	Debit	Credit	Balance Debit	Balance Credit
20XX Jul.	1	Balance	✓			9 0 0 00	
	31		S1	2 4 5 0 00		3 3 5 0 00	
	31		CR4		2 0 0 0 00	1 3 5 0 00	

6   Prepare a schedule of accounts receivable.

From the account balances in Hare Company's accounts receivable ledger, the following **schedule of accounts receivable** was prepared. Note that the total of the schedule agrees with the balance of the Accounts Receivable controlling account shown in the preceding section.

Hare Company
Schedule of Accounts Receivable
July 31, 20XX

Hall Company	7 5 0 00
Watson, Inc.	6 0 0 00
West Company	—
Total	1 3 5 0 00

7   Record credit card sales.

The Willoughby Men's Shop accepts two types of credit cards, VISA and American Express. On November 22, 20XX, VISA card sales totaled $400, and American Express sales totaled $300. The business is located in an area with a 6% retail sales tax. The discount rate charged on the VISA sales is 4%, and the discount rate charged on the American Express sales is 6%. These sales are recorded as follows. (Remember that VISA sales are recorded as cash sales, and American Express sales are recorded as sales on account.)

> To record the VISA sales: $400 × .06 (6% tax) = $24; $424 ($400 + $24) × .04 (4% discount rate) = bank discount of $16.96; $424 − $16.96 = $407.04 (amount of cash received)

+ asset →	1	20XX Nov.	22	Cash	4 0 7 04		1
+ expense →	2			Credit Card Expense	1 6 96		2
+ revenue →	3			Sales		4 0 0 00	3
+ liability →	4			Sales Tax Payable		2 4 00	4
	5			Recorded VISA card sales.			5

To record the American Express sales: $300 × .06 (6% tax) = $18; $318 ($300 + $18) × .06 (6% discount rate) = discount of $19.08; $318 − $19.08 = $298.92 (amount of cash to be received)

	20XX					
+ asset → 1	Nov.	22	Accounts Receivable—Credit Cards	2 9 8 92		1
+ expense → 2			Credit Card Expense	1 9 08		2
+ revenue → 3			Sales		3 0 0 00	3
+ liability → 4			Sales Tax Payable		1 8 00	4
5			Recorded American Express sales.			5

Terms and Concepts Review

• Key Terms and Definitions in English and Spanish
• Additional Quiz Questions

Key Terms

Accounts Receivable account, 338
Accounts Receivable—Credit Cards account, 355
accounts receivable ledger, 339
cash receipts journal, 345
cash register tape, 336
Credit Card Expense account, 354
credit period, 334
credit terms, 334
revolving charge plan, 334

Sales account, 337
Sales Discounts account, 343
sales journal, 338
sales order, 334
Sales Returns and Allowances account, 342
sales tax, 350
Sales Tax Payable account, 350
sales ticket, 336
schedule of accounts receivable, 348

Concepts Review

1. What is the source document for recording credit sales and cash sales?
2. Why is the Sales account an owner's equity account?
3. Which account is credited for a cash receipt from (a) a sale of merchandise; (b) a sale of supplies; and (c) a credit customer paying on account?
4. Compare the accounts receivable ledger with the accounts payable ledger. Which accounts are contained in each ledger?
5. What two types of postings are made from the sales journal?
6. Why is it a common practice to record sales returns in the Sales Returns and Allowances account rather than in the Sales account?
7. What type of balance does the Sales Returns and Allowances account have? What is the relationship of this account to the Sales account?
8. How does the seller of goods account for a cash discount?
9. What three types of postings are made from the cash receipts journal?
10. How does a schedule of accounts receivable serve as a check on the accuracy of the accounts receivable ledger?
11. Who is responsible for the collection and payment of sales tax?
12. What purpose is served by a three-column sales journal?
13. Why are bank credit card sales recorded as cash sales?
14. Who is responsible for the billing of customers in nonbank credit card sales and department store credit card sales?

Skills Review

Quick Practice

Quick Practice 8-1

Objective: To match payment terms with description

Common payment terms are (1) net cash; (2) 2/10,n/30; (3) n/EOM; (4) C.O.D.; (5) FOB shipping point; and (6) FOB destination point

Directions: Match the payment term by number with its correct description.

Payment Term	Description
(a) _____	A discount of 2% is allowed if an invoice is paid within 10 days of the date of the invoice. If payment is not made within 10 days, the total must be paid within 30 days of the date of the invoice.
(b) _____	Under these terms, the seller is responsible for all freight charges.
(c) _____	No credit is allowed by the seller. Payment must be made by the buyer at the time of purchase.
(d) _____	Under these terms, the buyer is responsible for all freight charges.
(e) _____	Payment for goods must be made by the end of the month in which the goods were purchased.
(f) _____	Under these terms, payment for goods must be made when goods are delivered to the buyer.

Quick Practice 8-2

Objective: To record credit sales in general journal form

The following credit sales were made by Tim Sether's Home Furnishings during October 20XX:

Date		Customer's Name	Amount
Oct.	1	Samuel duPlessis Outlet	$4,950
	15	Redeker Furnishings	3,850
	31	Shelton Industries	6,275

Directions: Record the transactions in a two-column general journal.

Quick Practice 8-3

Objective: To record sales in a sales journal

Directions: Record the credit sales in Quick Practice 8-2 into a sales journal page 8, starting with Invoice No. 371. Post to the subsidiary ledger after each entry. Total the sales journal, and post to the general ledger at the end of the month. Use account number 112 for Accounts Receivable and account number 411 for Sales.

Quick Practice 8-4

Objective: To record merchandise transactions in general journal form

The following merchandise transactions of Kevin Harold Appliances took place in January 20XX:

20XX

Jan. 2 Purchased merchandise on account from Cantoria Wholesalers, $9,000.

Jan. 3 Sold merchandise for cash, $6,000.

8 Sold merchandise on account to Dianna Johnson Co., $2,400.

12 Issued a credit memorandum to Dianna Johnson Co. for the return of damaged merchandise, $800.

22 Purchased merchandise for cash, $4,300.

31 Returned merchandise to Malcom Industries and received a cash refund, $3,300.

Directions: Record the transactions in a two-column general journal.

Learning Objective **5**

Check Figure
July 1 Cash 8,000 (debit);
Cheryl Granroth, Capital 8,000 (credit)

Quick Practice 8-5

Objective: To record cash receipts in general journal form

Cheryl Granroth Retailing had the following cash receipts during July 20XX. All credit sales carry terms of 2/10, n/3a.

Date	Amount	Received from	For
20XX			
Jul. 1	$8,000	Owner	Cash investment
3	600	Mike Gobbel	Sale of June 25
15	900	Walk-in customers	Cash sales
30	560	Shaw Co.	Sale of July 20
31	290	Hall Co.	Sale of July 1

Directions: Record Cheryl's cash receipts in a two-column general journal.

Learning Objective **5**

Check Figure
Total of Cash Debit Column = $10,350

Quick Practice 8-6

Objective: To record cash receipts in a cash receipts journal

Directions: Record the cash receipts in Quick Practice 8-5 in a cash receipts journal. Total and rule the journal, and prove the equality of debits and credits in the column totals.

Learning Objectives **2, 4**

Check Figure
Nov. 15 Cash 1,372 (debit);
Sales Discounts 28 (debit);
Accounts Receivable—
Killingsworth Enterprises
1,400 (credit)

Quick Practice 8-7

Objective: To record merchandise sales and sales discounts in general journal form

The following transactions were completed by Christina Simmons Enterprises during November 20XX:

20XX

Nov. 1 Sold merchandise to Martin, Inc., $2,300; terms, n/30.

5 Sold merchandise to Killingsworth Enterprises, $1,400; terms, 2/10,n/30.

6 Sold merchandise to Edwards Car Dealership, $1,600; terms, 2/10,n/30.

15 Received payment from Killingsworth Enterprises for the sale of November 5.

30 Received payment from Edwards Car Dealership for the sale of November 6.

30 Received payment from Martin Inc. for the sale of November 1.

Directions: Record the transactions in a two-column general journal.

Learning Objective **3**

Check Figure
(c) Sales Returns and
Allowances 100 (debit); Cash
100 (credit)

Quick Practice 8-8

Objective: To record returns and allowances

Directions: Record the following transactions in a two-column general journal:

(a) Received a credit memorandum for the return of merchandise purchased on account from Lasselle Company, $400.

(b) Issued a credit memorandum for the return of merchandise sold on account to Fritz Shop, $275.

(c) Issued a check for $100 to Kate Dins as a cash refund for damaged merchandise.

(d) Issued a credit memorandum for an allowance made to Dan Jenkins for defective merchandise sold on account, $380.

Learning Objective **2**

Check Figure
(a) $4,800 × .06 = $288

Quick Practice 8-9

Objective: To calculate and record sales tax

Marilyn Jensen, owner of Marilyn's Beauty Supplies, is located in a state with a 6% retail sales tax. During June 20XX, Marilyn reported cash sales of $4,800.

Directions:

(a) Calculate the amount of sales tax collected.

(b) Record a summary entry in general journal form for June cash sales and sales taxes collected.

(c) Record the entry to send the sales taxes to the taxing authority.

Learning Objective **2**

Check Figure
Sales Tax Payable column
total = $43.50

Quick Practice 8-10

Objective: To record retail sales in a three-column sales journal

Paul Bunyon Industries sells wood-cutting products to its regular customers on credit. The following credit sales were made during February 20XX. All sales carry terms of n/30 and are subject to a 5% sales tax.

20XX

Feb. 3 Sold a chain saw to Brad Smith, $470.

14 Sold axes and shovels to Nick Flint, $240.

27 Sold leather gloves and hard hats to Jade Cardoso, $160.

Directions: Record the sales in a three-column sales journal. Number sales starting with 91, and total and rule the journal.

Learning Objective **7**

Check Figure
(a) Credit Card Expense 52
(debit)

Quick Practice 8-11

Objective: To record credit card sales

Carla Bradley's Coin Shop had the following credit card sales that are subject to a 4% sales tax:

(a) Sold merchandise, $1,000, and accepted a VISA card. The discount rate is 5%.

(b) Sold merchandise, $600, and accepted a nonbank credit card. The discount rate is 6%.

Directions: Record the credit card sales in a two-column general journal.

Learning Objectives **2, 5**

Check Figure
(a) CR

Quick Practice 8-12

Objective: To identify journals in which transactions are recorded

Gerald Kwilecki Clothing uses four special journals and a general journal.

Directions: Use a check mark to indicate the journal in which the transactions on the next page should be recorded.

Transaction	P	S	CR	CP	G
(a) Performed services for cash.					
(b) Paid a creditor on account.					
(c) Corrected an error.					
(d) Purchased merchandise for cash.					
(e) Sold merchandise for cash.					
(f) Adjusted for supplies used.					
(g) Sold merchandise on account.					
(h) Purchased merchandise on account.					
(i) Owner withdrew merchandise.					
(j) Collected cash on account.					

Exercises

Learning Objective **2**

Check Figure
Total of sales journal = $5,335

Exercise 8-1

Objective: To record credit sales in a sales journal and post to the general and accounts receivables ledgers

Hamme Company made the following credit sales during June 20X2:

20X2
Jun. 5   Adams Co., $900.
    10   Heard, Inc., $500.
    12   Brown Co., $525.
    17   Heard, Inc., $1,060.
    19   Brown Co., $1,175.
    26   Mallory, Inc., $610.
    30   Adams Co., $565.

Directions: Starting with Invoice No. 477, record the sales on page 1 of a sales journal. Post to the subsidiary ledger after each entry. Total the sales journal, and post to the general ledger at the end of the month.

Learning Objectives **2, 3**

Check Figure
(g) cash 800 (debit) Purchases Returns and Allowance 800 (credit)

Exercise 8-2

Objective: To record merchandise transactions in general journal form

Directions: Record the following transactions of Sterling Company in general journal form:

(a) Sold merchandise on account to Smith Co., $8,000.
(b) Sold merchandise for cash, $5,000.
(c) Purchased merchandise on credit from Sutton Co., $6,500.
(d) Issued a credit memorandum to Paul Jones for the return of damaged merchandise, $300.
(e) Issued a check to Tami Owens for the return of merchandise that was the wrong model, $175.
(f) Returned merchandise to B & M Manufacturing Co. and received credit, $4,200.
(g) Returned merchandise to Mobley Co. and received a cash refund, $800.

Learning Objective **5**

Check Figure
Nov. 10 Cash 350 (debit)
Sales 350 (credit

Exercise 8-3

Objective: To record cash receipts in general journal form

Directions: Patty Boyle's cash receipts for November 20X1 follow. Record each in general journal form. All credit sales carry terms of 2/10,n/30.

Date 20X1		Amount	Received from	For
Nov.	1	$12,000	Owner	Cash investment
	3	500	Hall Co.	Cash sale
	7	200	Thomas Co.	Sale of October 28
	10	350	Walk-in customers	Cash sales
	15	700	James Smith	Sale of November 5
	20	850	Rosser Co.	Sale of October 25
	26	225	Wells Co.	Sale of our supplies
	28	800	Speer, Inc.	Sale of November 18

Learning Objective **5**

Check Figure
Total credits = $15,625

Exercise 8-4

Objective: To record cash receipts in a cash receipts journal

Directions: Record the cash receipts listed in Exercise 8-3 in a cash receipts journal. Total the journal, and prove the equality of the debits and credits in the column totals. Then, rule the journal.

Learning Objectives
2, 4, 5

Check Figure
No discount on the July 29 cash collection

Exercise 8-5

Objective: To record merchandise sales, sales discounts, and cash receipts in general journal form

The following transactions were completed by Twin Cities Products Company during July 20XX:

20XX

Jul. 3 Sold merchandise for cash, $7,200.
5 Sold merchandise to Parkside Grocery, $9,500; terms, n/30.
6 Sold merchandise to Derrek's Quick Stop Grocery, $900; terms, 2/10,n/30.
8 Sold merchandise to Bronson's Grocery Company, $2,100; terms, 2/10,n/30.
16 Received payment from Derrek's Quick Stop Grocery for the sale of July 6.
25 Received payment from Bronson's Grocery Company for the sale of July 8.
29 Received $1,000 on account from Parkside Grocery.

Directions: Record the transactions in general journal form.

Learning Objective **3**

Check Figure
Three debits to the Sales Returns and Allowances account

Exercise 8-6

Objective: To record returns and allowances

Directions: Record the following transactions in general journal form:

(a) Issued a credit memorandum for the return of merchandise sold on account to Lawson Company, $1,650.
(b) Received a credit memorandum for the return of equipment purchased on account from Zayer Equipment Company, $1,600.
(c) Issued a check for $225 to Glen Justice as a cash refund for damaged merchandise.
(d) Received a credit memorandum for the return of merchandise purchased on account from Morton Supply Company, $900.
(e) Issued a credit memorandum for an allowance made to Susan Watson for defective merchandise sold on account, $400.

Learning Objective **2**

Check Figure
Sales tax = $1,392

Exercise 8-7

Objective: To calculate and record sales tax

Culver's Restaurant is located in an area with a 6% retail sales tax. For the month just ended, Culver reported cash sales of $23,200.

Directions:
1. Calculate the amount of sales tax collected.

2. In general journal form, record a summary entry for the month's cash sales and sales tax collected.
3. In general journal form, record the entry to pay the sales tax to the taxing authority.

Learning Objective 2

Check Figure
Total of Accounts Receivable
Dr. column = $1,900.53

Exercise 8-8

Objective: To record retail sales in a three-column sales journal

The Churchwell Ski Shop is a small ski and accessory shop that sells merchandise on credit to its regular customers. The following credit sales were made during December 20X2. All sales carry terms of n/30 and are subject to a 6% sales tax.

20X2
Dec. 1   Sold skis to Walter Waddell, $538.
3   Sold a sweater and gloves to Aida Rodriguez, $195.
12   Sold skis to Mitch Worrell, $330.
21   Sold an overcoat to Kay Rodgers, $259.95.
28   Sold various items to Karen Kilmer, $280.
31   Sold a helmet and gloves to Martin Choi, $190.

Directions:
1. Record the sales in a three-column sales journal. Number sales starting with 225.
2. Total and rule the journal.

Learning Objective 7

Check Figure
(a) Credit Card Expense 42.40
(debit)

Exercise 8-9

Objective: To record credit card sales

Directions: Record the following credit card sales of O'Rourke Company in a two-column general journal. All sales are subject to a 6% retail sales tax.

(a) Sold merchandise, $1,000, and accepted a VISA card. The discount rate is 4%.
(b) Sold merchandise, $300, and accepted a nonbank credit card. The discount rate is 5%.

**Learning Objectives
2, 3, 4, 5**

Check Figure
Six transactions would be recorded in the general journal.

Exercise 8-10

Objective: To identify journals in which transactions are recorded

Directions: A form and several transactions follow. Use a check mark in your working papers to indicate the journal in which each transaction should be recorded, assuming that four special journals and the general journal are used.

Transaction	P	S	CR	CP	G
(a) Collected cash on account.					
(b) Purchased supplies for cash.					
(c) Owner invested several noncash assets.					
(d) Paid a creditor on account.					
(e) Purchased merchandise for cash.					
(f) Owner withdrew merchandise.					
(g) Performed services on credit.					
(h) Sold merchandise for cash.					
(i) Corrected an error.					
(j) Purchased equipment on credit.					
(k) Paid utilities expense.					
(l) Sold merchandise on credit.					
(m) Purchased merchandise on credit.					
(n) Adjusted for supplies used.					
(o) Performed services for cash.					

Case Problems

Group A

Problem 8-1A

Objective: To record credit sales and sales returns, post them, and prepare a schedule of accounts receivable

Houser Supply Company opened on November 12, 20X2. Houser's credit sales and related returns and allowances for the remainder of the month are shown below. Terms of all sales were 2/10,n/30, FOB destination.

20X2

Nov.15 Sold merchandise on account to Horton Co., $3,700, Invoice No. 1.

18 Sold merchandise on account to Duffy Co., $2,550, Invoice No. 2.

24 Sold merchandise on account to J.D. Wells Co., $4,400, Invoice No. 3.

25 Issued Credit Memorandum No. 1 for $400 to Horton Co. for merchandise returned.

26 Sold merchandise on account to Trent Co., $4,100, Invoice No. 4.

27 Sold merchandise on account to Zernik, Inc., $900, Invoice No. 5.

28 Sold merchandise on account to Duffy Co., $3,100, Invoice No. 6.

30 Issued Credit Memorandum No. 2 for $250 to Duffy Co. for merchandise returned.

30 Issued Credit Memorandum No. 3 for $150 to Zernik, Inc. for damages to merchandise caused by improper packing.

30 Sold merchandise on account to Trent Co., $1,300, Invoice No. 7.

Directions:

1. Open the following accounts in the accounts receivable ledger: Duffy Co.; Horton Co.; Trent Co.; J.D. Wells Co.; and Zernik, Inc.

2. Open the following accounts in the general ledger: Accounts Receivable, 112; Sales, 411; and Sales Returns and Allowances, 411.1.

3. Record the November transactions in the appropriate journal, either a one-column sales journal (page 1) or a general journal (page 1). Post to the accounts receivable ledger after each transaction, and remember to never record the same transaction in two separate journals.

4. Total the sales journal, and post the column total to the general ledger. Then, post from the general journal to the general ledger.

5. Prepare a schedule of accounts receivable.

6. Compare the balance of the Accounts Receivable controlling account with the total of the schedule of accounts receivable.

Problem 8-2A

Objective: To record sales in a three-column sales journal, total, and post to the accounts receivable and general ledgers

Lammer's Department Store opened on December 1, 20XX, and made the following sales during the month. The amounts do not include the 6% sales tax charged on each sale.

Date	Customer	Amount
20XX		
Dec. 3	Baker Co.	$ 730
7	Jane Cote	675
12	Milton Arlen	1,520
16	Mid-Island Store	2,455
22	Jane Cote	620
27	Milton Arlen	1,060
29	Baker Co.	410
30	Jane Cote	345
31	Milton Arlen	810

Directions:

1. Open an account in the accounts receivable ledger for each credit customer to whom a sale was made.
2. Open the following accounts in the general ledger: Accounts Receivable, 112; Sales Tax Payable, 212; and Sales, 411.
3. Record each sale on page 1 of a three-column sales journal. Begin with Invoice No. 1. Post to the accounts receivable ledger after making each entry.
4. Total and rule the sales journal, and post the column totals to the general ledger.
5. Prepare a schedule of accounts receivable, and verify its total against the balance of the Accounts Receivable account.

Learning Objective **5**

Check Figure
Total credits = $9,509.68

Problem 8-3A

Objective: To record cash receipts in a cash receipts journal

The cash receipts of Sargent's Variety Store for September 20X1 follow:

20X1

Sep. 2 Collected $720 from Phil Williams on account.

5 Jerry Sargent, the owner, invested an additional $2,000 in the business.

9 Collected the amount due from Edna Hansen for the sale of August 16, $285, less a 1% cash discount.

12 Collected $397.50 from Jean Evans on account.

15 Cash sales for the first half of the month amounted to $1,076.45.

19 Received a cash refund for an overcharge on a purchase of equipment, $35.

22 Collected the amount due from Avco Co. for the sale of September 12, $410, less a 2% cash discount.

23 Sold old equipment for cash, $375.

27 Collected the amount due from Sylvia Portland, $442.75, less a 3% cash discount.

29 Received a cash refund for the return of defective merchandise purchased this week, $75.

30 Cash sales for the second half of the month amounted to $3,692.98.

Directions:

1. Record the transactions in a cash receipts journal. Use page 19 of the journal.
2. Total the journal, and prove the equality of the debits and credits in the column totals. Then, rule the journal.

Problem 8-4A

Objective: To record sales-related transactions in special journals, post to the accounts receivable and general ledgers, and prepare a schedule of accounts receivable

LaProva Enterprises, a wholesale dealer of personal care supplies, opened for business on January 2, 20X1. Following are the sales-related transactions completed by LaProva during its first month of operations. All sales carry terms of 2/10,n/30. Number both sales invoices and credit memorandums starting with 101.

20X1

Jan.	2	Sold merchandise on account to Linda Sayers, $245.
	4	Sold merchandise on account to Marion Parks, $340.
	5	Issued a credit memorandum to Marion Parks for damaged merchandise, $50.
	9	Sold merchandise on account to Dave Langlin, $560.
	11	Received a check from Linda Sayers for the amount due today.
	12	Sold merchandise on account to Klasic Kuts, $500.
	14	Received a check from Marion Parks for the balance due on her account.
	15	Recorded cash sales for the first half of the month, $6,565.
	18	Sold merchandise on account to Dave Langlin, $605.
	19	Issued a credit memorandum to Dave Langlin for a shortage on the sale of January 18, $80.
	19	Received a check from Dave Langlin in payment of the amount due on the sale of January 9.
	20	Sold merchandise on account to Klasic Kuts, $500.
	21	Sold merchandise on account to Scissors Palace, $750.
	22	Received a check from Klasic Kuts in payment of the amount due on the sale of January 12.
	23	Sold merchandise on account to Marion Parks, $400.
	24	Issued a credit memorandum to Marion Parks as an allowance for damaged merchandise due to faulty packaging, $70.
	27	Sold merchandise on account to Scissors Palace, $300.
	28	Received a check from Dave Langlin for the balance due on his account.
	28	Sold merchandise on account to Michelle's, $600.
	31	Sold merchandise on account to Michelle's, $250.
	31	Recorded cash sales for the second half of the month, $6,170.

Directions:
1. Open the following accounts in the accounts receivable ledger: Klasic Kuts, 411 Herbison Drive, Riverside, GA 30301; Dave Langlin, 4101 Madison Road, Atlanta, GA 30303; Marion Parks, 211 Fourth Place South, Marietta, GA 31101; Michelle's, 511 Warm Springs Loop, Morrow, GA 30302; Linda Sayers, 31 Third Avenue, Atlanta, GA 30330; and Scissors Palace, 102 Shannon Mall Shopping Center, Atlanta, GA 30330.
2. Open the following accounts in the general ledger: Cash, 111; Accounts Receivable, 112; Sales, 411; Sales Returns and Allowances, 411.1; and Sales Discounts, 411.2.
3. Record LaProva's January transactions in the appropriate journal, either a one-column sales journal, a five-column cash receipts journal, or a general journal. Use page 1 for each journal. Post to the accounts receivable ledger after each entry.
4. Total and rule the special journals, and post the column totals to the general ledger. Post the individual entries from the general journal to the general ledger.
5. Prepare a schedule of accounts receivable as of January 31, and compare its total with the balance of the Accounts Receivable controlling account.

Learning Objectives
2, 3, 4, 5, 6

Check Figure
Ending balance of Accounts
Receivable = $1,350;
Ending balance of Accounts
Payable = $12,230

Problem 8-5A

Objective: To complete a comprehensive problem using five journals and three ledgers

The following transactions were completed by Pendleton Food Company during October 20X1. All credit sales carry terms of 2/10,n/30. (Note: Read all directions to the problem before journalizing and posting the October transactions.)

20X1

Oct. 1 Paid October rent, $1,500.
1 Received the balance of Bill Fahey's account, less a 2% discount.
2 Paid for radio advertising, $1,080.
3 Received the balance of Brad Craven's account, less a 2% discount.
3 Sold merchandise on account to Hardy's Food World, $3,900.
3 Purchased office equipment for cash, $3,100.
4 Paid S. Sanchez Co. for the October 1 balance; no discount.
6 Made the following credit purchases from S. Sanchez Co.: store supplies, $450; office supplies, $220; and merchandise, $1,060; terms, n/30.
6 Sold merchandise on account to Southside Grocery, $2,600.
7 Recorded cash sales for the week, $4,690.
7 Purchased merchandise on account from Belk's, $8,000; terms, 1/10,n/30.
7 Paid Zachary Products Co. for the October 1 balance, less a 2% discount.
8 Due to damage during shipment, the following items were returned for credit to S. Sanchez Co.: office supplies, $20; store supplies, $40; and merchandise, $60.
8 Paid Belk's for the October 1 balance, less a 2% discount.
9 Issued a check to a cash customer for the return of damaged merchandise, $85.
9 Purchased store equipment on account from Baker Supply Co., $6,620; terms, 2/10,n/30.
10 Received the balance owed by Adams Co., less a 2% discount.
13 Received payment from Hardy's Food World for the sale of October 3.
15 Recorded cash sales for the week, $6,010.
15 Paid salaries for the first half of the month, $2,100.
16 Received payment from Southside Grocery for the sale of October 6.
17 Paid Belk's the amount due on the purchase of October 7.
18 Purchased merchandise on account from Engel Co., $3,600; terms, 2/10,n/30.
19 Returned defective merchandise to Engel Co. and received credit, $350.
21 Purchased merchandise for cash, $1,000.
22 Sold at cost a computer printer that was no longer needed, $1,500.
22 Recorded cash sales for the week, $6,495.
23 Paid for miscellaneous expenses, $225.
25 Paid for repairs to delivery truck, $250.
26 Paid gas and oil expense, $125.
27 Purchased merchandise on account from Belk's, $4,000.
28 Paid Engel Co. for the purchase of October 18, less the return of October 19.
30 Sold merchandise on account to Southside Grocery, $1,350.
31 Recorded cash sales for the week, $9,600.
31 Paid salaries for the second half of the month, $2,200.
31 Paid utility bill, $872.

Directions:

1. Open the following accounts in the general ledger, and enter the balances as of October 1:

	Account	Balance
111	Cash	$ 9,300
112	Accounts Receivable	11,500
113	Store Supplies	3,500
114	Office Supplies	1,890
121	Store Equipment	18,750
122	Office Equipment	8,560
211	Accounts Payable	19,700
411	Sales	118,400
411.1	Sales Returns and Allowances	3,300
411.2	Sales Discounts	3,940
511	Purchases	46,700
511.1	Purchases Returns and Allowances	5,400
511.2	Purchases Discounts	3,000
611	Rent Expense	3,750
612	Salaries Expense	36,700
613	Utilities Expense	7,800
614	Repairs Expense	890
615	Advertising Expense	3,200
616	Gas and Oil Expense	1,500
618	Miscellaneous Expense	936

2. Open the following accounts in the accounts receivable ledger, and enter the balances as of October 1:

Account	Balance
Adams Co.	$4,100
Brad Craven	4,500
Bill Fahey	2,900
Hardy's Food World	-0-
Southside Grocery	-0-

3. Open the following accounts in the accounts payable ledger, and enter the balances as of October 1:

Account	Balance
Baker Supply Co.	$ -0-
Belk's	6,500
Engel Co.	-0-
S. Sanchez Co.	4,300
Zachary Products Co.	8,900

4. Record the October transactions using a sales journal (page 8), a cash receipts journal (page 7), a purchases journal (page 14), a cash payments journal (page 10), and a general journal (page 5). Post to the subsidiary ledgers after each entry. Start sales invoices with No. 377, purchases invoices with No. 364, and checks with No. 419. Remember that all credit sales carry terms of 2/10,n/30.

5. Post the individual entries from the general journal to the general ledger. Total, rule, and post the special journals.

6. Prepare schedules of accounts receivable and accounts payable, and verify the totals.

Group B

Learning Objectives
2, 3, 6

Check Figure
Balance of Accounts
Receivable account =
$24,065

Problem 8-1B

Objective: To record credit sales and sales returns, post them, and prepare a schedule of accounts receivable

Fiano Supply Company opened on December 10, 20X2. Its credit sales and related returns and allowances for the remainder of the month are as follows. Terms of all sales were 2/10,n/30, FOB destination.

20X2

Dec. 12 Sold merchandise on account to McCullum Co., $4,100, Invoice No. 1.

15 Sold merchandise on account to Carbone Co., $2,450, Invoice No. 2.

18 Sold merchandise on account to Goorbin, Inc., $5,300, Invoice No. 3.

21 Issued Credit Memorandum No. 1 for $350 to McCullum Co. for merchandise returned.

26 Sold merchandise on account to Burke Co., $4,300, Invoice No. 4.

28 Sold merchandise on account to Stone Ridge Co., $1,050, Invoice No. 5.

29 Sold merchandise on account to Carbone Co., $3,300, Invoice No. 6.

30 Issued Credit Memorandum No. 2 for $275 to Carbone Co. for merchandise returned.

30 Issued Credit Memorandum No. 3 for $160 to Stone Ridge Co. for damages to merchandise caused by improper packing.

31 Sold merchandise on account to Burke Co., $4,350, Invoice No. 7.

Directions:

1. Open the following accounts in the accounts receivable ledger: Burke Co.; Carbone Co.; Goorbin, Inc.; McCullum Co.; and Stone Ridge Co.

2. Open the following accounts in the general ledger: Accounts Receivable, 112; Sales, 411; and Sales Returns and Allowances, 411.1.

3. Record the December transactions in the appropriate journal, either a one-column sales journal (page 1) or a general journal (page 1). Post to the accounts receivable ledger after each transaction, and remember to never record the same transaction in two separate journals.

4. Total the sales journal, and post the column total to the general ledger. Then, post from the general journal to the general ledger.

5. Prepare a schedule of accounts receivable.

6. Compare the balance of the Accounts Receivable controlling account with the total of the schedule of accounts receivable.

Learning Objective **2**

Check Figure
Total of schedule of accounts
receivable = $10,880.90

Problem 8-2B

Objective: To record sales in a three-column sales journal, total, and post to the accounts receivable and general ledgers

Demarco's Department Store opened on August 1, 20XX, and made the following sales during the month. The amounts do not include the 6% sales tax charged on each sale.

Date	Customer	Amount
20XX		
Aug. 6	Sean Walsh	$1,060
10	Kris Cassereau	275
12	Juan Baez	955
15	Melody Meyer	1,620
19	Kris Cassereau	865
21	Melody Meyer	2,145
24	Sean Walsh	930
27	Juan Baez	810
30	Melody Meyer	1,605

Directions:

1. Open an account in the accounts receivable ledger for each credit customer to whom a sale was made.
2. Open the following accounts in the general ledger: Accounts Receivable, 112; Sales Tax Payable, 212; and Sales, 411.
3. Record each sale on page 1 of a three-column sales journal. Begin with Invoice No. 1. Post to the accounts receivable ledger after making each entry.
4. Total and rule the sales journal, and post the column totals to the general ledger.
5. Prepare a schedule of accounts receivable, and verify its total against the balance of the Accounts Receivable account.

Learning Objective **5**

Check Figure
Total Credits = $9,485.92

Problem 8-3B

Objective: To record cash receipts in a cash receipts journal

The cash receipts of Cantwell's Department Store for November 20X1 are as follows:

20X1

Nov. 3 Received a cash refund for the return of defective merchandise purchased this week, $295.75.

6 Collected the amount due from Wade Martin for the sale of October 24, $675.10, less a 1% cash discount.

8 Collected $247.95 from Jane Gillis for the sale of September 17.

10 Pete Cantwell, the owner, invested an additional $1,800 in the business.

12 Collected the amount due from Dana Kelly, $550, less a 3% cash discount.

15 Cash sales for the first half of the month amounted to $912.65.

20 Received $1,100 on account from A-One Resort.

22 Sold office supplies at cost, $165.

24 Received a cash refund for an overcharge on a purchase of equipment, $175.

29 Collected the amount due from Paul Arlen for the sale of November 9, $627.90, less a 2% cash discount.

30 Cash sales for the second half of the month amounted to $2,936.57.

Directions:

1. Record the transactions in a cash receipts journal. Use page 19 of the journal.
2. Total the journal, and prove the equality of the debits and credits in the column totals. Then, rule the journal.

Learning Objectives
2, 3, 4, 5, 6

Check Figure
Balance of Accounts
Receivable account = $3,880

Problem 8-4B

Objective: To record sales-related transactions in special journals, post to the accounts receivable and general ledgers, and prepare a schedule of accounts receivable

Graham Enterprises, a wholesale dealer of soft drinks, opened for business on March 1, 20X1. Following are the sales-related transactions completed by Graham during its first month of operations. All sales carry terms of 2/10,n/30. Number both sales invoices and credit memorandums starting with 101.

20X1

Mar. 1 Sold merchandise on account to Brenda Myers, $345.

3 Sold merchandise on account to Marvin Stark, $390.

5 Issued a credit memorandum to Marvin Stark for damaged merchandise, $35.

9 Sold merchandise on account to Bob Lawford, $600.

11 Received a check from Brenda Myers for the amount due today.

12 Sold merchandise on account to Country Corner Grocery, $600.

13 Received a check from Marvin Stark for the balance due on his account.

Mar. 15 Recorded cash sales for the first half of the month, $6,300.
18 Sold merchandise on account to Bob Lawford, $595.
19 Issued a credit memorandum to Bob Lawford for a shortage on the sale of March 18, $85.
19 Received a check from Bob Lawford in payment of the amount due on the sale of March 9.
20 Sold merchandise on account to Country Corner Grocery, $625.
22 Sold merchandise on account to Grand Rapids Produce Company, $990.
22 Received a check from Country Corner Grocery in payment of the amount due on the sale of March 12.
23 Sold merchandise on account to Marvin Stark, $420.
24 Issued a credit memorandum to Marvin Stark as an allowance for damaged merchandise due to faulty packaging, $95.
27 Sold merchandise on account to Grand Rapids Produce Company, $400.
28 Received a check from Bob Lawford for the balance due on his account.
28 Sold merchandise on account to Michael's Foods, $1,000.
31 Sold merchandise on account to Michael's Foods, $540.
31 Recorded cash sales for the second half of the month, $8,780.

Directions:

1. Open the following accounts in the accounts receivable ledger: Country Corner Grocery, 415 East Fulton, Grand Rapids, MI 49503; Grand Rapids Produce Company, 14 Rangeline Road, Grand Rapids, MI 49503; Bob Lawford, 12 Shimmel Road, Centerville, MI 49032; Michael's Foods, 144 Bostwick NE, Grand Rapids, MI 49503; Brenda Myers, 512 East Greenwood, Grand Rapids, MI 49503; and Marvin Stark, 312 Bankers Loop, Grand Rapids, MI 49503.

2. Open the following accounts in the general ledger: Cash, 111; Accounts Receivable, 112; Sales, 411; Sales Returns and Allowances, 411.1; and Sales Discounts, 411.2.

3. Record Graham's March transactions in the appropriate journal, either a one-column sales journal, a five-column cash receipts journal, or a general journal. Use page 1 for each journal. Post to the accounts receivable ledger after each entry.

4. Total and rule the special journals, and post the column totals to the general ledger. Post the individual entries from the general journal to the general ledger.

5. Prepare a schedule of accounts receivable as of March 31, and compare its total with the balance of the Accounts Receivable controlling account.

Learning Objectives
2, 3, 4, 5, 6

Check Figure
Ending balance of Accounts Receivable = $4,420; Ending balance of Accounts Payable = $11,404

Problem 8-5B

Objective: To complete a comprehensive problem using five journals and three ledgers

The following transactions were completed by Armstrong Distributing Company during May 20X1. All credit sales carry terms of 2/10,n/30. (Note: Read all directions to the problem before journalizing and posting the May transactions.)

20X1

May 1 Paid May rent, $2,100.
1 Received the balance of Will Facson's account, less a 2% discount.
2 Paid for advertising in the local paper, $610.
4 Received the balance of Trent Tarven's account, less a 2% discount.
4 Sold merchandise on account to Harry's Restaurant, $2,600.
4 Purchased office equipment for cash, $5,300.
5 Paid Rojas Co. for the May 1 balance; no discount.
5 Made the following credit purchases from Rojas Co.: store supplies, $490; office supplies, $330; and merchandise, $950; terms, n/30.
6 Sold merchandise on account to Eastway Foods, $3,500.

May 7   Recorded cash sales for the week, $2,300.

     7   Purchased merchandise on account from Prago Co., $9,100; terms, 3/10,n/30.

     7   Paid Zenith Products Co. for the May 1 balance, less a 2% discount.

     8   Due to damage during shipment, the following items were returned for credit to Rojas Co.: office supplies, $22; store supplies, $38; and merchandise, $66.

     8   Paid Prago Co. for the May 1 balance, less a 2% discount.

     9   Issued a check to a cash customer for the return of damaged merchandise, $55.

     9   Purchased store equipment on account from Tyler Supply Co., $6,860; terms, n/30.

   10   Received the balance owed by Aims Co., less a 2% discount.

   14   Received payment from Harry's Restaurant for the sale of May 4.

   15   Recorded cash sales for the week, $2,520.

   15   Paid salaries for the first half of the month, $4,600.

   16   Received payment from Eastway Foods for the sale of May 6.

   17   Paid Prago Co. for the purchase of May 7.

   18   Purchased merchandise on account from Ingalls Co., $4,100; terms, 2/10, n/30.

   19   Returned defective merchandise to Ingalls Co. and received credit, $450.

   21   Purchased merchandise for cash, $1,300.

   22   Sold at cost a computer that was no longer needed, $690.

   22   Recorded cash sales for the week, $2,495.

   23   Paid for miscellaneous expenses, $195.

   25   Paid for repairs to office copier, $65.

   26   Paid gas and oil expense, $110.

   27   Purchased merchandise on account from Prago Co., $2,900; terms, 2/10,n/30.

   28   Paid Ingalls Co. for the purchase of May 18, less the return of May 19.

   30   Sold merchandise on account to Eastway Foods, $4,420.

   31   Recorded cash sales for the week, $2,555.

   31   Paid salaries for the second half of the month, $4,600.

   31   Paid utility bill, $948.

Directions:

1. Open the following accounts in the general ledger, and enter the balances as of May 1:

	Account	Balance
111	Cash	$ 26,600
112	Accounts Receivable	11,800
113	Store Supplies	3,900
114	Office Supplies	1,950
121	Store Equipment	22,500
122	Office Equipment	11,320
211	Accounts Payable	22,200
411	Sales	112,400
411.1	Sales Returns and Allowances	2,400
411.2	Sales Discounts	3,460
511	Purchases	47,600
511.1	Purchases Returns and Allowances	1,810
511.2	Purchases Discounts	700
611	Rent Expense	4,400
612	Salaries Expense	36,800
613	Utilities Expense	3,500
614	Repairs Expense	540
615	Advertising Expense	450
616	Gas and Oil Expense	390
618	Miscellaneous Expense	512

2. Open the following accounts in the accounts receivable ledger, and enter the balances as of May 1:

Account	Balance
Aims Co.	$4,600
Eastway Foods	-0-
Will Facson	3,300
Harry's Restaurant	-0-
Trent Tarven	3,900

3. Open the following accounts in the accounts payable ledger, and enter the balances as of May 1:

Account	Balance
Ingalls Co.	$ –0–
Prago Co.	7,500
Rojas Co.	5,300
Tyler Supply Co.	–0–
Zenith Products Co.	9,400

4. Record the May transactions using a sales journal (page 6), a cash receipts journal (page 9), a purchases journal (page 12), a cash payments journal (page 8), and a general journal (page 3). Post to the subsidiary ledgers after each entry. Start sales invoices with No. 395, purchases invoices with No. 314, and checks with No. 515. Remember that all credit sales carry terms of 2/10,n/30.

5. Post the individual entries from the general journal to the general ledger. Total, rule, and post the special journals.

6. Prepare schedules of accounts receivable and accounts payable, and verify the totals.

Critical Thinking Problems

Challenge Problem

Check Figure
Ending balance of Accounts Receivable = $16,000; Ending balance of Accounts Payable = $17,163

James Collier Company started its new fiscal period on July 1, 20X2, and completed the following transactions during July. All credit sales are subject to terms of 2/10,n/30. (Note: Read all directions before journalizing and posting the July transactions.)

20X2

Jul. 1 Issued Check No. 720 for July rent, $1,200.

1 Received a check from Xavier Corp. in payment of balance due, less 2% discount.

2 Issued Check No. 721 for the cash purchase of office supplies, $325.

2 Issued Check No. 722 to Dwyar Products Co. for the balance owed, less 1% discount.

2 Received a check from Illinois Central Products Co. in payment of balance due, less 2% discount.

3 Purchased store equipment on account from Allan Co., $3,800.

3 Purchased merchandise on account from Faulk Co., $24,250; terms, 2/10,n/30.

5 Sold merchandise on account to Leland Co., $3,290, Sales Invoice No. 821.

7 Received a check from Tom Larkin in payment of balance due, less 2% discount.

7 Recorded cash sales, $15,800.

8 Received a check from Hanks Co. in payment of balance due, less 2% discount.

8 Issued Check No. 723 in payment of miscellaneous expenses, $235.

8 Sold merchandise on account to McFarland Co., $5,680, Sales Invoice No. 822.

Jul. 9 Issued Check No. 724 to Thompson Suppliers for the balance owed, less 2% discount.

9 Purchased merchandise on account from Dunlop Co., $5,000; terms, 2/10,n/30.

10 Issued Check No. 725 to Adams, Inc. for the balance owed; no discount.

11 Sold merchandise on account to Leland Co., $5,900, Sales Invoice No. 823.

11 Issued Check No. 726 for the cash purchase of store supplies, $428.

12 Issued Check No. 727 in payment of the telephone bill, $89.

13 Issued Check No. 728 to Faulk Co. for the purchase of July 3.

14 Sold merchandise on account to Illinois Central Products Co., $4,690, Sales Invoice No. 824.

15 Sold merchandise on account to Aims Corp., $5,200, Sales Invoice No. 825.

15 Received a check from Leland Co. for the sale of July 5.

16 Issued Credit Memorandum No. 12 to Illinois Central Products Co. for damaged merchandise, $80.

16 Recorded cash sales, $12,900.

17 Purchased merchandise on account from Elgin Co., $12,500; terms, 1/10,n/30.

18 Received a check from McFarland Co. for the sale of July 8.

19 Issued Check No. 729 to Dunlop Co. for the purchase of July 9.

19 Returned damaged merchandise to Elgin Co., receiving credit, $130.

20 Issued Check No. 730 for the cash purchase of merchandise, $2,500.

20 Received a check from Leland Co. for the sale of July 11.

21 Recorded cash sales, $11,900.

22 Issued Check No. 731 for the payment of repairs expense, $75.

23 Issued Check No. 732 for carpet cleaning, $50.

24 Received a check from Illinois Central Products Co. for the sale of July 14, less the return of July 16.

25 Purchased merchandise on account from Elgin Co., $8,600; terms, 1/10,n/30.

25 Sold merchandise on account to Aims Corp., $2,800, Sales Invoice No. 826.

25 Received a check from Aims Corp. for the sale of July 15.

26 Issued Check No. 733 in payment of the power bill, $967.

27 Issued Check No. 734 to Elgin Co. for the balance due on the purchase of July 17, less the return of July 19.

27 Issued Credit Memorandum No. 13 to Aims Corp. for a shortage on the sale of July 25, $30.

28 Purchased merchandise on account from McFadden Co., $6,000; terms, n/30.

29 Returned defective merchandise to McFadden Co., receiving credit, $230.

29 Issued Check No. 735 for advertising, $1,500.

30 Issued Check No. 736 to Allan Co. in payment of the July 3 purchase; no discount.

30 Issued Check No. 737 for the cash purchase of merchandise, $5,200.

30 Purchased the following on account from Wall Supply, Inc.: store equipment, $2,000; store supplies, $525; and office supplies, $318.

31 Received a check for return of damaged merchandise that had been purchased for cash on July 30, $225.

31 Recorded cash sales, $12,500.

31 Issued Check No. 738 in payment of monthly salaries, $5,300.

31 Issued Check No. 739 in payment of transportation charges for merchandise purchased during the month, $390.

31 Sold merchandise on account to Leland Co., $8,500, Sales Invoice No. 827.

31 Sold merchandise on account to Aims Corp. $3,450, Sales Invoice No. 828.

31 Returned damaged store supplies purchased on July 30 and received credit, $50.

31 James Collier, the owner, issued Check No. 740 to himself as a personal withdrawal, $2,000.

31 Sold merchandise on account to Tom Larkin, $1,280, Sales Invoice No. 829.

Directions:

1. Open the following accounts in the general ledger, entering the balances as of July 1:

	Account	Balance
111	Cash	$12,500
112	Accounts Receivable	31,150
113	Store Supplies	1,800
114	Office Supplies	790
115	Prepaid Insurance	1,200
119	Store Equipment	22,400
119.1	Accumulated Depreciation—Store Equipment	4,500
120	Office Equipment	12,900
120.1	Accumulated Depreciation—Office Equipment	3,200
211	Accounts Payable	18,420
311	James Collier, Capital	56,620
312	James Collier, Drawing	—
411	Sales	—
411.1	Sales Returns and Allowances	—
411.2	Sales Discounts	—
511	Purchases	—
511.1	Purchases Returns and Allowances	—
511.2	Purchases Discounts	—
512	Freight In	—
611	Salaries Expense	—
612	Rent Expense	—
613	Utilities Expense	—
614	Advertising Expense	—
615	Telephone Expense	—
616	Repairs Expense	—
622	Miscellaneous Expense	—

2. Open the following accounts in the accounts receivable ledger, entering the balances as of July 1:

Account	Balance
Aims Corp.	$ —
Hanks Co.	6,400
Illinois Central Products Co.	7,850
Leland Co.	—
McFarland Co.	—
Tom Larkin	4,600
Xavier Corp.	12,300

3. Open the following accounts in the accounts payable ledger, entering the balances as of July 1:

Account	Balance
Adams, Inc.	$6,900
Allan Co.	—
Dunlop Co.	—
Dwyar Products Co.	4,200
Elgin Co.	—
Faulk Co.	—
McFadden Co.	—
Thompson Suppliers	7,320
Wall Supply, Inc.	—

4. Record the July transactions in the appropriate journal, either a purchases journal (page 6), a cash payments journal (page 9), a cash receipts journal (page 7), a sales journal (page 11), or a general journal (page 14). Post to the subsidiary ledgers after each entry.
5. Total, prove (where needed), and rule each special journal.
6. Post to the general ledger.
7. Prepare a trial balance.
8. Prepare a schedule of accounts receivable.
9. Prepare a schedule of accounts payable.
10. Verify the agreement of the subsidiary ledgers with the related controlling accounts.

Communications

You have been asked by Havicus Company, a new small business, to take a look at their accounting system. You discover that Havicus is using a general journal to record all transactions. The company does, however, have three separate ledgers—general, customers', and creditors' ledgers.

Write a brief memo to Susan Havicus, the owner, explaining why it would be of value to her to use special journals rather than a single journal. Focus on the advantages of special journals.

Team Internet Project

Changing money from one currency to another is a very common financial activity today. For example, if you were to travel into Canada from the United States for any period of time, you would want to exchange U.S. dollars for Canadian dollars. To make this exchange, you would look up the current exchange rate between the two currencies in the financial pages of the newspaper, at a bank, or on the Internet. While the rate varies daily, you would find a rate such as 1 U.S. Dollar = $1.08243 Canadian Dollars (rate as of May 24, 2007).

Therefore, if you were converting 100 U.S. dollars to Canadian dollars, multiply 100 × 1.08243 and get $108.24 Canadian, rounded to the nearest cent. For 200 U.S. dollars, your answer would be $216.49 Canadian.

Search the Internet to convert 5,000 U.S. dollars into the currencies of the following countries as of the date or dates on which this activity is assigned:

Japanese yen
Chinese yuan renminbi
Russian ruble
South African rand
Argentine peso

Ethics

Thrift-Mart is a large discount department store located in a heavily populated area. The store has a total of 15 cash registers, each of which is on-line with the company's computer system.

Wendy Krislen-Adams, a new employee who is also studying computer science at the local community college, commented, "On-line cash registers double as computer terminals." This led you, the store manager, to realize that all cash register operators have access to all information in the company's computer system.

Write an explanation of the dangers of this type of access as well as what kind of safeguard(s) can be designed to keep cashiers from accessing other company information.

In the Real World	Target Corporation

Following are some data from the income statements (statements of operations) of Target Corporation for the years 2004, 2005, and 2006. Amounts are in millions.

Statements of Operations	2006	2005	2004
Sales	$59,490	$51,271	$45,682
Cost of sales	39,999	34,927	31,445
Operating expenses	12,819	11,185	9,797
Net earnings	2,787	2,408	3,198

Based on this information, answer the following questions:

(a) What are the amounts and directions of the changes in sales from 2004 to 2005 and from 2005 to 2006?

(b) How would you describe these changes?

Answers to Review Quizzes

Review Quiz 8-1

#			Dr.	Cr.	
1	(a)	Cash	4 00 00		1
2		Sales		4 00 00	2
3					3
4	(b)	Accounts Receivable	1 2 00 00		4
5		Sales		1 2 00 00	5
6					6
7	(c)	Cash	8 00 00		7
8		Equipment		8 00 00	8
9					9
10	(d)	Cash	2 00 00		10
11		Supplies		2 00 00	11

Review Quiz 8-2

			Sales Journal		Page 1	
	Date	Invoice No.	Customer's Name	P.R.	Accts. Rec. Dr. Sales Cr.	
	20X5					
1	May 1	1	Bill French		3 00 00	1
2	8	2	Lee Smith		8 00 00	2
3	18	3	Leah King		5 90 00	3
4	30	4	Charles Swift		5 00 00	4
5	30		Total		2 1 90 00	5

	Date		Account Title	P.R.	Debit	Credit	
			General Journal			**Page 1**	
	20X5						
1	May	3	Cash		5 0 0 00		1
2			Sales			5 0 0 00	2
3							3
4		12	Cash		6 7 0 00		4
5			Sales			6 7 0 00	5
6							6
7		25	Cash		4 0 0 0 00		7
8			Store Equipment			4 0 0 0 00	8

Review Quiz 8-3

			Account Title	P.R.	Debit	Credit	
1	(a)		Accounts Receivable—Camp Company	/	8 0 0 00		1
2			Sales			8 0 0 00	2
3							3
4	(b)		Sales Returns and Allowances		2 0 0 00		4
5			Accounts Receivable—Camp Company	/		2 0 0 00	5
6							6
7	(c)		Sales Returns and Allowances		4 0 0 00		7
8			Cash			4 0 0 00	8
9							9
10	(d)		Cash		6 0 0 00		10
11			Accounts Receivable—Camp Company	/		6 0 0 00	11
12							12
13							13

Review Quiz 8-4

(a) On the books of Wachal Company:

			Account Title	P.R.	Debit	Credit	
	20X2						
1	Jun.	10	Purchases		9 0 0 0 00		1
2			Accounts Payable—Entler Company	/		9 0 0 0 00	2
3							3
4		19	Accounts Payable—Entler Company	/	9 0 0 0 00		4
5			Purchases Discounts			2 7 0 00	5
6			Cash			8 7 3 0 00	6

(b) On the books of Entler Company:

			Account Title	P.R.	Debit	Credit	
	20X2						
1	Jun.	10	Accounts Receivable—Wachal Company	/	9 0 0 0 00		1
2			Sales			9 0 0 0 00	2
3							3
4		19	Cash		8 7 3 0 00		4
5			Sales Discounts		2 7 0 00		5
6			Accounts Receivable—Wachal	/		9 0 0 0 00	6
7			Company				7

Review Quiz 8-5

(a) The check mark means that the column total is not posted.

(b) The check mark means that a posting is made to the customer's account in the accounts receivable ledger.

(c) The check mark means that an individual posting is not necessary; the amount will be posted as part of the column total.

Review Quiz 8-6

	Date		Account Title	P.R.	Debit	Credit	
1	20X1 Aug.	1	Cash		5 30 00		1
2			Sales Tax Payable			30 00	2
3			Sales			5 00 00	3
4							4
5		4	Accounts Receivable—Eve Li	/	2 12 00		5
6			Sales Tax Payable			12 00	6
7			Sales			2 00 00	7
8							8
9		6	Cash		6 36 00		9
10			Sales Tax Payable			36 00	10
11			Sales			6 00 00	11
12							12
13		10	Accounts Receivable—Max Leatherwood	/	1 4 84 00		13
14			Sales Tax Payable			84 00	14
15			Sales			1 4 00 00	15
16							16
17		12	Sales Returns and Allowances		50 00		17
18			Sales Tax Payable		3 00		18
19			Accounts Rec.—Max Leatherwood	/		53 00	19
20							20
21		15	Sales Tax Payable		9 40 00		21
22			Cash			9 40 00	22

Page 10 — General Journal

Review Quiz 8-7

1	20X2 Apr.	8	Cash		1 0 17 60		1
2			Credit Card Expense		4 2 40		2
3			Sales			1 0 00 00	3
4			Sales Tax Payable			6 0 00	4
5							5
6		8	Accounts Receivable—Credit Cards		4 0 2 80		6
7			Credit Card Expense		2 1 20		7
8			Sales			4 0 0 00	8
9			Sales Tax Payable			2 4 00	9
10							10

Review Quiz 8-8

(a) Cash receipts journal
(b) General journal
(c) Cash payments journal
(d) Sales journal
(e) Cash receipts journal
(f) General journal
(g) Cash receipts journal
(h) General journal
(i) Cash payments journal

APPENDIX C

The Perpetual Inventory System

Learning Objectives

1 Differentiate between the periodic inventory system and the perpetual inventory system.
2 Record merchandising transactions using the perpetual inventory system.

Learning Objective

1 Differentiate between the periodic inventory system and the perpetual inventory system.

periodic inventory system an inventory system in which the Merchandise Inventory account shows the value of the most recent inventory count, usually at the beginning of the accounting period, and no attempt is made to balance the account until the next inventory is taken

perpetual inventory system an inventory system in which the Merchandise Inventory account is debited each time merchandise is purchased and credited each time merchandise is sold in order to keep a running balance of the entire inventory

ISBN 0-7638-2001-6

In Chapter 7, we learned how to record the cost of merchandise purchased in the Purchases account. When merchandise was sold, we recorded the selling price as a debit to Cash or Accounts Receivable and a credit to Sales. When recording sales, we made no attempt to identify the cost of the items sold or how much merchandise remained on hand after the sale. This is referred to as the **periodic inventory system**—a system where merchandise purchased is recorded in the Purchases account and the cost of items unsold is determined by a *periodic* inventory count, usually at the end of a month or year.

Another system is the perpetual inventory system. Under the **perpetual inventory system**, accounting records are maintained that continuously show the amount of inventory on hand. The cost of merchandise purchased is debited to an asset account entitled Merchandise Inventory. When merchandise is sold, the Merchandise Inventory account is decreased by the cost of the merchandise sold; thus, the balance of the account always (perpetually) shows the amount of the inventory on hand.

In the past, the perpetual system was used only by businesses with a relatively low sales volume of high-cost items, such as furniture, autos, and appliances. However, modern computer technology, with point-of-sale cash register terminals and electronic scanners, has allowed the use of the perpetual inventory system with almost any product. As computer prices fall and software becomes more flexible and abundant, it is likely that the perpetual system will continue to grow in popularity. Computerized accounting programs like Peachtree and QuickBooks have made it possible for even very small businesses with limited resources to use the perpetual inventory system.

Target, Sears, Best Buy, and most other large retail businesses, as well as many smaller merchandisers, use computerized perpetual inventory systems. In these systems, inventory items are entered on computer records when the items are purchased. When an item is sold, an optical scanner at the cash register is used to read a bar code, which records the item's selling price and removes its cost from inventory. Bar codes can be seen on most consumer products; for an example, see the back of this textbook.

At the heart of the perpetual inventory system is the maintenance of records that show a continuous or running balance for each inventory item. The Merchandise Inventory account serves as a controlling account, and a subsidiary ledger is set up with an account for each item in inventory. This

Remember

As you learned in Chapter 7, a controlling account is an account located in the general ledger that summarizes the balance of individual accounts set up in a subsidiary ledger.

is the same relationship as the Accounts Receivable account and the accounts receivable ledger or the Accounts Payable account and the accounts payable ledger.

When new merchandise is received, the Merchandise Inventory account (in the general ledger) is increased, and the individual inventory records in the subsidiary ledger are updated. When merchandise is sold, the Merchandise Inventory account is decreased, and the individual inventory records are updated. As a result, the Merchandise Inventory account always shows the total value of the inventory on hand, and the individual inventory records show the amount of each item on hand. At month-end, when all posting is complete, the balance of the Merchandise Inventory account will equal the total of the balances of the individual inventory records.

Recording Purchases of Merchandise

Learning Objective

2 Record merchandising transactions using the perpetual inventory system.

In the perpetual inventory system, as we have stressed, the Merchandise Inventory account is increased (debited) when merchandise is purchased. The credit is to Cash for cash purchases or Accounts Payable for credit purchases. To illustrate, Kathryn DeBice, owner of DeBice Home Products Company, uses the perpetual system. On July 15, 20XX, DeBice purchased a lawn tractor costing $800 on account from G. McFarlin Distributors; terms, 2/10,n/30. The purchase is recorded as follows:

		20XX						
+ asset →	1	Jul.	15	Merchandise Inventory		8 00 00		1
+ liability →	2			Accounts Payable—G. McFarlin				2
	3			Distributors	/		8 00 00	3
	4			Purchased merchandise on account.				4

Recording Sales of Merchandise

Under the perpetual system, two journal entries are required when merchandise is sold. The first entry records the sales price of the merchandise by making a debit to either Cash or Accounts Receivable and a credit to Sales. The second entry reduces the Merchandise Inventory account and transfers the cost of the items sold to the **Cost of Goods Sold account**. To illustrate these entries, assume that on July 21, 20XX, DeBice Home Products Company sold the lawn tractor (purchased on July 15) for $1,200 on account to Donna Harper. DeBice made the following entries:

Cost of Goods Sold account an expense account used in a perpetual inventory system to record the cost of merchandise sold to customers

		20XX						
+ asset →	1	Jul.	21	Accounts Receivable—Donna Harper	/	1 2 00 00		1
+ revenue →	2			Sales			1 2 00 00	2
	3			Sold merchandise on account.				3
	4							4
+ expense →	5		21	Cost of Goods Sold		8 00 00		5
– asset →	6			Merchandise Inventory			8 00 00	6
	7			Recorded the cost of goods sold.				7

As we can see, the $1,200 sales price of the tractor has been recorded, and its $800 cost has been transferred from the Merchandise Inventory account to the Cost of Goods Sold account. Merchandise Inventory is an asset account, and its end-of-period balance is reported on the balance sheet. Cost of Goods Sold is an expense account that shows the total cost of merchandise sold to customers during the accounting period; its balance is reported on the income statement. And along with all other expenses, Cost of Goods Sold is closed to Income Summary at the end of the accounting period.

Recording Returns of Merchandise Sold

As you recall, when merchandise sold on credit is returned by a customer to the seller, the Sales Returns and Allowances account is debited and Accounts Receivable is credited. Under the perpetual inventory system, the cost of the merchandise returned must also be transferred from the Cost of Goods Sold account back into the Merchandise Inventory account. To illustrate, assume that Donna Harper found that the lawn tractor she purchased on July 21 was too large for her yard. She thus decided to take DeBice Home Products Company up on their three-day, no-questions-asked return policy and on July 24 returned the tractor for full credit. To record the return, DeBice made the following entries:

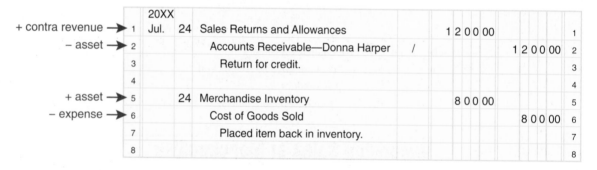

	20XX					
1	Jul.	24	Sales Returns and Allowances		1 2 0 0 00		1
2			Accounts Receivable—Donna Harper	/		1 2 00 00	2
3			Return for credit.				3
4							4
5		24	Merchandise Inventory		8 0 0 00		5
6			Cost of Goods Sold			8 0 0 00	6
7			Placed item back in inventory.				7
8							8

+ contra revenue → 1
− asset → 2

+ asset → 5
− expense → 6

The lawn tractor is now back in inventory and available for sale to another customer.

Recording Returns of Merchandise Purchased

Under the periodic inventory system, returns of merchandise to the supplier are recorded by crediting the Purchases Returns and Allowances account. The debit is either to Cash or Accounts Payable, depending on whether the purchase was for cash or on account. Under the perpetual inventory system, the cost of inventory returned to a supplier is credited to the Merchandise Inventory account. For example, on July 8, 20XX, DeBice Home Products Company returned for credit five bags of lawn fertilizer that had hardened during shipment. The cost per bag was $5, and the supplier was L.A. Lovering Company. DeBice recorded the return as follows:

		20XX								
– liability →	1	Jul.	8	Accounts Payable—L.A. Lovering Co.	/		2 5 00			1
– asset →	2			Merchandise Inventory (five bags × $5)					2 5 00	2
	3			Returned merchandise for credit.						3
	4									4

Recording Payment for Merchandise Purchased

On July 25, 20XX, DeBice paid for the lawn tractor that had been purchased on July 15. Remember that the purchase price was $800, and the invoice carried credit terms of 2/10,n/30. Thus, DeBice can deduct a purchases discount of $16 ($800 × .02). Under the periodic inventory system, a purchases discount is recorded as a credit to the Purchases Discounts account. However, under the perpetual system, a discount is credited to the Merchandise Inventory account because the discount decreases the cost of the merchandise. To illustrate this, let's look at DeBice's entry to record payment of the item:

		20XX								
– liability →	1	Jul.	25	Accounts Payable—G. McFarlin						1
	2			Distributors	/		8 0 0 00			2
– asset →	3			Cash					7 8 4 00	3
– asset →	4			Merchandise Inventory					1 6 00	4
	5			Paid for July 15 purchase.						5
	6									6

Recording Freight on Incoming Merchandise

Under the periodic inventory system, freight charges on incoming merchandise are debited to the Freight-In account. Under the perpetual system, freight is debited to the Merchandise Inventory account because freight increases the cost of merchandise. To illustrate, assume that on July 28, 20XX, DeBice Home Products Company purchased 200 bags of lawn fertilizer from L.A. Lovering Company. The cost per bag was $6, and the goods were shipped FOB shipping point with a freight charge of $190 added to the invoice. The purchase is recorded as follows:

		20XX								
+ asset →	1	Jul.	28	Merchandise Inventory (200 × $6 + $190)			1 3 9 0 00			1
+ liability →	2			Accounts Payable—L.A. Lovering Co.	/				1 3 9 0 00	2
	3			Purchased merchandise on account.						3
	4									4

The perpetual inventory system provides a higher degree of control than the periodic system because inventory records are always up to date. Having up-to-date records allows management to monitor inventory levels to make sure there is an ample supply of fast-selling items and a minimum supply of slow-selling items. Inventory represents a major investment for most merchandising businesses, and good inventory management is vital to the success of the firm.

Comparing the Periodic and Perpetual Inventory Systems

Figure C-1 presents a side-by-side comparison of entries under the periodic inventory system and the perpetual inventory system.

Figure C-1

Comparison of Periodic Inventory System and Perpetual Inventory System

	Purchased $20,000 of merchandise on account; terms 2/10,n/30.
	Returned merchandise purchased on June 2, $1,000.
	Paid for the June 2 purchase, less return of $1,000 and discount of $380 ($19,000 × .02).
	Sold merchandise on account, $10,000; terms, 2/10,n/45. The cost of the merchandise was $7,500.
	Received merchandise returns from the June 15 sale, $1,500. The cost of the items returned was $1,200.
	Received payment for the June 15 sale, less return of $1,500 and sales discount of $170 ($8,500 x .02).
	Purchased merchandise, $12,000; terms, 2/10,n/30; FOB shipping point, with freight charges of $350 added to the invoice.
	Recorded cash sales for the month, $30,000. The cost of items sold was $24,000.

Periodic Inventory System

	Date		Account Title	P.R.	Debit	Credit	
1	20XX Jun.	2	Purchases		20 0 0 0 00		1
2			Accounts Payable			20 0 0 0 00	2
3							3
4							4
5		6	Accounts Payable		1 0 0 0 00		5
6			Purchases Returns and Allowances			1 0 0 0 00	6
7							7
8							8
9		12	Accounts Payable		19 0 0 0 00		9
10			Cash			18 6 2 0 00	10
11			Purchases Discounts			3 8 0 00	11
12							12
13		15	Accounts Receivable		10 0 0 0 00		13
14			Sales			10 0 0 0 00	14
15							15
16							16
17							17
18		18	Sales Returns and Allowances		1 5 0 0 00		18
19			Accounts Receivable			1 5 0 0 00	19
20							20
21							21
22							22
23		25	Cash		8 3 3 0 00		23
24			Sales Discounts		1 7 0 00		24
25			Accounts Receivable			8 5 0 0 00	25
26							26
27		28	Purchases		12 0 0 0 00		27
28			Freight In		3 5 0 00		28
29			Accounts Payable			12 3 5 0 00	29
30							30
31		30	Cash		30 0 0 0 00		31
32			Sales			30 0 0 0 00	32
33							33
34							34
35							35

General Journal — Page 1

Perpetual Inventory System

			General Journal			Page 1	
	Date		Account Title	P.R.	Debit	Credit	
1	20XX Jun.	2	Merchandise Inventory		20 0 0 0 00		1
2			Accounts Payable			20 0 0 0 00	2
3							3
4							4
5		6	Accounts Payable		1 0 0 0 00		5
6			Merchandise Inventory			1 0 0 0 00	6
7							7
8							8
9		12	Accounts Payable		19 0 0 0 00		9
10			Cash			18 6 2 0 00	10
11			Merchandise Inventory			3 8 0 00	11
12							12
13		15	Accounts Receivable		10 0 0 0 00		13
14			Sales			10 0 0 0 00	14
15							15
16		15	Cost of Goods Sold		7 5 0 0 00		16
17			Merchandise Inventory			7 5 0 0 00	17
18							18
19		18	Sales Returns and Allowances		1 5 0 0 00		19
20			Accounts Receivable			1 5 0 0 00	20
21							21
22		18	Merchandise Inventory		1 2 0 0 00		22
23			Cost of Goods Sold			1 2 0 0 00	23
24							24
25		25	Cash		8 3 3 0 00		25
26			Sales Discounts		1 7 0 00		26
27			Accounts Receivable			8 5 0 0 00	27
28							28
29		28	Merchandise Inventory		12 3 5 0 00		29
30			Accounts Payable			12 3 5 0 00	30
31							31
32							32
33		30	Cash		30 0 0 0 00		33
34			Sales			30 0 0 0 00	34
35							35
36		30	Cost of Goods Sold		24 0 0 0 00		36
37			Merchandise Inventory			24 0 0 0 00	37
38							38

As you remember from earlier chapters, all business transactions can be recorded in a two-column general journal. However, special journals save journalizing and posting time. In the next section, we will look at special journals designed for a perpetual inventory system. Before we do that, however, let's look as a summary of the Merchandise Inventory account.

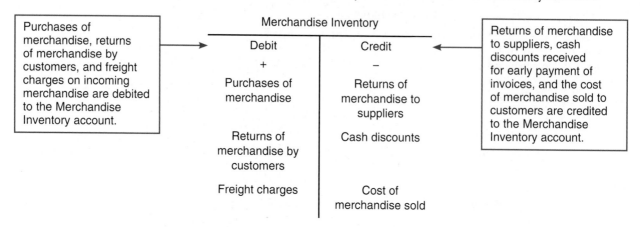

Using Special Journals with a Perpetual Inventory System

With only slight modification, the special journals we used in Chapters 7 and 8 with the periodic inventory system can be used to record transactions in a perpetual inventory system. To illustrate, let's look at the special journals used by DeBice Home Products Company.

Purchases Journal

DeBice's purchases journal for July 20XX is shown in Figure C-2. Notice that it has one money column entitled *Merchandise Inventory Debit/Accounts Payable Credit*. As we learned earlier, when using the perpetual inventory system, all purchases of merchandise on account involve a debit to Merchandise Inventory and a credit to Accounts Payable. Thus, one money column is all that is needed, as *only* credit purchases of merchandise are recorded in a one-column purchases journal.

Figure C-2

Purchases Journal for Use in a Perpetual Inventory System

	Date		Invoice No.	Account Credited	P.R.	Mer. Inv. Dr. / Accts. Pay. Cr.	
	20XX						
1	Jul.	1	301	John Blaylock Enterprises	✓	9 2 0 0 00	1
2		3	302	G. McFarlin Distributors	✓	3 8 0 0 00	2
3		5	303	J.A. Edwards Company	✓	5 5 6 0 00	3
4		6	304	L.A. Lovering Company	✓	1 2 5 0 00	4
5		15	305	G. McFarlin Distributors	✓	8 0 0 00	5
6		22	306	Westglenn Chemicals	✓	4 6 1 0 00	6
7		28	307	L.A. Lovering Company	✓	1 3 9 0 00	7
8		31		Total		26 6 1 0 00	8
9						(113) (211)	9

Purchases Journal   **Page 18**

Cash Payments Journal

DeBice's cash payments journal for July 20XX is shown in Figure C-3. Notice it contains a *Merchandise Inventory Credit* column, which is used to record cash discounts received on invoices paid within the discount period. The other columns are the same as the cash payments journal we used in Chapter 7 for the periodic inventory system.

Figure C-3

Cash Payments Journal for Use in a Perpetual Inventory System

> In the perpetual inventory system, cash discounts received for early payment of invoices are credited to the Merchandise Inventory account because discounts decrease the cost of inventory.

	Date	Ck. No.	Account Debited	P.R.	General Dr.	Accounts Payable Dr.	Merchandise Inventory Cr.	Cash Cr.	
1	20XX Jul. 1	115	Rent Expense	611	1 0 5 0 00			1 0 5 0 00	1
2	2	116	Repairs Expense	618	8 5 00			8 5 00	2
3	7	117	Office Supplies	115	1 2 5 00			1 2 5 00	3
4	11	118	John Blaylock Enterprises	✓		9 2 0 0 00	1 8 4 00	9 0 1 6 00	4
5	13	119	G. McFarlin Distributors	✓		3 8 0 0 00	7 6 00	3 7 2 4 00	5
6	15	120	Salaries Expense	612	3 8 5 0 00			3 8 5 0 00	6
7	15	121	J.A. Edwards Company	✓		5 6 5 0 00	1 1 3 00	5 5 3 7 00	7
8	16	122	L.A. Lovering Company	✓		1 2 5 0 00	1 2 50	1 2 3 7 50	8
9	25	123	G. McFarlin Distributors	✓		8 0 0 00	1 6 00	7 8 4 00	9
10	30	124	Utilities Expense	621	1 5 6 0 00			1 5 6 0 00	10
11	31	125	Salaries Expense	612	3 8 5 0 00			3 8 5 0 00	11
12	31		Totals		10 5 2 0 00	20 7 0 0 00	4 0 1 50	30 8 1 8 50	12
13					(✓)	(2 1 1)	(1 1 3)	(1 1 1)	13

Sales Journal

DeBice's sales journal for July 20XX is shown in Figure C-4 on the next page. Notice that there are two money columns: *Accounts Receivable Debit/Sales Credit* and *Cost of Goods Sold Debit/Merchandise Inventory Credit*. Each sale recorded in the sales journal results in one entry *at selling price* and another entry *at cost*. The entry at selling price is a debit to Accounts Receivable and a credit to Sales. The entry at cost is a debit to Cost of Goods Sold and a credit to Merchandise Inventory.

Figure C-4

Sales Journal for Use in
a Perpetual Inventory
System

	Date		Invoice No.	Customer's Name	P.R.	Accts. Rec. Dr./ Sales Cr.	Cost of Goods Sold Dr./ Mer. Inv. Cr.	
	Sales Journal						**Page 14**	
1	20XX Jul.	1	151	Three Sands Motel	✓	6 0 0 0 00	4 5 0 0 00	1
2		2	152	Ben's Lawn Care Service	✓	5 2 0 0 00	3 9 0 0 00	2
3		5	153	Barbara O'Malley	✓	1 5 0 0 00	1 1 2 5 00	3
4		8	154	Coco Shotz	✓	1 8 0 0 00	1 2 3 0 00	4
5		12	155	Drew Adkins	✓	6 8 0 0 00	5 1 0 0 00	5
6		18	156	Tri City Landscaping	✓	10 4 0 0 00	7 8 0 0 00	6
7		20	157	Betty Brown	✓	4 0 0 0 00	3 0 0 0 00	7
8		21	158	Donna Harper	✓	1 2 0 0 00	8 0 0 00	8
9		29	159	Lori Scott	✓	2 2 5 0 00	1 6 8 8 00	9
10		31		Totals		39 1 5 0 00	29 1 4 3 00	10
11						(112) (411)	(601) (113)	11

Cash Receipts Journal

DeBice's cash receipts journal for July 20XX is shown in Figure C-5. Notice that there are six money columns. One of these columns is entitled *Cost of Goods Sold Debit/Merchandise Inventory Credit*. As we learned earlier, cash sales of goods to customers under a perpetual inventory system require two entries, as follows:

- A debit to Cash and a credit to Sales for the selling price
- A debit to Cost of Goods Sold and a credit to Merchandise Inventory for the cost

To illustrate, look at the July 3 entry, highlighted in Figure C-5. A customer paid cash for 50 five-pound bags of lawn fertilizer at $9 a bag. We recorded the $450 selling price (50 bags × $9) by debiting Cash and crediting Sales. The total cost of the fertilizer (50 bags × $5 = $225) was recorded by debiting Cost of Goods Sold and crediting Merchandise Inventory.

Key Point ⊘

In the perpetual inventory system, all sales require two journal entries: one entry records the selling price of the merchandise, and the second entry transfers the cost of the items sold out of inventory into Cost of Goods Sold.

Figure C-5

Cash Receipts Journal
for Use in a Perpetual
Inventory System

	Date		Account Credited	P.R.	General Cr.	Sales Cr.	Cost of Goods Sold Dr./ Mer. Inv. Cr.	Accounts Receivable Cr.	Sales Discounts Dr.	Cash Dr.	
	Cash Receipts Journal									**Page 18**	
1	20XX Jul.	1	Whiddon's Lawn Co.	✓				2 4 0 0 00	4 8 00	2 3 5 2 00	1
2		2	Three Sands Motel	✓				1 4 5 0 00	2 9 00	1 4 2 1 00	2
3		3	Cash Sale	✓		4 5 0 00	2 2 5 00			4 5 0 00	3
4		6	Office Equipment	118	8 0 0 00					8 0 0 00	4
5		11	Three Sands Motel	✓				6 0 0 0 00	1 2 0 00	5 8 8 0 00	5
6		12	Ben's Lawn Care	✓				5 2 0 0 00	1 0 4 00	5 0 9 6 00	6
7		15	Barbara O'Malley	✓				1 5 0 0 00		1 5 0 0 00	7
8		18	Coco Shotz	✓				1 8 0 0 00		1 8 0 0 00	8
9		21	Cash Sale	✓		8 0 0 0 00	6 0 0 0 00			8 0 0 0 00	9
10		22	Drew Adkins	✓				6 8 0 0 00	1 3 6 00	6 6 6 4 00	10
11		28	Tri City Landscraping	✓				10 4 0 0 00	2 0 8 00	10 1 9 2 00	11
12		30	Betty Brown	✓				4 0 0 0 00		4 0 0 0 00	12
13		31	Cash Sale	✓		12 0 0 0 00	9 0 0 0 00			12 0 0 0 00	13
14		31	Totals		8 0 0 00	20 4 5 0 00	15 2 2 5 00	39 5 5 0 00	6 4 5 00	60 1 5 5 00	14
15					(✓)	(4 1 1)	(6 0 1) (1 1 3)	(1 1 2)	(4 1 1.2)	(1 1 1)	15

Summary

Interactive Summary in English and Spanish

1 Differentiate between the periodic inventory system and the perpetual inventory system.

The **periodic inventory system** is one in which merchandise purchased is debited to the Purchases account and no ongoing records are kept to show the cost of items sold, or how much inventory is on hand at any given time. Instead, inventory is counted "periodically," which is usually at the end of the accounting period.

In the **perpetual inventory system**, individual inventory records are set up that show a continuous, or running, balance for each inventory item. When new merchandise is purchased, the inventory records for the items received are updated (increased). When merchandise is sold, the inventory records of the items sold are updated (decreased). Thus, the inventory records always (perpetually) show the amount of merchandise that should be on hand.

2 Record merchandising transactions using the perpetual inventory system.

In the perpetual inventory system, the cost of merchandise purchased is debited to an asset account entitled Merchandise Inventory. When merchandise is sold, the cost of the items sold is credited to the Merchandise Inventory account and debited to an expense account entitled **Cost of Goods Sold**.

The Merchandise Inventory account serves as a controlling account and is thus located in the general ledger. The individual inventory records serve as a subsidiary stock ledger. At month end, when all posting is complete, the balance of the Merchandise Inventory account should agree with the total of the individual balances in the subsidiary stock ledger.

Terms Review

Key Terms and Definitions in English and Spanish

Key Terms

Cost of Goods Sold account, 391
periodic inventory system, 390
perpetual inventory system, 390

Skills Review

Exercises

Learning Objectives **1, 2**

Check Figure
None

Exercise C-1

Objective: To record merchandise transactions using the perpetual inventory system

The following transactions were incurred by C. Nash Company during March 20X1:

20X1

Mar. 12 Purchased merchandise on account from Bay Distributors, $12,000; terms, 2/10,n/30.

15 Returned $1,000 of defective items from the purchase of March 12.

21 Sold merchandise on account to Alli O'Malley, $6,500; terms 2/10,n/30. The cost of the items sold was $4,000.

22 Paid for the purchase of March 12, less the return of March 15 and less 2% cash discount.

Mar. 23 Accepted returns of $500 from the sale of March 21. The cost of the items returned was $350.

31 Received payment for the March 21 sale, less the return of March 23 and less 2% cash discount.

Directions: Record the transactions in a general journal.

Learning Objectives **1, 2**

Check Figure
July 15 Cost of Goods Sold = $15,200 ($15,500–$300 discount)

Exercise C-2

Objective: To record merchandise transactions using the perpetual inventory system

The following transactions were incurred by Fritz Company during July 20X2:

20X2

July 2 Purchased merchandise on account from James Company, $15,000; terms, 1/10,n/30; FOB shipping point with prepaid freight charges of $500 added to the invoice.

12 Paid for the purchase of July 2 (remember not to take the discount on the $500 freight charge).

15 Sold all merchandise from the July 2 purchase to Tim Green for $18,500; terms 2/10,n/30.

25 Collected payment from the sale of July 15.

Directions: Record the transactions in a general journal.

Learning Objective **2**

Check Figure
Total of the Cash Credit column of the cash payments journal = $27,324

Exercise C-3

Objective: To record transactions in special journals using the perpetual inventory system

The following purchases and cash payments were made by J.T. Lasselle Company during May 20X2:

20X2

May 1 Paid rent for the month, $1,200.

2 Purchased merchandise on account from J.T. Wilder Company, $5,000; terms, 2/10,n/30; FOB destination.

4 Purchased merchandise on account from S.E. Wright, $8,000; terms, 1/10,n/30; FOB shipping point. A freight charge of $400 was prepaid by the seller and added to the invoice.

8 Purchased merchandise on account from Whitehurst Company, $2,500; terms, 2/10,n/30; FOB destination.

10 Purchased merchandise on account from Covington Company, $1,800; terms, 2/15,n/45; FOB shipping point. A freight charge of $90 was prepaid by the seller and added to the invoice.

12 Paid for the purchase of May 2.

14 Paid for the purchase of May 4 (remember to take the discount only on the merchandise).

15 Paid salaries for the first half of the month, $4,200.

18 Paid for the purchase of May 8.

25 Paid for the purchase of May 10 (remember the freight charge is not subject to a discount).

31 Paid salaries for the second half of the month, $4,400.

Directions: Lasselle uses a one-column purchases journal and a four-column cash payments journal. Record the transactions in the appropriate journal. Purchase invoice numbers start with 102, and check numbers start with 300. Total and rule both journals.

Learning Objective **2**

Check Figure
Total of the Cash Debit column
of the cash receipts journal =
$22,260

Exercise C-4

Objective: To record transactions in special journals using the perpetual inventory system

The J.T. Lasselle Company's sales and cash receipts during May 20X2 are as follows:

20X2

May 1   Sold merchandise for cash, $2,000. The cost of the merchandise sold was $1,400.

4   Sold merchandise to James Stone, $800; terms, 2/10,n/30. The cost of the merchandise sold was $570.

6   Sold merchandise to Lee Bowick, $3,000; terms, 2/10,n/30. The cost of the merchandise sold was $2,400.

10   Sold merchandise to T.D. Sether, $3,200; terms, 2/10,n/30. The cost of the merchandise sold was $2,480.

12   Sold merchandise for cash, $4,000. The cost of the merchandise was $2,800.

14   Collected balance due from the sale to James Stone on May 4.

16   Collected balance due from the sale to Lee Bowick on May 6.

20   Sold merchandise for cash, $1,200. The cost of the merchandise sold was $810.

20   Collected balance due from the sale to T.D. Sether on May 10.

25   Sold merchandise to Ann Hawkins, $500; terms, n/30. The cost of the merchandise sold was $315.

28   Sold store supplies to a competitor at cost, $200.

31   Sold merchandise for cash, $8,000. The cost of the merchandise sold was $6,400.

Directions: Lasselle uses a two-column sales journal and a six-column cash receipts journal. Record the above transactions in the appropriate journal. Sales invoice numbers start with 278. Total and rule both journals.

Case Problems

Learning Objectives **1, 2**

Check Figure
Total of the Cash Debit column
of the cash receipts journal =
$32,370

Problem C-1

Objective: To record transactions in general and special journals using the perpetual inventory system

Del Lapree Company completed the following transactions during April 20X2:

20X2

Apr. 1   Sold merchandise for cash, $8,000. The cost of the merchandise sold was $6,800.

2   Paid rent for the month, $900. Check No. 100.

5   Sold merchandise to Shirl Mallory, $1,200; terms, 2/10,n/30; Invoice No. 102.The cost of the merchandise sold was $900.

8   Sold merchandise to Carl Mills, $1,500; terms, 2/10,n/30; Invoice No. 103. The cost of the merchandise sold was $1,110.

9   Issued Credit Memorandum No. 12 for $200 to Shirl Mallory for the return of damaged merchandise. The cost of the merchandise was $150.

10   Sold merchandise for cash, $6,000. The cost of the merchandise sold was $4,700.

10   Purchased merchandise from King Company, $3,000; terms, 3/10,n/45; Invoice No. 51.

12   Purchased merchandise from Sabens Suppliers, $4,000; terms, n/30; Invoice No. 52.

Apr. 15   Paid salaries for the first half of the month, $3,000, Check No. 101.

     15   Received payment from Shirl Mallory for the sale of April 5, less the return on April 9 and less discount.

     18   Received payment from Carl Mills for the sale of April 8, less discount.

     19   Purchased merchandise from K. Hendrick Enterprises, $9,000; terms, 1/10,n/30; Invoice No. 53.

     20   Sold merchandise to Larry Sweat, $4,000; terms, 2/10,/30; Invoice No. 104. The cost of the merchandise sold was $3,000.

     20   Paid King Company for the purchase of April 10, Check No. 102.

     23   Purchased merchandise from Taylor and Son, $5,000; terms, n/30; Invoice No. 54.

     25   Returned damaged merchandise to Taylor and Son, $400.

     25   Paid cash for repairs to equipment, $50, Check No. 103.

     29   Paid K. Hendrick Enterprises for the purchase of April 19, Check No. 104.

     30   Paid salaries for the second half of the month, $3,200, Check No. 105.

     30   Received payment from Larry Sweat for the sale of April 20.

     30   Sold merchandise for cash, $12,000. The cost of the merchandise sold was $9,200.

     30   Paid utility bill for the month, $1,245, Check No. 106.

     30   Sold merchandise to Shirl Mallory, $6,000; terms, 2/10,n/30; Invoice No. 105. The cost of the merchandise sold was $4,500.

Directions: Del Lapree uses a general journal and special journals. Record the transactions in the appropriate journal: general journal, page 18; purchases journal, page 12; cash payments journal, page 19; sales journal, page 22; and cash receipts journal, page 20. Total and rule each special journal.

Learning Objectives **1, 2**

Check Figure
Total of the schedule of
accounts receivable = $57,000

Problem C-2

Objective: To complete a comprehensive problem using five journals and three ledgers for a company using the perpetual inventory system

The following transactions were completed by M. Fritz Wholesale Food Company during November 20X3. All credit sales carry terms of 2/10,n/30.

Note: Read directions at the end of the problem before you start journalizing and posting.

20X3

Nov. 1   Paid rent, $1,500.

     2   Received the balance of Nika Hall's account, less a 2% discount.

     3   Received the balance of Kim Janicki's account, no discount.

     3   Sold merchandise on account to Handy Andy's Food World, $12,400. The cost of the merchandise was $10,500.

     3   Received the balance of Lori Lawson's Natural Foods account, less a 2% discount.

     4   Purchased office equipment for cash, $3,200.

     4   Paid H.H. Farless Company the balance owed on account, less 1% discount.

     5   Sold merchandise on account to Riverside Grocery, $28,500. The cost of the merchandise was $20,200.

     6   Purchased office supplies on account from White's Office Supply, $500; terms, n/30.

     7   Purchased merchandise on account from J.J. Bakker Food Processors, $60,000; terms, 2/10,n/30.

     7   Recorded cash sales for the week, $18,000. The cost of the merchandise was $13,500.

Nov. 8 Sold merchandise on account to Lori Lawson's Natural Foods, $5,000. The cost of the merchandise was $3,750.

9 Paid Taylor Company for the November 1 balance, less a 2% discount.

10 Purchased merchandise on account from H.H. Farless Company, $25,000; terms, 2/10,n/30.

12 Returned defective merchandise to H.H. Farless Company, $800.

13 Purchased store equipment on account from Sam DuPree Products Company, $12,000; terms, n/30.

13 Collected amount due from Handy Andy's Food World for the sale on November 3 (remember that all credit sales carry terms of 2/10,n/30).

14 Recorded cash sales for the week, $29,200. The cost of the merchandise was $21,900.

15 Collected amount due from Riverside Grocery for the sale on November 5, less discount.

15 Paid salaries for the first half of the month, $6,500.

16 Sold merchandise on account to Wilder Foods, $12,000. The cost of the merchandise was $9,800.

17 Paid J.J. Bakker Food Processors for the purchase on November 7, less discount.

18 Collected amount due from Lori Lawson's Natural Foods for the sale of November 8, less discount.

20 Paid H.H. Farless Company for the purchase on November 10, less the return on November 12 and less discount.

21 Recorded cash sales for the week, $30,400. The cost of the merchandise was $22,800.

22 Issued a check to a cash customer for the return of goods, $200. The cost of the merchandise was $150. (Note: Record the $200 cash refunded in the cash payments journal, but record the $150 return of merchandise to inventory in the general journal.)

23 Paid for miscellaneous expenses, $400.

24 Sold merchandise on account to Riverside Grocery, $24,000. The cost of the merchandise was $18,000.

26 Collected amount due from Wilder Foods for the sale of November 16, less discount.

27 Sold merchandise on account to Lori Lawson's Natural Foods, $12,400. The cost of the merchandise was $9,300.

28 Purchased merchandise on account from Tyler Meat Packers, $15,000; terms, n/30.

29 Sold merchandise on account to Kim Janicki, $4,000. The cost of the merchandise was $3,000.

29 Issued Credit Memorandum No. 1 for $600 to Lori Lawson's Natural Foods for the return of merchandise. The cost of the merchandise was $450.

29 Paid utility bill, $1,840.

30 Recorded cash sales for the week, $19,700. The cost of the merchandise was $14,775.

30 Paid salaries for the second half of the month, $6,500.

30 Purchased store supplies for cash, $498.

30 Paid for gas and oil expense for the month, $4,200.

30 Sold merchandise on account to Riverside Grocery, $17,200. The cost of the merchandise was $12,900.

30 Paid for repairs to delivery truck, $600.

30 Purchased merchandise on account from Taylor Company, $2,000; terms, n/30.

Directions:

1. Open the following accounts in the general ledger, and enter the balances as of November 1:

	Account	Balance
111	Cash	$ 48,300
112	Accounts Receivable	24,200
113	Merchandise Inventory	228,600
114	Store Supplies	4,000
115	Office Supplies	2,400
121	Store Equipment	65,000
122	Office Equipment	26,600
211	Accounts Payable	25,000
411	Sales	428,900
411.1	Sales Returns and Allowances	5,680
411.2	Sales Discounts	18,400
601	Cost of Goods Sold	501,000
611	Salaries Expense	122,000
612	Rent Expense	12,000
613	Utilities Expense	14,600
614	Gas and Oil Expense	28,300
615	Repairs Expense	3,810
620	Miscellaneous Expense	1,200

2. Open the following accounts in the accounts receivable ledger, and enter the balances as of November 1:

Account	Balance
Handy Andy's Food World	$ -0-
Kim Janicki	8,000
Lori Lawson's Natural Foods	10,200
Nika Hall	6,000
Riverside Grocery	-0-
Wilder Foods	-0-

3. Open the following accounts in the accounts payable ledger, and enter the balances as of November 1:

Account	Balance
H.H. Farless Company	$ 9,000
J.J. Bakker Food Processors	-0-
Sam DuPree Products Company	-0-
Taylor Company	16,000
Tyler Meat Packers	-0-
White's Office Supply	-0-

4. Record the November transactions in the appropriate journal as follows: general journal, page 14; sales journal, page 10; cash receipts journal, page 12; purchases journal, page 8; and cash payments journal, page 15. Sales invoices start with number 275, purchases invoices start with number 118, and check numbers start with 101. Post to the subsidiary ledgers after each entry.
5. Post the individual entries from the general journal and the general columns of special journals to the general ledger. Total, rule, and post the special journals.
6. Prepare a schedule of accounts receivable.
7. Prepare a schedule of accounts payable.

Work Sheet and Adjustments for a Merchandising Business

Learning Objectives

1 Make adjustments to the Merchandise Inventory account.
2 Make other needed adjustments and complete a work sheet for a merchandising business.

Our study of merchandising has taken us through purchasing and selling procedures, special journals, subsidiary ledgers, controlling accounts, returns and allowances, discounts, and transportation costs. We now reach the end-of-period summarizing and reporting procedures for a merchandising business. End-of-period activities for a merchandising business are similar to the end-of-period activities we studied for a service business in Chapters 4 and 5. In a merchandising business, however, consideration must be given to the amount of merchandise inventory on hand at the beginning and end of the accounting period. Additionally, the use of three ledgers—a general ledger and two subsidiary ledgers—means special checking (i.e., schedules of accounts receivable and accounts payable) that often is not done in service businesses.

Chart of Accounts for a Merchandising Business

Before embarking on our study of end-of-period activities for a merchandising business, let's look at the account titles with which we will be working. The full chart of accounts for Lakeside Electronics, as it appears on December 31, 20X1, is shown in Table 9-1.

Now that we have Lakeside's chart of accounts, the first step in the end-of-period activities is to prepare a trial balance of the general ledger and determine which accounts need adjusting.

As you recall, the trial balance is a form that shows the title and balance of each account in the general ledger. On December 31, 20X1, after all posting has been done, the trial balance of Lakeside appears as shown in Figure 9-1. You may notice that some accounts did not have balances when the trial balance was prepared; they are included because they will be needed during the adjusting process, which we will discuss next.

Table 9-1 Chart of Accounts for Lakeside Electronics

Account Category	Account Number	Account Title
Assets (100–199)	111	Cash
	112	Accounts Receivable
	113	Merchandise Inventory
	114	Store Supplies
	115	Office Supplies
	116	Prepaid Insurance
	119	Store Equipment
	119.1	Accumulated Depreciation— Store Equipment
	120	Office Equipment
	120.1	Accumulated Depreciation— Office Equipment
	121	Delivery Equipment
	121.1	Accumulated Depreciation— Delivery Equipment
Liabilities (200–299)	211	Accounts Payable
	212	Salaries Payable
	215	Notes Payable
Owner's Equity (300–399)	311	John Graham, Capital
	312	John Graham, Drawing
	313	Income Summary
Revenue (400–499)	411	Sales
	411.1	Sales Returns and Allowances
	411.2	Sales Discounts
Cost of Goods Sold (500–599)	511	Purchases
	511.1	Purchases Returns and Allowances
	511.2	Purchases Discounts
	512	Freight In
Expenses (600–799) Selling Expense	611	Sales Salaries Expense
	612	Advertising Expense
	613	Store Supplies Expense
	614	Depreciation Expense—Store Equipment
	619	Miscellaneous Selling Expense
General Expense	711	Rent Expense
	712	Office Salaries Expense
	713	Insurance Expense
	714	Depreciation Expense—Office Equipment
	715	Depreciation Expense—Delivery Equipment
	716	Utilities Expense
	717	Office Supplies Expense
	720	Interest Expense
	721	Miscellaneous General Expense

A contra account is listed as a subaccount of the account to which it is contra.

Determining Needed Adjustments

Remember

As you learned in Chapter 4, adjusting entries are a planned part of the accounting cycle; they do not result from errors.

Remember that the trial balance shows us that total debits in the ledger equal total credits. But also remember that a few accounts listed on the trial balance will need adjusting to bring their balances up to date. As we discussed in Chapter 4, adjustments are needed because certain changes occur during the accounting period, and it is usually not practical to attempt to keep up with these changes as they occur. For example, a prepaid item, such as supplies or insurance, is recorded as an asset when purchased. As time passes, however, the

Figure 9-1
Trial Balance

Lakeside Electronics Trial Balance December 31, 20X1		
Account Title	**Debit**	**Credit**
Cash	6 2 0 0 00	
Accounts Receivable	9 6 8 9 00	
Merchandise Inventory	66 0 0 0 00	
Store Supplies	2 0 1 5 00	
Office Supplies	6 6 7 00	
Prepaid Insurance	7 2 0 00	
Store Equipment	11 3 8 5 00	
Accumulated Depreciation—Store Equipment		4 5 0 0 00
Office Equipment	10 2 0 0 00	
Accumulated Depreciation—Office Equipment		7 1 0 0 00
Delivery Equipment	56 0 0 0 00	
Accumulated Depreciation—Delivery Equipment		13 8 0 0 00
Accounts Payable		14 0 2 5 00
Salaries Payable		—
Notes Payable		26 0 0 0 00
John Graham, Capital		75 5 8 1 00
John Graham, Drawing	18 0 0 0 00	
Income Summary	—	—
Sales		304 6 0 0 00
Sales Returns and Allowances	5 2 3 0 00	
Sales Discounts	3 4 6 1 00	
Purchases	144 9 1 8 00	
Purchases Returns and Allowances		6 6 9 2 00
Purchases Discounts		2 9 1 0 00
Freight In	1 1 6 0 00	
Sales Salaries Expense	68 2 0 0 00	
Advertising Expense	5 8 4 0 00	
Store Supplies Expense	—	
Depreciation Expense—Store Equipment	—	
Miscellaneous Selling Expense	2 1 0 0 00	
Rent Expense	5 7 0 0 00	
Office Salaries Expense	30 4 5 3 00	
Insurance Expense	—	
Depreciation Expense—Office Equipment	—	
Depreciation Expense—Delivery Equipment	—	
Utilities Expense	6 2 4 0 00	
Office Supplies Expense	—	
Interest Expense	1 3 0 00	
Miscellaneous General Expense	9 0 0 00	
Totals	455 2 0 8 00	455 2 0 8 00

value of the asset is consumed in the business, and therefore its cost gradually becomes an expense. Consequently, an adjustment must be made to record the portion of the prepayment that has been used up or has expired.

Additionally, there are usually other items—such as depreciation of long-term assets and unpaid salaries—that must be recorded to match revenue and expenses properly and to state the amount of assets and liabilities accurately.

The accountant for Lakeside Electronics determined that adjustments were needed for the following items as of December 31, 20X1: merchandise inventory, store supplies used, office supplies used, insurance expired, depreciation of equipment, and unpaid salaries.

To illustrate these adjustments, we will first record them in T accounts. T accounts, as you recall, are an excellent way to organize data and collect one's thoughts. We will then enter the adjustments on a work sheet. In Chapter 10, we will discuss financial statements, journalizing the adjustments, and closing entries.

inventory a count taken of the merchandise on hand at the end of an accounting period

Learning Objective

1 Make adjustments to the Merchandise Inventory account.

Merchandise Inventory account an asset account that shows the value of goods (inventory) on hand at a given moment (usually at the beginning or end of the accounting period)

beginning merchandise inventory the dollar value of merchandise that is on hand at the beginning of an accounting period

ending merchandise inventory the dollar value of merchandise that is on hand at the end of an accounting period

Adjustment for Merchandise Inventory

The cost of merchandise purchased during an accounting period is debited to the Purchases account. However, the Purchases account shows only the cost of merchandise purchased—not the value of merchandise on hand at the end of the accounting period. To determine the value of the goods on hand, it is necessary to take an **inventory**—a physical count to determine how much merchandise is unsold. The count can be done by a manual hard count or by electronic scanning equipment. The value of the goods on hand is then recorded in the **Merchandise Inventory account**, which is an asset account.

During the year, Lakeside constantly purchases, sells, and replaces merchandise. Rather than trying to keep up with this constant change in its inventory, Lakeside waits until the end of the year, takes an inventory of merchandise, and then adjusts the Merchandise Inventory account to show the value of the current inventory.

The adjustment for Merchandise Inventory is relatively simple. The Merchandise Inventory account is decreased by the value of the **beginning merchandise inventory** (the dollar value of inventory at the beginning of the period), and it is increased by the value of the **ending merchandise inventory** (the dollar value of inventory at the end of the period). To explore further, in Lakeside's trial balance (Figure 9-1), the Merchandise Inventory account shows a balance of $66,000. Since Lakeside adjusts the Merchandise Inventory account only at year-end, this figure does not represent the value of the goods currently on hand; it represents the value of the goods that were on hand when the period started.

A current count of merchandise (as of December 31) reveals that $72,400 worth of goods remain on hand. This is the up-to-date inventory, the amount we wish to show in the Merchandise Inventory account, and the amount we wish to list on the balance sheet.

How can we make the Merchandise Inventory account show the value of the latest inventory? A popular way is to simply remove the old inventory

The use of an electronic scanner speeds the inventory process by identifying the item, what category of merchandise it belongs to, and how many units are on hand.

figure from the Merchandise Inventory account and, in its place, record the new inventory figure. This is accomplished in two steps, as described below.

Remember

As you learned in Chapter 4, cash is never involved in an adjusting entry.

Step 1: Transfer the Beginning Inventory Figure from the Merchandise Inventory Account to the Income Summary Account

Analysis: Merchandise Inventory is an asset account, so it has a normal debit balance. Therefore, to decrease the account, we will credit the account for its balance. Our debit is to the Income Summary account. The adjustment is as follows:

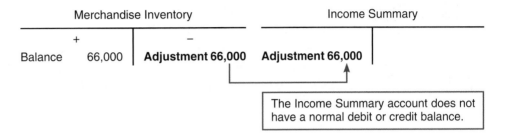

Merchandise Inventory		Income Summary	
+	−	−	
Balance 66,000	**Adjustment 66,000**	**Adjustment 66,000**	

The Income Summary account does not have a normal debit or credit balance.

Step 2: Record the Ending Inventory Figure in the Merchandise Inventory Account

Analysis: The current inventory figure is $72,400. The Merchandise Inventory account should be increased by this amount. The Merchandise Inventory account—an asset—is increased on the debit side. Our credit is to the Income Summary account.

Key Point ⟩

To adjust the Merchandise Inventory account, take out the old and put in the new.

Merchandise Inventory		Income Summary	
+	−	−	
Balance 66,000	Adjustment 66,000	Adjustment 66,000	**Adjustment 72,400**
Adjustment 72,400			

The old inventory figure, $66,000, has been removed from the Merchandise Inventory account; the new inventory figure, $72,400, has been recorded in the Merchandise Inventory account. This two-step procedure to adjust the Merchandise Inventory account is generally preferred by accountants because both the beginning and ending inventory figures appear on the income statement, which is prepared directly from the Income Statement columns of the work sheet. (We will discuss the income statement at greater length in Chapter 10.) We could have accomplished the same result by adjusting the Merchandise Inventory account for the difference between the beginning and ending inventory figures ($72,400 – $66,000 = $6,400). Under this method, we would have increased the Merchandise Inventory account by $6,400 (because the ending inventory was higher than the beginning), thus bringing its balance to $72,400—the amount of the ending inventory. This method, however, is considered less meaningful because the difference between the inventory figures, $6,400, does not appear as a separate figure on the income statement.

Before adjustment on December 31, 20XX, the Merchandise Inventory account of Tricia's Boutique shows a debit balance of $94,000. A current inventory count (as of December 31), however, shows that the new inventory figure is $97,000. Draw T accounts, and make the adjusting entries to (a) remove the balance of the beginning inventory from the Merchandise Inventory account and (b) record the value of the inventory on hand in the Merchandise Inventory account.

Check your answers on page 441.

Adjustment for Store Supplies Used

Learning Objective

2 Make other needed adjustments and complete a work sheet for a merchandising business.

Lakeside Electronics' remaining adjustments are very similar to those we made for Walker and Associates in Chapter 4. Our next adjustment is for the amount of store supplies used during the period. Referring to Lakeside's trial balance (page 409), we see that the Store Supplies account has a $2,015 balance, which represents the cost of supplies on hand at the beginning of the year, plus the cost of supplies purchased during the year. An inventory count on December 31 revealed that $500 worth of store supplies remain on hand. The value of store supplies used is computed as follows:

Balance of Store Supplies account, December 31	$2,015
Store supplies on hand, December 31	– 500
Store supplies used (amount of adjustment)	$1,515

Remember

Increases in expense accounts are recorded as debits.

Decreases in asset accounts are recorded as credits.

The value of store supplies used is no longer an asset; it has become an expense. Therefore, the adjustment for the store supplies used involves a debit to the Store Supplies Expense account and a credit to the Store Supplies account, as illustrated in the T accounts below.

Store Supplies Expense		Store Supplies	
+	–	+	–
Adjustment 1,515		Balance 2,015	Adjustment 1,515

Adjustment for Office Supplies Used

The adjustment for office supplies used is determined in the same manner as the adjustment for store supplies used. Again, we refer to Lakeside's trial balance and see that the Office Supplies account has a $667 balance. However, an inventory count on December 31 revealed that only $250 worth remain on hand. Thus, $417 ($667 – $250) is the value of office supplies used. Our adjusting entry involves a debit to the Office Supplies Expense account and a credit to the Office Supplies account, as shown below:

Office Supplies Expense		Office Supplies	
+	–	+	–
Adjustment 417		Balance 667	Adjustment 417

Adjustment for Insurance Expired

In Chapter 4, we learned that insurance paid in advance is considered an asset because it provides a benefit—insurance protection—that the company will receive in the future. As time passes, however, the prepayment expires and the asset becomes an expense. At the end of the accounting period, we must make an adjustment for the value of insurance expired during the period.

On December 31, Lakeside's Prepaid Insurance account shows a $720 balance. This balance represents a two-year prepayment, made on October 1, for comprehensive (fire, theft, etc.) coverage on merchandise and equipment. The amount of the adjustment at December 31 is determined as follows:

$$\frac{\$720}{24 \text{ months}} = \$30 \text{ monthly expiration}$$

$$\text{Oct. 1 to Dec. 31} = 3 \text{ months}$$

$$\$30 \times 3 \text{ mo.} = \$90 \text{ insurance expired}$$

The adjusting entry for insurance expired involves a debit to the Insurance Expense account and a credit to the Prepaid Insurance account. This entry is illustrated as follows:

Remember

Straight-line depreciation is calculated as follows: Cost of Asset – Trade-in value = Estimated years of usefulness

Insurance Expense			Prepaid Insurance		
+		–		+	–
Adjustment 90			Balance 720		**Adjustment** 90

Adjustment for Depreciation Expense

As you recall, long-term physical assets—such as equipment, buildings, machinery, and furniture—are purchased for use in the business. To match the cost of these assets against the revenue they produce (according to the *accrual basis* of accounting), a part of their cost should be transferred to an expense account during each period the assets are used. This is accomplished by debiting the Depreciation Expense account and crediting the Accumulated Depreciation account.

Lakeside has three types of depreciable assets: (1) store equipment, (2) office equipment, and (3) delivery equipment. Lakeside uses the *straight-line method* to figure depreciation. This means that the same amount of depreciation is recorded for each full period the asset is used. In prior years, Lakeside's accountant determined the straight-line amount for each type of asset. Since some new equipment was purchased during 20X1, the depreciation amounts were refigured. They are as follows:

Remember

As you learned in Chapter 4, depreciation is always recorded by debiting Depreciation Expense and crediting Accumulated Depreciation.

Asset	Cost	Depreciation Recorded in Prior Years	Depreciation for 20X1
Store Equipment	$11,385	$ 4,500	$ 900
Office Equipment	10,200	7,100	820
Delivery Equipment	56,000	13,800	9,200

Lakeside's adjusting entries for depreciation are recorded in the following T accounts:

Store Equipment

Depreciation Expense— Store Equipment		Accumulated Depreciation— Store Equipment	
+	−	−	+
Adjustment 900			Balance 4,500
			Adjustment 900

Office Equipment

Depreciation Expense— Office Equipment		Accumulated Depreciation— Office Equipment	
+	−	−	+
Adjustment 820			Balance 7,100
			Adjustment 820

Delivery Equipment

Depreciation Expense— Delivery Equipment		Accumulated Depreciation— Delivery Equipment	
+	−	−	+
Adjustment 9,200			Balance 13,800
			Adjustment 9,200

In each case, the Depreciation Expense account did not have a balance before recording the adjusting entry; the Accumulated Depreciation account did have a balance. This is because the Depreciation Expense account shows a cost only for a particular period; when that period is over, the balance of the account is closed to the Income Summary account (along with all other expenses). The account balance is thus reduced to zero, and the account is ready to record depreciation at the end of the next period. The Accumulated Depreciation account does *not* relate to a single period. It is a contra account used to *accumulate* depreciation over the life of the asset to which it relates.

Summing Up

- Under the accrual basis of accounting, revenue is recorded when it is earned, regardless of when cash is received; and expenses are recorded when they are incurred, regardless of when they are paid.
- The Accumulated Depreciation account is a *contra asset account* used to summarize the amount of depreciation recorded over the life of the asset to which it relates. It has a normal credit balance that is opposite the debit balance of the asset account.

Adjustment for Salaries Owed but Unpaid

accrued salaries earnings that are unpaid (and unrecorded) and owed to employees at the end of an accounting period; also referred to as accrued wages

Under the accrual basis of accounting, all salary expense incurred in an accounting period should be recorded in that period, even though payment may not have been made. Thus, at the end of an accounting period, a liability should be recorded for all salaries earned by employees but not yet paid by the employer. The liability for unpaid salaries is determined by calculating the salaries earned by employees from the last payday to the end of the accounting period. Accountants refer to the unpaid salaries as **accrued salaries** or accrued wages.

Lakeside's accounting year ends on December 31, 20X1. It is Lakeside's policy to pay employees every other Friday. The last payday was Friday, December 19. Therefore, at the close of business on December 31, seven workdays have passed since employees were last paid. This period can be illustrated as shown in Figure 9-2.

	Sun	Mon	Tue	Wed	Thu	Fri	Sat
December		1	2	3	4	5 Payday	6
	7	8	9	10	11	12	13
	14	15	16	17	18	19 Payday	20
	21	22	23	24	25 H	26	27
20X1	28	29	30	31			

	Sun	Mon	Tue	Wed	Thu	Fri	Sat
January					1	2 Payday	3
	4	5	6	7	8	9	10
	11	12	13	14	15	16 Payday	17
	18	19	20	21	22	23	24
20X2	25	26	27	28	29	30 Payday	31

H = Holiday

Figure 9-2
Calculating the Adjustment for Unpaid Salaries

Seven workdays since last payday

According to payroll records maintained by Lakeside's accountant, sales personnel earned $900 and office personnel earned $700 in the seven workdays between the last payday and the end of the period. Although these amounts will not be paid until the next regular payday (January 2, 20X2), they are an expense of 20X1. The use of the accrual basis, therefore, requires that they be recorded in 20X1. The adjusting entry involves debits to the expense accounts and a credit to the Salaries Payable account, as follows:

Key Point ⊚

The adjusting entry for an accrued expense *always* involves a debit to an expense account or accounts and a credit to a liability account.

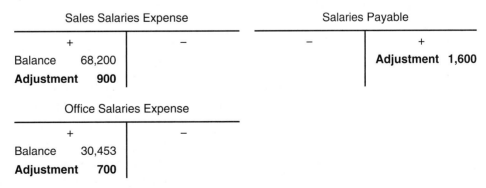

Sales Salaries Expense		Salaries Payable	
+	–	–	+
Balance 68,200			Adjustment 1,600
Adjustment 900			

Office Salaries Expense	
+	–
Balance 30,453	
Adjustment 700	

In addition to salaries, other expenses may be unpaid (and unrecorded) at the end of the accounting period. Utilities, for example, may have been used at the end of a period, but payment may not be due until sometime in the next period. These unpaid utilities need to be recorded to show the proper amount of utilities expense for the period.

Review Quiz **9-2**

Watkins Company ends its accounting year on December 31, 20XX. The accounting records showed the following data as of that date:

1. Merchandise Inventory: January 1 (beginning), $24,300; December 31 (ending), $25,600.
2. Balance of Store Supplies account, $600; inventory of store supplies on December 31, $250.
3. A three-year insurance policy for $3,600 was prepaid on November 1, 20XX.
4. Accrued (unpaid) salaries at December 31, $2,300.

Record Watkins's adjusting entries in general journal form.

Check your answer on page 441.

The End-of-Period Work Sheet

As you learned in Chapter 4, the work sheet is an informal working paper used by the accountant to organize data and make end-of-period work easier.

A work sheet summarizes data and makes preparing other reports faster and easier.

It is not a financial statement, and it will never be published. Nevertheless, it is an excellent tool that is widely used, particularly by large businesses that could have hundreds of adjustments.

In Chapter 4, we prepared a 10-column work sheet for Walker and Associates. Now, we will prepare a 10-column work sheet for Lakeside Electronics. As you remember from Chapter 4, the work sheet is completed one section at a time. Let's see how it is done for a merchandising business.

The Trial Balance and Adjustments Columns

You start the work sheet by entering the heading and then entering the trial balance in the first two columns. Your next step is to enter the adjustments in the Adjustments columns. We have seen each adjustment needed by Lakeside Electronics in T-account form. Let's now enter Lakeside's December trial balance and the adjustments on the work sheet, as shown in Figure 9-3. Each adjustment, as you have already learned, is labeled starting with (a). After all adjustments have been entered, the Adjustments columns are totaled to check the equality of debits and credits. The column totals are then ruled.

Figure 9-3

Trial Balance and Adjustments Columns of the Work Sheet

Lakeside Electronics
Work Sheet
For Year Ended December 31, 20X1

#	Account Title	Trial Balance Debit	Trial Balance Credit	Adjustments Debit	Adjustments Credit	#
1	Cash	6 2 0 0 00				1
2	Accounts Receivable	9 6 8 9 00				2
3	Merchandise Inventory	66 0 0 0 00		(b)72 4 0 0 00	(a)66 0 0 0 00	3
4	Store Supplies	2 0 1 5 00			(c) 1 5 1 5 00	4
5	Office Supplies	6 6 7 00			(d) 4 1 7 00	5
6	Prepaid Insurance	7 2 0 00			(e) 9 0 00	6
7	Store Equipment	11 3 8 5 00				7
8	Accumulated Depreciation—Store Equipment		4 5 0 0 00		(f) 9 0 0 00	8
9	Office Equipment	10 2 0 0 00				9
10	Accumulated Depreciation—Office Equipment		7 1 0 0 00		(g) 8 2 0 00	10
11	Delivery Equipment	56 0 0 0 00				11
12	Accumulated Depreciation—Delivery Equipment		13 8 0 0 00		(h) 9 2 0 0 00	12
13	Accounts Payable		14 0 2 5 00			13
14	Salaries Payable				(i) 1 6 0 0 00	14
15	Notes Payable		26 0 0 0 00			15
16	John Graham, Capital		75 5 8 1 00			16
17	John Graham, Drawing	18 0 0 0 00				17
18	Income Summary			(a) 66 0 0 0 00	(b)72 4 0 0 00	18
19	Sales		304 6 0 0 00			19
20	Sales Returns and Allowances	5 2 3 0 00				20
21	Sales Discounts	3 4 6 1 00				21
22	Purchases	144 9 1 8 00				22
23	Purchases Returns and Allowances		6 6 9 2 00			23
24	Purchases Discounts		2 9 1 0 00			24
25	Freight In	1 1 6 0 00				25
26	Sales Salaries Expense	68 2 0 0 00		(i) 9 0 0 00		26
27	Advertising Expense	5 8 4 0 00				27
28	Store Supplies Expense			(c) 1 5 1 5 00		28
29	Depreciation Expense—Store Equipment			(f) 9 0 0 00		29
30	Miscellaneous Selling Expense	2 1 0 0 00				30
31	Rent Expense	5 7 0 0 00				31
32	Office Salaries Expense	30 4 5 3 00		(i) 7 0 0 00		32
33	Insurance Expense			(e) 9 0 00		33
34	Depreciation Expense—Office Equipment			(g) 8 2 0 00		34
35	Depreciation Expense—Delivery Equipment			(h) 9 2 0 0 00		35
36	Utilities Expense	6 2 4 0 00				36
37	Office Supplies Expense			(d) 4 1 7 00		37
38	Interest Expense	1 3 0 00				38
39	Miscellaneous General Expense	9 0 0 00				39
40		455 2 0 8 00	455 2 0 8 00	152 9 4 2 00	152 9 4 2 00	40

The Adjusted Trial Balance Columns

The adjustments are now combined with the account balances in the Trial Balance columns, and the updated amounts are moved over to the Adjusted Trial Balance columns, as illustrated in Figure 9-4. To avoid confusion, each account is moved in order, starting with the Cash account and proceeding downward line by line. Amounts are moved over as follows:

1 If an account does not have an adjustment, simply carry over the Trial Balance figure to the appropriate Adjusted Trial Balance column. For example, the Cash account has a debit balance of $6,200. Since this amount was not adjusted, it is moved directly to the Adjusted Trial Balance Debit column. Remember that a debit remains a debit.

2 The Merchandise Inventory account has a $66,000 debit balance in the Trial Balance Debit column. However, a $66,000 credit adjustment was made to the account in the Adjustments columns. The $66,000 debit balance is balanced out by the $66,000 credit adjustment. Thus, the amount moved to the Adjusted Trial Balance column is the amount of the debit adjustment, $72,400.

3 If an account has a debit balance, and the adjustment is a credit, the difference between the two amounts is entered in the Adjusted Trial Balance Debit column. For example, the Store Supplies account has a debit balance of $2,015 and a credit adjustment of $1,515. Thus, the difference between the two amounts, $500, is entered in the Adjusted Trial Balance Debit column.

4 If an account has a debit balance, and the adjustment is also a debit, add the two figures and move the total to the Adjusted Trial Balance Debit column. For example, the Sales Salaries Expense account has a debit balance of $68,200 and a $900 debit adjustment. The two debits are added, and the total, $69,100, is entered in the Adjusted Trial Balance Debit column.

5 If an account has a credit balance, and the adjustment is also a credit, add the two figures and enter the total in the Adjusted Trial Balance Credit column. For example, the Accumulated Depreciation—Store Equipment account has a credit balance of $4,500 and a credit adjustment of $900. The two credits are added, and the total, $5,400, is entered in the Adjusted Trial Balance Credit column.

6 If an account does not have a balance in the Trial Balance columns, but there is an adjustment, the amount of the adjustment becomes the balance. It is carried over to the appropriate Adjusted Trial Balance column. For example, the Salaries Payable account did not have a balance. However, there was a $1,600 credit adjustment. Thus, $1,600 is moved to the Adjusted Trial Balance Credit column.

7 *Both* the $66,000 debit adjustment and the $72,400 credit adjustment to the Income Summary account are moved over to the Adjusted Trial Balance columns. We do this because both figures will appear on the income statement, which is prepared directly from the completed work sheet.

Figure 9-4

Work Sheet Through the Adjusted Trial Balance

Lakeside Electronics
Work Sheet
For Year Ended December 31, 20X1

	Account Title	Trial Balance Debit	Trial Balance Credit	Adjustments Debit	Adjustments Credit	Adjusted Trial Balance Debit	Adjusted Trial Balance Credit	
1	Cash	6 2 0 0 00				6 2 0 0 00		1
2	Accounts Receivable	9 6 8 9 00				9 6 8 9 00		2
3	Merchandise Inventory	66 0 0 0 00		(b)72 4 0 0 00	(a)66 0 0 0 00	72 4 0 0 00		3
4	Store Supplies	2 0 1 5 00			(c) 1 5 1 5 00	5 0 0 00		4
5	Office Supplies	6 6 7 00			(d) 4 1 7 00	2 5 0 00		5
6	Prepaid Insurance	7 2 0 00			(e) 9 0 00	6 3 0 00		6
7	Store Equipment	11 3 8 5 00				11 3 8 5 00		7
8	Accum. Depr.—Store Equip.		4 5 0 0 00		(f) 9 0 0 00		5 4 0 0 00	8
9	Office Equipment	10 2 0 0 00				10 2 0 0 00		9
10	Accum. Depr.—Off. Equip.		7 1 0 0 00		(g) 8 2 0 00		7 9 2 0 00	10
11	Delivery Equipment	56 0 0 0 00				56 0 0 0 00		11
12	Accum. Depr.—Del. Equip.		13 8 0 0 00		(h) 9 2 0 0 00		23 0 0 0 00	12
13	Accounts Payable		14 0 2 5 00				14 0 2 5 00	13
14	Salaries Payable		—		(i) 1 6 0 0 00		1 6 0 0 00	14
15	Notes Payable		26 0 0 0 00				26 0 0 0 00	15
16	John Graham, Capital		75 5 8 1 00				75 5 8 1 00	16
17	John Graham, Drawing	18 0 0 0 00				18 0 0 0 00		17
18	Income Summary	—	—	(a)66 0 0 0 00	(b)72 4 0 0 00	66 0 0 0 00	72 4 0 0 00	18
19	Sales		304 6 0 0 00				304 6 0 0 00	19
20	Sales Returns and Allow.	5 2 3 0 00				5 2 3 0 00		20
21	Sales Discounts	3 4 6 1 00				3 4 6 1 00		21
22	Purchases	144 9 1 8 00				144 9 1 8 00		22
23	Purchases Ret. and Allow.		6 6 9 2 00				6 6 9 2 00	23
24	Purchases Discounts		2 9 1 0 00				2 9 1 0 00	24
25	Freight In	1 1 6 0 00				1 1 6 0 00		25
26	Sales Salaries Expense	68 2 0 0 00		(i) 9 0 0 00		69 1 0 0 00		26
27	Advertising Expense	5 8 4 0 00				5 8 4 0 00		27
28	Store Supplies Expense	—		(c) 1 5 1 5 00		1 5 1 5 00		28
29	Depr. Exp.—Store Equip.	—		(f) 9 0 0 00		9 0 0 00		29
30	Miscellaneous Selling Exp.	2 1 0 0 00				2 1 0 0 00		30
31	Rent Expense	5 7 0 0 00				5 7 0 0 00		31
32	Office Salaries Expense	30 4 5 3 00		(i) 7 0 0 00		31 1 5 3 00		32
33	Insurance Expense	—		(e) 9 0 00		9 0 00		33
34	Depr. Exp.—Off. Equip.	—		(g) 8 2 0 00		8 2 0 00		34
35	Depr. Exp.—Del. Equip.	—		(h) 9 2 0 0 00		9 2 0 0 00		35
36	Utilities Expense	6 2 4 0 00				6 2 4 0 00		36
37	Office Supplies Expense	—		(d) 4 1 7 00		4 1 7 00		37
38	Interest Expense	1 3 0 00				1 3 0 00		38
39	Miscellaneous General Exp.	9 0 0 00				9 0 0 00		39
40		455 2 0 8 00	455 2 0 8 00	152 9 4 2 00	152 9 4 2 00	540 1 2 8 00	540 1 2 8 00	40
41								41

Income Summary is the only account for which you do not combine the debit and credit figures. Instead, you move both to the Adjusted Trial Balance as two distinct figures.

After all amounts have been moved over, the Adjusted Trial Balance columns are totaled to prove the equality of debits and credits. The column totals are then ruled. Lakeside's work sheet through the Adjusted Trial Balance is shown in Figure 9-4.

Summing Up

When extending amounts to the Adjusted Trial Balance columns, "likes" are added and "dislikes" are subtracted. If there are two debits or two credits, you add. If there is one debit and one credit, you subtract.

The Financial Statement Columns

Now that the Adjusted Trial Balance columns are complete, our next step is to move the updated amounts over to the appropriate financial statement columns, as shown in Figure 9-5 on pages 422–423. It is possible to complete one set of financial statement columns at a time. For a business with a large number of accounts, however, it is less confusing to start with the Cash account and move downward, line by line, extending each amount to the appropriate statement column. Amounts are moved as follows:

1. Assets and the owner's drawing account are moved to the Balance Sheet Debit column.

2. Accumulated depreciation, liabilities, and the owner's capital account are moved to the Balance Sheet Credit column.

3. Both amounts shown for the Income Summary account are moved to the Income Statement columns. Thus, $66,000 is moved to the Income Statement Debit column; and $72,400 is moved to the Income Statement Credit column.

4. Revenue and contra purchases accounts (Purchases Returns and Allowances and Purchases Discounts) are moved to the Income Statement Credit column.

5. Expenses, Purchases, and contra sales accounts (Sales Returns and Allowances and Sales Discounts) are moved to the Income Statement Debit column.

Before looking at how amounts are actually moved to the financial statement columns, let's take a moment to look at Table 9-2, which summarizes the above steps.

Table 9-2 Summary of Steps to Complete the Financial Statement Columns of a Work Sheet

Income Statement		Balance Sheet	
Debit	**Credit**	**Debit**	**Credit**
Income Summary	Income Summary	Assets	Accumulated Depreciation
Sales Returns and Allowances	Sales	Drawing	Liabilities
Sales Discounts	Purchases Returns and Allowances		Capital
Purchases	Purchases Discounts		
Freight In			
Expenses			

Now look at Figure 9-5 and, starting with the Cash account, trace how each amount is moved from the Adjusted Trial Balance to the appropriate financial statement column.

Completing the Work Sheet

Having extended all amounts to the appropriate financial statement columns, we can now complete the work sheet as follows:

1 Total the Income Statement Debit and Credit columns.

2 Total the Balance Sheet Debit and Credit columns.

3 Determine the amount of net income (or net loss) by finding the difference between the Income Statement Credit column and the Income Statement Debit column. If the Income Statement Credit column (revenue) is greater than the Income Statement Debit column (costs and expenses), there is a net income. On the other hand, if the Income Statement Debit column is greater than the Income Statement Credit column, there is a net loss.

4 Write the words Net income (or Net loss) in the Account Title column.

5 Enter the net income figure under the Income Statement Debit column and the Balance Sheet Credit column. If a net loss exists, the net loss figure is entered under the Income Statement Credit column and the Balance Sheet Debit column.

6 Retotal the Income Statement columns and the Balance Sheet columns as an arithmetic check.

7 Double rule the column totals.

Lakeside's completed work sheet is shown in Figure 9-5.

Review Quiz **9-3** The totals of the Income Statement columns and Balance Sheet columns of Massey Company's June 30 work sheet are as follows:

Income Statement		Balance Sheet	
Debit	**Credit**	**Debit**	**Credit**
$22,300	$40,400	$61,000	$42,900

Using a separate sheet of paper, balance the columns and state the amount of net income (or net loss) for the period.

Check your answers on page 441.

Figure 9-5
Completed Work Sheet

Lakeside Electronics
Work Sheet
For Year Ended December 31, 20X1

	Account Title	Trial Balance Debit	Trial Balance Credit	Adjustments Debit	Adjustments Credit	
1	Cash	6 200 00				1
2	Accounts Receivable	9 689 00				2
3	Merchandise Inventory	66 000 00		(b) 72 400 00	(a) 66 000 00	3
4	Store Supplies	2 015 00			(c) 1 515 00	4
5	Office Supplies	667 00			(d) 417 00	5
6	Prepaid Insurance	720 00			(e) 90 00	6
7	Store Equipment	11 385 00				7
8	Accumulated Depreciation—Store Equipment		4 500 00		(f) 900 00	8
9	Office Equipment	10 200 00				9
10	Accumulated Depreciation—Office Equipment		7 100 00		(g) 820 00	10
11	Delivery Equipment	56 000 00				11
12	Accumulated Depreciation—Delivery Equipment		13 800 00		(h) 9 200 00	12
13	Accounts Payable		14 025 00			13
14	Salaries Payable		—		(i) 1 600 00	14
15	Notes Payable		26 000 00			15
16	John Graham, Capital		75 581 00			16
17	John Graham, Drawing	18 000 00				17
18	Income Summary		—	(a) 66 000 00	(b) 72 400 00	18
19	Sales		304 600 00			19
20	Sales Returns and Allowances	5 230 00				20
21	Sales Discounts	3 461 00				21
22	Purchases	144 918 00				22
23	Purchases Returns and Allowances		6 692 00			23
24	Purchases Discounts		2 910 00			24
25	Freight In	1 160 00				25
26	Sales Salaries Expense	68 200 00		(i) 900 00		26
27	Advertising Expense	5 840 00				27
28	Store Supplies Expense	—		(c) 1 515 00		28
29	Depreciation Expense—Store Equipment	—		(f) 900 00		29
30	Miscellaneous Selling Expense	2 100 00				30
31	Rent Expense	5 700 00				31
32	Office Salaries Expense	30 453 00		(i) 700 00		32
33	Insurance Expense	—		(e) 90 00		33
34	Depreciation Expense—Office Equipment	—		(g) 820 00		34
35	Depreciation Expense—Delivery Equipment	—		(h) 9 200 00		35
36	Utilities Expense	6 240 00				36
37	Office Supplies Expense	—		(d) 417 00		37
38	Interest Expense	130 00				38
39	Miscellaneous General Expense	900 00				39
40		455 208 00	455 208 00	152 942 00	152 942 00	40
41	Net income					41
42						42

#	Adjusted Trial Balance Debit	Adjusted Trial Balance Credit	Income Statement Debit	Income Statement Credit	Balance Sheet Debit	Balance Sheet Credit	#
1	6 2 0 0 00				6 2 0 0 00		1
2	9 6 8 9 00				9 6 8 9 00		2
3	72 4 0 0 00				72 4 0 0 00		3
4	5 0 0 00				5 0 0 00		4
5	2 5 0 00				2 5 0 00		5
6	6 3 0 00				6 3 0 00		6
7	11 3 8 5 00				11 3 8 5 00		7
8		5 4 0 0 00				5 4 0 0 00	8
9	10 2 0 0 00				10 2 0 0 00		9
10		7 9 2 0 00				7 9 2 0 00	10
11	56 0 0 0 00				56 0 0 0 00		11
12		23 0 0 0 00				23 0 0 0 00	12
13		14 0 2 5 00				14 0 2 5 00	13
14		1 6 0 0 00				1 6 0 0 00	14
15		26 0 0 0 00				26 0 0 0 00	15
16		75 5 8 1 00				75 5 8 1 00	16
17	18 0 0 0 00				18 0 0 0 00		17
18	66 0 0 0 00	72 4 0 0 00	66 0 0 0 00	72 4 0 0 00			18
19		304 6 0 0 00		304 6 0 0 00			19
20	5 2 3 0 00		5 2 3 0 00				20
21	3 4 6 1 00		3 4 6 1 00				21
22	144 9 1 8 00		144 9 1 8 00				22
23		6 6 9 2 00		6 6 9 2 00			23
24		2 9 1 0 00		2 9 1 0 00			24
25	1 1 6 0 00		1 1 6 0 00				25
26	69 1 0 0 00		69 1 0 0 00				26
27	5 8 4 0 00		5 8 4 0 00				27
28	1 5 1 5 00		1 5 1 5 00				28
29	9 0 0 00		9 0 0 00				29
30	2 1 0 0 00		2 1 0 0 00				30
31	5 7 0 0 00		5 7 0 0 00				31
32	31 1 5 3 00		31 1 5 3 00				32
33	9 0 00		9 0 00				33
34	8 2 0 00		8 2 0 00				34
35	9 2 0 0 00		9 2 0 0 00				35
36	6 2 4 0 00		6 2 4 0 00				36
37	4 1 7 00		4 1 7 00				37
38	1 3 0 00		1 3 0 00				38
39	9 0 0 00		9 0 0 00				39
40	540 1 2 8 00	540 1 2 8 00	354 8 7 4 00	386 6 0 2 00	185 2 5 4 00	153 5 2 6 00	40
41			31 7 2 8 00			31 7 2 8 00	41
42			386 6 0 2 00	386 6 0 2 00	185 2 5 4 00	185 2 5 4 00	42

Mercury Finance Company Indicted in Accounting Fraud Scheme

The former treasurer of the now-defunct Mercury Finance Company was indicted for allegedly participating in a corporate accounting fraud scheme for slightly more than a year. The scheme ended about the same time that Mercury's stock collapsed in 1997. Bradley Vallem and others attempted to inflate and maintain the price of the company's common stock (common stock is similar to owner's capital but is used with a corporation) to obtain and maintain sufficient financing to fund Mercury's daily operations, thereby receiving personal benefits in the form of salaries, bonuses, and stock options.

Inflation of common stock value may increase salaries, bonuses, and stock options but can also cause the stock to collapse.

Vallem allegedly provided Mercury's outside auditors with a fraudulently altered list of Mercury's short-term debt in order to convince the auditors that the debt had genuinely been reduced by $30 million. He knew that this list did not reflect the $30 million that Mercury owed Mellon Bank. When the outside auditors uncovered the scheme, Vallem corrected the error in debt reporting but avoided reducing earnings by recording the $30 million in phony accounts receivable.

When Mercury's accounting fraud was discovered, shareholders lost nearly $2 billion in the market value (current market price) of its common stock.

Source: Patrick J. Fitzgerald, "Ex Mercury Accounting Treasurer Indicted in Accounting Fraud Scheme." U.S. Department of Justice, December 11, 2002.

For Discussion

1. What were the motives behind the Mercury Finance Company accounting fraud?
2. What parties are responsible for this accounting fraud?
3. Who are the stakeholders who lost in this accounting fraud?

Joining the Pieces

Procedures for Adjusting the Merchandise Inventory Account

Beginning inventory (January 1) = $66,000
Ending inventory (December 31) = $72,400

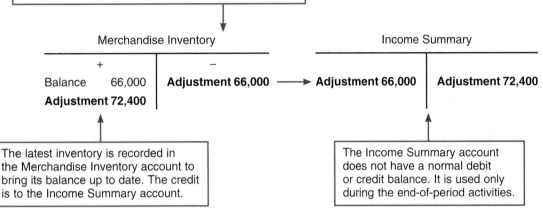

The Merchandise Inventory account must be reduced by the amount of the beginning inventory to make the account ready to record the ending inventory. The debit is to the Income Summary account

Merchandise Inventory			Income Summary	
+	−			
Balance 66,000	**Adjustment 66,000**	→	**Adjustment 66,000**	**Adjustment 72,400**
Adjustment 72,400				

The latest inventory is recorded in the Merchandise Inventory account to bring its balance up to date. The credit is to the Income Summary account.

The Income Summary account does not have a normal debit or credit balance. It is used only during the end-of-period activities.

Summary

Interactive Summary in English and Spanish

1 Make adjustments to the Merchandise Inventory account.

The Rose Bowl is a retail florist. On June 30, 20X1, the end of The Rose Bowl's accounting year, the **Merchandise Inventory account** had a balance of $46,000. However, a current count revealed that only $42,000 worth of merchandise remained on hand. The adjustment for merchandise is shown in T-account form as follows:

Merchandise Inventory		Income Summary	
Balance 46,000	**Adjustment 46,000**	**Adjustment 46,000**	**Adjustment 42,000**
Adjustment 42,000			

2 Make other needed adjustments and complete a work sheet for a merchandising business.

The Rose Bowl's June 30, 20X1, trial balance is shown in Figure 9-6.

In addition to the merchandise inventory adjustment presented in the preceding section, The Rose Bowl had the following adjustment data on June 30:

- A current count revealed that $400 worth of store supplies were on hand.
- Estimated depreciation on store equipment, $1,000.
- Estimated depreciation on trucks, $3,000.
- Accrued (unpaid) salaries, $400.

Using The Rose Bowl's trial balance and the above adjustment data, the work sheet shown in Figure 9-7 was prepared.

Figure 9-6

Trial Balance for
The Rose Bowl

Account Title	Debit	Credit
The Rose Bowl		
Trial Balance		
June 30, 20X1		
Cash	3 1 0 0 00	
Accounts Receivable	6 8 0 0 00	
Merchandise Inventory	46 0 0 0 00	
Store Supplies	6 0 0 00	
Store Equipment	25 0 0 0 00	
Accumulated Depreciation—Store Equipment		3 0 0 0 00
Trucks	38 0 0 0 00	
Accumulated Depreciation—Trucks		7 0 0 0 00
Accounts Payable		4 9 0 0 00
Sales Tax Payable		1 1 0 0 00
Salaries Payable		—
Rosemarie Hubley, Capital		83 5 0 0 00
Rosemarie Hubley, Drawing	25 0 0 0 00	
Income Summary	—	—
Sales		177 1 9 0 00
Sales Returns and Allowances	8 0 0 00	
Purchases	77 8 0 0 00	
Purchases Returns and Allowances		1 2 0 0 00
Purchases Discounts		6 0 0 00
Sales Salaries Expense	32 0 0 0 00	
Advertising Expense	4 8 0 0 00	
Depreciation Expense—Store Equipment	—	
Miscellaneous Selling Expense	8 0 0 00	
Store Supplies Expense	—	
Rent Expense	4 8 9 0 00	
Repairs Expense	6 0 0 00	
Transportation Expense	9 0 0 00	
Depreciation Expense—Trucks	—	
Utilities Expense	9 6 0 0 00	
Miscellaneous General Expense	1 8 0 0 00	
Totals	278 4 9 0 00	278 4 9 0 00

Figure 9-7
Work Sheet

The Rose Bowl
Work Sheet
For Year Ended June 30, 20X1

#	Account Title	Trial Balance Debit	Trial Balance Credit	Adjustments Debit	Adjustments Credit	Adjusted Trial Balance Debit	Adjusted Trial Balance Credit	Income Statement Debit	Income Statement Credit	Balance Sheet Debit	Balance Sheet Credit
1	Cash	3 1 00 00				3 1 00 00				3 1 00 00	
2	Accounts Receivable	6 8 00 00				6 8 00 00				6 8 00 00	
3	Merchandise Inventory	46 0 00 00		(b)42 0 00 00	(a)46 0 00 00	42 0 00 00				42 0 00 00	
4	Store Supplies	6 00 00			(c)2 00 00	4 00 00				4 00 00	
5	Store Equipment	25 0 00 00				25 0 00 00				25 0 00 00	
6	Acc. Depr.—Store Equip.		3 00 00		(d)1 00 00		4 00 00				4 00 00
7	Trucks	38 0 00 00				38 0 00 00				38 0 00 00	
8	Acc. Depr.—Trucks		7 00 00		(e)3 00 00		10 0 00 00				10 0 00 00
9	Accounts Payable		4 9 00 00				4 9 00 00				4 9 00 00
10	Sales Tax Payable		1 1 00 00				1 1 00 00				1 1 00 00
11	Salaries Payable		—		(f) 4 00 00		4 00 00				4 00 00
12	Rosemarie Hubley, Capital		83 5 00 00				83 5 00 00				83 5 00 00
13	Rosemarie Hubley, Drawing	25 0 00 00	—			25 0 00 00				25 0 00 00	
14	Income Summary			(a)46 0 00 00	(b)42 0 00 00	46 0 00 00	42 0 00 00	46 0 00 00	42 0 00 00		
15	Sales		177 1 90 00				177 1 90 00		177 1 90 00		
16	Sales Ret. and Allow.	8 00 00				8 00 00		8 00 00			
17	Purchases	77 8 00 00				77 8 00 00		77 8 00 00			
18	Purch. Ret. and Allow.		1 2 00 00				1 2 00 00		1 2 00 00		
19	Purchases Discounts		6 00 00				6 00 00		6 00 00		
20	Sales Salaries Expense	32 0 00 00		(f) 4 00 00		32 4 00 00		32 4 00 00			
21	Advertising Expense	4 8 00 00				4 8 00 00		4 8 00 00			
22	Depr. Exp.—Store Equip.			(d)1 00 00		1 00 00		1 00 00			
23	Misc. Selling Expense	8 00 00				8 00 00		8 00 00			
24	Store Supplies Expense			(c) 2 00 00		2 00 00		2 00 00			
25	Rent Expense	4 8 90 00				4 8 90 00		4 8 90 00			
26	Repairs Expense	6 00 00				6 00 00		6 00 00			
27	Transportation Expense	9 00 00				9 00 00		9 00 00			
28	Depr. Exp.—Trucks			(e)3 00 00		3 00 00		3 00 00			
29	Utilities Expense	9 6 00 00				9 6 00 00		9 6 00 00			
30	Misc. General Expense	1 8 00 00				1 8 00 00		1 8 00 00			
31		278 4 90 00	278 4 90 00	92 6 00 00	92 6 00 00	324 8 90 00	324 8 90 00	184 5 90 00	220 9 90 00	140 3 00 00	103 9 00 00
32	Net Income							36 4 00 00			36 4 00 00
33								220 9 90 00	220 9 90 00	140 3 00 00	140 3 00 00

Terms and Concepts Review

- Key Terms and Definitions in English and Spanish
- Additional Quiz Questions

Key Terms

accrued salaries, 415
beginning merchandise inventory, 410
ending merchandise inventory, 410

inventory, 410
Merchandise Inventory account, 410

Concepts Review

1. Why are adjustments needed?
2. The Purchases account shows only the cost of merchandise purchased—not what is on hand at the end of the accounting period. Explain.
3. Why is it necessary to adjust the Merchandise Inventory account at the end of an accounting period?
4. For which merchandise inventory—beginning or ending—is the Income Summary account debited? For which is it credited?
5. If the Supplies account shows a balance of $850 before adjustment and $300 is calculated to be on hand, what is (a) the amount of the adjustment for supplies used, (b) the amount of supplies expense to be reported on the income statement, and (c) the amount of supplies to be reported on the balance sheet?
6. What type of account is the Accumulated Depreciation account?
7. If salaries are paid weekly, payday is Friday, and the accounting period ends on a Wednesday, how many days' salary are accrued at the end of that accounting period?
8. Identify the column on the work sheet to which you extend the following amounts from the adjusted trial balance column:
   (a) assets, (b) contra assets, (c) liabilities, (d) revenue, (e) expenses.
9. How do adjustments for a merchandising business differ from those for a service business?

Skills Review

Quick Practice

Learning Objective 2

Check Figure
Store Supplies Expense
$1,065 (debit)

Quick Practice 9-1

Objective: To calculate the amount of supplies used

Samantha Hopf owns a retail store called Hopfs n' Brew. On January 1, 20XX, her Store Supplies account had a balance of $520. On April 15, $395 of store supplies were purchased. On December 5, $425 of store supplies were purchased. An inventory count on December 31 revealed that $275 of store supplies remain on hand.

Directions: Prepare the December 31, 20XX, adjusting entry for store supplies used.

Learning Objective 2

Check Figure
Insurance Expense $1,815
(debit)

Quick Practice 9-2

Objective: To calculate the amount of expired insurance

On February 1, 20XX, Daniel Odds n' Ends purchased a 2-year insurance policy for $3,960.

Directions: Prepare the December 31, 20XX, adjusting entry for insurance expired.

Quick Practice 9-3

Objective: To calculate the amount of the adjustment for accrued salaries

Stango Company has a five-day workweek and pays salaries of $65,000 on Monday for the preceding week.

Directions: Assuming Stango ends its accounting period on December 31, 20XX, prepare the adjusting entry for accrued salaries if that day falls on (a) Wednesday or (b) Thursday.

Quick Practice 9-4

Objective: To prepare the adjusting entry for depreciation of store equipment

On January 1, 20X7, store equipment was purchased for $44,000. The estimated life of the store equipment is six years, and the estimated trade-in value is $2,000. Thus, yearly depreciation will be $7,000.

Directions: Prepare the adjusting entry for depreciation expense for the year ending December 31, 20X7.

Learning Objective **1**

Check Figure
Dec. 31 Merchandise
Inventory $98,000 (debit);
Income Summary $98,000
(credit)

Quick Practice 9-5

Objective: To adjust the Merchandise Inventory account

Frank Company had a beginning merchandise inventory of $92,000 and an ending merchandise inventory of $98,000 for the year ended December 31, 20X1.

Directions: Prepare adjusting entries to update the Merchandise Inventory account.

Quick Practice 9-6

Objective: To record beginning and ending merchandise inventories on the work sheet

Swan Company had a beginning merchandise inventory of $53,000 and an ending merchandise inventory of $62,000 for the year ended December 31, 20XX.

Directions: Record the adjustments for the beginning and ending merchandise inventories on Swan Company's December 31, 20XX, work sheet. Use the letter (a) for the beginning merchandise inventory and the letter (b) for the ending merchandise inventory.

CHAPTER 9 REVIEW, PRACTICE, AND APPLY

Quick Practice 9-7

Objective: To record adjustments on a work sheet

Wray Company's partial worksheet for the year ended December 31, 20XX, is as follows:

Wray Company
Work Sheet (Partial)
For Year Ended December 31, 20XX

	Account Title	Trial Balance Debit	Trial Balance Credit	Adjustments Debit	Adjustments Credit	Adjusted Trial Balance Debit	Adjusted Trial Balance Credit	
3	Merchandise Inventory	36 0 0 0 00						3
4	Store Supplies	9 3 0 00						4
5	Office Supplies	6 1 0 00						5
6	Prepaid Insurance	1 6 0 0 00						6
7	Store Equipment	20 0 0 0 00						7
8	Accum. Depr.—Store Equipment		4 0 0 0 00					8
11	Salaries Payable							11
14	Income Summary							14
20	Sales Salaries Expense	18 0 0 0 00						20
21	Store Supplies Expense							21
22	Office Supplies Expense							22
23	Insurance Expense							23
24	Depr. Ex.—Store Equipment							24

Adjustment data:

(a) Beginning merchandise inventory, $36,000.
(b) Ending merchandise inventory, $33,000.
(c) Store supplies on hand, $355.
(d) Office supplies on hand, $270.
(e) Insurance expired, $1,200.
(f) Depreciation of store equipment, $1,000.
(g) Accrued salaries as of December 31, $900.

Directions: Enter the adjustments on the work sheet, identifying each adjustment by letter, and extend to the Adjusted Trial Balance columns.

Quick Practice 9-8

Objective: To identify work sheet columns

Directions: For each account listed, indicate whether it is extended to the (a) Income Statement Debit column, (b) Income Statement Credit column, (c) Balance Sheet Debit column, or (d) Balance Sheet Credit column.

1. Merchandise Inventory (ending)
2. Prepaid Insurance
3. Store Equipment
4. Accumulated Depreciation—Store Equipment
5. Salaries Payable

6. Sales
7. Sales Returns and Allowances
8. Purchases
9. Purchases Returns and Allowances
10. Freight In

Learning Objective **2**

Check Figure
Step 1 (d)

Quick Practice 9-9

Objective: To complete a work sheet

Directions: Arrange the steps in the proper order of how a work sheet should be completed after all accounts have been extended to the Income Statement and Balance Sheet columns.

(a) Determine the amount of net income (or net loss) by finding the difference between the Income Statement Credit column and the Income Statement Debit column.
(b) Write the words *Net Income* (or *Net Loss*) in the account title column.
(c) Double-rule the column totals.
(d) Total the Income Statement Debit and Credit columns.
(e) Enter the net income figure under the Income Statement Debit column and the Balance Sheet Credit column. If a net loss exists, the net loss figure is entered under the Income Statement Credit column and the Balance Sheet Debit column.
(f) Total the Balance Sheet Debit and Credit columns.
(g) Retotal the Income Statement columns and the Balance Sheet columns as an arithmetic check.

Exercises

Learning Objective **2**

Check Figure
(1) Expense for 20XX = $300

Exercise 9-1

Objective: To calculate the amount of expired insurance

Directions: Information about three insurance policies follows. Complete the table shown here and reproduced in your working papers. All policies were purchased on March 1, 20XX. It is now December 31, 20XX.

Policy Number	Premium	Term (Years)	Monthly Expiration	Expense for 20XX
(1)	$ 360	1	$_____	$_____
(2)	1,440	3	$_____	$_____
(3)	2,160	2	$_____	$_____

Learning Objective **2**

Check Figure
(a) $60,400

Exercise 9-2

Objective: To calculate the amount of the adjustment for accrued salaries

Directions: Paschal Company pays salaries of $151,000 on Monday for the preceding week. Calculate the amount of the adjustment for accrued salaries on December 31 if that day falls on (a) Tuesday, (b) Thursday, and (c) Friday. Assume a five-day workweek and the accounting period ending on December 31.

Learning Objective **2**

Check Figure
(a) Store supplies used = $820

Exercise 9-3

Objective: To record adjustments in T accounts

Directions: In separate pairs of T accounts, record each of the following adjustments. When beginning balances are given, insert them in the proper T accounts before making the adjustments.

(a) The Supplies account shows a balance of $1,290 prior to adjustment. Supplies of $470 are on hand.

(b) The Prepaid Insurance account shows a balance of $900 prior to adjustment. Of this amount, $300 has expired.

(c) Accrued salaries amount to $575.

(d) Depreciation of office equipment is $1,075.

Learning Objectives 1, 2

Check Figure
(b) Store Supplies used =
$56,040
(f) Accrued Salaries =
$36,000

Exercise 9-4

Objective: To record adjustments in T accounts

Directions: In separate pairs of T accounts, record each of the following adjustments. When beginning balances are given, insert them in the proper T accounts before making the adjustments.

(a) Merchandise inventory (beginning), January 1, $48,000.
Merchandise inventory (ending), December 31, $51,510.

(b) Store supplies on hand, $16,410; balance of Store Supplies account prior to adjustment, $72,450.

(c) Office supplies on hand, $3,125; balance of Office Supplies account prior to adjustment, $21,355.

(d) Insurance expired, $1,000.

(e) Depreciation of office equipment, $35,000.

(f) Weekly salaries of $60,000 (assume 5-day work week), unpaid for three days.

Learning Objective 2

Check Figure
1. (b)
3. (d)
9. (a)

Exercise 9-5

Objective: To identify work sheet columns

Directions: For each account listed, indicate whether it is extended to the (a) Income Statement Debit column; (b) Income Statement Credit column; (c) Balance Sheet Debit column; or (d) Balance Sheet Credit column.

1. Purchases Returns and Allowances
2. Accumulated Depreciation—Office Equipment
3. Accounts Payable
4. Sales Discounts
5. Owner, Drawing
6. Rent Expense
7. Prepaid Insurance
8. Merchandise Inventory (ending)
9. Freight In
10. Accounts Receivable
11. Owner, Capital
12. Purchases

Learning Objectives 1, 2

Check Figure
Net Loss = $12

Exercise 9-6

Objective: To prepare a work sheet

Directions: The December 31, 20XX, trial balance of Vitacco Company is shown on the next page. Using the adjustment data that are also listed, prepare a work sheet. The amounts are small so that you can concentrate on how to prepare a work sheet without arithmetic getting in the way.

Vitacco Company
Trial Balance
December 31, 20XX

Account Title	Debit	Credit
Cash	9 00	
Accounts Receivable	4 00	
Merchandise Inventory	10 00	
Supplies	7 00	
Prepaid Insurance	3 00	
Equipment	15 00	
Accumulated Depreciation—Equipment		6 00
Accounts Payable		4 00
Salaries Payable		—
Jack Vitacco, Capital		40 00
Jack Vitacco, Drawing	4 00	
Income Summary	—	—
Sales		38 00
Sales Returns and Allowances	2 00	
Purchases	20 00	
Purchases Returns and Allowances		1 00
Rent Expense	3 00	
Salaries Expense	10 00	
Supplies Expense	—	
Insurance Expense	—	
Depreciation Expense—Equipment	—	
Miscellaneous Expense	2 00	
Totals	89 00	89 00

Adjustment data:

(a) and (b) Merchandise inventory at December 31, $8.
  (c) Supplies on hand, $2.
  (d) Insurance expired, $1.
  (e) Accrued salaries, $3.
  (f) Depreciation of equipment, $3.

Case Problems

Group A

Learning Objective **2**

Check Figure
(a) $16,530

Problem 9-1A

Objective: To calculate amounts of adjustments

Directions: In each of the following situations, calculate the amount of the adjustment needed as of December 31, the end of the current accounting period.

(a) The Office Supplies account shows a balance of $7,295 on January 1 and a purchase of $16,755 on July 1. The December 31 inventory is $7,520.

(b) The Store Supplies account shows a balance of $11,475 on January 1 and purchases of $35,640 and $19,570 during the year. The December 31 inventory is $5,775.

(c) The Prepaid Insurance account shows a debit balance of $3,240, representing a 3-year premium paid on March 1 of the current year.

(d) Salaries of $72,000 are paid weekly on Monday for the preceding 5-day work week. This year, December 31 fell on a Tuesday.

Learning Objectives 1, 2

Check Figure
Balance of Office Supplies
Expense account = $21,480

Problem 9-2A

Objective: To record adjustments in T accounts

Directions: In each of the following unrelated transactions, record in T accounts opening balances, purchases, and adjustments as of December 31 of the current year.

(a) Merchandise inventory (beginning) on January 1 was $91,645. Merchandise inventory (ending) on December 31 is $87,365.

(b) The Office Supplies account shows a January 1 balance of $8,145, a July 1 purchase of $17,510, and a December 31 inventory of $4,175.

(c) The Store Supplies account shows a January 1 balance of $7,250, a March 1 purchase of $15,595, and a December 31 inventory of $8,165.

(d) The Prepaid Insurance account shows a payment for a 2-year policy on October 1 of this year in the amount of $1,800.

(e) Salaries of $18,000 are paid weekly on Monday for the preceding 5-day work week. This year, December 31 fell on a Tuesday.

(f) Depreciation expense on office equipment is $15,000.

Learning Objectives 1, 2

Check Figure
Net Income = $34,580

Problem 9-3A

Objective: To prepare a work sheet

Account balances and adjustment data for Moreira Carpet Shop follow:

Account	Balance
Cash	$ 6,725
Accounts Receivable	9,450
Merchandise Inventory (January 1)	13,165
Office Supplies	16,210
Store Supplies	14,575
Prepaid Insurance	2,400
Office Equipment	36,000
Accumulated Depreciation—Office Equipment	9,000
Store Equipment	84,000
Accumulated Depreciation—Store Equipment	25,200
Delivery Equipment	27,000
Accumulated Depreciation—Delivery Equipment	13,500
Accounts Payable	16,510
Salaries Payable	—
Joyce Moreira, Capital	88,220
Joyce Moreira, Drawing	24,000
Income Summary	—
Sales	469,600
Sales Returns and Allowances	21,540
Sales Discounts	9,310
Purchases	301,240
Purchases Returns and Allowances	19,565
Purchases Discounts	6,110
Freight In	14,590
Sales Salaries Expense	30,000
Store Supplies Expense	—
Advertising Expense	4,500
Depreciation Expense—Store Equipment	—
Depreciation Expense—Delivery Equipment	—
Rent Expense	12,000

Account	Balance
Office Salaries Expense	$ 15,000
Office Supplies Expense	—
Utilities Expense	6,000
Insurance Expense	—
Depreciation Expense—Office Equipment	—

Adjustment data:

(a) and (b) Merchandise inventory, December 31, $13,410.
   (c) Office supplies on hand, $2,190.
   (d) Store supplies on hand, $4,175.
   (e) Insurance expired, $800.
   (f) Salaries accrued: office, $180; sales, $360.
   (g) Depreciation of office equipment, $3,600.
   (h) Depreciation of store equipment, $8,400.
   (i) Depreciation of delivery equipment, $9,000.

Directions: Prepare a work sheet for the year ended December 31, 20X1.

Learning Objectives **1, 2**

Check Figure
Net Income = $18,297

Problem 9-4A

Objective: To prepare a work sheet

The June 30, 20X2 trial balance of Sandersville Technical Products Co. follows:

Sandersville Technical Products Co. Trial Balance June 30, 20X2		
Account Title	**Debit**	**Credit**
Cash	3 0 0 0 00	
Accounts Receivable	8 4 0 0 00	
Merchandise Inventory (July 1)	38 9 0 0 00	
Store Supplies	1 5 4 0 00	
Office Supplies	1 3 6 0 00	
Prepaid Insurance	1 8 0 0 00	
Store Equipment	11 0 9 5 00	
Accumulated Depreciation—Store Equipment		2 6 5 0 00
Office Equipment	10 5 0 0 00	
Accumulated Depreciation—Office Equipment		4 5 6 0 00
Delivery Equipment	47 8 0 0 00	
Accumulated Depreciation—Delivery Equipment		12 3 0 0 00
Building	85 7 0 0 00	
Accumulated Depreciation—Building		18 3 5 0 00
Land	38 8 0 0 00	
Accounts Payable		7 4 0 0 00
Salaries Payable		—
Notes Payable		42 0 0 0 00
Bob Lawson, Capital		150 3 0 3 00
Bob Lawson, Drawing	25 0 0 0 00	
Income Summary	—	—
Sales		202 5 0 0 00
Sales Returns and Allowances	3 5 9 0 00	
Sales Discounts	1 7 0 0 00	
Purchases	71 4 0 0 00	

Chapter 9 | Work Sheet and Adjustments for a Merchandising Business **435**

Purchases Returns and Allowances				2 4 5 0 00
Purchases Discounts				4 6 7 9 00
Sales Salaries Expense	38 0 0 0 00			
Advertising Expense	8 9 8 0 00			
Depreciation Expense—Store Equipment				
Store Supplies Expense				
Miscellaneous Selling Expense	1 2 1 5 00			
Office Salaries Expense	26 7 0 0 00			
Delivery Expense	7 8 4 0 00			
Utilities Expense	8 9 0 0 00			
Depreciation Expense—Office Equipment				
Depreciation Expense—Delivery Equipment				
Depreciation Expense—Building				
Repairs Expense	3 5 6 0 00			
Office Supplies Expense				
Insurance Expense				
Miscellaneous General Expense	1 4 1 2 00			
Totals	447 1 9 2 00		447 1 9 2 00	

Directions: Prepare a work sheet for the year ended June 30, 20X2. Use the following adjustment data:

(a) and (b) Merchandise inventory, June 30, 20X2, $36,710.
(c) Store supplies on hand, $455.
(d) Office supplies on hand, $915.
(e) Insurance expired, $875.
(f) Depreciation of store equipment, $2,400.
(g) Depreciation of office equipment, $2,000.
(h) Depreciation of delivery equipment, $4,000.
(i) Depreciation of building, $3,000.
(j) Accrued salaries: sales, $1,230; office, $810.

Group B

Learning Objective **2**

Check Figure
(a) $16,065

Problem 9-1B

Objective: To calculate amounts of adjustments

Directions: In each of the following situations, calculate the amount of the adjustment needed as of December 31, the end of the current accounting period.

(a) The Office Supplies account shows a balance of $5,575 on January 1 and a purchase of $17,210 on March 1. The December 31 inventory is $6,720.
(b) The Store Supplies account shows a balance of $12,675 on January 1 and purchases of $18,220 and $11,505 during the year. The December 31 inventory is $7,145.
(c) The Prepaid Insurance account shows a debit balance of $1,920, representing a 2-year premium paid on June 1 of the current year.
(d) Salaries of $80,000 are paid weekly on Monday for the preceding 5-day work week. This year, December 31 fell on a Thursday.

Problem 9-2B

Objective: To record adjustments in T accounts

Directions: In each of the following unrelated transactions, record in T accounts opening balances, purchases, and adjustments as of December 31 of the current year.

(a) Merchandise inventory (beginning) on January 1 was $85,240.
Merchandise inventory (ending) on December 31 is $89,610.

(b) The Office Supplies account shows a January 1 balance of $5,370, an October 1 purchase of $17,210, and a December 31 inventory of $2,945.

(c) The Store Supplies account shows a January 1 balance of $15,175, a March 18 purchase of $28,410, and a December 31 inventory of $17,555.

(d) The Prepaid Insurance account shows a payment for a three-year policy on June 1 of this year in the amount of $7,200.

(e) Salaries of $36,000 are paid weekly on Monday for the preceding 5-day work week. This year, December 31 fell on a Monday.

(f) Depreciation expense on store equipment is $50,000.

Problem 9-3B

Objective: To prepare a work sheet

Account balances and adjustment data for Wright's Variety Store follow.

Account	Balance
Cash	$ 9,165
Accounts Receivable	15,210
Merchandise Inventory (January 1)	27,895
Office Supplies	12,910
Store Supplies	16,805
Prepaid Insurance	3,600
Office Equipment	54,000
Accumulated Depreciation—Office Equipment	10,800
Store Equipment	72,000
Accumulated Depreciation—Store Equipment	21,600
Delivery Equipment	20,000
Accumulated Depreciation—Delivery Equipment	8,000
Accounts Payable	19,575
Salaries Payable	—
Betty Wright, Capital	121,045
Betty Wright, Drawing	9,600
Income Summary	—
Sales	421,000
Sales Returns and Allowances	15,210
Sales Discounts	7,900
Purchases	270,000
Purchases Returns and Allowances	13,975
Purchases Discounts	5,100
Freight In	4,100
Sales Salaries Expense	26,000
Store Supplies Expense	—
Advertising Expense	4,700
Depreciation Expense—Store Equipment	—
Depreciation Expense—Delivery Equipment	—
Rent Expense	12,000
Office Salaries Expense	32,000
Office Supplies Expense	—
Utilities Expense	8,000
Insurance Expense	—
Depreciation Expense—Office Equipment	—

Adjustment data:

(a) and (b) Merchandise inventory, December 31, $32,455.
  (c) Office supplies on hand, $3,750.
  (d) Store supplies on hand, $3,557.
  (e) Insurance expired, $1,200.
  (f) Salaries accrued: office, $350; sales, $300.
  (g) Depreciation of office equipment, $5,400.
  (h) Depreciation of store equipment, $7,200.
  (i) Depreciation of delivery equipment, $4,000.

Directions: Prepare a work sheet for the year ended December 31, 20X1.

Learning Objectives **1, 2**

Check Figure
Net Income = $60,053

Problem 9-4B

Objective: To prepare a work sheet

The December 31, 20X4, trial balance of Stouder Company follows:

Stouder Company
Trial Balance
December 31, 20X4

Account Title	Debit	Credit
Cash	4 0 0 0 00	
Accounts Receivable	9 2 0 0 00	
Merchandise Inventory (January 1)	41 3 0 0 00	
Store Supplies	1 4 5 6 00	
Office Supplies	1 2 8 0 00	
Prepaid Insurance	2 5 8 0 00	
Store Equipment	12 4 9 5 00	
Accumulated Depreciation—Store Equipment		3 2 1 6 00
Office Equipment	11 3 4 8 00	
Accumulated Depreciation—Office Equipment		3 8 9 0 00
Delivery Equipment	42 3 0 0 00	
Accumulated Depreciation—Delivery Equipment		5 1 2 0 00
Building	84 6 0 0 00	
Accumulated Depreciation—Building		16 9 0 0 00
Land	15 6 0 0 00	
Accounts Payable		8 3 0 0 00
Salaries Payable		—
Notes Payable		38 0 0 0 00
Sally Stouder, Capital		92 3 0 4 00
Sally Stouder, Drawing	28 0 0 0 00	
Income Summary	—	—
Sales		279 8 0 0 00
Sales Returns and Allowances	3 8 9 0 00	
Sales Discounts	2 3 4 5 00	
Purchases	90 8 0 0 00	
Purchases Returns and Allowances		2 5 6 0 00
Purchases Discounts		4 2 3 0 00
Sales Salaries Expense	49 5 0 0 00	
Advertising Expense	9 4 5 0 00	
Depreciation Expense—Store Equipment	—	
Store Supplies Expense	—	

Miscellaneous Selling Expense				1	4	5	6	00													
Office Salaries Expense			24	6	9	0	00														
Delivery Expense			6	7	8	5	00														
Utilities Expense			8	6	5	5	00														
Depreciation Expense—Office Equipment					—																
Depreciation Expense—Delivery Equipment					—																
Depreciation Expense—Building					—																
Repairs Expense			1	3	5	5	00														
Office Supplies Expense					—																
Insurance Expense					—																
Miscellaneous General Expense			1	2	3	5	00														
Totals	454	3	2	0	00	454	3	2	0	00											

Directions: Prepare a work sheet for the year ended December 31, 20X4. Use the following adjustment data:

(a) and (b) Merchandise inventory, December 31, 20X4, $33,500.
     (c) Store supplies on hand, $410.
     (d) Office supplies on hand, $945.
     (e) Insurance expired, $1,450.
     (f) Depreciation of store equipment, $2,200.
     (g) Depreciation of office equipment, $1,890.
     (h) Depreciation of delivery equipment, $4,800.
     (i) Depreciation of building, $3,800.
     (j) Accrued salaries: sales, $1,840; office, $1,215.

Critical Thinking Problems

Challenge Problem

Peterson's Apparel Shop's accounts follow in alphabetical order. Also shown are the adjustment data. Missing from the list are the accounts needed for adjusting entries.

Account	Balance
Accounts Payable	$ 37,300
Accounts Receivable	21,545
Accumulated Depreciation—Office Equipment	16,000
Accumulated Depreciation—Store Equipment	16,800
Advertising Expense	2,940
Laura Peterson, Capital	71,535
Laura Peterson, Drawing	15,200
Cash	11,110
Freight In	9,125
Merchandise Inventory (January 1)	19,465
Office Equipment	42,000
Office Salaries Expense	37,600
Office Supplies	8,420
Prepaid Insurance	1,620
Purchases	252,300
Purchases Discounts	5,100
Purchases Returns and Allowances	12,300
Rent Expense	14,000
Sales	412,700
Sales Discounts	8,100

Account	Balance
Sales Returns and Allowances	$ 15,700
Sales Salaries Expense	41,200
Store Equipment	56,000
Store Supplies	11,710
Utilities Expense	3,700

Adjustment data:

(a) and (b) Merchandise inventory, December 31, $18,340.

        (c) Office supplies on hand, $1,075.

        (d) Store supplies on hand, $3,975.

        (e) Insurance expired: the balance in the Prepaid Insurance account represents the premium paid on August 1, 20X1, for a 3-year policy.

        (f) Accrued salaries: sales, $550; office, $490.

        (g) Depreciation of office equipment, $4,000.

        (h) Depreciation of store equipment, 10% of cost.

Directions:

1. Arrange accounts in the proper order, and prepare a trial balance. Be sure to add the additional accounts that you will need in the proper place.
2. Complete a work sheet for the year ended December 31, 20X1.

Communications

Linda Marti is the chief accountant at Asher Company. When training a new employee to make adjustments, Linda was asked why it is necessary to adjust the Merchandise Inventory account for the value of the latest inventory. The employee reasoned that since all purchases of merchandise are recorded in the Purchases account, the balance of the Purchases account would show the cost of merchandise on hand at the end of the accounting period.

Write a note to Linda explaining why and how the Merchandise Inventory account shows the cost of merchandise on hand at the end of the accounting period.

Team Internet Project

Large-scale merchandising businesses report sales in many different categories. Choose a large national merchandiser, and search the Internet to find the different categories of revenue that are reported for a store in the chain.

Ethics

Wes Tucker is the accounting supervisor at Albany Products. Among his responsibilities are preparation of adjustments, completion of the work sheet, and preparation of financial statements. You are a new accounting clerk who is working along with Wes. As you look over Wes's adjusting entries, you notice that there is no adjustment for unpaid salaries. You ask Wes about this, and he replies, "Since salaries will be paid next week, why bother? Besides, with less expense, our profit will be higher, and since our firm shares profits with employees, we will all be better off." Write a memo to Wes explaining that he is following an unethical practice.

Following are some data from the income statements (statements of operations) of Target Corporation for the years 2004, 2005, and 2006. Amounts are in millions.

	2006	2005	2004
Statements of Operations			
Sales	$59,490	$51,271	$45,682
Cost of sales	39,999	34,927	31,445
Operating expenses	12,819	11,185	9,797
Net earnings	2,787	2,408	3,198

Based on the statements of operations data for Target, answer the following questions:

(a) What is the amount and direction of the change in net earnings from 2004 to 2005?
(b) What is the amount and direction of the change in net earnings from 2005 to 2006?
(c) How might you explain the large difference in your answers to parts (a) and (b)?

Answers to Review Quizzes

Review Quiz 9-1

Merchandise Inventory				Income Summary	
Balance 94,000	(a) Adjustment 94,000		(a) Adjustment 94,000	(b) Adjustment 97,000
(b) Adjustment 97,000					

Review Quiz 9-2

1			Adjusting Entries			1
2	20XX Dec.	31	Income Summary	24 3 00 00		2
3			Merchandise Inventory		24 3 00 00	3
4		31	Merchandise Inventory	25 6 00 00		4
5			Income Summary		25 6 00 00	5
6		31	Store Supplies Expense	3 50 00		6
7			Store Supplies		3 50 00	7
8		31	Insurance Expense	2 00 00		8
9			Prepaid Insurance		2 00 00	9
10		31	Salaries Expense	2 3 00 00		10
11			Salaries Payable		2 3 00 00	11

Review Quiz 9-3

	Income Statement		Balance Sheet	
	Debit	**Credit**	**Debit**	**Credit**
	$22,300	$40,400	$61,000	$42,900
Net Income	18,100			18,100
	$40,400	$40,400	$61,000	$61,000

D

Merchandise Inventory Adjustment and Work Sheet Using the Perpetual Inventory System

Learning Objectives

1 Make adjusting entries to record inventory shortages or overages.
2 Prepare a work sheet for a company using the perpetual inventory system.

Merchandise Inventory Adjustment

Learning Objective

1 Make adjusting entries to record inventory shortages or overages.

We learned in Appendix C that under the perpetual inventory system, individual inventory records are maintained for all items a business sells. When new merchandise is purchased, the inventory records are increased. When merchandise is sold, the inventory records are decreased. Thus, the business always (perpetually) knows how much inventory *should* be on hand. However, the system is not error proof and does not eliminate the need for taking periodic physical inventory counts. Usually once a year, businesses will take a physical inventory and compare the actual count of merchandise against the perpetual records. Through this comparison, any errors or loss of merchandise due to theft and breakage can be detected. For example, if merchandise has been shoplifted, the perpetual records will show that the item is still on hand (because no sale has been made). A physical inventory would compare the actual count of the items in stock against the perpetual inventory record, and the shortage would be discovered.

Inventory Short and Over account an account used to record differences between the inventory value shown in the perpetual records and the value determined by the period-end physical count; an account that does not have a normal debit or credit balance

If there is a difference between the physical count and the perpetual records, it is necessary to make an adjusting entry to correct the records. The **Inventory Short and Over account** is used to reconcile the perpetual records to the actual inventory count. For example, if at the end of 20X4, King Company's perpetual inventory records show an inventory value of $32,345 but a physical count shows that only $32,205 worth of merchandise is on hand, an inventory shortage of $140 exists. The following adjusting entry records the shortage:

		General Journal				Page 1	
	Date	Account Title	P.R.	Debit	Credit	
1	20X4 Dec. 31	Inventory Short and Over		1 4 0 00			1
2		Merchandise Inventory			1 4 0 00		2
3							3
4							4

no normal balance → (line 1)

– asset → (line 2)

In the case on the previous page, there was a shortage because the inventory on hand was less than that shown on the perpetual records. Inventory shortages are common. Overages, on the other hand, are far less common. When overages do occur, it is usually because of an error. If King Company's 20X4 inventory count shows that $32,400 worth of merchandise is on hand while the perpetual records show $32,345, there will be a $55 overage. This overage would be recorded as follows:

	General Journal					Page 1	
Date		Account Title	P.R.	Debit		Credit	
20X4							1
Dec. 31	Merchandise Inventory			5 5 00			1
	Inventory Short and Over					5 5 00	2
							3
							4

+ asset → 1 (pointing to Merchandise Inventory row)
no normal balance → 2 (pointing to Inventory Short and Over row)

The Inventory Short and Over account is like the Cash Short and Over account we studied in Chapter 6. If the account has a period-end debit balance (shortage), it is listed with other expenses on the income statement. If it has a credit balance (overage), it is listed with other revenue on the income statement.

Summing Up

The Inventory Short and Over account is used to bring the Merchandise Inventory account into agreement with the actual amount of merchandise on hand. This account works in a way that is similar to the Cash Short and Over account we used in Chapter 6 to bring the amount of cash in a cash register into agreement with the amount of sales rung up on the register.

Work Sheet for a Company Using the Perpetual Inventory System

In Chapter 9, we prepared a work sheet for a company using the periodic inventory system. We learned that the Merchandise Inventory account is adjusted to show the value of the latest inventory count. To review, the adjustment to update the Merchandise Inventory account using the periodic inventory system is:

Beginning inventory: Debit: Income Summary
                             Credit: Merchandise Inventory

Ending inventory: Debit: Merchandise Inventory
                             Credit: Income Summary

Under the perpetual inventory system, this adjustment is *not* needed because the inventory is updated each time goods are bought and sold. The only inventory adjustment needed is to record any shortages (or overages) in the Inventory Short and Over account (as we learned in the section above).

To illustrate a work sheet for a company using the perpetual inventory system, let's look at Figure D-1, which shows the December 31, 20X4, work sheet of King Company. Notice that the adjustment for merchandise inventory assumes a shortage of $140. Also notice that all other adjustments are the same as those we used in the periodic inventory system.

Figure D-1
Work Sheet of a Company Using the Perpetual Inventory System

King Company
Work Sheet
For Year Ended December 31, 20X4

#	Account Title	Trial Balance Debit	Trial Balance Credit	Adjustments Debit	Adjustments Credit	Adjusted Trial Balance Debit	Adjusted Trial Balance Credit	Income Statement Debit	Income Statement Credit	Balance Sheet Debit	Balance Sheet Credit
1	Cash	18 000 00				18 000 00				18 000 00	
2	Petty Cash	300 00				300 00				300 00	
3	Accounts Receivable	30 000 00				30 000 00				30 000 00	
4	Merchandise Inventory	32 345 00			(a) 1 40 00	32 205 00				32 205 00	
5	Store Supplies	6 200 00			(b) 2 900 00	3 300 00				3 300 00	
6	Office Supplies	3 800 00			(c) 1 400 00	2 400 00				2 400 00	
7	Prepaid Insurance	1 080 00			(d) 90 00	990 00				990 00	
8	Store Equipment	98 400 00				98 400 00				98 400 00	
9	Accum. Depr.—Store Equip.		14 760 00		(e) 4 920 00		19 680 00				19 680 00
10	Office Equipment	37 500 00				37 500 00				37 500 00	
11	Accum. Depr.—Office Equip.		7 500 00		(f) 2 500 00		10 000 00				10 000 00
12	Accounts Payable		12 600 00				12 600 00				12 600 00
13	Salaries Payable				(h) 1 800 00		1 800 00				1 800 00
14	Notes Payable		32 000 00				32 000 00				32 000 00
15	M.M. King, Capital		143 885 00				143 885 00				143 885 00
16	M.M. King, Drawing	25 000 00				25 000 00				25 000 00	
17	Sales		281 300 00				281 300 00		281 300 00		
18	Sales Returns and Allow.	2 800 00				2 800 00		2 800 00			
19	Sales Discounts	2 050 00				2 050 00		2 050 00			
20	Cost of Goods Sold	103 500 00				103 500 00		103 500 00			
21	Inventory Short and Over			(a) 1 40 00		1 40 00		1 40 00			
22	Sales Salaries Expense	58 000 00		(g) 1 100 00		59 100 00		59 100 00			
23	Advertising Expense	9 500 00				9 500 00		9 500 00			
24	Store Supplies Expense			(b) 2 900 00		2 900 00		2 900 00			
25	Depr. Exp.—Store Equip.			(e) 4 920 00		4 920 00		4 920 00			
26	Rent Expense	15 000 00				15 000 00		15 000 00			
27	Office Salaries Expense	31 000 00		(g) 7 00 00		31 700 00		31 700 00			
28	Depr. Expense—Office Equip.			(f) 2 500 00		2 500 00		2 500 00			
29	Utilities Expense	14 200 00				14 200 00		14 200 00			
30	Office Supplies Expense			(c) 1 400 00		1 400 00		1 400 00			
31	Insurance Expense			(d) 90 00		90 00		90 00			
32	Interest Expense	2 810 00				2 810 00		2 810 00			
33	Miscellaneous Expense	5 600 00				5 600 00		5 600 00			
34		492 045 00	492 045 00	13 750 00	13 750 00	501 265 00	501 265 00	253 170 00	281 300 00	248 095 00	219 965 00
35	Net Income							28 130 00			28 130 00
36								281 300 00	281 300 00	248 095 00	248 095 00

Summary

Interactive Summary in English and Spanish

1 Make adjusting entries to record inventory shortages or overages.

The perpetual inventory system is designed to track inventory coming into and going out of a business. However, the system is not error proof and a period-end physical inventory count is still needed to compare the actual amount of merchandise on hand with amounts shown on the inventory records. An account entitled **Inventory Short and Over** is used to reconcile the perpetual records with the actual account. For example, assume that Geneva Taylor, owner of the G.T. Shoppe, took a physical inventory count as of December 31, 20X5 and determined that $208,000 worth of inventory remained on hand. However, her perpetual inventory records show that $208,920 of merchandise should be on hand. As a result, her inventory is $920 short ($208,920 - $208,000). Geneva made the following adjusting entry to bring her perpetual inventory records into agreement with the actual amount of merchandise on hand:

In this entry, we recorded an inventory shortage, which common. Inventory

	General Journal							**Page 1**	
	Date		Account Title	P.R.	Debit		Credit		
1			Adjusting entries						1
2	20X5 Dec.	31	Inventory Short and Over		9 2 0 00				2
3			Merchandise Inventory				9 2 0 00		3
4									4

no normal balance → 2
– asset → 3

overages, on the other hand, are rare and usually result from error. To illustrate an overage, let's assume that Geneva's inventory count revealed that $208,200 worth of merchandise is on hand. Since her perpetual records show that $208,000 should be one hand, the inventory is over by $200. We can record the overage as follows:

The Inventory Short and Over account does not have a normal debit or credit

	General Journal							**Page 1**	
	Date		Account Title	P.R.	Debit		Credit		
1			Adjusting entries						1
2	20X5 Dec.	31	Merchandise Inventory		2 0 0 00				2
3			Inventory Short and Over				2 0 0 00		3
4									4

+ asset → 2
no normal balance → 3

balance and is similar to the Cash Short and Over account we used in Chapter 6 to reconcile the difference between the amount of cash in a cash register and the amount of sales rung up on the register.

2 Prepare a work sheet for a company using the perpetual inventory system.

With the exception of the Merchandise Inventory adjustment, the work sheet for a company using the perpetual inventory system is the same as that of one using the periodic inventory system. A work sheet for a company using the perpetual inventory system is illustrated on Page 445.

Key Terms

Inventory Short and Over account, 442

Skills Review

Exercises

Learning Objective **1**

Check Figure
Inventory Short and Over =
$148 (debit)

Exercise D-1

Objective: To record an inventory shortage

On December 31, 20X2, K Company's perpetual inventory records show that $93,458 worth of goods should be on hand. However, an inventory count shows that the actual value of goods on hand is $93, 310.

Directions: Make the adjusting entry to record the inventory shortage.

Learning Objective **1**

Check Figure
Inventory Short and Over =
$72 (credit)

Exercise D-2

Objective: To record an inventory overage

On June 30, 20XX, Blaylock Company's perpetual inventory records show that $55,700 worth of goods should be on hand. An inventory count reveals $55,772 worth of goods on hand. After the accuracy of the inventory count was verified, the company concluded that the overage could only have come from a recording error.

Directions: Make the adjusting entry to reconcile the perpetual inventory records with the physical count.

Exercise D-3

Objective: To prepare a work sheet using the perpetual inventory system

The April 30, 20X2, trial balance of Ingersol follows:

Ingersol Company Trial Balance April 30, 20X2		
Account Title	**Debit**	**Credit**
Cash	12 0 0 0 00	
Accounts Receivable	26 0 0 0 00	
Merchandise Inventory	38 4 0 0 00	
Store Supplies	3 2 0 0 00	
Office Supplies	2 3 4 0 00	
Prepaid Insurance	9 6 0 00	
Store Equipment	38 0 0 0 00	
Accumulated Depreciation—Store Equipment		5 7 0 0 00
Office Equipment	24 0 0 0 00	
Accumulated Depreciation—Office Equipment		4 8 0 0 00
Accounts Payable		9 6 0 0 00
Salaries Payable		—
Notes Payable		25 0 0 0 00
Jay Ingersol, Capital		95 3 0 0 00
Jay Ingersol, Drawing	18 0 0 0 00	
Sales		176 3 0 0 00
Sales Returns and Allowances	2 2 0 0 00	
Cost of Goods Sold	72 5 2 0 00	
Inventory Short and Over	—	—
Sales Salaries Expense	36 0 0 0 00	
Advertising Expense	4 5 0 0 00	
Store Supplies Expense	—	
Depreciation Expense—Store Equipment	—	
Rent Expense	9 0 0 0 00	
Office Salaries Expense	20 8 0 0 00	
Depreciation Expense—Office Equipment	—	
Utilities Expense	8 4 0 0 00	
Office Supplies Expense	—	
Insurance Expense	—	
Miscellaneous Expense	3 8 0 00	
Totals	316 7 0 0 00	316 7 0 0 00

Directions: Prepare a work sheet for the year ended April 30, 20X2, using the following adjustment data:

(a) Perpetual inventory records show an inventory value of $38,400. An inventory count shows a value of $38,205.

(b) Store supplies on hand, $1,200.

(c) Office supplies on hand, $540.

(d) Insurance expired, $80.

(e) Depreciation of store equipment, $2,900.

(f) Depreciation of office equipment, $1,600.

(g) Accrued salaries: sales, $1,210; office, $630.

Financial Statements and Closing Entries for a Merchandising Business

Learning Objectives

1 Prepare financial statements for a merchandising business.
2 Journalize adjusting and closing entries for a merchandising business.
3 Prepare a post-closing trial balance.
4 Make reversing entries for accrued (unpaid) salaries.

In Chapter 9, we discussed the end-of-period adjustments necessary for a merchandising business, and we prepared a work sheet for Lakeside Electronics. In this chapter, we will prepare financial statements, journalize and post adjusting and closing entries, and prepare a post-closing trial balance.

Preparing Financial Statements for a Merchandising Business

Learning Objective

1 Prepare financial statements for a merchandising business.

Remember

Financial statements are prepared in this order:
• Income statement
• Statement of owner's equity
• Balance sheet

As we discussed in Chapter 4, a completed work sheet supplies all the information needed to prepare financial statements. As you have learned, the financial statements are prepared in the following order: (1) the income statement, (2) the statement of owner's equity, and (3) the balance sheet.

- The income statement summarizes revenue and expenses and shows the amount of net income (or net loss) for an accounting period.
- The statement of owner's equity summarizes the changes in owner's equity during the accounting period.
- The balance sheet lists a firm's assets, liabilities, and owner's equity as of a certain date.

In this section, we will use the financial statement columns of Lakeside's work sheet to prepare a classified income statement, a statement of owner's equity, and a classified balance sheet. Figure 10-1 shows the financial statement columns of the work sheet for Lakeside Electronics that we presented in Chapter 9.

Figure 10-1

Financial Statement Columns of a Work Sheet

Lakeside Electronics
Work Sheet
For Year Ended December 31, 20X1

#	Account Title	Income Statement Debit	Income Statement Credit	Balance Sheet Debit	Balance Sheet Credit
1	Cash			6 2 0 0 00	
2	Accounts Receivable			9 6 8 9 00	
3	Merchandise Inventory			72 4 0 0 00	
4	Store Supplies			5 0 0 00	
5	Office Supplies			2 5 0 00	
6	Prepaid Insurance			6 3 0 00	
7	Store Equipment			11 3 8 5 00	
8	Accumulated Depreciation—Store Equipment				5 4 0 0 00
9	Office Equipment			10 2 0 0 00	
10	Accumulated Depreciation—Office Equipment				7 9 2 0 00
11	Delivery Equipment			56 0 0 0 00	
12	Accumulated Depreciation—Delivery Equipment				23 0 0 0 00
13	Accounts Payable				14 0 2 5 00
14	Salaries Payable				1 6 0 0 00
15	Notes Payable				26 0 0 0 00
16	John Graham, Capital				75 5 8 1 00
17	John Graham, Drawing			18 0 0 0 00	
18	Income Summary	66 0 0 00	72 4 0 0 00		
19	Sales		304 6 0 0 00		
20	Sales Returns and Allowances	5 2 3 0 00			
21	Sales Discounts	3 4 6 1 00			
22	Purchases	144 9 1 8 00			
23	Purchases Returns and Allowances		6 6 9 2 00		
24	Purchases Discounts		2 9 1 0 00		
25	Freight In	1 1 6 0 00			
26	Sales Salaries Expense	69 1 0 0 00			
27	Advertising Expense	5 8 4 0 00			
28	Store Supplies Expense	1 5 1 5 00			
29	Depreciation Expense—Store Equipment	9 0 0 00			
30	Miscellaneous Selling Expense	2 1 0 0 00			
31	Rent Expense	5 7 0 0 00			
32	Office Salaries Expense	31 1 5 3 00			
33	Insurance Expense	9 0 0 00			
34	Depreciation Expense—Office Equipment	8 2 0 00			
35	Depreciation Expense—Delivery Equipment	9 2 0 0 00			
36	Utilities Expense	6 2 4 0 00			
37	Office Supplies Expense	4 1 7 00			
38	Interest Expense	1 3 0 00			
39	Miscellaneous General Expense	9 0 0 00			
40		354 8 7 4 00	386 6 0 2 00	185 2 5 4 00	153 5 2 6 00
41	Net Income	31 7 2 8 00			31 7 2 8 00
42		386 6 0 2 00	386 6 0 2 00	185 2 5 4 00	185 2 5 4 00

The Classified Income Statement

An income statement summarizes revenues and expenses and shows how much net income (or net loss) a firm has for an accounting period. Up to this point, we have shown nonclassified income statements, which simply contain a listing of revenues and expenses. A nonclassified income statement is better suited to the needs of a service business. Determining net income or net loss for a merchandising business is a more involved process. Consequently, it is easier to understand the income statement if we divide it into sections. A **classified income statement** is an income statement divided into sections, as follows:

The income statement reports the results of a company's operations to stockholders, lenders, and taxing authorities.

- Revenue
- Cost of Goods Sold
- Operating Expenses
- Income from Operations
- Other Income and Expenses

classified income statement an income statement divided into the following sections: revenue, cost of goods sold, operating expenses, income from operations, and other income and expenses

We will discuss the content of each of these sections shortly. Before we do that, however, let's talk in general terms about the format of the income statement for a merchandising business. The following is a skeleton outline used when a classified income statement is prepared:

	Net Sales for the Period
−	Cost of Goods Sold
=	Gross Profit
−	Operating Expenses
=	Income from Operations
+	Other Income
−	Other Expenses
=	Net Income

This outline is so important to fully understanding the income statement of a merchandising business that you should firmly entrench it in your mind. It will be followed each time we prepare an income statement.

As well, you should fully understand the concepts of *gross* and *net*. **Gross profit**, also called gross margin, is the profit before subtracting the expenses of doing business. It results from subtracting the cost of items sold (the **cost of goods sold**) from their net sales price. **Net sales** is obtained by subtracting the amount of sales returns and allowances and the amount of sales discounts from the amount of sales. When expenses are subtracted from gross profit, we obtain the amount of *income from operations*, which will be discussed in detail shortly. Then, we add other (nonoperating) income and subtract other (nonoperating) expenses to find the net income.

gross profit the profit before subtracting the expenses of doing business; calculated by subtracting cost of goods sold from net sales; also referred to as gross margin

cost of goods sold the cost of merchandise sold to customers during the accounting period

net sales the amount obtained by subtracting the amount of sales returns and allowances and the amount of sales discounts from the amount of sales

Let's now closely examine the sections of the classified income statement. (Remember, the data you need to prepare Lakeside's income statement can be found on the partial work sheet shown in Figure 10-1 on page 450.)

The Revenue Section

The revenue section provides a figure for net sales, which is the balance of the Sales account, less the balances of the contra sales accounts (Sales Returns and Allowances and Sales Discounts), as shown in Figure 10-2.

Figure 10-2
Net Sales

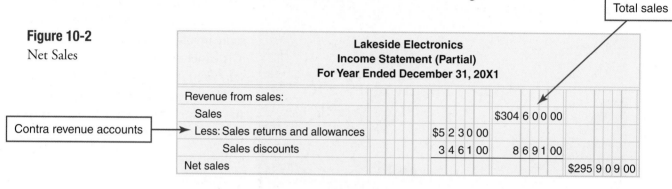

Total sales

Contra revenue accounts

Lakeside Electronics Income Statement (Partial) For Year Ended December 31, 20X1			
Revenue from sales:			
Sales			$304 6 0 0 00
Less: Sales returns and allowances	$5 2 3 0 00		
Sales discounts	3 4 6 1 00	8 6 9 1 00	
Net sales			$295 9 0 9 00

The Cost of Goods Sold Section

The cost of merchandise sold to customers during a period is subtracted from the net sales figure for the same period to get the amount of *gross profit*. In most merchandising businesses, the volume of sales is too large to permit a determination of the cost of items as they are being sold. Consequently, a simple formula is generally used. The formula to calculate cost of goods sold is as follows:

Beginning Merchandise Inventory
+ Net Purchases of Merchandise
= Cost of Goods Available for Sale
− Ending Merchandise Inventory
= Cost of Goods Sold

Notice that to calculate cost of goods sold, you will need both the beginning and ending inventory figures as well as the net purchases for the period. You can find the inventory figures in the Income Statement columns of the work sheet. (The beginning inventory will be the debit to the Income Summary account, and the ending inventory will be the credit to the Income Summary account.) You calculate the amount of net purchases as follows:

Total Purchases
− Purchases Returns and Allowances
− Purchases Discounts
+ Freight In
= Net Purchases

Remember

Purchases, Purchases Returns and Allowances, Purchases Discounts, and Freight In fall under the category of cost accounts. Cost accounts are like expense accounts in that both are presented on the income statement as a subtraction from sales revenue. They differ in that, unlike expenses, cost accounts are not directly subtracted from sales but are used in the calculation of cost of goods sold.

◁ Key Point

Notice that Purchases Returns and Allowances and Purchases Discounts decrease the cost of purchases; the amount of Freight In increases the cost of purchases.

Continuing with our example of Lakeside Electronics, the cost of goods sold section of the income statement appears as shown in Figure 10-3.

Figure 10-3
Cost of Goods Sold

Lakeside Electronics
Income Statement (Partial)
For Year Ended December 31, 20X1

Net sales				$295 9 0 9 00
Cost of goods sold:				
Merchandise inventory, January 1			$ 66 0 0 0 00	
Purchases		$144 9 1 8 00		
Less: Purchases ret. and allow.	$6 6 9 2 00			
Purchases discounts	2 9 1 0 00	9 6 0 2 00		
		$135 3 1 6 00		
Add: Freight in		1 1 6 0 00		
Net purchases			136 4 7 6 00	
Goods available for sale			$202 4 7 6 00	
Less: Merch. inv., December 31			72 4 0 0 00	
Cost of goods sold				130 0 7 6 00
Gross profit				$165 8 3 3 00

Contra purchases accounts

Remember

Net Sales
– Cost of Goods Sold
= Gross Profit

Notice that the cost of goods sold is subtracted from net sales to get the gross profit for the period: $295,909 – $130,076 = $165,833.

Review Quiz 10-1

Cost data related to three businesses are shown below. Calculate the cost of goods sold for each company.

(a)
Beginning Merchandise Inventory	$30,000
Purchases of Merchandise During the Period	70,000
Purchases Returns and Allowances	2,800
Purchases Discounts	1,450
Ending Merchandise Inventory	32,000

(b)
Beginning Merchandise Inventory	-0-
Purchases of Merchandise During the Period	$90,000
Purchases Discounts	2,400
Ending Merchandise Inventory	26,000

(c)
Beginning Merchandise Inventory	$88,000
Purchases of Merchandise During the Period	99,400
Freight In	3,400
Purchases Returns and Allowances	4,200
Purchases Discounts	900
Ending Merchandise Inventory	61,000

Check your answers on page 495.

The Operating Expenses Section

operating expenses the normal and expected expenses of operating a business

selling expenses operating expenses directly related to the sale of a firm's merchandise

Operating expenses, as the name implies, are the regular expenses of operating the business. Lakeside Electronics has broken down its operating expenses into *selling expenses* and *general expenses*, which is a common practice that allows closer analysis and monitoring of the types of expenses. Let's look at these groups in a little more detail.

- **Selling expenses** are all expenses directly related to the sale of merchandise, such as:

- Sales Salaries Expense
- Advertising Expense
- Store Supplies Expense
- Depreciation Expense—Store Equipment
- Miscellaneous Selling Expense

general expenses
expenses related to running a firm's office, overall administration of the business, or any other operating activities that do not involve the sale of merchandise; also referred to as administrative expenses

- **General expenses** (also called administrative expenses) are expenses related to the business's office, the overall administration of the business, or any other operating expenses that cannot be tied directly to sales activity, such as:
  - Office Salaries Expense
  - Rent Expense
  - Depreciation Expense—Office Equipment
  - Depreciation Expense—Delivery Equipment
  - Utilities Expense
  - Office Supplies Expense
  - Insurance Expense
  - Miscellaneous General Expense

Now let's look at the operating expenses section of Lakeside's income statement shown in Figure 10-4.

Figure 10-4
Operating Expenses

Lakeside Electronics Income Statement (Partial) For Year Ended December 31, 20X1			
Gross profit			$165 8 3 3 00
Operating expenses:			
Selling expenses:			
Sales salaries expense	$69 1 0 0 00		
Advertising expense	5 8 4 0 00		
Store supplies expense	1 5 1 5 00		
Depr. exp.—store equipment	9 0 0 00		
Miscellaneous selling expense	2 1 0 0 00		
Total selling expenses		$79 4 5 5 00	
General expenses:			
Rent expense	$ 5 7 0 0 00		
Office salaries expense	31 1 5 3 00		
Insurance expense	9 0 00		
Depr. exp.—office equipment	8 2 0 00		
Depr. exp.—delivery equipment	9 2 0 0 00		
Utilities expense	6 2 4 0 00		
Office supplies expense	4 1 7 00		
Miscellaneous general expense	9 0 0 00		
Total general expenses		54 5 2 0 00	
Total operating expenses			133 9 7 5 00

The Income from Operations Section

income from operations gross profit minus operating expenses; also referred to as operating income

Gross profit minus total operating expenses equals income from operations. **Income from operations** (also called operating income) is a measure of a firm's ongoing operations, or its regular operations. Lakeside's income from operations section is shown in Figure 10-5.

Figure 10-5
Income from Operations

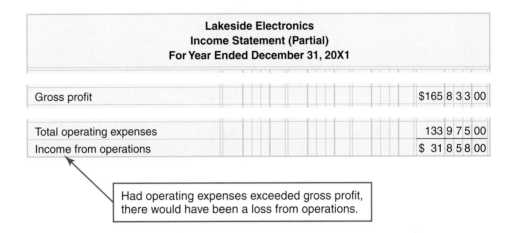

Lakeside Electronics Income Statement (Partial) For Year Ended December 31, 20X1		
Gross profit		$165 8 3 3 00
Total operating expenses		133 9 7 5 00
Income from operations		$ 31 8 5 8 00

> Had operating expenses exceeded gross profit, there would have been a loss from operations.

The Other Income and Expenses Section

other income revenue earned that is not directly associated with the normal operation of the business, such as income from vending machine sales and interest earned

other expenses expenses that are not directly associated with the normal operation of the business, such as interest expense

Some businesses have income and expenses that are not a part of normal operations. Food stores, for example, often receive income from vending machine sales and video games. Likewise, department stores sometimes earn rent income by renting unused space to other businesses. Since this income is not a part of regular operations, it should not be included as part of the business's regular sales of merchandise. Instead, the income is listed at the bottom of the income statement as **other income**.

Expenses that are not part of the regular expenses of operating the business should not be listed with the operating expenses. Instead, the expenses should be shown in a separate section called **other expenses**. A common example of a nonoperating expense is interest expense—interest is an expense of borrowing money, not of operating the business. Another common nonoperating expense is recurring losses from factors such as vandalism and accidents.

Lakeside did not have any nonoperating income; however, the firm incurred interest expense of $130 related to a note payable. Since this expense is not a part of normal operations, it is presented on the income statement as shown in Figure 10-6.

Figure 10-6
Other Expenses

Lakeside Electronics Income Statement (Partial) For Year Ended December 31, 20X1		
Income from operations		$31 8 5 8 00
Other expenses:		
Interest expense		1 3 0 00
Net income		$31 7 2 8 00

Review Quiz **10-2**

The following data are for the Tasty World Ice Cream Factory:

Account	Balance
Sales	$69,500
Sales Returns and Allowances	300
Beginning Merchandise Inventory	9,000
Purchases	22,000
Purchases Discounts	600
Ending Merchandise Inventory	9,500
Operating Expenses (Total)	18,200
Interest Expense (Other Expense)	1,400

Determine the following:

(a) The amount of net sales
(b) The cost of goods sold
(c) The amount of gross profit
(d) The amount of income (or loss) from operations
(e) The amount of net income (or net loss)

Check your answers on page 495.

The Completed Income Statement

Now let's now look at Lakeside's completed income statement, which is shown in Figure 10-7.

The Statement of Owner's Equity

classified balance sheet a balance sheet that divides the assets and liabilities sections into the following subsections: current assets and plant assets; current liabilities and long-term liabilities

Using the partial work sheet presented in Figure 10-1, we can find all the data we need to complete the statement of owner's equity. The statement of owner's equity has been called the link between the income statement and the balance sheet. This is because the net income (or net loss) figure from the income statement is entered on the statement of owner's equity as a necessary part of updating the owner's capital; the updated capital figure is then entered on the balance sheet. Figure 10-8 shows Lakeside's statement of owner's equity for the year ended December 31, 20X1.

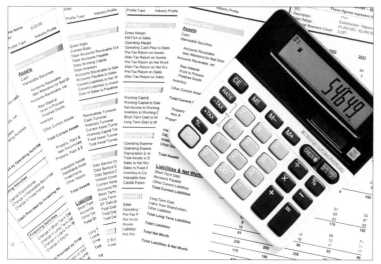

Financial statements help management assess performance and make decisions as well as report a company's profit (or loss) and financial condition to the outside world.

The Classified Balance Sheet

The principal objective of the balance sheet is to present the reader with as much information as possible about the financial condition of a business at a particular point in time. Until now, the balance sheets we have prepared have been divided into three sections: (1) assets, (2) liabilities, and (3) owner's equity. By grouping items into classifications within these sections, we can prepare a **classified balance sheet**, which presents the reader with more detail.

Figure 10-7

Completed Income
Statement

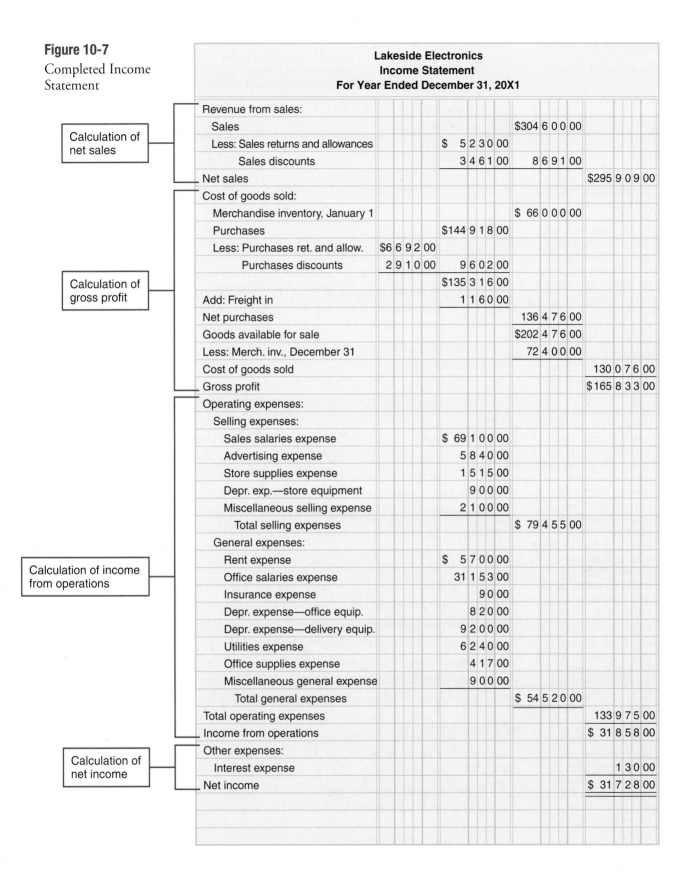

Lakeside Electronics Income Statement For Year Ended December 31, 20X1				
Revenue from sales:				
Sales			$304 600 00	
Less: Sales returns and allowances		$ 5 230 00		
Sales discounts		3 461 00	8 691 00	
Net sales				$295 909 00
Cost of goods sold:				
Merchandise inventory, January 1			$ 66 000 00	
Purchases		$144 918 00		
Less: Purchases ret. and allow.	$6 692 00			
Purchases discounts	2 910 00	9 602 00		
		$135 316 00		
Add: Freight in		1 160 00		
Net purchases			136 476 00	
Goods available for sale			$202 476 00	
Less: Merch. inv., December 31			72 400 00	
Cost of goods sold				130 076 00
Gross profit				$165 833 00
Operating expenses:				
Selling expenses:				
Sales salaries expense		$ 69 100 00		
Advertising expense		5 840 00		
Store supplies expense		1 515 00		
Depr. exp.—store equipment		900 00		
Miscellaneous selling expense		2 100 00		
Total selling expenses			$ 79 455 00	
General expenses:				
Rent expense		$ 5 700 00		
Office salaries expense		31 153 00		
Insurance expense		900 00		
Depr. expense—office equip.		820 00		
Depr. expense—delivery equip.		9 200 00		
Utilities expense		6 240 00		
Office supplies expense		417 00		
Miscellaneous general expense		900 00		
Total general expenses			$ 54 520 00	
Total operating expenses				133 975 00
Income from operations				$ 31 858 00
Other expenses:				
Interest expense				130 00
Net income				$ 31 728 00

Calculation of
net sales

Calculation of
gross profit

Calculation of income
from operations

Calculation of
net income

Figure 10-8

Statement of Owner's Equity

From income statement →

Lakeside Electronics Statement of Owner's Equity For Year Ended December 31, 20X1			
John Graham, capital, January 1			$75 5 8 1 00
Net income for period	$31 7 2 8 00		
Less: Withdrawals	18 0 0 0 00		
Increase in capital			13 7 2 8 00
John Graham, capital, December 31			$89 3 0 9 00

current assets cash and other assets that through normal operations are expected to be sold, coverted to cash, used up, or expired, usually within one year of the balance sheet date

liquidity refers to how quickly an asset can be turned into cash, used up, or expire; used in reference to assets, which are listed on the balance sheet in the order of their liquidity

plant assets assets that are expected to be used in the business for more than one year, are acquired for use in the operation of a business, are not intended for resale to customers, and are tangible; examples include land, buildings, machinery and equipment, furniture, and automobiles; also referred to as fixed assets; property, plant, and equipment; or long-term assets

stability a reference to how long an asset will last; an organizing quality of a plant asset for listing on the balance sheet

current liabilities short-term debt that is due for payment within one year; examples include accounts payable, salaries payable, sales tax payable, and the current portion of notes payable

long-term liabilities debt that will not come due for payment within one year; examples include long-term notes payable and mortgages payable

Assets

On the classified balance sheet, assets are usually classified as either *current* or *plant*. **Current assets** are cash and any other assets that through normal business operations are expected to be sold, converted to cash, used up, or expired, usually within one year. Examples of current assets, other than cash, include accounts receivable, merchandise inventory, supplies, and prepaid insurance. Current assets are listed on the balance sheet according to their **liquidity**, that is, how quickly they will be turned into cash, or how quickly they will be used up or expire. Therefore, cash is listed first and usually is followed by accounts receivable, merchandise inventory, supplies, and prepaid items.

Plant assets are assets that are expected to be used in the business for more than one year. Examples of plant assets include land, buildings, machinery, furniture, computers, and automobiles. Plant assets are usually listed on the balance sheet according to their **stability** (how long they will last). Less stable assets (such as office equipment) are listed first, followed by more stable assets. Land is the most stable asset; therefore, it is typically listed last. Plant assets are also called *fixed assets*; *property*, *plant*, and *equipment*; or *long-term assets*.

Liabilities

Liabilities are presented on the classified balance sheet as either *current* or *long-term*. **Current liabilities** are debts that are due for payment within one year. Examples usually include accounts payable, salaries payable, sales tax payable, notes payable, and the current portion of long-term notes payable.

Long-term liabilities are debts that will not come due for payment within one year. Examples include long-term notes payable and mortgages payable.

Owner's Equity

The balance sheet also requires an up-to-date amount for the owner's capital. This amount will be supplied by the statement of owner's equity.

When we combine the assets, liabilities, and owner's equity information, we get Lakeside's balance sheet, dated as of December 31, 20X1, as shown in Figure 10-9.

Now that we have presented each of Lakeside's financial statements, let's pause to look at some key figures on Lakeside's balance sheet.

Figure 10-9
Classified Balance
Sheet

> The balance sheet is dated as of the last day of the fiscal period.

Lakeside Electronics
Balance Sheet
December 31, 20X1

Assets			
Current assets:			
Cash		$ 6 2 0 0 00	
Accounts receivable		9 6 8 9 00	
Merchandise inventory		72 4 0 0 00	
Store supplies		5 0 0 00	
Office supplies		2 5 0 00	
Prepaid insurance		6 3 0 00	
Total current assets			$ 89 6 6 9 00
Plant assets:			
Store equipment	$11 3 8 5 00		
Less: Accumulated depreciation	5 4 0 0 00	$ 5 9 8 5 00	
Office equipment	$10 2 0 0 00		
Less: Accumulated depreciation	7 9 2 0 00	2 2 8 0 00	← book value
Delivery equipment	$56 0 0 0 00		
Less: Accumulated depreciation	23 0 0 0 00	33 0 0 0 00	
Total plant assets			41 2 6 5 00
Total assets			$130 9 3 4 00
Liabilities			
Current liabilities:			
Accounts payable	$14 0 2 5 00		
Salaries payable	1 6 0 0 00		
Total current liabilities		$15 6 2 5 00	
Long-term liabilities:			
Notes payable		26 0 0 0 00	
Total liabilities			$ 41 6 2 5 00
Owner's Equity			
John Graham, capital			89 3 0 9 00
Total liabilities and owner's equity			$130 9 3 4 00

Working Capital and the Current Ratio

The balance sheet alone tells us much about the financial condition of a business. Most accountants, however, perform certain analyses so that the balance sheet will be of maximum benefit as a decision-making tool. We will deal with financial statement analysis in detail in a later chapter. For now, we are interested in two important questions about the business:

- Does the business have enough capital to operate and continue growing?
- Can the business meet its debts as they fall due?

To help answer these questions, it is common to look at a firm's *working capital* and its *current ratio*, both of which can easily be determined by looking at a classified balance sheet.

Working Capital

working capital current assets minus current liabilities; a measure of a company's ability to meet short-term obligations

Working capital is the amount of current assets minus the amount of current liabilities, which can be stated in a simple formula, as follows:

Working capital = Current assets – Current liabilities

As we discussed in the preceding section, current assets consist of cash and other assets that will be realized in cash within one year, and current liabilities are debts to be paid within one year. Sufficient current assets must be available to pay current liabilities as they fall due. Thus, working capital represents the funds available to replace inventory and to acquire credit. The larger the working capital, the better able the business is to pay its debts. For Lakeside Electronics, we can calculate working capital as follows:

Current assets	$89,669
– Current liabilities	15,625
= Working capital	$74,044

Take This Into Account

Capital (or owner's equity) is simply the difference between total assets and total liabilities. Working capital can be thought of as a current version of total capital.

Total assets – Total liabilities = Owner's capital

Current assets – Current liabilities = Working capital

To be of maximum benefit, working capital should be computed at the end of each period, and any significant change should be subjected to close scrutiny by management. Without adequate working capital, a business can fail, a point that is well illustrated by the failure of W.T. Grant Corporation in the late 1970s. W.T. Grant was a large chain of discount department stores that at the time of its closing was earning a profit and had millions of dollars in long-term assets. However, the company had insufficient working capital and was forced into bankruptcy when severe cash flow problems prevented the timely repayment of debt.

Current Ratio

current ratio current assets divided by current liabilities; a measure of a company's ability to pay current liabilities from current assets

Closely tied in with working capital is the **current ratio**, which is the ratio of current assets to current liabilities. The current ratio gives an indication of the ability of a business to pay its current liabilities and is calculated as follows:

$$\text{Current ratio} = \frac{\text{Current assets}}{\text{Current liabilities}}$$

We can calculate Lakeside's current ratio as follows:

$$\frac{\text{Current assets}}{\text{Current liabilities}} = \frac{\$89,669}{\$15,625} = 5.7{:}1$$

Lakeside's current ratio is 5.7:1, which is read as *5.7 to 1*. This means that Lakeside has approximately $5.70 in current assets for each $1 in current liabilities. While it is difficult to say exactly what is a good current ratio (because of differences in the financial makeup of businesses), a current ratio of 2:1 is generally considered acceptable. Since Lakeside's current ratio is much better than this, it is likely that the firm will be able to pay its debts as they fall due.

Review Quiz **10-3**

Selected data from the classified balance sheet of Miller Company follow:

Account	Balance
Cash	$ 9,000
Accounts Receivable	12,000
Merchandise Inventory	64,000
Prepaid Insurance	1,000
Store Supplies	800
Store Equipment	18,000
Display Equipment	32,000
Computer	7,800
Accounts Payable	5,800
Sales Tax Payable	1,400
Salaries Payable	800
Note Payable (due in five years)	9,400

What is the (a) amount of current assets, (b) amount of current liabilities, (c) working capital, and (d) current ratio? Does it seem that the firm will be able to pay its current liabilities as they fall due? Explain.

Check your answers on page 495.

Journalizing Adjusting and Closing Entries for a Merchandising Business

Learning Objective

2 Journalize adjusting and closing entries for a merchandising business.

Now that we have prepared Lakeside's financial statements, our next step in the accounting cycle is to journalize adjusting and closing entries, which we will do in this section.

Journalizing Adjusting Entries

You will recall from Chapter 4 that the work sheet is a useful tool for accountants. However, the work sheet is not a journal, and no posting is ever made from it to the ledger. Therefore, to get the adjusting entries into the ledger, formal journal entries must be made. This is a simple process, however, because the adjustments already appear on the work sheet. You simply copy them into the journal. In Figure 10-10, we have reproduced the Adjustments columns of Lakeside's work sheet. Starting with the first adjustment—adjustment (a)—very carefully copy each adjustment into the journal, as shown in Figure 10-11 on page 463.

Figure 10-10
Trial Balance and Adjustments
Columns of the Work Sheet

Lakeside Electronics
Work Sheet
For Year Ended December 31, 20X1

	Account Title	Trial Balance Debit	Trial Balance Credit	Adjustments Debit	Adjustments Credit	
1	Cash	6 2 0 0 00				1
2	Accounts Receivable	9 6 8 9 00				2
3	Merchandise Inventory	66 0 0 0 00		(b)72 4 0 0 00	(a) 66 0 0 0 00	3
4	Store Supplies	2 0 1 5 00			(c)1 5 1 5 00	4
5	Office Supplies	6 6 7 00			(d) 4 1 7 00	5
6	Prepaid Insurance	7 2 0 00			(e) 9 0 00	6
7	Store Equipment	11 3 8 5 00				7
8	Accum. Depr.—Store Equipment		4 5 0 0 00		(f) 9 0 0 00	8
9	Office Equipment	10 2 0 0 00				9
10	Accum. Depr.—Office Equipment		7 1 0 0 00		(g) 8 2 0 00	10
11	Delivery Equipment	56 0 0 0 00				11
12	Accum. Depr.—Delivery Equipment		13 8 0 0 00		(h)9 2 0 0 00	12
13	Accounts Payable		14 0 2 5 00			13
14	Salaries Payable				(i) 1 6 0 0 00	14
15	Notes Payable		26 0 0 0 00			15
16	John Graham, Capital		75 5 8 1 00			16
17	John Graham, Drawing	18 0 0 0 00			(b)	17
18	Income Summary	—	—	(a)66 0 0 0 00	72 4 0 0 00	18
19	Sales		304 6 0 0 00			19
20	Sales Returns and Allowances	5 2 3 0 00				20
21	Sales Discounts	3 4 6 1 00				21
22	Purchases	144 9 1 8 00				22
23	Purchases Returns and Allowances		6 6 9 2 00			23
24	Purchases Discounts		2 9 1 0 00			24
25	Freight In	1 1 6 0 00				25
26	Sales Salaries Expense	68 2 0 0 00		(i) 9 0 0 00		26
27	Advertising Expense	5 8 4 0 00				27
28	Store Supplies Expense	—		(c)1 5 1 5 00		28
29	Depr. Expense—Store Equipment	—		(f) 9 0 0 00		29
30	Miscellaneous Selling Expense	2 1 0 0 00				30
31	Rent Expense	5 7 0 0 00				31
32	Office Salaries Expense	30 4 5 3 00		(i) 7 0 0 00		32
33	Insurance Expense	—		(e) 9 0 00		33
34	Depr. Expense—Office Equipment	—		(g) 8 2 0 00		34
35	Depr. Expense—Delivery Equipment	—		(h)9 2 0 0 00		35
36	Utilities Expense	6 2 4 0 00				36
37	Office Supplies Expense	—		(d) 4 1 7 00		37
38	Interest Expense	1 3 0 00				38
39	Miscellaneous General Expense	9 0 0 00				39
40		455 2 0 8 00	455 2 0 8 00	152 9 4 2 00	152 9 4 2 00	40
41	Net income					41

Figure 10-11

Adjusting Entries

	Date		Account Title	P.R.	Debit	Credit	
1			Adjusting Entries				1
2	20X1 Dec.	31	Income Summary		66 0 0 0 00		2
3			Merchandise Inventory			66 0 0 0 00	3
4							4
5		31	Merchandise Inventory		72 4 0 0 00		5
6			Income Summary			72 4 0 0 00	6
7							7
8		31	Store Supplies Expense		1 5 1 5 00		8
9			Store Supplies			1 5 1 5 00	9
10							10
11		31	Office Supplies Expense		4 1 7 00		11
12			Office Supplies			4 1 7 00	12
13							13
14		31	Insurance Expense		9 0 00		14
15			Prepaid Insurance			9 0 00	15
16							16
17		31	Depr. Expense—Store Equipment		9 0 0 00		17
18			Accum. Depr.—Store Equipment			9 0 0 00	18
19							19
20		31	Depr. Expense—Office Equipment		8 2 0 00		20
21			Accum. Depr.—Office Equipment			8 2 0 00	21
22							22
23		31	Depr. Expense—Delivery Equipment		9 2 0 0 00		23
24			Accum. Depr.—Delivery Equipment			9 2 0 0 00	24
25							25
26		31	Sales Salaries Expense		9 0 0 00		26
27			Office Salaries Expense		7 0 0 00		27
28			Salaries Payable			1 6 0 0 00	28

Annotations at left of the figure:

- no normal balance → 2
- – asset → 3
- + asset → 5
- no normal balance → 6
- + expense → 8
- – asset → 9
- + expense → 11
- – asset → 12
- + expense → 14
- – asset → 15
- + expense → 17
- + contra asset → 18
- + expense → 20
- + contra asset → 21
- + expense → 23
- + contra asset → 24
- + expense → 26
- + expense → 27
- + liability → 28

Callout box: Adjusting entries are dated as of the last day of the accounting period.

Journalizing Closing Entries

In Chapter 5, we discussed closing entries for a service business. As we noted there, the objectives of the closing process are as follows:

- To reduce the balances of the temporary accounts to zero and thus make the accounts ready for entries in the next accounting period
- To update the balance of the owner's capital account

Remember that with the exception of the owner's drawing account, *all* temporary accounts are income statement accounts. Therefore, to start the closing process, let's refer to the Income Statement columns of Lakeside's work sheet (Figure 10-1 on page 450). The first amounts shown are those in the Income Summary account. These amounts are the beginning and ending inventory figures; they were entered in the Income Statement columns because they are needed in the calculation of cost of goods sold. Since these figures are a part of the adjusting process, they are not considered when closing.

Therefore, we start with the next account listed—the Sales account—and proceed downward, line by line, closing each account to Income Summary.

As we discussed in Chapter 5, the closing process is accomplished in the following four steps:

Step **1** Close the Sales account and other income statement accounts with credit balances to the Income Summary account.

Step **2** Close each expense account and other income statement accounts with debit balances to the Income Summary account.

Step **3** Close the Income Summary account to the owner's capital account.

Step **4** Close the balance of the owner's drawing account to the owner's capital account.

Step 1: Close the Sales Account and Other Income Statement Accounts with Credit Balances to the Income Summary Account

Lakeside has three income statement accounts with credit balances: (1) Sales, (2) Purchases Returns and Allowances, and (3) Purchases Discounts. The credit balance of each account is closed by making an equal debit. Our credit is to the Income Summary account. This entry appears as follows:

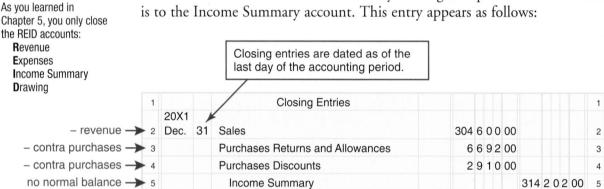

Remember

As you learned in Chapter 5, you only close the REID accounts:
Revenue
Expenses
Income Summary
Drawing

Step 2: Close Each Expense Account and Other Income Statement Accounts with Debit Balances to the Income Summary Account

All amounts remaining on the income statement are debits. Therefore, to close, we make equal credits. To balance the entry, we will make a compound debit to the Income Summary account, as follows:

				Debit		Credit	
no normal balance →	7	31	Income Summary	288 8 7 4 00			7
– contra revenue →	8		Sales Returns and Allowances			5 2 3 0 00	8
– contra revenue →	9		Sales Discounts			3 4 6 1 00	9
– cost account →	10		Purchases			144 9 1 8 00	10
– cost account →	11		Freight In			1 1 6 0 00	11
– expense →	12		Sales Salaries Expense			69 1 0 0 00	12
– expense →	13		Advertising Expense			5 8 4 0 00	13
– expense →	14		Store Supplies Expense			1 5 1 5 00	14
– expense →	15		Depr. Expense—Store Equipment			9 0 0 00	15
– expense →	16		Miscellaneous Selling Expense			2 1 0 0 00	16
– expense →	17		Rent Expense			5 7 0 0 00	17
– expense →	18		Office Salaries Expense			31 1 5 3 00	18
– expense →	19		Insurance Expense			9 0 0 00	19
– expense →	20		Depr. Expense—Office Equipment			8 2 0 00	20
– expense →	21		Depr. Expense—Delivery Equipment			9 2 0 00	21
– expense →	22		Utilities Expense			6 2 4 0 00	22
– expense →	23		Office Supplies Expense			4 1 7 00	23
– expense →	24		Interest Expense			1 3 0 00	24
– expense →	25		Miscellaneous General Expense			9 0 0 00	25

Step 3: Close the Income Summary Account to the Owner's Capital Account

Remember that when revenue and expenses have been closed to the Income Summary account, this account will show the amount of net income or net loss for the period. We can see this if we pause at this point and draw a T account for Income Summary.

Income Summary

Adjustment 66,000	Adjustment 72,400
(Expenses) 288,874	(Revenue) 314,202

Now, if we balance the Income Summary account, we will find a familiar figure—the amount of net income:

Debit Column:
$ 66,000
288,874
$354,874

Credit Column:
$ 72,400
314,202
$386,602

$386,602
– 354,874
$ 31,728 ←——— credit balance = net income

As we can see, to determine net income we subtract the Debit column total from the Credit column total. At this stage of the closing process, the balance of the Income Summary account will always show the amount of net income, or net loss, for the period.

If the Income Summary account had a debit balance, it would mean a net loss had occurred.

The Income Summary account has now served its purpose for this accounting period. All revenue, cost, and expense accounts have been closed. The account was also used to adjust the Merchandise Inventory account to reflect the ending inventory. Therefore, we now close the Income Summary account. Since the balance of the account is a credit (net income), we close it by making an equal debit. Our credit is to John Graham, Capital. Remember that net income increases capital. Thus, we transfer the amount of net income to the credit side (increase side) of the owner's capital account. This entry appears as shown below.

no normal balance →	26	31	Income Summary	3 1 7 2 8 00		26
+ owner's equity →	27		John Graham, Capital		3 1 7 2 8 00	27

Step 4: Close the Balance of the Owner's Drawing Account to the Owner's Capital Account

The owner's drawing account is used to record owner withdrawals during a single accounting period. When that period is over, the drawing account has served its purpose. Therefore, its balance is closed to the owner's capital account. Since the drawing account has a debit balance, it is closed by making an equal credit. Our debit is to the owner's capital account.

– owner's equity →	29	31	John Graham, Capital	18 0 0 0 00		29
– drawing →	30		John Graham, Drawing		18 0 0 0 00	30

We have now closed all temporary accounts in the ledger of Lakeside Electronics. After these closing entries are posted, the only accounts that will have balances are assets, contra assets, liabilities, and owner's capital. The balances of these accounts will be up to date and will agree with the amounts reported on the financial statements. The temporary accounts will have zero balances and will be ready for entries in the next accounting period. The balance of the owner's capital account will correspond exactly to the capital figure reported on the statement of owner's equity. Let's take a quick look at how the John Graham, Capital account looks at this moment.

Account John Graham, Capital							Account No. 311	
Date	Item	P.R.	Debit	Credit	Balance			
					Debit		Credit	
20X1 Jan. 1	Balance	✓					75 5 8 1 00	
Dec. 31	Closing	GJ4		31 7 2 8 00			107 3 0 9 00	
31	Closing	GJ4	18 0 0 0 00				89 3 0 9 00	

If we now compare the balance of John's capital account with the total of the statement of owner's equity (Figure 10-8), we will find that the two amounts agree. This completes the closing process.

Summary of the Steps in the Closing Process

Now that we have walked through the steps in the closing process for a merchandising business, let's look at a summary of those steps, shown in Figure 10-12.

Figure 10-12
Steps in the Closing Process

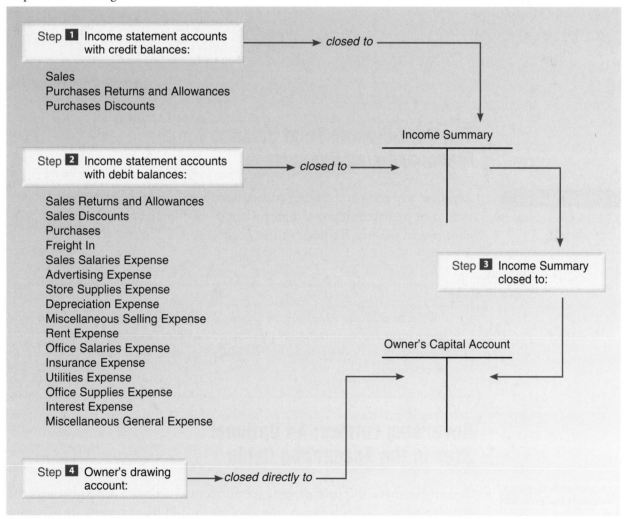

	Account Title	Income Statement		Balance Sheet		
		Debit	Credit	Debit	Credit	
14						14
15	LeeAnn Gatewood, Drawing			12 0 0 0 00		15
16	Income Summary	20 0 0 0 00	21 2 0 0 00			16
17	Sales		70 0 0 0 00			17
18	Sales Returns and Allowances	8 0 0 00				18
19	Sales Discounts	1 2 0 0 00				19
20	Purchases	38 0 0 0 00				20
21	Purchases Discounts		2 9 0 00			21
22	Rent Expense	4 0 0 0 00				22
23	Salaries Expense	9 0 0 0 00				23
24	Depreciation Expense	8 0 0 00				24
25	Supplies Expense	9 5 00				25
26	Telephone Expense	1 9 5 00				26
27	Utilities Expense	1 4 0 0 00				27
28	Miscellaneous Expense	1 2 6 00				28
29		75 6 1 6 00	91 4 9 0 00			29

Check your answer on page 498.

The Post-Closing Trial Balance for a Merchandising Business

Learning Objective

3 Prepare a post-closing trial balance.

After the adjusting and closing entries have been posted, another trial balance should be prepared to prove that the ledger is still in balance. Lakeside's post-closing trial balance is shown in Figure 10-13.

> **Summing Up**
>
> The only accounts appearing on the post-closing trial balance are the permanent accounts (assets, contra assets, liabilities, and owner's equity) because the temporary accounts (revenue, expenses, and drawing) have been closed.

Reversing Entries: An Optional Step in the Accounting Cycle

Learning Objective

4 Make reversing entries for accrued (unpaid) salaries.

Remember that an unpaid expense (or an accrued expense) occurs because the accounting period ends before the expense is due for payment. In Chapter 4 and again in Chapter 9, we made an adjusting entry for salaries that were unpaid when the accounting period ended. In both cases, we debited

Figure 10-13

The Post-Closing Trial
Balance

	Lakeside Electronics **Post-Closing Trial Balance** **December 31, 20X1**		
Account Title		**Debit**	**Credit**
Cash		6 2 0 0 00	
Accounts Receivable		9 6 8 9 00	
Merchandise Inventory		72 4 0 0 00	
Store Supplies		5 0 0 00	
Office Supplies		2 5 0 00	
Prepaid Insurance		6 3 0 00	
Store Equipment		11 3 8 5 00	
Accumulated Depreciation—Store Equipment			5 4 0 0 00
Office Equipment		10 2 0 0 00	
Accumulated Depreciation—Office Equipment			7 9 2 0 00
Delivery Equipment		56 0 0 0 00	
Accumulated Depreciation—Delivery Equipment			23 0 0 0 00
Accounts Payable			14 0 2 5 00
Salaries Payable			1 6 0 0 00
Notes Payable			26 0 0 0 00
John Graham, Capital			89 3 0 9 00
Totals		167 2 5 4 00	167 2 5 4 00

Salaries Expense (to show the proper amount of expense for the period), and we credited Salaries Payable (because the salaries will be paid in the next accounting period). But what entry do we make when the salaries are paid in the next accounting period?

To answer this question, let's look back at the adjusting entry we made for accrued salaries in Chapter 9. We learned that on December 31, 20X1, Lakeside Electronics had $900 in sales salaries and $700 in office salaries that were unpaid. We made the following adjusting entry to record these amounts:

1	20X1		Adjusting Entries		1
2	Dec.	31	Sales Salaries Expense	9 0 0 00	2
3			Office Salaries Expense	7 0 0 00	3
4			Salaries Payable	1 6 0 0 00	4

+ expense → (rows 2)
+ expense → (row 3)
+ liability → (row 4)

This entry was then posted to the ledger, and the proper amount of expenses were reported on the income statement. The balance sheet showed the liability for unpaid salaries. The next regular payday was on the following Friday—January 2, 20X2. On that date, Lakeside made payment for the payroll period. However, this payroll period is different from regular payroll periods because part of the salaries were earned by employees in the last accounting period (20X1) and part were earned in the new accounting period (20X2). We can break this down as shown in Figure 10-14. (To simplify the example, let's not worry about office salaries for the moment.)

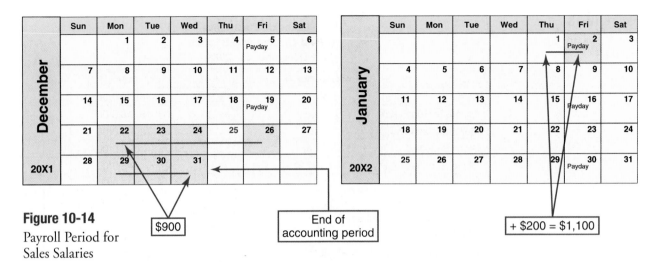

Figure 10-14
Payroll Period for Sales Salaries

To show the proper amount of sales salaries for each accounting period, we must split the $1,100 sales payroll that is now being paid between the $900 that was accrued at the end of 20X1 and the $200 that was incurred during the first two days of 20X2. The entry to do this appears as shown below:

				Debit	Credit	
		20X2				
+ expense →	1	Jan.	2 Sales Salaries Expense	2 00 00		1
– liability →	2		Salaries Payable	9 00 00		2
– asset →	3		Cash		1 1 00 00	3

After the entry is posted, the ledger accounts appear as shown in Figure 10-15.

Figure 10-15
General Ledger Accounts Showing Payment of Sales Salaries

General Ledger

Account **Salaries Payable** Account No. **212**

Date		Item	P.R.	Debit	Credit	Balance Debit	Balance Credit
20X1							
Dec.	31	Adjusting	GJ3		9 00 00		9 00 00
20X2							
Jan.	2		GJ4	9 00 00		—	—

Account **Sales Salaries Expense** Account No. **611**

Date		Item	P.R.	Debit	Credit	Balance Debit	Balance Credit
20X1							
Dec.	1	Balance	✓			68 2 00 00	
	31	Adjusting	GJ3	9 00 00		69 1 00 00	
	31	Closing	GJ4		69 1 00 00	—	—
20X2							
Jan.	2		GJ4	2 00 00		2 00 00	

The Sales Salaries Expense account shows a $200 balance on January 2, 20X2, which is the correct amount of expense as of this date. The balance of the Salaries Payable account is zero because the liability for payment ended when the January 2 payroll was paid.

In making the above entry, the accountant had to *look back* in the records to find out how much of the $1,100 sales payroll applied to the current accounting period and how much was accrued at the end of the last period.

This may seem like a simple task, but think of the problems the accountant could have if the company had many employees who were paid on different schedules, such as weekly, monthly, or bimonthly.

Is there anything the accountant can do so that an entry such as this does not have to be split between the two periods? The answer is yes. Use of an optional technique called **reversing entries** allows the accountant to make the same entry to record the payment of accrued expenses that would have been made had two separate accounting periods not been involved. Reversing entries are made on the first day of the next accounting period, and they are the exact opposite (the reverse) of the adjusting entries made to record the accrued expenses. To illustrate, let's assume that Lakeside decided to use reversing entries. Accordingly, the following entry was made on January 1, 20X2.

reversing entries a technique that allows the accountant to make the same entry to record the payment of accrued expenses that would have been made had two separate accounting periods not been involved; always recorded on the first day of the new accounting period

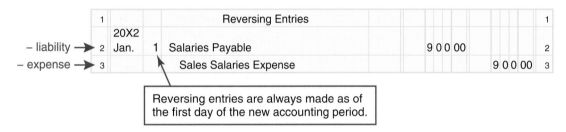

After this entry is posted, the ledger accounts appear as shown in Figure 10-16.

Figure 10-16

General Ledger Accounts Showing Reversing Entries

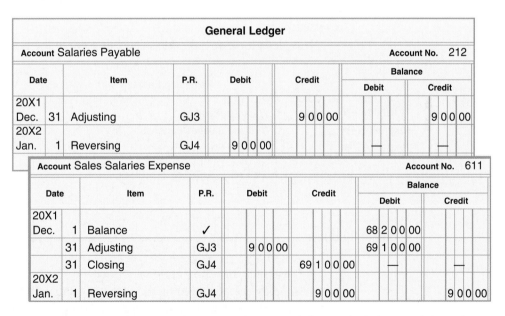

Notice that the reversing entry eliminated the credit balance of the Salaries Payable account, and a *credit* balance was created in the Sales Salaries Expense account. In effect, the balance of the liability account has been transferred to the Sales Salaries Expense account. So, on Friday, January 2, we can make our regular payroll entry, as shown below:

Now look at what happens to the Sales Salaries Expense account when this entry is posted:

Account Sales Salaries Expense							Account No.	611
Date	Item	P.R.	Debit	Credit	Balance			
					Debit		Credit	
20X1 Dec. 1	Balance	✓			68 2 0 0 00			
31	Adjusting	GJ3	9 0 0 00		69 1 0 0 00			
31	Closing	GJ4		69 1 0 0 00	—		—	
20X2 Jan. 1	Reversing	GJ4		9 0 0 00			9 0 0 00	
2		GJ5	1 1 0 0 00		2 0 0 00			

As we can see, the Sales Salaries Expense account now has a $200 debit balance, which is the proper amount of expense for the January 2, 20X2, payroll. Why did this happen when we did not split the entry? In effect, the reversing entry transferred the $900 unpaid expense for 20X1 to the credit side of the Sales Salaries Expense account. Thus, when the $1,100 debit was posted, the $900 credit balance offset the debit posting and created the proper balance in the account ($200 debit).

You may be thinking, "How do I remember which adjusting entries to reverse?" The answer to the question is simple. Most adjusting entries are not reversed. The *only* adjusting entry we have studied thus far that would be reversed is for accrued expenses—none of the other adjusting entries would be reversed.

Now, let's look at Lakeside's reversing entry for both types of salaries.

		Reversing Entries			
1					1
	20X2				
– liability → 2	Jan. 1	Salaries Payable	1 6 0 0 00		2
– expense → 3		Sales Salaries Expense		9 0 0 00	3
– expense → 4		Office Salaries Expense		7 0 0 00	4
5					5

Summing Up

- Reversing entries are optional journal entries that are intended to simplify the bookkeeping for transactions that involve accrued expenses.
- Reversing entries are always made as of the first day of the next accounting period—never on the last day of the period.
- In this chapter, the only adjusting entry suitable for reversing is the one for accrued expenses (unpaid salaries).

Anderson Company made the following adjusting entries as of December 31, 20X3. Make the appropriate reversing entry.

1			Adjusting Entries			1
	20X3					
2	Dec.	31	Income Summary	42 0 0 0 00		2
3			Merchandise Inventory		42 0 0 0 00	3
4						4
5		31	Merchandise Inventory	43 2 0 0 00		5
6			Income Summary		43 2 0 0 00	6
7						7
8		31	Insurance Expense	8 0 0 00		8
9			Prepaid Insurance		8 0 0 00	9
10						10
11		31	Supplies Expense	6 9 0 00		11
12			Supplies		6 9 0 00	12
13						13
14		31	Salaries Expense	8 1 0 00		14
15			Salaries Payable		8 1 0 00	15

Check your answer on page 498.

Interim Statements

We should stress that the fiscal period for most businesses consists of 12 consecutive months. At the end of the fiscal period, financial statements are prepared and the adjusting and closing entries are posted to the ledger. But owners and managers do not want to wait until the end of the year to see how well the company is doing financially. Consequently, many businesses prepare **interim statements**, which are statements that are prepared during the fiscal year for periods of *less* than 12 months, such as monthly, quarterly, and semiannually. For example, Coca-Cola, like most other large corporations, issues quarterly reports to its stockholders. These statements provide up-to-date information about the results of operations for the period covered by the statements.

To prepare interim statements, the accountant assembles adjustment data for the interim period. The adjustments are then entered on a work sheet, and the interim statements are prepared from the completed work sheet. However, adjusting and closing entries are not journalized; thus they are not entered in the ledger. These entries are recorded only at the end of the fiscal year.

interim statements
financial statements prepared during the fiscal year for periods of less than 12 months, such as monthly, quarterly, and semiannually

Small Trucking Firm Bookkeeper in Wire Fraud Scheme

Sue Nelson worked for a small trucking firm as a bookkeeper. She began a life of luxury on her salary of $35,000 a year, but her supervisor, Jim Walsh, did not notice. What Jim *did* notice when reviewing employee salaries was that Sue's salary was listed at $36,000 a year and he was certain she had been hired at $1,000 a year less.

Jim checked Sue's personnel file, and sure enough, her pay record had been altered. Becoming suspicious, he looked further and saw many suspicious wire transfers out of the company's bank account. Jim decided the case needed professional investigation, and he hired John Wallace, CPA.

Business owners should install effective internal controls to safeguard assets, especially cash.

Even though only the owner could sign checks, Sue was responsible for all other accounting for the business, including handling wire transfers. She would authorize a wire transfer to her own bank account and cover it by spreading the amount between one or more expense accounts. Sue was aware that no one but herself reconciled the bank account, so when the bank statements arrived, she would tear up any evidence.

The crime would have been prevented or at least stopped as soon as it began if the company had a second person review the bank statements. Most company embezzlement starts small, and as the perpetrators realize they are undetected, they continue to steal larger amounts.

Sue was indicted and spent several years in prison. She was a beautiful prisoner, however, because she used much of the money for head-to-toe cosmetic surgery!

Source: Robert Griffin, "Protecting Your Small Business from Fraud." *Oakland Business Review,* October 2004.

For Discussion

1. What internal control was violated in this accounting fraud?
2. What should the owner do to prevent this form of accounting fraud in the future?
3. Why is it important for an owner of a small business to become involved with the daily operations including the accounting records?

Joining the Pieces

Steps in the Accounting Cycle for a Merchandising Business

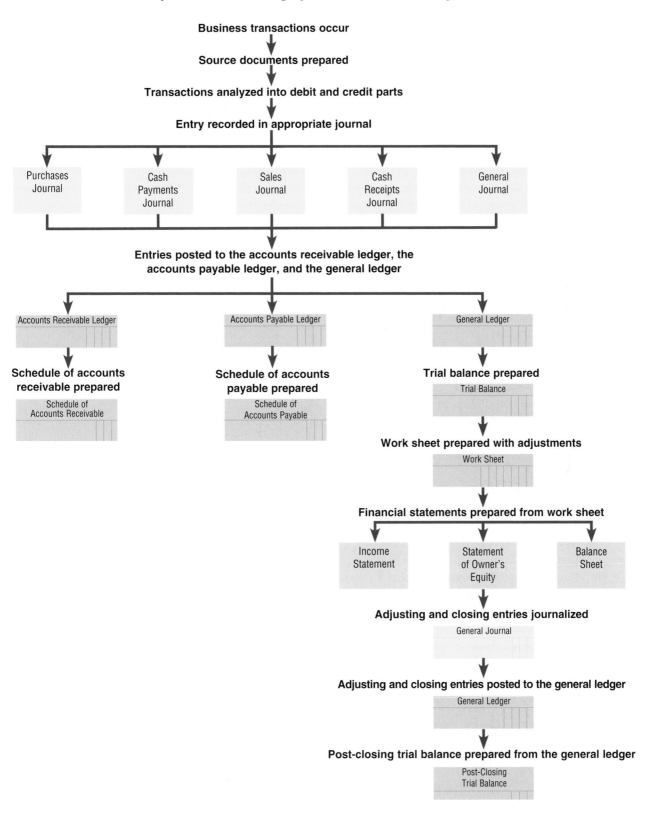

Summary  Interactive Summary in English and Spanish

1 Prepare financial statements for a merchandising business.

Figure 10-17

The Rose Bowl's
Work Sheet

In the Summary for Chapter 9, we prepared a work sheet for The Rose Bowl. The financial statement columns of The Rose Bowl's work sheet are reproduced in Figure 10-17.

The Rose Bowl
Work Sheet
For Year Ended June 30, 20X1

	Account Title	Income Statement Debit	Income Statement Credit	Balance Sheet Debit	Balance Sheet Credit	
1	Cash			3 1 0 0 00		1
2	Accounts Receivable			6 8 0 0 00		2
3	Merchandise Inventory			42 0 0 0 00		3
4	Store Supplies			4 0 0 00		4
5	Store Equipment			25 0 0 0 00		5
6	Accumulated Depreciation—Store Equipment				4 0 0 0 00	6
7	Trucks			38 0 0 0 00		7
8	Accumulated Depreciation—Trucks				10 0 0 0 00	8
9	Accounts Payable				4 9 0 0 00	9
10	Sales Tax Payable				1 1 0 0 00	10
11	Salaries Payable				4 0 0 00	11
12	Rosemarie Hubley, Capital				83 5 0 0 00	12
13	Rosemarie Hubley, Drawing			25 0 0 0 00		13
14	Income Summary	46 0 0 0 00	42 0 0 0 00			14
15	Sales		177 1 9 0 00			15
16	Sales Returns and Allowances	8 0 0 00				16
17	Purchases	77 8 0 0 00				17
18	Purchases Returns and Allowances		1 2 0 0 00			18
19	Purchases Discounts		6 0 0 00			19
20	Sales Salaries Expense	32 4 0 0 00				20
21	Advertising Expense	4 8 0 0 00				21
22	Depreciation Expense—Store Equipment	1 0 0 0 00				22
23	Miscellaneous Selling Expense	8 0 0 00				23
24	Store Supplies Expense	2 0 0 00				24
25	Rent Expense	4 8 9 0 00				25
26	Repairs Expense	6 0 0 00				26
27	Transportation Expense	9 0 0 00				27
28	Depreciation Expense—Trucks	3 0 0 0 00				28
29	Utilities Expense	9 6 0 0 00				29
30	Miscellaneous General Expense	1 8 0 0 00				30
31		184 5 9 0 00	220 9 9 0 00	140 3 0 0 00	103 9 0 0 00	31
32	Net income	36 4 0 0 00			36 4 0 0 00	32
33		220 9 9 0 00	220 9 9 0 00	140 3 0 0 00	140 3 0 0 00	33

The following **classified income statement** (Figure 10-18), statement of owner's equity (Figure 10-19), and **classified balance sheet** (Figure 10-20) were prepared from The Rose Bowl's work sheet.

Figure 10-18

Classified Income Statement

The dates of the income statement and statement of owner's equity cover a specific period of time.

The Rose Bowl
Income Statement
For Year Ended June 30, 20X1

Revenue from sales:					
Sales				$177 1 9 0 00	
Less: Sales returns and allow.				8 0 0 00	
Net sales					$176 3 9 0 00
Cost of goods sold:					
Merch. inventory, July 1, 20X0				$ 46 0 0 0 00	
Purchases			$77 8 0 0 00		
Less: Purchases returns and allow.	$1 2 0 0 00				
Purchases discounts	6 0 0 00	1 8 0 0 00			
Net purchases				76 0 0 0 00	
Goods available for sale				$122 0 0 0 00	
Less: Merch. inv., June 30, 20X1				42 0 0 0 00	
Cost of goods sold					80 0 0 0 00
Gross profit					$ 96 3 9 0 00
Operating expenses:					
Selling expenses:					
Sales salaries expense		$32 4 0 0 00			
Advertising expense		4 8 0 0 00			
Depr. expense—store equip.		1 0 0 0 00			
Misc. selling expense		8 0 0 00			
Store supplies expense		2 0 0 00			
Total selling expenses			$ 39 2 0 0 00		
General expenses:					
Rent expense		$ 4 8 9 0 00			
Repairs expense		6 0 0 00			
Transportation expense		9 0 0 00			
Depr. expense—trucks		3 0 0 0 00			
Utilities expense		9 6 0 0 00			
Misc. general expense		1 8 0 0 00			
Total general expenses			20 7 9 0 00		
Total operating expenses					59 9 9 0 00
Net income					$ 36 4 0 0 00

Figure 10-19

Statement of Owner's Equity

The Rose Bowl Statement of Owner's Equity For Year Ended June 30, 20X1			
Rosemarie Hubley, capital, July 1, 20X0			$83 5 0 0 00
Net income for period	$36 4 0 0 00		
Less: Withdrawals	25 0 0 0 00		
Increase in capital			11 4 0 0 00
Rosemarie Hubley, capital, June 30, 20X1			$94 9 0 0 00

Figure 10-20

Classified Balance Sheet

> The balance sheet is dated as of the last day of the accounting period.

The Rose Bowl Balance Sheet June 30, 20X1			
Assets			
Current assets:			
Cash		$ 3 1 0 0 00	
Accounts receivable		6 8 0 0 00	
Merchandise inventory		42 0 0 0 00	
Store supplies		4 0 0 00	
Total current assets			$ 52 3 0 0 00
Plant assets:			
Store equipment	$25 0 0 0 00		
Less: Accumulated depreciation	4 0 0 0 00	$21 0 0 0 00	
Trucks	$38 0 0 0 00		
Less: Accumulated depreciation	10 0 0 0 00	28 0 0 0 00	
Total plant assets			49 0 0 0 00
Total assets			$101 3 0 0 00
Liabilities			
Current liabilities:			
Accounts payable		$ 4 9 0 0 00	
Sales tax payable		1 1 0 0 00	
Salaries payable		4 0 0 00	
Total liabilities			$ 6 4 0 0 00
Owner's Equity			
Rosemarie Hubley, capital			94 9 0 0 00
Total liabilities and owner's equity			$101 3 0 0 00

2 Journalize adjusting and closing entries for a merchandising business.

The adjusting and closing entries shown in Figure 10-21 and Figure 10-22 were prepared from The Rose Bowl's work sheet.

Figure 10-21
Adjusting Entries

			General Journal					Page 5	

		Date	Account Title	P.R.	Debit	Credit	
	1		Adjusting Entries				1
no normal balance →	2	20X1 Jun. 30	Income Summary		46 0 0 0 00		2
– asset →	3		Merchandise Inventory			46 0 0 0 00	3
	4						4
+ asset →	5	30	Merchandise Inventory		42 0 0 0 00		5
no normal balance →	6		Income Summary			42 0 0 0 00	6
	7						7
+ expense →	8	30	Store Supplies Expense		2 0 0 00		8
– asset →	9		Store Supplies			2 0 0 00	9
	10						10
+ expense →	11	30	Depreciation Expense—Store Equipment		1 0 0 0 00		11
+ contra asset →	12		Accumulated Depr.—Store Equipment			1 0 0 0 00	12
	13						13
+ expense →	14	30	Depreciation Expense—Trucks		3 0 0 0 00		14
+ contra asset →	15		Accumulated Depr.—Trucks			3 0 0 0 00	15
	16						16
+ expense →	17	30	Sales Salaries Expense		4 0 0 00		17
+ liability →	18		Salaries Payable			4 0 0 00	18

Figure 10-22
Closing Entries

			General Journal					Page 6	

		Date	Account Title	P.R.	Debit	Credit	
	1		Closing Entries				1
– revenue →	2	20X1 Jun. 30	Sales		177 1 9 0 00		2
– contra purchases →	3		Purchases Returns and Allowances		1 2 0 0 00		3
– contra purchases →	4		Purchases Discounts		6 0 0 00		4
no normal balance →	5		Income Summary			178 9 9 0 00	5
	6						6
no normal balance →	7	30	Income Summary		138 5 9 0 00		7
– contra revenue →	8		Sales Returns and Allowances			8 0 0 00	8
– cost account →	9		Purchases			77 8 0 0 00	9
– expense →	10		Sales Salaries Expense			32 4 0 0 00	10
– expense →	11		Advertising Expense			4 8 0 0 00	11
– expense →	12		Depreciation Expense—Store Equip.			1 0 0 0 00	12
– expense →	13		Miscellaneous Selling Expense			8 0 0 00	13
– expense →	14		Store Supplies Expense			2 0 0 00	14
– expense →	15		Rent Expense			4 8 9 0 00	15
– expense →	16		Repairs Expense			6 0 0 00	16
– expense →	17		Transportation Expense			9 0 0 00	17
– expense →	18		Depreciation Expense—Trucks			3 0 0 0 00	18
– expense →	19		Utilities Expense			9 6 0 0 00	19
– expense →	20		Miscellaneous General Expense			1 8 0 0 00	20
	21						21
no normal balance →	22	30	Income Summary		36 4 0 0 00		22
+ owner's equity →	23		Rosemarie Hubley, Capital			36 4 0 0 00	23
	24						24
– owner's equity →	25	30	Rosemarie Hubley, Capital		25 0 0 0 00		25
– drawing →	26		Rosemarie Hubley, Drawing			25 0 0 0 00	26

3 Prepare a post-closing trial balance.

A post-closing trial balance is a trial balance of the general ledger prepared after adjusting and closing entries have been posted. Figure 10-23 shows the trial balance that was prepared after The Rose Bowl's adjusting and closing entries were posted. Notice that only the permanent accounts are shown, as all temporary accounts have been closed.

Figure 10-23

Post-Closing Trial Balance

The Rose Bowl — Post-Closing Trial Balance — June 30, 20X1		
Account Title	Debit	Credit
Cash	3 1 0 0 00	
Accounts Receivable	6 8 0 0 00	
Merchandise Inventory	42 0 0 0 00	
Store Supplies	4 0 0 00	
Store Equipment	25 0 0 0 00	
Accumulated Depreciation—Store Equipment		4 0 0 0 00
Trucks	38 0 0 0 00	
Accumulated Depreciation—Trucks		10 0 0 0 00
Accounts Payable		4 9 0 0 00
Sales Tax Payable		1 1 0 0 00
Salaries Payable		4 0 0 00
Rosemarie Hubley, Capital		94 9 0 0 00
Totals	115 3 0 0 00	115 3 0 0 00

4 Make reversing entries for accrued (unpaid) salaries.

Reversing entries are entries made at the beginning of the next accounting period, and they are the exact reverse of certain adjusting entries made at the end of the preceding period. Reversing entries are not required as part of the accounting cycle, and they should be prepared only when they will save time in the next accounting period. In this chapter, we worked with only one type of adjusting entry that should be reversed—accrued (unpaid) salaries. Accrued salaries are salaries incurred at the end of one period that will not be paid until the next accounting period. When unpaid salaries are paid in the next accounting period, the entry will have to be split between the part of the payment that pertains to the preceding period (salaries payable) and the part that pertains to the current period (salaries expense). Reversing the adjusting entry for accrued salaries (and all accrued expenses) allows the accountant to make routine entries when the expense is paid. That is, the entry does not have to be split between two amounts. The Rose Bowl had only one accrued expense, unpaid salaries in the amount of $400. We can save time when this amount is paid in the next accounting period by making the following reversing entry:

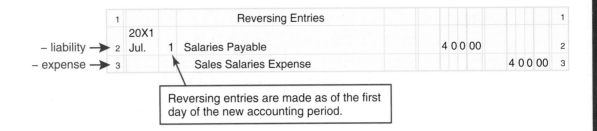

			Reversing Entries					1
– liability →	2	20X1 Jul.	1	Salaries Payable	4 0 0 00			2
– expense →	3			Sales Salaries Expense			4 0 0 00	3

Reversing entries are made as of the first day of the new accounting period.

Terms and Concepts Review

• Key Terms and Definitions in English and Spanish
• Additional Quiz Questions

Key Terms

classified balance sheet, 456
classified income statement, 451
cost of goods sold, 451
current assets, 458
current liabilities, 458
current ratio, 460
general expenses, 454
gross profit, 451
income from operations, 455
interim statements, 473
liquidity, 458

long-term liabilities, 458
net sales, 451
operating expenses, 453
other expenses, 455
other income, 455
plant assets, 458
reversing entries, 471
selling expenses, 453
stability, 458
working capital, 460

Concepts Review

1. What are the sections of the classified income statement?
2. Explain the difference between gross profit and net income.
3. Identify each of the following as either a selling expense or a general expense: (a) store supplies expense, (b) depreciation expense—office equipment, (c) rent expense, (d) advertising expense, (e) insurance expense, (f) utilities expense.
4. Explain how the statement of owner's equity serves as a link between the income statement and the balance sheet.
5. Explain the order of the current assets on the balance sheet.
6. What are other terms for plant assets?
7. How does time distinguish between current and long-term liabilities?
8. "The calculations for working capital and the current ratio use the same information but in different ways." Explain this statement.
9. Are all temporary accounts income statement accounts? Explain.
10. What figures appearing in the Income Summary account are not the result of closing entries?
11. What is the purpose of a post-closing trial balance?
12. How does the use of reversing entries make accounting for accrued expenses easier?
13. Are all adjusting entries reversed? Explain.
14. What is an interim statement?

Skills Review

Quick Practice

Learning Objective 1

Check Figure
3. Gross Profit

Quick Practice 10-1

Objective: To arrange the parts of a classified income statement in proper order

Directions: Arrange the following parts of the classified income statement in proper order.

a. Income from Operations
b. Other Expenses
c. Net Income
d. Cost of Goods Sold
e. Net Sales for the Period
f. Operating Expenses
g. Gross Profit
h. Other Income

Learning Objective 1

Check Figure
Net sales = $260,417

Quick Practice 10-2

Objective: To prepare the revenue section of a classified income statement

Directions: Using the following account balances of Kendall Kandlemakers, prepare the revenue section of the income statement for the year ended December 31, 20XX.

Account	Amount
Sales	$271,191
Sales Returns and Allowances	6,183
Sales Discounts	4,591

Learning Objective 1

Check Figure
Cost of goods sold = $120,417

Quick Practice 10-3

Objective: To prepare the cost of goods sold section of a classified income statement

Kendall Kandlemakers had the following account balances on December 31, 20XX:

Account	Amount
Merchandise Inventory, January 1, 20XX	$ 61,395
Purchases	139,360
Freight In	1,140
Purchases Returns and Allowances	5,628
Purchases Discounts	2,600
Merchandise Inventory, December 31, 20XX	73,250

Directions: Prepare the cost of goods sold section of Kendall Kandlemakers' income statement for the year ended December 31, 20XX.

Learning Objective 1

Check Figure
Gross profit = $140,000

Quick Practice 10-4

Objective: To prepare a classified income statement through gross profit

Directions: Using your solutions to Quick Practice 10-2 and 10-3, prepare an income statement through gross profit for Kendall Kandlemakers for the year ended December 31, 20XX.

Learning Objective 1

Check Figure
Total operating expenses = $111,455

Quick Practice 10-5

Objective: To prepare the operating expenses section of a classified income statement

Kendall Kandlemakers had the following operating expenses for the year ended December 31, 20XX.

Account	Amount
Rent Expense	$23,000
Sales Salaries Expense	24,200
Store Supplies Expense	1,100
Repairs Expense	800
Depreciation Expense—Store Equipment	1,800
Miscellaneous General Expense	770
Advertising Expense	35,000
Depreciation Expense—Office Equipment	2,200
Miscellaneous Selling Expense	685
Office Salaries Expense	21,900

Directions: Classify the operating expenses as selling expenses and general expenses, and prepare the total operating expenses section of Kendall Kandlemakers' income statement for the year ended December 31, 20XX.

Learning Objective **1**

Check Figure
Net income = $27,345

Quick Practice 10-6

Objective: To prepare a classified income statement

Kendall Kandlemakers had interest expense of $1,200 for the year ended December 31, 20XX.

Directions: Using your solutions to Quick Practice 10-2 through 10-5, prepare a classified income statement for Kendall Kandlemakers for the year ended December 31, 20XX.

Learning Objective **2**

Check Figure
3. Net income = $24,500

Quick Practice 10-7

Objective: To prepare closing entries using the financial statement columns of a work sheet

Diona Wagner's Hairstyling
Work Sheet (Partial)
For Year Ended December 31, 20XX

	Account Title	Income Statement Debit	Income Statement Credit	Balance Sheet Debit	Balance Sheet Credit	
1	Diona Wagner, Drawing			40 0 0 0 00		1
2	Income Summary	36 0 0 0 00	33 0 0 0 00			2
3	Sales		430 0 0 0 00			3
4	Sales Returns and Allowances	23 0 0 0 00				4
5	Sales Discounts	8 5 0 0 00				5
6	Purchases	290 0 0 0 00				6
7	Freight In	15 0 0 0 00				7
8	Purchases Returns and Allowances		20 0 0 0 00			8
9	Purchases Discounts		7 0 0 0 00			9
10	Sales Salaries Expense	30 0 0 0 00				10
11	Advertising Expense	20 0 0 0 00				11
12	Rent Expense	25 0 0 0 00				12
13	Office Salaries Expense	18 0 0 0 00				13
14						14
15						15

Directions:

1. Set up a T account for Income Summary, and enter the amounts appearing on the Income Statement columns of Wagner's partial work sheet, like this:

Income Summary

36,000	33,000

2. Journalize closing entries, posting after each entry to the T account you set up in Direction 1.
3. What is the amount of net income (or net loss) for the year?

Learning Objective **1**

Check Figure
1. (a)
6. (b)

Quick Practice 10-8

Objective: To classify balance sheet items

Directions: Classify each of the following items as a (a) current asset, (b) plant asset, (c) current liability, or (d) long-term liability.

1. Merchandise Inventory
2. Office Equipment
3. Notes Payable (due in eight months)
4. Store Supplies
5. Notes Payable (due in seven years)
6. Accumulated Depreciation—Office Equipment
7. Accounts Payable
8. Accounts Receivable

Learning Objective **1**

Check Figure
(a) $35,360

Quick Practice 10-9

Objective: To calculate working capital and the current ratio

Directions: Using the following account balances of Pualani Chang, owner of Pualani Pizzas, calculate (a) working capital and (b) the current ratio.

Account	Amount
Cash	$ 8,700
Accounts Receivable	14,600
Merchandise Inventory	31,000
Prepaid Insurance	1,300
Supplies	1,860
Store Equipment	90,000
Accounts Payable	18,000
Salaries Payable	4,100
Notes Payable (due in nine years)	30,000

Exercises

Exercise 10-1

Learning Objective 1

Check Figure
Cost of goods sold = $108,805

Objective: To calculate cost of goods sold

Directions: From the following data, calculate Maxon Company's cost of goods sold for 20X1.

Item	Amount
Beginning merchandise inventory	$ 47,610
Purchases during the period	114,750
Freight in	3,375
Purchases returns and allowances	14,875
Purchases discounts	3,145
Ending merchandise inventory	38,910

Exercise 10-2

Learning Objective 1

Check Figure
Net income = $22,930

Objective: To calculate income statement amounts

Directions: From the following data, calculate (a) net sales, (b) cost of goods sold, (c) gross profit, and (d) net income or net loss.

Item	Amount
Sales	$437,600
Sales returns and allowances	21,600
Sales discounts	9,520
Beginning merchandise inventory	37,510
Purchases	307,300
Ending merchandise inventory	43,710
Operating expenses	82,450

Exercise 10-3

Learning Objective 1

Check Figure
(a) Gross Profit = $39,300

Objective: To calculate missing financial statement items

Directions: Calculate the missing items in the following table:

	Sales	Sales Returns and Allowances	Net Sales	Beginning Inventory	Net Purchases	Goods Available for Sale	Ending Inventory	Cost of Goods Sold	Gross Profit
(a)	$122,000		$118,900		$ 72,100	$ 98,600	$19,000		
(b)		$900	110,400	$38,000	65,200		31,000		
(c)	87,500		81,230		118,000	145,000		$73,400	

Exercise 10-4

Learning Objectives 1, 2

Check Figure
Balance sheet totals = $115,850

Objective: To prepare financial statements and journalize closing entries

Directions: The financial statement columns of the December 31, 20X4, work sheet for McGaw Company are on page 486. Prepare (1) an income statement, (2) a statement of owner's equity, and (3) a balance sheet, and (4) journalize closing entries.

McGaw Company
Work Sheet
For Year Ended December 31, 20X4

	Account Title	Income Statement Debit	Income Statement Credit	Balance Sheet Debit	Balance Sheet Credit	
1	Cash			8 7 2 5 00		1
2	Accounts Receivable			9 4 5 0 00		2
3	Merchandise Inventory			12 4 1 0 00		3
4	Office Supplies			6 9 6 5 00		4
5	Office Equipment			147 0 0 0 00		5
6	Accumulated Depreciation—Office Equipment				68 7 0 0 00	6
7	Accounts Payable				16 5 1 0 00	7
8	Salaries Payable				5 4 0 00	8
9	Darin McGaw, Capital				90 2 2 0 00	9
10	Darin McGaw, Drawing			24 0 0 0 00		10
11	Income Summary	13 1 6 5 00	12 4 1 0 00			11
12	Sales		469 6 0 0 00			12
13	Sales Returns and Allowances	21 5 4 0 00				13
14	Sales Discounts	9 3 1 0 00				14
15	Purchases	301 2 4 0 00				15
16	Freight In	14 5 9 0 00				16
17	Purchases Returns and Allowances		19 5 6 5 00			17
18	Purchases Discounts		6 1 1 0 00			18
19	Sales Salaries Expense	30 3 6 0 00				19
20	Advertising Expense	4 5 0 0 00				20
21	Rent Expense	12 0 0 0 00				21
22	Office Salaries Expense	15 1 8 0 00				22
23	Office Supplies Expense	25 4 2 0 00				23
24	Utilities Expense	6 8 0 0 00				24
25	Depreciation Expense—Office Equipment	21 0 0 0 00				25
26		475 1 0 5 00	507 6 8 5 00	208 5 5 0 00	175 9 7 0 00	26
27	Net Income	32 5 8 0 00			32 5 8 0 00	27
28		507 6 8 5 00	507 6 8 5 00	208 5 5 0 00	208 5 5 0 00	28

Learning Objective **1**

Check Figure
Capital, December 31 = $120,470

Exercise 10-5

Objective: To prepare a statement of owner's equity

Directions: From the following data, prepare a statement of owner's equity for French Trading Company, owned by Rhonda French, for the year ended December 31, 20XX.

Item	Amount
Capital, January 1	$110,610
Net income for the year	47,360
Withdrawals for the year	37,500

Learning Objective **1**

Check Figure
1. (c)
7. (b)

Exercise 10-6

Objective: To classify balance sheet items

Directions: Classify each of the items in this exercise as one of the following: (a) current asset, (b) plant asset, (c) current liability, or (d) long-term liability.

1. Notes Payable (due in six months)
2. Store Supplies

3. Accounts Payable
4. Prepaid Insurance
5. Accumulated Depreciation—Store Equipment
6. Salaries Payable
7. Office Equipment
8. Notes Payable (due in five years)
9. Accounts Receivable
10. Merchandise Inventory

Learning Objective **1**

Check Figure
(a) $17,400; (b) 2.2:1

Exercise 10-7

Objective: To calculate working capital and the current ratio

Directions: From the following data, calculate (a) working capital and (b) the current ratio.

Account	Amount
Cash	$ 8,200
Accounts Receivable	5,200
Merchandise Inventory	17,000
Prepaid Insurance	750
Supplies	250
Office Equipment	17,900
Accounts Payable	11,200
Salaries Payable	2,800
Notes Payable (due in three years)	11,300

Learning Objective **2**

Check Figure
Account balance = $66,200
on the credit side

Exercise 10-8

Objective: To place items on the correct side of the Income Summary account

Directions: Set up a T account for Income Summary. Enter the following data on the correct side of the account. Do you need all the items?

Item	Amount
Revenue for the period	$158,500
Beginning merchandise inventory	13,900
Expenses for the period	95,700
Owner's withdrawals	10,600
Ending merchandise inventory	17,300
Owner's beginning capital balance	107,500

Case Problems

Group A

Learning Objective **1**

Check Figure
Net income = $27,000

Problem 10-1A

Objective: To prepare a classified income statement from account balances

The following are account balances after adjustments for Cindy Logan Clothing Store for the year ended December 31, 20XX:

Account	Balance
Advertising Expense	$ 6,100
Depreciation Expense—Office Equipment	13,000
Depreciation Expense—Store Equipment	16,000
Freight In	5,200
Insurance Expense	7,000
Merchandise Inventory, December 31	37,600
Merchandise Inventory, January 1	42,400
Office Salaries Expense	28,300

Account	Balance
Office Supplies Expense	$ 4,750
Purchases	219,550
Purchases Returns and Allowances	13,465
Purchases Discounts	6,300
Rent Expense	26,200
Sales	395,140
Sales Returns and Allowances	15,505
Sales Discounts	7,400
Sales Salaries Expense	23,000
Store Supplies Expense	5,300
Utilities Expense	5,800

Directions: Prepare a classified income statement.

Learning Objective **1**

Check Figure
Balance sheet totals =
$115,534

Problem 10-2A

Objective: To prepare and analyze a classified balance sheet

Adjusted account balances for Goffinet's Variety Store appear as follows on December 31, 20X1:

Account	Adjusted Balance
Accounts Payable	$16,025
Accounts Receivable	11,819
Accumulated Depreciation—Office Equipment	11,455
Accumulated Depreciation—Store Equipment	16,805
Cash	5,750
Merchandise Inventory	32,600
Notes Payable (due within this year)	7,000
Notes Payable (due beyond this year)	17,000
Office Equipment	37,625
Office Supplies	3,725
Prepaid Insurance	4,500
Salaries Payable	3,600
Store Equipment	42,595
Store Supplies	5,180
Renee Goffinet, Capital	71,909

Directions:

1. Prepare a classified balance sheet.
2. Calculate the firm's (a) working capital and (b) current ratio (to the nearest tenth).

Problem 10-3A

Objective: To prepare financial statements from a work sheet

The financial statement columns of Goforty Company's December 31, 20XX, work sheet follow:

Goforty Company
Work Sheet
For Year Ended December 31, 20XX

	Account Title	Income Statement Debit	Income Statement Credit	Balance Sheet Debit	Balance Sheet Credit	
1	Cash			5 8 9 5 00		1
2	Accounts Receivable			6 2 5 5 00		2
3	Merchandise Inventory			11 2 7 0 00		3
4	Store Supplies			3 7 1 0 00		4
5	Office Supplies			5 1 6 5 00		5
6	Prepaid Insurance			1 2 0 0 00		6
7	Store Equipment			21 0 0 0 00		7
8	Accumulated Depreciation—Store Equipment				6 3 0 0 00	8
9	Office Equipment			12 0 0 0 00		9
10	Accumulated Depreciation—Office Equipment				5 0 0 0 00	10
11	Accounts Payable				8 2 4 5 00	11
12	Salaries Payable				6 0 0 00	12
13	June Goforty, Capital				37 4 9 0 00	13
14	June Goforty, Drawing			7 0 0 0 00		14
15	Income Summary	12 5 4 0 00	11 2 7 0 00			15
16	Sales		194 3 7 5 00			16
17	Sales Returns and Allowances	14 5 0 5 00				17
18	Sales Discounts	3 1 7 5 00				18
19	Purchases	110 5 4 0 00				19
20	Freight In	2 5 5 0 00				20
21	Purchases Returns and Allowances		9 3 1 0 00			21
22	Purchases Discounts		2 1 4 0 00			22
23	Store Supplies Expense	9 4 2 5 00				23
24	Sales Salaries Expense	12 0 0 0 00				24
25	Depreciation Expense—Store Equipment	2 1 0 0 00				25
26	Rent Expense	4 8 0 0 00				26
27	Office Supplies Expense	18 0 0 0 00				27
28	Office Salaries Expense	10 0 0 0 00				28
29	Depreciation Expense—Office Equipment	1 0 0 0 00				29
30	Insurance Expense	6 0 0 00				30
31		201 2 3 5 00	217 0 9 5 00	73 4 9 5 00	57 6 3 5 00	31
32	Net Income	15 8 6 0 00			15 8 6 0 00	32
33		217 0 9 5 00	217 0 9 5 00	73 4 9 5 00	73 4 9 5 00	33

Directions:

1. Prepare a classified income statement for the year ended December 31, 20XX.
2. Prepare a statement of owner's equity for the year ended December 31, 20XX.
3. Prepare a classified balance sheet as of December 31, 20XX.

Problem 10-4A

Objective: To prepare closing entries from a work sheet

Directions: From the work sheet in Problem 10-3A, prepare closing entries on page 1 of a general journal.

Problem 10-5A

Objective: To prepare closing entries from account balances

The following are adjusted account balances of B.C. Lamb's Wallpaper Store as of December 31, 20X5. Beginning merchandise inventory is $19,300; ending is $21,400.

Account	Adjusted Balance
Advertising Expense	$ 4,100
Depreciation Expense—Office Equipment	12,000
Depreciation Expense—Store Equipment	8,000
B.C. Lamb, Capital	180,450
B.C. Lamb, Drawing	13,600
Insurance Expense	5,200
Office Salaries Expense	24,600
Office Supplies Expense	3,275
Purchases	92,600
Purchases Returns and Allowances	5,942
Purchases Discounts	2,520
Rent Expense	36,000
Sales	229,300
Sales Returns and Allowances	8,345
Sales Discounts	2,150
Sales Salaries Expense	37,600
Store Supplies Expense	3,675
Utilities Expense	4,920

Directions: Prepare closing entries on page 4 of a general journal.

Problem 10-6A

Objective: To record adjusting and reversing entries

Directions:

1. In each of the following unrelated situations, record the appropriate adjusting entry as of December 31, 20X2:
   (a) The Office Supplies account shows a balance before adjustment of $15,300. Office supplies of $7,900 are on hand.
   (b) The Prepaid Insurance account shows a payment of $3,780 on October 1, 20X2, for a three-year policy.
   (c) Salaries of $48,000 are paid on Monday for the preceding 5-day work week. This year, December 31 fell on a Tuesday.
2. Prepare reversing entries as needed.
3. Record the weekly salary payment on Monday, January 6, 20X3, for the week ended January 3, 20X3.
4. Assuming that the company does not use reversing entries, prepare the entry to pay the salaries on January 6, 20X3.

Problem 10-1B

Objective: To prepare a classified income statement from account balances

The following are the account balances after adjustments for Brayden Department Store for the year ended December 31, 20XX.

Account	Balance
Advertising Expense	$ 7,100
Depreciation Expense—Office Equipment	16,000
Depreciation Expense—Store Equipment	21,000
Freight In	6,200
Insurance Expense	6,100
Merchandise Inventory, December 31	17,200
Merchandise Inventory, January 1	19,600
Office Salaries Expense	31,500
Office Supplies Expense	5,610
Purchases	275,100
Purchases Returns and Allowances	13,400
Purchases Discounts	6,100
Rent Expense	29,200
Sales	445,100
Sales Returns and Allowances	21,350
Sales Discounts	8,900
Sales Salaries Expense	44,200
Store Supplies Expense	7,155
Utilities Expense	7,000

Directions: Prepare a classified income statement.

Problem 10-2B

Objective: To prepare and analyze a classified balance sheet

Adjusted account balances for Schmidt Company appear as follows on December 31, 20XX:

Account	Adjusted Balance
Accounts Payable	$27,350
Accounts Receivable	18,210
Accumulated Depreciation—Office Equipment	15,350
Accumulated Depreciation—Store Equipment	10,600
Cash	9,450
Interest Payable	350
Leslie Schmidt, Capital	66,710
Merchandise Inventory	27,110
Notes Payable (due in three years)	8,600
Office Equipment	36,500
Office Supplies	5,145
Prepaid Insurance	2,710
Salaries Payable	3,800
Store Equipment	28,600
Store Supplies	5,035

Directions:

1. Prepare a classified balance sheet.
2. Calculate the firm's (a) working capital and (b) current ratio (to the nearest tenth).

Learning Objective **1**

Check Figure
Balance sheet totals =
$120,165

Problem 10-3B

Objective: To prepare financial statements from a work sheet

The financial statement columns of Francis Company's December 31, 20XX, work sheet follow:

Francis Company
Work Sheet
For Year Ended December 31, 20XX

	Account Title	Income Statement Debit	Income Statement Credit	Balance Sheet Debit	Balance Sheet Credit	
1	Cash			3 7 2 5 00		1
2	Accounts Receivable			11 6 8 0 00		2
3	Merchandise Inventory			16 9 1 0 00		3
4	Store Supplies			4 5 0 0 00		4
5	Office Supplies			3 7 5 0 00		5
6	Prepaid Insurance			6 0 0 00		6
7	Store Equipment			85 0 0 0 00		7
8	Accumulated Depreciation—Store Equipment				36 0 0 0 00	8
9	Office Equipment			45 0 0 0 00		9
10	Accumulated Depreciation—Office Equipment				15 0 0 0 00	10
11	Accounts Payable				21 4 5 0 00	11
12	Salaries Payable				2 0 0 0 00	12
13	Debbie Francis, Capital				116 3 2 0 00	13
14	Debbie Francis, Drawing			12 0 0 0 00		14
15	Income Summary	12 4 0 0 00	16 9 1 0 00			15
16	Sales		196 5 0 0 00			16
17	Sales Returns and Allowances	11 1 1 0 00				17
18	Sales Discounts	3 1 2 0 00				18
19	Purchases	98 5 0 0 00				19
20	Freight In	2 5 0 0 00				20
21	Purchases Returns and Allowances		6 3 7 0 00			21
22	Purchases Discounts		2 1 0 0 00			22
23	Store Supplies Expense	5 1 2 5 00				23
24	Sales Salaries Expense	36 0 0 0 00				24
25	Depreciation Expense—Store Equipment	12 0 0 0 00				25
26	Rent Expense	6 0 0 0 00				26
27	Office Supplies Expense	6 2 5 0 00				27
28	Office Salaries Expense	31 0 0 0 00				28
29	Depreciation Expense—Office Equipment	5 0 0 0 00				29
30	Insurance Expense	4 8 0 00				30
31		229 4 8 5 00	221 8 8 0 00	183 1 6 5 00	190 7 7 0 00	31
32	Net Loss		7 6 0 5 00	7 6 0 5 00		32
33		229 4 8 5 00	229 4 8 5 00	190 7 7 0 00	190 7 7 0 00	33

Directions:

1. Prepare a classified income statement for the year ended December 31, 20XX.
2. Prepare a statement of owner's equity for the year ended December 31, 20XX.
3. Prepare a classified balance sheet as of December 31, 20XX.

Problem 10-4B

Objective: To prepare closing entries from a work sheet

Directions: From the work sheet in Problem 10-3B, prepare closing entries on page 1 of a general journal.

Problem 10-5B

Objective: To prepare closing entries from account balances

The following are adjusted account balances of Adkins' Variety Store as of December 31, 20X1. Beginning merchandise inventory is $29,210; ending is $25,495.

Account	Adjusted Balance
Advertising Expense	$ 3,275
Jennifer Adkins, Capital	79,210
Jennifer Adkins, Drawing	11,650
Depreciation Expense—Delivery Equipment	5,700
Depreciation Expense—Office Equipment	10,200
Depreciation Expense—Store Equipment	12,600
Insurance Expense	7,300
Office Salaries Expense	31,900
Office Supplies Expense	7,210
Purchases	207,645
Purchases Returns and Allowances	17,620
Purchases Discounts	4,155
Rent Expense	14,400
Sales	305,650
Sales Returns and Allowances	11,250
Sales Discounts	6,055
Sales Salaries Expense	65,200
Store Supplies Expense	2,300
Utilities Expense	5,275

Directions: Prepare closing entries on page 2 of a general journal.

Problem 10-6B

Objective: To record adjusting and reversing entries

Directions:

1. In each of the following unrelated situations, record the appropriate adjusting entry as of December 31, 20X3:
   (a) The Office Supplies account shows a balance before adjustment of $17,700. Office supplies of $3,145 are on hand.
   (b) The Prepaid Insurance account shows a payment of $1,680 on April 1, 20X3, for a two-year policy.
   (c) Salaries of $64,000 are paid on Monday for the preceding 5-day work week. This year, December 31 fell on a Wednesday.
2. Prepare reversing entries as needed.
3. Record the weekly salary payment on Monday, January 5, 20X4, for the week ended January 2, 20X4.
4. Assuming that the company does not use reversing entries, prepare the entry to pay the salaries on January 5, 20X4.

Critical Thinking Problems

Challenge Problem

The completed work sheet for Hatfield's Department Store is shown on pages 496–497.

Directions:

1. Open a general ledger account for each account listed in the Trial Balance columns. Enter the balances as of December 31, 20X2.
2. Prepare a classified income statement.
3. Prepare a statement of owner's equity.
4. Prepare a classified balance sheet. The notes payable are due in three years.
5. Calculate working capital and the current ratio rounded to the nearest tenth.
6. Journalize and post adjusting entries.
7. Journalize and post closing entries.
8. Prepare a post-closing trial balance.
9. Journalize reversing entries (if needed). Date the entries January 1, 20X3.
10. Comment on the financial condition of the company.

Communications

Kimberly Lybarger is an accounting teacher at a local community college. After studying the material in this chapter, several students asked her the same question: "Cost of goods sold, operating expenses, and other expenses are all deductions from revenue. Why are they not simply listed in one section called 'Expenses' instead of reported separately on the income statement?"

Write a response that answers the students' question.

Team Internet Project

Currency exchange works both ways. In the Chapter 8 Team Internet Project activity, you converted from U.S. dollars to currencies of other countries by multiplying the conversion rate by U.S. dollars. In this activity, work is in the opposite direction—the following purchase transactions are in the currency of the other country and need to be converted back to U.S. dollars. Just as you multiplied to get the answers in Chapter 8, you will divide here in this chapter. Divide the number of units of currency of the other country by the conversion rate to obtain the number of dollars. The purchases are as follows:

From a European firm for 600 euros
From a Malaysian firm for 500 ringgits
From an Egyptian firm for 2,000 pounds
From a Brazilian firm for 700 reals
From an Indian firm for 30,000 rupees

Search the Internet to find the exchange rates, and do the conversions.

Ethics

Mark Watson is a business owner who is very interested in showing a good current ratio. Therefore, he instructs his bookkeeper to list all notes payable on the balance sheet as long-term liabilities. Write an explanation as to why this is an unacceptable accounting practice.

Following are some data from the income statements (statements of operations) of Target Corporation for the years 2004, 2005, and 2006. Amounts are in millions.

	2006	2005	2004
Statements of Operations			
Sales	$59,490	$51,271	$45,682
Cost of sales	39,999	34,927	31,445
Operating expenses	12,819	11,185	9,797
Net earnings	2,787	2,408	3,198

Based on the statements of operations data for Target, answer the following questions:

(a) What is the amount of gross profit for each of the three years?
(b) How would you describe the trend in gross profit for the three years?

Answers to Review Quizzes

Review Quiz 10-1

(a) $63,750
(b) $61,600
(c) $124,700

Review Quiz 10-2

(a) $69,200
(b) $20,900
(c) $48,300
(d) $30,100, income from operations
(e) $28,700, net income

Review Quiz 10-3

(a) $86,800
(b) $8,000
(c) $78,800
(d) 10.85:1 (or 10.85 to 1)

Yes. The company should be able to pay its current liabilities as they fall due. For every $1 of current liabilities, Miller has $10.85 in current assets. A current ratio of 2:1 is considered acceptable.

Hatfield's Department Store
Work Sheet
For Year Ended December 31, 20X2

Account Title	Trial Balance Debit	Trial Balance Credit	Adjustments Debit	Adjustments Credit	Adjusted Trial Balance Debit	Adjusted Trial Balance Credit	Income Statement Debit	Income Statement Credit	Balance Sheet Debit	Balance Sheet Credit	
1 Cash	8 3 5 0 00				8 3 5 0 00				8 3 5 0 00		1
2 Accounts Receivable	7 4 2 5 00				7 4 2 5 00				7 4 2 5 00		2
3 Merchandise Inventory	25 4 6 0 00		(b)30 2 1 5 00	(a)25 4 6 0 00	30 2 1 5 00				30 2 1 5 00		3
4 Office Supplies	12 3 5 0 00			(c)7 1 9 0 00	5 1 6 0 00				5 1 6 0 00		4
5 Store Supplies	11 3 0 0 00			(d)8 4 0 0 00	2 9 0 0 00				2 9 0 0 00		5
6 Prepaid Insurance	3 9 0 0 00			(e)2 2 0 0 00	1 7 0 0 00				1 7 0 0 00		6
7 Office Equipment	42 0 0 0 00				42 0 0 0 00				42 0 0 0 00		7
8 Acc. Depr.—Off. Equip.		12 0 0 0 00		(g)3 0 0 0 00		15 0 0 0 00				15 0 0 0 00	8
9 Store Equipment	90 0 0 0 00				90 0 0 0 00				90 0 0 0 00		9
10 Acc. Depr.—Store Equip.		28 4 0 0 00		(h)6 2 0 0 00		34 6 0 0 00				34 6 0 0 00	10
11 Delivery Equipment	32 0 0 0 00				32 0 0 0 00				32 0 0 0 00		11
12 Acc. Depr.—Del. Equip.		18 5 0 0 00		(i)6 5 0 0 00		25 0 0 0 00				25 0 0 0 00	12
13 Accounts Payable		11 4 2 5 00				11 4 2 5 00				11 4 2 5 00	13
14 Salaries Payable				(f)9 8 5 00		9 8 5 00				9 8 5 00	14
15 Notes Payable		25 0 0 0 00				25 0 0 0 00				25 0 0 0 00	15
16 John Hatfield, Capital		71 2 6 0 00				71 2 6 0 00				71 2 6 0 00	16
17 John Hatfield, Drawing	39 0 0 0 00				39 0 0 0 00				39 0 0 0 00		17
18 Income Summary			(a)25 4 6 0 00	(b)30 2 1 5 00	25 4 6 0 00	30 2 1 5 00	25 4 6 0 00	30 2 1 5 00			18
19 Sales		524 8 0 0 00				524 8 0 0 00		524 8 0 0 00			19
	524 8 0 0 00	524 8 0 0 00									

Line	Account	Trial Balance Dr	Trial Balance Cr	Adjustments Dr	Adjustments Cr	Adjusted Trial Balance Dr	Adjusted Trial Balance Cr	Income Statement Dr	Income Statement Cr	Balance Sheet Dr	Balance Sheet Cr
20	Sales Returns and Allow.	22,400.00				22,400.00		22,400.00			
21	Sales Discounts	8,200.00				8,200.00		8,200.00			
22	Purchases	306,500.00				306,500.00		306,500.00			
23	Purch. Ret. and Allow.		20,300.00				20,300.00		20,300.00		
24	Purchases Discounts		5,950.00				5,950.00		5,950.00		
25	Freight In	13,650.00				13,650.00		13,650.00			
26	Sales Salaries Expense	41,000.00		(f) 360.00		41,360.00		41,360.00			
27	Store Supplies Expense			(d) 8,400.00		8,400.00		8,400.00			
28	Advertising Expense	6,700.00				6,700.00		6,700.00			
29	Depr. Exp.—Store Equip.			(h) 6,200.00		6,200.00		6,200.00			
30	Depr. Exp.—Del. Equip.			(i) 6,500.00		6,500.00		6,500.00			
31	Rent Expense	20,000.00				20,000.00		20,000.00			
32	Office Salaries Expense	18,000.00		(f) 625.00		18,625.00		18,625.00			
33	Office Supplies Expense			(c) 7,190.00		7,190.00		7,190.00			
34	Utilities Expense	7,800.00				7,800.00		7,800.00			
35	Depr. Exp.—Office Equip.			(g) 3,000.00		3,000.00		3,000.00			
36	Insurance Expense			(e) 2,200.00		2,200.00		2,200.00			
37	Miscellaneous Expense	1,200.00				1,200.00		1,200.00			
38	Interest Expense	400.00				400.00		400.00			
39		717,635.00		90,150.00	90,150.00	764,535.00	764,535.00	505,785.00	581,265.00	258,750.00	183,270.00
40	Net income							75,480.00			75,480.00
41								581,265.00	581,265.00	258,750.00	258,750.00

Review Quiz 10-4

1			Closing Entries				1
2	20XX Jul.	31	Sales	70 0 0 0 00			2
3			Purchases Discounts	2 9 0 00			3
4			Income Summary		70 2 9 0 00		4
5							5
6		31	Income Summary	55 6 1 6 00			6
7			Sales Returns and Allowances		8 0 0 00		7
8			Sales Discounts		1 2 0 0 00		8
9			Purchases		38 0 0 0 00		9
10			Rent Expense		4 0 0 0 00		10
11			Salaries Expense		9 0 0 0 00		11
12			Depreciation Expense		8 0 0 00		12
13			Supplies Expense		9 5 00		13
14			Telephone Expense		1 9 5 00		14
15			Utilities Expense		1 4 0 0 00		15
16			Miscellaneous Expense		1 2 6 00		16
17							17
18		31	Income Summary	15 8 7 4 00			18
19			LeeAnn Gatewood, Capital		15 8 7 4 00		19
20							20
21		31	LeeAnn Gatewood, Capital	12 0 0 0 00			21
22			LeeAnn Gatewood, Drawing		12 0 0 0 00		22

Review Quiz 10-5

1			Reversing Entries				1
2	20X4 Jan.	1	Salaries Payable	8 1 0 00			2
3			Salaries Expense		8 1 0 00		3

Comprehensive Review Problem II

Mills Sporting Goods Store

(P) (Q)

You have now completed the accounting cycle for a merchandising business and are ready to try to put it all together in this second comprehensive review problem.

You are keeping the accounting records for Cindi Mills, owner of Mills Sporting Goods Store. You begin with the balances in her accounts and go through the accounting cycle for two months.

Directions:

1. Open accounts in the general ledger with the following balances as of January 1, 20X1:

	Account	Balance
111	Cash	$ 6,560
112	Accounts Receivable	2,955
113	Office Supplies	825
114	Store Supplies	1,915
115	Merchandise Inventory	13,540
116	Prepaid Insurance	750
121	Office Equipment	9,500
121.1	Accumulated Depreciation—Office Equipment	2,600
122	Store Equipment	16,600
122.1	Accumulated Depreciation—Store Equipment	4,000
123	Delivery Equipment	13,000
123.1	Accumulated Depreciation—Delivery Equipment	7,000
211	Accounts Payable	3,880
311	Cindi Mills, Capital	48,165
312	Cindi Mills, Drawing	
313	Income Summary	
411	Sales	
412	Sales Returns and Allowances	
413	Sales Discounts	
511	Purchases	
512	Purchases Returns and Allowances	
513	Purchases Discounts	
514	Freight In	
611	Salaries Expense	
612	Rent Expense	
613	Utilities Expense	
614	Office Supplies Expense	
615	Store Supplies Expense	
616	Insurance Expense	
617	Depreciation Expense—Office Equipment	
618	Depreciation Expense—Store Equipment	
619	Depreciation Expense—Delivery Equipment	

2. Open accounts in the accounts receivable ledger with the following balances as of January 1, 20X1:

Customer Name	Balance
Henry Galvin	$1,025
Lee Maddox	755
Neagle Co.	1,175
Smitz, Inc.	-0-

3. Open accounts in the accounts payable ledger with the following balances as of January 1, 20X1:

Creditor Name	Balance
W. Bedford Co.	$1,365
Jones Co.	-0-
Lemke Brothers	1,540
Wohlers, Inc.	975

4. Record the January transactions in a general journal (page 12), a one-column sales journal (page 26), a purchases journal (page 10), a five-column cash receipts journal (page 11), or a four-column cash payments journal (page 9). All credit sales carry terms of 2/10,n/30. Freight on all purchases is charged to the Freight In account.

20X1

Jan. 2 Paid rent for the month, $1,070, Check No. 234.

2 Sold merchandise to Smitz, Inc., $765, Invoice No. 176.

4 Collected the balance due from Henry Galvin, less 2% discount.

5 Sold merchandise to Henry Galvin, $1,670, Invoice No. 177.

6 Collected the balance due from Neagle Co., less 2% discount.

7 Issued a credit memorandum to Henry Galvin for the return of defective merchandise sold on January 5, $210.

7 Purchased merchandise from Lemke Brothers, $1,045; terms 2/10,n/30; Invoice No. 187.

8 Paid W. Bedford Co. the balance due, less 2% discount; Check No. 235.

9 Paid Wohlers, Inc., the balance due, less 1% discount; Check No. 236.

10 Returned defective merchandise purchased on January 7 from Lemke Brothers, receiving a credit memorandum for $105.

10 Collected the balance due from Lee Maddox, less 2% discount.

11 Paid Lemke Brothers the January 1 balance; no discount; Check No. 237.

12 Received a check from Smitz, Inc., for the amount due from the sale of January 2.

14 Purchased merchandise from Jones Co., $2,550; terms, 2/10,n/30; Invoice No. 188.

15 Received a check from Henry Galvin for the amount due from the sale of January 5, less the return of January 7.

15 Recorded cash sales for the first half of January, $1,665.

15 Cindi invested an additional $3,000 cash in the firm.

16 Purchased office equipment from Wohlers, Inc., $4,400; terms, 2/30,n/60; Invoice No. 189.

17 Sold merchandise to Lee Maddox, $950, Invoice No. 178.

17 Paid Lemke Brothers the amount due from the purchase of January 7, less the return of January 10; Check No. 238.

18 Purchased office supplies from W. Bedford Co., $860; terms, n/30; Invoice No. 190.

19 Returned defective office supplies to W. Bedford Co., receiving a credit memorandum for $110.

20 Purchased store supplies from Jones Co., $555; terms, n/30; Invoice No. 191.

22 Cindi invested a used truck valued at $4,700 in the business.

23 Sold merchandise to Neagle Co., $820, Invoice No. 179.

24 Paid the balance due to Jones Co. from the purchase of January 14; Check No. 239.

24 Cindi wrote Check No. 240 to pay her home phone bill, $205.

25 Sold merchandise to Smitz, Inc., $1,995, Invoice No. 180.

26 Sold store supplies to another firm at cost for cash, $110.

27 Issued a credit memorandum to Smitz, Inc., for a shortage from the sale of January 25, $75.

27 Purchased merchandise from Jones Co., $750; terms, 2/10,n/30; Invoice No. 192.

29 Paid January's electric bill, $595, Check No. 241.

31 Recorded cash sales for the second half of January, $2,445.

31 Paid freight on January purchases, $450, Check No. 242.

31 Paid salaries for January, $4,450, Check No. 243.

5. Total all special journals.
6. Post all items that need to be posted.
7. Prepare a trial balance on a work sheet as of January 31, 20X1.
8. Prepare schedules of accounts receivable and accounts payable.
9. Complete the work sheet. Adjustment data for January 31 are as follows:
   (a) Office supplies on hand, $830.
   (b) Store supplies on hand, $750.
   (c) Insurance expired, $20.
   (d) Depreciation of office equipment, $90.
   (e) Depreciation of store equipment, $125.
   (f) Depreciation of delivery equipment, $250.
   (g) Merchandise inventory (beginning), $13,540.
   (h) Merchandise inventory (ending), $12,210.
10. Record and post adjusting entries as of January 31.
11. Record and post closing entries as of January 31.
12. Prepare a January 31 post-closing trial balance.
13. Prepare an income statement for the month of January. All salaries are sales salaries.
14. Prepare a statement of owner's equity for the month of January.
15. Prepare a January 31 balance sheet.
16. Record the following February transactions:

20X1

Feb. 1 Paid rent for the month, $1,070, Check No. 244.

2 Purchased merchandise from Lemke Brothers, $740; terms, 2/10,n/30; Invoice No. 193.

3 Returned merchandise purchased from Lemke Brothers on February 2, receiving a credit memorandum for $75.

3 Collected the balance due from Lee Maddox.

4 Collected the balance due from Smitz, Inc., for the sale of January 25 less the credit of January 27 and less the 2% discount.

5 Cindi took home $40 of office supplies for her personal use.

6 Sold merchandise to Henry Galvin, $2,140, Invoice No. 181.

6 Paid Jones Co. the balance due on purchases of $555 and $750, less a 2% discount on the $750 purchase; Check No. 245.

7 Collected the balance due from Neagle Co.

8 Issued a credit memorandum to Henry Galvin for damaged merchandise sold on February 6, $195.

9 Purchased merchandise for cash, $375, Check No. 246.

11 Paid Lemke Brothers for the balance due from the purchase of February 2, less the return of February 3; Check No. 247.

11	Returned $20 of the merchandise purchased on February 9, receiving a cash refund.
12	Sold merchandise to Lee Maddox, $1,185, Invoice No. 182.
13	Cindi wrote Check No. 248 for personal expenses, $350.
14	Recorded cash sales for the first half of the month, $3,095.
15	Paid Wohlers, Inc., the balance due, less 2% discount; Check No. 249.
16	Received a check from Henry Galvin for the amount due from the sale of February 6, less the return of February 8.
17	Sold office supplies for cash, $85.
17	Paid W. Bedford Co. the balance due for the purchase of January 18, less the return of January 19; Check No. 250.
19	Purchased store supplies from W. Bedford Co. $340; terms, n/30; Invoice No. 194.
20	Returned $30 of the store supplies purchased on February 19, receiving credit.
21	Purchased merchandise from Lemke Brothers, $940; terms, 2/10,n/30; Invoice No. 195.
22	Sold merchandise to Neagle Co., $1,095; Invoice No. 183.
24	Purchased merchandise from Jones Co., $1,045; terms, 2/10,n/30; Invoice No. 196.
25	Sold merchandise to Smitz, Inc., $1,755, Invoice No. 184.
26	Purchased store equipment from Wohlers, Inc., $2,700; terms, 2/30,n/60; Invoice No. 197.
27	Paid the electric bill for February, $550, Check No. 251.
28	Recorded cash sales for the second half of the month, $2,985.
28	Paid freight on February purchases, $435, Check No. 252.
28	Paid salaries for February, $4,450, Check No. 253.

17. Total all special journals.
18. Post all items that need to be posted.
19. Prepare a trial balance on a work sheet as of February 28, 20X1.
20. Prepare schedules of accounts receivable and accounts payable.
21. Complete the work sheet. Adjustment data for February 28 are as follows:
    (a) Office supplies on hand, $355.
    (b) Store supplies on hand, $275.
    (c) Insurance expired, $20.
    (d) Depreciation of office equipment, $90.
    (e) Depreciation of store equipment, $125.
    (f) Depreciation of delivery equipment, $250.
    (g) Merchandise inventory (beginning), $12,210.
    (h) Merchandise inventory (ending), $12,780.
22. Record and post adjusting entries as of February 28.
23. Record and post closing entries as of February 28.
24. Prepare a February 28 post-closing trial balance.
25. Prepare an income statement for the month of February. All salaries are sales salaries.
26. Prepare a statement of owner's equity for the month of February.
27. Prepare a February 28 balance sheet.

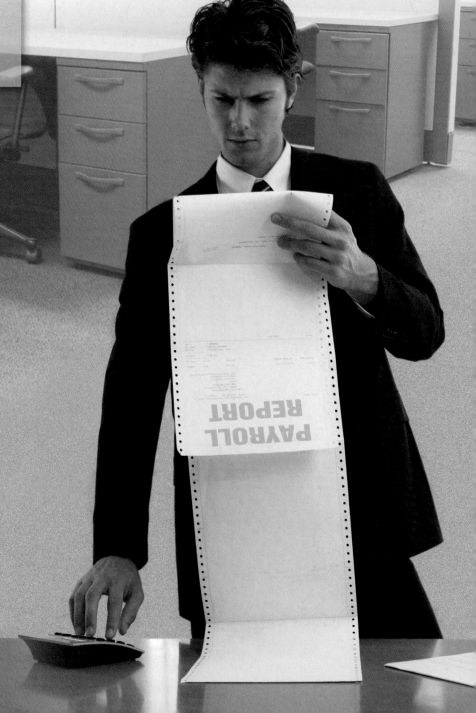

PART III

Accounting for Payroll

The Social Security Administration is a federal government organization that oversees the Federal Insurance Contributions Act (Social Security) deductions from our paychecks and the distribution of funds from the amounts collected to those who receive benefits. The U.S. Treasury Department does the accounting for the Social Security Administration. Four separate accounts or trust funds are kept for these amounts:

- The OASI account for Old-Age and Survivors Insurance, our retirement pensions.
- The DI account for Disability Insurance to pay for disability benefits. OASI and DI together make up the OASDI account that you will learn about in Chapter 11.
- The HI account for Hospitalization Insurance, or basic Medicare. You will also learn more about this account in Chapter 11.
- The SMI account for Supplementary Medical Insurance, or Medicare for doctors and prescriptions.

Alexander Hamilton was the first Secretary of the Treasury. His statue welcomes visitors to the Treasury Department building in Washington, DC.

While we read much about the future of Social Security in the United States, it is worthwhile to get some specific data about the particular funds. You will find these data in the In the Real World section of Chapter 11.

For further information about the Social Security Administration, look up *www.ssa.gov.*

CHAPTER 11

Accounting for Payroll
Employee Earnings and Deductions

Learning Objectives

1 Describe the importance of payroll records.
2 Calculate gross earnings for employees.
3 Explain the nature of payroll deductions.
4 Calculate payroll deductions and net pay.
5 Complete a payroll register and use it to record and pay the payroll.
6 Make accounting entries for employee earnings and deductions and for payment of the payroll.

Our study of accounting has now taken us through the accounting cycle for both a service business and a merchandising business. For each type of business, we recorded salaries earned by employees in an account entitled Salaries Expense. We have also learned that salaries unpaid (accrued) at the end of an accounting period must be recorded to show the proper amount of expenses for the period. We are now concerned with how the amount of earnings is determined. In this chapter, we will learn how to determine and account for the earnings of employees. We will also learn about various taxes and other deductions that are taken from the pay of employees. We will continue our study of payroll in Chapter 12 by looking at the payroll taxes imposed on the employer.

Learning Objective

1 Describe the importance of payroll records.

Accurate and current records are very important, especially for payroll accounting. In many companies, the cost of payroll alone amounts to 50% to 60% of all operating expenses. Due to the significant amount of this expense, companies must have an accurate and efficient means of keeping up with payroll information.

There are two primary reasons for maintaining accurate and up-to-date payroll records. First, we must accumulate the information needed to calculate the pay of each employee for each payroll period. Second, we must provide information needed to complete the various payroll reports that are required by federal and state regulations.

Employer/Employee Relationships

employee a person who works under the direct control of an employer on a continuing basis

independent contractor a person who agrees to complete a specific job or task and determines the ways and methods of achieving that job or task

Our first task in learning about payroll is to distinguish between an employee and an independent contractor. An **employee** is under the direct control of an employer on a continuing basis. This means that an employer is able to tell an employee when to work, how to work, and where to work. An **independent contractor**, on the other hand, agrees to perform and complete a specific job or task and is left to determine the ways and methods of achieving that job or task. In other words, an independent contractor is hired for a specific purpose and, since there is no permanent working relationship, is not on the payroll of the employer. Examples of independent contractors are architects, certified public accountants, attorneys, plumbers, and exterminators.

Take This Into Account

The distinction between an employee and an independent contractor is important because payroll accounting applies *only* to the employees of a firm. Most employers are required to deduct taxes and other amounts from the pay of employees; independent contractors are paid on a fee basis and are personally responsible for paying their own taxes.

salaried employee an individual who works for a fixed amount of pay for a definite period of time, such as a week, a month, or a year

salary a fixed amount paid to employees for a certain period of time, such as a week, month, or year

hourly worker an individual who works for a fixed hourly rate, usually referred to as a wage

wage a fixed hourly rate paid to an employee

Fair Labor Standards Act an act passed by Congress in 1938 that, as amended, establishes standards for minimum wage, overtime pay, child labor, required payroll record keeping and equal pay for equal work regardless of sex; also referred to as the Wages and Hours Law

minimum wage the lowest hourly rate that can be paid to employees who are covered by the Fair Labor Standards Act

How Employees Are Paid

We can distinguish between different types of employees on the basis of how they are paid. There are generally two types of employees, *salaried* and *hourly*. A **salaried employee** works for a fixed amount (**salary**) for a definite period of time, such as a week, a month, or a year. Examples of salaried employees include managers, teachers, public officials, and administrative service personnel.

An **hourly worker** works for a fixed hourly rate, which is commonly called a **wage.** In practice, however, the terms *salary* and *wage* are often used interchangeably.

Fair Labor Standards Act

Employees who receive an hourly wage are generally covered by the **Fair Labor Standards Act** (commonly called the Wages and Hours Law), which establishes standards for the minimum wage, overtime pay, child labor, required payroll record keeping, and equal pay for equal work regardless of sex. The Act is administered by the Wage and Hour Division of the U.S. Department of Labor and applies *only* to firms engaged in interstate commerce. Employees covered by the Act are guaranteed a *minimum wage* and *overtime pay* if they work more than 40 hours in one week.

The **minimum wage** is the lowest hourly rate that can be paid to employees covered by the Act. The minimum wage is raised periodically to

overtime pay a mini-
mum of one and one-half
times the regular rate
of pay for hours worked
over 40 in a week;
commonly referred to as
time-and-a-half

time-and-a-half the
common rate for over-
time pay

reflect cost-of-living increases. At this writing, it is $6.55 an hour. **Overtime pay** means a *minimum* of one and one-half times the regular rate of pay for all hours worked over 40 during a week. The overtime rate is commonly referred to as **time-and-a-half**.

> ! Take This Into Account
>
> In May 2007, Congress raised the federal minimum wage from $5.15 per hour to the current $6.55 per hour in three increments. The law defined the increases according to the following schedule: July 24, 2007, $5.85; July 24, 2008, $6.55; July 24, 2009, $7.25.

While the Fair Labor Standards Act requires a minimum overtime rate of time-and-a-half, many companies have gone beyond the minimum overtime rate and pay double time for weekend work and for work on holidays. Some companies also pay overtime if an employee works more than 8 hours in one day even if total hours for the week do not exceed 40. We should stress, however, that this is a matter of company policy (or union contract), not the law. We should also stress that certain workers, such as executive, administrative, and professional employees, are exempt from the minimum wage and overtime provisions of the Fair Labor Standards Act. Thus, when such workers (often referred to as *exempt employees*) work more than 40 hours in a week, they usually do not receive overtime pay.

Piece-Rate Plans

piece-rate plan a
method of payment
in which workers are
paid for each unit they
produce rather than by
hours worked

Some employees (usually factory workers) are paid on a **piece-rate plan**; that is, they receive a certain rate of pay for each unit they complete. For example, assume that a factory worker is paid $.08 for each unit produced. Further assume that during the last workweek, the employee produced 4,800 units. The employee's earnings for that week are calculated as follows:

Number of units produced × Rate per unit = Earnings for the period
        4,800   × $.08   = $384

Calculating Gross Earnings

Learning Objective

2 Calculate gross earnings
for employees.

gross earnings an em-
ployee's earnings before
any amount is deducted
by the employer

Gross earnings are an employee's earnings before any amount is deducted by the employer. The calculation of gross earnings for a salaried employee is rather simple. The employee is usually hired for an annual salary; the annual salary is then divided by the number of pay periods in the year. How many checks the employee receives in the year will depend on the pay period selected by the employer. The most common pay periods are weekly, biweekly (every other week), semimonthly (twice a month), and monthly. To illustrate, assume that an employee is hired at an annual salary of $28,080. We can calculate gross earnings per pay period as follows:

Type of Pay Period	Number of Pay Periods in a Year	Gross Earnings per Pay Period
Weekly	52	$ 540 ($28,080 ÷ 52)
Biweekly	26	1,080 ($28,080 ÷ 26)
Semimonthly	24	1,170 ($28,080 ÷ 24)
Monthly	12	2,340 ($28,080 ÷ 12)

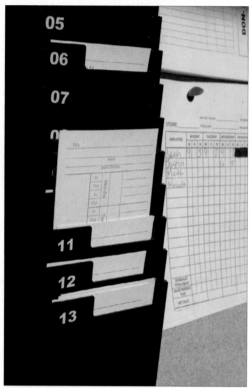

The use of time cards is one way to track an employee's hours.

The calculation of gross earnings for an hourly worker is different. We need information about the number of hours the employee worked, the hourly rate of pay, and overtime rates. Hours worked can be tracked manually by filling out a time card or electronically by entering information into a computer terminal or scanning an employee's name badge. To illustrate, let's take two examples. For our first example, we will use Sam Morgan, who is an hourly worker earning $9 an hour. During the last workweek, Sam worked a total of 40 hours. (Note: Since Sam's total hours for the week did not exceed 40, he will not receive overtime pay for this period.) His gross earnings for the week are calculated as follows:

Hours worked	×	Rate per hour	=	Gross earnings
40	×	$9	=	$360

For our second example, we will use Anne Sheppard, who is an hourly worker earning $10 an hour. During her last workweek, Anne worked a total of 44 hours. Her gross earnings for the week are calculated as follows:

Regular hours	×	Regular rate	
40	×	$10	= $400

Overtime hours	×	Overtime rate	
4	×	$15 ($10 × 1.5)	= 60

| Gross earnings | | | = $460 |

Another way to calculate Anne's gross earnings is to multiply her total number of hours worked by $10 and then add the overtime pay. This method looks like this:

Total hours	×	Regular rate	
44	×	$10	= $440

Overtime hours	×	One-half time	
4	×	$5 ($10 × .5)	= 20

| Gross earnings | | | = $460 |

For covered employees, overtime is paid only for hours worked over 40 in a week. The overtime rate is at least 1.5 times the regular rate. However, it is the policy of many employers to pay double time for some work (such as weekends or holidays) and overtime for more than eight hours in one day, even if total hours for the week don't exceed 40.

Review Quiz **11-1** Joy Jackson worked 45 hours this week. Her hourly wage is $8.00, and she receives overtime pay at a rate of time-and-a-half. Calculate her gross earnings.

Check your answer on page 538.

Payroll Deductions

3 Explain the nature of payroll deductions.

payroll deduction an amount withheld (deducted) from the pay of an employee

As anyone who has received a paycheck knows, the amount actually paid to employees (take-home pay) rarely equals the amount of gross earnings. The reason for the difference is payroll deductions. A **payroll deduction** is an amount an employer withholds (deducts) from an employee's earnings before payment is made.

Payroll deductions may be mandatory or voluntary. Mandatory deductions are required by law. Federal law requires employers to withhold Social Security taxes and federal income taxes. An employer is also required to withhold certain taxes for state (and sometimes local) taxing agencies.

Voluntary deductions are those employers agree to make for the benefit of employees, such as amounts for insurance premiums, charities, retirement plans, and union dues. Let's look closer at the various deductions and how they are calculated.

FICA Tax (Social Security)

4 Calculate payroll deductions and net pay.

Federal Insurance Contributions Act (FICA) an act that requires contributions by both the employer and the employee to the federal Social Security system; includes two component parts: OASDI (Old-Age, Survivors, and Disability Insurance) and HI (Hospital Insurance), or Medicare

OASDI taxable wage base the maximum amount of earnings during a calendar year that is subject to OASDI taxes

Most workers in the United States are covered by the **Federal Insurance Contributions Act (FICA)**, which is commonly referred to as Social Security. FICA taxes are used to finance (1) the federal Old-Age, Survivors, and Disability Insurance (OASDI) program and (2) the Hospital Insurance (HI) plan, or Medicare. A unique aspect of the FICA tax is that *both* the employee and the employer contribute equal amounts. We will discuss the employer's share of FICA in Chapter 12. For now, let's concentrate on the employee's share.

The OASDI Taxable Wage Base

The **OASDI taxable wage base** is the maximum amount of earnings during a calendar year that is subject to OASDI taxes. At the time of this writing, the taxable OASDI base is $102,000. Should an employee's earnings reach or exceed this amount, no additional OASDI taxes will be withheld for the remainder of the year. There is no maximum wage base for HI taxes, however. That is, all earnings are subject to HI regardless of the amount. To help clarify this, let's assume that Jerry Kholer is a sales rep whose earnings for 20X3 are

$102,800 as of the November 15 payroll. Since Jerry has exceeded the OASDI taxable base of $102,000, he will pay no more OASDI taxes for the rest of the year. However, since there is no wage limit for HI taxes, he will continue to pay this tax for the rest of the year.

The FICA Tax Rates

Under the Social Security Act, as amended, a separate tax rate is used to calculate OASDI and HI. At this writing, the OASDI rate is 6.2% (of the first $102,000 earned during the year); the HI rate is 1.45% of all earnings. To illustrate, let's return to our earlier example of Sam Morgan. Remember that Sam earned $360 during his last workweek. Further, Sam's earnings have not reached $102,000 during the year. His FICA tax for the pay period is calculated as follows:

OASDI	$360 × .062 (6.2%)	= $22.32
HI	360 × .0145 (1.45%)	= 5.22
Total FICA tax		$27.54

Review Quiz **11-2** Complete the following information:

Employee	Earnings before This Pay Period	Earnings This Pay Period	FICA OASDI	HI
A	$ 15,400	$ 412	$_____	$_____
B	101,600	1,250	$_____	$_____
C	69,300	825	$_____	$_____
D	32,400	618	$_____	$_____

Check your answers on page 538.

Federal Income Tax

The federal government's main source of revenue is the income tax imposed on personal incomes. Unless specifically exempted, all income (legal and illegal) is subject to the personal income tax. The amount of personal income tax to be withheld depends on three factors:

- the employee's gross earnings
- the employee's marital status
- the number of withholding allowances claimed by the employee

The calculation of gross earnings was discussed earlier. An employee's marital status, for withholding purposes, is either *married* or *single*. Thus, a divorced person who has not remarried is considered to be single, as is a widow or widower who has not remarried.

A **withholding allowance**, also called an *exemption*, is an amount of earnings not subject to taxation. A withholding allowance is allowed for the employee, for his or her spouse (if the spouse is not also working and claiming an allowance), and for each dependent for whom the taxpayer provides support.

At the start of a new job, or when personal information changes, an employee is required to complete an **Employee's Withholding Allowance Certificate (Form W-4)**, which is kept on file by the employer. The Form

withholding allowance an amount of earnings that is not subject to taxation; also referred to as an exemption

Employee's Withholding Allowance Certificate (Form W-4) a form filled out by each employee showing marital status and number of withholding allowances claimed

Figure 11-1
Form W-4

W-4 indicates the employee's marital status and the number of withholding allowances claimed. Figure 11-1 shows Sam Morgan's Form W-4.

········· **Cut here and give Form W-4 to your employer. Keep the top part for your records.** ·········

Form **W-4** Department of the Treasury Internal Revenue Service	**Employee's Withholding Allowance Certificate** ▶ Whether you are entitled to claim a certain number of allowances or exemption from withholding is subject to review by the IRS. Your employer may be required to send a copy of this form to the IRS.	OMB No. 1545-0074 20**X3**

1 Type or print your first name and middle initial. **Sam L.**	Last name **Morgan**	2 Your social security number 422 ¦ 22 ¦ 6222

Home address (number and street or rural route) **1244 Oak Street**	3 ☐ Single ☑ Married ☐ Married, but withhold at higher Single rate. **Note.** If married, but legally separated, or spouse is a nonresident alien, check the "Single" box.
City or town, state, and ZIP code **Ames, NJ 07003**	4 If your last name differs from that shown on your social security card, check here. You must call 1-800-772-1213 for a replacement card. ▶ ☐

5	Total number of allowances you are claiming (from line **H** above **or** from the applicable worksheet on page 2)	5	2
6	Additional amount, if any, you want withheld from each paycheck	6	$
7	I claim exemption from withholding for 20X3, and I certify that I meet **both** of the following conditions for exemption.		

- Last year I had a right to a refund of **all** federal income tax withheld because I had **no** tax liability **and**
- This year I expect a refund of **all** federal income tax withheld because I expect to have **no** tax liability.

If you meet both conditions, write "Exempt" here . . . . ▶ | 7 |

Under penalties of perjury, I declare that I have examined this certificate and to the best of my knowledge and belief, it is true, correct, and complete.

Employee's signature (Form is not valid unless you sign it.) ▶ *Sam L. Morgan*   Date ▶ January 2, 20X3

8	Employer's name and address (Employer: Complete lines 8 and 10 only if sending to the IRS.)	9 Office code (optional)	10 Employer identification number (EIN)

For Privacy Act and Paperwork Reduction Act Notice, see page 2.	Cat. No. 10220Q	Form **W-4** (20X3)

---

wage bracket method a method that uses government-issued tables to compute the amount of federal income tax to be withheld from employees

Employer's Tax Guide (Circular E) an Internal Revenue Service publication containing federal income withholding tables for various payroll periods for married and single persons

Various methods are available for calculating the amount of federal income tax to be withheld. Many employers use the **wage bracket method**, in which government-issued tax tables are used to determine the amount of the tax. An Internal Revenue Service publication entitled the **Employer's Tax Guide (Circular E)** provides tax tables for weekly, biweekly, semimonthly, monthly, and daily or miscellaneous payroll periods for married and single persons. Two wage bracket tables, Single Persons—Weekly Payroll Period and Married Persons—Weekly Payroll Period, are shown in Figures 11-2 and 11-3 on pages 514 and 515.

To see how to use the tables, let's return again to our example of Sam. Sam's Form W-4 (Figure 11-1) indicates that he is married and claiming two exemptions. He is paid weekly, and his earnings for the pay period are $360. Therefore, to determine the amount of federal income tax to be withheld, we refer to the Married Persons—Weekly Payroll Period table in Figure 11-3 on page 515. Since Sam's earnings fall in the bracket of "At least $360 but less than $370" and he has two exemptions, his federal income tax withholding is $8.

Summing Up

The OASDI tax has a ceiling; that is, if your earnings reach the taxable wage base (currently $102,000), you will cease to pay the tax for the rest of the year. However, there is no ceiling on HI and the federal income tax—the more you make, the more taxes you pay.

Figure 11-2
Weekly Wage Bracket Table Used to Find Federal Income Tax Withholding for Single Persons

SINGLE Persons—WEEKLY Payroll Period

If the wages are—		And the number of withholding allowances claimed is—										
At least	But less than	0	1	2	3	4	5	6	7	8	9	10
		The amount of income tax to be withheld is—										
$0	$55	$0	$0	$0	$0	$0	$0	$0	$0	$0	$0	$0
55	60	1	0	0	0	0	0	0	0	0	0	0
60	65	1	0	0	0	0	0	0	0	0	0	0
65	70	2	0	0	0	0	0	0	0	0	0	0
70	75	2	0	0	0	0	0	0	0	0	0	0
75	80	3	0	0	0	0	0	0	0	0	0	0
80	85	3	0	0	0	0	0	0	0	0	0	0
85	90	4	0	0	0	0	0	0	0	0	0	0
90	95	4	0	0	0	0	0	0	0	0	0	0
95	100	5	0	0	0	0	0	0	0	0	0	0
100	105	5	0	0	0	0	0	0	0	0	0	0
105	110	6	0	0	0	0	0	0	0	0	0	0
110	115	6	0	0	0	0	0	0	0	0	0	0
115	120	7	0	0	0	0	0	0	0	0	0	0
120	125	7	1	0	0	0	0	0	0	0	0	0
125	130	8	1	0	0	0	0	0	0	0	0	0
130	135	8	2	0	0	0	0	0	0	0	0	0
135	140	9	2	0	0	0	0	0	0	0	0	0
140	145	9	3	0	0	0	0	0	0	0	0	0
145	150	10	3	0	0	0	0	0	0	0	0	0
150	155	10	4	0	0	0	0	0	0	0	0	0
155	160	11	4	0	0	0	0	0	0	0	0	0
160	165	11	5	0	0	0	0	0	0	0	0	0
165	170	12	5	0	0	0	0	0	0	0	0	0
170	175	12	6	0	0	0	0	0	0	0	0	0
175	180	13	6	0	0	0	0	0	0	0	0	0
180	185	13	7	0	0	0	0	0	0	0	0	0
185	190	14	7	1	0	0	0	0	0	0	0	0
190	195	14	8	1	0	0	0	0	0	0	0	0
195	200	15	8	2	0	0	0	0	0	0	0	0
200	210	16	9	3	0	0	0	0	0	0	0	0
210	220	18	10	4	0	0	0	0	0	0	0	0
220	230	19	11	5	0	0	0	0	0	0	0	0
230	240	21	12	6	0	0	0	0	0	0	0	0
240	250	22	13	7	0	0	0	0	0	0	0	0
250	260	24	14	8	1	0	0	0	0	0	0	0
260	270	25	16	9	2	0	0	0	0	0	0	0
270	280	27	17	10	3	0	0	0	0	0	0	0
280	290	28	19	11	4	0	0	0	0	0	0	0
290	300	30	20	12	5	0	0	0	0	0	0	0
300	310	31	22	13	6	0	0	0	0	0	0	0
310	320	33	23	14	7	1	0	0	0	0	0	0
320	330	34	25	15	8	2	0	0	0	0	0	0
330	340	36	26	17	9	3	0	0	0	0	0	0
340	350	37	28	18	10	4	0	0	0	0	0	0
350	360	39	29	20	11	5	0	0	0	0	0	0
360	370	40	31	21	12	6	0	0	0	0	0	0
370	380	42	32	23	13	7	1	0	0	0	0	0
380	390	43	34	24	14	8	2	0	0	0	0	0
390	400	45	35	26	16	9	3	0	0	0	0	0
400	410	46	37	27	17	10	4	0	0	0	0	0
410	420	48	38	29	19	11	5	0	0	0	0	0
420	430	49	40	30	20	12	6	0	0	0	0	0
430	440	51	41	32	22	13	7	0	0	0	0	0
440	450	52	43	33	23	14	8	1	0	0	0	0
450	460	54	44	35	25	15	9	2	0	0	0	0
460	470	55	46	36	26	17	10	3	0	0	0	0
470	480	57	47	38	28	18	11	4	0	0	0	0
480	490	58	49	39	29	20	12	5	0	0	0	0
490	500	60	50	41	31	21	13	6	0	0	0	0
500	510	61	52	42	32	23	14	7	1	0	0	0
510	520	63	53	44	34	24	15	8	2	0	0	0
520	530	64	55	45	35	26	16	9	3	0	0	0
530	540	66	56	47	37	27	18	10	4	0	0	0
540	550	67	58	48	38	29	19	11	5	0	0	0
550	560	69	59	50	40	30	21	12	6	0	0	0
560	570	70	61	51	41	32	22	13	7	1	0	0
570	580	72	62	53	43	33	24	14	8	2	0	0
580	590	73	64	54	44	35	25	16	9	3	0	0
590	600	75	65	56	46	36	27	17	10	4	0	0
750	760	112	96	80	70	60	51	41	32	22	13	7
760	770	115	99	83	71	62	52	43	33	24	14	8
770	780	117	101	85	73	63	54	44	35	25	16	9
780	790	120	104	88	74	65	55	46	36	27	17	10
790	800	122	106	90	76	66	57	47	38	28	19	11
800	810	125	109	93	77	68	58	49	39	30	20	12
810	820	127	111	95	79	69	60	50	41	31	22	13
820	830	130	114	98	82	71	61	52	42	33	23	14
830	840	132	116	100	84	72	63	53	44	34	25	15
840	850	135	119	103	87	74	64	55	45	36	26	17

Figure 11-3
Weekly Wage Bracket Table Used to Find Federal Income Tax Withholding for Married Persons

MARRIED Persons—WEEKLY Payroll Period

If the wages are—		And the number of withholding allowances claimed is—										
At least	But less than	0	1	2	3	4	5	6	7	8	9	10
		The amount of income tax to be withheld is—										
$0	$125	$0	$0	$0	$0	$0	$0	$0	$0	$0	$0	$0
125	130	0	0	0	0	0	0	0	0	0	0	0
130	135	0	0	0	0	0	0	0	0	0	0	0
135	140	0	0	0	0	0	0	0	0	0	0	0
140	145	0	0	0	0	0	0	0	0	0	0	0
145	150	0	0	0	0	0	0	0	0	0	0	0
150	155	0	0	0	0	0	0	0	0	0	0	0
155	160	0	0	0	0	0	0	0	0	0	0	0
160	165	1	0	0	0	0	0	0	0	0	0	0
165	170	1	0	0	0	0	0	0	0	0	0	0
170	175	2	0	0	0	0	0	0	0	0	0	0
175	180	2	0	0	0	0	0	0	0	0	0	0
180	185	3	0	0	0	0	0	0	0	0	0	0
185	190	3	0	0	0	0	0	0	0	0	0	0
190	195	4	0	0	0	0	0	0	0	0	0	0
195	200	4	0	0	0	0	0	0	0	0	0	0
200	210	5	0	0	0	0	0	0	0	0	0	0
210	220	6	0	0	0	0	0	0	0	0	0	0
220	230	7	1	0	0	0	0	0	0	0	0	0
230	240	8	2	0	0	0	0	0	0	0	0	0
240	250	9	3	0	0	0	0	0	0	0	0	0
250	260	10	4	0	0	0	0	0	0	0	0	0
260	270	11	5	0	0	0	0	0	0	0	0	0
270	280	12	6	0	0	0	0	0	0	0	0	0
280	290	13	7	0	0	0	0	0	0	0	0	0
290	300	14	8	1	0	0	0	0	0	0	0	0
300	310	15	9	2	0	0	0	0	0	0	0	0
310	320	16	10	3	0	0	0	0	0	0	0	0
320	330	17	11	4	0	0	0	0	0	0	0	0
330	340	18	12	5	0	0	0	0	0	0	0	0
340	350	19	13	6	0	0	0	0	0	0	0	0
350	360	20	14	7	1	0	0	0	0	0	0	0
360	370	21	15	8	2	0	0	0	0	0	0	0
370	380	22	16	9	3	0	0	0	0	0	0	0
380	390	23	17	10	4	0	0	0	0	0	0	0
390	400	24	18	11	5	0	0	0	0	0	0	0
400	410	25	19	12	6	0	0	0	0	0	0	0
410	420	26	20	13	7	1	0	0	0	0	0	0
420	430	27	21	14	8	2	0	0	0	0	0	0
430	440	28	22	15	9	3	0	0	0	0	0	0
440	450	29	23	16	10	4	0	0	0	0	0	0
450	460	31	24	17	11	5	0	0	0	0	0	0
460	470	32	25	18	12	6	0	0	0	0	0	0
470	480	34	26	19	13	7	0	0	0	0	0	0
480	490	35	27	20	14	8	1	0	0	0	0	0
490	500	37	28	21	15	9	2	0	0	0	0	0
500	510	38	29	22	16	10	3	0	0	0	0	0
510	520	40	30	23	17	11	4	0	0	0	0	0
520	530	41	32	24	18	12	5	0	0	0	0	0
530	540	43	33	25	19	13	6	0	0	0	0	0
540	550	44	35	26	20	14	7	1	0	0	0	0
550	560	46	36	27	21	15	8	2	0	0	0	0
560	570	47	38	28	22	16	9	3	0	0	0	0
570	580	49	39	30	23	17	10	4	0	0	0	0
580	590	50	41	31	24	18	11	5	0	0	0	0
590	600	52	42	33	25	19	12	6	0	0	0	0
600	610	53	44	34	26	20	13	7	1	0	0	0
610	620	55	45	36	27	21	14	8	2	0	0	0
620	630	56	47	37	28	22	15	9	3	0	0	0
630	640	58	48	39	29	23	16	10	4	0	0	0
640	650	59	50	40	31	24	17	11	5	0	0	0
650	660	61	51	42	32	25	18	12	6	0	0	0
660	670	62	53	43	34	26	19	13	7	0	0	0
670	680	64	54	45	35	27	20	14	8	1	0	0
680	690	65	56	46	37	28	21	15	9	2	0	0
1,190	1,200	142	132	123	113	104	94	85	75	66	56	47
1,200	1,210	143	134	124	115	105	96	86	77	67	58	48
1,210	1,220	145	135	126	116	107	97	88	78	69	59	50
1,220	1,230	146	137	127	118	108	99	89	80	70	61	51
1,230	1,240	148	138	129	119	110	100	91	81	72	62	53
1,240	1,250	149	140	130	121	111	102	92	83	73	64	54
1,250	1,260	151	141	132	122	113	103	94	84	75	65	56
1,260	1,270	152	143	133	124	114	105	95	86	76	67	57
1,270	1,280	154	144	135	125	116	106	97	87	78	68	59
1,280	1,290	155	146	136	127	117	108	98	89	79	70	60

In Review Quiz 11-1, you calculated the gross weekly earnings of Joy Jackson. Now calculate her FICA tax and federal income tax, assuming she is married, claims zero withholding allowances, and has not exceeded the OASDI taxable wage base.

Check your answer on page 538.

State and Local Income Taxes

Most state governments also require an employer to withhold an income tax from the earnings of employees. The rates charged vary so greatly from state to state that it would not be practical to attempt to list them here. The withholding process, however, is very similar to that for federal income tax. The state provides the employer with tax tables similar to the federal tax tables shown in Figures 11-2 and 11-3. And like the federal income tax, the state income tax is also based on an employee's marital status, the amount of earnings, and the number of withholding allowances claimed.

Some county and city governments also require a tax on earnings. Although the tax may be called something other than an income tax (such as an occupational tax), such taxes are income taxes, and the withholding process is basically the same as that for the federal and state income taxes.

Other Deductions

In addition to the required withholdings (FICA, federal income tax, and state income tax), employees may voluntarily agree to have other amounts withheld from their pay. Examples include amounts donated to charities (such as the United Way), amounts for health and life insurance or union dues, or amounts invested in U.S. savings bonds or retirement plans. These types of withholdings are for the benefit and convenience of the employee and must be authorized in writing by the employee. Once amounts are withheld, the employer becomes responsible for remitting them to the proper agencies. If union dues are withheld, for example, the employer incurs a legal liability and must remit to the union the amount withheld. We will look at how the employer accounts for these deductions later in the chapter.

Calculating Net Earnings (Take-Home Pay)

net earnings gross earnings minus payroll deductions; also referred to as net pay or take-home pay

Net earnings (or net pay) is the amount of earnings after all payroll deductions have been made; it is the actual amount of the employee's paycheck, or take-home pay.

To illustrate the calculation of net earnings, let's continue with our example of Sam Morgan. We have calculated Sam's gross earnings as $360, his OASDI tax deduction as $22.32, his HI tax deduction as $5.22, and his federal income tax deduction as $8. In addition to these deductions, assume that Sam has a state income tax withholding of $5, medical insurance deduction of $15, savings bonds deduction of $10, and union dues deduction of $5. His net (take-home) pay is calculated as follows:

Gross earnings		$360.00
Less deductions:		
FICA—OASDI	$22.32	
FICA—HI	5.22	
Federal income tax	8.00	
State income tax	5.00	
Medical insurance	15.00	
Savings bonds	10.00	
Union dues	5.00	
Total deductions		70.54
Net earnings		$289.46

Figure 11-4 summarizes how net pay is determined.

Figure 11-4
How Net Pay Is
Determined

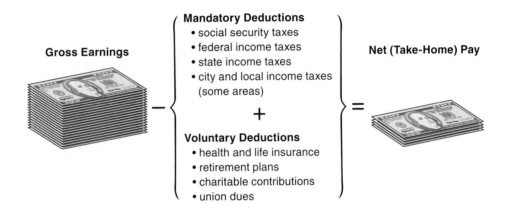

Review Quiz **11-4** How is Joy Jackson doing? She has gross earnings of $380, an OASDI tax deduction of $23.56, an HI tax deduction of $5.51, a federal income tax deduction of $23, a state income tax deduction of $11.40, a medical insurance deduction of $15, and a savings bonds deduction of $25. What is the amount of her net earnings?

Check your answer on page 538.

Payroll Record Keeping

To provide management with up-to-date payroll information and to comply with various federal, state, and local laws, an employer must maintain payroll records that will supply the following information for each employee:

- Name, address, and Social Security number
- The amount of gross earnings for each payroll
- The period of employment covered by each payroll
- The year-to-date (*cumulative*) gross earnings
- The amount of taxes and other deductions
- The date each payroll was paid

To keep accurate and timely records, a business must have a payroll system that can deal with a large number of employees who have various pay periods, various wage rates, and various types of deductions. This is accomplished by using a payroll register and employees' earnings records, which we will discuss next.

The Payroll Register

The **payroll register** is a summary of the gross earnings, deductions, and net pay for all employees for a specific payroll period. The design of the payroll register depends on the number of employees and the method of processing payroll data. The complete payroll register for Northwest Company—the company for which Anne Sheppard, Joy Jackson, and Sam Morgan work—is shown in Figure 11-5 for the payroll period ending on November 18, 20X3.

Notice that the payroll register contains *Taxable Earnings* columns. These columns are used to show two things: (1) how much of an employee's earnings for this payroll period are subject to employer's unemployment tax (discussed in Chapter 12) and (2) how much of an employee's earnings for this payroll period are subject to FICA taxes. Remember that there is a taxable wage base for OASDI. By looking in the Cumulative Earnings column, we can see that William Adams's cumulative earnings (before this pay date) are $102,100. As a result, his earnings for this pay period are not subject to OASDI. (Remember that the current OASDI taxable base is $102,000.) No other employee has reached or exceeded the OASDI taxable base.

Figure 11-5

Payroll Register for Northwest Company

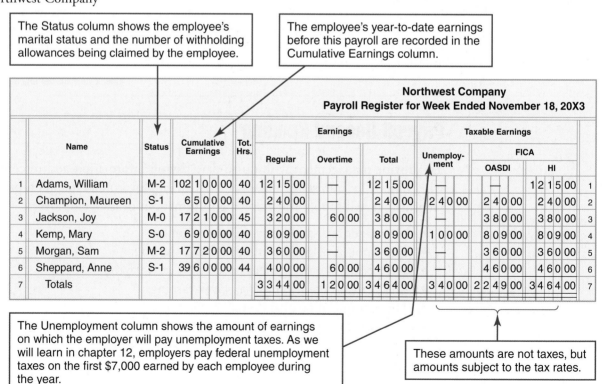

| Name | Status | Cumulative Earnings | Tot. Hrs. | Earnings | | | Taxable Earnings | | |
				Regular	Overtime	Total	Unemployment	FICA OASDI	HI
1 Adams, William	M-2	102 100 00	40	1215 00	—	1215 00	—	—	1215 00
2 Champion, Maureen	S-1	6500 00	40	240 00	—	240 00	240 00	240 00	240 00
3 Jackson, Joy	M-0	17 210 00	45	320 00	60 00	380 00	—	380 00	380 00
4 Kemp, Mary	S-0	6900 00	40	809 00	—	809 00	100 00	809 00	809 00
5 Morgan, Sam	M-2	17 720 00	40	360 00	—	360 00	—	360 00	360 00
6 Sheppard, Anne	S-1	39 600 00	44	400 00	60 00	460 00	—	460 00	460 00
7 Totals				3344 00	120 00	3464 00	340 00	2249 00	3464 00

Northwest Company
Payroll Register for Week Ended November 18, 20X3

The Status column shows the employee's marital status and the number of withholding allowances being claimed by the employee.

The employee's year-to-date earnings before this payroll are recorded in the Cumulative Earnings column.

The Unemployment column shows the amount of earnings on which the employer will pay unemployment taxes. As we will learn in chapter 12, employers pay federal unemployment taxes on the first $7,000 earned by each employee during the year.

These amounts are not taxes, but amounts subject to the tax rates.

cross-footing the addition of columns of figures in different ways to check the accuracy of the totals

After all information has been entered in the payroll register, it is totaled, as shown in Figure 11-5. Before payroll checks are prepared, the accuracy of the payroll register should be proved by cross-footing the column totals. **Cross-footing**, or adding the columns in different ways to check for accuracy, can be done as follows:

$$\text{Total earnings} - \text{Deductions} = \text{Net pay}$$
$$\$3,464.00 - \$801.79 = \$2,662.21$$

or

$$\text{Total earnings} - \text{Net pay} = \text{Deductions}$$
$$\$3,464.00 - \$2,662.21 = \$801.79$$

Employee's Earnings Record

employee's earnings record a record maintained for each employee that contains basic employee information and a summary of payroll data for that employee

As we stated earlier, employers are required to maintain a record of earnings and deductions for each employee. Consequently, a separate earnings record is prepared for each employee at the beginning of each calendar year. It is necessary that certain information about an employee be available in the earnings record. An **employee's earnings record** includes basic information such as the employee's name, address, Social Security number, and pay structure. Figure 11-6 illustrates the employee's earnings record that Northwest Company maintains for Sam Morgan.

	Deductions								Payments		Expense Account Debited		
	FICA		Federal Income Tax	State Income Tax	Medical Insurance	Savings Bonds	Union Dues	Total	Ck. No.	Net Amount	Sales Salaries Expense	Office Salaries Expense	
	OASDI	HI											
1		17 62	1 26 00	58 45	15 00	10 00	5 00	2 32 07	141	9 82 93	1 2 1 5 00		1
2	1 4 88	3 48	1 3 00	7 20	12 00			50 56	142	1 89 44		2 40 00	2
3	2 3 56	5 51	2 3 00	1 1 40	15 00	25 00		1 03 47	143	2 76 53	3 80 00		3
4	5 0 16	1 1 73	1 25 00	36 27				2 23 16	144	5 85 84		8 09 00	4
5	2 2 32	5 22	8 00	5 00	15 00	10 00	5 00	70 54	145	2 89 46		3 60 00	5
6	2 8 52	6 67	4 6 00	1 3 80	12 00	10 00	5 00	1 21 99	146	3 38 01	4 6 0 00		6
7	1 3 9 44	50 23	3 41 00	1 32 12	69 00	55 00	15 00	8 01 79		2 6 62 21	2 0 55 00	1 4 09 00	7

These columns show the amounts withheld from the pay of employees.

Take-home pay

Name of Employee	Morgan, Sam								Social Security Number	422-22-6222		

Address	1244 Oak Street	City or Town	Ames, NJ 07003

Date of Birth	10-14-58	Married ☒ or Single ☐	Number of Exemptions 2	Phone No. 555-1212	Clock No. 025

Position	Clerk	Rate $9.00/hr.	Date 1-2-X3	Date Started 1-2-X3	Date Terminated

Remarks		Reason	

FOURTH QUARTER 20X3

WEEK	Hours Worked		Total Earnings	DEDUCTIONS									Gross Earnings Year to Date
	Reg.	Over Time		FICA Taxes		Federal Income Tax	State Income Tax	Union Dues	Savings Bonds	Medical Insurance	Net Pay		
				OASDI	HI								
40	40	—	360 00	22 32	5 22	8 00	5 00	5 00	10 00	15 00	289 46		14,235 00
41	40	2	387 00	23 99	5 61	10 00	6 00	5 00	10 00	15 00	311 40		14,622 00
QUARTER TOTALS			4,940 00	306 28	71 63	117 00	71 50	65 00	130 00	195 00	3,983 59		19,562 00
YEARLY TOTALS			19,562 00	1,212 84	283 65	468 00	286 00	260 00	510 00	780 00	15,761 51		19,562 00

Figure 11-6

Employee's Earnings Record

As you can see, the earnings record contains a good deal of information about an employee. The lower portion of the record contains a summary of earnings and deductions for all payrolls during the year. The column headings are self-explanatory; they come from our earlier discussion of gross earnings and deductions. The column heading at the extreme right deserves special notice. The Gross Earnings Year to Date column helps the payroll clerk keep track of total earnings and comply with the maximum amount of earnings subject to the OASDI part of FICA and other maximum wage levels for federal and state purposes.

CAUTION

Don't confuse the employee's earnings record and the payroll register. The payroll register shows payroll data for *all* employees for a single payroll period; the employee's earnings record shows a summary of payroll data for *each* employee for all payroll periods during a year.

Payroll Systems

There are two basic types of payroll systems: manual and computerized. The payroll system we have worked with in this chapter is manual. Many businesses today use electronic equipment to calculate and record the payroll more quickly and efficiently. Let's see how both systems work.

Manual Payroll System

In a manual payroll system, the payroll register is prepared first, and the information is transferred to the employee's earnings record. This is usually done using the "write-it-once" principle. This means that while information is being entered by hand on the payroll register, it is also being entered on an employee's earnings record. This is often accomplished by the use of a *pegboard system*, in which one record is placed over the other record, and information is entered on both records (using carbonless paper) at the same time. This allows both documents to be completed with "one writing," which saves time and reduces the possibility of errors.

A totally manual payroll system is rare today. Even very small businesses often use machines to at least partially complete their payroll. However, many small businesses process some, or all, of their payroll information by hand.

Computerized Payroll System

Payroll records, and the payroll process itself, are highly repetitive. Pay period after pay period, the payroll clerk records data in the payroll register and transfers the information to the employees' earnings records. This repetitive process lends itself well to computerization. As computers have become faster, cheaper, and smaller, a great number of computerized payroll systems have become available for even the smallest of business firms.

Many payroll software systems available in the marketplace can save the payroll personnel hours of tedious, repetitive payroll calculations. And with improved technology and increased production, the cost of a system—the computer and the software—has become reasonable. Today, there exists an array of relatively inexpensive payroll programs that run on desktop computers. Such systems have limited applications, but they are adequate for the needs of many smaller and medium-sized businesses. Larger businesses often own large computers (mainframes) and employ computer programmers who write and maintain the payroll system. Some businesses rent time (*time-shared system*) on a large computer that is owned by another company. This permits the use of a large computer without the heavy investment necessary to purchase the system.

Computerized payroll programs increase processing speed and accuracy as well as generate payroll reports automatically.

Recording the Payroll

The payroll register provides all the information necessary to record the payroll. We can use the payroll register as a special journal and post the column totals directly to the ledger. Or we can use the payroll register as an information source for recording the payroll in either the general journal or the cash payments journal. Let's assume that we are using the payroll register as an information source and not as a special journal.

In recording employee earnings and the deductions from earnings, separate accounts should be maintained for the earnings and for each deduction. In previous chapters, we have recorded the earnings of employees in an account entitled Salaries Expense (other commonly used terms are *Wages Expense*, *Payroll Expense*, and *Salaries and Commissions Expense*).

In recording the deductions from employee earnings, it helps to think of the employer as an agent who is responsible for withholding these amounts and then passing them on to the proper agency. In effect, the employer is liable for each amount withheld until it is passed on to the appropriate agency. Thus, *each deduction is recorded in an appropriate liability account.*

To help understand the actual recording of the payroll, let's look at T accounts of the major accounts used in the process.

The Salaries Expense Account

Salaries Expense account an expense account used to record the gross amount of the payroll; also referred to as Wages Expense account, Payroll Expense account, and Salaries and Commissions Expense account

The **Salaries Expense account** is an operating expense account used to record the *gross amount* of the payroll. Sometimes, the account is broken down into separate accounts such as Sales Salaries Expense and Office Salaries Expense. In such a case, the gross salaries in each classification are recorded in the appropriate account. Let's look at the Salaries Expense account in T-account form:

Salaries Expense

Debit	Credit
+	–
To record the gross amount of the payroll each pay period	

Expense accounts are always debited to show an increase.

The FICA Tax Payable—OASDI Account and FICA Tax Payable—HI Account

FICA Tax Payable—OASDI account a liability account used to record (1) the amount of OASDI taxes withheld from employee earnings and (2) the amount of OASDI taxes matched by the employer; an account credited when OASDI taxes are withheld from employees (and matched by the employer) and debited when the taxes are sent in

Remember that FICA has two parts: OASDI and HI. The **FICA Tax Payable—OASDI account** is a liability account used to record the amount of OASDI tax withheld from the earnings of employees and is also used to record the liability for the employer's share of OASDI taxes. The account is credited when OASDI taxes are withheld, and it is debited when OASDI taxes are sent in. In T-account form, we can describe the account as follows:

FICA Tax Payable—OASDI

Debit	Credit
–	+
To record payment of OASDI tax previously withheld from employees or imposed on the employer	To record OASDI tax withheld from employees or imposed on the employer

Liability accounts are always credited to show an increase and debited to show a decrease.

The **FICA Tax Payable—HI account** is a liability account used to record the amount of HI (Medicare) taxes withheld from the earnings of employees and imposed on the employer. The account is credited when HI taxes are withheld, and it is debited when the taxes are sent in. In T-account form, it looks like this:

FICA Tax Payable—HI	
Debit	Credit
–	+
To record payment of HI tax previously withheld from employees or imposed on the employer	To record HI tax withheld from employees or imposed on the employer

The Federal Income Tax Payable Account

The **Federal Income Tax Payable account** is a liability account used to record the amount of federal income taxes withheld from the earnings of employees. The account is credited when income taxes are withheld and debited when the taxes are sent in. In T-account form, we can describe the account as follows:

Federal Income Tax Payable	
Debit	Credit
–	+
To record payment of federal income tax previously withheld from the earnings of employees	To record federal income tax withheld from the earnings of employees

Other Amounts Withheld

Other amounts withheld should be recorded in an appropriate liability account. For example, state income tax withheld should be recorded in the State Income Tax Payable account. Likewise, union dues withheld should be recorded in the Union Dues Payable account. These accounts, and similar liability accounts, are credited when amounts are withheld and debited when payment is made to the appropriate agency.

Now that we have looked at the major accounts involved in recording the payroll, let's look at the entry to record the payroll. By referring to the column totals of Northwest Company's payroll register (Figure 11-5), we can make the general journal entry shown in Figure 11-7.

This entry would now be posted to the appropriate general ledger accounts. If we were using the payroll register as a special journal, the column totals would be posted directly to the appropriate general ledger accounts. We would then write the number of the account to which a posting was made directly below the column total.

Figure 11-7

Journal Entry for Employee Earnings and Deductions

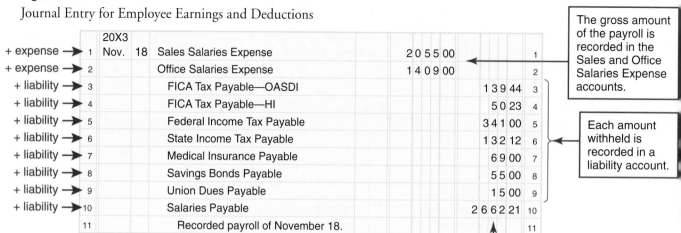

	20X3					
+ expense → 1	Nov.	18	Sales Salaries Expense	2 0 5 5 00		1
+ expense → 2			Office Salaries Expense	1 4 0 9 00		2
+ liability → 3			FICA Tax Payable—OASDI		1 3 9 44	3
+ liability → 4			FICA Tax Payable—HI		5 0 23	4
+ liability → 5			Federal Income Tax Payable		3 4 1 00	5
+ liability → 6			State Income Tax Payable		1 3 2 12	6
+ liability → 7			Medical Insurance Payable		6 9 00	7
+ liability → 8			Savings Bonds Payable		5 5 00	8
+ liability → 9			Union Dues Payable		1 5 00	9
+ liability →10			Salaries Payable		2 6 6 2 21	10
11			Recorded payroll of November 18.			11

The gross amount of the payroll is recorded in the Sales and Office Salaries Expense accounts.

Each amount withheld is recorded in a liability account.

The net amount of the payroll is recorded in the Salaries Payable account. The Cash account would be credited if payment were made immediately. However, recording the net amount in the Salaries Payable account allows the payroll to be recorded before the paychecks are prepared.

Review Quiz 11-5 Information from the payroll register of Northwest Company for the payroll period ended February 6, 20X3, is shown below. In general journal form, make the necessary entry to record employee earnings and deductions.

Northwest Company
Payroll Register for Week Ended February 6, 20X3

	Name	Status	Cumulative Earnings	Tot. Hrs.	Earnings Regular	Earnings Overtime	Earnings Total	Taxable Earnings Unemployment	Taxable Earnings FICA OASDI	Taxable Earnings FICA HI	
1	Adams, William	M-2	3 2 0 0 00	40	6 1 5 00	—	6 1 5 00	6 1 5 00	6 1 5 00	6 1 5 00	1
2	Champion, Maureen	S-1	9 4 0 00	40	2 4 0 00	—	2 4 0 00	2 4 0 00	2 4 0 00	2 4 0 00	2
3	Jackson, Joy	M-0	1 6 4 0 00	40	3 2 0 00	—	3 2 0 00	3 2 0 00	3 2 0 00	3 2 0 00	3
4	Morgan, Sam	M-2	1 8 8 0 00	40	3 6 0 00	—	3 6 0 00	3 6 0 00	3 6 0 00	3 6 0 00	4
5	Sheppard, Anne	S-1	2 7 1 5 00	44	4 0 0 00	6 0 00	4 6 0 00	4 6 0 00	4 6 0 00	4 6 0 00	5
6	Totals				1 9 3 5 00	6 0 00	1 9 9 5 00	1 9 9 5 00	1 9 9 5 00	1 9 9 5 00	6

	Deductions FICA OASDI	Deductions FICA HI	Federal Income Tax	State Income Tax	Medical Insurance	Savings Bonds	Union Dues	Total	Payments Ck. No.	Payments Net Amount	Expense Account Debited Sales Salaries Expense	Expense Account Debited Office Salaries Expense	
1	3 8 13	8 92	3 6 00	1 8 45	1 5 00	1 0 00	5 00	1 3 1 50	47	4 8 3 50	6 1 5 00		1
2	1 4 88	3 48	1 3 00	7 20	1 2 00	—	—	5 0 56	48	1 8 9 44		2 4 0 00	2
3	1 9 84	4 64	1 7 00	1 1 40	1 5 00	2 5 00	—	9 2 88	49	2 2 7 12	3 2 0 00		3
4	2 2 32	5 22	8 00	5 00	1 5 00	1 0 00	5 00	7 0 54	50	2 8 9 46		3 6 0 00	4
5	2 8 52	6 67	4 6 00	1 3 80	1 2 00	1 0 00	5 00	1 2 1 99	51	3 3 8 01	4 6 0 00		5
6	1 2 3 69	2 8 93	1 2 0 00	5 5 85	6 9 00	5 5 00	1 5 00	4 6 7 47		1 5 2 7 73	1 3 9 5 00	6 0 0 00	6

Check your answer on page 539.

Making Payment to Employees

Many employees today are paid electronically by direct deposit to their bank accounts. Employers generally prefer this method of payment because it is cheaper than preparing physical checks. However, as of November 20X3, since Northwest has only six employees, each employee is paid by check out of the company's regular checking account. Larger companies often maintain a special checking account just for the payroll. When this practice is followed, one check for the net amount of the payroll is written on the company's regular checking account. The check is then deposited in the separate payroll account. Individual checks for employees are then written on the special account. When all checks have been cashed by employees, the payroll account should have a zero balance.

Regardless of how employees are paid, the entry to record the payment is the same. The following general journal entry was made to record the payment of Northwest Company's November 18 payroll:

	20X3				
– liability ➤ 1	Nov.	18	Salaries Payable	2 6 6 2 21	1
– asset ➤ 2			Cash	2 6 6 2 21	2
3			Paid payroll of November 18.		3

In a business that uses special journals, the entry to record payment of the payroll would be made in the cash payments journal.

Summing Up

The sequence of steps for recording the payroll is as follows:

Step **1** Record the payroll information in the payroll register.
Step **2** Use the payroll register as an information source to record a journal entry for employee earnings and deductions.
Step **3** Record a journal entry for payment of the payroll.

Review Quiz **11-6** Referring to the journal entry you made to record Northwest Company's payroll in Review Quiz 11-5, make the entry to record payment of this payroll.

Check your answer on page 539.

Tax Evasion by Residential Property Project Manager

On August 5, 2008, Edward Barrier, of St. Louis, Missouri, was sentenced to 30 months in prison for tax evasion. According to court documents, during the years 2002 through 2005, Barrier was self-employed as a project manager supervising the development of high-end residential property in the St. Louis area. Barrier was paid substantial sums of money during these years for identifying properties for development. His total income for the four-year period was $2.46 million. However, Barrier did not report any of the income or file any federal income tax returns for those years.

Cash transactions are harder to monitor and easier to hide. Barrier attempted to evade paying taxes by doing business in cash.

His total tax liability for the four years, after allowing for expenses and deductions, totaled $796,514. Barrier was audited by the Internal Revenue Service (IRS), and additional taxes were assessed against him for tax years 1987 through 1994. Normally, the IRS will not audit an individual tax return after three years, unless fraud or other irregularities are suspected. Since this was the case, Barrier's earlier tax returns were examined. Barrier failed to pay the taxes due and stopped filing tax returns. After the audit, the IRS sent Barrier numerous notices regarding his tax liabilities; however, he did not pay any of the taxes nor did he dispute the assessment. Instead, according to the U.S. Attorney, Barrier attempted to evade the payment of these taxes by doing business in cash, not acquiring any assets in his own name, residing with his mother, placing titles to vehicles in the name of an unregistered business entity, and limiting his use of bank accounts.

In 2002, Barrier also began structuring cash transactions in an attempt to prevent detection of his income by the IRS. He allegedly took the checks he earned from his property and construction management services to the bank on which the checks were drawn. He then obtained a combination of cash and cashier's checks from that bank. Barrier usually obtained an amount of cash under $10,000 and structured over $700,000 in these types of transactions between August 2002 and January 2006.

The taxes due, including the unpaid liabilities for the years 2002 and 2005, and the liabilities assessed for the years 1987 through 1994 totaled $1 million. Barrier was responsible for paying these taxes in addition to serving 30 months in prison.

Source: Internal Revenue Service, "Missouri Residential Property Project Manager Sentenced for Tax Evasion," *Examples of Tax Fraud Investigations*, www.irs.gov/compliance/enforcement/article/0,,id=174636,00.html, October 30, 2008.

For Discussion

1. Often, individuals who do not report or underreport income are fined, assessed interest, and required to pay unpaid taxes. Why do cases such as Edward Barrier often result in jail time as well?
2. What is the probable reason Barrier failed to report income and file tax returns?
3. What was Barrier's objective when he resorted to cash transactions only and not placing assets in his name?
4. Was there a reason for Barrier obtaining an amount of cash under $10,000 when depositing checks?

Joining the Pieces

Procedures for Recording the Payroll

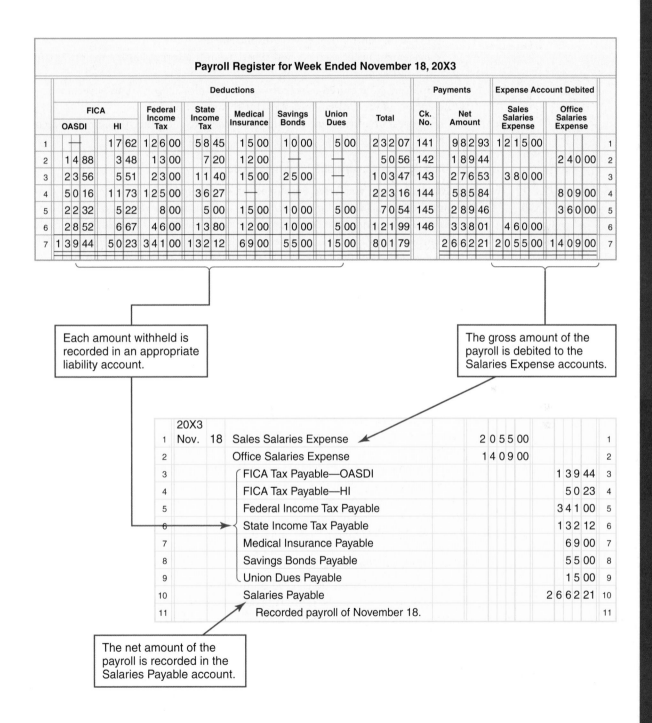

Payroll Register for Week Ended November 18, 20X3

| | Deductions | | | | | | | | Payments | | Expense Account Debited | | |
| | FICA | | Federal Income Tax | State Income Tax | Medical Insurance | Savings Bonds | Union Dues | Total | Ck. No. | Net Amount | Sales Salaries Expense | Office Salaries Expense | |
	OASDI	HI											
1		17 62	126 00	58 45	15 00	10 00	5 00	232 07	141	982 93	1215 00		1
2	14 88	3 48	13 00	7 20	12 00			50 56	142	189 44		240 00	2
3	23 56	5 51	23 00	11 40	15 00	25 00		103 47	143	276 53	380 00		3
4	50 16	11 73	125 00	36 27				223 16	144	585 84		809 00	4
5	22 32	5 22	8 00	5 00	15 00	10 00	5 00	70 54	145	289 46		360 00	5
6	28 52	6 67	46 00	13 80	12 00	10 00	5 00	121 99	146	338 01	460 00		6
7	139 44	50 23	341 00	132 12	69 00	55 00	15 00	801 79		2662 21	2055 00	1409 00	7

Each amount withheld is recorded in an appropriate liability account.

The gross amount of the payroll is debited to the Salaries Expense accounts.

	20X3					
1	Nov.	18	Sales Salaries Expense	2055 00		1
2			Office Salaries Expense	1409 00		2
3			FICA Tax Payable—OASDI		139 44	3
4			FICA Tax Payable—HI		50 23	4
5			Federal Income Tax Payable		341 00	5
6			State Income Tax Payable		132 12	6
7			Medical Insurance Payable		69 00	7
8			Savings Bonds Payable		55 00	8
9			Union Dues Payable		15 00	9
10			Salaries Payable		2662 21	10
11			Recorded payroll of November 18.			11

The net amount of the payroll is recorded in the Salaries Payable account.

Summary

Interactive Summary in English and Spanish

1 Describe the importance of payroll records.

Payroll records are important from several perspectives:

- Payroll is a significant expense of doing business, and accurate records are necessary to maintain control over payroll disbursements.
- Management needs accurate and timely payroll information for analysis, planning, and decision making.
- Employers are required to report various payroll data to various government agencies, and records are necessary for this reporting task.
- Employees of a firm must be paid in an accurate and timely fashion, and records assist in accomplishing this task.

2 Calculate gross earnings for employees.

Gross earnings for a **salaried employee** are usually stated by the employer on a weekly, monthly, or annual basis. Gross earnings for an **hourly worker** are calculated by multiplying the hourly rate of pay times the number of hours worked. If an employee works more than 40 hours in one week, the employee is usually paid time-and-a-half for hours in excess of 40. For example, Glenn Turkow is married, claims two **withholding allowances**, and worked 50 hours last week at a rate of $12.00 an hour. His gross earnings are calculated as follows:

Regular pay	= $12.00 × 40 hours	= $480.00
Overtime pay	= $18.00 ($12.00 × 1.5) × 10 hours	= 180.00
Gross earnings	=	$660.00

3 Explain the nature of payroll deductions.

A **payroll deduction** is an amount withheld by the employer from the earnings of employees for various taxes and other purposes. In this chapter, we discussed three required deductions: (1) **Federal Insurance Contributions Act (FICA)** taxes, (2) federal income taxes, and (3) state income taxes. We also discussed certain deductions that are not required by law but result from an agreement between the employer and the employee. Deductions of this kind include those for medical insurance, pension plans, savings bonds, union dues, and loan repayments.

4 Calculate payroll deductions and net pay.

We calculate payroll deductions based on the gross earnings of employees. The FICA tax has two components: (1) the **OASDI taxable wage** (Old-Age, Survivors, and Disability Insurance) and (2) HI (Hospital Insurance) plan, or Medicare. The current OASDI rate is 6.2% of the first $102,000 of wages earned during the year. If an employee's earnings exceed this taxable wage base, no additional OASDI taxes are withheld for the rest of the year. The HI rate is 1.45% of all earnings during the year (no limit).

Federal and state income taxes are found by using tables provided by federal and state agencies. It is very important to use the proper table for single or married persons and for the proper payroll period; that is, weekly, biweekly, semimonthly, or monthly.

Other payroll deductions, such as union dues, pension plans, and medical insurance, are usually fixed at the beginning of a year, and the proper amounts are deducted each pay period. Remember that employers are required to obtain written permission from employees before these amounts can be withheld.

To illustrate how to calculate payroll deductions and net pay, let's return to our earlier example of Glenn Turkow. For the workweek ending March 15, 20X3, Glenn earned $660. Amounts deducted by Glenn's employer were as follows:

FICA:

OASDI ($660 × .062)	=	$ 40.92
HI ($660 × .0145)	=	9.57
Federal income tax	=	43.00
State income tax	=	9.00
Medical insurance	=	15.00
Total deductions		$117.49

Glenn's net pay for the period is now calculated by subtracting his total deductions from his gross earnings:

Gross earnings	–	Payroll deductions	=	Net pay
$660.00	–	$117.49	=	$542.51

5 Complete a payroll register and use it to record and pay the payroll.

The **payroll register** is a form that summarizes, for all employees, the number of hours worked and the amount of gross earnings, deductions, and net pay for a single pay period. The payroll register can be prepared manually or with the assistance of a computer. The data provided by the payroll register are used to prepare the entry to record the payroll and to prepare the **employee's earnings record.**

To review how to prepare a payroll register, let's look at the January 17, 20X3, payroll information of Logan's Blades, a comic book and collectible card exchange.

Employee	Status	Hourly Pay	Hours This Week	Earnings
Kaye Merrill	S-1	$8.00	42	$344.00
Lee Mitchell	M-2	9.00	44	414.00
Bill Stanton	S-0	7.65	10	76.50
Dori Winchell	M-1	8.25	40	330.00

Using this information, we can prepare the payroll register shown in Figure 11-8. The Cumulative Earnings column was filled in by looking at each employee's earnings record.

6 Make accounting entries for employee earnings and deductions and for payment of the payroll.

The payroll register prepared by Logan's Blades is not a journal. Thus, it is necessary to use information from the payroll register to make an accounting entry for employee earnings and deductions. The entry appears in general journal form as follows:

+ expense → 1	20X3 Jan.	17	Sales Salaries Expense	8 3 4 50	1
+ expense → 2			Office Salaries Expense	3 3 0 00	2
+ liability → 3			FICA Tax Payable—OASDI		7 2 20	3
+ liability → 4			FICA Tax Payable—HI		1 6 89	4
+ liability → 5			Federal Income Tax Payable		5 6 00	5
+ liability → 6			State Income Tax Payable		2 4 50	6
+ liability → 7			Medical Insurance Payable		4 5 00	7
+ liability → 8			Savings Bonds Payable		1 0 00	8
+ liability → 9			Union Dues Payable		5 00	9
+ liability →10			Salaries Payable		9 3 4 91	10
11			Recorded payroll of January 17.			11

Now, assuming that the employees are paid out of the company's regular checking account, we can make the following entry to record the payment:

	20X3					
– liability → 1	Jan.	17	Salaries Payable	9 3 4 91		1
– asset → 2			Cash		9 3 4 91	2
3			Paid payroll of January 17.			3

In the two entries we made to record the payroll and its payment, the debit and credit to the Salaries Payable account cancel each other out. Had we chosen, we could have combined the two entries by crediting Cash (rather than Salaries Payable) when the payroll was recorded. However, entering the net amount of the payroll in the Salaries Payable account makes it possible to record the payroll before the checks are actually prepared. If special journals were being used to record payment of the payroll, the entry would be made in the cash payments journal.

Figure 11-8

Payroll Register for Logan's Blades

Logan's Blades
Payroll Register for Week Ended January 17, 20X3

	Name	Status	Cumulative Earnings	Tot. Hrs.	Earnings			Taxable Earnings			
					Regular	Overtime	Total	Unemploy-ment	FICA OASDI	FICA HI	
1	Merrill, Kaye	S-1	8 0 0 00	42	3 2 0 00	2 4 00	3 4 4 00	3 4 4 00	3 4 4 00	3 4 4 00	1
2	Mitchell, Lee	M-2	7 2 0 00	44	3 6 0 00	5 4 00	4 1 4 00	4 1 4 00	4 1 4 00	4 1 4 00	2
3	Stanton, Bill	S-0	1 7 0 00	10	7 6 50	—	7 6 50	7 6 50	7 6 50	7 6 50	3
4	Winchell, Dori	M-1	3 3 0 00	40	3 3 0 00	—	3 3 0 00	3 3 0 00	3 3 0 00	3 3 0 00	4
5	Totals				1 0 8 6 50	7 8 00	1 1 6 4 50	1 1 6 4 50	1 1 6 4 50	1 1 6 4 50	5

	Deductions								Payments		Expense Account Debited		
	FICA OASDI	FICA HI	Federal Income Tax	State Income Tax	Medical Insurance	Savings Bonds	Union Dues	Total	Ck. No.	Net Amount	Sales Salaries Expense	Office Salaries Expense	
1	2 1 33	4 99	2 8 00	1 2 00	1 5 00	1 0 00	—	9 1 32	153	2 5 2 68	3 4 4 00		1
2	2 5 67	6 00	1 3 00	6 00	1 5 00	—	5 00	7 0 67	154	3 4 3 33	4 1 4 00		2
3	4 74	1 11	3 00	1 00	—	—	—	9 85	155	6 6 65	7 6 50		3
4	2 0 46	4 79	1 2 00	5 50	1 5 00	—	—	5 7 75	156	2 7 2 25		3 3 0 00	4
5	7 2 20	1 6 89	5 6 00	2 4 50	4 5 00	1 0 00	5 00	2 2 9 59		9 3 4 91	8 3 4 50	3 3 0 00	5

• Key Terms and Definitions in English and Spanish
• Additional Quiz Questions

Key Terms

cross-footing, 519
employee, 508
employee's earnings record, 519
Employee's Withholding Allowance
    Certificate (Form W-4), 512
Employer's Tax Guide (Circular E), 513
Fair Labor Standards Act, 508
Federal Income Tax Payable account, 523
Federal Insurance Contributions Act
    (FICA), 511
FICA Tax Payable—HI account, 523
FICA Tax Payable—OASDI account, 522
gross earnings, 509
hourly worker, 508
independent contractor, 508

minimum wage, 508
net earnings, 516
OASDI taxable wage base, 511
overtime pay, 509
payroll deduction, 511
payroll register, 518
piece-rate plan, 509
salaried employee, 508
Salaries Expense account, 522
salary, 508
time-and-a-half, 509
wage, 508
wage bracket method, 513
withholding allowance, 512

Concepts Review

1. Why are payroll records important?
2. What is the difference between an employee and an independent contractor?
3. What is the difference between a salary and a wage?
4. Distinguish between the terms *gross earnings* and *net earnings*.
5. What are the components of FICA tax?
6. What purpose does Form W-4 (Employee's Withholding Allowance Certificate) serve?
7. Name some deductions that an employee might want to have withheld from a paycheck in addition to the required deductions.
8. What is the difference in purpose between the payroll register and the employee's earnings record?
9. Is the payroll register a journal? Explain your answer.
10. Why are amounts withheld from employee earnings credited to liability accounts?

Skills Review

Quick Practice

Quick Practice 11-1

Learning Objective 2

Check Figure
Amy's gross earnings = $602.00

Objective: To calculate gross earnings

Payroll data for two workers follow:

Employee	Hours Worked	Hourly Rate	Overtime Rate
Amy Hassan	42.0	$14.00	1.5
Rick Jiminez	49.0	$11.00	2.0

Directions: Calculate the gross earnings for each employee.

Quick Practice 11-2

Learning Objective 2

Check Figure
Gross earnings = $570.00

Objective: To calculate gross earnings

Marlene Schwartz worked nine hours a day for the five working days last week. Her hourly rate is $12.00, with time-and-a-half for overtime hours.

Directions: Calculate Marlene's gross earnings.

Learning Objective **4**

Check Figure
OASDI for Jose = $55.80

Quick Practice 11-3

Objective: To calculate FICA taxes

Wage data for two employees follow:

Employee	Cumulative Earnings	Gross Earnings This Pay Period	FICA OASDI	HI
Jose Rios	$ 78,600	$ 900	$_____	$_____
Lori Sweat	101,800	1,500	$_____	$_____

Directions: For each employee, calculate this period's OASDI and HI taxes.

Learning Objective **4**

Check Figure
Martin's withholding tax = $47

Quick Practice 11-4

Objective: To determine federal income taxes

Martin Oglethorpe earns $475 this week and has a withholding status of S-1. Jennifer Pulaski earns $683 this week and has a withholding status of M-4.

Directions: Using the appropriate tables, determine the amount of federal income tax to be withheld from each worker's paycheck.

Learning Objective **4**

Check Figure
Net pay = $476.48

Quick Practice 11-5

Objective: To calculate net earnings

Steve O'Hara has gross earnings of $595 this week. He is married and claims two exemptions. So far this year, he has earned $6,250 and has a medical insurance deduction of $40 taken from each paycheck.

Directions: Calculate his net earnings for the week.

Learning Objective **6**

Check Figure
Salaries Payable = $13,920 (credit)

Quick Practice 11-6

Objective: To make a journal entry to record a payroll

The following information is taken from the payroll records of Benning Company for the week ending May 19, 20X9:

Gross pay	$20,000
OASDI tax	1,240
HI tax	290
Federal income tax	3,500
State income tax	600
Medical insurance	450

Directions: Prepare the general journal entry to record the payroll.

Learning Objective **6**

Check Figure
Amount = $13,920

Quick Practice 11-7

Objective: To make a journal entry to pay a payroll

Directions: Based on your answer to Quick Practice 11-6, prepare the May 22, 20X9, general journal entry to pay the payroll.

Exercises

Learning Objective **2**

Check Figure
Bob Darby = $486.88

Exercise 11-1

Objective: To calculate gross earnings

Directions: The following payroll information pertains to four employees of Apex Corporation. Calculate the weekly gross earnings of each person.

Employee	Hours Worked	Hourly Rate	Overtime Rate
Bob Darby	47.5	$ 9.50	1.5
Sam Jones	47.0	10.00	1.5
Joy Smith	40.0	12.00	1.5
Ben White	57.0	7.25	2.0

Exercise 11-2

Objective: To calculate total hours worked and gross earnings

Directions: Tammy Bayto worked the following hours last week: Monday, 8; Tuesday, 10.5; Wednesday, 9; Thursday, 12; Friday, 7. What are Tammy's gross earnings for the week if her hourly rate is $14.50 and she earns time-and-a-half for hours over 40 a week?

Exercise 11-3

Objective: To compute FICA taxes

Directions: Data about four employees are presented below. For each, calculate the OASDI and HI taxes using the rates and the taxable limit presented in the chapter.

Employee	Cumulative Earnings	Gross Earnings This Pay Period	FICA OASDI	HI
David Mack	$ 38,500	$1,060	$_____	$_____
Jules Caray	61,000	1,820	$_____	$_____
Megan Slats	102,800	3,200	$_____	$_____
Kevin Sharp	101,900	3,050	$_____	$_____

Exercise 11-4

Objective: To determine federal income taxes

Directions: Using the wage bracket tables presented in this chapter, determine the federal income tax to be withheld from each person's gross earnings for the week.

Employee	Gross Earnings	Status	Withholding Tax
(a)	$328.45	M-2	$_____
(b)	535.00	M-3	$_____
(c)	524.38	S-1	$_____
(d)	335.56	S-0	$_____
(e)	465.00	S-2	$_____

Exercise 11-5

Objective: To calculate net earnings

Directions: Leighan Sweat is an employee whose hourly rate is $9.60. During the current week, she worked 48 hours. Her time is regulated by the Fair Labor Standards Act. She is married and claims three exemptions. So far this year, she has earned $8,200. She has a medical insurance deduction of $12.50 taken from her paycheck each week. Calculate her net earnings for the week.

Exercise 11-6

Objective: To make journal entries for payroll

Directions: From the following information taken from the payroll register totals for Windsor Company, prepare general journal entries to record (a) employee earnings and deductions and (b) payment of the payroll.

Office salaries	$120,000
Sales salaries	180,000
OASDI tax	18,600
HI tax	4,350
Federal income tax	45,000
Medical insurance deductions	4,700
Union dues	5,600

Case Problems

Group A

Learning Objectives **2, 4**

Check Figure
Hugo's net pay = $331.84

Problem 11-1A

Objective: To calculate gross earnings, payroll deductions, and net pay

Directions: Use the wage bracket tables and FICA tax rates presented in the chapter to supply the missing information for each employee listed in this problem. No employee has reached or exceeded the OASDI taxable wage base. Overtime pay is at the rate of one and one-half times the regular pay.

Employee	Status	Hours Worked	Hourly Rate	Gross Earnings	FICA OASDI	HI	Federal Income Tax	Net Pay
Hugo Arn	M-2	44.0	$ 8.00	$____	$____	$____	$____	$____
Jeff Bell	S-1	39.0	12.00	$____	$____	$____	$____	$____
Katy Dodd	M-0	46.0	8.75	$____	$____	$____	$____	$____
Brenda Frank	M-4	39.5	9.50	$____	$____	$____	$____	$____
Arthur Gibbs	S-0	42.0	7.25	$____	$____	$____	$____	$____
Terry Mann	S-2	40.0	8.00	$____	$____	$____	$____	$____
Harold Ross	M-1	44.0	10.00	$____	$____	$____	$____	$____

Learning Objectives **5, 6**

Check Figure
Salaries Payable = $1,564.66

Problem 11-2A

Objective: To complete a payroll register and record the payroll

A partial payroll register for Fox Facts, a data processing firm, is presented in the *Study Guide/Working Papers.*

Directions:

1. Complete the payroll register.
2. Use the completed payroll register as an information source to record employee earnings and deductions in general journal form.
3. Make a general journal entry to record the payment of the payroll.

Learning Objectives
4, 5, 6

Check Figure
Total of Net Amount column = $1,734.69

Problem 11-3A

Objective: To calculate net pay, complete a payroll register, and record the payroll

The following payroll information is for Ron-Ann's, a retail florist and gift shop, for the week ended June 14, 20X3:

Employee	Cumulative Earnings	Earnings This Period	Status	Dept.*	Deductions Medical Insurance	Savings Bonds
John Casper	$ 7,790	$328	S-1	O	$12	$10
George Hines	8,600	355	M-1	S	24	10
Gena Jones	9,200	425	M-2	S	35	25
Jena Miller	6,200	285	S-0	O	0	0
Bill Stokes	6,400	310	S-2	S	24	0
Martha Teal	11,900	510	M-1	O	24	20

*O = Office Salaries; S = Sales Salaries

Directions:

1. Enter the data in a payroll register and complete the register.
2. Record employee earnings and deductions and payment of the payroll in general journal form.

Problem 11-4A

Objective: To make accounting entries for payroll

Hines Department Store has the following payroll information for the week ended November 21, 20X3:

	Dept.	Name	Cumulative Earnings	Total Earnings	FICA OASDI	FICA HI	Federal Income Tax	State Income Tax	Medical Insurance	
1	S	Sandra Day	25 241 00	340 00	21 08	4 93	19 00	9 20	16 00	1
2	O	Ben Ellis	17 215 00	290 00	17 98	4 21	37 00	11 00	—	2
3	O	Jan Greene	6 820 00	215 00	13 33	3 12	10 00	3 40	12 00	3
4	S	Elisa Iverson	37 200 00	420 00	26 04	6 09	21 00	12 00	16 00	4
5	S	Robert Tagen	31 680 00	458 00	28 40	6 64	25 00	14 50	16 00	5
6	O	Tina Watson	4 200 00	312 00	19 34	4 52	23 00	8 90	—	6

Directions:

1. Record employee earnings and deductions in general journal form.
2. Record the payment of the payroll in general journal form.

Group B

Problem 11-1B

Objective: To calculate gross earnings, payroll deductions, and net pay

Directions: Use the wage bracket tables and FICA tax rates presented in the chapter to supply the missing information for each employee listed in this problem. No employee has reached or exceeded the OASDI taxable wage base. Overtime pay is at the rate of one and one-half times the regular pay.

Employee	Status	Hours Worked	Hourly Rate	Gross Earnings	FICA OASDI	FICA HI	Federal Income Tax	Net Pay
Carl Beal	S-1	46.0	$ 8.70	$_____	$_____	$_____	$_____	$_____
Tim Davis	M-3	44.0	13.50	$_____	$_____	$_____	$_____	$_____
Gary Grey	M-2	40.0	9.25	$_____	$_____	$_____	$_____	$_____
Pat Long	S-1	38.5	8.40	$_____	$_____	$_____	$_____	$_____
Kay Norris	M-0	40.0	7.25	$_____	$_____	$_____	$_____	$_____
Hal Reid	M-1	42.0	9.00	$_____	$_____	$_____	$_____	$_____
Guy Steale	S-2	45.0	9.50	$_____	$_____	$_____	$_____	$_____

Problem 11-2B

Objective: To complete a payroll register and record the payroll

A partial payroll register for Nathan's Bones, a computer and software dealer, is presented in the *Study Guide/Working Papers.*

Directions:

1. Complete the payroll register.
2. Use the completed payroll register as an information source to record employee earnings and deductions in general journal form.
3. Make a general journal entry to record the payment of the payroll.

Learning Objectives
4, 5, 6

Check Figure
Total of Net Amount column =
$1,966.71

Problem 11-3B

Objective: To calculate net pay, complete a payroll register, and record the payroll

The following payroll information is for Save-Mart, a small discount department store, for the week ended June 15, 20X4:

Employee	Cumulative Earnings	Earnings This Period	Status	Dept.*	Deductions Medical Insurance	Deductions Savings Bonds
Kay Norris	$ 9,600	$405	M-0	O	$12	$ 0
Al O'Malley	8,210	335	M-2	S	18	10
Joe Peters	7,800	325	S-1	O	12	10
Ted Reeves	1,200	410	M-2	S	18	0
Jay Sparks	11,400	430	M-3	S	25	21
Lori Veal	13,900	530	M-1	S	21	25

*O = Office Salaries; S = Sales Salaries

Directions:

1. Enter the data in a payroll register and complete the register.
2. Record employee earnings and deductions and payment of the payroll in general journal form.

Learning Objective **5, 6**

Check Figure
Salaries Payable = $1,647.25

Problem 11-4B

Objective: To make accounting entries for payroll

Art's Department Store has the following payroll information for the week ended October 22, 20X5:

	Dept.	Name	Cumulative Earnings	Total Earnings	FICA OASDI	FICA HI	Federal Income Tax	State Income Tax	Medical Insurance	
1	S	William Ashe	21 4 56 00	3 1 8 00	1 9 72	4 61	1 6 00	6 00	1 2 00	1
2	O	Jason Helmes	5 4 20 00	2 7 5 00	1 7 05	3 99	1 7 00	7 30	—	2
3	S	Kathy Komendantov	39 6 00 00	4 9 0 00	3 0 38	7 11	6 0 00	1 1 00	8 00	3
4	S	Tyler Milkin	24 3 00 00	3 1 2 00	1 9 34	4 52	1 0 00	7 60	1 2 00	4
5	S	Regina Musselman	18 2 10 00	2 7 6 00	1 7 11	4 00	1 3 00	5 00	8 00	5
6	O	Mark Pitts	—	3 5 2 00	2 1 82	5 10	2 0 00	8 10	—	6

Directions:

1. Record employee earnings and deductions in general journal form.
2. Record the payment of the payroll in general journal form.

Critical Thinking Problems

Challenge Problem

Judy Lyle is an account executive for a regional stock brokerage firm. During 20X2, Judy received a weekly salary of $650. She also received a commission of 2% on total sales and a year-end 12% bonus that is based on her yearly salary. In 20X2, her yearly sales amounted to $735,000.

Directions: Using the tax tables, OASDI taxable wage base, and other information presented in this chapter, calculate the following:

1. Judy's gross earnings for the year.
2. Judy's federal income tax for the year. She is married and claims one withholding allowance. Assume a federal income tax rate of 20% on her commission and bonus.
3. Judy's FICA taxes for the year.

Communications

Mike Moore is a new employee of Furtell Industries. When Mike received his first paycheck, he noticed that in addition to deductions for federal and state income tax, two additional amounts were withheld: OASDI and HI. Mike has heard of Social Security, but he had never heard of either of these two taxes. Write a note explaining to Mike what these taxes are and how they are calculated.

Team Internet Project

A current trend in accounting is to use software as a helpful tool. Commonly used software titles are Peachtree and QuickBooks, but there are many other products on the market, each of which serves different functions. Search the Internet and prepare a list, not of software titles, but of software product types. In other words, what are the different purposes of accounting software?

Ethics

Marie Leclair is a new employee who is in the process of filling in her paperwork for your company. As the human resource manager, you are looking over her employment application and find that she states that she is 19 and single. You then look at her Form W-4 and find that she has listed herself as married with three children. You ask her about the difference between the two forms, and she replies, "Oh yes, I know, but I can save taxes by claiming to be married with three kids. Besides, it's my right to fill out the form as I want to."

Write how you would respond to Marie's reply.

In the Real World			Social Security Administration	

Following are some data about the four funds described in the introduction to Part III. Amounts are in billions.

	OASI	DI	HI	SMI
Assets (end of 2005)	$1,663.0	$195.6	$285.8	$ 24.0
Income during 2006	642.2	102.6	211.5	225.5
Outgo during 2006	461.0	94.5	191.9	216.4
Net increase in assets	181.3	8.2	19.6	9.1
Assets (end of 2006)	1,844.3	203.8	305.4	33.1

Based on the information presented, answer the following questions:

(a) What were the total assets for all four funds at the end of 2005?
(b) What were the total assets for all four funds at the end of 2006?
(c) By how much did the total assets for all four funds increase from 2005 to 2006?

Answers to Review Quizzes

Review Quiz 11-1

$380 (40 × $8 = $320; 5 × $12 = $60; $320 + $60)

Review Quiz 11-2

	FICA	
Employee	OASDI	HI
A	$25.54	$ 5.97
B	24.80	18.13
C	51.15	11.96
D	38.32	8.96

Review Quiz 11-3

FICA:
$$\text{OASDI} = \$380 \times .062 = \$23.56$$
$$\text{HI} = 380 \times .0145 = \underline{5.51}$$
$$\$29.07$$
Federal income tax = $23

Review Quiz 11-4

Gross earnings		$380.00
Less deductions:		
FICA—OASDI	$23.56	
FICA—HI	5.51	
Federal income tax	23.00	
State income tax	11.40	
Medical insurance	15.00	
Savings bonds	25.00	
Total deductions		103.47
Net earnings		$276.53

Review Quiz 11-5

	20X3								
1	Feb.	6	Sales Salaries Expense	1 3 9 5 00			1
2			Office Salaries Expense	6 0 0 00			2
3			FICA Tax Payable—OASDI		1 2 3 69		3
4			FICA Tax Payable—HI		2 8 93		4
5			Federal Income Tax Payable		1 2 0 00		5
6			State Income Tax Payable		5 5 85		6
7			Medical Insurance Payable		6 9 00		7
8			Savings Bonds Payable		5 5 00		8
9			Union Dues Payable		1 5 00		9
10			Salaries Payable		1 5 2 7 53		10
11			Recorded payroll of February 6.				11

Review Quiz 11-6

	20X3					
1	Feb.	6	Salaries Payable	1 5 2 7 53		1
2			Cash		1 5 2 7 53	2
3			Paid payroll of February 6.			3

Accounting for Payroll
Employer Taxes and Reports

Learning Objectives

1 Describe and calculate payroll taxes imposed on the employer.
2 Record the employer's payroll taxes.
3 Record the deposit of employees' federal income taxes and FICA taxes and report these taxes to the government (Forms 8109 and 941).
4 Record and report payment of the employer's federal and state unemployment taxes (Form 940).
5 Report employee earnings and tax deductions to the federal government at the end of the year (Forms W-2 and W-3).
6 Describe and account for workers' compensation insurance.

In Chapter 11, we looked at the payroll taxes imposed on employees. We learned that employers must calculate and withhold these taxes from the earnings of employees. The payroll taxes, however, were not an expense of the employer. The employer simply had the responsibility of withholding them and then passing them on to the appropriate agency in a timely manner.

In this chapter, we continue our study of payroll accounting by looking at the payroll taxes imposed on employers. We will also look at the journal entries needed when the employer sends in taxes and other amounts that were withheld from the pay of employees.

Employer's Payroll Taxes

Learning Objective

1 Describe and calculate payroll taxes imposed on the employer.

All employers are required to pay certain taxes to federal and state authorities on behalf of employees. The three basic payroll taxes imposed on most employers are:
- FICA (both OASDI and HI)
- Federal unemployment taxes
- State unemployment taxes

Since payroll taxes are a necessary part of operating a business, they are recorded in the **Payroll Tax Expense account**, an operating expense account. We can describe this account in T-account form as follows:

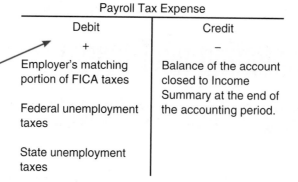

Payroll Tax Expense	
Debit	Credit
+	–
Employer's matching portion of FICA taxes	Balance of the account closed to Income Summary at the end of the accounting period.
Federal unemployment taxes	
State unemployment taxes	

Now, let's look in greater detail at the payroll taxes imposed on employers.

FICA Tax

Remember from our discussion in Chapter 11 that the FICA tax is a matching tax paid equally by the employee and the employer. Remember also that FICA consists of two parts: Old-Age, Survivors, and Disability Insurance (OASDI) and the Hospital Insurance (HI) plan, or Medicare.

As we discussed in Chapter 11, the current OASDI rate is 6.2% of the first $102,000 earned in a year, and the HI rate is 1.45% of all earnings. To illustrate how to calculate these taxes, we will continue with our Chapter 11 example of Northwest Company. The taxable earnings columns of Northwest's November 18, 20X3, payroll register are shown in Figure 12-1. Notice that the FICA columns in the Taxable Earnings section show that $2,249 of employee earnings this pay period are subject to OASDI taxes and that $3,464 are subject to HI taxes. Using the current rates, we can calculate these taxes as follows:

OASDI taxable earnings × OASDI rate = Tax

$2,249.00 × .062 = $139.44

Total earnings × HI rate = Tax

$3,464.00 × .0145 = $50.23

If you refer to the taxes withheld by Northwest Company in Chapter 11, you will see that the same amount of FICA taxes withheld from the pay of employees is now being imposed on the employer.

Federal Unemployment Tax

The **Federal Unemployment Tax Act (FUTA)** requires the payment of taxes to provide benefits for workers during periods of temporary unemployment. Unlike FICA, this tax is paid *only* by the employer; it *cannot* be withheld from the pay of employees. The FUTA rate, like the FICA rate, is set by federal legislation. The current rate is 6.2% of the first $7,000 of wages paid to each employee during the calendar year. However, the employer may take a credit of up to 5.4% for timely contributions to state unemployment funds. And since all states have unemployment funds, this leaves an effective FUTA rate of only 0.8% (6.2% – 5.4%).

To calculate Northwest's FUTA tax for the payroll of November 18, refer to the partial payroll register in Figure 12-1. Look at the total of the Unemployment column in the Taxable Earnings section. This total, $340, is the amount of earnings this pay period that are subject to FUTA. We thus multiply this amount by the effective FUTA rate of 0.8% (.008):

$340 × .008 = $2.72

Figure 12-1

Partial Payroll Register for Northwest Company

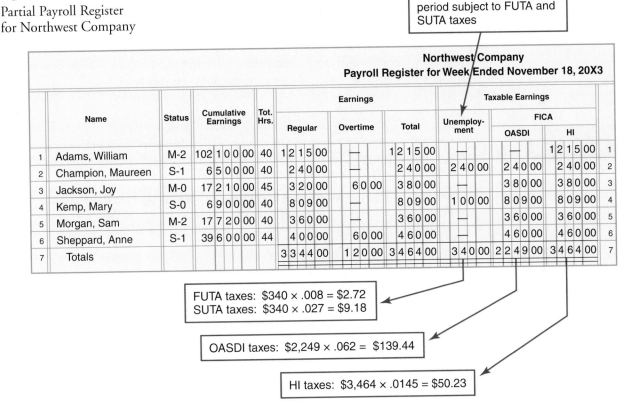

Amount of earnings this pay period subject to FUTA and SUTA taxes

Northwest Company
Payroll Register for Week Ended November 18, 20X3

	Name	Status	Cumulative Earnings	Tot. Hrs.	Earnings			Taxable Earnings			
					Regular	Overtime	Total	Unemployment	FICA		
									OASDI	HI	
1	Adams, William	M-2	102 1 0 0 00	40	1 2 1 5 00	—	1 2 1 5 00	—	—	1 2 1 5 00	1
2	Champion, Maureen	S-1	6 5 0 0 00	40	2 4 0 00	—	2 4 0 00	2 4 0 00	2 4 0 00	2 4 0 00	2
3	Jackson, Joy	M-0	17 2 1 0 00	45	3 2 0 00	6 0 00	3 8 0 00	—	3 8 0 00	3 8 0 00	3
4	Kemp, Mary	S-0	6 9 0 0 00	40	8 0 9 00	—	8 0 9 00	1 0 0 00	8 0 9 00	8 0 9 00	4
5	Morgan, Sam	M-2	17 7 2 0 00	40	3 6 0 00	—	3 6 0 00	—	3 6 0 00	3 6 0 00	5
6	Sheppard, Anne	S-1	39 6 0 0 00	44	4 0 0 00	6 0 00	4 6 0 00	—	4 6 0 00	4 6 0 00	6
7	Totals				3 3 4 4 00	1 2 0 00	3 4 6 4 00	3 4 0 00	2 2 4 9 00	3 4 6 4 00	7

FUTA taxes: $340 × .008 = $2.72
SUTA taxes: $340 × .027 = $9.18

OASDI taxes: $2,249 × .062 = $139.44

HI taxes: $3,464 × .0145 = $50.23

State Unemployment Tax

All states and the District of Columbia have passed unemployment compensation laws that, along with FUTA, provide benefits to qualified unemployed workers. State unemployment taxes are usually referred to as **State Unemployment Tax Act (SUTA)** taxes. SUTA taxes are paid to the state in which the employer conducts business.

The taxable base for SUTA taxes varies from state to state. For this text, we will assume that the taxable base for SUTA taxes is the first $7,000 earned by each employee in a calendar year. The rate for SUTA, however, can vary from employer to employer, depending on the employer's record of

State Unemployment Tax Act (SUTA) a law that requires employers to pay unemployment taxes (for the benefit of employees) to the states in which they conduct business unemployment claims and the state's recent experience with unemployment claims. Most states have a **merit-rating system** that provides a lower rate as an incentive for employers to stabilize employment. Under this system, it is possible for an employer who has laid off few workers to pay considerably less than the maximum rate. For example, Northwest Company is located in New Jersey. At the time of this writing, the employer SUTA rate in New Jersey ranges from a minimum of 0.6% to the maximum of 5.4%. We will assume that Northwest Company's rate is 2.7% (.027). Thus, the SUTA tax for Northwest's November 18 payroll is $9.18:

$340 × .027 = $9.18

Take This Into Account

The funds collected by the federal government as a result of the employer FUTA tax are used primarily to pay the cost of administering both the federal and state unemployment programs. The FUTA tax is not used to pay weekly benefits to unemployed workers. Instead, payments are made by each state in accordance with the state's unemployment tax law.

Review Quiz   12-1   Assuming the current FICA rates, a FUTA rate of 0.8%, and a SUTA rate of 2.7%, calculate the employer's payroll taxes for the following payroll:

Employee	Year-to-Date Earnings	Earnings This Pay Period
Walt King	$14,500.00	$396.00
Carol Maris	6,750.00	318.00
Jill Mimms	33,000.00	675.00
Bill Todd	5,400.00	215.50
Chuck Wade	6,900.00	200.00

Check your answers on page 575.

Recording Employer's Payroll Taxes

Learning Objective

2 Record the employer's payroll taxes.

As stated earlier, the employer's payroll taxes are debited to an expense account entitled Payroll Tax Expense. The journal entry for payroll taxes should be prepared separately from the journal entry for salaries expense. This helps ensure that both salaries expense and payroll tax expense are recognized properly. Let's look again at the payroll taxes imposed on Northwest Company's November 18 payroll:

FICA:		
OASDI	$139.44	
HI	50.23	$189.67
FUTA		2.72
SUTA		9.18
Total		$201.57

The following general journal entry shows the recording of Northwest's payroll taxes for the pay period ended November 18, 20X3.

	20X3						
+ expense → 1	Nov.	18	Payroll Tax Expense	2 0 1 57			1
+ liability → 2			FICA Tax Payable—OASDI		1 3 9 44		2
+ liability → 3			FICA Tax Payable—HI		5 0 23		3
+ liability → 4			FUTA Tax Payable		2 72		4
+ liability → 5			SUTA Tax Payable		9 18		5
6			Recorded employer's payroll taxes.				6

Notice that even though all employer payroll taxes are debited to a single expense account, the amount of *each* tax is credited to a separate liability account. This is done to record the employer's obligation to pay the different taxes. For a clearer understanding, let's look at each of the liability accounts.

FICA Tax Payable—OASDI Account

The FICA Tax Payable—OASDI account is the same account we introduced in Chapter 11 to record the employees' share of OASDI taxes. Since the employer must match the OASDI taxes paid by the employees, the same account is used to record both the employees' and the employer's share. The account is credited to record OASDI taxes imposed on the employer and debited when the taxes are sent in.

FICA Tax Payable—OASDI

Debit	Credit
–	+
Payment of OASDI taxes previously withheld from employees or imposed on the employer	OASDI taxes: (1) withheld from employees *and* (2) imposed on the employer

FICA Tax Payable—HI Account

As with the OASDI taxes, HI taxes are shared equally by the employees and employer. Thus, the same account we used in Chapter 11 to record HI taxes withheld from employees is used by the employer. It is credited to record HI taxes imposed on the employer and debited when the taxes are sent in.

FICA Tax Payable—HI

Debit	Credit
–	+
Payment of HI taxes previously withheld from employees or imposed on the employer	HI taxes: (1) withheld from employees *and* (2) imposed on the employer

FUTA Tax Payable Account

The **FUTA Tax Payable account** is a current liability account used to record the employer's obligation for federal unemployment taxes. The account is credited when taxes are imposed on the employer and debited when the taxes are sent in.

FUTA Tax Payable	
Debit	Credit
–	+
Payment of FUTA taxes	FUTA taxes imposed on the employer

SUTA Tax Payable Account

The **SUTA Tax Payable account** is a current liability account used to record the employer's obligation for state unemployment taxes. The account is credited when taxes are imposed on the employer and debited when the taxes are sent in.

SUTA Tax Payable	
Debit	Credit
–	+
Payment of SUTA taxes	SUTA taxes imposed on the employer

Review Quiz **12-2** Using the payroll information in Review Quiz 12-1, make the general journal entry needed to record the employer's payroll taxes. The date of the payroll is November 18, 20X3.

Check your answer on page 575.

The timely and accurate filing of required tax reports is a very important part of payroll accounting.

Filing Reports and Making Payroll Tax Payments

As we indicated earlier, employers are responsible for filing reports and making payroll tax payments on a timely basis. To file tax reports, employers must have an **employer identification number (EIN)**, which is a nine-digit number issued by the Internal Revenue Service (IRS). The EIN must be listed on all reports filed with the IRS and the Social Security Administration (SSA). An EIN is to a business what a Social Security number is to an individual.

Learning Objective

3 Record the deposit of employees' federal income taxes and FICA taxes and report these taxes to the government (Forms 8109 and 941).

Form 941, Employer's Quarterly Federal Tax Return a quarterly report that summarizes FICA taxes (employer and employee shares) and federal income taxes withheld during the quarter

lookback period a 12-month period ending on June 30 of the prior year; employers look at the amount of FICA taxes (employee and employer shares) and withheld income taxes during the lookback period to determine their deposit status for the current year

Figure 12-2

Lookback Period for 2010

Employers must file reports and make payments in three areas: (1) FICA taxes and federal income taxes, (2) federal unemployment taxes, and (3) state unemployment taxes. In the following discussion, we will examine these three areas and the accounting entries needed when payments are made.

FICA and Federal Income Taxes

The employer's responsibility in this area extends to FICA taxes withheld from the pay of employees, the employer's share of FICA taxes, and income taxes withheld from employees. To summarize the amounts of these taxes, the employer must file **Form 941, Employer's Quarterly Federal Tax Return** with the IRS at the end of each calendar quarter. If during the quarter in question the employer's total tax liability is less than $2,500, payment may be sent with Form 941. However, if the total taxes exceed $2,500, employers are not permitted to send payment directly to the IRS at the end of the quarter. Instead, the taxes must be deposited by electronic funds transfers or in a Federal Reserve bank or other authorized bank. When taxes are deposited in a local bank, the IRS is notified of the deposit and sends for the funds.

When to Deposit Taxes

Employers can electronically deposit FICA taxes and federal income taxes withheld from employees by using the Electronic Federal Tax Payment System (EFTPS) or by mailing or delivering a check, money order, or cash to a Federal Reserve bank or other authorized bank. There are two deposit schedules—monthly or semiweekly—for determining when taxes must be deposited. Determining which schedule to use is based on the employer's total tax liability reported during a 12-month lookback period. The **lookback period** for any year is the 12-month period beginning on July 1 *two years* prior to the current year and ending on June 30 *one year* prior to the current year. Although this sounds complicated, it is really quite simple. Figure 12-2 illustrates the lookback period for the year 2010. As we can see, the lookback period for 2010 starts on July 1, 2008, and ends on June 30, 2009.

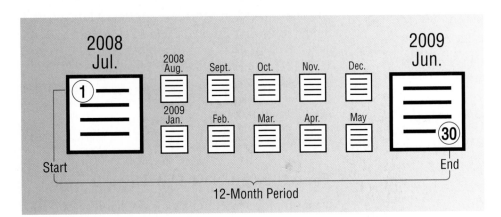

Keep in mind that the lookback period is always 12 months long; it always starts on July 1 and ends on June 30. Thus, it is only necessary to determine the

years for those dates. This involves only simple subtraction. To determine the start of the lookback period, subtract two years from the current year:

Start of lookback period = July 1 of current year – 2 years

To determine the end of the lookback period, subtract one year from the current year:

End of lookback period = June 30 of current year – 1 year

Now, what is the lookback period for 2011?

Start of lookback period = July 1 of current year – 2 years
                         = July 1, 2011 – 2 years = July 1, 2009

End of lookback period = June 30 of current year – 1 year
                         = June 30, 2011 – 1 year = June 30, 2010

Thus, the 2011 lookback period is July 1, 2009, to June 30, 2010.

Monthly Deposit Schedule

An employer is a monthly depositor for the current year if the total taxes (FICA and withheld federal income taxes) for the lookback period were $50,000 or less. For example, assume that Alexandra Company reported a total tax liability of $45,000 for the 2009 lookback period. Since this amount does not exceed $50,000, Alexandra is a monthly depositor for 2009.

Under the monthly deposit schedule, taxes must be deposited by the 15th day of the following month. Thus, FICA taxes and federal income taxes withheld during January must be deposited by February 15.

Semiweekly Deposit Schedule

If an employer's total taxes during the lookback period were more than $50,000, the semiweekly deposit schedule is required. Under the semiweekly deposit schedule, taxes on payroll payments made on Wednesday, Thursday, or Friday must be deposited by the following Wednesday. Taxes on payroll payments made on Saturday, Sunday, Monday, or Tuesday must be deposited by the following Friday. Table 12-1 summarizes these rules.

Table 12-1 Semiweekly Deposit Schedule

IF the payday falls on a:	THEN deposit taxes by the following:
Wednesday, Thursday, or Friday	Wednesday
Saturday, Sunday, Monday, or Tuesday	Friday

The $100,000 Next-Day Deposit Rule

If an employer accumulates a tax liability of $100,000 or more on any day during a deposit period, the taxes must be deposited the next business day. For example, a large company such as Coca-Cola or General Motors could easily accumulate a tax liability (employees' and employer's FICA taxes and withheld income taxes) of well over $100,000 in a single payroll. For these employers, the monthly and semiweekly deposit schedules don't apply; they must deposit the taxes the next business day.

Accounting for Taxes Deposited

Form 8109, Federal Tax Deposit Coupon a form that must be filled out when FICA taxes and withheld federal income taxes are deposited in an authorized bank

When any deposit of taxes is made, the employer should complete and submit to the bank a **Form 8109, Federal Tax Deposit Coupon**, shown in Figure 12-3.

To illustrate the accounting entry for recording the payment of FICA and employee federal income taxes, let's assume that on April 14, 20X3, Northwest Company deposited the following taxes in a local bank:

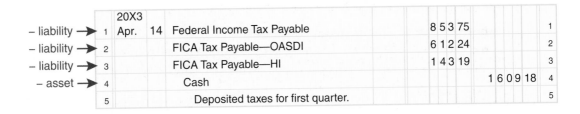

Federal income tax withheld from employees		$853.75
FICA tax:		
OASDI	$612.24	
HI	143.19	755.43
Total amount deposited		$1,609.18

Northwest's accountant made the following general journal entry to record the payment:

– liability →	1	20X3 Apr.	14	Federal Income Tax Payable	8 5 3 75		1
– liability →	2			FICA Tax Payable—OASDI	6 1 2 24		2
– liability →	3			FICA Tax Payable—HI	1 43 19		3
– asset →	4			Cash		1 6 09 18	4
	5			Deposited taxes for first quarter.			5

As we mentioned earlier, employers must file Form 941 at the end of each calendar quarter. This form is a quarterly summary of FICA taxes (employee and employer's shares) and federal income taxes withheld. Remember that when the cumulative amount of these taxes reaches $2,500, deposits in an authorized bank are required. As a result, any amount sent with Form 941 should be under $2,500. Figure 12-4 on the next page illustrates the Form 941 prepared by Sondra Smith, owner of Northwest Company, at the end of the first calendar quarter, 20X3.

Figure 12-3

Form 8109, Federal Tax Deposit Coupon

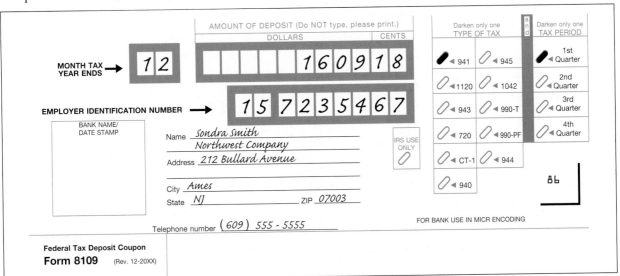

Figure 12-4

Form 941,
Employer's Quarterly
Federal Tax Return

Form **941 for 20X3:** Employer's QUARTERLY Federal Tax Return   990107

(Rev. January 20X3)   Department of the Treasury — Internal Revenue Service

OMB No. 1545-0029

(EIN)
Employer identification number   1   5   –   7   2   3   5   4   6   7

Name (not your trade name)   **Sondra Smith**

Trade name (if any)   **Northwest Company**

Address   **212 Bullard Avenue**
      Number   Street   Suite or room number
      Ames   **NJ**   **07003**
      City   State   ZIP code

Report for this Quarter of 20X3
(Check one.)

☑ **1:** January, February, March

☐ **2:** April, May, June

☐ **3:** July, August, September

☐ **4:** October, November, December

Read the separate instructions before you fill out this form. Please type or print within the boxes.

Part 1: Answer these questions for this quarter.

1 Number of employees who received wages, tips, or other compensation for the pay period
including: *Mar. 12* (Quarter 1), *June 12* (Quarter 2), *Sept. 12* (Quarter 3), *Dec. 12* (Quarter 4)   **1**   6

2 Wages, tips, and other compensation . . . .   **2**   11,277 . 42

3 Total income tax withheld from wages, tips, and other compensation . . . .   **3**   1,950 . 00

4 If no wages, tips, and other compensation are subject to social security or Medicare tax . . ☐ Check and go to line 6.

5 Taxable social security and Medicare wages and tips:

	Column 1		Column 2
5a Taxable social security wages	11,277 . 42	× .124 =	1,398 . 40
5b Taxable social security tips	0 . 00	× .124 =	0 . 00
5c Taxable Medicare wages & tips	11,277 . 42	× .029 =	327 . 05

5d Total social security and Medicare taxes (*Column 2*, lines 5a + 5b + 5c = line 5d) . .   **5d**   1,725 . 45

6 Total taxes before adjustments (lines 3 + 5d = line 6) . . . .   **6**   3,675 . 45

7 TAX ADJUSTMENTS (Read the instructions for line 7 before completing lines 7a through 7h.):

7a Current quarter's fractions of cents . . . .   0 . 00

7b Current quarter's sick pay . . . .   0 . 00

7c Current quarter's adjustments for tips and group-term life insurance   0 . 00

7d Current year's income tax withholding (attach Form 941c) . .   0 . 00

7e Prior quarters' social security and Medicare taxes (attach Form 941c)   0 . 00

7f Special additions to federal income tax (attach Form 941c) . . .   0 . 00

7g Special additions to social security and Medicare (attach Form 941c)   0 . 00

7h TOTAL ADJUSTMENTS (Combine all amounts: lines 7a through 7g.) . . . . .   **7h**   0 . 00

8 Total taxes after adjustments (Combine lines 6 and 7h.) . . . .   **8**   3,675 . 45

9 Advance earned income credit (EIC) payments made to employees . . . . . .   **9**   0 . 00

10 Total taxes after adjustment for advance EIC (line 8 – line 9 = line 10) . . . . .   **10**   3,675 . 45

11 Total deposits for this quarter, including overpayment applied from a prior quarter . .   **11**   3,675 . 45

12 Balance due (If line 10 is more than line 11, write the difference here.) . . . . . .   **12**   0 . 00
Follow the Instructions for Form 941-V, Payment Voucher.

13 Overpayment (If line 11 is more than line 10, write the difference here.)   0 . 00   Check one ☐ Apply to next return.
                                                                             ☐ Send a refund.

▶ You **MUST** fill out both pages of this form and **SIGN** it.   Next ➡

For Privacy Act and Paperwork Reduction Act Notice, see the back of the Payment Voucher.   Cat. No. 17001Z   Form **941** (Rev. 1-20X3)

Name *(not your trade name)*
Sondra Smith

Employer identification number (EIN)
15-7235467

Part 2: Tell us about your deposit schedule and tax liability for this quarter.

If you are unsure about whether you are a monthly schedule depositor or a semiweekly schedule depositor, see *Pub. 15 (Circular E)*, section 11.

14 [N] [J] Write the state abbreviation for the state where you made your depositsOR write "MU" if you made your deposits in *multiple* states.

15 Check one: ☐ Line 10 is less than $2,500. Go to Part 3.

☑ You were a monthly schedule depositor for the entire quarter. Fill out your tax liability for each month. Then go to Part 3.

Tax liability:	Month 1	1,120 . 03
	Month 2	946 . 24
	Month 3	1,609 . 18
Total liability for quarter		3,675 . 45	Total must equal line 10.

☐ You were a semiweekly schedule depositor for any part of this quarter. Fill out *Schedule B (Form 941): Report of Tax Liability for Semiweekly Schedule Depositors,* and attach it to this form.

Part 3: Tell us about your business. If a question does NOT apply to your business, leave it blank.

16 If your business has closed or you stopped paying wages . . . . ☐ Check here, and

enter the final date you paid wages [/ /]

17 If you are a seasonal employer and you do not have to file a return for every quarter of the year . . ☐ Check here.

Part 4: May we speak with your third-party designee?

Do you want to allow an employee, a paid tax preparer, or another person to discuss this return with the IRS? (See the instructions for details.)

☐ Yes. Designee's name [   ]

Select a 5-digit Personal Identification Number (PIN) to use when talking to IRS. [ ][ ][ ][ ][ ]

☑ No.

Part 5: Sign here. You MUST fill out both pages of this form and SIGN it.

Under penalties of perjury, I declare that I have examined this return, including accompanying schedules and statements, and to the best of my knowledge and belief, it is true, correct, and complete.

X Sign your name here *Sondra Smith*

Print your name here **Sondra Smith**

Print your title here **Owner**

Date 4 / 14 / X3

Best daytime phone (609) 555 – 5555

Part 6: For paid preparers only *(optional)*

Paid Preparer's Signature		
Firm's name		
Address		EIN
		ZIP code
Date [/ /] Phone ( ) –		SSN/PTIN

☐ Check if you are self-employed.

Page **2**

Form **941** (Rev. 1-20X3)

Table 12-2 summarizes the steps for determining the tax deposit schedule for FICA and withheld income taxes.

Table 12-2 Summary of Steps to Determine Tax Deposit Schedule for FICA and Withheld Federal Income Taxes

1. Identify the lookback period for the current year.
2. Add the total taxes reported on line 8 of Forms 941 filed during the lookback period.
3. Determine if you are a monthly or semiweekly schedule depositor:

IF the total taxes reported on Forms 941 during the look period were:	THEN you are a:
$50,000 or less	Monthly schedule depositor
More than $50,000	Semiweekly schedule depositor

If you accumulate $100,000 or more in taxes during any deposit period, a deposit is required the next business (banking) day.

Federal Unemployment Taxes

Learning Objective

4 Record and report payment of the employer's federal and state unemployment taxes (Form 940).

If the amount of federal unemployment taxes (FUTA) is more than $500 in any quarter, the total must be deposited in an authorized bank by the last day of the first month following the close of the quarter involved. If the amount is $500 or less, no deposit is required. However, this amount must be added to the FUTA tax in the following quarter, and if the cumulative total is over $500, a deposit must be made.

In addition to the quarterly reports that are made when FUTA taxes are deposited, employers also must file **Form 940, Employer's Annual Federal Unemployment Tax Return**, by January 31, following the end of the year. This form summarizes the quarterly reports and deposits. Figure 12-5 illustrates Northwest's Form 940 for 20X3.

Form 940, Employer's Annual Federal Unemployment Tax Return a form filed by the employer by January 31, summarizing quarterly FUTA deposits made during the preceding year

To illustrate the accounting entry needed when FUTA taxes are paid, assume that on January 31, 20X4, Northwest Company issued a check for $248 to pay its FUTA taxes for the previous year (since the company's total FUTA tax liability was less than $500, no deposits were made during the year). The following general journal entry records the payment:

– liability → 1	20X4 Jan.	31	FUTA Tax Payable	2 4 8 00	1
– asset → 2			Cash		2 4 8 00	2
3			Paid undeposited FUTA taxes.		3

This entry records the payment of taxes owed at the end of a year. The same entry is made when quarterly FUTA taxes are deposited during the year. Table 12-3 on the next page shows a summary of when to deposit FUTA taxes.

Form **940 for 20X3:** Employer's Annual Federal Unemployment (FUTA) Tax Return   850107
Department of the Treasury — Internal Revenue Service

OMB No. 1545-0028

(EIN)
Employer identification number   1 5 – 7 2 3 5 4 6 7

Name *(not your trade name)*   Sondra Smith

Trade name *(if any)*   Northwest Company

Address   212 Bullard Avenue
Number   Street   Suite or room number

Ames   NJ   07003
City   State   ZIP code

Type of Return
(Check all that apply.)

a. Amended
b. Successor employer
c. No payments to employees in 20X3
d. Final: Business closed or stopped paying wages

Read the separate instructions before you fill out this form. Please type or print within the boxes.

Part 1: Tell us about your return. If any line does NOT apply, leave it blank.

1   If you were required to pay your state unemployment tax in ...

    1a **One state only,** write the state abbreviation . . . . **1a**   N J

    - OR -

    1b **More than one state** (You are a multi-state employer) . . . . **1b** ☐ Check here. Fill out Schedule A.

    ~~Skip line 2 for 20X3 and go to line 3.~~

2   ~~If you paid wages in a state that is subject to CREDIT REDUCTION~~ . . . . **2** ☐ ~~Check here. Fill out Schedule A (Form 940), Part 2.~~

Part 2: Determine your FUTA tax before adjustments for 2007. If any line does NOT apply, leave it blank.

3   Total payments to all employees . . . . **3**   128,300 . 00

4   Payments exempt from FUTA tax . . . . **4**   0 . 00

    Check all that apply: **4a** ☐ Fringe benefits   **4c** ☐ Retirement/Pension   **4e** ☐ Other
                4b ☐ Group term life insurance   **4d** ☐ Dependent care

5   Total of payments made to each employee in excess of $7,000 . . . . . . **5**   97,300 . 00

6   Subtotal (line 4 + line 5 = line 6) . . . . **6**   97,300 . 00

7   Total taxable FUTA wages (line 3 – line 6 = line 7) . . . . **7**   31,000 . 00

8   FUTA tax before adjustments (line 7 × .008 = line 8) . . . . **8**   248 . 00

Part 3: Determine your adjustments. If any line does NOT apply, leave it blank.

9   If ALL of the taxable FUTA wages you paid were excluded from state unemployment tax, multiply line 7 by .054 (line 7 × .054 = line 9). Then go to line 12 . . . . **9**   0 . 00

10   If SOME of the taxable FUTA wages you paid were excluded from state unemployment tax, OR you paid ANY state unemployment tax late (after the due date for filing Form 940), fill out the worksheet in the instructions. Enter the amount from line 7 of the worksheet onto line 10 . . **10**   0 . 00

    ~~Skip line 11 for 20X3 and go to line 12.~~

11   ~~If credit reduction applies, enter the amount from line 3 of Schedule A (Form 940)~~ . . . . . **11**   .

Part 4: Determine your FUTA tax and balance due or overpayment for 2007. If any line does NOT apply, leave it blank.

12   Total FUTA tax after adjustments (lines 8 + 9 + 10 = line 12) . . . . **12**   248 . 00

13   FUTA tax deposited for the year, including any payment applied from a prior year . . . . **13**   0 . 00

14   Balance due (If line 12 is more than line 13, enter the difference on line 14.)
    ● If line 14 is more than $500, you must deposit your tax.
    ● If line 14 is $500 or less and you pay by check, make your check payable to the United States Treasury and write your EIN, *Form 940,* and *20X3* on the check . . . . **14**   248 . 00

15   Overpayment (If line 13 is more than line 12, enter the difference on line 15 and check a box below.) . . . . **15**   0 . 00

    Check one ☐ Apply to next return.
             ☐ Send a refund.

▶ You **MUST** fill out both pages of this form and **SIGN** it.

Next ➡

For Privacy Act and Paperwork Reduction Act Notice, see the back of Form 940-V, Payment Voucher.   Cat. No. 11234O   Form **940** (20X3)

Figure 12-5

Continued

850207

Name (not your trade name)	Employer identification number (EIN)
Sondra Smith	15-7235467

Part 5: Report your FUTA tax liability by quarter only if line 12 is more than $500. If not, go to Part 6.

16 Report the amount of your FUTA tax liability for each quarter; do NOT enter the amount you deposited. If you had no liability for a quarter, leave the line blank.

16a 1st quarter (January 1 – March 31) . . . . 16a | 198 . 00

16b 2nd quarter (April 1 – June 30) . . . . 16b | 21 . 00

16c 3rd quarter (July 1 – September 30) . . . . 16c | 16 . 00

16d 4th quarter (October 1 – December 31) . . . . 16d | 13 . 00

17 Total tax liability for the year (lines 16a + 16b + 16c + 16d = line 17) 17 | 248 . 00   Total must equal line 12.

Part 6: May we speak with your third-party designee?

Do you want to allow an employee, a paid tax preparer, or another person to discuss this return with the IRS? See the instructions for details.

☐ Yes. Designee's name _____

Select a 5-digit Personal Identification Number (PIN) to use when talking to IRS ☐ ☐ ☐ ☐ ☐

☑ No.

Part 7: Sign here. You MUST fill out both pages of this form and SIGN it.

Under penalties of perjury, I declare that I have examined this return, including accompanying schedules and statements, and to the best of my knowledge and belief, it is true, correct, and complete, and that no part of any payment made to a state unemployment fund claimed as a credit was, or is to be, deducted from the payments made to employees.

✗ Sign your name here *Sondra Smith*

Print your name here | Sondra Smith
Print your title here | Owner

Date 1 / 31 / X4

Best daytime phone (609) 555 – 5555

Part 8: For PAID preparers only (optional)

If you were paid to prepare this return and are not an employee of the business that is filing this return, you may choose to fill out Part 8.

Paid Preparer's name | _____

Preparer's SSN/PTIN | _____

Paid Preparer's signature | _____

Date | / /

☐ Check if you are self-employed.

Firm's name | _____

Firm's EIN | _____

Street address | _____

City | _____ State | _____

ZIP code | _____

Table 12-3 When to Deposit FUTA Taxes

Quarter	Ending	Due Date
Jan.–Feb.–Mar.	Mar. 31	Apr. 30
Apr.–May–Jun.	Jun. 30	Jul. 31
Jul.–Aug.–Sept.	Sept. 30	Oct. 31
Oct.–Nov.–Dec.	Dec. 31	Jan. 31

State Unemployment Taxes

Each state provides its own special forms and specifies how state unemployment taxes are paid. Generally, the amount of state unemployment taxes imposed on employers must be remitted to the proper state office by the end of the month following the close of the calendar quarter in which wages and salaries were earned by employees. To illustrate the accounting entry needed when state unemployment taxes are remitted, assume that on April 27, 20X3, Northwest Company issued a check for $489 to New Jersey in payment of state unemployment taxes on earnings of employees during the first quarter of 20X3. The following general journal entry records the payment:

– liability →	1	20X3 Apr.	27	SUTA Tax Payable	4 8 9 00		1
– asset →	2			Cash		4 8 9 00	2
	3			Paid SUTA for first quarter, 20X3.			3

Form W-2: Wage and Tax Statement

Learning Objective

5 Report employee earnings and tax deductions to the federal government at the end of the year (Forms W-2 and W-3).

Form W-2, Wage and Tax Statement a form issued by the employer to each employee by January 31 that contains a summary of the employee's earnings and tax deductions for the past year

Form W-3, Transmittal of Wage and Tax Statements an annual form employers file with the Social Security Administration to summarize employee earnings and tax deductions; filed with copy A of each employee's Form W-2

In the sections above, we discussed the reports that employers must file with the government. Employers must also report to employees. By January 31 of each year, employers are required to furnish copies of **Form W-2, Wage and Tax Statement**, to each person who was employed in any part of the previous year. The employer is also required to send a copy of each employee's Form W-2 directly to the Social Security Administration. This allows the IRS to check on employees and employers as to whether the employees are reporting the proper amount of income on their personal income tax returns and whether the employers are properly reporting and submitting the tax amounts withheld from the earnings of employees. Figure 12-6 shows the Form W-2 that Sam Morgan received from Northwest Company at the end of 20X3. Notice that the information shown on Sam's Form W-2 was taken from his employee's earnings record illustrated in Figure 11-6 on page 520.

Form W-3: Transmittal of Wage and Tax Statements

Along with Copy A of each employee's Form W-2, employers must file **Form W-3, Transmittal of Wage and Tax Statements**, with the Social Security Administration by the last day of February following each year. This form, which is illustrated in Figure 12-7 on page 556, summarizes the earnings and tax deductions of all employees of the firm for the previous year.

Figure 12-6

Completed Form W-2

22222	Void ☐	a Employee's social security number 422-22-6222	For Official Use Only ▶ OMB No. 1545-0008	

b Employer identification number (EIN) 15-7235467		1 Wages, tips, other compensation $19,562.00	2 Federal income tax withheld $468.00

c Employer's name, address, and ZIP code **Northwest Company** 212 Bullard Ave. Ames, NJ 07003	3 Social security wages $19,562.00	4 Social security tax withheld $1,212.84
	5 Medicare wages and tips $19,562.00	6 Medicare tax withheld $283.65
	7 Social security tips	8 Allocated tips

d Control number	9 Advance EIC payment	10 Dependent care benefits

e Employee's first name and initial **Sam**	Last name **Morgan**	Suff.	11 Nonqualified plans	12a See instructions for box 12 Code

1244 Oak Street Ames, NJ 07003	13 Statutory employee ☐	Retirement plan ☐	Third-party sick pay ☐	12b Code
	14 Other			12c Code
				12d Code

f Employee's address and ZIP code			

15 State NJ	Employer's state ID number 28677	16 State wages, tips, etc. $19,562.00	17 State income tax $286.00	18 Local wages, tips, etc.	19 Local income tax	20 Locality name

Figure 12-7

Form W3, Transmittal of Wage and Tax Statements

DO NOT STAPLE

33333	a Control number	For Official Use Only ▶ OMB No. 1545-0008	

b Kind of Payer ▶	941 [X] CT-1	Military ☐ Hshld. emp. ☐	943 ☐ Medicare govt. emp. ☐	944 ☐ Third-party sick pay ☐	1 Wages, tips, other compensation $128,300.00	2 Federal income tax withheld $14,245.00
					3 Social security wages $122,600.00	4 Social security tax withheld $7,601.20

c Total number of Forms W-2 6	d Establishment number 6	5 Medicare wages and tips $128,300.00	6 Medicare tax withheld $1,860.35

e Employer identification number (EIN) 15-7235467	7 Social security tips	8 Allocated tips

f Employer's name **Northwest Company** Sondra Smith 212 Bullard Avenue Ames, NJ 07003	9 Advance EIC payments	10 Dependent care benefits
	11 Nonqualified plans	12 Deferred compensation
	13 For third-party sick pay use only	
	14 Income tax withheld by payer of third-party sick pay	

g Employer's address and ZIP code		
h Other EIN used this year		

15 State NJ	Employer's state ID number 28677	16 State wages, tips, etc. $128,300.00	17 State income tax $4,460.00
		18 Local wages, tips, etc.	19 Local income tax

Contact person	Telephone number (609) 555-5555	For Official Use Only
Email address	Fax number ( )	

Under penalties of perjury, I declare that I have examined this return and accompanying documents, and, to the best of my knowledge and belief, they are true, correct, and complete.

Signature ▶ *Sondra Smith*   Title ▶ *Owner*   Date ▶ *1-11-X4*

Form **W-3 Transmittal of Wage and Tax Statements**   20X3   Department of the Treasury Internal Revenue Service

Based on its May 31, 20XX, payroll, Augusta Company owed the following payroll taxes:

FICA:
OASDI	$568.00
HI	132.00
FUTA	57.00
SUTA	189.00

(a) Record the deposit of the OASDI and HI taxes, assuming they were deposited on June 15.
(b) Record the deposit of the FUTA tax, assuming a June 30 deposit.
(c) Record the June 30 payment of the SUTA tax.

Check your answers on page 575.

Paying Other Amounts Withheld

Previously, we stated that through agreement between the employee and the employer, deductions other than those required can be made from the earnings of employees. We have seen that when an employer makes such a deduction, an appropriate liability account is credited. For example, Northwest Company's November 18 payroll register (Figure 11-5 on pages 518-519) shows that $55 was withheld from employees' pay to go toward the purchase of U.S. savings bonds. When enough has been accumulated to purchase a certain amount of bonds, the company will make the purchase and deliver the bonds to the employees. When the deduction was made, the U.S. Savings Bonds Payable account was credited. When the bonds are purchased, this account will be debited, and the Cash account will be credited. To illustrate this entry, let's assume that on February 12, 20X3, Northwest purchased savings bonds for $125, an amount that was withheld during January and the first payroll in February. The following general journal entry records the payment:

		20X3				
– liability →	1	Feb.	12	U.S. Savings Bonds Payable	1 2 5 00		1
– asset →	2			Cash		1 2 5 00	2
	3			Purchased savings bonds.			3

Summing Up

The sequence of steps for recording the payroll is:

1. Record the payroll information in the payroll register.
2. Use the payroll register as an information source to record accounting entries for employee earnings and deductions and the payment of the payroll.
3. Use the Taxable Earnings columns of the payroll register to calculate the employer's payroll taxes and then record an accounting entry for these taxes.
4. Record an accounting entry whenever an amount withheld from employee earnings or a payroll tax owed by the employer is paid. Debit the appropriate liability account and credit the Cash account.

Workers' Compensation Insurance

Learning Objective

6 Describe and account for workers' compensation insurance.

workers' compensation insurance the insurance employers must carry to provide protection for employees who suffer job-related illness or injury; payments recorded in the Worker's Compensation Insurance Expense account

Most state governments require employers to carry **workers' compensation insurance** to provide protection for employees who suffer a job-related illness or injury. The entire cost of workers' compensation insurance is usually paid by the employer. The cost depends on several factors, including (1) the number of employees a company has, (2) the company's accident history, and (3) risk factors associated with the job. The third factor, risk, relates to the likelihood that the job will lead to injury. For example, the insurance premium for workers in a steel foundry would probably be higher than the premium for office workers.

Workers' compensation insurance can generally be obtained from private insurance companies or directly from the state in which the company is located. The employer usually pays the premium at the beginning of the year, using estimated payroll figures for the year. At year-end, the actual amount of the payroll is compared with the estimate made at the beginning of the year. An adjustment is then made for the difference between the estimated premium and the actual premium. If the employer has overpaid, a credit is received from the state or private insurance company. If, on the other hand, the employer has underpaid, an additional premium is paid.

To illustrate how to account for workers' compensation insurance, let's assume that on January 2, 20X3, Northwest Company estimates its total 20X3 payroll to be $312,000. Let's further assume that Northwest's insurance premium rate is 0.2% (.002). Accordingly, Northwest's estimated premium is $624, calculated as follows:

Workers' compensation insurance provides protection to workers who are injured while on the job. The cost of coverage is paid by the employer and depends on the number of employees and the type of work they do.

Estimated payroll		Premium rate		Estimated insurance premium
$312,000	×	.002	=	$624.00

The following journal entry shows the payment:

+ expense → 1	20X3 Jan.	2	Workers' Comp. Insurance Expense	6 2 4 00		1
– asset → 2			Cash		6 2 4 00	2
3			Paid estimated premium for the year.			3

Now, let's assume that at the end of the year Northwest's actual payroll was $330,000. Since this amount is more than Northwest's beginning-of-the-year estimate ($312,000), the company owes an additional premium. We calculate the additional premium as follows:

Actual payroll × **Premium rate** = **Insurance premium**

$330,000	×	.002	=	$660.00

Less estimated premium	624.00
Additional premium due	$ 36.00

We now make the following adjusting entry to record the additional expense:

1			Adjusting Entries			1
2	20X3 Dec.	31	Workers' Comp. Insurance Expense	3 6 00		2
3			Workers' Comp. Insurance Payable		3 6 00	3

+ expense → (row 2)
+ liability → (row 3)

After this entry is posted, the Workers' Compensation Insurance Expense account appears as follows:

Workers' Compensation Insurance Expense

Debit		Credit
+		–
January 2	624.00	
December 31	36.00	
Balance	660.00	

In this example, it was necessary to record additional workers' compensation insurance expense because the actual payroll for the year exceeded the amount that had been estimated. But what happens when the reverse is true—that is, the actual payroll is less than the amount estimated? In that case, the company would have overpaid its premium and would thus be entitled to a credit or a refund. To illustrate this situation, let's assume that Northwest's actual payroll for 20X3 turned out to be only $300,000. The amount of the refund is determined as follows:

Actual payroll × **Premium rate** = **Insurance premium**

$300,000	×	.002	=	$600.00

Estimated premium paid	$624.00
Less actual premium owed	600.00
Credit due	$ 24.00

We now make the following adjusting entry to record the credit due:

1			Adjusting Entries			1
2	20X3 Dec.	31	Workers' Comp. Insurance Receivable	2 4 00		2
3			Workers' Comp. Insurance Expense		2 4 00	3

+ asset → (row 2)
– expense → (row 3)

The Workers' Compensation Insurance Expense account would then appear as follows:

Workers' Compensation Insurance Expense

Debit		Credit	
+		−	
January 2	624.00	December 31	24.00
Balance	600.00		

The balance of the account is now $600, which is the correct amount of the expense for the year. This balance will now be closed to Income Summary, along with the balances of all other expense accounts. By the way, this adjusting entry involved a credit to an expense account. This does not happen often, but it was necessary here because too much expense had been estimated (and thus recorded). So, to show the proper amount of expense for the year, the Workers' Compensation Insurance Expense account had to be credited to reduce its balance.

Review Quiz **12-4**

In January 20X2, the accountant for Whitehurst Company estimated its total payroll for the year to be $425,000. At the end of the year, the actual amount of the payroll was $442,000. Assuming a workers' compensation premium rate of 1.5% (.015), record:

(a) The January 2 payment of the estimated premium.
(b) The December 31 adjusting entry showing the additional premium due.

Check your answers on page 576.

Minneapolis Business Owner Sentenced

Douglas G. Radtke, the owner of two Twin Cities construction companies, was sentenced for tax fraud on April 29, 2004. Also sentenced were his son, Scott Radtke, and project manager, Michael T. Donohoe. Douglas Radtke received 36 months in prison and had to pay $20,114 for conspiracy, seven counts of failure to collect and pay tax, and two counts of mail fraud. Scott Radtke was sentenced to 24 months in prison for conspiracy and three counts of mail fraud. Donohoe received 18 months in prison for conspiracy, filing a false tax return, and three counts of mail fraud. Jointly, all of them had to pay $132,012 to Wilson McShane Corp. and $47,873 to Berkley Risk Administrator's Company.

The three defendants were engaged in a payroll, tax, and worker's compensation fraud scheme from December 1995 to January 2000. They employed people who agreed to work for "cash checks." Cash checks are not subject to any withholding taxes or fringe benefits. The problem with cash checks is that they cannot equal more than $600. To get around this rule, the executives of the firm would write the checks for $599.99, using the employee's Social Security number. If the employee was to receive more pay than $599.99, that employee had to provide the names and Social Security numbers of friends and relatives, to whom they would write additional cash checks.

The Radtkes and Donohoe wrote over 500 cash checks for a total of about $175,000 over the four-year span of their fraud. Fraudulent Employer's Quarterly Federal Tax Returns were submitted to the IRS by their accountant, and Donohoe filed fraudulent U.S. individual income tax returns in an effort to conceal the scheme.

Payroll tax fraud includes scheming ways to avoid paying Social Security or other withholding taxes.

Source: FY2004 Examples of Employment Tax Investigations, www.irs.gov. Filed July 18, 2005.

For Discussion

1. What is a cash check?
2. What is the primary motive of the employer to write a cash check for less than $600 to the employees?
3. Identify the parties in the case who were involved in this payroll tax fraud.

Joining the Pieces

Deposit Rules for Federal Taxes Withheld and FICA taxes

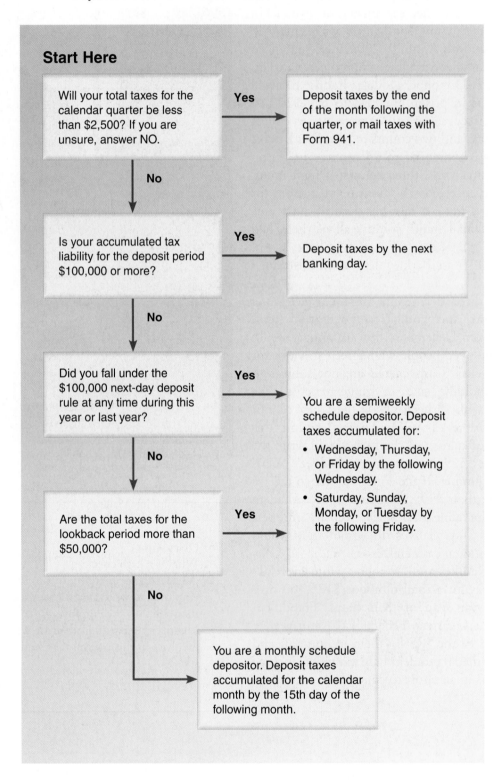

Start Here

Will your total taxes for the calendar quarter be less than $2,500? If you are unsure, answer NO. — **Yes** → Deposit taxes by the end of the month following the quarter, or mail taxes with Form 941.

No ↓

Is your accumulated tax liability for the deposit period $100,000 or more? — **Yes** → Deposit taxes by the next banking day.

No ↓

Did you fall under the $100,000 next-day deposit rule at any time during this year or last year? — **Yes** → You are a semiweekly schedule depositor. Deposit taxes accumulated for:
- Wednesday, Thursday, or Friday by the following Wednesday.
- Saturday, Sunday, Monday, or Tuesday by the following Friday.

No ↓

Are the total taxes for the lookback period more than $50,000? — **Yes** → (see semiweekly schedule depositor box above)

No ↓

You are a monthly schedule depositor. Deposit taxes accumulated for the calendar month by the 15th day of the following month.

Summary

1 Describe and calculate payroll taxes imposed on the employer.

Employers are responsible for at least three payroll taxes: (1) FICA (Social Security), (2) federal unemployment taxes, and (3) state unemployment taxes.

Employer FICA tax. In addition to withholding, reporting, and remitting the FICA (OASDI and HI) taxes imposed on employees, employers must also match these taxes dollar for dollar. Thus, the Social Security program is funded by equal contributions from employees and employers. To review how to calculate the employer's part of FICA, assume the following payroll data for Gigabite Food Company for the pay period ending October 15, 20X0:

Total payroll for week	$195,000
Part of payroll subject to OASDI	126,000

Notes:

At this writing, the OASDI rate is 6.2% of the first $102,000 of earnings by each employee during the year. Employers and employees pay the same rate based on the same annual wage limit. The current HI rate is 1.45% of all earnings (no annual wage limit).

Calculations:

OASDI:	$126,000 × .062	=	$ 7,812.00
HI:	$195,000 × .0145	=	2,827.50
Total FICA			$10,639.50

Federal unemployment taxes. All employers are covered by the **Federal Unemployment Tax Act (FUTA),** which requires the payment of taxes to provide benefits for workers during periods of temporary unemployment. At this writing, the FUTA rate is 6.2% of the first $7,000 of annual earnings for each employee. A credit of up to 5.4% can be taken against the FUTA rate for state unemployment taxes paid by the employer. This leaves an effective FUTA rate of 0.8% (6.2% − 5.4%).

According to payroll records, there were only four recently hired employees who had not reached the $7,000 annual wage limit when the October 15 payroll was recorded. Their total wages amounted to $2,800. Thus, Gigabite's FUTA taxes for the week are:

$2,800 × .008 = $22.40

State unemployment taxes. All states have passed legislation requiring employers to pay unemployment taxes for the benefit of employees. These taxes are usually referred to as **State Unemployment Tax Act (SUTA)** taxes. The wage base for SUTA taxes can vary from state to state. The SUTA rate also varies from state to state and from employer to employer, depending on the recent experience of the state and the employer with unemployment claims. Most states have a **merit-rating system** that provides a lower rate as an incentive for employers to stabilize employment. Gigabite Foods has a SUTA rate of 3% of the first $7,000 of annual earnings by each employee. Thus, if the taxable wages are $2,800, the same amount as that subject to FUTA, the current period's SUTA taxes are:

$2,800 × .03 = $84.00

The total of Gigabite's payroll taxes for the current payroll is:

FICA:		
OASDI	$7,812.00	
HI	2,827.50	$10,639.50
FUTA		22.40
SUTA		84.00
Total		$10,745.90

2 Record the employer's payroll taxes.

Gigabite records its payroll taxes by debiting an operating expense account entitled **Payroll Tax Expense** for the total amount of the taxes. A credit is made to a separate liability account for each tax. Notice that the same liability accounts are used to record both the employees' and employer's shares of the FICA taxes.

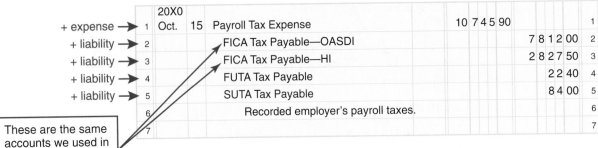

	20X0					
+ expense → 1	Oct.	15	Payroll Tax Expense	10 7 4 5 90		1
+ liability → 2			FICA Tax Payable—OASDI		7 8 1 2 00	2
+ liability → 3			FICA Tax Payable—HI		2 8 2 7 50	3
+ liability → 4			FUTA Tax Payable		2 2 40	4
+ liability → 5			SUTA Tax Payable		8 4 00	5
6			Recorded employer's payroll taxes.			6
7						7

These are the same accounts we used in Chapter 11 to record the employees' part of FICA.

3 Record the deposit of employees' federal income taxes and FICA taxes and report these taxes to the government (Forms 8109 and 941).

If during any calendar quarter the total of employees' income tax withheld and FICA taxes (employee and employer shares) reaches or exceeds $2,500, the employer does not send the taxes directly to the Internal Revenue Service (IRS). Instead, the taxes must be deposited in a Federal Reserve bank or other authorized bank. The IRS will then send for the taxes. When to deposit taxes is based on the amount of an employer's total FICA taxes and withheld income taxes during a 12-month lookback period. The **lookback period** for any year is the 12-month period starting on July 1 two years prior to the current year, and ending on June 30 one year prior to the current year. An employer is a monthly depositor for the current year if total taxes (FICA and withheld income taxes) were $50,000 or less. If an employer's total taxes exceeded $50,000, the semiweekly deposit schedule is required. Under the semiweekly deposit schedule, taxes on payroll payments made on Wednesday, Thursday, or Friday must be deposited by the following Wednesday. Taxes on payroll payments made on Saturday, Sunday, Monday, or Tuesday must be deposited by the following Friday. If an employer accumulates a tax liability of $100,000 or more on any day during a deposit period, the taxes must be deposited the next business day. When a deposit is made, an entry is recorded by debiting the appropriate liability accounts and crediting Cash. To illustrate this entry, assume that on November 7, 20X0, Gigabite Food Company deposited the following taxes in a local bank:

Federal income tax withheld from employees		$15,400
FICA tax:		
OASDI	$6,365	
HI	1,489	7,854
Total amount deposited		$23,254

The following journal entry shows the payment:

		20X0						
– liability →	1	Nov.	7	Federal Income Tax Payable	15 4 0 0 00			1
– liability →	2			FICA Tax Payable—OASDI	6 3 6 5 00			2
– liability →	3			FICA Tax Payable—HI	1 4 8 9 00			3
– asset →	4			Cash		23 2 5 4 00		4
	5			Deposited taxes for payroll				5
	6			of November 7.				6

Employers must prepare various reports to provide payroll information to the federal government. All reports must contain the **employer identification number (EIN)**, which is a nine-digit identifying number issued by the IRS. At the end of each calendar quarter, the employer must prepare and file **Form 941, Employer's Quarterly Federal Tax Return**, which summarizes the payment of FICA taxes and federal income taxes withheld. Payment of these taxes can only be made with Form 941 if the total amount of taxes for the quarter is under $2,500. If the amount of the FICA taxes (employees' and employer's shares) and federal income taxes withheld is $2,500 or more during any quarter, the taxes must be deposited in an authorized bank. When a deposit is made, the employer fills out a **Form 8109, Federal Tax Deposit Coupon.** A copy of Form 8109 will go to the IRS, and the IRS will send for the money.

4 Record and report payment of employer's federal and state unemployment taxes (Form 940).

If the amount of federal unemployment taxes (FUTA) is more than $500 in any quarter, the total must be deposited in an authorized bank by the last day of the first month following the close of the quarter involved. If the amount is $500 or less, no deposit is required; however, this amount must be added to the FUTA tax in the following quarter. If the cumulative total is over $500, a deposit is required. The journal entry to record the deposit involves a debit to the **FUTA Tax Payable account** and a credit to Cash.

Each state provides rules and guidelines for paying state unemployment taxes (SUTA). As a general rule, the amount of SUTA taxes must be remitted to the proper state office by the end of the month following the close of the quarter in which the wages and salaries were earned by employees. The entry to record the payment involves a debit to the **SUTA Tax Payable account** and a credit to Cash.

To review the accounting entries needed when FUTA and SUTA taxes are sent in, assume the following transactions for Gigabite Food Company when less than $500 of the FUTA taxes were due:

Transaction:
January 15, 20X1: Mailed a check for $156 to the federal government for FUTA taxes incurred during the fourth quarter of 20X0.

Entry:

		20X1						
– liability →	1	Jan.	15	FUTA Tax Payable	1 5 6 00			1
– asset →	2			Cash		1 5 6 00		2
	3			Deposited FUTA taxes.				3

Transaction:
January 15, 20X1: Mailed a check for $312 to the state government for SUTA taxes incurred during the fourth quarter of 20X0.

Entry:

– liability →	1	20X1 Jan.	15	SUTA Tax Payable		3 1 2 00			1
– asset →	2			Cash			3 1 2 00		2
	3			Paid fourth quarter SUTA taxes.					3

After the end of each year (by January 31), employers must file **Form 940, Employer's Annual Federal Unemployment Tax Return** to summarize the quarterly deposits of FUTA taxes made during the year. Form 940 also shows the amount of SUTA tax that the employer paid to the state in which it is located.

5 **Report employee earnings and tax deductions to the federal goverment at the end of the year (Forms W-2 and W-3).**

By January 31 of each year, an employer must furnish each employee (who worked any part of the year) with a **Form W-2, Wage and Tax Statement**, which reports the employee's earnings and taxes for the previous year. The information on the W-2s is summarized on **Form W-3, Transmittal of Wage and Tax Statements**, which is sent to the Social Security Administration (SSA) along with Copy A of each employee's W-2.

6 **Describe and account for workers' compensation insurance.**

Most state governments require employers to carry **workers' compensation insurance** to provide protection for employees who suffer a job-related illness or injury. The entire cost of this insurance is usually paid by the employer. The cost depends on the number of company employees, its accident history, and overall risk factors associated with working conditions. The employer pays a premium at the beginning of each year, using estimated payroll figures for the year. Recording this payment involves a debit to the Workers' Compensation Insurance Expense account and a credit to the Cash account.

At the end of the year, the workers' compensation insurance rate is applied to the actual payroll. If the employer underestimated the payroll and has not paid enough, an adjusting entry is made to show the additional expense and the additional amount that must be paid. If, on the other hand, the employer overestimated the payroll and paid too much, an adjusting entry is made to record the reduction in the expense and the credit to be received.

Terms and Concepts Review

- Key Terms and Definitions in English and Spanish
- Additional Quiz Questions

Key Terms

employer identification number (EIN), 546

Federal Unemployment Tax Act (FUTA), 542

Form 8109, Federal Tax Deposit Coupon, 549

Form 940, Employer's Annual Federal Unemployment Tax Return, 552

Form 941, Employer's Quarterly Federal Tax Return, 547

Form W-2, Wage and Tax Statement, 555

Form W-3, Transmittal of Wage and Tax Statements, 555

FUTA Tax Payable account , 546

lookback period, 547

merit-rating system, 544

Payroll Tax Expense account, 542

State Unemployment Tax Act (SUTA), 543

SUTA Tax Payable account, 546

workers' compensation insurance, 558

Concepts Review

1. An employee has a Social Security number. What comparable number does an employer have?
2. What is meant by the employer "matching" FICA tax withheld?
3. Why is the FUTA rate said to be an "effective" rate of 0.8%?
4. What is meant by a merit-rating system for state unemployment tax?
5. Why isn't the Salaries Expense account debited for the total of payroll taxes, since these taxes are part of the payroll cost of employees?
6. Explain the meaning of a lookback period.
7. What is the lookback period for the year 2009?
8. What protection is provided by workers' compensation insurance?
9. Why is an adjusting entry always needed for workers' compensation insurance?
10. Indicate when each of the following accounts is (a) debited and (b) credited: Payroll Tax Expense, FICA Tax Payable—OASDI, FICA Tax Payable—HI, FUTA Tax Payable, SUTA Tax Payable.

Skills Review

Quick Practice

Quick Practice 12-1

Learning Objective **1**

Check Figure
OASDI = $37.20

Objective: To calculate employer payroll taxes

Ellen Boardman earned $600 this week. Her prior earnings this year amount to $6,000.

Directions: Calculate the employer's payroll taxes on this week's salary. Use the standard rates for FICA-OASDI, FICA-HI, FUTA, and 2% for SUTA.

Quick Practice 12-2

Learning Objective **1**

Check Figure
FUTA = $3.20

Objective: To calculate employer payroll taxes when limits are exceeded

Joel Converse earned $900 this week. His prior earnings this year amount to $6,600.

Directions: Calculate the employer's payroll taxes using the rates indicated in Quick Practice 12-1 and taxable FUTA and SUTA limits of $7,000.

Quick Practice 12-3

Learning Objective **1**

Check Figure
SUTA = $792

Objective: To calculate employer payroll taxes

Ricci Company's payroll amounts to $22,000 gross for the week ended April 17, 20X9. No employee has reached any of the taxable limits.

Directions: Using standard rates for FICA-OASDI, FICA-HI, FUTA and a rate of 3.6% for SUTA, calculate each of the employer's taxes on the payroll.

Quick Practice 12-4

Learning Objective **2**

Check Figure
Payroll Tax Expense $2,651
(debit)

Objective: To record employer payroll taxes

Directions: Using your answers to Quick Practice 12-3, prepare the April 17, 20X9, general journal entry to record the employer's payroll taxes.

Quick Practice 12-5

Objective: To calculate and record employer payroll taxes

Marion Company's payroll data for the week ended June 2, 20X9, is as follows:

Gross earnings of employees	$100,000
OASDI taxable earnings	90,000
FUTA/SUTA taxable earnings	20,000

Directions: Using a SUTA rate of 2.1% and standard rates given in the chapter for the other payroll taxes, calculate and record in general journal form the employer's taxes for the week.

Quick Practice 12-6

Objective: To record the payment of tax liabilities

On May 14, 20X9, the accountant for DeLong Company deposited the following taxes in a local bank:

Employees' federal income tax withheld	$600
OASDI—employee and employer shares	200
HI—employee and employer shares	80

Directions: Prepare the entry in general journal form to record the payment of the taxes.

Quick Practice 12-7

Objective: To calculate and record estimated workers' compensation insurance

In January 20X9, the accountant for Clayton Corporation estimated that its total payroll for the year would be $400,000. The premium rate for workers' compensation insurance is 0.4%.

Directions: Calculate and record in general journal form the entry to pay the estimated premium on January 3, 20X9.

Quick Practice 12-8

Objective: To calculate and record additional workers' compensation insurance

Directions: If in Quick Practice 12-7 the actual payroll turned out to be $410,000, prepare the December 31, 20X9, adjusting journal entry to record the additional premium due for workers' compensation insurance.

Quick Practice 12-9

Objective: To calculate and record a credit for workers' compensation insurance

Directions: If in Quick Practice 12-7 the actual payroll turned out to be $380,000, prepare the December 31, 20X9, adjusting journal entry to record the credit for workers' compensation insurance.

Exercises

Exercise 12-1

Objective: To calculate employer payroll taxes

Directions: For each of the following employees, calculate the taxable earnings for FICA—OASDI, FICA—HI, FUTA, and SUTA for the current week. Then, calculate the total taxable earnings and the employer's liability for each of these taxes. Use rates of 6.2% for FICA—OASDI and 1.45% for FICA—HI and a tax base of $102,000 for OASDI . Assume rates of 0.8% for FUTA and 3.1% for SUTA and a tax base of $7,000.

Employee	Current Week's Gross Earnings	Prior Gross Earnings This Year
Jim Burns	$700	$6,850
Helen Carrol	650	6,200
Barbara Harold	900	8,400

Learning Objective **2**

Check Figure
Payroll Tax Expense = $203.33 (debit)

Exercise 12-2

Objective: To record employer payroll taxes

Directions: Using the data from Exercise 12-1, prepare a general journal entry to record the employer's payroll tax expense for the week and the liabilities for FICA taxes and unemployment taxes. The date of the entry is April 3, 20X1.

Learning Objectives **1, 2**

Check Figure
Payroll Tax Expense = $1,922.25 (debit)

Exercise 12-3

Objective: To calculate and record employer payroll taxes

PCQ Company had total payroll wages of $16,500 for the week ended March 15, 20X2. PCQ has a FUTA rate of 0.8% and a SUTA rate of 3.2%. All wages during the pay period are subject to both FICA taxes and both unemployment taxes.

Directions: Calculate the taxes, and prepare a general journal entry to record the employer's payroll tax expense for the week.

Learning Objectives **1, 2**

Check Figure
Payroll Tax Expense = $11,361.65 (debit)

Exercise 12-4

Objective: To calculate and record employer payroll taxes

Portland Company's payroll for the week ended December 14, 20X4, is as follows:

Gross earnings of employees	$138,900
FICA—OASDI taxable earnings	126,300
FUTA taxable earnings	37,000
SUTA taxable earnings	37,000

Directions: Using the FICA rates presented in the chapter, a FUTA rate of 0.8%, and a SUTA rate of 3.3%, calculate the taxes and prepare a general journal entry for the employer's payroll tax expense for the week.

Learning Objective **3**

Check Figure
Cash = $1,599 (credit)

Exercise 12-5

Objective: To record the payment of payroll tax liabilities

On May 12, 20X1, the accountant for Americus Appliance Company deposited the following taxes in a local bank:

Employees' federal income tax withheld	$815
OASDI taxes (employees' share)	318
OASDI taxes (employer's share)	318
HI taxes (employees' share)	74
HI taxes (employer's share)	74

Directions: Prepare the general journal entry to record the payment of these taxes.

Learning Objective **6**

Check Figure
Estimated premium = $2,750

Exercise 12-6

Objective: To calculate workers' compensation insurance

In January 20X1, the accountant for Quinlan Company estimated its total payroll for the year to be $550,000. The workers' compensation premium rate was 0.5%.

Directions: (a) Calculate the estimated premium for the year. (b) Assuming that the actual payroll was $560,000, calculate the amount of additional premium due at the end of the year. (c) Assuming that the actual payroll was $530,000, calculate the amount of the credit due at the end of the year.

Learning Objective 6

Check Figure
(b) Workers' Compensation
Insurance Expense = $50
(debit)

Exercise 12-7

Objective: To account for workers' compensation insurance

Directions: Use the information given in Exercise 12-6 to prepare general journal entries for (a) the payment of the estimated premium on January 3, (b) an adjustment on December 31 for additional premium due, and (c) an adjustment on December 31 for the credit due.

Case Problems

Group A

Learning Objectives 1, 2

Check Figure
Payroll Tax Expense =
$342.90 (debit)

Problem 12-1A

Objective: To calculate and record employer's payroll taxes

Selected information about six employees follows:

Employee	Current Week's Gross Pay	Prior Weeks' Gross Pay
Ben Cassidy	$465.50	$4,900.75
Carl Erer	555.75	5,680.30
Lily Leung	300.30	3,109.35
Herb McMahon	425.80	4,850.10
Ray Ramirez	641.90	6,754.70
Ned Thomas	790.70	8,010.40

Directions:

1. Calculate the amount of taxable earnings for FICA—OASDI, FICA—HI, FUTA, and SUTA for each employee and for the total payroll this week. Then, calculate the amount of each tax owed by the employer. Use the rates and wage limits presented in the chapter, with a rate of 4.2% for SUTA.
2. Prepare the general journal entry to record the employer's payroll taxes for the week. The date of the entry is March 10, 20X3.

**Learning Objectives
1, 2, 3, 4**

Check Figure
2. (Jan. 31) Payroll Tax
Expense = $3,012.50 (debit)

Problem 12-2A

Objective: To calculate, record, and pay employer's payroll taxes

Marchant Company presents the following data for its payrolls for the months of January, February, and March 20X1:

Month	Gross Salaries	Unemployment Taxable Salaries
January	$25,000	$25,000
February	27,000	27,000
March	32,000	18,000

Directions:

1. Calculate the amounts that the employer owes for both FICA taxes and both unemployment taxes for each month. Assume a SUTA rate of 3.6%. All salaries are subject to FICA taxes.
2. Prepare each month's payroll tax expense entry.
3. Prepare the February 15 entry to deposit the January FICA taxes (employer and employee shares) along with federal income taxes withheld at 20% of the gross payroll.
4. Prepare the April 25 entry to deposit the FUTA tax for the first quarter and the entry on the same date to pay the SUTA tax for the first quarter.

Problem 12-3A

Objective: To journalize and post employer's payroll taxes

The Wesley Company pays its employees semimonthly. Payroll tax rates for the employer are the standard ones, including a SUTA rate of 2.0%. The balances of certain payroll-related accounts are as follows as of April 1, 20X2:

Number	Title	Balance
215	FICA Tax Payable—OASDI	$1,840.00
216	FICA Tax Payable—HI	435.00
217	Federal Income Tax Payable	3,500.00
218	State Income Tax Payable	1,500.00
219	FUTA Tax Payable	240.00
220	SUTA Tax Payable	600.00
221	Union Dues Payable	300.00
551	Payroll Tax Expense	1,987.50

Directions:

1. Open the accounts listed, and enter the April 1, 20X2, balances.
2. Record the following April transactions in a general journal, page 6, and post only to the accounts you have opened.

20X2

Apr. 15 Deposited all of the FICA and federal income taxes due for March, according to the April 1 balances of accounts 215, 216, and 217.

15 Prepared the semimonthly payroll as follows:

Gross salaries	$5,000.00
FICA—OASDI	310.00
FICA—HI	72.50
Federal income tax	650.00
State income tax	250.00
Union dues	500.00

15 Paid the semimonthly payroll.

20 Sent in the union dues withheld through April 1.

25 Deposited the FUTA tax April 1 balance.

27 Sent in the SUTA tax April 1 balance.

30 Sent in the April 1 amount due for state income tax.

30 Prepared the semimonthly payroll. The same amounts apply as on April 15.

30 Paid the semimonthly payroll.

30 Recorded the employer's tax expense for both FICA taxes and both unemployment taxes on the April payrolls.

Problem 12-4A

Objective: To account for workers' compensation insurance

In January 20X2, the accountant for Scanlon Company estimated that its total payroll for the year would be $798,500. The firm has a premium rate of 0.4% for workers' compensation insurance.

(a) Calculate the estimated premium for the year.
(b) Prepare a general journal entry to record payment of the estimated premium on January 2, 20X2.
(c) If the actual payroll for the year is $805,600, prepare the December 31, 20X2, adjusting entry.
(d) If the actual payroll for the year is $783,600, prepare the December 31, 20X2, adjusting entry.

Group B

Problem 12-1B

Objective: To calculate and record employer's payroll taxes

Selected information about six employees follows:

Employee	Current Week's Gross Pay	Prior Weeks' Gross Pay
Ed Delgado	$485.50	$5,200.75
Mae Jniene	779.45	7,645.80
Kim Minakawa	334.25	3,705.55
Roy O'Brien	445.80	4,650.40
Al Sanchez	682.90	6,659.20
Sid Zhang	524.30	5,340.10

Directions:

1. Calculate the amount of taxable earnings for FICA—OASDI, FICA—HI, FUTA, and SUTA for each employee and for the total payroll this week. Then, calculate the amount of each tax owed by the employer. Use the rates and wage limits presented in the chapter, with a rate of 2.4% for SUTA.
2. Prepare the general journal entry to record the employer's payroll taxes for the week. The date of the entry is March 6, 20X1.

Problem 12-2B

Objective: To calculate, record, and pay employer's payroll taxes

Malden Company presents the following data for its payrolls for the months of January, February, and March 20X1:

Month	Gross Salaries	Unemployment Taxable Salaries
January	$35,000	$35,000
February	39,000	34,000
March	42,000	1,000

Directions:

1. Calculate the amounts that the employer owes for both FICA taxes and both unemployment taxes for each month. Assume a SUTA rate of 3.4%. All salaries are subject to FICA taxes.
2. Prepare each month's payroll tax expense entry.
3. Prepare the February 15 entry to deposit the January FICA taxes (employer and employee shares) along with federal income taxes withheld at 20% of the gross payroll.
4. Prepare the April 25 entry to deposit the FUTA tax for the first quarter and the entry on the same date to pay the SUTA tax for the first quarter.

Problem 12-3B

Objective: To journalize and post employer's payroll taxes

The Albright Company pays its employees semimonthly. Payroll tax rates for the employer are the standard ones, including a SUTA rate of 3.0%. The balances of certain payroll-related accounts are as follows as of April 1, 20X2:

Number	Title	Balance
215	FICA Tax Payable—OASDI	$2,760.00
216	FICA Tax Payable—HI	652.50
217	Federal Income Tax Payable	5,750.00
218	State Income Tax Payable	2,250.00
219	FUTA Tax Payable	360.00
220	SUTA Tax Payable	1,350.00
221	Union Dues Payable	450.00
551	Payroll Tax Expense	3,416.25

Directions:

1. Open the accounts listed, and enter the April 1, 20X2, balances.
2. Record the following April transactions in a general journal, page 6, and post only to the accounts that you have opened.

20X2

Apr. 15 Deposited all of the FICA and federal income taxes due for March, according to the April 1 balances of accounts 215, 216, and 217.

15 Prepared the semimonthly payroll as follows:

Gross salaries	$7,500.00
FICA—OASDI	465.00
FICA—HI	108.75
Federal income tax	975.00
State income tax	375.00
Union dues	750.00

15 Paid the semimonthly payroll.
20 Sent in the union dues withheld through April 1.
25 Deposited the FUTA tax April 1 balance.
27 Sent in the SUTA tax April 1 balance.
30 Sent in the April 1 amount due for state income tax.
30 Prepared the semimonthly payroll. The same amounts apply as on April 15.
30 Paid the semimonthly payroll.
30 Recorded the employer's tax expense for both FICA taxes and both unemployment taxes on the April payrolls.

Learning Objective **6**

Check Figure
(a) Estimated Insurance Premium = $4,128.50

Problem 12-4B

Objective: To account for workers' compensation insurance

In January 20X2, the accountant for Ruggieri Company estimated that its total payroll for the year would be $825,700. The firm has a premium rate of 0.5% for workers' compensation insurance.

(a) Calculate the estimated premium for the year.
(b) Prepare the journal entry to record payment of the estimated premium on January 2, 20X2.
(c) If the actual payroll for the year is $811,500, prepare the December 31, 20X2, adjusting entry.
(d) If the actual payroll for the year is $829,450, prepare the December 31, 20X2, adjusting entry.

Critical Thinking Problems

Challenge Problem

Check Figure
None

Lori Sweat is an employee with a gross salary of $105,600 for 20X1. She is paid monthly. Calculate the employer's FICA—OASDI (at 6.2%), FICA—HI (at 1.45%), FUTA (at 0.8%), and SUTA (at 3.7%) taxes for each month of the year. Then, prepare the January, February, November, and December 20X1 general journal entries to record the employer's payroll taxes on Lori's salary. Use the OASDI, FUTA, and SUTA wage bases presented in the chapter.

Communications

Ella Hirsch, a new payroll clerk you have just hired, is very confused by the variety of payroll forms that the employer must prepare. Write a brief memo to her to explain the use of the following forms: 940, 941, 8109, W-2, and W-3.

Team Internet Project

As mentioned in the chapter, unemployment insurance rates vary a lot from state to state. To explore this a bit, search the Internet and find and then list the rules for unemployment insurance taxes for any five different states. Include the tax rates, the taxable wage limits, and the businesses covered.

Ethics

Arthur McNeill is the owner of the Newfound Company. The company has experienced a large number of layoffs in recent years and has a high (5.4%) rate for state unemployment tax. As a result, the amount of SUTA tax is substantial. Arthur decides to temporarily save some money and earn some interest by sending in the tax amount annually instead of quarterly.

Write a note explaining why, in addition to being in violation of the law by not sending in quarterly payments, Arthur's behavior is unethical, given the purpose of the tax.

In the Real World — Social Security Administration

Look again at the data presented at the end of Chapter 11. Amounts are in billions.

	OASI	DI	HI	SMI
Assets (end of 2005)	$1,663.0	$195.6	$285.8	$ 24.0
Income during 2006	642.2	102.6	211.5	225.5
Outgo during 2006	461.0	94.5	191.9	216.4
Net increase in assets	181.3	8.2	19.6	9.1
Assets (end of 2006)	1,844.3	203.8	305.4	33.1

Now, add in these bits of information:

Account	Number of People Receiving Benefits
OASI	40.5 million
DI	8.6 million
HI and SMI	43.2 million

If you divide the amount labeled "outgo" in any category by the number of people receiving benefits, you can figure the average benefit per person. So, for OASI, divide 461,000,000,000 by 40,500,000 and get $11,383 per person, rounded to the nearest dollar. Each person receiving a pension in 2006 got an average of that amount.

Why is there concern about money being available for retirement and other funds in the future when it seems as if there is an increase in the total assets of the funds in 2006?

Answers to Review Quizzes

Review Quiz 12-1

Employee	FICA—OASDI	FICA—HI	FUTA	SUTA
Walt King	$ 24.55	$ 5.74	-0-	-0-
Carol Maris	19.72	4.61	$2.00	$ 6.75
Jill Mimms	41.85	9.79	-0-	-0-
Bill Todd	13.36	3.12	1.72	5.82
Chuck Wade	12.40	2.90	.80	2.70
Totals	$111.88 +	$26.16 +	$4.52 +	$15.27 = $157.83

Review Quiz 12-2

	20X3						
1	Nov.	18	Payroll Tax Expense	1 5 7 83			1
2			FICA Tax Payable—OASDI		1 1 1 88		2
3			FICA Tax Payable—HI		2 6 16		3
4			FUTA Tax Payable		4 52		4
5			SUTA Tax Payable		1 5 27		5
6			Recorded employer's payroll taxes.				6

Review Quiz 12-3

(a)

	20XX					
1	June	15	FICA Tax Payable—OASDI	5 6 8 00		1
2			FICA Tax Payable—HI	1 3 2 00		2
3			Cash		7 0 0 00	3
4			Deposited FICA taxes.			4

(b)

	20XX					
1	June	30	FUTA Tax Payable	5 7 00		1
2			Cash		5 7 00	2
3			Deposited FUTA taxes.			3

(c)

	20XX					
1	June	30	SUTA Tax Payable	1 8 9 00		1
2			Cash		1 8 9 00	2
3			Paid SUTA taxes.			3

Review Quiz 12-4

(a)

	20X2						
1	Jan.	2	Workers' Comp. Insurance Expense	6 3 7 5 00			1
2			Cash		6 3 7 5 00		2
3			Paid estimated premium for the year.				3

(b)

			Adjusting Entries			
1						1
2	20X2 Dec.	31	Workers' Comp. Insurance Expense	2 5 5 00		2
3			Workers' Comp. Insurance Payable		2 5 5 00	3

Comprehensive Review Problem III

Carlson Company (P) (Q)

The purpose of this problem is to follow a payroll system for two weeks. It includes preparing a payroll register and all related accounting entries for payroll.

Assumed tax rates are as follows:

FICA:	OASDI	6.2% on the first $102,000
	HI	1.45% on all earnings
FUTA:		0.8% on the first $7,000
SUTA:		2.4% on the first $7,000
Federal income tax:		See tax tables on pages 514–515
State income tax:		5%

Carlson Company pays its employees every week and pays time-and-a-half for all hours over 40 a week. Earnings through the April 12, 20X1, payroll and the classification of the company's workers are as follows:

Sales:

Tom Craig	$11,300	S-1
Pat Guidry	6,800	S-0
Jim Iannone	6,400	M-0

Office:

Mary Perez	$ 9,700	S-0
Liz Wesley	14,200	M-1

Directions: Record the following transactions in a general journal, pages 46 and 47. Prepare payroll registers as requested, and use them as the basis for some of your accounting entries.

Apr. 15 Deposited March FICA and federal income taxes in a bank. FICA—OASDI tax amounted to $500, while FICA—HI tax amounted to $100. Federal income tax withheld amounted to $1,350.

  18 Wrote a check to pay for bonds purchased with March savings bond deductions, $90.

  19 Recorded and paid the weekly payroll. Prepare a payroll register, journalize the payroll, and record its payment. Use the following data:

Name	Status	Hours	Rate per Hour	Savings Bonds	Union Dues	Ck. No.
Tom Craig	S-1	42	$10	$10	$ 5.00	63
Pat Guidry	S-0	30	6	—	—	64
Jim Iannone	M-0	45	9	5	5.00	65
Mary Perez	S-0	40	11	—	7.50	66
Liz Wesley	M-1	46	12	10	12.50	67

  19 Recorded the employer's payroll taxes on the April 19 payroll.

  20 Paid March union dues to the union, $120.

  25 Sent in March state income tax withheld, $415.

  26 Recorded and paid the weekly payroll. Prepare a payroll register, journalize the payroll, and record its payment. All basic data are the same as for April 19 except for the hours worked and the check numbers. Hours worked are 44, 30, 47, 42, and 40, respectively. Check numbers continue with No. 68. Remember to calculate the up-to-date cumulative earnings by adding last

week's total earnings for each employee to the cumulative earnings the employee had last week.

26   Recorded the employer's payroll taxes on the April 26 payroll.

30   Paid FUTA tax for the first quarter. Taxable wages for this tax amounted to $13,000 in the quarter.

30   Paid SUTA tax for the first quarter. Taxable wages were $13,000.

Glossary

A

accelerated method of depreciation a depreciation method that allows for larger amounts of depreciation in early years and smaller amounts in later years; the double declining-balance method is an example

account an individual form used to record increases and decreases in a specific asset, liability, or owner's equity item

accountancy the profession of accounting

accountant one who records, plans, summarizes, analyzes, and interprets financial information

accounting clerk one who sorts, records, and files accounting data; usually considered an entry-level job

accounting cycle the sequence of steps and procedures used to process and summarize accounting data during an accounting period

accounting equation the equation that expresses the relationship between the accounting elements in a simple mathematical form: assets = liabilities + owner's equity; also referred to as the basic accounting equation

accounting period a period for which accounting records are maintained, typically a year but can be as short as a month

accounting the process of recording, summarizing, analyzing, and interpreting financial (money-related) activities to permit individuals and organizations to make informed judgments and decisions

accounts payable ledger a subsidiary ledger that lists the individual accounts of creditors; also referred to as the creditors' ledger

accounts payable the liability that results from purchasing goods or services on credit

Accounts Receivable account an asset account that shows the total dollar amount due from credit customers

accounts receivable ledger a subsidiary ledger containing only accounts of credit customers; also referred to as the customers' ledger

accounts receivable the asset arising from selling goods or services on credit to customers

accounts receivable turnover a measure that indicates how quickly a firm is collecting its accounts receivable; calculated by dividing net credit sales by average net accounts receivable

Accounts Receivable—Credit Cards account an asset account used to record the amount due from nonbank credit card sales

accrual basis of accounting the basis of accounting that requires that revenue is recorded when earned, no matter when cash is received, and that expenses are recorded when incurred, no matter when cash is paid

accruals expenses incurred and revenue earned in the current accounting period but not recorded as of the end of the period

accrued expenses expenses that build up or accumulate during the current period but will not be paid until the next period; also referred to as accrued liabilities

accrued revenue revenue that has been earned in the current accounting period but will not be received until the next period; also referred to as accrued assets

accrued salaries earnings that are unpaid (and unrecorded) and owed to employees at the end of an accounting period; also referred to as accrued wages

accumulated depreciation the total depreciation from the start of the life of a plant asset to any point in time

acid-test ratio the ratio of quick assets to current liabilities; a measure of a company's instant debt-paying ability; also referred to as the quick ratio

addition a capital expenditure that literally adds on to an existing plant asset; the cost of an addition is debited to a plant asset account

adequate disclosure principle states that financial statements or the explanatory notes and schedules that go with the statements must disclose all relevant data about the financial position of a company

adjusting entry an entry made at the end of an accounting period to bring the balance of an account up to date

aging schedule a schedule in which accounts receivable are grouped into age categories and an estimated bad debts rate is applied to each age category

aging the receivables a way of estimating bad debts expense when using the balance sheet approach

Allowance for Doubtful Accounts account a contra-asset account used to record the estimated amount of uncollectible accounts; also referred to as the Allowance for Bad Debts account or the Allowance for Uncollectible Accounts account

allowance method a method of accounting for bad debts in which the amount estimated to be uncollectible is established at the end of an accounting period and recorded in an adjusting entry

American Bankers Association (ABA) transit number a number printed on checks and deposit slips that identifies the bank and the area in which the bank is located as well as other information

amortization the periodic write-off of the cost of an intangible asset

apportionment the process of dividing operating expenses among departments

appropriation of retained earnings a portion of retained earnings earmarked for a specific purpose, such as plant expansion or the retirement of debt; the amount appropriated may not be used for cash or stock dividends

articles of incorporation an application filed with a state government when incorporating a business

articles of partnership an agreement made between partners that sets forth the terms of their partnership, such as the amount of cash or other assets each is to invest, the amount of time each is to devote to running the business, and how the net income or loss will be divided; also referred to as a partnership agreement

asset an item with a money value owned by a business

asset turnover a measure of the amount of sales generated by the assets of a firm; calculated by dividing net sales by total assets (excluding investments)

auditor an accountant who reviews a company's accounting systems, operations, and financial reports; also referred to as an external auditor

authorized stock the maximum number of shares that a corporation is permitted to sell; this amount appears in the corporate charter

auxiliary record a nonessential business record that is helpful in maintaining records that are essential

average collection period for accounts receivable a rough measure of the length of time accounts receivable have been outstanding; calculated by dividing 365 days by the accounts receivable turnover

B

bad debt an account receivable that for one reason or another cannot be collected; also referred to as an uncollectible account

Bad Debts Expense an operating expense account used to record losses from uncollectible receivables; also referred to as the Uncollectible Accounts Expense

balance form of account a standard ledger account form expanded to include two balance columns for keeping a running, or continuous, balance; also called the four-column account form

balance sheet a listing of the firm's assets, liabilities, and owner's equity at a specific point in time; also referred to as statement of financial position and position statement

balance sheet approach a method of estimating the bad debts expense under the allowance method in which the expense is based on aging the accounts receivable; also referred to as the percent of receivables approach

balance the difference between total debits and total credits to an account; determined by footing (adding) the debit side, footing the credit side, and subtracting the smaller total from the larger

bank checking account an amount of cash on deposit with a bank that the bank must pay at the written order of the depositor

bank discount interest deducted in advance by a bank

bank reconciliation the process of bringing the cash balance reported on the bank statement into agreement with the balance in the depositor's checkbook; also referred to as reconciling the bank statement

bank statement the bank's summary of checking account transactions, usually prepared monthly and mailed to the depositor (or made available online)

banker's year a 360-day year used by many companies and financial institutions for ease in calculation of interest; also referred to as the commercial year

bankruptcy a condition in which a firm does not have sufficient cash to pay its creditors

beginning merchandise inventory the dollar value of merchandise that is on hand at the beginning of an accounting period

betterment a capital expenditure that improves a plant asset, such as placing siding on a building; the cost of a betterment is debited to a plant asset account

blank endorsement an endorsement consisting only of a depositor's signature that allows anyone who possesses a check to cash it

board of directors people elected by a corporation's stockholders to oversee the business and appoint the officers

bond An interest-bearing security that represents debt to the losing corporation

bond certificate a certificate of ownership of a bond(s); issued by corporations as evidence of debt to shareholders

bond indenture an agreement, or contract, between the corporation and its bondholders; also referred to as a trust indenture

bond issue the total number of bonds that a corporation issues; each bond in the issue usually has a face value of $1,000 (or multiple thereof)

bond sinking fund a special cash fund that is set up to accumulate cash over the life of the bonds to enable the issuing corporation to pay off the bond issue when it comes due

bondholders investors who own bonds issued by a corporation or governmental unit

Bonds Payable account a long-term liability account used to record the face value of bonds issued

bonus to the existing partners a plan for admitting a new partner in which part of a new partner's investment is credited to the existing partners' capital accounts

bonus to the new partner a plan for admitting a new partner in which a part of the capital of each existing partner is transferred to the new partner

book of final entry the ledger to which amounts are transferred (posted) from the journal

book of original entry the journal in which transactions are first formally recorded

book value the difference between an asset's cost and its accumulated depreciation

bookkeeper one whose primary job is to record financial information

boot in an exchange of plant assets, the difference between the price of the new asset and the trade-in allowance granted for the old asset

Branch account an account on the home office books that shows the amount the branch owes for merchandise received

branch any location of a business other than its home office

break-even point the point in operations where total sales dollars equal total fixed and variable costs; the point of zero profit or loss

budget a formal statement of management's financial plans for the future

budgeted balance sheet a balance sheet that estimates each element of financial condition at a specified future time

budgeted income statement an income statement that estimates net income for the next fiscal period, based on all income statement budgets

business an organization that operates with the objective of earning a profit

business entity concept the principle stating that, for accounting purposes, a business is a distinct economic entity or unit that is separate from its owner and from any other business; requires that transactions of a business be recorded separately from the personal transactions of the business owner

bylaws a set of policies that act as a corporation's constitution

C

canceled check a check that has been paid by the bank out of the depositor's account

capital expenditure an expenditure for a plant asset that benefits more than one accounting period; examples include additions, betterments, and extraordinary repairs; capital expenditures increase either the value or the life of the asset and are debited to either a plant asset account or its Accumulated Depreciation account, depending on the type of expenditure

capital expenditures budget a budget used for long-term planning of when plant assets will need to be replaced

capital stock shares of ownership in a corporation

career a planned sequence of increasingly more challenging and better-paying positions that begin with an entry-level job

career ladder a diagram showing the stages of advancement in a career field

cash an asset including currency (paper money), coins, checks, and money orders made payable to the business

cash basis of accounting a basis of accounting where revenue is recorded only when cash is received, and expenses are recorded only when cash is paid

cash budget a budget that estimates the expected cash to be received and spent over a period of time

cash discount a discount offered by a seller to encourage early payment by a buyer; to the seller, referred to as a sales discount; to the buyer, referred to as a purchases discount

cash dividend a dividend paid in cash

Cash Dividends account a contra capital account used to record cash dividends declared during an accounting period; its balance is closed to Retained Earnings at the end of the accounting period

cash equivalent a highly liquid, short-term investment that can be turned to cash with little or no delay

cash flows cash receipts and cash payments from operating activities, investing activities, and financing activities

cash overage an amount of cash in the cash register that is more than the amount indicated by the cash sales; recorded in the Cash Short and Over account

cash payments journal a special journal used to record all cash payments, including those made by check; also referred to as the cash disbursements journal

cash receipts journal a special journal used to record all receipts of cash, regardless of the source

cash register tape a variation of the sales ticket; the total of the tape serves as the source document for later journal entries

Cash Short and Over account an account used to bring the Cash account into agreement with the actual amount of cash on hand and can be used by businesses that have many cash transactions and thus often have small amounts of cash over or under what the cash register shows

cash shortage an amount of cash in the cash register that is less than the amount indicated by the cash sales; recorded in the Cash Short and Over account

centralized branch accounting a system of accounting for branches in which all records for each branch are kept on the home office books

certified bookkeeper (CB) a bookkeeper with at least two years of experience and who has passed a four-part examination administered by the American Institute of Professional Bookkeepers (AIPB) and has signed a code of ethics

certified public accountant (CPA) an accountant who has met a state's education and experience requirement and has passed a comprehensive examination prepared by the American Institute of Certified Public Accountants (AICPA)

Change Fund account an asset account in which the amount of the change fund is recorded

change fund an amount of money that is maintained in the cash register for making change for cash customers; recorded in the Change Fund account

chart of accounts a directory or listing of accounts in the ledger

charter issued by a state to the incorporators of a company; a contract between the state and the incorporators, authorizing the corporation to conduct business; also referred to as certificate of incorporation

check a written order directing a bank to pay a specified sum of money to a designated person or business

check stub part of a check that remains in the checkbook as a permanent record of the check; often referred to as a stub

checkbook a bound book of checks with stubs; the depositor's record of the checking account

classified balance sheet a balance sheet that divides the assets and liabilities sections into the following subsections: current assets and plant assets, and current liabilities and long-term liabilities

classified income statement an income statement divided into the following sections: revenue, cost of goods sold, operating expenses, income from operations, and other income and expenses

clearing account an account used to summarize the balances of other accounts

closely held corporation a corporation that is typically owned by a small group of investors or a family

closing entries entries made at the end of an accounting period to transfer the balances of the temporary accounts to the owner's capital account

closing process the process of transferring the balances of temporary accounts to the owner's capital account

combined journal a multicolumn journal used by small businesses to help save journalizing and posting time that has two special columns for recording debits and credits to cash, various other special columns for recording transactions that occur often, and two general columns for recording transactions that occur less often; also referred to as a combination journal

Common Stock account a stockholder's equity (paid-in capital) account used to record the par value of common shares issued

Common Stock Dividends Distributable account a stockholders' equity account used to record the total par value of shares to be issued in a stock dividend

common stock shares of ownership in a corporation; the class of stock that usually has voting rights

comparative financial statements side-by-side comparison of a company's financial statements for two or more accounting periods

compound entry an entry requiring three or more accounts

consignee a business or person accepting possession but not title of goods to sell for others on a commission basis

consignment a procedure in which one business (the consignee) accepts goods from another business (the consignor) for sale on a commission basis; goods acquired on consignment should be counted in the inventory of the consignor

consignor a business or person delivering goods to a consignee to be sold on a commission basis

consistency principle the accounting principle that requires a firm to continue to use a method once chosen, rather than switch from method to method arbitrarily or for temporary advantage

contingent liability a possible liability, such as on a discounted note of a customer, that may become a real liability if certain events occur

contra asset account an account whose balance is opposite the asset to which it relates; an account with a credit balance, because it is opposite to an asset account having a debit balance

contract interest rate the rate of interest stated on the bond certificate; also referred to as the face interest rate

contribution margin ratio the percentage of each dollar of sales available to cover the fixed costs and provide operating income

contribution margin the excess of sales revenue over variable costs

controller the chief accountant or chief financial officer for an organization

corporation a form of business organization owned by investors or stockholders that has a separate legal existence from its owners

correcting entry an entry used to correct certain types of errors in the ledger

cost accounting the field of accounting that is used to determine the dollar value of goods that are manufactured

cost accounts accounts that are presented on the income statement; used to determine the cost of goods sold to customers

cost an input into the manufacturing of a product; three common inputs in manufacturing are (1) raw materials, (2) direct labor, and (3) factory overhead

cost behavior the way a cost changes in relation to a change in activity level

cost of goods manufactured the total cost of goods produced during an accounting period

cost of goods manufactured budget a budget that estimates cost of goods manufactured for the next fiscal period

cost of goods sold budget a budget that estimates cost of goods sold for the next fiscal period

cost of goods sold the cost of merchandise sold to customers during the accounting period; an amount determined by the formula: Beginning Merchandise Inventory + Net Purchases of Merchandise = Cost of Goods Available for Sale – Ending Merchandise Inventory = Cost of Goods Sold

cost of production report a report that summarizes all of the units and costs transferred into and out of a production department in a process cost accounting system

cost percentage in the retail method, the dollar value of goods available for sale at cost divided by the dollar value of goods available for sale at retail

cost principle the principle that states that an asset should be recorded at its actual cost, even if the true market value of the asset is more or less than the price paid

cost-volume-profit (CVP) analysis the study of the relationships among costs, selling prices, production volume, expenses, and profits

coupon bonds bonds for which the owners are not registered with the issuing corporation; ownership of such bonds is transferred by delivery of the bonds, and interest payments are received by presenting an interest coupon to a bank; also referred to as bearer bonds

credit balance a balance that occurs when the amounts on the credit side of an account is greater than the amounts on the debit side

Credit Card Expense account an expense account that is used to record discounts paid when receipts for credit card sales are deposited with the bank that issued the card (such as VISA or MasterCard) or with the credit card company that issued the card (such as American Express)

credit memorandum a written statement that indicates a seller's willingness to reduce the amount owed by a buyer

credit period the amount of time a seller allows a credit customer to pay for a purchase

credit terms the terms for payment set by a seller of goods or services; includes the amount of time before payment is due and the rate of discount (if any) for paying early

credit the allowance of cash, goods, or services in the present, with payment expected in the future

creditor a business or person to whom a debt is owed

cross-footing the addition of columns of figures in different ways to check the accuracy of the totals

cross-reference a ledger account number in the posting reference (P.R.) column of the journal and the journal page number in the P.R. column of the ledger account

cumulative preferred stock preferred stock in which unpaid dividends accumulate from year to year; unpaid dividends must be paid in full before any amount can be paid to the holders of common stock

current assets cash and other assets that through normal operations are expected to be sold, converted to cash, used up, or expired usually within one year of the balance sheet date

current liability short-term debt that is due for payment within one year; examples include accounts payable, salaries payable, sales tax payable, and the current portion of notes payable

current ratio current assets divided by current liabilities; a measure of a company's ability to pay current liabilities from current assets

D

date of declaration the date on which the board of directors of a corporation formally declares that a dividend will be paid

date of payment the date on which dividend checks are mailed out to stockholders

date of record the date associated with reviewing the stockholders' records to determine the ownership of shares outstanding; anyone who buys stock after the date of record will not receive the dividend for that period

debenture bonds bonds that are issued based on the general credit of the issuing corporation; no specific assets are pledged as security for the debt

debit balance a balance that occurs when the amounts on the debit side of an account is greater than the amounts on the credit side

debit memorandum the buyer's written request to a seller for credit for a merchandise return or allowance

debt securities investments in debt instruments (bonds and notes) issued by a corporation or a governmental unit

decentralized branch accounting a system of accounting for branches in which each branch keeps its own records and prepares its own financial statements

deferrals expenses and revenue that have been recorded in the current accounting period but are not incurred or earned until a future period

deferred expense an advance payment for goods or services that benefit more than one accounting period; also referred to as prepaid expense or a deferred charge

deferred revenue the advance receipt of revenue that will not be earned until a future accounting period; also referred to as unearned revenue or deferred credits

deficit a debit balance in the Retained Earnings account

departmental margin analysis the determination of the actual financial contribution of a specific department to a firm

departmental margin the gross profit of a department minus the direct expenses of that department

depletion the expense resulting from the using up of a natural resource

deposit in transit a deposit made and appearing in the checkbook but not appearing on the bank statement; also referred to as an outstanding deposit

deposit slip a form that is prepared when coin, currency, or checks are deposited in a bank account indicating the depositor's name and account number and summarizes the amount deposited; also referred to as a deposit ticket

depositor the business or person under whose name a checking account is opened

depreciation an allocation process in which the cost of a long-term asset (except land) is divided over the periods in which the asset is used in the production of the business's revenue; always recorded by debiting the Depreciation Expense account and crediting the Accumulated Depreciation account

depreciation expense the expense that results from the allocation process of depreciation

depreciation schedule a table that lists for a plant asset the amount of depreciation for each year and the accumulated depreciation and book value of that plant asset at the end of each year

direct expense an expense that is associated with a specific department; an expense that benefits only that department and that would not exist if the department did not exist

direct labor cost budget a budget that estimates direct labor costs for the next fiscal period

direct labor rate variance the difference between the actual cost per hour and the budgeted cost per hour

direct labor the cost of those employees who work directly to produce the product

direct labor time variance the difference between the number of direct labor hours used and the budgeted direct labor hours; also referred to as labor efficiency

direct labor variance the difference between actual direct labor costs and budgeted direct labor costs

direct materials materials that are an identifiable part of a manufactured product

direct materials price variance the difference between the actual price paid for direct materials and the budgeted price

direct materials purchases budget a budget that shows the dollar amount of direct materials that must be purchased to meet production requirements

direct materials quantity variance the difference between the actual quantity of direct materials used and the budgeted quantity

direct materials variance the difference between actual direct materials costs and budgeted direct materials costs

direct method a format for preparing the statement of cash flows that discloses each major class of cash inflow and cash outflow from operating activities, showing the amount of cash received or paid for revenues and expenses reported on the income statement; the method recommended by the FASB

direct write-off method a method of accounting for bad debts in which the expense is recorded only when a customer's account is determined to be uncollectible; also referred to as the direct charge-off method

discount occurs when a share of stock or bond sells for less than its par or face value; many states prohibit the practice of issuing stock at a discount

Discount on Bonds Payable account a contra liability account used to record the discount when bonds are issued at an amount below face value

discount period the time from the date of discounting a customer's note until the due date of the note; also referred to as term of discount

discounting a note payable the act of borrowing from a bank on one's own note with the interest being deducted at the time of borrowing

dishonored note a note that is not paid by its maker on the due date

distributive share the share of net income or net loss received by each partner

dividend a distribution of corporate earnings to the stockholders of the company

dividend yield a measure of profitability that tells the investor the rate earned on an investment; calculated by dividing a stock's dividend per share by its market price per share

dividends in arrears passed dividends on cumulative preferred stock

Dividends Payable account a current liability account used to record the amount of cash dividends declared

double declining-balance method a depreciation method that allows greater depreciation in the early years of the life of a plant asset and less depreciation in later years; achieved by applying a constant rate to each year's decreasing book value

double-entry accounting a system in which each transaction is recorded as having at least two effects on the accounting elements; the sum of all debits must equal the sum of all credits

drawee the bank on which a check is drawn

drawer a person or business who writes a check

drawing account a temporary owner's equity account used to record a business owner's withdrawals of cash or other assets from the business for personal use

dual effect the principle stating that all business transactions are recorded as having *at least* two effects on the basic accounting elements (assets, liabilities, and owner's equity)

due date the date on which a note must be paid; also referred to as the maturity date

E

earned capital capital that arises from profitable operations of the corporation; usually referred to as retained earnings

earnings per share on common stock (EPS) the amount of net income available to the owner of each share of common stock; calculated by dividing net income (less preferred dividend requirements) by the number of common shares outstanding

electronic funds transfer (EFT) the movement of cash by electronic communication rather than by paper documents (money, checks, money orders, etc.)

employee a person who works under the direct control of an employer on a continuing basis

employee's earnings record a record maintained for each employee that contains basic employee information and a summary of payroll data for that employee

Employee's Withholding Allowance Certificate (Form W-4) a form filled out by each employee showing marital status and number of withholding allowances claimed

employer identification number (EIN) an identifying number each business with employees must have if during any part of the year it employs one or more people; the business's equivalent of an individual's Social Security number

Employer's Tax Guide (Circular E) an Internal Revenue Service publication containing federal income withholding tables for various payroll periods for married and single persons

ending merchandise inventory the dollar value of merchandise that is on hand at the end of an accounting period

endorsement a signature or stamp on the back of a check or promissory note that transfers ownership of the check to the bank or another person

entry-level job a job requiring education but not necessarily work experience

equipment a physical asset used by a business in its operations

equity securities investments in stocks issued by corporations

equivalent units a measure of the number of units that could have been completed using the costs incurred during the period

estimated useful life (EUL) the amount of time that an asset is expected to be in use or the amount of output it is expected to produce

ethics principles of moral conduct that guide the behavior of individuals and businesses

ex-dividends a way of quoting stock sold between the date of record and the date of payment to signify that a purchaser will not receive the current dividend

expenses the costs of operating a business; does not provide a future benefit to the business and is thus a reduction in owner's equity

extension the amount found by multiplying the unit cost of an item by the quantity

external auditor an accountant who reviews a company's accounting systems, operations, and financial reports; also referred to as an auditor

extraordinary repair a capital expenditure that prolongs the life of a plant asset, such as new wiring in a building; the cost of an extraordinary repair is debited to the Accumulated Depreciation account

F

factory overhead all costs of running a factory other than direct materials and direct labor; includes utilities, rent, depreciation, and indirect labor

factory overhead budget a budget that estimates the factory overhead costs for the next fiscal period

Factory Overhead Control account a cost account used to record indirect production costs

factory overhead variance the difference between the actual factory overhead costs and the budgeted factory overhead costs

Fair Labor Standards Act an act passed by Congress in 1938, that as amended, establishes standards for minimum wage, overtime pay, child labor, required payroll record keeping, and equal pay for equal work regardless of sex; also referred to as the Wages and Hours Law

favorable variance a variance that exists when actual costs are less than budgeted costs

Federal Income Tax Payable account a liability account used to record the amount of federal income taxes withheld from the earnings of employees; credited when taxes are withheld and debited when the taxes are sent in

Federal Insurance Contributions Act (FICA) an act that requires contributions by both the employer and the employee to the federal Social Security system; includes two component parts: OASDI (Old-Age, Survivors, and Disability Insurance) and HI (Hospital Insurance), or Medicare

Federal Unemployment Tax Act (FUTA) an act requiring employers to pay into a fund designed to assist workers who are temporarily unemployed

FICA Tax Payable—HI account a liability account used to record (1) the amount of HI taxes withheld from employees' earnings and (2) matched by the employer; an account credited when HI taxes are withheld (or imposed on the employer) and debited when the taxes are sent in

FICA Tax Payable—OASDI account a liability account used to record (1) the amount of OASDI taxes withheld from employee earnings and (2) the amount of OASDI taxes matched by the employer; an account credited when OASDI taxes are withheld from employees (and matched by the employer) and debited when the taxes are sent in

financial statements summaries of financial activities

financing activities transactions that involve cash receipts or payments from changes in long-term liabilities and stockholders' equity—such as selling stock to stockholders and paying dividends as well as borrowing from creditors and repaying the loans

Finished Goods Inventory account an asset account that shows the cost of finished goods that have not been sold to customers

finished goods inventory record a subsidiary record of finished goods that have not been sold to customers; controlled by the Finished Goods Inventory account

finished goods inventory the inventory of goods that are completed but unsold at the end of an accounting period

first-in, first-out (FIFO) method an inventory costing method that assumes the first goods purchased (first-in) are the first goods sold (first-out), leaving the most recent goods purchased as the ending inventory

fiscal period the period of time that covers a complete accounting cycle

fiscal year a fiscal period covering 12 months but not necessarily coinciding with the calendar year

fixed cost a cost that does not change as production changes; a cost that occurs even without any production

flexible budget a budget that is actually a series of budgets for different levels of production activity

FOB (free on board) destination a shipping term that means that the seller is responsible for all freight costs until the goods reach their destination

FOB (free on board) shipping point a shipping term that means that the buyer is responsible for all freight costs while the goods are in transit

footing the total of the debit column or credit column of an account

forensic accountant an accountant who integrates accounting, auditing, and investigative skills for a specific job or task

Form 8109, Federal Tax Deposit Coupon a form that must be filled out when FICA taxes and withheld federal income taxes are deposited in an authorized bank

Form 940, Employer's Annual Federal Unemployment Tax Return a form filed by the employer by January 31, summarizing quarterly FUTA deposits made during the preceding year

Form 941, Employer's Quarterly Federal Tax Return a quarterly report that summarizes FICA taxes (employer and employee shares) and federal income taxes withheld during the quarter

Form W-2, Wage and Tax Statement a form issued by the employer to each employee by January 31 that contains a summary of the employee's earnings and tax deductions for the past year

Form W-3, Transmittal of Wage and Tax Statements an annual form employers file with the Social Security Administration to summarize employee earnings and tax deductions; filed with copy A of each employee's Form W-2

Freight In account cost account in which charges for freight on incoming merchandise are recorded; also referred to as Transportation

full endorsement an endorsement using the phrase "Pay to the order of" followed by the name of the business or person to whom the check is being transferred, thus allowing only the specified business or person to cash the check

FUTA Tax Payable account a current liability account used to record the employer's obligation for federal unemployment taxes

G

general accounting for manufacturing a system in which costs are gathered throughout the year and transferred periodically to a summary account

general expenses expenses related to running a firm's office, overall administrative expenses of the business or any other operating activities that do not involve the sale of merchandise; also referred to as administrative expenses

general journal the basic form of journal that has two money columns

general ledger the main ledger; the ledger containing the accounts needed to prepare the financial statements

generally accepted accounting principles (GAAP) accounting guidelines governing how financial information is measured, recorded, processed, and reported

gross earnings an employee's earnings before any amount is deducted by the employer

gross profit method a method for estimating the cost of the ending inventory by using a modified version of the cost of goods sold formula

gross profit the profit before subtracting the expenses of doing business; calculated by subtracting cost of goods sold from net sales; also referred to as gross margin

H

high-low method a method of separating the variable and fixed cost components of mixed costs by using the highest and lowest activity levels (and the cost at each level)

Home Office account an account on the books of the branch that serves as an owner's equity account

home office the main location of a business

horizontal analysis the comparison of each item in a company's financial statements in the current period with the same item from a previous accounting period or periods

hourly worker an individual who works for a fixed hourly rate, usually referred to as a wage in the Worker's Compensation Insurance Expense account

I

income from operations gross profit minus operating expenses; also referred to as operating income

income statement a summary of a business's revenue and expenses for a specific period of time, such as a month or a year; also referred to as earnings statement, operating statement, statement of operations, and profit and loss (P & L) statement

income statement approach a method of estimating the bad debts expense under the allowance method in which the expense is based on a percent of credit sales; also referred to as the percentage of sales method

Income Summary account a clearing account used to summarize the balances of revenue and expense accounts that is used only at the end of an accounting period and is opened and closed during the closing process

incorporators a group of persons who file an application to form a corporation

independent contractor a person who agrees to complete a specific job or task and determines the ways and methods of achieving that job or task

indirect expense an expense of operating a business that is not associated with a specific department; an expense that benefits an entire business and would continue to exist even if a specific department were eliminated

indirect labor the cost of those employees who work in the factory but not on the product itself

indirect materials materials that are used in the production process but are not an identifiable part of the finished product

indirect method a format for the statement of cash flows that adjusts the net income figure in order to calculate net cash flows from operating activities

individual job sheet individual a record that shows the costs accumulated for each job

intangible asset a long-term asset used in a business that lacks physical substance; examples include patents, copyrights, trademarks, and franchises

interest allowance a method of sharing net income that recognizes differences in partners' investments

interest the charge for credit

interim financial statements financial statements, such as a balance sheet and an income statement, that are prepared for a period of time less than a fiscal year

interim statements financial statements prepared during the fiscal year for periods of less than 12 months such as monthly, quarterly, and semiannually

internal auditor an accountant who works for a specific organization and reviews the records and operations of that organization

internal control the procedures used within a company to protect its assets

internal transactions adjusting entries that update the ledger without involving parties outside the business

inventory a count taken of the merchandise on hand at the end of an accounting period

inventory sheet a form on which a physical inventory is recorded

Inventory Short and Over account An account used to record differences between the inventory value shown in the perpetual records and the value determined by the period-end physical account; an account that does not have a normal debit or credit balance

investing activities transactions that increase and decrease the non-current assets that a business owns

invoice the bill the seller of goods sends to the buyer of the goods that identifies and describes the goods and how they will be delivered; to the seller, referred to as the sales invoice; to the buyer, referred to as a purchase invoice

issued stock shares that have been issued to stockholders

issuing a note on account the act of issuing a note to a creditor in return for an extension of time to pay an existing account payable

J

job an activity or task performed for pay

job order cost accounting a cost accounting system in which costs are kept track of by individual jobs, or batches of similar items being produced at one time

journal a record in which business transactions are recorded in the order that they occur (chronological order, by order of date)

journalizing the process of recording transactions in a journal

just-in-time (JIT) inventory system an inventory system designed to reduce storage costs and improve efficiency by ordering just enough raw materials to meet daily production needs and finishing just enough goods to be shipped to customers at the end of each day

L

Land Improvements account an asset account to which the cost of improvements to real estate, such as sidewalks, driveways, fences, and parking lots (all of which have a limited life), are debited

last-in, first-out (LIFO) method an inventory costing method that assumes the last goods purchased (last-in) are the first goods sold (first-out), leaving the earliest goods as the ending inventory

ledger a grouping of all accounts a company uses

legal capital the amount of earnings that a corporation must retain before a dividend can be paid to stockholders; usually equals the par value of the stock outstanding

leverage the use of borrowed funds to earn a greater return than the cost of the borrowed funds

liability a debt owed to a creditor, a party outside of the business

limited liability company (LLC) a type of business organization that combines features of a corporation and those of a partnership or sole proprietorship

limited liability means that stockholders of a corporation are not personally liable for the debts of the company

liquidation schedule a table that shows the three steps in liquidation

liquidation the process of winding up a business

liquidity refers to how quickly an asset can be turned into cash, used up, or expire; used in reference to assets, which are listed on the balance sheet in the order of their liquidity

list price the price appearing in a price catalog issued by the seller

long-term investment an investment that management intends to hold for more than one year

long-term liability debt that will not come due for payment within one year; examples include long-term notes payable and mortgages payable

lookback period a 12-month period ending on June 30 of the prior year; employers look at the amount of FICA taxes (employee and employer shares) and withheld income taxes during the lookback period to determine their deposit status for the current year

lower of cost or market (LCM) rule an alternate way to value an inventory in which the cost of the merchandise on hand is compared with the market price (current cost to replace), and the lower value is used

M

maker the person who has received credit and issues a note

manufacturing business a business that produces a product to sell to its customers to earn a profit

margin of safety the amount of sales above break-even sales

market interest rate the prevailing rate of interest in the bond market; also referred to as the effective interest rate

market value the amount for which a stock can be bought (or sold) at a given time

matching principle a rule of accounting that requires that revenue and expenses be recorded in the accounting period in which they occur; a rule stating that an accurate net income or net loss for an accounting period be reported by offsetting revenue earned by the expenses that were necessary to produce that revenue

materials ledger record a subsidiary record of raw materials kept as a perpetual inventory

math error an addition or subtraction mistake

maturity date the date on which the principal must be repaid to bondholders

maturity value the principal plus the interest on a note; the amount that must be paid to the payee on the maturity date of the note

memorandum entry a notation, without amounts, in the journal that is used to report the effect of a stock split; an optional practice

merchandise goods held for sale to customers; also referred to as merchandise inventory and stock in trade

Merchandise Inventory account an asset account that shows the value of goods (inventory) on hand at a given moment (usually at the beginning or end of the accounting period)

merchandise inventory goods held for sale to customers in the normal course of business

merchandise inventory turnover a measure of the number of times a firm's average inventory is sold during the year; calculated by dividing cost of goods sold by the average inventory

merchandising business a business that purchases goods produced by others and then sells them to customers to earn a profit; also referred to as a trading business

merit-rating system a system set up by the states to provide a lower SUTA rate for employers who maintain stable employment

minimum wage the lowest hourly rate that can be paid to employees who are covered by the Fair Labor Standards Act

mixed costs costs that have both variable and fixed characteristics

Modified Accelerated Cost Recovery System (MACRS) an accelerated depreciation method required for calculating depreciation for income tax purposes

modified cash basis of accounting a basis of accounting where revenue is recorded only when cash is received and expenses are recorded only when cash is paid; however, adjustments are made for expenditures for items having an economic life of more than one year—such as equipment, prepaid insurance, and large purchases of supplies

moving average the average cost method applied to the perpetual inventory system; a new average unit cost is calculated each time an item is purchased

N

natural business year a fiscal year ending at a business's lowest point of activity

natural resource a long-term asset that is acquired to extract or remove resources from the ground; examples include oil wells, coal mines, and forests; also referred to as a wasting assets

negotiable able to be transferred by endorsement to another party

net earnings gross earnings minus payroll deductions; also referred to as net pay or take-home pay

net income excess of revenue over total expenses; also referred to as net profit or net earnings; the opposite of net loss

net loss excess of total expenses over revenue; the opposite of net income

net realizable value the difference between the balance in the Accounts Receivable account and the Allowance for Doubtful Accounts account; the actual amount of receivables that the firm expects to collect; also referred to as net receivables

net sales the amount obtained by subtracting the amount of sales returns and allowances and the amount of sales discounts from the amount of sales

noncumulative preferred stock preferred stock in which undeclared dividends do not accumulate; in a year in which the board of directors does not declare a dividend, it is lost forever

noninterest-bearing note a note that has no interest charge

nonoperating expense an expense, such as interest expense, that is not related to the day-to-day operations of the business

nonoperating revenue revenue, such as interest income, that is earned from a source other than the normal operations of the business

nonparticipating preferred stock preferred stock in which the dividend is limited to a fixed amount; most preferred stock is issued as non-participating

no-par value stock stock without a fixed dollar amount assigned to each share

normal balance the increase side of an account or where you would expect to find the balance of that account

note payable a formal written promise to pay a specified amount at a definite future date

not-for-profit accountant an accountant who works for a governmental unit or a nonprofit organization

NSF check a check drawn against an account in which there are not sufficient funds; also referred to as an uncollectible, or bad check

number of days in merchandise inventory a measure of the number of days that it takes a firm to sell its inventory; calculated by dividing 365 days by the merchandise inventory turnover

O

OASDI taxable wage base the maximum amount of earnings during a calendar year that is subject to OASDI taxes

operating activities transactions that enter into the calculation of net income; affect the income statement

operating expenses budget a budget that estimates operating expenses for the next fiscal period

operating expenses the normal and expected expenses of operating a business

other expenses expenses that are not directly associated with the normal operation of the business, such as interest expense

other income revenue earned that is not directly associated with the normal operation of the business, such as income from vending machine sales and interest earned

outstanding check a check that was recorded in the checkbook but does not appear on the bank statement because it did not reach the bank's accounting department in time to be included on the statement

outstanding stock the number of shares actually in the hands of the stockholders; also referred to as outstanding shares

overapplied overhead when factory overhead charged to production is greater than actual factory overhead charges; causes a credit balance in the Factory Overhead Control account

overtime pay a minimum of one and one-half times the regular rate of pay for hours worked over 40 in a week; commonly referred to as time-and-a-half

owner's equity the difference between assets and liabilities; also referred to as capital, proprietorship, and net worth

P

paid vouchers file a file of vouchers that have been paid, organized by payment date

paid-in capital capital that comes from stockholders through the purchase of the company's stock capital

Paid-In Capital in Excess of Par-Common account a stockholders' equity (paid-in capital) account used to record the premium when par value common stock is issued for an amount greater than par value

Paid-In Capital in Excess of Par-Preferred account a stockholders' equity (paid-in capital) account used to record the premium when par value preferred stock is issued for an amount greater than par value

par value stock stock for which a fixed dollar amount is designated in the corporate charter as the face value of each share

participating preferred stock preferred stock that is allowed to receive dividends of *more than* the stated rate if a sufficient amount remains after both preferred and common stockholders have received a dividend

partnership a business co-owned by two or more people

payee the business or person to whom a check or note is made payable

Payroll account a holding account in which the gross amount of the payroll is recorded until the payroll can be analyzed to determine what part is direct labor, what part is indirect labor, and what part is sales and office salaries

payroll deduction an amount withheld (deducted) from the pay of an employee

payroll register a summary of the gross earnings, deductions, and net pay for all employees for a specific payroll period

Payroll Tax Expense account an operating expense account used to record the total payroll taxes imposed on the employer

periodic inventory system an inventory system in which the Merchandise Inventory account shows the value of the most recent inventory count, usually at the beginning of the accounting period; no attempt is made to adjust the balance of this account until the next inventory is taken

permanent account accounts such as assets, liabilities, and owner's capital whose balances will be carried into the next accounting period; accounts whose balances are not closed; also referred to as real accounts

perpetual inventory records records used in the perpetual system to record purchases and sales of an item of inventory and to keep a running balance of that item

perpetual inventory system an inventory system in which the Merchandise Inventory account is debited each time merchandise is purchased and credited each time merchandise is sold in order to keep a running balance of the entire inventory

Petty Cash account an asset account in which the amount of the petty cash fund is recorded

petty cash fund a small amount of cash kept in the office for making small payments for items such as postage and office supplies; recorded in the Petty Cash account

petty cash payments record a nonessential business record used to record payments from the petty cash fund and is summarized and used as a basis for a journal entry at the end of the month; a type of auxiliary record

petty cash voucher a form showing the amount of the payment, the purpose, and the account to be debited used when payment is made from the petty cash fund

petty cashier the person designated to disburse money from the petty cash fund; recorded in the Petty Cash account

physical inventory a count of merchandise on hand at the end of a period

piece-rate plan a method of payment in which workers are paid for each unit they produce, rather than by hours worked

plant assets assets that are expected to be used in the business for more than one year; are acquired for use in the operation of a business, are not intended for resale to customers, and are tangible; examples include land, buildings, machinery and equipment, furniture, and automobiles; also referred to as *fixed assets; property, plant, and equipment*; or *long-term assets*

post-closing trial balance a trial balance prepared after closing entries have been posted and consisting only of permanent accounts; also referred to as an after-closing trial balance

posting error an incorrect transfer from the journal to an account or from the ledger to the trial balance

posting the process of transferring transactions from the journal to the ledger

preemptive right the right of common stockholders to maintain their proportionate ownership share of the corporation if the corporation issues additional shares of stock

preferred stock a class of stock that a corporation can issue in addition to common; such stockholders have special rights or privileges not available to holders of common stock: prior claim to dividends and a prior claim to assets if the corporation were to cease operations and liquidate its assets

Preferred Stock account a stockholders' equity (paid-in capital) account used to record the par value of preferred shares issued

premium a fee paid for insurance coverage that will benefit the business in the future; a bond sold for more than face value

Premium on Bonds Payable account a long-term liability account used to record the premium when bonds are issued at an amount above face value

premium the amount by which the issue price of stock exceeds the par value

price/earnings (P/E) ratio a measure of the future prospects of a stock; calculated by dividing the market price per share of stock by earnings per share

principal the amount of money borrowed or the amount of credit extended; also referred to as the face or par value; the amount that must be repaid when a bond matures

principle of materiality the principle that proper accounting procedures have to be strictly followed only for events and transactions that would have an effect on a business's financial statements

principle of objective evidence the principle that source documents should form the foundation for recording business transactions

private accountant an accountant who is employed by a specific company

proceeds the difference between the maturity value of a discounted note and the bank discount charged

process cost accounting a cost accounting system in which costs are accumulated as goods in production move through the various production departments

production budget a budget that estimates the number of units to be produced in the upcoming fiscal period

profit center any segment of a business that incurs expenses while producing revenue

profitability the ability of a business to earn a reasonable return on the owners' investments

promissory note a written promise to pay a sum of money at a definite time in the future; also referred to as a note

protest fee a fee charged by a bank to the payee of a note when the note is dishonored by its maker

public accountant an accountant who works on a fee basis for individuals and organizations

Public Company Accounting Oversight Board (PCAOB) a not-for-profit corporation created by the Sarbanes-Oxley Act of 2002 to oversee the auditors of public companies in order to protect the interest of investors and further the public's interest in the preparation of fair and reliable financial reports

publicly held corporation a corporation whose ownership is spread over many investors and whose stock is usually listed on an organized stock exchange

purchase order a written or online form sent from a buyer of goods to the seller specifying the quantity and description of the goods to be purchased

purchase requisition a written request for goods to be purchased; usually prepared by a department head or manager and sent to a firm's purchasing department

Purchases account a temporary owner's equity account used to record the cost of merchandise purchased for resale; also referred to as the Merchandise Purchases account or the Purchases of Merchandise account

purchases discount buyer's term for the discounts offered by a seller to encourage early payment

Purchases Discounts account a contra purchases account used to record discounts received for prompt payment of merchandise invoices

purchases invoice the buyer's copy of the bill that identifies and describes the sold goods and how they will be delivered

purchases journal a special journal used only to record credit purchases of merchandise; sometimes a multicolumn journal used to record all credit purchases, not just merchandise

Purchases Returns and Allowances account a contra purchases account used to record returns and allowances on merchandise purchases

purchases returns and allowances returns of merchandise purchases or price reductions received for damaged or irregular merchandise

Q

quick assets current assets that can be converted to cash right away; usually only cash, current receivables, and marketable securities

R

rate the annual percent charged on the principal

ratio a fractional relationship of one number to another

ratio of owner's equity to total liabilities a measure of the position of a company in the eyes of its creditors; calculated by dividing owner's equity by total liabilities

ratio of plant assets to long-term liabilities a measure of the margin of safety for those who hold notes and bonds of a company; calculated by dividing plant assets by long-term liabilities

Raw Materials Inventory account an asset account that shows the cost of raw materials purchased and on hand

raw materials inventory the inventory of goods not yet put into production at the end of an accounting period

raw materials materials used in the manufacturing process; also referred to as direct materials

realization principle a principle that states that revenue should be recorded when it is earned, even though cash may not be collected until later

realization the step in liquidation in which all noncash assets are converted into cash

receiving report a form prepared by a buyer to verify that goods have been received and accepted

reciprocal accounts accounts in sets of interrelated records, such as those for a home office and a branch, that match in dollar amount but have opposite balances

recording error a mistake made in a journal entry

Recovery of Bad Debts account a miscellaneous revenue account used to record the amount of a bad debt recovered in a period after the period in which the account was written off

registered bonds bonds for which the names and addresses of the bondholders are registered with the issuing corporation

reinstate to reopen a customer's account that was previously written off as uncollectible

responsibility accounting a management tool that uses the organization's accounting system to hold people responsible for their work

restrictive endorsement an endorsement using a phrase "For deposit only," which limits or restricts any further transfer of the check

retail business a business such as a grocery store, drugstore, and restaurant, that sells directly to consumers

retail method a method for estimating the cost of the ending inventory by using a cost percentage derived from cost and retail prices of the goods available for sale

retained earnings past earnings that have not been paid out as dividends to stockholders

retained earnings statement a statement that shows the changes that have taken place in retained earnings over a specific period of time, such as a month or a year

return on stockholders' equity a measure of the return on each dollar invested by stockholders; calculated by dividing net income by average stockholders' equity

return on total assets a measure of the profitability of a firm's assets; calculated by dividing the sum of net income and interest expense by average total assets

revenue expenditure an expenditure for a plant asset that benefits only the current accounting period; examples include repairs and maintenance expenses; debited to an expense account

revenue income earned from carrying out the major activities of a firm

reversing entries a technique that allows the accountant to make the same entry to record the payment of accrued expenses that would have been made had two separate accounting periods not been involved; always recorded on the first day of the new accounting period

revolving charge plan a payment system in which customers pay a percentage of their account plus finance charges on a monthly basis

salaried employee an individual who works for a fixed amount of pay for a definite period of time, such as a week, a month, or a year

S

Salaries Expense account an expense account used to record the gross amount of the payroll; also referred to as Wages Expense account, Payroll Expense account, and Salaries and Commissions Expense account

salary a fixed amount paid to employees for a certain period of time, such as a week, month, or year

salary allowance a method of sharing net income that recognizes how much work was done by each partner

Sales account a revenue account used to record the price of merchandise sold to customers

sales budget a budget that estimates the total dollar volume of sales revenue for the upcoming period

sales discounts a seller's term for the discounts offered to encourage early payment by a buyer

Sales Discounts account a contra revenue account with a normal debit balance used to record cash discounts granted to credit customers for prompt payment

sales invoice the seller's copy of the bill that identifies and describes the sold goods and how they will be delivered

sales journal a special journal used only to record credit sales of merchandise

sales order a document prepared when an order is received from a customer

Sales Returns and Allowances account a contra revenue account with a normal debit balance used to record returns from and allowances to customers

sales tax a tax on the retail price of goods sold, collected by the merchant and paid to the governmental body that levies the tax

Sales Tax Payable account a liability account used to record sales taxes on retail purchases

sales ticket a form prepared by the seller when a cash sale is made that describes the goods sold, identifies the customer, and serves as a source document for recording the sale; also referred to as the sales slip

salvage value the amount that an asset is expected to be worth at the end of its productive life; also referred to as scrap value, trade-in value, and residual value

Sarbanes-Oxley Act of 2002 a law, passed by Congress, requiring companies to certify the accuracy of their financial information and intended to restore the public's confidence in the financial statements of companies; often referred to as Sarbanes-Oxley or SOX

schedule of accounts payable a listing of the individual creditor account balances in the accounts payable ledger

schedule of accounts receivable a listing of the balances in the accounts receivable ledger

secured bonds bonds that have a specific asset (or assets) pledged as security for the debt; also referred to as mortgage trust bonds

segmentation the division of an organization into parts

selling expenses operating expenses directly related to the sale of a firm's merchandise

serial bonds a bond issue in which the bonds mature periodically over a number of years

service business a business that performs services for customers to earn a profit

service charge an account maintenance fee charged by the bank and deducted directly from the depositor's balance; also referred to as a bank fee

shift in assets a change that occurs when one asset is exchanged for another asset, such as when supplies are purchased for cash; occurs when one asset goes up in amount and another goes down

Shipments from Home Office account a branch account that shows the total amount of merchandise received from the home office; acts like a purchases account

Shipments to Branch account a home office account that shows the total amount of merchandise shipped to the branch; acts like a sales account

signature card a form kept by a bank documenting personal information and the signature of the person(s) authorized to write checks on a bank account

Sinking Fund Cash account an asset account in which cash deposited in a bond sinking fund is recorded

Sinking Fund Income account a revenue account used to record earnings from bond sinking fund investments

Sinking Fund Investments account an asset account used to record investments made from a bond sinking fund

slide a type of posting error caused by an incorrectly placed decimal point, such as entering 100 for 1,000 or 24.50 for 245

sole proprietorship a business owned by one person

source documents business documents or papers that prove business transactions occurred; the basis for journal entries

special journal a journal used by businesses to record transactions that are similar in nature; examples are the purchases journal and the cash payments journal; also referred to as a special-purpose journal

specific identification method an inventory costing method in which units are identified as coming from specific purchases and are assigned a cost based on the price of those purchases

stability a reference to how long an asset will last; an organizing quality of a plant asset for listing on the balance sheet

standard cost accounting a system of cost accounting in which manufacturing costs are budgeted and later compared with actual costs to determine the efficiency of the planning process

standard form of account a form of account with separate debit and credit sides

State Unemployment Tax Act (SUTA) a law that requires employers to pay unemployment taxes (for the benefit of employees) to the states in which they conduct business

stated value a value that is sometimes assigned to no-par stock; there is little difference between accounting for par value stock and for stated value stock

statement of cash flows a financial statement that provides information about the cash flows from operating activities, investing activities, and financing activities during an accounting period and the net increase or decrease in cash that occurred

statement of cost of goods manufactured a statement used by a manufacturer to show the total cost of goods manufactured during an accounting period; also referred to as a cost of goods manufactured statement or a manufacturing statement

statement of owner's equity a summary of the changes that have occurred in owner's equity during a specific period of time, such as a month or year; also referred to as a capital statement

stock certificate a document issued to a purchaser of stock when the stock has been paid for in full; represents proof of ownership

stock dividend a proportional distribution of additional shares of a corporation's own stock to stockholders of record

Stock Dividends account a contra capital account used to record the market value of stock issued as a dividend; its balance is closed to Retained Earnings at the end of the accounting period

stock split the issuance of additional shares of stock to stockholders based on the number of shares previously owned; usually declared to bring down the market value of the stock; accompanied by a proportionate reduction in par or stated value

stockholders those who own shares of stock in a corporation; also referred to as shareholders

stockholders' equity the owners' claim against the assets of the corporation; represents the excess of total assets over total liabilities; is divided into paid-in capital and earned capital (or retained earnings); also referred to as shareholders' equity

straight-line method a popular method of calculating depreciation that yields the same amount of depreciation for each full period an asset is used

straight-line rate the annual percent of depreciation in the straight-line method; calculated by dividing 100% by the estimated years of life

Subscriptions Income account a revenue account showing the amount earned on subscription sales

subsidiary ledger a ledger that contains only one type of account such as the accounts payable ledger

sum-of-the-years'-digits method an accelerated depreciation method used to calculate depreciation using a fraction consisting of a constant denominator (the sum of the digits of the years making up the estimated useful life of the asset) and a changing numerator (the number of the years remaining in the useful life of the asset)

supplies short-term physical assets needed in the operation of a business

SUTA Tax Payable account a current liability account used to record the employer's obligation for state unemployment taxes

T

T account skeleton version of the standard form of an account

tangible capable of being touched; the quality of a physical asset

Tax Reform Act of 1986 an act passed by Congress in 1986 to simplify the income tax code, broaden the tax base, and eliminate many tax shelters

temporary account accounts whose balances are not carried over from one accounting period to another but instead are closed to the owner's capital account at period-end; revenue, expense, and drawing accounts; also referred to as nominal accounts

temporary investment an investment that can be turned into cash with little delay; also referred to as a marketable security

temporary owner's equity accounts accounts whose balances will be transferred to the owner's capital account at the end of the accounting period; examples include expense accounts, revenue accounts, and the owner's drawing account

term bonds a bond issue in which all of the bonds mature at one point in time

time the number of years, months, or days for which a note is issued; also referred to as the term

time-and-a-half the common rate for overtime pay

times interest earned (TIE) a measure of a company's ability to meet its interest payments; calculated by dividing the sum of net income, interest expense, and income taxes by interest expense

to credit to enter an amount on the right, or credit, side of the account; abbreviated as Cr.

to debit to enter an amount on the left, or debit, side of the account; abbreviated as Dr.

to replenish the petty cash fund the action of replacing the amount paid from the petty cash fund, usually done at the end of the month

trade discounts percentage reductions from the list price of merchandise

transaction any activity that changes the value of a firm's assets, liabilities, or owner's equity

transposition a type of posting error caused by the reversal of digits, such as entering 240 for 420

treasury stock shares of a company's stock that have been (1) issued as fully paid, (2) later reacquired, and (3) not retired or reissued

trend percentages measure used to compare financial data over a period of years, in which one year is selected as the base year, and every other year's amount is expressed as a percent of the base year's amount

trial balance a listing of all ledger accounts and their balances to test the equality of debits and credits in the ledger at the end of an accounting period, usually at the end of each month

U

underapplied overhead when factory overhead charged to production is less than actual factory overhead charges; causes a debit balance in the Factory Overhead Control account

Unearned Subscriptions Income account a liability account showing the dollar amount of subscriptions due to subscribers of a publication

unfavorable variance a variance that exists when actual costs exceed budgeted costs

unit contribution margin the sales price of an item minus the variable cost per unit

units-of-production method a depreciation method in which cost is allocated over the estimated productive life of a plant asset, and life is expressed by such measures as hours, units, or miles

unpaid vouchers file a file of vouchers to be paid, organized by date due so vouchers can be paid promptly

V

variable cost a cost that varies in total as production varies but remains the same per unit regardless of how many units are produced

variance the difference between an actual and a budgeted (standard) cost

vertical analysis the expression of each item in a company's financial statement as a percent of a base figure, in order to see the relative importance of each item; for the income statement, the base is net sales; for the balance sheet, the base is total assets

voucher a receipt or document showing authorization of a payment; recorded in the Vouchers Payable account

voucher system a method of accounting for cash payments in which all payments are authorized in advance

Vouchers Payable account a liability account in which unpaid vouchers are recorded

W

wage a fixed, hourly rate paid to an employee

wage bracket method a method that uses government-issued tables to compute the amount of federal income tax to be withheld from employees

weighted-average method an inventory costing method in which it is assumed that all units have the same average price; calculated by dividing the total cost of goods available for sale by the total units available for sale; also referred to as the average cost method

wholesalers a business that purchases goods in bulk from manufacturers and sells the goods to retailers, other wholesalers, schools and other nonprofit institutions, and, at times, directly to consumers

withdrawal the removal of business assets for the owner's personal use

withholding allowance an amount of earnings that is not subject to taxation; also referred to as an exemption

work sheet an informal working a paper used by the accountant to organize data for the financial statements and lessen the possibility of overlooking an adjustment

workers' compensation insurance the insurance employers must carry to provide protection for employees who suffer job-related illness or injury; payments recorded

working capital current assets minus current liabilities; a measure of a company's ability to meet short-term obligations

Work-in-Process Inventory account an asset account used to record production costs as goods are moved through the production process

work-in-process inventory the inventory of goods that are partially completed at the end of an accounting period

Z

zero proof test a test performed using the plus and minus bars of a calculator; passing this test indicates that two equal columns have a zero difference

Index

Account Title	Financial Statement	Classification	Permanent or Temporary	Normal Balance
Accounts Receivable	Balance Sheet	Current Asset	Permanent	Debit
Cash	Balance Sheet	Current Asset	Permanent	Debit
Merchandise Inventory	Balance Sheet	Current Asset	Permanent	Debit
Notes Receivable	Balance Sheet	Current Asset	Permanent	Debit
Petty Cash	Balance Sheet	Current Asset	Permanent	Debit
Prepaid Insurance	Balance Sheet	Current Asset	Permanent	Debit
Prepaid Rent	Balance Sheet	Current Asset	Permanent	Debit
Stock Subscriptions Receivable	Balance Sheet	Current Asset	Permanent	Debit
Supplies	Balance Sheet	Current Asset	Permanent	Debit
Allowance for Doubtful Accounts	Balance Sheet	Contra Current Asset	Permanent	Credit
Buildings	Balance Sheet	Plant Asset	Permanent	Debit
Equipment	Balance Sheet	Plant Asset	Permanent	Debit
Land	Balance Sheet	Plant Asset	Permanent	Debit
Land Improvements	Balance Sheet	Plant Asset	Permanent	Debit
Machinery	Balance Sheet	Plant Asset	Permanent	Debit
Accumulated Depreciation	Balance Sheet	Contra Plant Asset	Permanent	Credit
Copyrights	Balance Sheet	Intangible Asset	Permanent	Debit
Goodwill	Balance Sheet	Intangible Asset	Permanent	Debit
Patents	Balance Sheet	Intangible Asset	Permanent	Debit
Accounts Payable	Balance Sheet	Current Liability	Permanent	Credit
Dividends Payable	Balance Sheet	Current Liability	Permanent	Credit
Federal Income Tax Payable	Balance Sheet	Current Liability	Permanent	Credit
FICA Tax Payable—HI	Balance Sheet	Current Liability	Permanent	Credit
FICA Tax Payable—OASDI	Balance Sheet	Current Liability	Permanent	Credit
FUTA Tax Payable	Balance Sheet	Current Liability	Permanent	Credit
Interest Payable	Balance Sheet	Current Liability	Permanent	Credit
Notes Payable	Balance Sheet	Current Liability	Permanent	Credit
Salaries Payable	Balance Sheet	Current Liability	Temporary	Credit
Sales Tax Payable	Balance Sheet	Current Liability	Permanent	Credit
SUTA Tax Payable	Balance Sheet	Current Liability	Permanent	Credit
Unearned Revenue	Balance Sheet	Current Liability	Permanent	Credit
Bonds Payable	Balance Sheet	Long-Term Liability	Permanent	Credit
Mortgage Note Payable	Balance Sheet	Long-Term Liability	Permanent	Credit
Premium on Bonds Payable	Balance Sheet	Long-Term Liability	Permanent	Credit
Discount on Bonds Payable	Balance Sheet	Contra Long-Term Liability	Permanent	Debit
(Owner's Name), Capital	Statement of Owner's Equity; Balance Sheet	Owner's Equity	Permanent	Credit
Common Stock	Balance Sheet	Stockholders' Equiy	Permanent	Credit
Common Stock Dividends Distributable	Balance Sheet	Stockholders' Equiy	Permanent	Credit
Common Stock Subscribed	Balance Sheet	Stockholders' Equiy	Permanent	Credit
Paid-In Capital from Treasury Stock	Balance Sheet	Stockholders' Equity	Permanent	Credit
Paid-In Capital in Excess of Par—Common	Balance Sheet	Stockholders' Equity	Permanent	Credit